HOLT
ELEMENTS OF
LITERATURE

Introductory Course

HOLT, RINEHART AND WINSTON

A Harcourt Education Company

Orlando • **Austin** • New York • San Diego • Toronto • London

EDITORIAL

Editorial Vice President: Ralph Tachuk
Executive Book Editors: Juliana Koenig, Katie Vignery
Senior Book Editors: Jennifer Johnson, Kathryn Rogers
Senior Product Manager: Don Wulbrecht
Managing Editor: Marie Price
Editorial Staff: Gail Coupland, Randy Dickson, Ann Michelle Gibson, Kerry Johnson, Karen Kolar, Evan Wilson, Sari Wilson
Copyediting Manager: Michael Neibergall
Copyediting Supervisors: Kristen Azzara, Mary Malone
Copyeditors: Christine Altgelt, Elizabeth Dickson, Emily Force, Leora Harris, Anne Heausler, Julia Thomas Hu, Kathleen Scheiner, Nancy Shore
Associate Managing Editor: Elizabeth LaManna
Editorial Support: Christine Degollado, Betty Gabriel, Danielle Greer, Mark Koenig, Erik Netcher, Janet Jenkins, Gloria Shahan, Emily Stern
Editorial Permissions: Ann Farrar, Susan Lowrance

Index: Tamsin Nutter

ART, DESIGN, AND PRODUCTION

Director: Athena Blackorby
Senior Design Director: Betty Mintz
Series Design: Kirchoff/Wohlberg, Inc.
Design and Electronic Files: Paul Caullett
Photo Research: Mary Monaco, Susan Sato
Production Manager: Carol Trammel
Sr. Production Coordinator: Carol Marunas
Prepress: Anthology, Inc.
Manufacturing: R. R. Donnelley & Sons Company, Willard, Ohio

COVER

Photo Credits: (inset) *Landscape With Horses* (1934) by John Ward Lockwood. Oil on canvas (30" × 40⅛"). Courtesy of The Anschutz Collection. Photograph by William J. O'Connor. (background) Photograph of horses © Will and Deni McIntyre/Getty Images.

Requests for permission to make copies of any part of the work should be mailed to the following address: Permissions Department, Holt, Rinehart and Winston, 10801 N. MoPac Expressway, Building 3, Austin, Texas 78759-5415.

Acknowledgments appear on pages 933–935, which are an extension of the copyright page.

Printed in the United States of America

ISBN 0-03-035713-6   2 3 4 5 048 07 06

Language Arts Standards

The following chart lists the **North Carolina Course of Study for English Language Arts**. The Course of Study describes what you are expected to learn and do in sixth grade.

As you review the chart, you will find that the Course of Study is divided into six competency goals. Each appears in a yellow box. Below each goal are the objectives. They appear in yellow boxes in the left column. Underneath each objective, is an explanation. The right column gives specific examples of how *Elements of Literature* helps meet the objective.

COMPETENCY GOAL I

The learner will use language to express individual perspectives drawn from personal or related experience.

1.01 Narrate an expressive account (e.g., fictional or autobiographical) which:

• uses a coherent organizing structure appropriate to purpose, audience, and context.
• tells a story or establishes the significance of an event or events.
• uses remembered feelings and specific details.
• uses a range of appropriate strategies (e.g., dialogue, suspense, movement, gestures, expressions).

When telling a story, whether it is a true one or a fictional one, you must use different strategies to make the scenes come alive for your readers.

EXAMPLE: Writing Your Own Stories

This book gives you many opportunities to write stories. For example, the Writing Workshop on pages 108–113 takes you through writing a short story; on pages 292–297, you are asked to write about an important experience in your life.

COMPETENCY GOAL 1

1.02 **Explore expressive materials that are read, heard, and/or viewed by:**

- **monitoring comprehension for understanding of what is read, heard and/or viewed.**
- **analyzing the characteristics of expressive works.**
- **determining the effect of literary devices and/or strategies on the reader/viewer/listener.**
- **making connections between works, self and related topics.**
- **comparing and/or contrasting information.**
- **drawing inferences and/or conclusions.**
- **determining the main idea and/or significance of events.**
- **generating a learning log or journal.**

- **creating an artistic interpretation that connects self to the work.**
- **discussing print and non-print expressive works formally and informally.**

To address this standard, you will read and effectively respond in discussion and writing to expressive texts, such as essays and poems.

EXAMPLE: Responding to Texts

The personal essay writing assignment on page 197 asks you to connect a theme in the essay "Summer Diamond Girl" to your own life.

The After You Read pages in the textbook have you discuss both fiction and nonfiction texts (for example, pages 156 and 434).

1.03 **Interact appropriately in group settings by:**

- **listening attentively.**
- **showing empathy.**
- **contributing relevant comments connecting personal experiences to content.**
- **monitoring own understanding of the discussion and seeking clarification as needed.**

In a group discussion, you will need to listen to what other people are saying and express your views. In order to follow what is being said, you may need to ask questions.

EXAMPLE: Participating in Classroom Discussions

The Thinking Critically and Extending Interpretations questions on the Response and Analysis pages give you practice in discussion. See, for example, the questions on page 705.

See "Making Assertions About a Text," page 569, for help in supporting your views about a text you have read.

See also tips for listening on pages 907 and 910–911 in the Speaking and Listening Handbook.

COMPETENCY GOAL 1

1.04 Reflect on learning experiences by:

- describing personal learning growth and changes in perspective.
- identifying changes in self throughout the learning process.
- interpreting how personal circumstances and background shape interaction with text.

You are required to reflect on your learning experiences in order to allow you to take more of an active role in what you learn.

EXAMPLE: Making Personal Connections with a Text

Features such as the Writing assignment on page 329 help you relate to your own life what you have read. This specific feature asks that you compare the experience of the main character in "The Gold Cadillac" to your own experience of injustice. A model of a chart in which you can organize your notes is provided.

COMPETENCY GOAL 2

The learner will explore and analyze information from a variety of sources.

2.01 Explore informational materials that are read, heard, and/or viewed by:

- monitoring comprehension for understanding of what is read, heard and/or viewed.
- studying the characteristics of informational works.
- restating and summarizing information.
- determining the importance and accuracy of information.
- making connections between works, self and related topics/information.
- comparing and/or contrasting information.
- drawing inferences and/or conclusions.
- generating questions.

You are required to show an understanding of informational material and an ability to summarize and evaluate it.

EXAMPLE: Analyzing Informational Materials

The Informational Text features throughout the textbook will help you read and analyze informational works. For example, you will learn how to understand the characteristics of a magazine on page 53. On pages 727–729, you will learn how to recognize propaganda in advertisements that you see, hear, or read.

In addition, you will learn the skills of summarizing on page 4 and inferring on page 690.

COMPETENCY GOAL 2

2.02 Use multiple sources of print and non-print information in designing and developing informational materials (such as brochures, newsletters, and infomercials) through:

- exploring a variety of sources from which information may be attained (e.g., books, Internet, electronic databases, CD-ROM).
- distinguishing between primary and secondary sources.
- analyzing the effects of the presentation and/or the accuracy of information.

Make sure you know how to use sources for finding information and can judge the reliability of the information they provide.

EXAMPLE: Conducting Research

The Communications Handbook on pages 893–898 provides you with research strategies and resources you can use when searching for the information in books, in library databases, in periodicals, and on the World Wide Web. It also provides a guide for evaluating the sources you find for authority, accuracy, and objectivity.

See also the Writing Workshop "Informative Report" on pages 518–523 for information on finding and evaluating sources.

COMPETENCY GOAL 3

The learner will examine the foundation of argument.

3.01 Explore argumentative works that are read, heard, and/or viewed by:

- monitoring comprehension for understanding what is read, heard, and/or viewed.
- analyzing the characteristics of argumentative works.
- determining the importance of author's word choice and focus.
- summarizing author's purpose and stance.
- making connections between works, self and related topics.
- drawing inferences.
- responding to public documents (such as but not limited to editorials and school and community policies).
- distinguishing between fact and opinion.

You must respond to a persuasive message and show you can recognize the specific techniques used and evaluate their effectiveness.

EXAMPLE: Analyzing Persuasive Techniques and Propaganda Techniques

See page 265 for a lesson on evaluating evidence, such as distinguishing between fact and opinion.

Pages 724–726 provide a lesson on analyzing persuasive techniques. The Media Handbook section on "Analyzing Propaganda on TV," pages 918–921, will also help you analyze any persuasive message.

COMPETENCY GOAL 3

3.02 **Explore the problem solution process by:**

- **studying examples (in literature and other text) that present problems coherently, describe the solution clearly, sequence reasons to support the solution, and show awareness of audience.**
- **preparing individual and/or group essays and presentations that focus on the diagnosis of a problem and possible solutions.**

Have you ever read about or noticed a problem and said to yourself, "I have the perfect solution"? You put your ideas into action by putting them in writing or by presenting them orally.

EXAMPLE: Reading and Writing a Problem-Solution Essay

The article "What Will Our Towns Look Like?" on pages 54–55 includes a problem (pollution) and solutions (new inventions).

The Writing Workshop on pages 206–211 leads you step-by-step through the process of writing a persuasive essay on a problem you have identified. The workshop gives you strategies for convincing your audience your solution is the right one. A model essay is also provided.

3.03 **Study arguments that evaluate through:**

- **exploring examples that show a firm control of sound judgments, audience awareness, clear idea/theme, and the use of relevant and coherent reasons for support.**
- **preparing individual and/or group essays and presentations that use evaluative techniques.**

When you read a persuasive piece of writing, you will ask the writer to prove his or her position. Know how to tell if the writer does prove his or her case, and be able to explain how he or she does it. Also, be prepared to present well-supported arguments in a paper or a presentation.

EXAMPLE: Evaluating Assertions and Evidence

The informational text on page 553, "Lincoln's Humor," includes support for a central argument on a topic. Your job will be to evaluate that evidence to see if it adequately supports the author's assertions. This process of evaluation is something you can use to strengthen your own essays.

COMPETENCY GOAL 4

The learner will use critical thinking skills and create criteria to evaluate print and non-print materials.

4.01 Determine the purpose of the author or creator by:

- monitoring comprehension for understanding or what is read, heard and/or viewed
- exploring any bias, apparent or hidden messages, emotional factors, and/or propaganda techniques.
- identifying and exploring the underlying assumptions of the author/creator.
- analyzing the effects of author's craft on the reader/viewer/listener.

Be able to recognize and analyze false or misleading arguments when reading persuasive materials.

EXAMPLE: Recognizing Bias and Propaganda Techniques Used on Television

The chart in the Media Handbook on pages 919–920 outlines several common propaganda techniques and gives examples of each, as well as clues you can use to identify the techniques and evaluate them. You can apply this process to the analysis of propaganda and bias in any medium.

4.02 Analyze the communication and develop (with teacher assistance) and apply appropriate criteria to evaluate the quality of the communication by:

- using knowledge of language structure and literary or media techniques.
- drawing conclusions based on evidence, reasons, or relevant information.
- considering the implications, consequences, or impact of those conclusions.

To evaluate a piece of writing means to judge it. For each evaluation you give for a text, you are required to provide evidence to support your assertion.

EXAMPLE: Making Assertions About a Text

The Informational Text link "Making Assertions About a Text" on pages 569–571 will help you draw conclusions about something you have read. It will also help you to find evidence to support your conclusions.

COMPETENCY GOAL 4

4.03 Recognize and develop a stance of a critic by:

- **considering alternative points of view or reasons.**
- **remaining fair-minded and open to other interpretations.**
- **constructing a critical response/review of a work/topic.**

When taking a stance on an issue, you are required to look at the topic from different points of view.

EXAMPLE: Supporting a Position

The Writing Workshop on pages 762–767 asks you to explore an issue and take your own position on it. You will consider other points of view in order to address counterarguments (page 764).

COMPETENCY GOAL 5

The learner will respond to various literary genres using interpretive and evaluative processes.

5.01 Increase fluency, comprehension, and insight through a meaningful and comprehensive reading program by:

- **using effective reading strategies to match type of text.**
- **reading self-selected literature and other materials of individual interest.**
- **reading literature and other materials selected by the teacher.**
- **discussing literature in teacher-student conferences and small group discussions.**
- **taking an active role in whole class seminars.**
- **discussing and analyzing the effects on texts of such literary devices as figurative language, dialogue, flashback and sarcasm.**
- **interpreting text by explaining elements such as plot, theme, point of view, characterization, mood, and style.**
- **investigating examples of distortion and stereotypes.**
- **recognizing underlying messages in order to identify recurring theme(s) across works.**

- **extending understanding by creating products for different purposes, different audiences and within various contexts.**
- **exploring relationships between and among characters, ideas, concepts and/or experiences.**

Not every text is the same, and your reading of different texts will involve different strategies. You must practice a variety of reading strategies to become a skilled reader.

EXAMPLE: Mastering Reading Skills

You will improve your reading skills by studying the many features in the book that treat specific reading skills in depth, providing instruction, strategies for use, and examples. These skills are revisited regularly in the book for you to keep in practice. See, for example, summarizing on pages 4, 226, and 456, or the KWL chart on page 544.

Another way to improve reading skills is by reading self-selected literature. The Read On features in this book (see pages 680–681, for example) give suggestions for nonfiction and fiction you can read on your own.

COMPETENCY GOAL 5

5.02 **Study the characteristics of literary genres (fiction, nonfiction, drama, and poetry) through:**

- **reading a variety of literature and other text (e.g., novels, autobiographies, myths, essays, magazines, plays, pattern poems, blank verse).**
- **interpreting what impact genre-specific characteristics have on the meaning of the work.**
- **exploring how the author's choice and use of a genre shapes the meaning of the literary work.**
- **exploring what impact literary elements have on the meaning of the text such as the influence of setting or the problem and its resolution.**

Texts may be grouped into categories depending on their form and style. These categories are called genres and they include the poem, the short story, and the essay. Each genre has its own unique characteristics. You must become familiar with these characteristics to help you better understand the text you are reading.

EXAMPLE: Exploring Literary Genres

This book explores a number of genres, including the short story (see, "Dragon, Dragon," page 5), the novella (see "The Gold Cadillac," page 316), folktales (see "Two Frogs and the Milk Vat," page 223), drama (see "The Hitchhiker," page 87), poetry (see "The Bridegroom," page 63), autobiography (see "Storm," page 426), biography (see "The Mysterious Mr. Lincoln," page 545), essay (see "Lincoln's Humor," page 553), and magazine article (see "Trial by Fire," page 717).

COMPETENCY GOAL 6

The learner will apply conventions of grammar and language usage.

6.01 Demonstrate an understanding of conventional written and spoken expression by:

- using a variety of sentence types correctly, punctuating them properly, and avoiding fragments and run-ons.
- using appropriate subject-verb agreement and verb tense that are appropriate for the meaning of the sentence.
- demonstrating the different roles of the parts of speech in sentence construction.
- using pronouns correctly, including clear antecedents and correct case.
- using phrases and clauses correctly (e.g., prepositional phrases, appositives, dependent and independent clauses).
- determining the meaning of unfamiliar vocabulary words by using context clues, a dictionary, a glossary, a thesaurus, and/or structural analysis (roots, prefixes, suffixes) of words.
- extending vocabulary knowledge by learning and using new words.
- exploring the role and use of dialects and of standard English to appreciate appropriate usage in different contexts.
- developing an awareness of language conventions and usage during oral presentations.

You must use conventional written and spoken expressions to reach different audiences and to communicate your message clearly.

EXAMPLE: Using Appropriate Language

Use the Language Handbook, pages 811–890, as a grammar resource.

The activities in the Speaking and Listening Handbook provide practice in choosing words that fit your purpose and audience. See page 902 for an example.

The Vocabulary Development activities (see page 330, for example) teach skills you can use to learn new words and use them appropriately.

COMPETENCY GOAL 6

6.02 Identify and edit errors in spoken and written English by:

- reviewing and using common spelling rules, applying common spelling patterns, and developing and mastering an individualized list of words that are commonly misspelled.
- applying proofreading symbols when editing.
- producing final drafts that demonstrate accurate spelling and the correct use of punctuation and capitalization.
- developing an awareness of errors in everyday speech.

Misspellings and incorrect punctuation can cause a reader to miss out on your message. Learn to use a dictionary to look up words you don't know how to spell. Also, become familiar with grammar rules. Understanding grammar will not only make you a better writer, it will also make you a better speaker.

EXAMPLE: Correcting Your Work

Consult the Spelling Handbook on pages 891–892 for the lists "Fifty Spelling Demons" and "One Hundred Spelling Words."

In addition, the Language Handbook on pages 811–890 provides instruction and practice for different grammar skills.

All of the Writing Workshops (for example, pages 108–113) give instruction in editing errors and include a revision model that shows how to use proofreading marks.

The North Carolina End-of-Grade Test of Reading Comprehension, Grade 6 and the Writing Assessment, Grade 7

This year, you will take the **North Carolina End-of-Grade Test of Reading Comprehension.** This test will measure your readiness for the reading tasks required in the seventh grade. Because good reading skills are necessary to succeed in all your school subjects, this is a very important test.

You will not take the **Writing Assessment** this year. However, practicing for this test now will help you become familiar with the testing process and will help you succeed in writing tasks throughout the year.

Taking the End-of-Grade Test of Reading Comprehension

In the End-of-Grade Test of Reading Comprehension, Grade 6, you will be asked to read and answer multiple-choice questions about nine reading selections. You will read:

- two fiction selections
- one nonfiction selection
- one drama selection
- two poems
- three informational selections

TYPES OF QUESTIONS

The multiple-choice questions on the End-of-Grade Test of Reading Comprehension will measure the following skills.

Cognition. The word *cognition* means "the process of knowing." This category includes the skills you use to get to know a selection. How do you get to know a selection? First, you use vocabulary skills, such as using context clues to figure out word meanings and to understand what the selection says. Next, you find the main points and summarize to understand the meaning of the passage. Finally, you consider the selection as a whole by determining its purpose and how it is organized.

Interpretation. Your interpretation of a selection is the deeper meaning you see in it. To find a text's deeper meaning, you must often read between the lines by making inferences and drawing conclusions. You may also need to clarify ideas from the selection, explain their significance, extend them, or adapt them.

Critical Stance. When you take a critical stance toward a selection, you look at it from the outside to see how it works. You look to see how the writer has created a mood or drawn characters. You identify the literary devices the writer has used and think about how well they work. You may also compare and contrast ideas or characters within the selection.

Connections. Once you have gotten to know a selection, explored its deeper meanings, and examined it to see how it works, you are ready to connect it with other selections and your own knowledge and experience.
   To make connections, you ask yourself questions such as the following.

- How does the selection change or add to my knowledge of the subject?

- How is the selection similar to or different from other selections of the same type?

- How does the information in the selection confirm or contradict my own experiences?

SCORING

After you have taken the test, you will receive a scale score ranging from 228–283. Based on your scale score, you will be assigned one of the following achievement levels.

Level 1, scale score 228–241

This score means that students need more skills to work at the next grade level.

Level 2, scale score 242–251

This score means that students need more practice of the skills necessary to work at the next grade level. Students at this level are minimally prepared for next year's work.

Level 3, scale score 252–263

This score means that students have all the knowledge and skills they need to work at the next grade level. Students at this level are ready for next year's work.

Level 4, scale score 264–283

This score means that students have mastered more skills and knowledge than what is expected at the next grade level. Students at this level are also ready for next year's work.

TIPS FOR TAKING A READING TEST

Multiple-choice questions are the most common type of question you will find on a reading test. Here are some tips that can help you do well on multiple-choice questions.

Budget your time. Plan your time so that you will have enough time to get through the reading *and* all of the questions. Estimate how long you can spend on each passage and set of questions.

Read everything carefully. Stay focused and alert as you read. Pay careful attention to

- the **reading passage**
- the **directions,** which tell you what to do
- the **entire question,** including all of the answer choices

Re-read strategically after you have read the questions. You proabably don't need to re-read the whole passage. Instead, scan or read quickly for material that is directly related to the question. Study any graphics or photos that accompany the passages for useful information that may help you answer the questions.

Trust yourself. Make up your mind only after you have read each answer choice carefully. (Remember that you are often looking for the *best* choice among several possible answers.) If you are not certain of a correct answer, try to eliminate answers that you know are wrong.

Push ahead. When taking a test on paper forms rather than on a computer, skip questions that you cannot answer and return to them later.

Mark your answer carefully. Make sure that you clearly mark each answer in the right place on your answer sheet.

Review your work. If you are able to do so, go back and answer any questions that you skipped. Erase any stray marks.

PRACTICE READING TEST

The following practice test includes one nonfiction selection, one informational piece, and one fiction selection. Each passage is followed by sample questions like those you might find on North Carolina's End-of-Grade Test of Reading Comprehension.

   After reading each passage, choose the best answer to each question. You may refer to the passages as often as necessary.

Directions: Read the selection, an excerpt from the autobiography of Willie Mays. Then, answer questions 1 through 5.

Willie Mays was a Major League Baseball player during the 1950s, 60s, and 70s. Many people consider him to be one of the finest baseball players who ever lived. In this excerpt from his autobiography, Mays talks about baseball and his father.

5   My father told me that I was able to walk when I was only six months old. And wouldn't you know it, he got me walking after a baseball. Getting a baseball was just about the first thing I was able to do. He put two chairs close to each other and then put a baseball on one. I was clinging to the other. He walked me through two or three times. "See the ball," he said.

10   "See the ball." Then he turned me loose—and I went for the ball myself. When he knew I could chase a ball, he gave me batting lessons. He handed me a rubber ball and a little stick maybe two feet long, and sat me in the middle of the floor. I'd play with the ball all day long, hitting it with the stick, then crawling or toddling after it across the room. My dad was

15   determined that if I wanted to, I would become a baseball player and not end up in the steel mills the way he did—although he was an outstanding player for the mill teams.

        He was never too tired to play. When I was five years old he'd take me outside and bounce the ball on the sidewalk to me and yell, "Catch it," and

20   we'd do that for hours. He was a very good baseball player. He was quick, really quick, and got the nickname Cat. He played in Birmingham's Industrial League, which often attracted six thousand fans a game. He took me to as many games as he could, and I was allowed to sit on the bench next to the grown-ups. There, I'd hear them discuss strategy—how you'd play a

25   right-handed pull hitter who was batting against a guy with a slow curve. Or how big a lead you could afford to take off first when you had a southpaw with a quick delivery on the mound. So baseball really came naturally to me, more so than to most other kids. My father never pushed me into becoming a baseball player. He just exposed me to it and it happened all by itself from

30   there. . . .

continued

continued

Even though my father didn't push me into baseball, it was the only thing that made sense. "Don't work in the mills," he would tell me. "You don't make any money there."

CONNECTIONS

1. Why did Willie Mays's father think baseball was a good career for his son?
   A Willie wasn't good at school.
   B There were few opportunities for African Americans at the time.
   C Baseball players made millions at the time, especially with endorsements.
   D He knew Willie would become famous.

EXPLANATION: Think of what you know about Willie Mays and the time when he lived. Then, look at the answer choices. Eliminate A, since the passage doesn't say whether Willie was good at school or not. Eliminate C because baseball players did not make millions of dollars when Mays played. Eliminate D because the passage doesn't say anything about Willie's father believing that Willie would become famous. It is true that when Willie Mays lived there were few opportunities for African Americans, so the correct answer is B.

COGNITION

2. What did Willie mean when he said that his father "just exposed" him to baseball?
   A His father pushed him very hard to become a baseball player.
   B His father pushed him very hard to learn the game quickly.
   C His father tried to keep him from learning to play baseball.
   D His father let him hang around the game and learn it at his own pace.

EXPLANATION: Look at the surrounding sentences for clues to the meaning of the word *exposed*. You can eliminate A and B. Willie states in the previous sentence that his father never pushed him into baseball. You can also rule out C, since Willie's father taught Willie baseball skills. D is the correct answer.

CRITICAL STANCE

3. Which theme **best** fits this passage?
   A fathers and sons
   B overcoming fear
   C battling injustice
   D how babies learn

EXPLANATION: To find the best match, check each answer choice. Eliminate B and C, since neither *fear* nor *injustice* plays a role in the passage. Mays does describe learning to walk (D), but he also describes experiences from later in life. The entire excerpt focuses on the relationship between a son and his father. A is the correct answer.

INTERPRETATION

4. Which statement is **best** supported by this passage?
   A Mays did well at all sports.
   B Mays became a star in his very first year in the league.
   C Mays's family was not wealthy.
   D Mays's family moved frequently.

EXPLANATION: The correct answer is not stated directly in the passage. It is, however, suggested by the details. Since no details hint that Mays moved from place to place or excelled in sports other than baseball, eliminate A and D. Although the italicized sentences before the excerpt suggest that Mays became a star, they do not provide information about *when* this happened (B). One key detail should lead you to conclude that the family was probably not wealthy: Mays's father, who worked in the steel mills, states that people "don't make any money there." C is the correct answer.

COGNITION

5. What do you think Mays's **main** purpose in this passage is?
   A to warn people that sometimes parents push their children too hard
   B to describe how he began playing baseball
   C to describe the difficulties he had learning to play baseball
   D to encourage kids to be more active

EXPLANATION: Mays makes it clear that his father did not push him, so A is incorrect. You can eliminate D, since the passage does not contain an appeal for readers to be active. Since Mays describes learning baseball as natural and easy, C is a poor choice. The correct answer is B.

Directions: Read the selection, an excerpt from a magazine article. Then, answer questions 1 through 3.

To get all the benefits of sports, children need to stay interested and have fun. In one survey, "Having fun" was the top reason children played team sports. "Not having fun" was the second most common reason for quitting a team (after "Lost interest"). Here's how to help your children stay on the

5 field:

"Let your children choose which sports they want to play, and once they choose, give them an out in case they lose interest," says Robert M. Malina, Ph.D., director of the Institute for the Study of Youth Sports at Michigan State University. "If your child says, 'I don't want to play anymore,' simply

10 say, 'Okay,' and don't pressure him to continue," Dr. Malina adds.

Do not set unrealistic goals for your child. Remember that the number of children who become sports superstars is very few compared with the number of children who play team sports.

Keep the emphasis on having fun and playing your best, not on winning.

15 "Winning doesn't become important for children until around age 10 or 11," says Dr. Malina. "Even then, having fun is still the primary goal. After a game, ask your children, 'Did you have fun? What do you think you did best? Where do you think you need improvement? Who did you really like playing with?' Wait before asking, 'Did you win?' Or don't ask it at all."

20 Be an encouraging spectator. Do not try to coach your child from the sidelines while she plays.

Make sure the coach is trained to work with young children, gives everyone on the team plenty of chances to play and emphasizes the fun of playing. A good coach does not yell at children for making mistakes, but instead

25 encourages children when they play well or try hard.

From "Why Kids Quit" by Laura Flynn McCarthy from *Family Life*, September 1998, p. 54. Copyright © 1998 by **Time Inc.** Reproduced by permission of the publisher.

CRITICAL STANCE

1. Why should readers trust the advice given in the magazine article?
   A It has been printed in a magazine.
   B It is based on interviews with children who enjoy sports.
   C The writer's tone is confident.
   D It is backed by quotations from an expert.

EXPLANATION: Neither the fact that information has been published nor the writer's confidence is a sufficient reason to trust a writer's advice, so A and C can be eliminated. B is incorrect because the article does not mention interviews with children. The writer quotes Dr. Robert M. Malina, an expert in youth sports. D is the correct answer.

INTERPRETATION

2. According to the article, what is the most common reason children quit team sports?
   A They're not having fun.
   B They lose interest.
   C They get upset when they lose too many games.
   D They don't like pressure from parents.

EXPLANATION: Although C and D are both possible, neither is mentioned as a reason that kids quit. A and B are mentioned as reasons. However, the passage indicates that losing interest (B) is the most common reason. B is the correct answer.

COGNITION

3. Which sentence **best** sums up the article's main idea?
   A For kids to have fun at sports, they need good coaching.
   B Kids should have fun at sports, without pressure to play or win.
   C Parents should try to make sure their kids play sports.
   D Wait before asking kids, "Did you win?"

EXPLANATION: The best answer covers the most important ideas in the article. C contradicts the article. A and D involve only single details. Only B covers all of the article's most important ideas. B is the correct answer.

Directions: Read the selection. Then, answer questions 1 through 5.

from Boar Out There
Cynthia Rylant

1   Everyone in Glen Morgan knew there was a wild boar in the woods over by the Miller farm. The boar was out beyond the splintery rail fence and past the old black Dodge that somehow had ended up in the woods and was missing most of its parts.

2   Jenny would hook her chin over the top rail of the fence, twirl a long green blade of grass in her teeth and whisper, "Boar out there."

3   And there were times she was sure she heard him. She imagined him running heavily through the trees, ignoring the sharp thorns and briars that raked his back and sprang away trembling.

4   She thought he might have a golden horn on his terrible head. The boar would run deep into the woods, then rise up on his rear hooves, throw his head toward the stars and cry a long, clear, sure note into the air. The note would glide through the night and spear the heart of the moon. The boar had no fear of the moon, Jenny knew, as she lay in bed, listening.

5   One hot summer day she went to find the boar. No one in Glen Morgan had ever gone past the old black Dodge and beyond, as far as she knew. But the boar was there somewhere, between those awful trees, and his dark green eyes waited for someone.

6   Jenny felt it was she.

7   Moving slowly over damp brown leaves, Jenny could sense her ears tingle and fan out as she listened for thick breathing from the trees. She stopped to pick a teaberry leaf to chew, stood a minute, then went on.

8   Deep in the woods she kept her eyes to the sky. She needed to be reminded that there was a world above and apart from the trees—a world of space and air, air that didn't <u>linger</u> all about her, didn't press deep into her skin, as forest air did.

9   Finally, leaning against a tree to rest, she heard him for the first time. She forgot to breathe, standing there listening to the stamping of hooves, and she choked and coughed.

10   Coughed!

11   And now the pounding was horrible, too loud and confusing for Jenny. Horrible. She stood stiff with wet eyes and knew she could always pray, but for some reason didn't.

12   He came through the trees so fast that she had no time to scream or run. And he was there before her.

13   His large gray-black body shivered as he waited just beyond the shadow of the tree she held for support. His nostrils glistened, and his eyes; but astonishingly, he was silent. He shivered and glistened and was absolutely silent.

14   Jenny matched his silence, and her body was rigid,[1] but not her eyes. They traveled along his scarred, bristling back to his thick hind legs. Tears spilling and flooding her face, Jenny stared at the boar's ragged ears, caked with blood. Her tears dropped to the leaves, and the only sound between them was his slow breathing.

15   Then the boar snorted and jerked. But Jenny did not move.

16   High in the trees a bluejay yelled, and, suddenly, it was over. Jenny stood like a rock as the boar wildly flung his head and in terror bolted[2] past her.

17   Past her. . . .

18   And now, since that summer, Jenny still hooks her chin over the old rail fence, and she still whispers, "Boar out there." But when she leans on the fence, looking into the trees, her eyes are full and she leaves wet patches on the splintery wood. She is sorry for the torn ears of the boar and sorry that he has no golden horn.

19   But mostly she is sorry that he lives in fear of bluejays and little girls, when everyone in Glen Morgan lives in fear of him.

---

1.   **rigid:** stiff, unmoving.
2.   **bolted:** suddenly ran quickly away.

From *Every Living Thing* by Cynthia Rylant. Copyright © 1985 by Cynthia Rylant. Reproduced by permission of **Atheneum Books for Young Readers, an imprint of Simon & Schuster Children's Publishing Division.**

INTERPRETATION

1. Which statement **best** explains why Jenny goes alone in search of the wild boar?
   A She wants to kill the boar.
   B She wants to tame the wild boar.
   C She is curious about the boar.
   D She thinks of the boar as her friend.

EXPLANATION: You can eliminate A and B because there is no mention of these thoughts in the selection. D is also wrong because Jenny is afraid of the boar. The correct answer is C. Although Jenny is afraid, she is also curious and goes to search for the boar.

CRITICAL STANCE

2. Based on the information in the text, which of the following is **most similar** to the relationship below?
   feelings of the townspeople toward the boar : feelings of Jenny toward the boar
   A curious : friendly
   B fearful : sympathetic
   C cautious : unkind
   D hurtful : unhappy

EXPLANATION: In the fifth paragraph, you learn that no one in the town goes beyond the old black Dodge because that is where the boar lives. Therefore, the townspeople must be fearful of the boar. By the end of the story (paragraph 18), you know that Jenny feels sorry for the boar, so the correct answer is B.

INTERPRETATION

3. Which word **best** describes how Jenny feels about the boar at the end?
   A frightened
   B angry
   C disgusted
   D sympathetic

EXPLANATION: Jenny's attitude toward the boar changes from fear at the beginning of the story to sympathy at the end. In paragraphs 18 and 19, she is sorry for the boar. The correct answer is D.

CRITICAL STANCE

4. In paragraph 16, the author says, "Jenny stood like a rock." This is an example of which type of figurative language?
   A simile
   B foreshadowing
   C personification
   D understatement

EXPLANATION: You can recognize the figure of speech as a simile because it compares two unlike things using the word *like*. The correct answer is A.

COGNITION

5. In paragraph 8, what does the word "linger" mean?

   A   continue to stay

   B   surround

   C   blow

   D   threaten

EXPLANATION: Context clues do not help much in this case, although if Jenny is listening for the breathing of the boar, she would not be able to hear it if the wind was blowing (C). B and D do not fit well in the sentence. For example, you would not say "air that didn't threaten all about her" (D). The correct answer is A.

Taking the Writing Assessment

The next Writing Assessment you will take will be in grade seven. For this test, you will be asked to write a short essay in response to a prompt. This essay will be an argumentative essay in which you will define a problem and propose a solution or evaluate an issue and present an opinion. Your essay will be scored based on its **content** and on your use of **writing conventions.** You will receive a score for content, a score for conventions, and a total writing score. Take a look at the rubric below and the one on page NC27 to understand the different scores you might receive.

CONTENT RUBRIC

The following rubric tells you which content elements scorers will look for in your paper.

A 4-point paper

- has a clear topic or subject. This topic may not be stated in a topic sentence, but the whole paper focuses on the topic.

- is organized to reflect the way the ideas or events in the paper go together.

- logically relates ideas or events to one another and has no gaps in logic or information.

- contains only information that clearly supports the topic.

- uses plenty of specific details to support the topic.

- uses appropriate, precise vocabulary and a variety of correct sentence structures.

A 3-point paper

- has a fairly clear topic or subject. This may not be stated in a topic sentence, but almost all of the paper focuses on the topic.

- is mostly organized to reflect the way the ideas or events in the paper go together.

- logically relates ideas or events to one another and has few gaps in logic or information.

- contains information that supports the topic.

- uses some specific details to support the topic.

- generally uses appropriate, precise vocabulary and a variety of correct sentence structures.

A 2-point paper

- has a vague topic or subject. Some of the paper focuses on the topic.

- is generally not organized to reflect the way the ideas or events in the paper go together.

- may not logically relate ideas or events to one another and has major gaps in logic or information.

- may contain a large amount of information that does not support the topic.

- uses general, undeveloped details to support the topic.

- generally does not use appropriate, precise vocabulary or a variety of correct sentence structures.

A 1-point paper

- has an unclear or confusing topic or subject. The paper may not focus on the topic.

- is not organized to reflect the way the ideas or events in the paper go together.

- does not logically relate ideas or events to one another and has major gaps in logic or information.

- may contain a large amount of information that does not support the topic.

- uses few details. These details do not support the topic or are confusing.

- does not use appropriate, precise vocabulary and may not use a variety of correct sentence structures.

A NS (non-scorable) paper

- cannot be read.

- is blank.

- is written in a foreign language.

- restates the prompt.

- is off-topic or incoherent.

CONVENTIONS RUBRIC

Your paper will also be scored for your use of English writing conventions according to the following rubric.

A 2-point paper

- uses correctly formed sentences.

- shows correct agreement, tense, and case.

- uses correct capitalization, punctuation, and spelling.

A 1-point paper

- uses some correctly formed sentences.

- sometimes shows correct agreement, tense, and case.

- uses some correct capitalization, punctuation, and spelling.

A 0-point paper

- does not use correctly formed sentences.

- does not show correct agreement, tense, and case.

- does not use correct capitalization, punctuation, and spelling.

STEPS FOR TAKING THE WRITING ASSESSMENT

Here are some steps and a suggested timetable you can use when responding to the writing prompt on the Writing Assessment, Grade 7. You'll probably find these steps in the writing process comfortable and familiar.

Watch Your Time

Prewriting	10 min.
Drafting	25 min.
Revising	15 min.
Proofreading	10 min.
Writing the Final Draft	15 min.

STEP 1   **Analyze the writing prompt.** Read the prompt and think about what it means.

STEP 2   **Plan what you will say.** You have about seventy-five minutes to work on your paper, so take about ten minutes for prewriting. Make notes on scratch paper. Use a cluster diagram or other graphic organizer to list main ideas and supporting details. Number your major points in the order you think you will use them.

STEP 3   **Draft your paper.** Allow twenty-five minutes for drafting your paper. Pay special attention to creating a strong opening paragraph and a definite closing. Strive to express your ideas as clearly as you can and in an order your readers will understand. Also, include relevant details to support and elaborate each major point. Vary the kinds of sentences (simple, compound, complex) you use.

STEP 4   **Revise your paper.** Allow fifteen minutes for re-reading and revising your first draft. Make sure you have clearly expressed a main idea. Look for places where you can add transitions or combine sentences to make your sentences flow smoothly together. Strengthen your paper by inserting additional supporting details.

STEP 5   **Proofread your paper.** Take at least ten minutes to search for and correct errors in grammar, usage, and mechanics.

STEP 6   **Write the final paper.** Allow about fifteen minutes to copy your final draft into the response booklet. Make sure your handwriting is readable! If you need to make major corrections, neatly cross out words and rewrite them correctly.

A SAMPLE WRITING PROMPT

As stated previously, the writing prompt on the grade seven Writing Assessment asks you to write an **argumentative essay.** In this essay, you will offer a solution to a problem or present your position for an issue. Whether you write a problem/solution essay or an evaluative essay, you will need to support your ideas with evidence. Don't worry about research. The prompt will present a familiar problem or issue that does not require research. Below you will find a sample prompt. As you read the prompt, look for clue words that tell you if you should write a problem/solution essay or an evaluative essay.

> Your community has never had a need for laws to regulate dogs. Now, however, packs of dogs are roaming the streets. The dogs destroy property and could be dangerous to people and other animals. Your town council or neighborhood association will meet to discuss the problem tonight.
>
> Write a speech to present to your town council or neighborhood association recommending a solution for the dog problem.

As you write your speech, be sure to:
- Focus on a solution to the problem of packs of dogs.
- Consider the purpose, audience, and context of your speech.
- Present your ideas in a logical manner.
- Include relevant and specific details.
- Edit your speech for correct grammar and usage.

PREWRITING: ORGANIZING YOUR IDEAS

Gather your ideas. First, brainstorm possible solutions for the problem presented in the prompt. You might want to use a cluster diagram. Write the problem in the center, and then write possible solutions around it. Write all the solutions that you can think of—even those that seem far-fetched. You will evaluate them next.

Choose a solution. Now review all of your possible solutions and choose the best solution for the problem. Ask yourself the following questions to assess each possible solution.

- **Is it effective?** Will the solution actually solve the current problem? Will it keep the problem from happening in the future?

- **Is it fair?** Does the solution respect the rights of everyone involved? For instance, outlawing dogs takes away people's right to have dogs as pets. Impounding and destroying all loose dogs is unfair because family pets that manage to get out of their fences would be destroyed along with stray dogs. Asking residents to securely fasten trash containers is not reasonable because dogs can turn over and spill trash that is in a secure container. Asking people to carry pepper spray is not fair because it violates people's right to feel safe in their streets.

- **Is it practical?** How easy is the solution to implement? How much money will it cost? How will it be paid for?

DRAFTING: GETTING IT DOWN ON PAPER

Time to write. Now it is time to draft your speech. First, define the problem. Then, present your solution. Use the questions you asked yourself during prewriting to tell why your solution is effective, fair, and practical. To end your essay, restate your solution and ask your audience to adopt it.

REVISING AND PROOFREADING: POLISHING YOUR DRAFT

The final step. Before you write your final speech, read it a couple of times. Make sure that your points are clear and expressed with style. Also, proofread your first draft to catch mistakes in grammar, usage, mechanics, and spelling. Remember that scorers of the Writing Assessment will be looking for correct

- sentence formation

- agreement, tense, and case

- capitalization, punctuation, and spelling

WRITING THE FINAL DRAFT

Here is one writer's final draft in response to the prompt on page NC29. This essay would likely receive high content and conventions scores based on North Carolina's criteria.

Pleasant Hills Must Pass a Leash Law

We can all agree that our community faces a serious problem when it comes to dogs roaming the streets unattended. We all know what it is like to wake up on Wednesday morning to find that all our garbage and recycling has been spilled out onto the street. We know what it is like to begin walking to a park or store only to find a pack of growling dogs in our path. We all know what it is like to feel threatened by unfamiliar dogs coming up to your dog while you are taking a walk. The problem of stray dogs must be addressed, and I believe the best way to solve it is by passing a leash law.

The leash law can solve our problem if it is strictly enforced. All stray dogs would be rounded up and their owners identified. The owners of stray dogs would be ticketed and fined. To effectively discourage dog owners from allowing their pets to run loose, the fine must be substantial. If the fine is large enough, dog owners will repair fences and take other steps to keep their dogs at home to avoid paying the fine.

Unlike some other possible solutions to the problem, a leash law would be fair. It would not punish responsible dog owners, who walk their dogs on a leash or contain them in the backyards, or the dogs themselves. After all, Rover can't help it if his master leaves the gate open. Instead, it would punish only dog owners who allow their dogs to run free. It would protect residents' rights to be safe in their neighborhoods and to own dogs as pets.

Finally, a leash law is a practical solution to our problem. We could start enforcing it with a volunteer animal control committee. Members of this committee would round up the stray dogs, identify their owners, and write tickets. The fines paid by owners of stray dogs could be used to hire a part-time dogcatcher who would take over from the volunteers. In this way, the leash law would pay for itself.

No one in Pleasant Hill has been bitten by a stray dog—yet. Let's act quickly before anyone is injured. Please pass a leash law today.

CHARACTERISTICS OF AN EXCELLENT PAPER

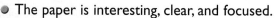

When you have finished your paper, how can you tell whether it will earn a high score? Evaluate your writing by comparing it with the characteristics of an excellent paper below.

- The paper is interesting, clear, and focused.

- The ideas are thoroughly explained and supported with appropriate details and examples.

- The organization of ideas is strong and moves the reader smoothly and naturally through the paper.

- Language use is mature and effective.

- Knowledge of language and its rules adds to the effectiveness of the paper.

HOLT
ELEMENTS OF
LITERATURE

Introductory
Course

HOLT, RINEHART AND WINSTON

A Harcourt Education Company

Orlando • **Austin** • New York • San Diego • Toronto • London

EDITORIAL
Project Directors: Kathleen Daniel, Mescal Evler
Executive Editor: Juliana Koenig
Senior Book Editor: Jennifer Johnson
Senior Product Manager: Don Wulbrecht
Managing Editor: Marie Price
Associate Managing Editor: Elizabeth LaManna
Editorial Staff: Kerry Johnson, Evan Wilson, Sari Wilson
Copyediting Manager: Michael Neibergall
Copyediting Supervisor: Mary Malone
Copyeditors: Christine Altgelt, Elizabeth Dickson, Emily Force, Leora Harris, Anne Heausler,
    Julia Thomas Hu, Kathleen Scheiner, Nancy Shore
Editorial Support: Christine Degollado, Betty Gabriel, Janet Jenkins, Mark Koenig, Erik Netcher,
    Gloria Shahan
Editorial Permissions: Mark Koenig, Sally Garland

Index: Tamsin Nutter

ART, DESIGN, AND PRODUCTION
Director: Athena Blackorby
Senior Design Director: Betty Mintz
Designer: Paul Caullett
Senior Picture Researcher: Mary Monaco
Picture Researcher: Susan Sato
Production Coordinator: Carol Marunas

Cover
Photo Credits: (inset) *Landscape With Horses* (1934) by John Ward Lockwood. Oil on canvas
    (30" × 40⅛"). Courtesy of The Anschutz Collection. Photograph by William J. O'Connor.
    (background) Photograph of horses © Will and Deni McIntyre/Getty Images.

7 048 05

Program Author

Kylene Beers established the reading pedagogy for *Elements of Literature*. A former middle-school teacher, Dr. Beers has turned her commitment to helping readers having difficulty into the major focus of her research, writing, speaking, and teaching. Dr. Beers is currently Senior Reading Researcher at the Child Study Center of the School Development Program at Yale University and was formerly a Research Associate Professor at the University of Houston. Dr. Beers is also currently the editor of the National Council of Teachers of English journal *Voices from the Middle*. She is the author of *When Kids Can't Read: What Teachers Can Do* and the co-editor of *Into Focus: Understanding and Creating Middle School Readers*. Dr. Beers is the 2001 recipient of the Richard Halle Award from the NCTE for outstanding contributions to middle-level literacy education. She has served on the review boards of the *English Journal* and *The Alan Review*. Dr. Beers currently serves on the board of directors of the International Reading Association's Special Interest Group on Adolescent Literature.

Special Contributors

Flo Ota De Lange and **Sheri Henderson** helped plan and organize the program and played key roles in developing and preparing the informational materials. They also wrote Test Smarts.

Flo Ota De Lange is a former teacher with a thirty-year second career in psychotherapy, during which she studied learning processes in children and adults. These careers have led to her third career, as a writer.

Sheri Henderson brings to the program twenty years of experience as a middle-school research practitioner and full-time reading and language arts teacher at La Paz Intermediate School in Saddleback Valley Unified School District in California. She regularly speaks at statewide and national conferences.

Since 1991, DeLangeHenderson LLC has published forty-three titles designed to integrate the teaching of literature with standards requirements and state and national tests.

Writers

John Malcolm Brinnin, author of six volumes of poetry that have received many prizes and awards, was a member of the American Academy and Institute of Arts and Letters. He was a critic of poetry and a biographer of poets and was for a number of years Director of New York's famous Poetry Center. His teaching career, begun at Vassar College, included long terms at the University of Connecticut and Boston University, where he succeeded Robert Lowell as Professor of Creative Writing and Contemporary Letters. Mr. Brinnin wrote *Dylan Thomas in America: An Intimate Journal* and *Sextet: T. S. Eliot & Truman Capote & Others.*

John Leggett is a novelist, biographer, and teacher. He went to the Writer's Workshop at the University of Iowa in the spring of 1969, expecting to work there for a single semester. In 1970, he assumed temporary charge of the program, and for the next seventeen years he was its director. Mr. Leggett's novels include *Wilder Stone, The Gloucester Branch, Who Took the Gold Away?, Gulliver House,* and *Making Believe.* He is also the author of the highly acclaimed biography *Ross and Tom: Two American Tragedies* and of a biography of William Saroyan, *A Daring Young Man.* Mr. Leggett lives in California's Napa Valley.

Joan Burditt is a writer and editor who has a master's degree in education with a specialization in reading. She taught for several years in Texas, where her experience included work in programs for readers having difficulty. Since then she has developed and written instructional materials for middle-school language arts texts.

Madeline Travers Hovland, who taught middle school for several years, is a writer of educational materials. She studied English at Bates College and received a master's degree in education from Harvard University.

Richard Kelso is a writer and editor whose children's books include *Building a Dream: Mary Bethune's School; Walking for Freedom: The Montgomery Bus Boycott; Days of Courage: The Little Rock Story;* and *The Case of the Amistad Mutiny.*

Mara Rockliff is a writer and editor with a degree in American civilization from Brown University. She has written dramatizations of classic stories for middle-school students, collected in a book called *Stories for Performance.* She has also published feature stories in national newspapers and is currently writing a novel for young adults.

Fannie Safier has worked as a teacher in New York City schools. She has been writing and editing educational materials for more than thirty years.

Program Consultants

READING CONSULTANT

Judith L. Irvin served as a reading consultant for the content-area readers: *The Ancient World; A World in Transition;* and *The United States: Change and Challenge.* Dr. Irvin is a Professor of Education at Florida State University. She writes a column, "What Research Says to the Middle Level Practitioner," for the *Middle School Journal* and serves as the literacy expert for the *Middle Level News,* published by the California League of Middle Schools. Her several books include the companion volumes *Reading and the Middle School Student: Strategies to Enhance Literacy* and *Reading and the High School Student: Strategies to Enhance Literacy* (with Buehl and Klemp).

SENIOR PROGRAM CONSULTANT

Carol Jago is the editor of CATE's quarterly journal, *California English.* She teaches English at Santa Monica High School, in Santa Monica, and directs the California Reading and Literature Project at UCLA. She also writes a weekly education column for the *Los Angeles Times.* She is the author of several books, including two in a series on contemporary writers in the classroom: *Alice Walker in the Classroom* and *Nikki Giovanni in the Classroom.* She is also the author of *With Rigor for All: Teaching the Classics to Contemporary Students* and *Beyond Standards: Excellence in the High School English Classroom.*

CRITICAL REVIEWERS

Dr. Julie M. T. Chan
Director of Literacy
   Instruction
Newport-Mesa Unified
   School District
Costa Mesa, California

Kathy Dubose
Murchison Junior High
   School
Austin, Texas

Pamela Dukes
Boude Storey Middle
   School
Dallas, Texas

Diana Edie
Bret Harte Middle
   School
Hayward, California

Debra Hardick
Bennet Middle School
Manchester, Connecticut

Cheri Howell
Reading Specialist
Covina-Valley Unified
   School District
Covina, California

José M. Ibarra-Tiznado
ELL Program Coordinator
Bassett Unified School
   District
La Puente, California

Dr. Ronald Klemp
Instructor
California State
   University, Northridge
Northridge, California

Colette F. McDonald
HB DuPont Middle
   School
Hockessin, Delaware

Jennifer Oehrlein
Tewinkle Middle School
Costa Mesa, California

Jeff Read
Oak Grove Middle
   School
Clearwater, Florida

Constance Ridenour
Ford Middle School
Brook Park, Ohio

Judith Shane
Carr Intermediate
   School
Santa Ana, California

Fern M. Sheldon
K–12 Curriculum and
   Instruction Specialist
Rowland Unified School
   District
Rowland Heights,
   California

Karen Simons
Slausen Middle School
Ann Arbor, Michigan

**FIELD-TEST
PARTICIPANTS**

Kristina Chow
Martha Baldwin School
Alhambra, California

Katrina Hunt
Ida Price Middle School
San Jose, California

Candice Phillips
South Hills Middle
   School
Pittsburgh,
   Pennsylvania

CONTENTS IN BRIEF

Collection 1

Plot: Moments of Truth

LITERARY FOCUS
Analyzing Plot and Setting

INFORMATIONAL FOCUS
Analyzing Structural Features
of Media

Collection 2

Characters: The People You'll Meet

LITERARY FOCUS
Analyzing Character

INFORMATIONAL FOCUS
Taking Notes and Outlining

Collection 3

Theme: The Heart of the Matter

LITERARY FOCUS
Analyzing Theme

INFORMATIONAL FOCUS
Evaluating Evidence

Collection 4

Forms of Fiction

LITERARY FOCUS
Identifying and Analyzing
Forms of Fiction

INFORMATIONAL FOCUS
Analyzing Comparison
and Contrast

A10   Contents

Zora Neale Hurston

Collection 5

Biography and Autobiography: Unforgettable Personalities

LITERARY FOCUS
Analyzing First- and
Third-Person Narration

INFORMATIONAL FOCUS
Connecting and Clarifying
Main Ideas

Collection 6

The Writer's Craft: Metaphors, Symbols, and Images

LITERARY FOCUS
Analyzing Literary Devices

INFORMATIONAL FOCUS
Making Assertions About a Text

Collection 7

POETRY

LITERARY FOCUS
Analyzing Sound Effects and Figures of Speech

Vocabulary Development

Identifying and Interpreting Figurative Language 656

Collection 8

Literary Criticism: You Be the Judge

LITERARY FOCUS
Responding Critically to Literature

INFORMATIONAL FOCUS
Preparing Applications;
Analyzing Faulty Reasoning

Resource Center

SKILLS, WORKSHOPS, AND FEATURES

SKILLS

ELEMENTS OF LITERATURE ESSAYS

READING SKILLS AND STRATEGIES LESSONS

LITERARY SKILLS

READING SKILLS FOR LITERARY TEXTS

READING SKILLS FOR INFORMATIONAL TEXTS

VOCABULARY SKILLS

WORKSHOPS

WRITING WORKSHOPS

FEATURES

GRAMMAR LINKS

SKILLS REVIEW

TEST SMARTS

LANGUAGE HANDBOOK

SPELLING HANDBOOK

COMMUNICATIONS HANDBOOK

SPEAKING AND LISTENING HANDBOOK

MEDIA HANDBOOK

SELECTIONS BY GENRE

FICTION

SHORT STORIES

DRAMA

POETRY

NONFICTION

INFORMATIONAL TEXTS

INFORMATIONAL ARTICLES

MAGAZINE ARTICLES

WEB PAGES/WEB-SITE ARTICLES

INTERVIEWS

APPLICATION FORMS

Elements of Literature on the Internet

TO THE STUDENT

At the *Elements of Literature* Internet site, you can read texts by professional writers and learn the inside stories behind your favorite authors. You can also build your word power and analyze messages in the media. As you move through *Elements of Literature*, you will find the best online resources at **go.hrw.com.**

Here's how to log on:

1. Start your Web browser, and enter **go.hrw.com** in the Address or Location field.

Back   Forward   Reload   Home   Search

Location: http://go.hrw.com

2. Note the keyword in your textbook.

INTERNET

More About Plot and Setting

Keyword: LE5 6-1

3. Enter the keyword, and click "go."

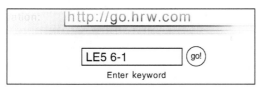

http://go.hrw.com

LE5 6-1   go!

Enter keyword

FEATURES OF THE SITE

More About the Writer
Author biographies provide the inside stories behind the lives and works of great writers.

More About the Literary Element
Graphic organizers present visual representations of literary concepts.

Interactive Reading Model
Interactive Reading Workshops guide you through high-interest informational articles and allow you to share your opinions through pop-up questions and polls.

More Writer's Models
Interactive Writer's Models present annotations and reading tips to help you with your own writing. Printable Professional Models and Student Models provide you with quality writing by real writers and students from across the country.

Vocabulary Activity
Interactive vocabulary-building activities help you build your word power.

Projects and Activities
Projects and activities help you extend your study of literature through writing, research, art, and public speaking.

Speeches
Video clips from historical speeches provide you with the tools you need to analyze elements of great speechmaking.

Media Tutorials
Media tutorials help you dissect messages in the media and learn to create your own multimedia presentations.

Battle scene from the comic opera *The Seafarer* by Paul Klee. Watercolor.

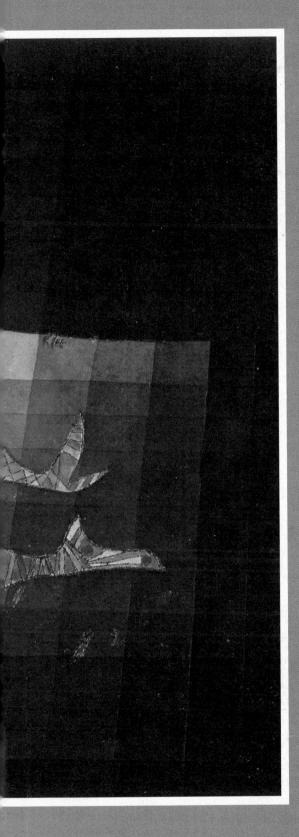

Plot: Moments of Truth

Literary Focus:
Analyzing Plot
and Setting

Informational Focus:
Analyzing
Structural Features
of Media

INTERNET

Collection
Resources
Keyword: LE5 6-1

Elements of Literature
Plot and Setting *by* Madeline Travers Hovland

Plot: The Story's Structure

Plot is the series of events in a story. Plot answers the question "What happened?"

1 The first part of the plot tells you about the story's basic situation. It often answers these questions:

- Who is the main **character**?

- What is the character's basic problem, or **conflict**?

A **conflict** is a struggle. One kind of conflict involves two characters opposing each other. Another kind of conflict involves a character struggling with a **setting**—a flood, a drought, a hurricane, a mountain, a dying space station. Conflict might also involve a character against a whole group of other people. Conflict can even result from a struggle inside a character—for confidence, for example, or for self-control.

Here's the beginning of a story in which the setting creates the problem:

As the hot July sun slipped below the horizon, a cooling darkness filled Central Valley. Lisa had just fallen asleep when the windows of the trailer rattled like a snake giving warning. The trailer swayed back and forth. Lisa could hear the baby screaming. Papa yelled, "Outside! Get out! Get out! It's an earthquake!"

2 As the story continues, the characters take action to solve their life-threatening problem. **Complications** arise, which means new problems come up. All of this creates suspense. We worry, "What will happen to the little family?"

The earth groaned, and a river of mud slid down the canyon. The family huddled together in the dark. Mama tore up a sheet to make a sling for Papa's broken arm. Papa shined his flashlight on the wreck that used to be the trailer. "It could explode," he warned. "Don't get any closer."

The baby kept screaming. Lisa's mother said, "I have nothing to feed him. What are we going to do?" Suddenly the earth rumbled again. Lisa looked back at the trailer and saw fallen electric wires dangling all around it.

3 When you read a good story, you become more and more involved with the plot as the characters try to solve their problems. You want to know what will happen next and how the conflict will turn out. At last you reach the **climax,** the most exciting moment of the story. This is the point where you find out how the conflict will be resolved.

North Carolina Competency Goal
5.01

INTERNET
More About Plot and Setting
Keyword: LE5 6-1

Literary Skills
Understand plot structure and the way setting influences plot.

Lisa stumbled down the side of the canyon. She could hear a siren coming closer. The lights of a helicopter shone on her like a spotlight. "Stop! Help us!" she cried, frantically waving her arms. The copter clattered to the ground.

4 In the **resolution,** the final part of the plot, the characters' problems are solved one way or another and the story ends. In this story we may find the family in their grandmother's home, a safe distance from the scene of the quake. We may see the family returning to their ruined home weeks after the earthquake and starting to rebuild their lives. What other resolutions can you think of?

Setting and Conflict

Setting is where and when the action of a story takes place. Some stories could take place almost anywhere, but in most stories, setting plays a more important role. Writers often use setting to create atmosphere: scary, peaceful, gloomy. In many stories, setting controls the action; it is so crucial to the plot that the story could not take place anywhere else.

In many stories the characters are in conflict with the setting. This is what happens in the little story you just read. In that story the family must struggle to survive an earthquake. Their very lives are threatened by their setting.

We see this kind of conflict a lot in the movies. You might have seen characters fight to survive on a cold mountain with no food. You might have seen

a movie about people marooned in a rowboat in the middle of the Pacific Ocean or trapped by a raging forest fire. All of these are conflicts with settings.

In these stories, if the characters can survive the threat posed by the setting, the story is resolved happily. If the setting is more powerful than the human characters, then the story's resolution is very sad indeed.

Practice

The main events of a **plot** can be charted in a diagram like this one:

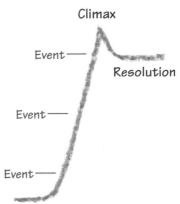

Fill out a diagram like this one, tracing the plot of a movie or book you know well. Try to find a story in which a character struggles with a setting that threatens his or her life.

Reading Skills and Strategies

Summarizing the Plot: Retelling

by Kylene Beers

During dinner, a five-year-old told his mom about the story his teacher had read to him at school: "It was about a girl, and she had this purse, and it was purple, and she wanted to play with it, but the teacher said no, and then she did, and then she was in trouble, and then she drew a picture, and then the teacher found it, and then she was sad, and then they danced, and everyone was happy, the end!"

The mom laughed and told him he did a good job of telling her about the story. He nodded and kept eating.

What Is Retelling?

The mom was right: Her little boy's **summary** was a good one—for a five-year-old. However, it wouldn't be a good summary for someone in middle school. It has events out of order and suffers from the "and then this happened" syndrome.

North Carolina Competency Goal 2.01

You can eliminate the habit of stringing events together with a series of *and then's* by using a strategy called **retelling.** Retelling will help you to cover critical points in a story, keep them in order, and connect them in a logical way.

Using the Strategy

SKILLS FOCUS

Reading Skills Retell story events.

Before you read "Dragon, Dragon," study the **Retelling Tips** at the right. Think about the prompts in the margins of the story as you read. After you finish, use the **Retelling Guide** on page 16 to help you give an oral summary of this story.

Retelling Tips

- Start by telling the title and author of the story.

- Identify the characters.

- Tell the main events, keeping them in the right order.

- Explain the conflict, or main problem.

- Explain how the story ends.

- Tell what you liked or didn't like about the story.

- Use words like *first, next, then, later,* and *finally* to help keep everything in order.

- Use words and phrases like *but, however,* or *on the other hand* when something happens that contradicts something that's already happened.

DRAGON, DRAGON

John Gardner ❶

There was once a king whose kingdom was plagued[1] by a dragon. The king did not know which way to turn. The king's knights were all cowards who hid under their beds whenever the dragon came in sight, so they were of no use to the king at all. And the king's wizard could not help either because, being old, he had forgotten his magic spells. Nor could the wizard look up the spells that had slipped his mind, for he had unfortunately misplaced his wizard's book many years before. The king was at his wit's end. ❷

Every time there was a full moon, the dragon came out of his lair and ravaged[2] the countryside. He frightened maidens and stopped up chimneys and broke store windows and set people's clocks back and made dogs bark until no one could hear himself think.

He tipped over fences and robbed graves and put frogs in people's drinking water and tore the last chapters out of novels and changed house numbers around.

He stole spark plugs out of people's cars and put firecrackers in people's cigars and stole the clappers from all the church bells and sprung every bear trap for miles around so the bears could wander wherever they pleased.

And to top it all off, he changed around all the roads in the kingdom so that people could not get anywhere except by starting out in the wrong direction.

---

1. **plagued** v.: troubled.
2. **ravaged** v.: violently destroyed.

As you read, you'll find this open-book sign at certain points in the story: . Stop at these points, and think about what you've just read. Sometimes a part of the retelling will be there for you. At other times you'll do the retelling.

RETELL

❶ Stop and notice the title and author. What's the chance that this story is about a dragon?

RETELL

❷ Where's this story set? Name four characters introduced in this paragraph.

" Dragon, dragon, how do you do?
I've come from the king to murder you."

RETELL

❸ In one sentence,
describe the problem
that this king and his
kingdom face.

"That," said the king in a fury, "is enough!" And he called a meeting
of everyone in the kingdom. ❸

Now it happened that there lived in the kingdom a wise old cobbler
who had a wife and three sons. The cobbler and his family came to the
king's meeting and stood way in back by the door, for the cobbler had
a feeling that since he was nobody important, there had probably been
some mistake, and no doubt the king had intended the meeting for
everyone in the kingdom except his family and him.

"Ladies and gentlemen," said the king when everyone was present, "I've put up with that dragon as long as I can. He has got to be stopped."

All the people whispered amongst themselves, and the king smiled, pleased with the impression he had made.

But the wise cobbler said gloomily, "It's all very well to talk about it—but how are you going to do it?"

And now all the people smiled and winked as if to say, "Well, King, he's got you there!"

The king frowned.

"It's not that His Majesty hasn't tried," the queen spoke up loyally.

"Yes," said the king, "I've told my knights again and again that they ought to slay that dragon. But I can't *force* them to go. I'm not a tyrant."

"Why doesn't the wizard say a magic spell?" asked the cobbler.

"He's done the best he can," said the king.

The wizard blushed and everyone looked embarrassed. "I used to do all sorts of spells and chants when I was younger," the wizard explained. "But I've lost my spell book, and I begin to fear I'm losing my memory too. For instance, I've been trying for days to recall one spell I used to do. I forget, just now, what the deuce it was for. It went something like—

> *Bimble,*
> *Wimble,*
> *Cha, Cha*
> *CHOOMPF!"* ❹

Suddenly, to everyone's surprise, the queen turned into a rosebush. "Oh dear," said the wizard.

"Now you've done it," groaned the king.

"Poor Mother," said the princess.

"I don't know what can have happened," the wizard said nervously, "but don't worry, I'll have her changed back in a jiffy." He shut his eyes and racked his brain for a spell that would change her back.

But the king said quickly, "You'd better leave well enough alone. If you change her into a rattlesnake, we'll have to chop off her head." ❺

Meanwhile the cobbler stood with his hands in his pockets, sighing at the waste of time. "About the dragon . . . ," he began.

RETELL

❹ Everyone is at the king's castle. The king is explaining why he can't get rid of the dragon. Why haven't the knights fought the dragon? What about the wizard? Finish this sentence: The king says that the knights haven't fought the dragon because _____, and the wizard hasn't used a magic spell because _____.

RETELL

❺ Why does the queen turn into a rosebush? People don't seem very upset. What does that tell you about how seriously you should take this story?

"Oh yes," said the king. "I'll tell you what I'll do. I'll give the princess's hand in marriage to anyone who can make the dragon stop."

"It's not enough," said the cobbler. "She's a nice enough girl, you understand. But how would an ordinary person support her? Also, what about those of us that are already married?"

"In that case," said the king, "I'll offer the princess's hand or half the kingdom or both—whichever is most convenient."

The cobbler scratched his chin and considered it. "It's not enough," he said at last. "It's a good enough kingdom, you understand, but it's too much responsibility."

"Take it or leave it," the king said.

"I'll leave it," said the cobbler. And he shrugged and went home.

But the cobbler's eldest son thought the bargain was a good one, for the princess was very beautiful, and he liked the idea of having half the kingdom to run as he pleased. So he said to the king, "I'll accept those terms, Your Majesty. By tomorrow morning the dragon will be slain." ❻ 📖

"Bless you!" cried the king.

"Hooray, hooray, hooray!" cried all the people, throwing their hats in the air.

The cobbler's eldest son beamed with pride, and the second eldest looked at him enviously. The youngest son said timidly, "Excuse me, Your Majesty, but don't you think the queen looks a little unwell? If I were you, I think I'd water her."

"Good heavens," cried the king, glancing at the queen, who had been changed into a rosebush, "I'm glad you mentioned it!"

Now the cobbler's eldest son was very clever and was known far and wide for how quickly he could multiply fractions in his head. He was perfectly sure he could slay the dragon by somehow or other playing a trick on him, and he didn't feel that he needed his

RETELL

❻ You should be able to remember meeting the king, finding out what the dragon is doing to the kingdom, discovering why the knights and wizard won't help, and finding out about the king's offer. What is his offer? If you can't remember one of these things, re-read the text up to this point.

wise old father's advice. But he thought it was only polite to ask, and so he went to his father, who was working as usual at his cobbler's bench, and said, "Well, Father, I'm off to slay the dragon. Have you any advice to give me?"

The cobbler thought a moment and replied, "When and if you come to the dragon's lair, recite the following poem.

Dragon, dragon, how do you do?
I've come from the king to murder you.

Say it very loudly and firmly, and the dragon will fall, God willing, at your feet."

"How curious!" said the eldest son. And he thought to himself, "The old man is not as wise as I thought. If I say something like that to the dragon, he will eat me up in an instant. The way to kill a dragon is to outfox him." And keeping his opinion to himself, the eldest son set forth on his quest.

When he came at last to the dragon's lair, which was a cave, the eldest son slyly disguised himself as a peddler and knocked on the door and called out, "Hello there!"

"There's nobody home!" roared a voice.

The voice was as loud as an earthquake, and the eldest son's knees knocked together in terror.

"I don't come to trouble you," the eldest son said meekly. "I merely thought you might be interested in looking at some of our brushes. Or if you'd prefer," he added quickly, "I could leave our catalog with you and I could drop by again, say, early next week."

"I don't want any brushes," the voice roared, "and I especially don't want any brushes next week."

"Oh," said the eldest son. By now his knees were knocking together so badly that he had to sit down. ❼

Suddenly a great shadow fell over him, and the eldest son looked up. It was the dragon. The eldest son drew his sword, but the dragon lunged[3] and swallowed him in a single gulp, sword and all, and the eldest son found himself in the dark of the dragon's belly. "What a fool I was not to listen to my wise old father!" thought the eldest son. And he began to weep bitterly.

"Well," sighed the king the next morning, "I see the dragon has not been slain yet."

---

3. **lunged** (lunjd) *v.:* plunged forward suddenly.

RETELL

❼ Now you've met the first person who's going to go after the dragon. What advice did his father give him? Do you think he's going to succeed? If not, predict how many other people will try.

"I'm just as glad, personally," said the princess, sprinkling the queen. "I would have had to marry that eldest son, and he had warts."

Now the cobbler's middle son decided it was his turn to try. The middle son was very strong and was known far and wide for being able to lift up the corner of a church. He felt perfectly sure he could slay the dragon by simply laying into him, but he thought it would be only polite to ask his father's advice. So he went to his father and said to him, "Well, Father, I'm off to slay the dragon. Have you any advice for me?"

The cobbler told the middle son exactly what he'd told the eldest.

"When and if you come to the dragon's lair, recite the following poem.

Dragon, dragon, how do you do?
I've come from the king to murder you.

Say it very loudly and firmly, and the dragon will fall, God willing, at your feet."

"What an odd thing to say," thought the middle son. "The old man is not as wise as I thought. You have to take these dragons by surprise." But he kept his opinion to himself and set forth.

When he came in sight of the dragon's lair, the middle son spurred his horse to a gallop and thundered into the entrance, swinging his sword with all his might.

But the dragon had seen him while he was still a long way off, and being very clever, the dragon had crawled up on top of the door so that when the son came charging in, he went under the dragon and on to the back of the cave and slammed into the wall. Then the dragon chuckled and got down off the door, taking his time, and strolled back to where the man and the horse lay unconscious from the terrific blow. Opening his mouth as if for a yawn, the dragon swallowed the middle son in a single gulp and put the horse in the freezer to eat another day.

"What a fool I was not to listen to my wise old father," thought the middle son when he came to in the dragon's belly. And he too began to weep bitterly. ❽

That night there was a full moon, and the dragon ravaged the countryside so terribly that several families moved to another kingdom.

"Well," sighed the king in the morning, "still no luck in this dragon business, I see."

"I'm just as glad, myself," said the princess, moving her mother, pot and all, to the window, where the sun could get at her. "The cobbler's middle son was a kind of humpback."

RETELL

❽ What happened to the second son? Think of how you could explain what happened to the first two sons in one or two sentences. Don't use the phrase *and then*.

Now the cobbler's youngest son saw that his turn had come. He was very upset and nervous, and he wished he had never been born. He was not clever, like his eldest brother, and he was not strong, like his second-eldest brother. He was a decent, honest boy who always minded his elders.

He borrowed a suit of armor from a friend of his who was a knight, and when the youngest son put the armor on, it was so heavy he could hardly walk. From another knight he borrowed a sword, and that was so heavy that the only way the youngest son could get it to the dragon's lair was to drag it along behind his horse like a plow.

When everything was in readiness, the youngest son went for a last conversation with his father.

"Father, have you any advice to give me?" he asked.

"Only this," said the cobbler. "When and if you come to the dragon's lair, recite the following poem.

Dragon, dragon, how do you do?
I've come from the king to murder you.

Say it very loudly and firmly, and the dragon will fall, God willing, at your feet."

"Are you certain?" asked the youngest son uneasily.

"As certain as one can ever be in these matters," said the wise old cobbler.

And so the youngest son set forth on his quest. He traveled over hill and dale and at last came to the dragon's cave. ❾

The dragon, who had seen the cobbler's youngest son while he was still a long way off, was seated up above the door, inside the cave, waiting and smiling to himself. But minutes passed and no one came thundering in. The dragon frowned, puzzled, and was tempted to peek out. However, reflecting that patience seldom goes unrewarded, the dragon kept his head up out of sight and went on waiting. At last, when he could stand it no longer, the dragon craned[4] his neck and looked. There at the entrance of the cave stood a trembling young man in a suit of armor twice his size, struggling with a sword so heavy he could lift only one end of it at a time.

At sight of the dragon, the cobbler's youngest son began to tremble so violently that his armor rattled like a house caving in. He heaved with all his might at the sword and got the handle up level with his chest, but even now the point was down in the dirt. As loudly and firmly as he could manage, the youngest son cried—

Dragon, dragon, how do you do?
I've come from the king to murder you!

"What?" cried the dragon, flabbergasted. "You? *You?* Murder *Me???*" All at once he began to laugh, pointing at the little cobbler's son. "*He he he ho ha!*" he roared, shaking all over, and tears filled his eyes. "*He he he ho ho ho ha ha!*" laughed the dragon. He was laughing so hard he had to hang onto his sides, and he fell off the door and landed on his back, still laughing, kicking his legs helplessly, rolling from side to side, laughing and laughing and laughing.

The cobbler's son was annoyed. "I *do* come from the king to murder you," he said. "A person doesn't like to be laughed at for a thing like that."

"*He he he!*" wailed the dragon, almost sobbing, gasping for breath. "Of course not, poor dear boy! But really, *he he,* the *idea* of it, *ha ha*

---

4. **craned** *v.*: stretched (the neck) as a crane does.

Using the Strategy

RETELL

❾ Now you've met the third son. Describe him.

ha! And that simply ri*dic*ulous *poem!*" Tears streamed from the dragon's eyes, and he lay on his back perfectly helpless with laughter.

"It's a good poem," said the cobbler's youngest son loyally. "My father made it up." And growing angrier he shouted, "I want you to stop that laughing, or I'll—I'll—" But the dragon could not stop for the life of him. And suddenly, in a terrific rage, the cobbler's son began flopping the sword end over end in the direction of the dragon. Sweat ran off the youngest son's forehead, but he labored on, blistering mad, and at last, with one supreme heave, he had the sword standing on its handle a foot from the dragon's throat. Of its own weight the sword fell, slicing the dragon's head off.

"*He he ho huk,*" went the dragon—and then he lay dead. ❿

The two older brothers crawled out and thanked their younger brother for saving their lives. "We have learned our lesson," they said.

Then the three brothers gathered all the treasures from the dragon's cave and tied them to the back end of the youngest brother's horse and tied the dragon's head on behind the treasures and started home. "I'm glad I listened to my father," the youngest son thought. "Now I'll be the richest man in the kingdom."

There were hand-carved picture frames and silver spoons and boxes of jewels and chests of money and silver compasses and maps telling where there were more treasures buried when these ran out. There was also a curious old book with a picture of an owl on the cover, and inside, poems and odd sentences and recipes that seemed to make no sense.

When they reached the king's castle, the people all leaped for joy to see that the dragon was dead, and the princess ran out and kissed the youngest brother on the forehead, for secretly she had hoped it would be him.

"Well," said the king, "which half of the kingdom do you want?"

"My wizard's book!" exclaimed the wizard. "He's found my wizard's book!" He opened the book and ran his finger along under the words and then said in a loud voice, "Glmuzk, shkzmlp, blam!"

Instantly the queen stood before them in her natural shape, except she was soaking wet from being sprinkled too often. She glared at the king.

"Oh dear," said the king, hurrying toward the door. ⓫

Using the Strategy

RETELL

❿ How does the third son slay the dragon?

RETELL

⓫ Think of a few sentences that explain what happens once the dragon is dead. You might start it this way, "Once the dragon is dead, the two other brothers crawl out of his stomach. After that, they _____."

14   Collection 1 / Plot: Moments of Truth

Meet the Writer

John Gardner

A Twister of Tales

With characters like the hero who is so weak and puny he can't lift the sword and the wizard who can't remember his magic, **John Gardner** (1933–1982)

poked fun at old-fashioned fairy tales. The story you've just read is from *Dragon, Dragon, and Other Tales* (1975), his first collection for young readers. Gardner became famous with *Grendel* (1971), a novel for adults that offers a twist on the well-known English epic *Beowulf*. The epic is about the hero Beowulf, who battles and finally defeats the monster Grendel. Gardner twists this tale by telling his story from the monster's point of view.

When Gardner was young, his favorite storytellers were Charles Dickens and Walt Disney, the producer of animated films. Gardner believed that both created wonderful cartoon images, told stories that were as direct as fairy tales, and knew the value of broad comedy spiced up with a little weeping. Gardner kept a bust of Dickens in his study "to keep me honest."

Gardner was only forty-nine years old when he died in a motorcycle accident.

For Independent Reading

For more twisted fairy tales, read the other stories in *Dragon, Dragon, and Other Tales.* For twisted verses, look for Gardner's *A Child's Bestiary,* a popular collection of humorous poems about animals.

Practice the Strategy

Retelling: Summarizing the Plot

Remember how the five-year-old retold the story he had heard at school? Well, here's a portion of a better retelling of that story.

> "We heard a story called *Lilly's Purple Plastic Purse* by Kevin Henkes. The story takes place mostly in a kindergarten class. The main characters are Lilly, a girl who is in kindergarten, and her teacher. The story begins when Lilly's grandmother gives her a beautiful purple plastic purse for her birthday. Next, Lilly takes her special purse to school. Then she wants to play with it, but her teacher tells her to put it away."

Talk with a friend about how this retelling is different from the one on page 4. Then, look at the Retelling Guide on the right. Can you identify which parts of the guide are followed in the partial retelling above? What words are used in this retelling instead of *and then*?

PRACTICE 1

Using the tips on page 4 and the Retelling Guide, retell "Dragon, Dragon." Be sure to think about how you will connect the story's main events. Avoid the word *and*! Instead, use some of the connection words found on page 4. Here are some others you might find useful: *additionally, furthermore, then, as a result, following that, after that,* and *in conclusion.*

Retelling Guide

1. **Introduction**
   Begin with the title and the author of the story. Then, tell where and when the story is set.

2. **Characters**
   Tell the characters' names, and explain how the characters are related or connected to one another. Explain what the main character wants or is trying to do.

3. **Conflict**
   What is the main character's conflict, or problem? In other words, what's keeping the main character from getting what he or she wants?

4. **Complications**
   Describe the main events—what happens as the characters try to solve the conflict.

5. **Climax**
   Describe the climax, the most suspenseful moment in the story, when you discover at last how the main character will overcome the conflict (or be defeated).

6. **Resolution**
   Tell what happens after the climax. How does the story end?

7. **Personal Response**
   Add your own thoughts about the story.

Ask a partner to listen as you give a retelling of "Dragon, Dragon" and to rate what you say on a **Retelling Checklist** (like the one that follows).

Retelling Checklist

Name _____

Text _____

Directions: Use the following checklist to have someone rate your retelling. Ask the listener to decide if your retelling covers each question listed below a little, some, a lot, or not at all. Work on those things that you skipped or only covered a little.

0	1	2	3
Not at all	A little	Some	A lot

Does this retelling . . .

1. have a good beginning that states the title, author, and when and where the story takes place?
2. tell who the characters are and how they are related to one another?
3. include the main events?
4. keep those main events in the correct sequence?
5. explain how the main conflict, or problem, is resolved?
6. provide any personal comments about the story?

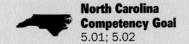 You can use the retelling strategy with the stories in this collection. If you want to review the elements of any plot, try **retelling.**

SKILLS FOCUS

Reading Skills
Retell story events.

North Carolina Competency Goal
5.01; 5.02

Just Once

Make the Connection
Quickwrite ✏️

Have you ever dreamed of walking onstage to accept an Oscar? Do you long to be a basketball star? Would you give anything to be the best dancer at your school? We aim for many different goals in life. One dream that many of us share is to hear the crowd cheering, just once, just for us. You may have to fight your way to that moment of glory. Tell what you are willing to do—and not willing to do—to be a star.

Literary Focus
Conflict

In this story, Bryan "the Moose" Crawford, a high school football player, longs to hear the crowd roaring his name. His campaign to make this happen creates conflict. **Conflict** is the struggle that pulls us into a story and won't let us go until we find out who (or what) wins.

Reading Skills 📖
Retelling

You can use a strategy called **retelling** to find the conflict and the important events in the plot. As you read this story, you'll see open-book signs (📖) alongside the text. At those points, stop and retell what has just happened. Focus on the major events that keep the plot moving. Jot down your retellings.

North Carolina Competency Goal
1.04; 4.01; 5.01; 5.02

INTERNET
Vocabulary Activity
Keyword: LE5 6-1

SKILLS FOCUS

Literary Skills
Understand conflict.

Reading Skills
Retell story events.

Vocabulary Development

This story is easy to read, but it does contain a few words that might be new to you. See if you can make up a sentence of your own for each of the following words:

devastating (dev'ə·stāt'iṇ) v. used as adj.: causing great damage. *The Moose's devastating attack punched a hole through the opposing team's line.*

nurturing (nʉr'chər·iŋ) v.: promoting the growth of; nursing. *The Moose's teammates suspected that he had been nurturing his dream for a while.*

anonymous (ə·nän'ə·məs) adj.: unknown; unidentified. *The Moose was tired of being anonymous.*

tolerant (täl'ər·ənt) adj.: patient; accepting of others. *A less tolerant coach might have become angry.*

ponder (pän'dər) v.: think over carefully. *Coach Williams walked off to ponder the Moose's request.*

JUST ONCE

Thomas J. Dygard

Everybody liked the Moose. To his father and mother he was Bryan—as in Bryan Jefferson Crawford—but to everyone at Bedford City High he was the Moose. He was large and strong, as you might imagine from his nickname, and he was pretty fast on his feet—sort of nimble, you might say—considering his size. He didn't have a pretty face but he had a quick and easy smile—"sweet," some of the teachers called it; "nice," others said.

But on the football field, the Moose was neither sweet nor nice. He was just strong and fast and a little bit <u>devastating</u> as the left tackle of the Bedford City Bears. When the Moose blocked somebody, he stayed blocked. When the Moose was called on to open a hole in the line for one of the Bears' runners, the hole more often than not resembled an open garage door.

Now in his senior season, the Moose had twice been named to the all-conference team and was considered a cinch for all-state. He spent a lot of his spare time, when he wasn't in a classroom or on the football field, reading letters from colleges eager to have the Moose pursue higher education—and football—at their institution.

But the Moose had a hang-up.

He didn't go public with his hang-up until the sixth game of the season. But, looking back, most of his teammates agreed that probably the Moose had been <u>nurturing</u> the hang-up secretly for two years or more.

The Moose wanted to carry the ball.

For sure, the Moose was not the first interior lineman in the history of football, or even the history of Bedford City High, who banged heads up front and wore bruises like badges of honor—and dreamed of racing down the field with the ball to the end zone[1] while everybody in the bleachers screamed his name.

But most linemen, it seems, are able to stifle the urge. The idea may pop into their minds from time to time, but in their hearts they know they can't run fast enough, they know they can't do that fancy dancing to elude tacklers, they know they aren't trained to read blocks. They know that their strengths and talents are best utilized in the line. Football is, after all, a team sport, and everyone plays the position where he most helps the team. And so these linemen, or most of them, go back to banging heads without saying the first word about the dream that flickered through their minds.

Not so with the Moose.

That sixth game, when the Moose's hang-up first came into public view, had ended with the Moose truly in all his glory as the Bears' left tackle. Yes, glory—but uncheered and sort of <u>anonymous</u>. The Bears were trailing 21–17 and had the ball on Mitchell High's five-yard line, fourth down,[2] with time running out. The rule in such a situation is simple—the best back carries the ball behind the best blocker—and it is a rule seldom violated by those in control of their faculties.[3] The Bears,

---

1. **end zone** *n.*: area between the goal line and the end line (the line marking the boundary of the playing area) at each end of a football field.
2. **fourth down:** In football the team holding the ball is allowed four downs, or attempts to carry the ball forward at least ten yards.
3. **faculties** *n.*: mental powers.

Vocabulary

devastating (dev′ə·stāt′iŋ) *v.* used as *adj.*: causing great damage.

nurturing (nʉr′chər·iŋ) *v.*: promoting the growth of; nursing.

anonymous (ə·nän′ə·məs) *adj.*: unknown; unidentified.

of course, followed the rule. That meant Jerry Dixon running behind the Moose's blocking. With the snap of the ball, the Moose knocked down one lineman, bumped another one aside, and charged forward to flatten an approaching linebacker. Jerry did a little jig behind the Moose and then ran into the end zone, virtually untouched, to win the game.

After circling in the end zone a moment while the cheers echoed through the night, Jerry did run across and hug the Moose, that's true. Jerry knew who had made the touchdown possible.

But it wasn't the Moose's name that everybody was shouting. The fans in the bleachers were cheering Jerry Dixon.

It was probably at that precise moment that the Moose decided to go public. ❶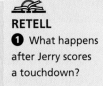

RETELL
❶ What happens after Jerry scores a touchdown?

In the dressing room, Coach Buford Williams was making his rounds among the cheering players and came to a halt in front of the Moose. "It was your great blocking that did it," he said.

"I want to carry the ball," the Moose said.

Coach Williams was already turning away and taking a step toward the next player due an accolade[4] when his brain registered the fact that the Moose had said something strange. He was expecting the Moose to say, "Aw, gee, thanks, Coach." That was what the Moose always said when the coach issued a compliment. But the Moose had said something else. The coach turned back to the Moose, a look of disbelief on his face. "What did you say?"

"I want to carry the ball."

---

4. **accolade** (ak′ə·lād′) *n.:* something said or done to express praise.

"I WANT TO CARRY THE BALL," THE MOOSE SAID.

Coach Williams was good at quick recoveries, as any high school football coach had better be. He gave a tolerant smile and a little nod and said, "You keep right on blocking, son."

This time Coach Williams made good on his turn and moved away from the Moose.

The following week's practice and the next Friday's game passed without further incident. After all, the game was a road game over at Cartwright High, thirty-five miles away. The Moose wanted to carry the ball in front of the Bedford City fans.

Vocabulary
tolerant (tӓl′ər·ənt) *adj.:* patient; accepting of others.

"SON, YOU'RE A GREAT LEFT TACKLE, A GREAT BLOCKER. LET'S LEAVE IT THAT WAY."

Then the Moose went to work.

He caught up with the coach on the way to the practice field on Wednesday. "Remember," he said, leaning forward and down a little to get his face in the coach's face, "I said I want to carry the ball."

Coach Williams must have been thinking about something else because it took him a minute to look up into the Moose's face, and even then he didn't say anything.

"I meant it," the Moose said.

"Meant what?"

"I want to run the ball."

"Oh," Coach Williams said. Yes, he remembered. "Son, you're a great left tackle, a great blocker. Let's leave it that way." ❷ 🔖

The Moose let the remaining days of the practice week and then the game on Friday night against Edgewood High pass while he reviewed strategies. The review led him to Dan Blevins, the Bears' quarterback. If the signal caller would join in, maybe Coach Williams would listen.

"Yeah, I heard," Dan said. "But, look, what about Joe Wright at guard, Bill Slocum at right tackle, even Herbie Watson at center. They might all want to carry the ball. What are we going to do—take turns? It doesn't work that way."

So much for Dan Blevins.

The Moose found that most of the players in the backfield agreed with Dan. They couldn't

🔖 **RETELL**
❷ How does Coach Williams respond to the Moose's request?

"JUST ONCE," THE MOOSE PLEADED.

see any reason why the Moose should carry the ball, especially in place of themselves. Even Jerry Dixon, who owed a lot of his glory to the Moose's blocking, gaped in disbelief at the Moose's idea. The Moose, however, got some support from his fellow linemen. Maybe they had dreams of their own, and saw value in a precedent.[5]

As the days went by, the word spread—not just on the practice field and in the corridors of Bedford City High, but all around town. The players by now were openly taking sides. Some thought it a jolly good idea that the Moose carry the ball. Others, like Dan Blevins, held to the purist[6] line—a left tackle plays left tackle, a ball carrier carries the ball, and that's it.

Around town, the vote wasn't even close. Everyone wanted the Moose to carry the ball.

"Look, son," Coach Williams said to the Moose on the practice field the Thursday before the Benton Heights game, "this has gone far enough. Fun is fun. A joke is a joke. But let's drop it."

"Just once," the Moose pleaded.

Coach Williams looked at the Moose and didn't answer.

The Moose didn't know what that meant.

The Benton Heights Tigers were duck soup for the Bears, as everyone knew they would be. The Bears scored in their first three possessions and led 28–0 at the half.

The hapless[7] Tigers had yet to cross the fifty-yard line under their own steam.

All the Bears, of course, were enjoying the way the game was going, as were the Bedford City fans jamming the bleachers.

Coach Williams looked irritated when the crowd on a couple of occasions broke into a chant: "Give the Moose the ball! Give the Moose the ball!" ❸

On the field, the Moose did not know whether to grin at hearing his name shouted by the crowd or to frown because the sound of his name was irritating the coach. Was the crowd going to talk Coach Williams into putting the

> 🏟 **RETELL**
> ❸ What's happening on the field and in the bleachers?

---

5. **precedent** (pres′ə·dənt) *n.:* action or statement that can serve as an example.
6. **purist** (pyoor′ist) *n.* used as *adj.:* someone who insists that rules be followed strictly.

---

7. **hapless** *adj.:* unlucky.

Moose in the backfield? Probably not; Coach Williams didn't bow to that kind of pressure. Was the coach going to refuse to give the ball to the Moose just to show the crowd—and the Moose and the rest of the players—who was boss? The Moose feared so.

In his time on the sideline, when the defensive unit was on the field, the Moose, of course, said nothing to Coach Williams. He knew better than to break the coach's concentration during a game—even a runaway victory—with a comment on any subject at all, much less his desire to carry the ball. As a matter of fact, the Moose was careful to stay out of the coach's line of vision, especially when the crowd was chanting "Give the Moose the ball!"

By the end of the third quarter the Bears were leading 42–0.

Coach Williams had been feeding substitutes into the game since halftime, but the Bears kept marching on. And now, in the opening minutes of the fourth quarter, the Moose and his teammates were standing on the Tigers' five-yard line, about to pile on another touchdown.

The Moose saw his substitute, Larry Hinden, getting a slap on the behind and then running onto the field. The Moose turned to leave.

Then he heard Larry tell the referee, "Hinden for Holbrook."

Holbrook? Chad Holbrook, the fullback?

Chad gave the coach a funny look and jogged off the field.

Larry joined the huddle and said, "Coach says the Moose at fullback and give him the ball."

Dan Blevins said, "Really?"

"Really."

The Moose was giving his grin—"sweet," some of the teachers called it; "nice," others said.

"I want to do an end run," the Moose said.

Dan looked at the sky a moment, then said, "What does it matter?"

The quarterback took the snap from center, moved back and to his right while turning, and extended the ball to the Moose.

The Moose took the ball and cradled it in his right hand. So far, so good. He hadn't fumbled. Probably both Coach Williams and Dan were surprised.

He ran a couple of steps and looked out in front and said aloud, "Whoa!"

Where had all those tacklers come from?

The whole world seemed to be peopled with players in red jerseys—the red of the Benton Heights Tigers. They all were looking straight at the Moose and advancing toward him. They looked very determined, and not friendly at all. And there were so many of them. The Moose had faced tough guys in the line, but usually one at a time, or maybe two. But this—five or six. And all of them heading for him.

The Moose screeched to a halt, whirled, and ran the other way.

Dan Blevins blocked somebody in a red jersey breaking through the middle of the line, and the Moose wanted to stop running and thank him. But he kept going.

His reverse had caught the Tigers' defenders going the wrong way, and the field in front of the Moose looked open. But his blockers were going the wrong way, too. Maybe that was why the field looked so open. What did it matter, though, with the field clear in front of him? This was going to be a cakewalk;[8] the Moose was going to score a touchdown.

_____

8. **cakewalk** *n.*: easy job.

Then, again—"Whoa!"

Players with red jerseys were beginning to fill the empty space—a lot of them. And they were all running toward the Moose. They were kind of low, with their arms spread, as if they wanted to hit him hard and then grab him.

A picture of Jerry Dixon dancing his little jig and wriggling between tacklers flashed through the Moose's mind. How did Jerry do that? Well, no time to <u>ponder</u> that one right now.

The Moose lowered his shoulder and thundered ahead, into the cloud of red jerseys. Something hit his left thigh. It hurt. Then something pounded his hip, then his shoulder. They both hurt. Somebody was hanging on to him and was a terrible drag. How could he run with somebody hanging on to him? He knew he was going down, but

PLAYERS WITH RED JERSEYS WERE BEGINNING TO FILL THE EMPTY SPACE . . .

maybe he was across the goal. He hit the ground hard, with somebody coming down on top of him, right on the small of his back.

The Moose couldn't move. They had him pinned. Wasn't the referee supposed to get these guys off?

Vocabulary
ponder (pän′dər) *v.*: think over carefully.

Finally the load was gone and the Moose, still holding the ball, got to his knees and one hand, then stood.

He heard the screaming of the crowd, and he saw the scoreboard blinking.

He had scored.

His teammates were slapping him on the shoulder pads and laughing and shouting.

The Moose grinned, but he had a strange and distant look in his eyes.

He jogged to the sideline, the roars of the crowd still ringing in his ears.

"OK, son?" Coach Williams asked.

The Moose was puffing. He took a couple of deep breaths. He relived for a moment the first sight of a half dozen players in red jerseys, all with one target—him. He saw again the menacing horde of red jerseys that had risen up just when he'd thought he had clear sailing to the goal. They all zeroed in on him, the Moose, alone.

The Moose glanced at the coach, took another deep breath, and said, "Never again." ❹

RETELL
❹ How is the Moose's conflict resolved?

Meet the Writer

Thomas J. Dygard

"I'm Not a Writer. I'm a Rewriter."

For **Thomas J. Dygard** (1931–1996), writing and editing newspaper articles was a full-time job; writing novels was the hobby he loved most. Dygard wrote seventeen novels, all sports related, for young people. In spite of his years of working with words, he said he always considered writing a challenge.

❝ My mistakes in my writing are so common that I'd bet I've thrown more pieces of paper in a wastebasket than any person alive. I'm not a writer. I'm a rewriter. As for having learned it all, I know that I haven't, and I also know that I never will. ❞

For Independent Reading

Dygard wrote several novels about football. One, *Winning Kicker*, is about a girl who makes the team as a place kicker and the problems that arise. For more Dygard on football, try *Game Plan* and *Second Stringer*.

First Thoughts

1. Respond to "Just Once" by completing one or more of these sentences:

- If I were in the Moose's shoes, I'd . . .
- I thought this story was . . .
- I was confused by . . .

Thinking Critically

2. What is the **setting** of the story? Could a story like this take place in any other setting? Explain.

3. What does the Moose expect to happen when he carries the ball? How is his dream different from reality?

4. Describe the **conflict** the Moose faces when the crowd chants, "Give the Moose the ball!" (page 23). What does he want? What is keeping him from getting it?

5. **Theme** is what the story reveals to us about life. What would you say is this story's theme, or underlying message about life? Is it the same lesson that the Moose learns? Explain.

Extending Interpretations

6. Is this a "boy's story," or does it appeal to both boys and girls? Conduct a survey of your classmates to find out what they think. Then, state and explain your own opinion.

WRITING

Making a Life Map

As a high school senior, the Moose longs to hear the cheers of the crowd. People want different things at different times in their lives. Draw a life map as a kind of road or journey showing a person at one end and the goal at the other end. Draw some of the forces that the person may have to overcome along the way. Then, write a paragraph explaining your map. (It does not have to be a map of the kind of life *you* want.) Look back at your Quickwrite notes for ideas for your map.

Reading Check

Use the following story map to outline the main parts of this story's **plot**.

```
┌──────────────┐   ┌──────────────┐
│  Characters  │   │   Setting    │
└──────┬───────┘   └──────┬───────┘
       │                  │
       ▼                  ▼
     ┌────────────────────┐
     │  Problem/Conflict  │
     └─────────┬──────────┘
               │
               ▼
     ┌────────────────────┐
     │  Major Events      │
     │  1.                │
     │  2.                │
     │  [Add as many as   │
     │   you need.]       │
     └─────────┬──────────┘
               │
               ▼
     ┌────────────────────┐
     │  Ending/Resolution │
     └────────────────────┘
```

North Carolina Competency Goal
1.02; 1.04; 4.01; 4.02; 5.01; 5.02

INTERNET
Projects and Activities
Keyword: LE5 6-1

SKILLS FOCUS

Literary Skills
Analyze conflict; analyze setting.

Reading Skills
Summarize plot events.

Writing/Art Skills
Draw a map; write an explanation.

Using Context to Determine Meaning

PRACTICE

Get into the habit of monitoring the text you are reading for unfamiliar words. If you find an unknown word, try to use the words and sentences around it—its **context**—to guess at the word's meaning. In the paragraph below, each underlined word has at least one **context clue.** Copy the paragraph, and circle the clues that would help a reader guess the words' meanings.

> The coach read aloud the <u>anonymous</u> note, wondering who had written it. "Please take some time to <u>ponder</u> our request carefully. You may think that it would have a <u>devastating</u> effect, but we're sure it won't ruin the sports program. It's time to be <u>tolerant</u> and fair. After all, we've been <u>nurturing</u> our dream for months. Please let girls try out for the team."

> **Word Bank**
>
> devastating
> nurturing
> anonymous
> tolerant
> ponder

Grammar Link

North Carolina Competency Goal
5.01;
5.02; 6.01

Troublesome Verbs

The **past tense** and **past participle** of most verbs are formed by adding *–d* or *–ed*, but **irregular verbs** change in sneaky ways. You just have to memorize them. (The past participle is the form you use with the helping verbs *has, have,* and *had.*)

Here are some irregular verbs from "Just Once":

Base Form	Past	Past Participle
rise	rose	(have) risen
say	said	(have) said
see	saw	(have) seen
think	thought	(have) thought

PRACTICE

In the following sentences, find the incorrect verb forms, and replace them with the correct forms.

1. The Moose rised from the field and seen a cloud of red jerseys.

2. The Moose thinked he wanted to hear the fans cheer for him.

3. Yesterday the Moose sayed to the coach, "I want to carry the ball."

For more help, see Irregular Verbs, 3c, in the Language Handbook.

SKILLS FOCUS

Vocabulary Skills
Use context clues.

Grammar Skills
Recognize irregular verbs.

The Stone

Make the Connection
Quickwrite ✏

Write a brief response to this question: Would you like to remain forever at the age you are now? Think about the pros and cons of always being eleven years old (or twelve, or any other age).

Literary Focus
Moral Lessons: Advice for Living

A **moral lesson** is a lesson about the right and wrong ways to behave. In "The Stone" the main character, Maibon, learns an important lesson about life. The old fables and fairy tales were meant to teach children (and others) useful lessons about the right and wrong ways to behave. In this story, a famous fantasy writer adopts the style and purpose of those old fairy tales.

Reading Skills 📖
Making Predictions

When you **make predictions**, you make educated guesses about what will happen next in a story. To make predictions as you read "The Stone," follow these steps:

- Look for clues in the story that suggest what might happen next.

- Use your knowledge of what usually happens in stories, especially fairy tales and stories about wishes.

- Think about how the characters might act, using what you've already learned about them and what you know about people in real life.

After you make a prediction, keep it in mind as you continue reading, and check to see whether it was correct. Don't worry if you were wrong—it's always fun to be surprised!

Vocabulary Development

Every time you read, you have a chance to add words to your vocabulary. The words that follow are underlined and defined in the story. See if you can use each one in a sentence of your own.

delved (delvd) v.: dug. *Delved* also means "searched." *Maibon's shovel no longer delved as well as it had when it was new.*

gaped (gāpt) v.: stared with the mouth open, as in wonder. *Maibon gaped at the trapped dwarf.*

plight (plīt) n.: bad situation. *Doli needed Maibon to help him out of his plight.*

obliged (ə·blījd') v.: forced. *Doli was obliged to grant Maibon's wish.*

jubilation (jōō'bə·lā'shən) n.: rejoicing; great joy. *Modrona did not share Maibon's jubilation over the magic stone.*

rue (rōō) v.: feel sorrow or regret for. *Doli thought that Maibon would soon rue the day he wished for the stone.*

mired (mīrd) v.: sunk or stuck, as if in mud. *The stone caused Maibon to get mired in time.*

fallow (fal'ō) adj.: left unplanted. *Maibon was very happy when his field, once fallow, became covered in blades of wheat.*

North Carolina Competency Goal
1.04; 4.01; 5.01; 5.02

INTERNET

Vocabulary Activity
•
More About Alexander

Keyword: LE5 6-1

Literary Skills
Understand moral lessons.

Reading Skills
Make predictions.

THE STONE

Lloyd Alexander

There was a cottager named Maibon, and one day he was driving down the road in his horse and cart when he saw an old man hobbling along, so frail and feeble he doubted the poor soul could go many more steps. Though Maibon offered to take him in the cart, the old man refused; and Maibon went his way home, shaking his head over such a pitiful sight, and said to his wife, Modrona:

"Ah, ah, what a sorry thing it is to have your bones creaking and cracking, and dim eyes, and dull wits. When I think this might come to me, too! A fine, strong-armed, sturdy-legged fellow like me? One day to go tottering and have his teeth rattling in his head and live on porridge like a baby? There's no fate worse in all the world."

"There is," answered Modrona, "and that would be to have neither teeth nor porridge.

Get on with you, Maibon, and stop borrowing trouble. Hoe your field or you'll have no crop to harvest, and no food for you, or me, or the little ones."

Sighing and grumbling, Maibon did as his wife bade him. Although the day was fair and cloudless, he took no pleasure in it. His ax blade was notched, the wooden handle splintery; his saw had lost its edge; and his hoe, once shining new, had begun to rust. None of his tools, it seemed to him, cut or chopped or delved as well as they once had done.

"They're as worn-out as that old codger[1] I saw on the road," Maibon said to himself. He squinted up at the sky. "Even the sun isn't as bright as it used to be and doesn't warm me half as well. It's gone threadbare as my cloak. And no wonder, for it's been there longer than I can remember. Come to think of it, the moon's been looking a little wilted around the edges, too.

"As for me," went on Maibon, in dismay, "I'm in even a worse state. My appetite's faded, especially after meals. Mornings, when I wake, I can hardly keep myself from yawning. And at night, when I go to bed, my eyes are so heavy I can't hold them open. If that's the way things are now, the older I grow, the worse it will be!"

In the midst of his complaining, Maibon glimpsed something bouncing and tossing back and forth beside a fallen tree in a corner of the field. Wondering if one of his piglets had squeezed out of the sty and gone rooting for acorns, Maibon hurried across the turf. Then he dropped his ax and gaped in astonishment.

There, struggling to free his leg, which had been caught under the log, lay a short, thickset

figure: a dwarf with red hair bristling in all directions beneath his round, close-fitting leather cap. At the sight of Maibon, the dwarf squeezed shut his bright red eyes and began holding his breath. After a moment the dwarf's face went redder than his hair; his cheeks puffed out and soon turned purple. Then he opened one eye and blinked rapidly at Maibon, who was staring at him, speechless.

"What," snapped the dwarf, "you can still see me?"

"That I can," replied Maibon, more than ever puzzled, "and I can see very well you've got yourself tight as a wedge under that log, and all your kicking only makes it worse."

At this the dwarf blew out his breath and shook his fists. "I can't do it!" he shouted. "No matter how I try! I can't make myself

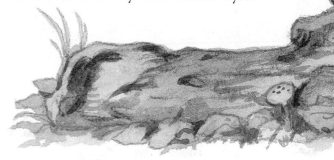

invisible! Everyone in my family can disappear—poof! Gone! Vanished! But not me! Not Doli! Believe me, if I could have done, you never would have found me in such a plight. Worse luck! Well, come on. Don't stand there goggling like an idiot. Help me get loose!"

At this sharp command Maibon began tugging and heaving at the log. Then he

---

1. **codger** *n.:* informal term meaning "elderly man."

Vocabulary
delved (delvd) *v.:* dug. *Delved* also means "searched."
gaped (gāpt) *v.:* stared with the mouth open, as in wonder or surprise.
plight (plīt) *n.:* bad situation.

of it with you ham-handed, heavy-footed oafs. Time was, you humans got along well with us. But nowadays you no sooner see a Fair Folk than it's grab, grab, grab! Gobble, gobble, gobble! Grant my wish! Give me this, give me that! As if we had nothing better to do!

"Yes, I'll give you a favor," Doli went on. "That's the rule; I'm <u>obliged</u> to. Now, get on with it."

Hearing this, Maibon pulled and pried and chopped away at the log as fast as he could and soon freed the dwarf.

Doli heaved a sigh of relief, rubbed his shin, and cocked a red eye at Maibon, saying:

"All right. You've done your work; you'll have your reward. What do you want? Gold, I suppose. That's the usual. Jewels? Fine clothes? Take my advice, go for something practical. A hazelwood twig to help you find water if your well ever goes dry? An ax that never needs sharpening? A cook pot always brimming with food?"

"None of those!" cried Maibon. He bent down to the dwarf and whispered eagerly, "But I've heard tell that you Fair Folk have magic stones that can keep a man young forever. That's what I want. I claim one for my reward."

Doli snorted. "I might have known you'd pick something like that. As to be expected, you humans have it all muddled. There's nothing can make a man young again. That's even beyond the best of our skills. Those stones you're babbling about? Well, yes, there are such things. But greatly overrated. All they'll do is keep you from growing any older."

"Just as good!" Maibon exclaimed. "I want no more than that!"

stopped, wrinkled his brow, and scratched his head, saying:

"Well, now, just a moment, friend. The way you look, and all your talk about turning yourself invisible—I'm thinking you might be one of the Fair Folk."

"Oh, clever!" Doli retorted. "Oh, brilliant! Great clodhopper! Giant beanpole! Of course I am! What else! Enough gabbling. Get a move on. My leg's going to sleep."

"If a man does the Fair Folk a good turn," cried Maibon, his excitement growing, "it's told they must do one for him."

"I knew sooner or later you'd come round to that," grumbled the dwarf. "That's the way

---

Vocabulary
obliged (ə·blījd′) *v.*: forced.

Doli hesitated and frowned. "Ah—between the two of us, take the cook pot. Better all around. Those stones—we'd sooner not give them away. There's a difficulty——"

"Because you'd rather keep them for yourselves," Maibon broke in. "No, no, you shan't cheat me of my due. Don't put me off with excuses. I told you what I want, and that's what I'll have. Come, hand it over and not another word."

Doli shrugged and opened a leather pouch that hung from his belt. He spilled a number of brightly colored pebbles into his palm, picked out one of the larger stones, and handed it to Maibon. The dwarf then jumped up, took to his heels, raced across the field, and disappeared into a thicket.

Laughing and crowing over his good fortune and his cleverness, Maibon hurried back to the cottage. There he told his wife what had happened and showed her the stone he had claimed from the Fair Folk.

"As I am now, so I'll always be!" Maibon declared, flexing his arms and thumping his chest. "A fine figure of a man! Oho, no gray beard and wrinkled brow for me!"

Instead of sharing her husband's jubilation, Modrona flung up her hands and burst out:

"Maibon, you're a greater fool than ever I supposed! And selfish into the bargain! You've turned down treasures! You didn't even ask that dwarf for so much as new jackets for the children! Nor a new apron for me!

You could have had the roof mended. Or the walls plastered. No, a stone is what you ask for! A bit of rock no better than you'll dig up in the cow pasture!"

Crestfallen[2] and sheepish, Maibon began thinking his wife was right and the dwarf had indeed given him no more than a common field stone.

"Eh, well, it's true," he stammered; "I feel no different than I did this morning, no better or worse, but every way the same. That red-headed little wretch! He'll rue the day if I ever find him again!"

So saying, Maibon threw the stone into the fireplace. That night he grumbled his way to bed, dreaming revenge on the dishonest dwarf.

Next morning, after a restless night, he yawned, rubbed his eyes, and scratched his chin. Then he sat bolt upright in bed, patting his cheeks in amazement.

"My beard!" he cried, tumbling out and hurrying to tell his wife. "It hasn't grown! Not by a hair! Can it be the dwarf didn't cheat me after all?"

"Don't talk to me about beards," declared his wife as Maibon went to the fireplace, picked out the stone, and clutched it safely in both hands. "There's trouble enough in the

---

2. **crestfallen** *adj.:* discouraged.

Vocabulary
jubilation (jōō′bə·lā′shən) *n.:* rejoicing; great joy.
rue (rōō) *v.:* feel sorrow or regret for.

chicken roost. Those eggs should have hatched by now, but the hen is still brooding on her nest."

"Let the chickens worry about that," answered Maibon. "Wife, don't you see what a grand thing's happened to me? I'm not a minute older than I was yesterday. Bless that generous-hearted dwarf!"

"Let me lay hands on him and I'll bless him," retorted Modrona. "That's all well and good for you. But what of me? You'll stay as you are, but I'll turn old and gray, and worn and wrinkled, and go doddering into my grave! And what of our little ones? They'll grow up and have children of their own. And grandchildren, and great-grandchildren. And you, younger than any of them. What a foolish sight you'll be!"

But Maibon, gleeful over his good luck, paid his wife no heed and only tucked the stone deeper into his pocket. Next day, however, the eggs had still not hatched.

"And the cow!" Modrona cried. "She's long past due to calve, and no sign of a young one ready to be born!"

"Don't bother me with cows and chickens," replied Maibon. "They'll all come right, in time. As for time, I've got all the time in the world!"

Having no appetite for breakfast, Maibon went out into his field. Of all the seeds he had sown there, however, he was surprised to see not one had sprouted. The field, which by now should have been covered with green shoots, lay bare and empty.

"Eh, things do seem a little late these days," Maibon said to himself. "Well, no hurry. It's that much less for me to do. The wheat isn't growing, but neither are the weeds."

Some days went by and still the eggs had not hatched, the cow had not calved, the wheat had not sprouted. And now Maibon saw that his apple tree showed no sign of even the smallest, greenest fruit.

"Maibon, it's the fault of that stone!" wailed his wife. "Get rid of the thing!"

"Nonsense," replied Maibon. "The season's slow, that's all."

Nevertheless, his wife kept at him and kept at him so much that Maibon at last, and very reluctantly, threw the stone out the cottage window. Not too far, though, for he had it in the back of his mind to go later and find it again.

Next morning he had no need to go looking for it, for there was the stone, sitting on the window ledge.

"You see?" said Maibon to his wife. "Here it is, back again. So it's a gift meant for me to keep."

"Maibon!" cried his wife. "Will you get rid of it! We've had nothing but trouble since you brought it into the house. Now the baby's fretting and fuming. Teething, poor little thing. But not a tooth to be seen! Maibon, that stone's bad luck and I want no part of it!"

Protesting it was none of his doing that the stone had come back, Maibon carried it into the vegetable patch. He dug a hole, not a very deep one, and put the stone into it.

Next day, there was the stone, above ground, winking and glittering.

"Maibon!" cried his wife. "Once and for all, if you care for your family, get rid of that cursed thing!"

Seeing no other way to keep peace in the household, Maibon regretfully and unwillingly took the stone and threw it down the well, where it splashed into the water and sank from sight.

But that night, while he was trying vainly to sleep, there came such a rattling and clattering that Maibon clapped his hands over his ears, jumped out of bed, and went stumbling into the yard. At the well the bucket was jiggling back and forth and up and down at the end of the rope, and in the bottom of the bucket was the stone.

Now Maibon began to be truly distressed, not only for the toothless baby, the calfless cow, the fruitless tree, and the hen sitting desperately on her eggs, but for himself as well.

"Nothing's moving along as it should," he groaned. "I can't tell one day from another. Nothing changes, there's nothing to look forward to, nothing to show for my work. Why sow if the seeds don't sprout? Why plant if there's never a harvest? Why eat if I don't get hungry? Why go to bed at night, or get up in the morning, or do anything at all? And the way it looks, so it will stay for ever and ever! I'll shrivel from boredom if nothing else!"

"Maibon," pleaded his wife, "for all our sakes, destroy the dreadful thing!"

Maibon tried now to pound the stone to dust with his heaviest mallet, but he could not so much as knock a chip from it. He put it against his grindstone without so much as scratching it. He set it on his anvil and belabored it with hammer and tongs, all to no avail.

At last he decided to bury the stone again, this time deeper than before. Picking up his shovel, he hurried to the field. But he suddenly halted and the shovel dropped from his hands. There, sitting cross-legged on a stump, was the dwarf.

"You!" shouted Maibon, shaking his fist. "Cheat! Villain! Trickster! I did you a good turn, and see how you've repaid it!"

The dwarf blinked at the furious Maibon. "You mortals are an ungrateful crew. I gave you what you wanted."

"You should have warned me!" burst out Maibon.

"I did," Doli snapped back. "You wouldn't listen. No, you yapped and yammered, bound to have your way. I told you we didn't like to give away those stones. When you mortals get hold of one, you stay just as you are—but so does everything around you. Before you know it, you're mired in time like a rock in the mud. You take my advice. Get rid of that stone as fast as you can."

"What do you think I've been trying to do?" blurted Maibon. "I've buried it, thrown it down the well, pounded it with a hammer—it keeps coming back to me!"

"That's because you really didn't want to give it up," Doli said. "In the back of your mind and the bottom of your heart, you didn't want to change along with the rest of the world. So long as you feel that way, the stone is yours."

"No, no!" cried Maibon. "I want no more of it. Whatever may happen, let it happen. That's better than nothing happening at all. I've had my share of being young; I'll take

---

Vocabulary

mired (mīrd) v.: sunk or stuck, as if in mud.

my share of being old. And when I come to the end of my days, at least I can say I've lived each one of them."

"If you mean that," answered Doli, "toss the stone onto the ground right there at the stump. Then get home and be about your business."

Maibon flung down the stone, spun around, and set off as fast as he could. When he dared at last to glance back over his shoulder, fearful the stone might be bouncing along at his heels, he saw no sign of it, or of the redheaded dwarf.

Maibon gave a joyful cry, for at that same instant the <u>fallow</u> field was covered with green blades of wheat, the branches of the apple tree bent to the ground, so laden they were with fruit. He ran to the cottage, threw his arms around his wife and children, and told them the good news. The hen hatched her chicks; the cow bore her calf. And Maibon laughed with glee when he saw the first tooth in the baby's mouth.

Never again did Maibon meet any of the Fair Folk, and he was just as glad of it. He and his wife and children and grandchildren lived many years, and Maibon was proud of his white hair and long beard as he had been of his sturdy arms and legs.

"Stones are all right in their way," said Maibon. "But the trouble with them is, they don't grow."

Vocabulary
fallow (fal′ō) *adj.:* left unplanted.

Lloyd Alexander

A Hungry Reader

Even as a child, **Lloyd Alexander** (1924–   ), the prize-winning fantasy writer, loved books.

66 I was always a hungry reader—in more ways than one. I gobbled up stories and never had my fill. At the same time, I wanted a real taste of whatever food the people in the stories were eating. Reading about the Mad Tea Party in *Alice in Wonderland,* I pleaded for a cup of tea, bread and butter, and treacle. . . . When Robin Hood and his Merry Men dined on venison washed down with flagons of brown October ale, I could only make believe with a hamburger and a glass of root beer. . . . Our neighborhood grocer never sold— nor had we money to buy—anything like the rich feasts at *King Arthur's Round Table.* Instead of the roast goose of *A Christmas Carol,* I gnawed a chicken leg.

    In time . . . I lost the habit of eating what I read about, but never my hunger for reading. I think the stories we love as children stay with us, somewhere in our hearts, to feed our imaginations. We never outgrow our need for them, any more than we outgrow our need for food. But, to me, the books I love are better than a feast. 99

For Independent Reading

"The Stone" is just one of the stories in Lloyd Alexander's book *The Foundling and Other Tales of Prydain.* Alexander has also written about the fantasy world of Prydain in a whole series of books called the *Prydain Chronicles.* One book in this series, *The High King,* won a Newbery Award.

After You Read   Response and Analysis

First Thoughts

1. Look back at your notes for the Quickwrite on page 29. Did reading this story change your opinion? Why or why not?

Thinking Critically

2. Maibon's troubles start when he sees an old man. Shortly after he meets the old man, his wife accuses him of "borrowing trouble." What do you think she means? Do you agree with her? Explain.

3. When did you begin to suspect that Maibon's wish wasn't going to turn out the way he expected? Make a list of the clues that helped you **predict** that Maibon's wish would be a mistake.

4. What **conflict** does Maibon have about getting rid of the stone? When does his "moment of truth" come?

5. At the end, Maibon says, "Stones are all right in their way. But the trouble with them is, they don't grow." What lesson has Maibon learned? How would you express the **moral lesson** of this story?

Extending Interpretations

6. What is the **setting** of this story? How would the story be different if it were set on a modern-day farm? What if it were set in a big modern city?

WRITING

Writing a Short Story with a Moral Lesson

On page 33, Doli advises Maibon to wish for something practical and then gives him several suggestions. Choose a suggestion, and write a short story about how that wish could go wrong. (For instance, would the cook pot produce *only* as much food as Maibon's family needed? Would it always produce the same kind of food?) You can use Maibon and his wife as characters or invent new ones if you prefer. Be sure your moral lesson is clear.

> **Reading Check**
> Draw a comic strip of four or five panels to show the **main events** in this story. Compare your comic-strip version of events with a partner's. Did you choose the same events?

North Carolina Competency Goal
1.02; 1.04; 4.01; 4.02; 5.01; 5.02

INTERNET
Projects and Activities
Keyword: LE5 6-1

SKILLS FOCUS

Literary Skills
Analyze moral lessons.

Reading Skills
Make predictions.

Writing Skills
Write a short story.

The Stone   **39**

Making Sense of Synonyms

Synonyms are words with the same or nearly the same meanings. For example, *stone* and *rock* are synonyms. Synonyms are not always interchangeable, though.

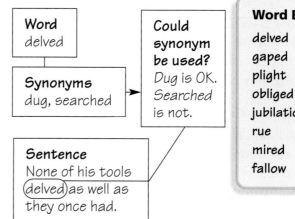

Word Bank

delved
gaped
plight
obliged
jubilation
rue
mired
fallow

PRACTICE

Fill out a chart like the one opposite for each word in the Word Bank. Go back to the story, and locate the sentence where the word is used. See if a synonym could be used in the story in place of the word the writer chose.

Grammar Link

Watch Your *Don't*s and *Doesn't*s

When Maibon has the stone, his beard doesn't grow and the hen's eggs don't hatch; his baby's tooth doesn't come in and the seeds don't sprout. The words *don't* and *doesn't* are contractions of *do not* and *does not.* Use *don't* with all plural subjects and with the pronouns *I* and *you.*

EXAMPLES   I don't [do not] make silly wishes.

You don't [do not] make silly wishes.

Most wishes don't [do not] come true.

Use *doesn't* with all singular subjects except *I* and *you.*

EXAMPLES   Maibon doesn't [does not] want to grow old.

He doesn't [does not] appreciate his life.

It doesn't [does not] make him happy anymore.

PRACTICE

Choose the correct verb for each sentence.

1. Maibon doesn't/don't like growing old.

2. When he makes his wish, the seeds doesn't/don't grow anymore.

3. At first, he doesn't/don't understand why.

4. His wife doesn't/don't want him to keep the stone.

5. The trouble with the stone is it doesn't/don't grow.

For more help, see Agreement of Subject and Verb, 2b, in the Language Handbook.

All Summer in a Day

Make the Connection
Quickwrite ✏️

In this story the children of Venus (that is, Venus as Ray Bradbury imagines it) lead lives that are very different from the lives of kids on Earth. One thing is the same, though: Someone who differs from the rest of the crowd is treated like an outsider.

How does it feel to be an outsider? Why do people sometimes refuse to accept someone into their group? Jot down your thoughts on these questions.

Literary Focus
Setting

Setting is the time and place of a story. Setting can tell us about the weather, the time of day, and the historical period (past, present, or future). Setting can also tell us how people live, what they eat, how they dress, and where they work. In some stories, like this one, setting plays such an important part that it shapes the action from beginning to end.

Reading Skills 📖
Making Inferences

An **inference** is a kind of guess. When you **make inferences** as you read, you look for clues in the story, and then you relate them to your own experience. You try to fill in the gaps by guessing about things the writer doesn't tell you directly. At certain points in this story, you'll see open-book signs alongside the text. When you see one, stop and make an inference about what you have just read.

You can make an inference about the **setting** of this story right now—just read the title. What do you think it means?

Vocabulary Development

These are the words you'll be learning as you read this story. Are any other words in the story new to you?

slackening (slak′ən·iŋ) v. used as *adj.:* lessening; slowing down. *The rain had fallen in huge, heavy drops for hours, but now it was slackening.*

surged (sʉrjd) v.: moved in a wave. *The children surged toward Margot.*

resilient (ri·zil′yənt) *adj.:* springy; quick to recover. *The vegetation was resilient beneath their feet.*

savored (sā′vərd) v.: delighted in. *The pale children savored the warm sunshine.*

North Carolina Competency Goal
1.04; 4.01; 5.01; 5.02

INTERNET

Vocabulary Activity
•
More About Bradbury

Keyword: LE5 6-1

Reflex (detail) (1988) by William Baggett.

Literary Skills
Understand setting and the way it influences plot.

Reading Skills
Make inferences.

All Summer in a Day

Ray Bradbury

"Ready."

"Ready."

"Now?"

"Soon."

"Do the scientists really know? Will it happen today, will it?"

"Look, look; see for yourself!"

The children pressed to each other like so many roses, so many weeds, intermixed, peering out for a look at the hidden sun.

It rained.

It had been raining for seven years; thousands upon thousands of days compounded and filled from one end to the other with rain, with the drum and gush of water, with the sweet crystal fall of showers and the concussion[1] of storms so heavy they were tidal waves come over the islands. A thousand

---

1. **concussion** *n.:* violent shaking or shock.

Reflex (1988) by William Baggett.

forests had been crushed under the rain and grown up a thousand times to be crushed again. And this was the way life was forever on the planet Venus, and this was the schoolroom of the children of the rocket men and women who had come to a raining world to set up civilization and live out their lives.

"It's stopping, it's stopping!"

"Yes, yes!"

Margot stood apart from them, from these

children who could never remember a time when there wasn't rain and rain and rain. They were all nine years old, and if there had been a day, seven years ago, when the sun came out for an hour and showed its face to the stunned world, they could not recall. Sometimes, at night, she heard them stir, in remembrance, and she knew they were dreaming and remembering gold or a yellow crayon or a coin large enough to buy the world with. She knew they thought they remembered a warmness, like a blushing in the face, in the body, in the arms and legs and trembling hands. But then they always awoke to the tatting drum, the endless shaking down of clear bead necklaces upon the roof, the walk, the gardens, the forests, and their dreams were gone. ❶

📖 **INFER**
❶ How do the children feel about the weather on Venus? Base your inference on their dreams.

All day yesterday they had read in class about the sun. About how like a lemon it was, and how hot. And they had written small stories or essays or poems about it.

I think the sun is a flower
That blooms for just one hour.

That was Margot's poem, read in a quiet voice in the still classroom while the rain was falling outside.

"Aw, you didn't write that!" protested one of the boys.

"I did," said Margot. *"I did."*

"William!" said the teacher.

But that was yesterday. Now the rain was slackening, and the children were crushed in the great thick windows.

"Where's teacher?"

"She'll be back."

"She'd better hurry; we'll miss it!"

They turned on themselves like a feverish wheel, all tumbling spokes.

Margot stood alone. She was a very frail girl who looked as if she had been lost in the rain for years and the rain had washed out the blue from her eyes and the red from her mouth and the yellow from her hair. She was an old photograph dusted from an album, whitened away, and if she spoke at all her voice would be a ghost. Now she stood, separate, staring at the rain and the loud wet world beyond the huge glass.

"What're *you* looking at?" said William.

Margot said nothing.

"Speak when you're spoken to." He gave her a shove. But she did not move; rather she let herself be moved only by him and nothing else.

They edged away from her; they would not look at her. She felt them go away. And this was because she would play no games with them in the echoing tunnels of the underground city. If they tagged her and ran, she stood blinking after them and did not follow. When the class sang songs about happiness and life and games, her lips barely moved. Only when they sang about the sun and the summer did her lips move as she watched the drenched windows.

And then, of course, the biggest crime of all was that she had come here only five years ago from Earth, and she remembered the sun and the way the sun was and the sky was when she was four in Ohio. And they, they had been on Venus all their lives, and they had been only two years old when last the sun came out and had long since forgotten the color and heat of it and the way it really was. But Margot remembered.

Vocabulary
slackening (slak′ən·iŋ) *v.* used as *adj.*: lessening; slowing

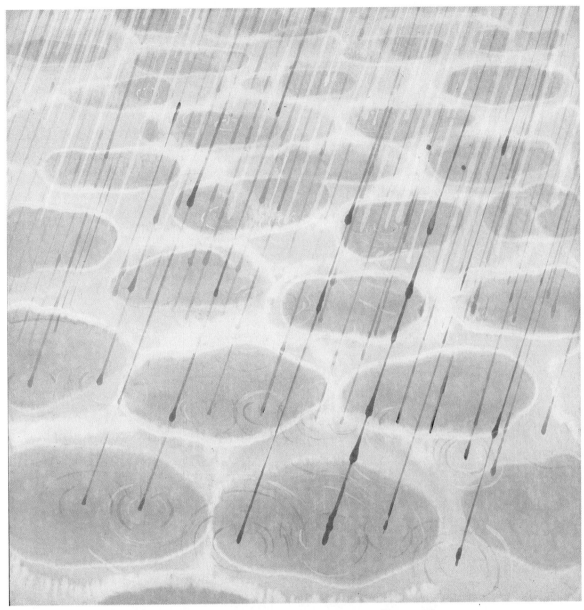

Japanese Rain on Canvas (1972) by David Hockney. Acrylic on canvas (48″ × 48″).
© David Hockney.

"It's like a penny," she said once, eyes closed. "No, it's not!" the children cried.

"It's like a fire," she said, "in the stove."

"You're lying; you don't remember!" cried the children.

But she remembered and stood quietly apart from all of them and watched the patterning windows. And once, a month ago, she had refused to shower in the school shower rooms, had clutched her hands to her ears and over her head, screaming the water mustn't touch her head. So after that, dimly, dimly, she sensed it, she was different, and they knew her difference and kept away.

There was talk that her father and mother were taking her back to Earth next year; it

Large Sun by David Finn.

seemed vital to her that they do so, though it would mean the loss of thousands of dollars to her family. And so, the children hated her for all these reasons of big and little consequence.[2] They hated her pale snow face, her waiting silence, her thinness, and her possible future. ❷ 📖

"Get away!" The boy gave her another push. "What're you waiting for?"

Then, for the first time, she turned and looked at him. And what she was waiting for was in her eyes.

"Well, don't wait around here!" cried the boy savagely. "You won't see nothing!"

Her lips moved.

"Nothing!" he cried. "It was all a joke, wasn't it?" He turned to the other children. "Nothing's happening today. Is it?"

They all blinked at him and then, understanding, laughed and shook their heads. "Nothing, nothing!"

"Oh, but," Margot whispered, her eyes helpless. "But this is the day, the scientists predict, they say, they know, the sun . . ."

"All a joke!" said the boy, and seized her roughly. "Hey everyone, let's put her in a closet before teacher comes!"

"No," said Margot, falling back.

They surged about her, caught her up and bore her, protesting, and then pleading, and then crying, back into a tunnel, a room, a closet, where they slammed and locked the door. They stood looking at the door and saw it tremble from her beating and throwing herself against it. They heard her muffled cries. Then, smiling, they turned

📖 **INFER**
❷ How is Margot different from the other children?

and went out and back down the tunnel, just as the teacher arrived.

"Ready, children?" She glanced at her watch.

"Yes!" said everyone.

"Are we all here?"

"Yes!"

The rain slackened still more.

They crowded to the huge door.

The rain stopped.

It was as if, in the midst of a film concerning an avalanche, a tornado, a hurricane, a volcanic eruption, something had, first, gone wrong with the sound apparatus, thus muffling and finally cutting off all noise, all of the blasts and repercussions and thunders, and then, second, ripped the film from the projector and inserted in its place a peaceful tropical slide which did not move or tremor. The world ground to a standstill. The silence was so immense and unbelievable that you felt your ears had been stuffed or you had lost your hearing altogether. The children put their hands to their ears. They stood apart. The door slid back and the smell of the silent, waiting world came in to them.

The sun came out.

It was the color of flaming bronze and it was very large. And the sky around it was a blazing blue tile color. And the jungle burned with sunlight as the children, released from their spell, rushed out, yelling, into the springtime.

"Now, don't go too far," called the teacher after them. "You've only two hours, you know. You wouldn't want to get caught out!"

But they were running and turning their faces up to the sky and feeling the sun on

2. **consequence** *n.:* importance.

Vocabulary
surged (sʉrjd) *v.:* moved forward, as if in a wave.

their cheeks like a warm iron; they were taking off their jackets and letting the sun burn their arms.

"Oh, it's better than the sun lamps, isn't it?"

"Much, much better!"

They stopped running and stood in the great jungle that covered Venus, that grew and never stopped growing, tumultuously,[3] even as you watched it. It was a nest of octopuses, clustering up great arms of fleshlike weed, wavering, flowering in this brief spring. It was the color of rubber and ash, this jungle, from the many years without sun. It was the color of stones and white cheeses and ink, and it was the color of the moon.

The children lay out, laughing, on the jungle mattress and heard it sigh and squeak under them, <u>resilient</u> and alive. They ran among the trees, they slipped and fell, they pushed each other, they played hide-and-seek and tag, but most of all they squinted at the sun until tears ran down their faces; they put their hands up to that yellowness and that amazing blueness and they breathed of the fresh, fresh air and listened and listened to the silence which suspended them in a blessed sea of no sound and no motion. They looked at everything and <u>savored</u> everything. Then, wildly, like animals escaped from their caves, they ran and ran in shouting circles. They ran for an hour and did not stop running. ❸

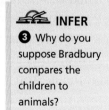

INFER

❸ Why do you suppose Bradbury compares the children to animals?

And then—

In the midst of their running, one of the girls wailed.

Everyone stopped.

The girl, standing in the open, held out her hand.

"Oh, look, look," she said, trembling.

They came slowly to look at her opened palm.

In the center of it, cupped and huge, was a single raindrop.

She began to cry, looking at it.

They glanced quietly at the sky.

"Oh. Oh."

A few cold drops fell on their noses and their cheeks and their mouths. The sun faded behind a stir of mist. A wind blew cool around them. They turned and started to walk back toward the underground house, their hands at their sides, their smiles vanishing away.

A boom of thunder startled them, and like leaves before a new hurricane, they tumbled upon each other and ran. Lightning struck ten miles away, five miles away, a mile, a half-mile. The sky darkened into midnight in a flash.

They stood in the doorway of the underground for a moment until it was raining hard. Then they closed the door and heard the gigantic sound of the rain falling in tons and avalanches, everywhere and forever.

"Will it be seven more years?"

"Yes. Seven."

Then one of them gave a little cry.

"Margot!"

"What?"

"She's still in the closet where we locked her."

"Margot."

They stood as if someone had driven them, like so many stakes, into the floor.

Vocabulary

resilient (ri·zil′yənt) *adj.:* springy; quick to recover.

savored (sā′vərd) *v.:* delighted in.

---

3. **tumultuously** *adv.:* wildly; violently.

Sunset, Casco Bay by John Marin.
The Roland P. Murdock Collection. Wichita Art Museum, Wichita, Kansas. © 2005 Estate of John Marin/Artists Rights Society (ARS), New York.

They looked at each other and then looked away. They glanced out at the world that was raining now and raining and raining steadily. They could not meet each other's glances. Their faces were solemn and pale. They looked at their hands and feet, their faces down.

"Margot."

One of the girls said, "Well . . . ?"

No one moved.

"Go on," whispered the girl.

They walked slowly down the hall in the sound of cold rain. They turned through the doorway to the room in the sound of the storm and thunder, lightning on their faces, blue and terrible. They walked over to the closet door slowly and stood by it.

Behind the closet door was only silence.

They unlocked the door, even more slowly, and let Margot out. ❹

PREDICT

❹ What will happen now?

Meet the Writer

Ray Bradbury

Space-Age Storyteller

Ray Bradbury (1920–   ) has been called the world's greatest science fiction writer. It is not a label Bradbury agrees with. He describes himself more simply: "I am a storyteller. That's all I've ever tried to be."

Although Bradbury's stories are often set in outer space, his characters and their emotions are human and down-to-earth. For more than fifty years, Bradbury has produced fiction that reflects his deeply felt concern about the future of humanity.

Bradbury encourages young people to try to imagine the wonders the future will hold—just as he did when he was in school:

> 66 Everything confronting us in the next thirty years will be science-fictional, that is, impossible a few years ago. The things you are doing right now, if you had told anyone you'd be doing them when you were children, they would have laughed you out of school. . . . I was the only person at Los Angeles High School who knew the Space Age was coming. Totally alone among four thousand students, I insisted we were going to get the rocket off the ground, and that made me the class kook, of course. I said, 'Well, we're going to do it anyway.' 99

For Independent Reading

Bradbury's stories are collected in books such as *The Illustrated Man*, *R Is for Rocket*, *Twice Twenty-Two*, and *The Stories of Ray Bradbury*. Try starting with "Mars Is Heaven," "The Fog Horn," "The Sound of Summer Running," and "The Flying Machine." If you're interested in reading a Bradbury novel, try *Dandelion Wine*.

First Thoughts

1. How do you feel about what the other children do to Margot in Bradbury's story? Explain.

Thinking Critically

2. Differences between people often cause **conflicts,** or clashes. What causes the conflict between Margot and the other children? Why does Margot keep to herself?

3. From her behavior throughout the story, what do you **infer** Margot will say or do when she is let out of the closet?

4. The characters in a story behave in certain ways for certain reasons. Why would the children lock Margot in the closet when they know how much the sun means to her? Think back to your Quickwrite notes as you answer this question.

5. Why is the **setting** of this story (including the weather) so important to the plot? Hint: Would there be a story if the weather on Venus were like the weather in San Diego?

Extending Interpretations

6. Bradbury's ending leaves some questions unanswered. Do you think he should have shown what happens when Margot gets out of the closet, or do you like the story as it is? Explain.

7. Do you think the hardships faced by pioneers (like the ones in this story) are worth it? Would you volunteer to be a colonist on a distant planet? Why or why not?

WRITING
Describing Extreme Weather

What's the most extreme weather you've ever had to face? Tell about what happened to you that day or night. (If nothing much happened, use your imagination.) Describe what you saw, heard, tasted, felt, and smelled on your bad-weather day. Be sure to identify your setting.

Reading Check

a. The children in this story live on Venus. In terms of what happens in the story, what is the most important feature of this setting?

b. Why are the children so excited at the beginning of the story?

c. How is Margot different from the other children?

d. What happens while Margot is in the closet?

e. How is the conflict in the story resolved at the end?

INTERNET

Projects and Activities
Keyword: LE5 6-1

SKILLS FOCUS

Literary Skills
Analyze setting and the way it influences plot.

Reading Skills
Make inferences.

Writing Skills
Write a description.

North Carolina Competency Goal
1.02; 5.01; 5.02

Monitoring Comprehension

A strategy called **semantic mapping** can help you learn new words you come across in your reading. (The word *semantic* means "having to do with the meaning of words.")

PRACTICE

Using the semantic map for *surged* below as a model, map the other words in the Word Bank. Before you begin, find each word in the story, and note how it's used. You can find related words for your maps in a **dictionary,** a **thesaurus,** or a **synonym finder,** another kind of reference book.

Word Bank

slackening
surged
resilient
savored

surged — Definition: moved in a wave — Words with related meanings: flooded, rushed — Examples: Rivers surge. Energy surges.

Grammar Link

North Carolina Competency Goal
5.01; 5.02; 6.01

SKILLS FOCUS

Vocabulary Skills
Make semantic maps.

Grammar Skills
Practice subject-verb agreement.

Subject-Verb Agreement: Search for the Subject

Once you find the subject of a sentence, you can decide whether you need a singular or a plural verb. Here are some tips for you:

- In a question the subject often comes *after* the verb. To find the subject, change the question to a statement.

   What <u>was/were</u> the children's deepest fear?

   The children's deepest fear <u>was</u> . . .

- The subject of a sentence is *rarely* part of a prepositional phrase. Cross out any prepositional phrases before looking for the subject.

   The <u>sound</u> of raindrops <u>was</u> upsetting to the children.

PRACTICE

Find the subject of each sentence, and then choose the correct verb.

1. The mood of the children <u>match/matches</u> the day.
2. What <u>do/does</u> Margot and the others think about the sun?
3. How friendly <u>are/is</u> Margot with the other children?
4. The dream of Margot and the others <u>is/are</u> to see the sun.

For more help, see Agreement of Subject and Verb, 2b, in the Language Handbook.

Understanding the Features of a Magazine

Reading Focus

Structural Features of a Magazine

Fantasies like "All Summer in a Day" ask us to imagine "what if?" Informational materials—such as newspapers, magazines, and some Internet Web pages—help us think about what actually is. They offer fact, not fiction.

Like most types of informational materials, magazines have special structural features that give you an overview of what's inside.

- **The cover.** The cover's art and main headline usually announce the lead article and other feature articles. The cover of *Archaeology's dig* magazine (see photo) tells you that the lead story is "Pyramid Power!" and that the issue includes articles on Hercules and King Arthur.

- **The contents page.** This page, at the front of the magazine, lists articles and tells you what pages they're on. The contents page is sometimes called simply "Inside This Issue." *Archaeology's dig* calls its contents page "dig into this!"

Before you read your next **magazine article,** take a minute to notice the way it's structured.

- **The title.** Most magazine articles have titles that are written to catch the reader's interest.

- **The subtitle.** An article may have a subtitle, a secondary title that tells you more about the article.

- **Headings.** Headings are words or phrases used to break up the text of an article into sections. They're often printed in a size or color intended to stand out. You can sometimes **outline** the main points of an article by listing the headings.

- **Illustrations.** Many articles are illustrated with drawings, photographs, maps, graphs, and tables. Illustrations are often used to help you picture something described in an article and to provide more information. They may be accompanied by brief printed explanations, called **captions.**

■ Look for these features as you read the magazine article on page 54.

North Carolina Competency Goal
5.01; 5.02

INTERNET
Interactive Reading Model
Keyword: LE5 6-1

SKILLS FOCUS

Reading Skills
Understand the structural features of a magazine.

What Will Our Towns Look Like?

(If We Take Care of Our Planet)

The **title** is often a catchy phrase intended to grab your attention.

The **subtitle** tells you more about the article.

A **caption** explains what is shown in an illustration.

New inventions will help us build clean, green places to live.

Fantastic inventions made daily life easier in the past century but often at the expense of our natural resources. Gas-powered cars got us everywhere in a flash, but they polluted our air. Electric heat and light made our homes warm and welcoming but also burned up limited coal and oil. Factories revolutionized the way we worked, but industrial waste trashed rivers, streams, and oceans.

Lifestyle changes on the horizon for the next one hundred years may actually improve our planet's health. We can use cleaner energy and fewer chemicals while working, playing, and bringing up families in the towns of tomorrow. This is not an impossible dream. Most of the innovations shown here already exist or are being developed. If we put our minds to it, our towns can preserve Earth's natural riches and still be lovely places to call home. Here's how things might be—if we make the environment a top concern.

Work/Transportation

More grownups will work in their homes **1** and keep in touch with co-workers through computers. Others will make a short trip to a nearby office park **2**. A few will ride swift electric trains **3** to the nearest city. Cars and trucks **4** will run on clean, hydrogen-powered fuel cells. Most entertainment and stores will be close by, so we'll often travel on old-fashioned, earth-friendly bicycles **5**.

Food

We'll grow fruits, grains, and vegetables close to home, either in our gardens **6** or on nearby organic farms **7**. Since the farms will use natural forms of pest control, such as predatory insects, there will be far fewer chemicals in the food supply.

Illustrations help you picture things described in the article.

Headings break up the text into sections.

Shopping

Even if online stores are here to stay, there will still be a mall ⑧ . But it will be small, with sidewalks and bike racks instead of a giant parking lot. An airy place in which a flood of natural light will cut down on energy use, the mall will be one big recycling operation; when you're through using any product you buy there, the store will be required to take it back for recycling.

Energy

Our power will come from sources cleaner than coal, oil, and gas. Some energy will flow from windmills ⑨ , but much of it will be generated in our own homes. Rooftop solar panels ⑩ will supply electricity to our appliances and to a basement fuel cell, which will produce hydrogen. When the sun is not shining, the cell will use the hydrogen to make electricity.

Waste

Plumbing lines will empty into enclosed marshes ⑪ , where special plants, fish, snails, and bacteria will naturally purify wastewater. Clean water will flow back into streams and reservoirs.

—from *Time for Kids*

Analyzing the Structure and Purpose of a Magazine Article

What Will Our Towns Look Like?

Test Practice

1. The article makes all of the following points *except* —
   A Lifestyle changes may help the environment.
   B Factories have made our daily lives harder.
   C Industrial wastes pollute streams, rivers, and oceans.
   D Coal and oil are burned to produce electric heat and light.

2. "New inventions will help us build clean, green places to live" is —
   F the magazine title
   G a caption
   H a heading
   J an illustration

3. In a special magazine issue on life in the twenty-first century, which article would you *not* expect to see?
   A "Next Stop: Mars"
   B "Staying Active After 150"
   C "Egypt's Early Pyramids"
   D "Robots Replace Teachers"

4. The article makes all of the following predictions *except* —
   F Malls will be smaller than they are today.
   G Malls will have bike racks instead of huge parking lots.
   H Malls will be lit by natural light.
   J There will be no malls in the future.

5. This article was written mainly to —
   A describe what life in the towns of the future will be like—if we take care of the environment
   B point out how desperate our environmental situation is
   C encourage people to grow their own food
   D suggest ways to clean up our water supply

North Carolina Competency Goal
2.01

Constructed Response

1. Write down the **title, subtitle,** and **headings** of this article. (You should have seven in all.)

2. What are numbers 6 and 7 in the article's illustration? Where would you find out what the numbers mean?

3. How will lifestyle changes in the next hundred years affect the planet?

SKILLS FOCUS

Reading Skills
Analyze the structure and purpose of a magazine article.

Understanding the Features of a Web Site

Reading Focus

Structural Features of a Web Site

"All Summer in a Day" is a work of fiction, but Venus is a real place. Like most writers who use real settings, Ray Bradbury includes factual information about the setting in his story.

In the past, if a writer wanted to research Venus, he or she would probably look in a reference or science book. Today we have another important source of information literally at our fingertips—the Internet.

Using the Internet

There are several ways to find information on the Internet. You can go directly to a **Web site** if you know the URL (uniform resource locator), the address of the site. To find information about Venus, you might want to try the Web site of NASA (the National Aeronautics and Space Administration). NASA is the U.S. government agency that conducts space exploration. The information on Venus on pages 58 and 59 comes from NASA's Web site. There is an example of NASA's home page on page 116.

Sometimes you have to use a **search engine** when you do research. Using a search engine gives you access to a gigantic library of information. Because the computer can search very quickly, you get results faster than if you searched through books in a library.

A search will usually produce a list of **Web sites** relating to the topic of your search. Often you can just click on the site name and go directly to the site. If you get too many results, you have to refine your search by choosing more specific search terms.

Online Skills: Getting Information

Most Web sites share some **basic structural features.** Knowing how to recognize the following features can help you find information online. When you are at a Web site, keep these points in mind.

- Most of what a site offers is shown on the site's **home page.** Start out by finding and reading basic information about the site, usually at the top or center of the home page.

- Look for a **table of contents,** a list of the site's other pages. The table of contents often appears on the side of the home page. You can generally reach the other pages of a site by clicking on the items listed in the table of contents.

- Look for **links,** Web sites related to the one you're exploring. You can often reach a link by clicking on its name. Not every Web site offers links, but you can usually find a "links" page in the table of contents.

■ How many of these Web site features can you find in the pages from NASA's Web site (pages 58–59)?

North Carolina Competency Goal
1.04; 2.01; 4.01; 4.02; 5.01

INTERNET
Media Tutorials
Keyword: LE5 6-1

SKILLS FOCUS

Reading Skills
Understand the structural features of a Web site.

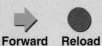

Back   Forward   Reload   Home   Search

Location:

FEATURES   HOME   SEARCH   FEEDBACK   SITE MAP   NASA

Mercury • Venus • Earth • Mars • Jupiter • Saturn • Uranus • Neptune • Pluto • Asteroids • Comets

Romanticized as the morning and evening star, Venus is actually a caldron of blistering heat and noxious gases!

SOLAR SYSTEM BODIES: VENUS

SCIENCE GOALS –

NEWS –

MISSIONS –

TECHNOLOGY –

RESEARCH –

EDUCATION –

Features: This band at the top of the page outlines the structure of the Web site.

Contents: This list tells you what other topics the site covers.

Venus, second planet from the sun, has sometimes been called Earth's sister planet because the two are so similar in size and mass. But there the similarities end. Venus is covered by thick, rapidly spinning clouds that trap surface heat, creating a scorched greenhouselike world with temperatures hot enough to melt lead, and pressure so intense that standing on Venus would feel like the pressure felt 900 m (3,000 ft.) deep in Earth's oceans.

These clouds reflect sunlight as well as trap in heat. Because Venus reflects so much sunlight, it is usually the brightest planet in the sky.

The atmosphere consists mainly of carbon dioxide (the same gas that produces fizzy sodas), virtually no water vapor, and droplets of sulfuric acid—not a great place for people or plants! In addition, the thick atmosphere allows the sun's heat in but does not allow it to escape, resulting in surface temperatures over 450°C (more than 800°F), hotter than the surface of the planet Mercury, which is closest to the sun. The high density of the atmosphere results in a surface pressure ninety times that of Earth, which is why probes that have landed on Venus have only survived several hours before being crushed ▶

PROFILE

Distance from the Sun (semimajor axis of orbit)
108,208,930 km
0.72333199 A.U.

Mean Equatorial Radius
6,051.8 km
(0.9488 of Earth's radius)

Mean Temperature at Solid Surface
730K

Major Atmospheric Constituents
CO_2, N_2

Natural Satellites
None

Back
 Forward
 Reload
 Home
 Search

Location:

FEATURES | HOME | SEARCH | FEEDBACK | SITE MAP | NASA

Mercury • Venus • Earth • Mars • Jupiter • Saturn • Uranus • Neptune • Pluto • Asteroids • Comets

Romanticized as the morning and evening star, Venus is actually a caldron of blistering heat and noxious gases!

SOLAR SYSTEM BODIES: VENUS

 SCIENCE GOALS –

 NEWS –

 MISSIONS –

 TECHNOLOGY –

 RESEARCH –

EDUCATION –

by the incredible pressure. In the upper layers, the clouds move faster than hurricane-force winds on Earth.

Much of the surface is covered by vast lava flows. In the north, an elevated region named Ishtar Terra is a lava-filled basin larger than the continental United States. Near the equator, the Aphrodite Terra highlands, more than half the size of Africa, extend for almost 10,000 km (6,200 mi.). Volcanic flows have also produced long, sinuous channels extending for hundreds of miles.

Over 100,000 small shield volcanoes dot the surface, along with hundreds of larger volcanoes. Maxwell Montes, a mountain taller than Mount Everest, sits at one end of Ishtar Terra. Giant calderas over 100 km (62 mi.) in diameter are found on Venus. Calderas are basinlike depressions in the surface that occur after the collapse of the center of a volcano.

Venus's interior is probably very similar to that of Earth, holding an iron core about 3,000 km (1,900 mi.) in radius and a molten rocky mantle comprising the majority of the planet. Recent results from the Magellan spacecraft suggest that Venus's crust is stronger and thicker than had previously been thought.

RELATED LINKS

• *Exploring the Planets— Venus*

• *Missions to Venus*

• *NASA Planetary Photojournal: Venus*

• *National Space Science Data Center*

• *The Nine Planets*

Links: Clicking on an item in this list takes you to another Web site and more information.

Analyzing the Structure and Purpose of a Web Site

Solar System Bodies: Venus

Test Practice

1. The main **purpose** of this **Web page** is to —
   A criticize scientific studies of Venus
   B describe the characteristics of Venus
   C explain how living things could survive on Venus
   D encourage scientific probes of Venus

2. Which of the following is a **fact** about Venus—something that can be proved?
   F Venus is the second planet from the sun.
   G Venus is a hideous planet.
   H Venus is more interesting than Earth.
   J People will never colonize Venus.

3. What part of this **Web page** tells you that Venus has no natural satellites?
   A The table of contents
   B Profile
   C Site Map
   D News

4. In this **Web site,** where would you find information on missions to Venus?
   F Features and the table of contents
   G Feedback and Home
   H Related Links and Profile
   J The table of contents and Related Links

5. Which of the following statements best sums up the **main idea** of this **Web page**?
   A Although Venus is similar to Earth in some ways, human beings could not survive the extreme conditions there.
   B Venus should be romanticized as the evening star.
   C Venus is Earth's sister planet.
   D Venus's atmosphere consists mainly of carbon dioxide.

North Carolina Competency Goal
1.02; 1.04; 2.01; 4.01; 4.02; 5.01

Reading Skills
Analyze the structure and purpose of a Web site.

Constructed Response

1. In what ways is Venus like Earth?

2. Why have probes that have landed on Venus survived only a few hours?

3. Find three places on the Web page where the writer describes a feature of Venus by **comparing** it to something we are familiar with on Earth.

After You Read   Vocabulary Development

Using Context Clues

When scientists write for the public, they often try to help readers understand specialized words. You can figure out the meanings of some of those words from clues in the text or in the word itself.

Look for definitions in the text.

"Giant <u>calderas</u> over 100 km (62 mi.) in diameter are found on Venus. Calderas are basinlike depressions in the surface that occur after the collapse of the center of a volcano."

Look for clues in the word itself.

"Venus is actually a caldron of blistering heat and <u>noxious</u> gases!"

> A definition is given in the second sentence.

> Noxious looks and sounds like obnoxious, which means "unpleasant or nasty."

PRACTICE

Study the context of the underlined word in each item below. Then, use **context clues** to select the best definition of the word. Do all the sentences contain context clues?

1. "Venus is covered by thick, rapidly spinning clouds that trap surface heat, creating a <u>scorched</u> greenhouselike world with temperatures hot enough to melt lead . . ."
   A damaged by intense heat
   B moist and warm
   C brightly lit

2. "The atmosphere consists mainly of <u>carbon dioxide</u> (the same gas that produces fizzy sodas) . . ."
   A a virus
   B a drink
   C a gas

3. "Volcanic flows have also produced long, <u>sinuous</u> channels extending for hundreds of miles."
   A winding
   B small
   C straight

North Carolina Competency Goal
6.01

Vocabulary Skills
Use context clues.

The Bridegroom

Make the Connection

Quickwrite ✏️

Suppose you knew someone who had witnessed a horrifying crime and was afraid to talk about it. Write a few sentences telling what you would advise the witness to do.

Literary Focus

Climax

The most exciting and suspenseful part of a plot is called the **climax**. This is when we find out for certain how the characters' problems are going to be resolved. You probably have seen movies in which the climax takes the form of a terrifying life-or-death struggle between the good character and the bad one. As you read this poem about violence and betrayal, you will feel the buildup of suspense before the climax is reached. What will happen to the young girl?

North Carolina Competency Goal
1.04; 4.01; 5.01; 5.02

SKILLS FOCUS

Literary Skills
Understand climax.

Reading Skills
Understand cause and effect.

Background
Literature and Folklore

"The Bridegroom" is based on an old folk tale about a young woman who witnesses a terrible crime. She is silent about the crime—until she realizes she is to become the next victim.

Reading Skills 📖

Understand Cause and Effect

A plot is a series of causes and their effects. A **cause** makes something happen. An **effect** is the result of a cause. That cause might be an event, a decision, or a situation. To find a cause, ask yourself, "Why did this happen?" To find an effect, ask, "What's the result of this event?" In this poem, for example, you learn at the start that Natasha has been missing for three days. You ask yourself, "Why did this happen?" Look for the answer later in the poem.

Set design for *Firebird* by Natalia Goncharova.
Victoria & Albert Museum, London. © 2005 Artists Rights Society (ARS), New York/ADAGP, Paris.

The Bridegroom

Alexander Pushkin
translated by D. M. Thomas

Troika on St. Petersburg Street
by Carl von Hampein.

The Bridegroom

For three days Natasha,
The merchant's daughter,
Was missing. The third night,
She ran in, distraught.°

5   Her father and mother
Plied° her with questions.
She did not hear them,
She could hardly breathe.

Stricken with foreboding°

10   They pleaded, got angry,
But still she was silent;
At last they gave up.
Natasha's cheeks regained
Their rosy color.

15   And cheerfully again
She sat with her sisters.

Once at the shingle-gate°
She sat with her friends
—And a swift troika°

20   Flashed by before them;
A handsome young man
Stood driving the horses;
Snow and mud went flying,
Splashing the girls.

25   He gazed as he flew past,
And Natasha gazed.
He flew on. Natasha froze.
Headlong she ran home.
"It was he! It was he!"

30   She cried. "I know it!
I recognized him! Papa,
Mama, save me from him!"

Full of grief and fear,
They shake their heads, sighing.

4. distraught (di·strôt′) *adj.:* extremely troubled.

6. plied (plīd) *v.:* addressed urgently and persistently.

9. foreboding (fôr·bōd′iŋ) *n.:* feeling that something bad will happen.

17. shingle-gate: gate to the beach (a shingle is a pebbly beach).

19. troika (troi′kə) *n.:* Russian sleigh or carriage drawn by three horses.

Morning by S. Koslov. Painted box.
Collection of the Manufacturer of Miniatures.

35   Her father says: "My child,
        Tell me everything.
        If someone has harmed you,
        Tell us . . . even a hint."
        She weeps again and
40   Her lips remain sealed.
        The next morning, the old
        Matchmaking woman
        Unexpectedly calls and
        Sings the girl's praises;
45   Says to the father: "You
        Have the goods and I
        A buyer for them:
        A handsome young man.

"He bows low to no one,
He lives like a lord
With no debts nor worries;
He's rich and he's generous,
Says he will give his bride,
On their wedding-day,
A fox-fur coat, a pearl,
Gold rings, brocaded° dresses.

56. **brocaded** (brō·kād′əd) *v.*
used as *adj.*: having a raised
design woven into the fabric.

"Yesterday, out driving,
He saw your Natasha;
Shall we shake hands
And get her to church?"
The woman starts to eat
A pie, and talks in riddles,
While the poor girl
Does not know where to look.

"Agreed," says her father;
"Go in happiness
To the altar, Natasha;
It's dull for you here;
A swallow should not spend
All its time singing,
It's time for you to build
A nest for your children."

Natasha leaned against
The wall and tried
To speak—but found herself
Sobbing; she was shuddering
And laughing. The matchmaker
Poured out a cup of water,
Gave her some to drink,
Splashed some in her face.

Her parents are distressed.
Then Natasha recovered,
And calmly she said:
"Your will be done. Call

85　My bridegroom to the feast,
　　Bake loaves for the whole world,
　　Brew sweet mead° and call
　　The law to the feast."

　　"Of course, Natasha, angel!
90　You know we'd give our lives
　　To make you happy!"
　　They bake and they brew;
　　The worthy guests come,
　　The bride is led to the feast,
95　Her maids sing and weep;
　　Then horses and a sledge

　　With the groom—and all sit.
　　The glasses ring and clatter,
　　The toasting-cup is passed

100　From hand to hand in tumult,°
　　The guests are drunk.

　　BRIDEGROOM
　　"Friends, why is my fair bride
　　Sad, why is she not
105　Feasting and serving?"

　　The bride answers the groom:
　　"I will tell you why
　　As best I can. My soul
　　Knows the rest, day and night
110　I weep; an evil dream
　　Oppresses me." Her father
　　Says: "My dear child, tell us
　　What your dream is."

　　"I dreamed," she says, "that I
115　Went into a forest,
　　It was late and dark;
　　The moon was faintly

87. mead (mēd) *n.:* alcoholic drink made of fermented honey and water.

100. tumult (tŏŏ′mult) *n.:* noisy commotion.

Shining behind a cloud;
I strayed from the path;
120　Nothing stirred except
The tops of the pine trees.

"And suddenly, as if
I was awake, I saw
A hut. I approach the hut
125　And knock at the door
—Silence. A prayer on my lips
I open the door and enter.
A candle burns. All
Is silver and gold."

130　BRIDEGROOM
"What is bad about that?
It promises wealth."

BRIDE
"Wait, sir, I've not finished.
135　Silently I gazed
On the silver and gold,
The cloths, the rugs, the silks,
From Novgorod, and I
Was lost in wonder.

140　"Then I heard a shout
And a clatter of hoofs . . .
Someone has driven up
To the porch. Quickly
I slammed the door and hid
145　Behind the stove. Now
I hear many voices . . .
Twelve young men come in,

"And with them is a girl,
Pure and beautiful.
150　They've taken no notice
Of the ikons,° they sit

151. ikons (ī′känz)
n.: images of Christ,
the Virgin, and saints,
used in the Eastern
Orthodox Church
(also spelled *icons*).

Cupolas and Swallows by Konstantin Yuon.

To the table without
Praying or taking off
Their hats. At the head,
155 The eldest brother,
At his right, the youngest;
At his left, the girl.
Shouts, laughs, drunken clamor . . .”°

158. clamor (klam′ər) *n.:* loud noise.

BRIDEGROOM
160 “That betokens merriment.”

BRIDE
“Wait, sir, I've not finished.
The drunken din goes on
And grows louder still.
165 Only the girl is sad.

“She sits silent, neither
Eating nor drinking;
But sheds tears in plenty;
The eldest brother

170 Takes his knife and, whistling,
Sharpens it; seizing her by
The hair he kills her
And cuts off her right hand.”

"Why," says the groom, "this
175 Is nonsense! Believe me,
My love, your dream is not evil."
She looks him in the eyes.
"And from whose hand
Does this ring come?"
180 The bride said. The whole throng
Rose in the silence.

With a clatter the ring
Falls, and rolls along
The floor. The groom blanches,°
185 Trembles. Confusion . . .
"Seize him!" the law commands.
He's bound, judged, put to death.
Natasha is famous!
Our song at an end.

184. blanches (blanch′iz) *v.*:
turns white; becomes pale.

Alexander Pushkin

The Father of Russian Literature

Russians read, admire, and quote **Alexander Pushkin** (1799–1837) as the English do William Shakespeare. A master of poetry, drama, and fiction, Pushkin is often called the father of modern Russian literature. Even in his earliest writings, Pushkin focused on Russian settings and folk tales. "The Bridegroom," first published in 1825 (under the Russian title "Zhenikh"), is one of many Pushkin works based on motifs from Russian folklore. As his talents developed, Pushkin became known for his realistic characters and simple, natural language, which were unlike the characters and language of any Russian writer before him.

Alexander Pushkin (19th century) by W. Troponin.

Pushkin was born in Moscow to a noble family that had lost most of its wealth. He was especially proud of his African great-grandfather, Abram Hannibal, who served as a general under the Russian ruler Peter the Great.

Pushkin's love of stories and reading began early. His father had a large library, and the boy's beloved nanny kept young Pushkin entertained with old tales. He had his first poem published at age fifteen. By the time he left school, Pushkin was viewed as a rival to the leading writers of the day.

Pushkin's first job, at eighteen, was at the foreign office in the Russian capital of St. Petersburg. However, he was soon banned from the city for writing poetry critical of Russia's czar. Officials of the Russian government kept tabs on Pushkin for the rest of his life.

In 1831, Pushkin married a beautiful woman named Natalya Goncharova. She became friends with a French nobleman, Baron Georges d'Anthes. D'Anthes was so in love with Pushkin's wife that he married her sister in order to be closer to her. In 1837, Pushkin challenged d'Anthes to a duel over his wife's honor. Like one of his own Romantic characters, Pushkin was fatally wounded in the duel. All Russia mourned the loss of a national hero.

First Thoughts

1. Why do you think Natasha doesn't immediately tell her parents what has happened? When she does tell, why do you think she describes her experience as a dream?

Thinking Critically

2. Look back at your notes for the Quickwrite on page 62. Would your advice have worked for Natasha? Why or why not? ✏️

3. What is the central **conflict,** or problem, in this poem?

4. Natasha invites the authorities to her wedding party. What do we later find out is the cause of this unusual action?

5. What moment would you say is the **climax** of this poem? Describe what you visualize happening at that moment.

Extending Interpretations

6. Some parts of Natasha's story are not explained in the poem. We don't know why she went into the forest at night or how she escaped from the hut without being seen. How would you explain these parts of the plot?

7. Could the main events of this poem happen today? Why or why not?

WRITING

Retelling the Story

"The Bridegroom" is based on an old folk tale. Fill out a plot chart like the one on page 3 for "The Bridegroom," or jot down some notes about key elements of the plot. Then, retell the poem as a prose story. If you wish, you can change the time and setting of the story.

Reading Check 📖

a. Natasha goes into the woods. What is the **effect** of her action?

b. Natasha runs home terrified when the young man goes by in his carriage. What do we learn later is the **cause** of her terror?

c. What are the "goods" that the matchmaker speaks of? Who is the "buyer"?

d. Natasha tells the story of her dream at her wedding banquet. What is the **effect** of this story on her guests?

e. Who killed the girl in the hut?

North Carolina Competency Goal
1.02; 1.04; 4.01; 4.02; 5.01; 5.02

SKILLS FOCUS

Literary Skills
Analyze climax.

Reading Skills
Analyze cause and effect.

Writing Skills
Retell the story.

Comparing Literature

Literary Focus
Suspense

You have just opened a book. It begins, "It was a dark and stormy night. I pulled back the curtain and looked out at the rainy darkness. A bolt of lightning flashed brightly. A dog howled in the distance. I had a strange feeling that something dangerous was out there waiting for me." Do you wonder what the narrator is afraid of? Do you want to find out what will happen to the narrator? Is your heart beating a little faster?

If so, you are feeling suspense. **Suspense** is the anxious curiosity you feel about what will happen next in a story. Suspense makes us eager to keep reading long after we should be asleep.

Some common elements of suspense stories are listed on the right. How many do you recognize?

Reading Skills
Comparing and Contrasting

You are about to read two plays, *In the Fog* and *The Hitchhiker*. Although these plays tell different stories, they are both full of suspense. You may even find that they use some of the same elements of suspense, such as mysterious characters and deserted roads. However, these plays also have important differences. For one thing, *In the Fog* is meant to be performed on a stage, but *The Hitchhiker* is meant to be read over the radio.

To **compare** and **contrast** the plays, you will look for ways in which they are similar and ways in which they are different. After each play, you'll find a chart (see page 85). Copy the chart, and use it to record details from the plays. You'll refer to the information in your chart when you write a comparison-contrast essay at the end of this lesson.

> ## Elements of Suspense
>
> - plot twists and surprise endings
> - a dark night
> - a deserted road
> - fog
> - knocks on the door
> - foreshadowing
> - thunder or lightning
> - strange footprints
> - mysterious characters or events
> - a creaky door
> - a howling dog or wolf
> - a shot in the dark
> - strong winds or violent rains

North Carolina Competency Goal
1.02

SKILLS FOCUS

Literary Skills
Understand suspense.

Reading Skills
Compare and contrast plays.

Before You Read

You are driving down a dark, lonely road in the Pennsylvania hills. The fog rolls in, and you can no longer see the roadside markers. You are turned around, confused. You think you are lost. Read on to see how a character in just such a situation responds—and what strange events begin to happen. Watch how this writer builds suspense and carries it through to a climactic and surprising end.

In the Fog

Milton Geiger

Characters

A Doctor	A Wounded Man
Eben	A Gas Station Attendant
Zeke	

Sets: A signpost on Pennsylvania Route 30. A rock or stump in the fog. A gas station pump.

Night. At first we can only see fog drifting across a dark scene devoid of[1] detail. Then, out of the fog, there emerges toward us a white roadside signpost with a number of white painted signboards pointing to right and to left. The marker is a Pennsylvania State Route—marked characteristically "PENNA-30." Now a light as from a far headlight sweeps the signs.

An automobile approaches. The car pulls up close. We hear the car door open and slam and a man's footsteps approaching on the concrete. Now the signs are lit up again by a more localized, smaller source of light. The light grows stronger as the man, offstage, approaches. The DOCTOR enters, holding a flashlight before him. He scrutinizes[2] the road marker. He flashes his light up at the arrows. We see the legends on the markers. Pointing off right there are markers that read: York, Columbia, Lancaster; pointing left the signs read: Fayetteville, McConnellsburg, Pennsylvania Turnpike.

The DOCTOR's face is perplexed and annoyed as he turns his flashlight on a folded road map. He is a bit lost in the fog. Then his flashlight fails him. It goes out! ❶

VISUALIZE

❶ Consider the stage directions you just read. Which details create a sense of mystery and suspense?

Doctor. Darn! (*He fumbles with the flashlight in the gloom. Then a voice is raised to him from offstage.*)

Eben (*offstage, strangely*). Turn around, mister. . . .

[*The* DOCTOR *turns sharply to stare offstage.*]

---

1. **devoid** (di·void′) **of:** without.
2. **scrutinizes** (skro͞ot″n·īz′iz) *v.:* examines carefully.

Zeke (*offstage*). You don't have to be afraid, mister. . . .

[*The* DOCTOR *sees two men slowly approaching out of the fog. One carries a lantern below his knees. The other holds a heavy rifle. Their features are utterly indistinct as they approach, and the rifleman holds up his gun with quiet threat.*]

Eben. You don't have to be afraid.

Doctor (*more indignant than afraid*). So you say! Who are you, man?

Eben. We don't aim to hurt you none.

Doctor. That's reassuring. I'd like to know just what you mean by this? This gun business! Who *are* you?

Zeke (*mildly*). What's your trade, mister?

Doctor. I . . . I'm a doctor. Why?

Zeke (*to* EBEN). Doctor.

Eben (*nods; then to* DOCTOR). Yer the man we want.

Zeke. Ye'll do proper, we're thinkin'.

Eben. So ye'd better come along, mister.

Zeke. Aye.

Doctor. Why? Has—anyone been hurt?

Eben. It's for you to say if he's been hurt nigh to the finish.

Zeke. So we're askin' ye to come along, doctor. ❷

[*The* DOCTOR *looks from one to another in indecision and puzzlement.*]

Eben. In the name o' mercy.

Zeke. Aye.

Doctor. I want you to understand—I'm not afraid of your gun! I'll go to your man all right. Naturally, I'm a doctor. But I demand to know who you are.

Zeke (*patiently*). Why not? Raise yer lantern, Eben. . . .

Eben (*tiredly*). Aye.

[EBEN *lifts his lantern. Its light falls on their faces now, and we see that they are terrifying. Matted beards, clotted with blood; crude head bandages, crusty with dirt and dry blood. Their hair, stringy and disheveled. Their faces are lean and hollow cheeked; their eyes sunken and tragic. The* DOCTOR *is shocked for a moment—then bursts out—*]

ANALYZE

❷ **Foreshadowing** hints at what is to come. What details in this scene foreshadow danger ahead?

PREDICT

❸ What do you think happened to Zeke and Eben?

Doctor. Good heavens!—

Zeke. That's Eben; I'm Zeke.

Doctor. What's happened? Has there been an accident or . . . what? ❸

Zeke. Mischief's happened, stranger.

Eben. Mischief enough.

Doctor (*looks at rifle at his chest*). There's been gunplay—hasn't there?

Zeke (*mildly ironic*). Yer tellin' us there's been gunplay!

Doctor. And I'm telling you that I'm not at all frightened! It's my duty to report this, and report it I will!

Zeke. Aye, mister. You do that.

Doctor. You're arrogant about it now! You don't think you'll be caught and dealt with. But people are losing patience with you men. . . . You . . . you moonshiners!³ Running wild . . . a law unto yourselves . . . shooting up the countryside!

Zeke. Hear that, Eben? Moonshiners.

Eben. Mischief's happened, mister, we'll warrant⁴ that. . . .

Doctor. And I don't like it!

Zeke. Can't say we like it better'n you do, mister. . . .

Eben (*strangely sad and remote*). What must be, must.

Zeke. There's no changin' or goin' back, and all 'at's left is the wishin' things were different. ❹

Eben. Aye.

Doctor. And while we talk, your wounded man lies bleeding, I suppose—worthless though he may be. Well? I'll have to get my instrument bag, you know. It's in the car.

[EBEN *and* ZEKE *part to let* DOCTOR *pass between them. The* Doctor *reenters, carrying his medical bag.*]

Doctor. I'm ready. Lead the way.

[EBEN *lifts his lantern a bit and goes first.* ZEKE *prods the* DOCTOR *ever so gently and apologetically but firmly with the rifle muzzle. The* DOCTOR *leaves.* ZEKE *strides off slowly after them.* ❺

  A wounded man is lying against a section of stone fence. He, too, is bearded, though very young, and his shirt is dark with blood. He

ANALYZE

❹ Mystery helps create **suspense**. What mysterious, unexplained things do Zeke and Eben do and say?

RETELL

❺ Stop and identify the main characters. Describe in your own words the doctor's situation. What dangers does he face?

---

3. **moonshiners** *n.*: people who distill liquor illegally.
4. **warrant** (wôr′ənt) *v.*: declare positively.

breathes but never stirs otherwise. EBEN *enters, followed by the* DOCTOR *and* ZEKE.]

Zeke. Ain't stirred a mite since we left 'im.

Doctor. Let's have that lantern here! (*The* DOCTOR *tears the man's shirt for better access to the wound. Softly*) Dreadful! Dreadful . . . !

Zeke's voice (*off scene*). Reckon it's bad in the chest like that, hey?

Doctor (*taking pulse*). His pulse is positively racing . . . ! How long has he been this way?

Zeke. A long time, mister. A long time. . . .

Doctor (*to* EBEN). You! Hand me my bag.

[EBEN *puts down lantern and hands bag to the* DOCTOR. *The* DOCTOR *opens bag and takes out a couple of retractors.*[5] ZEKE *holds lantern close now.*] ❻

Doctor. Lend me a hand with these retractors. (*He works on the man.*) All right . . . when I tell you to draw back on the retractors— draw back.

Eben. Aye.

Zeke. How is 'e, mister?

Doctor (*preoccupied*). More retraction. Pull them a bit more. Hold it. . . .

Eben. Bad, ain't he?

Doctor. Bad enough. The bullet didn't touch any lung tissue far as I can see right now. There's some pneumothorax[6] though. All I can do now is plug the wound. There's some cotton and gauze wadding in my bag. Find it. . . .

[ZEKE *probes about silently in the bag and comes up with a small dark box of gauze.*]

Doctor. That's it. (*Works a moment in silence*) I've never seen anything quite like it.

Eben. Yer young, doctor. Lots o' things you've never seen.

Doctor. Adhesive tape!

PREDICT

❻ Who do you think the injured person is? What do you think will happen to the doctor?

"It's my duty to report this, and report it I will!"

---

5. **retractors** (ri·trak′tərz) *n.:* surgical instruments for holding back the flesh at the edge of a wound.

6. **pneumothorax** (n$\overline{oo}$′mō·thôr′aks′) *n.:* air or gas in the chest cavity.

[ZEKE *finds a roll of three-inch tape and hands it to the* DOCTOR, *who tears off long strips and slaps them on the dressing and pats and smooths them to the man's chest.* EBEN *replaces equipment in* DOCTOR's *bag and closes it with a hint of the finality to come. A preview of dismissal, so to speak.*]

Doctor (*at length*). There. So much for that. Now then— (*takes man's shoulders*) give me a hand here.
Zeke (*quiet suspicion*). What fer?

Doctor. We've got to move this man.

Zeke. What fer?

Doctor (*stands; indignantly*). We've got to get him to a hospital for treatment; a thorough cleansing of the wound; irrigation.[7] I've done all I can for him here.

Zeke. I reckon he'll be all right 'thout no hospital. ❼

---

7. **irrigation** *n.:* here, flushing out a wound with water or other fluid.

COMPARE AND CONTRAST

❼ Compare the doctor's and Zeke's attitudes toward the injured man. Why might Zeke and Eben not want to take the man to a hospital?

Doctor. Do you realize how badly this man's hurt!

Eben. He won't bleed to death, will he?

Doctor. I don't think so—not with that plug and pressure dressing. But bleeding isn't the only danger we've got to—

Zeke (*interrupts*). All right, then. Much obliged to you.

Doctor. This man's dangerously hurt!

Zeke. Reckon he'll pull through now, thanks to you.

Doctor. I'm glad you feel that way about it! But I'm going to report this to the Pennsylvania State Police at the first telephone I reach!

Zeke. We ain't stoppin' ye, mister.

Eben. Fog is liftin', Zeke. Better be done with this, I say.

Zeke (*nods, sadly*). Aye. Ye can go now, mister . . . and thanks. (*Continues*) We never meant a mite o' harm, I can tell ye. If we killed, it was no wish of ours.

Eben. What's done is done. Aye.

Zeke. Ye can go now, stranger. . . .

[EBEN *hands* ZEKE *the* DOCTOR's *bag.* ZEKE *hands it gently to the* DOCTOR.]

Doctor. Very well. You haven't heard the last of this, though!

Zeke. That's the truth, mister. We've killed, aye; and we've been hurt for it. . . .

Eben. Hurt bad.

[*The* DOCTOR's *face is puckered with doubt and strange apprehension.*]

Zeke. We're not alone, mister. We ain't the only ones. (*Sighs*) Ye can go now, doctor . . . and our thanks to ye. . . .

[*The* DOCTOR *leaves the other two, still gazing at them in strange enchantment and wonder and a touch of indignation.*] ❽

Eben's voice. Thanks, mister. . . .

Zeke's voice. In the name o' mercy. . . . We thank you. . . .

Eben. In the name o' mercy.

Zeke. Thanks, mister. . . .

Eben. In the name o' kindness. . . .

COMPARE AND CONTRAST

❽ How has the doctor's attitude toward Zeke and Eben changed? Do you think he has more sympathy for them than he did at first? Explain.

[*The two men stand with their wounded comrade at their feet—like a group statue in the park. The fog thickens across the scene. Far off the long, sad wail of a locomotive whimpers in the dark.*

The scene now shifts to a young ATTENDANT *standing in front of a gasoline pump taking a reading and recording it in a book as he prepares to close up. He turns as he hears the car approach on the gravel drive.*

The DOCTOR *enters.*] ❾

Attendant (*pleasantly*). Good evening, sir. (*Nods off at car*) Care to pull 'er up to this pump, sir? Closing up.

Doctor (*impatiently*). No. Where's your telephone, please? I've just been held up!

Attendant. Pay station[8] inside, sir. . . .

Doctor. Thank you! (*The* DOCTOR *starts to go past the* ATTENDANT.)

Attendant. Excuse me, sir. . . .

Doctor (*stops*). Eh, what is it, what is it?

Attendant. Uh . . . what sort of looking fellows were they?

Doctor. Oh—two big fellows with a rifle; faces and heads bandaged and smeared with dirt and blood. Friend of theirs with a gaping hole in his chest. I'm a doctor, so they forced me to attend him. Why?

Attendant. *Those* fellers, huh?

Doctor. Then you know about them!

Attendant. I guess so.

Doctor. They're armed and they're desperate!

Attendant. That was about two or three miles back, would you say?

Doctor (*fumbling in pocket*). Just about— I don't seem to have the change. I wonder if you'd spare me change for a quarter . . . ? ❿

Attendant (*makes change from metal coin canister at his belt*). Certainly, sir. . . .

Doctor. What town was that back there, now?

Attendant (*dumps coins in other's hand*). There you are, sir.

Doctor (*impatient*). Yes, thank you. I say—what town was that back there, so I can tell the police?

Attendant. That was . . . Gettysburg, mister. . . .

Doctor. Gettysburg . . . ?

---

8. **pay station:** pay telephone.

Comparing Literature

PREDICT

❾ The doctor stated that he was going to report Zeke and Eben to the police. Do you think he will do so now? Why do you think Zeke and Eben seemed unconcerned about being reported?

IDENTIFY

❿ How does the attendant react to the doctor's story? Does his reaction surprise you? Why or why not?

Attendant. Gettysburg and Gettysburg battlefield. . . . (*Looks off*) When it's light and the fog's gone, you can see the gravestones. Meade's men . . . Pickett's men, Robert E. Lee's. . . .[9]

[*The* DOCTOR *is looking off with the* ATTENDANT; *now he turns his head slowly to stare at the other man.*]

Attendant (*continues*). On nights like this—well—you're not the first those men've stopped . . . or the last. (*Nods off*) Fill 'er up, mister?

Doctor. Yes, fill 'er up. . . . ⓫

INFER

⓫ What important information does the attendant give the doctor? What conclusions can you draw about Zeke and Eben?

---

9. **Meade's men . . . Lee's:** The Battle of Gettysburg was a turning point in the American Civil War. On July 1–3, 1863, the Confederacy's forces, under Robert E. Lee, met the Union forces, under George Gordon Meade. The climax of the battle came when 15,000 Confederate soldiers, led by George Pickett, charged Cemetery Ridge and were repelled. The North suffered about 23,000 casualties, the South about 20,000.

After You Read · *In the Fog*

First Thoughts

1. Respond to *In the Fog* by completing the following sentence:
   - I was surprised when . . .

Thinking Critically

2. What do you think would have happened if the doctor had refused to go with his captors?

3. When the fog lifts, Eben and Zeke tell the doctor he can go. Look back through the play and find other mentions of the fog. What importance do you think the fog has in this play? Use details from the play to support your interpretations.

4. Before the doctor leaves Zeke and Eben, Zeke says, "If we killed, it was no wish of ours." Now that you have finished the play, does this line make more sense to you? Explain what you think Zeke means by this statement.

Comparing Literature

5. After you read the next play, you will write a comparison-contrast essay. You can begin to plan your essay by filling in a chart like the one below, focusing on *In the Fog*. This chart will be repeated on page 104, where you will fill in details about *The Hitchhiker*.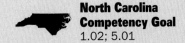

Reading Check

Use the following story map to outline the main parts of this play's plot. Keep your notes for the assignment on page 105.

Characters:	Setting:

Problem or Conflict:

Major Events:
1.
2.
(Add as many as you need)

Climax:

Ending/Resolution:

Comparing Elements of Suspense		
	In the Fog	The Hitchhiker
Props and Sound Effects		
Setting		
Ghost characters		
Human characters		

SKILLS FOCUS

Literary Skills
Analyze suspense.

Reading Skills
Compare and contrast plays.

North Carolina Competency Goal
1.02; 5.01

Before You Read

In the 1930s and 1940s, Americans gathered around the radio the way we now gather around the television. Like television shows, radio shows came in many varieties: There were adventure series, detective stories, comedies, and even soap operas (in fact, soap operas began on the radio). However, radio was different from television in important ways. Without pictures that showed what was happening, *dialogue* and *sound effects* had to tell the story and create mood. The rest was left to the listener's imagination!

The Hitchhiker is a popular and suspenseful radio play from the golden age of radio. As you read *The Hitchhiker,* use your imagination to "watch" the hair-raising events unfold.

The Hitchhiker

Lucille Fletcher

Characters

Ronald Adams	A Girl
His Mother	A Telephone Operator
The Gray Man	A Long-Distance Operator
A Mechanic	An Albuquerque Operator
Henry	A New York Operator
Henry's Wife	Mrs. Whitney

(Opposite) *Brooklyn Bridge* (detail) by W. Louis Sonntag, Jr.
© Museum of the City of New York.

The time of the play is the early 1940s.

[Sound: *Automobile wheels humming over concrete road.* Music: *Something weird and shuddery.*]

Adams. I am in an auto camp[1] on Route Sixty-six just west of Gallup, New Mexico. If I tell it, perhaps it will help me. It will keep me from going mad. But I must tell this quickly. I am not mad now. I feel perfectly well, except that I am running a slight temperature. My name is Ronald Adams. I am thirty-six years of age, unmarried, tall, dark, with a black moustache. I drive a 1940 Ford V-8, license number 6V-7989. I was born in Brooklyn. All this I know. I know that I am at this moment perfectly sane. That it is not I who have gone mad—but something else—something utterly beyond my control. But I must speak quickly. At any moment the link with life may break. This may be the last thing I ever tell on earth . . . the last night I ever see the stars. . . . ❶

IDENTIFY

❶ Which details in Adams's first speech make you want to read on?

[Music: *In.*]

Adams. Six days ago I left Brooklyn, to drive to California. . . .
Mother. Goodbye, Son. Good luck to you, my boy. . . .
Adams. Goodbye, Mother. Here—give me a kiss, and then I'll go. . . .
Mother. I'll come out with you to the car.
Adams. No. It's raining. Stay here at the door. Hey—what is this? Tears? I thought you promised me you wouldn't cry.
Mother. I know, dear. I'm sorry. But I—do hate to see you go.
Adams. I'll be back. I'll only be on the Coast three months. ❷
Mother. Oh, it isn't that. It's just—the trip. Ronald—I wish you weren't driving.
Adams. Oh—Mother. There you go again. People do it every day.
Mother. I know. But you'll be careful, won't you? Promise me you'll be extra careful. Don't fall asleep—or drive fast—or pick up any strangers on the road. . . .
Adams. Lord, no. You'd think I was still seventeen to hear you talk—
Mother. And wire me as soon as you get to Hollywood, won't you, Son?
Adams. Of course I will. Now don't you worry. There isn't anything going to happen. It's just eight days of perfectly simple driving on smooth, decent, civilized roads, with a hot dog or a hamburger stand every ten miles. . . . (*Fade*)

IDENTIFY

❷ A **flashback** is a scene that breaks the normal time order of the plot. When does this scene take place? How do you know? Pay attention, and see if you can figure out how much of this play is told in flashback.

---

1. **auto camp:** a campground with places for drivers to park their cars.

[Sound: *Auto hum.* Music: *In.*]

Adams. I was in excellent spirits. The drive ahead of me, even the loneliness, seemed like a lark.[2] But I reckoned without *him.*

[Music: *Changes to something weird and empty.*] ❸

Adams. Crossing Brooklyn Bridge that morning in the rain, I saw a man leaning against the cables. He seemed to be waiting for a lift. There were spots of fresh rain on his shoulders. He was carrying a cheap overnight bag in one hand. He was thin, nondescript, with a cap pulled down over his eyes. He stepped off the walk and if I hadn't swerved, I'd have hit him.

[Sound: *Terrific skidding.* Music: *In.*]

Adams. I would have forgotten him completely, except that just an hour later, while crossing the Pulaski Skyway[3] over the Jersey flats, I saw him again. At least, he looked like the same person. He was standing now, with one thumb pointing west. I couldn't figure out how he'd got there, but I thought probably one of those fast trucks had picked him up, beaten me to the Skyway, and let him off. I didn't stop for him. Then—late that night, I saw him again.

[Music: *Changing.*]

Adams. It was on the new Pennsylvania Turnpike between Harrisburg and Pittsburgh. It's two hundred and sixty-five miles long, with a very high speed limit. I was just slowing down for one of the tunnels—when I saw him—standing under an arc light by the side of the road. I could see him quite distinctly. The bag, the cap, even the spots of fresh rain spattered over his shoulders. He hailed me this time. . . .
Voice (*very spooky and faint*). Hall-ooo. . . . (*Echo as through tunnel*) Hall-ooo . . . !
Adams. I stepped on the gas like a shot. That's lonely country through the Alleghenies,[4] and I had no intention of stopping. Besides, the coincidence, or whatever it was, gave me the willies.[5] I stopped at the next gas station. ❹

---

2. **lark** *n.:* good time; spree.
3. **Pulaski Skyway:** long-span bridge connecting the cities of Newark and Jersey City, New Jersey.
4. **Alleghenies** (al′ə·gā′nēz): the Allegheny mountain range, a part of the Appalachian Mountains that runs through Pennsylvania, Maryland, West Virginia, and Virginia.
5. **willies** *n.:* feeling of nervousness; jitters.

Comparing Literature

ANALYZE

❸ How do the music directions give a clue that something is strange about the hitchhiker?

COMPARE AND CONTRAST

❹ Think back to the setting of *In the Fog.* What things are similar about the setting of these two plays so far? What things are different?

[Sound: *Auto tires screeching to stop . . . horn honk.*]

Mechanic. Yes, sir.
Adams. Fill her up.
Mechanic. Certainly, sir. Check your oil, sir?
Adams. No, thanks.

[Sound: *Gas being put into car . . . bell tinkle, etc.*]

Mechanic. Nice night, isn't it?
Adams. Yes. It—hasn't been raining here recently, has it?
Mechanic. Not a drop of rain all week.
Adams. Hm. I suppose that hasn't done your business any harm.
Mechanic. Oh—people drive through here all kinds of weather. Mostly business, you know. There aren't many pleasure cars out on the Turnpike this season of the year.
Adams. I suppose not. (*Casually*) What about hitchhikers?
Mechanic (*half laughing*). Hitchhikers *here*?

Portal and tunnel on Pennsylvania Turnpike.

Adams. What's the matter? Don't you ever see any?

Mechanic. Not much. If we did, it'd be a sight for sore eyes.

Adams. Why?

Mechanic. A guy'd be a fool who started out to hitch rides on this road. Look at it. It's two hundred and sixty-five miles long, there's practically no speed limit, and it's a straightaway. Now what car is going to stop to pick up a guy under those conditions? Would you stop?

Adams. No. (*Slowly, with puzzled emphasis*) Then you've never seen anybody?

Mechanic. Nope. Mebbe they get the lift before the Turnpike starts—I mean, you know just before the tollhouse—but then it'd be a mighty long ride. Most cars wouldn't want to pick up a guy for that long a ride. And you know—this is pretty lonesome country here—mountains, and woods. . . . You ain't seen anybody like that, have you? ❺

Adams. No. (*Quickly*) Oh no, not at all. It was—just a—technical question.

Mechanic. I see. Well—that'll be just a dollar forty-nine—with the tax. . . . (*Fade*)

[Sound: *Auto hum up.* Music: *Changing.*]

Adams. The thing gradually passed from my mind, as sheer coincidence. I had a good night's sleep in Pittsburgh. I did not think about the man all next day—until just outside Zanesville, Ohio, I saw him again.

[Music: *Dark, ominous note.*]

Adams. It was a bright sunshiny afternoon. The peaceful Ohio fields, brown with the autumn stubble, lay dreaming in the golden light. I was driving slowly, drinking it in, when the road suddenly ended in a detour. In front of the barrier, *he* was standing.

[Music: *In.*]

Adams. Let me explain about his appearance before I go on. I repeat. There was nothing sinister about him. He was as drab as a mud fence. Nor was his attitude menacing. He merely stood there, waiting, almost drooping a little, the cheap overnight bag in his hand. He looked as though he had been waiting there for hours. Then he looked up. He hailed me. He started to walk forward.

IDENTIFY

❺ What does the mechanic tell Adams that adds to the mystery of the hitchhiker?

Voice (*far-off*). Hall-ooo . . . Hall-ooo. . . .

Adams. I had stopped the car, of course, for the detour. And for a few moments, I couldn't seem to find the new road. I knew he must be thinking that I had stopped for him.

Voice (*closer*). Hall-ooo . . . Hallll . . . ooo. . . .

[Sound: *Gears jamming . . . sound of motor turning over hard . . . nervous accelerator.*]

Voice (*closer*). Halll . . . oooo. . . .

Adams (*panicky*). No. Not just now. Sorry. . . .

Voice (*closer*). Going to California?

[Sound: *Starter starting . . . gears jamming.*]

Adams (*as though sweating blood*). No. Not today. The other way. Going to New York. Sorry . . . sorry. . . .

[Sound: *Car starts with squeal of wheels on dirt . . . into auto hum.* Music: *In.*]

Adams. After I got the car back onto the road again, I felt like a fool. Yet the thought of picking him up, of having him sit beside me, was somehow unbearable. Yet, at the same time, I felt, more than ever, unspeakably alone. **❻**

[Sound: *Auto hum up.*]

COMPARE AND CONTRAST

❻ In *In the Fog,* the doctor meets men on the side of the road. Even though the men are armed, the doctor is unafraid. How is Adams's reaction to the hitchhiker different from the doctor's reaction to the men he meets?

Gas (1940) by Edward Hopper.
The Museum of Modern Art, New York.

Adams. Hour after hour went by. The fields, the towns ticked off, one by one. The lights changed. I knew now that I was going to see him again. And though I dreaded the sight, I caught myself searching the side of the road, waiting for him to appear.

[Sound: *Auto hum up . . . car screeches to a halt . . . impatient honk two or three times . . . door being unbolted.*]

Sleepy Man's Voice. Yep? What is it? What do you want?

Adams (*breathless*). You sell sandwiches and pop here, don't you?

Voice (*cranky*). Yep. We do. In the daytime. But we're closed up now for the night.

Adams. I know. But—I was wondering if you could possibly let me have a cup of coffee—black coffee.

Voice. Not at this time of night, mister. My wife's the cook and she's in bed. Mebbe further down the road—at the Honeysuckle Rest. . . .

[Sound: *Door squeaking on hinges as though being closed.*]

Adams. No—no. Don't shut the door. (*Shakily*) Listen—just a minute ago, there was a man standing here—right beside this stand—a suspicious-looking man. . . .

Woman's Voice (*from distance*). Hen-ry? Who is it, Hen-ry?

Henry. It's nobuddy, Mother. Just a feller thinks he wants a cup of coffee. Go back to bed.

Adams. I don't mean to disturb you. But you see, I was driving along—when I just happened to look—and there he was. . . .

Henry. What was he doing?

Adams. Nothing. He ran off—when I stopped the car.

Henry. Then what of it? That's nothing to wake a man in the middle of his sleep about. (*Sternly*) Young man, I've got a good mind to turn you over to the sheriff.

Adams. But—I—

Henry. You've been taking a nip, that's what you've been doing. And you haven't got anything better to do than to wake decent folk out of their hard-earned sleep. Get going. Go on.

Adams. But—he looked as though he were going to rob you.

Henry. I ain't got nothin' in this stand to lose. Now—on your way before I call out Sheriff Oakes. (*Fade*) ❼

RETELL

❼ Who is the **main character** of this play? What does he want? List the main events that have happened so far. What **complications** have developed?

[Sound: *Auto hum up.*]

Adams. I got into the car again, and drove on slowly. I was beginning to hate the car. If I could have found a place to stop . . . to rest a little. But I was in the Ozark Mountains of Missouri now. The few resort places there were closed. Only an occasional log cabin, seemingly deserted, broke the monotony[6] of the wild wooded landscape. I *had* seen him at that roadside stand: I knew I would see him again—perhaps at the next turn of the road. I knew that when I saw him next, I would run him down. . . .

[Sound: *Auto hum up.*]

Adams. But I did not see him again until late next afternoon. . . .

[Sound: *Of railroad warning signal at crossroads.*]

Adams. I had stopped the car at a sleepy little junction[7] just across the border into Oklahoma— to let a train pass by—when he appeared, across the tracks, leaning against a telephone pole.

[Sound: *Distant sound of train chugging . . . bell ringing steadily.*]

Adams (*very tense*). It was a perfectly airless, dry day. The red clay of Oklahoma was baking under the southwestern sun. Yet there were spots of fresh rain on his shoulders. I couldn't stand that. Without thinking, blindly, I started the car across the tracks.

[Sound: *Train chugging closer.*]

Adams. He didn't even look up at me. He was staring at the ground. I stepped on the gas hard, veering the wheel sharply toward him. I could hear the train in the distance now, but didn't care. Then something went wrong with the car. It stalled right on the tracks.

6. **monotony** (mə·nät′′n·ē) *n.:* tiresome sameness.
7. **junction** (juŋk′shən) *n.:* point where two sets of railroad tracks join.

[Sound: *Train chugging closer. Above this, sound of car stalling.*]

Adams. The train was coming closer. I could hear its bell ringing, and the cry of its whistle. Still he stood there. And now—I knew that he was beckoning—beckoning me to my death.

[Sound: *Train chugging close. Whistle blows wildly. Then train rushes up and by with pistons going, etc.*]

Adams. Well—I frustrated him that time. The starter had worked at last. I managed to back up. But when the train passed, he was gone. I was all alone in the hot, dry afternoon. ❽

[Sound: *Train retreating. Crickets begin to sing. Music: In.*]

PREDICT

❽ What do you think will happen to Adams? What clues **foreshadow** his future?

Railroad Crossing (1922–1923) by Edward Hopper. Oil on canvas, 29½" × 40¹⁄₁₆". Whitney Museum of American Art, New York; Josephine N. Hopper Bequest (70.1189).

Adams. After that, I knew I had to do something. I didn't know who this man was or what he wanted of me. I only knew that from now on, I must not let myself be alone on the road for one moment.

[Sound: *Auto hum up. Slow down. Stop. Door opening.*]

Adams. Hello, there. Like a ride?
Girl. What do you think? How far you going?
Adams. Amarillo . . . I'll take you to Amarillo.
Girl. Amarillo, Texas?
Adams. I'll drive you there.
Girl. Gee!

[Sound: *Door closed—car starts.* Music: *In.*]

Girl. Mind if I take off my shoes? My dogs[8] are killing me.
Adams. Go right ahead.
Girl. Gee, what a break this is. A swell car, a decent guy, and driving all the way to Amarillo. All I been getting so far is trucks.
Adams. Hitchhike much?
Girl. Sure. Only it's tough sometimes, in these great open spaces, to get the breaks.
Adams. I should think it would be. Though I'll bet if you get a good pickup in a fast car, you can get to places faster than—say, another person, in another car.
Girl. I don't get you.
Adams. Well, take me, for instance. Suppose I'm driving across the country, say, at a nice steady clip of about forty-five miles an hour. Couldn't a girl like you, just standing beside the road, waiting for lifts, beat me to town after town—provided she got picked up every time in a car doing from sixty-five to seventy miles an hour?
Girl. I dunno. Maybe she could and maybe she couldn't. What difference does it make?
Adams. Oh—no difference. It's just a—crazy idea I had sitting here in the car.
Girl (*laughing*). Imagine spending your time in a swell car thinking of things like that!
Adams. What would you do instead?
Girl (*admiringly*). What would I do? If I was a good-looking fellow like yourself? Why—I'd just *enjoy* myself—every minute of the time.

---

8. **dogs** *n.:* slang word for feet.

I'd sit back, and relax, and if I saw a good-looking girl along the side of the road . . . (*Sharply*) Hey! Look out!

Adams (*breathlessly*). Did you see him too?

Girl. See who?

Adams. That man. Standing beside the barbed-wire fence.

Girl. I didn't see—anybody. There wasn't nothing but a bunch of steers—and the barbed-wire fence. What did you think you was doing? Trying to run into the barbed-wire fence?

Adams. There was a man there, I tell you . . . a thin, gray man, with an overnight bag in his hand. And I was trying to—run him down.

Girl. Run him down? You mean—kill him?

Adams. He's a sort of—phantom. I'm trying to get rid of him—or else prove that he's real. But (*desperately*) you say you didn't see him back there? You're sure?

Girl (*queerly*). I didn't see a soul. And as far as that's concerned, mister . . .

Adams. Watch for him the next time, then. Keep watching. Keep your eyes peeled on the road. He'll turn up again—maybe any minute now. (*Excitedly*) There. Look there—

[Sound: *Auto sharply veering and skidding.* GIRL *screams.* Sound: *Crash of car going into barbed-wire fence. Frightened lowing of steer.*]

Girl. How does this door work? I—I'm gettin' outta here.

Adams. Did you see him that time?

Girl (*sharply*). No. I didn't see him that time. And personally, mister, I don't expect never to see him. All I want to do is to go on living—and I don't see how I will very long driving with you—

Adams. I'm sorry. I—I don't know what came over me. (*Frightened*) Please—don't go. . . .

Girl. So if you'll excuse me, mister—

Adams. You can't go. Listen, how would you like to go to California? I'll drive you to California.

Girl. Seeing pink elephants[9] all the way? No thanks.

Adams (*desperately*). I could get you a job there. You wouldn't have to be a waitress. I have friends there—my name is Ronald Adams—you can check up. ❾

[Sound: *Door opening.*]

---

9. **pink elephants:** imaginary objects seen by someone who is drunk or delirious.

INFER

❾ What does Adams learn about the hitchhiker in this scene with the girl? What does the girl learn about Adams?

Girl. Uhn-hunh. Thanks just the same.

Adams. Listen. Please. For just one minute. Maybe you think I am half cracked. But this man. You see, I've been seeing this man all the way across the country. He's been following me. And if you could only help me—stay with me—until I reach the Coast—

Girl. You know what I think you need, big boy? Not a girlfriend. Just a good dose of sleep. . . . There, I got it now.

[Sound: *Door opens . . . slams.*]

Adams. No. You can't go.

Girl (*screams*). Leave your hands offa me, do you hear! Leave your—

Adams. Come back here, please, come back.

[Sound: *Struggle . . . slap . . . footsteps running away on gravel . . . lowing of steer.*]

Adams. She ran from me, as though I were a monster. A few minutes later, I saw a passing truck pick her up. I knew then that I was utterly alone.

[Sound: *Lowing of steer up.*]

Adams. I was in the heart of the great Texas prairies. There wasn't a car on the road after the truck went by. I tried to figure out what to do, how to get hold of myself. If I could find a place to rest. Or even, if I could sleep right here in the car for a few hours, along the side of the road. . . . I was getting my winter overcoat out of the back seat to use as a blanket (*Hall-ooo*) when I saw him coming toward me (*Hall-ooo*), emerging from the herd of moving steers. . . .

Voice. Hall-ooo . . . Hall-ooo. . . .

[Sound: *Auto starting violently . . . up to steady hum.* Music: *In.*]

Adams. I didn't wait for him to come any closer. Perhaps I should have spoken to him then, fought it out then and there. For now he began to be everywhere. Whenever I stopped, even for a moment— for gas, or oil, for a drink of pop, a cup of coffee, a sandwich—he was there.

[Music: *Faster.*]

Adams. I saw him standing outside the auto camp in Amarillo that night, when I dared to slow down. He was sitting near the drinking fountain in a little camping spot just inside the border of New Mexico.

[Music: *Faster.*]

Adams. He was waiting for me outside the Navajo reservation, where I stopped to check my tires. I saw him in Albuquerque, where I bought twelve gallons of gas. . . . I was afraid now, afraid to stop. I began to drive faster and faster. I was in lunar landscape now—the great arid mesa[10] country of New Mexico. I drove through it with the indifference of a fly crawling over the face of the moon. ❿

[Music: *Faster.*]

Adams. But now he didn't even wait for me to stop. Unless I drove at eighty-five miles an hour over those endless roads—he waited for me at every other mile. I would see his figure, shadowless, flitting before me, still in its same attitude, over the cold and lifeless ground, flitting over dried-up rivers, over broken stones cast up by old glacial upheavals, flitting in the pure and cloudless air. . . .

[Music: *Strikes sinister note of finality.*]

---

10. **mesa** (mā′sə) *n.* used as *adj.*: elevated flat-topped land formation with steep sides.

Comparing Literature

COMPARE AND CONTRAST

❿ What did Adams want when he left Brooklyn? What does he want now?

U.S. Highway 1, Number 5 (1962) by Allan D'Arcangelo.
The Museum of Modern Art, New York. © Estate of Allan D'Arcangelo/Licensed by VAGA, New York.

Adams. I was beside myself when I finally reached Gallup, New Mexico, this morning. There is an auto camp here—cold, almost deserted at this time of year. I went inside, and asked if there was a telephone. I had the feeling that if only I could speak to someone familiar, someone that I loved, I could pull myself together.

[Sound: *Nickel put in slot.*]

Operator. Number, please?

Adams. Long distance.

Operator. Thank you.

[Sound: *Return of nickel; buzz.*]

Long Distance. This is long distance.
Adams. I'd like to put in a call to my home in Brooklyn, New York. I'm Ronald Adams. The number is Beechwood 2-0828.[11]
Long Distance. Thank you. What is your number?
Adams. 312.
Albuquerque Operator. Albuquerque.
Long Distance. New York for Gallup. (*Pause*)
New York Operator. New York.
Long Distance. Gallup, New Mexico, calling Beechwood 2-0828. (*Fade*)
Adams. I had read somewhere that love could banish demons. It was the middle of the morning. I knew Mother would be home. I pictured her, tall, white-haired, in her crisp housedress, going about her tasks. It would be enough, I thought, merely to hear the even calmness of her voice. . . . ⓫
Long Distance. Will you please deposit three dollars and eighty-five cents for the first three minutes? When you have deposited a dollar and a half, will you wait until I have collected the money?

[Sound: *Clunk of six coins.*]

Long Distance. All right, deposit another dollar and a half.

[Sound: *Clunk of six coins.*]

---

11. **Beechwood 2-0828**: phone number. At the time of this story, phone numbers in the United States began with two letters (called an exchange), followed by five numbers. Names (called exchange names) like Beechwood were used to tell callers which two letters to dial—usually the first two letters of the name (e.g., *BE* for *Beechwood*).

PREDICT

⓫ Do you think Adams will reach his mother? Will the phone call really help him feel calmer? Explain.

Long Distance. Will you please deposit the remaining eighty-five cents?

[Sound: *Clunk of four coins.*]

Long Distance. Ready with Brooklyn—go ahead, please.

Adams. Hello.

Mrs. Whitney. Mrs. Adams's residence.

Adams. Hello. Hello—Mother?

Mrs. Whitney (*very flat and rather proper*). This is Mrs. Adams's residence. Who is it you wished to speak to, please?

Adams. Why—who's this?

Mrs. Whitney. This is Mrs. Whitney.

Adams. Mrs. Whitney? I don't know any Mrs. Whitney. Is this Beechwood 2-0828?

Mrs. Whitney. Yes.

Adams. Where's my mother? Where's Mrs. Adams?

Mrs. Whitney. Mrs. Adams is not at home. She is still in the hospital.

Adams. The hospital!

Mrs. Whitney. Yes. Who is this calling, please? Is it a member of the family?

Adams. What's she in the hospital for?

Mrs. Whitney. She's been prostrated[12] for five days. Nervous breakdown. But who is this calling?

Adams. Nervous breakdown? But—my mother was never nervous.

Mrs. Whitney. It's all taken place since the death of her oldest son, Ronald.

Adams. Death of her oldest son, Ronald . . . ? Hey—what is this? What number is this?

Mrs. Whitney. This is Beechwood 2-0828. It's all been very sudden. He was killed just six days ago in an automobile accident on the Brooklyn Bridge.

Operator (*breaking in*). Your three minutes are up, sir. (*Pause*) Your three minutes are up, sir. (*Pause*) Your three minutes are up, sir. (*Fade*) Sir, your three minutes are up. Your three minutes are up, sir.

Adams (*in a strange voice*). And so, I am sitting here in this deserted auto camp in Gallup, New Mexico. I am trying to think. I am trying to get hold of myself. Otherwise, I shall go mad. . . . Outside it is night—

---

12. **prostrated** (präs′trā′tid) *v.*: overcome by exhaustion or grief; weak.

the vast, soulless night of New Mexico. A million stars are in the sky. Ahead of me stretch a thousand miles of empty mesa, mountains, prairies—desert. Somewhere among them, he is waiting for me. Somewhere I shall know who he is, and who . . . I . . . am. . . . **⓬**
[Music: *Up.*]

INFER

⓬ What really happened on the Brooklyn Bridge? How do we discover the truth?

The Scream (1893) by Edvard Munch.
National Gallery © 2005 The Munch Museum/The Munch-Ellingsen Group/Artists Rights Society (ARS), New York.

Meet the Writer

Lucille Fletcher

In an interview, **Lucille Fletcher** (1912–2000) shared the secret to writing convincing suspense stories:

> 66 Writing suspense stories is like working on a puzzle. You bury the secret, lead the reader down the path, put in false leads, and throughout the story remain completely logical. Each word must have meaning and be written in a fine literary style. 99

The Hitchhiker holds our attention because it contains all of these elements, as well as a kernel of truth. The idea for the play originated during a drive to California. As Fletcher, a Brooklyn native, was leaving New York, she saw a strange man on the Brooklyn Bridge. The same stranger later appeared on the Pulaski Skyway. It's no accident, then, that Fletcher has the gray man who haunts Ronald Adams in *The Hitchhiker* appear on both of these bridges.

Fletcher had wanted to become a writer since her childhood, but it was only when she was typing radio plays at CBS that she realized she could write radio plays of her own.

For Independent Reading

If you're ready for another dose of suspense, try Lucille Fletcher's most popular

Lucille Fletcher, as pictured in her college yearbook in 1933.

work, *Sorry, Wrong Number.* This play features a troubled woman who is tormented when she overhears a chilling conversation on the phone. The Mystery Writers of America presented Fletcher with the Edgar Allan Poe Award for this haunting thriller, which was also made into a popular movie starring Barbara Stanwyck.

First Thoughts

1. Respond to *The Hitchhiker* by completing the following sentence: *The most surprising thing about this play is . . .*

Thinking Critically

2. When does Adams first see the hitchhiker? How do his feelings about the hitchhiker change over the course of the play?

3. Whom or what do you think the hitchhiker represents?

4. In a way, this play doesn't end at all. Instead, Adams and the reader are kept in suspense. What do you think Adams will do after the end of the play? Use details from the play to support your answer.

Reading Check

Check your comprehension by **retelling** this play to a partner. Start with the title, author, and main character. See how many of the play's **settings** you can recall. Next, tell what the main **conflict** or problem is. Then, tell the main events, in the order in which they occur. Be sure to state which events are **flashbacks.** Finally, describe the **climax**—the most suspenseful moment in the story. Have your partner fill out a Retelling Checklist (see page 17) to give you feedback on your retelling.

Comparing Literature

5. Add information on *The Hitchhiker* to the chart below. Use this chart as you write the comparison-contrast essay on the next page.

North Carolina Competency Goal
1.02; 5.01

Comparing Elements of Suspense		
	In the Fog	The Hitchhiker
Props and sound effects		
Setting		
Ghost characters		
Human characters		

SKILLS FOCUS

Literary Skills
Analyze suspense.

Reading Skills
Compare and contrast plays.

Writing a Comparison-Contrast Essay

Assignment

Write an essay comparing and contrasting *In the Fog* and *The Hitchhiker*. To plan your essay, review the chart you completed earlier. The chart will help you focus on elements in the plays that are very similar or very different. You do not have to write about all of these elements. Pick the elements in the plays that interest you most.

Use the workshop on writing a **comparison-contrast essay,** pages 404–409, for help with this assignment.

There are two ways you can organize your essay:

1. You can organize by the plays. That means that you will discuss one play at a time, explaining how certain elements are used in that play. Your first paragraph should introduce the plays and the topic of your essay. Your second and third paragraphs might be outlined as shown below.

> **Paragraph 2:** How certain elements are used in *In the Fog*
>   A. Setting of *In the Fog*
>   B. Ghost characters in *In the Fog*
> **Paragraph 3:** How certain elements are used in
>   *The Hitchhiker*
>   A. Setting of *The Hitchhiker*
>   B. Ghost characters in *The Hitchhiker*

2. You can also organize by the elements. That means you will discuss one element at a time, explaining how it is used in each play. Your second and third paragraphs might be outlined as follows:

> **Paragraph 2:** The setting of each play
>   A. *In the Fog*
>   B. *The Hitchhiker*
> **Paragraph 3:** The ghost characters in each play
>   A. *In the Fog*
>   B. *The Hitchhiker*

At the end of your essay, tell which play you prefer and why. Which play was more suspenseful? Which play challenged you more as a reader? Use examples from the plays to explain your responses.

SKILLS FOCUS

North Carolina Competency Goal
1.02; 1.04; 4.01; 4.02; 5.01

Writing Skills
Write a comparison-contrast essay.

Earth

Oliver Herford

If this little world tonight
    Suddenly should fall through space
In a hissing, headlong flight,
    Shrivelling from off its face,
5   As it falls into the sun,
    In an instant every trace
Of the little crawling things—
    Ants, philosophers, and lice,
Cattle, cockroaches, and kings,
10   Beggars, millionaires, and mice,
Men and maggots all as one
    As it falls into the sun. . . .
Who can say but at the same
    Instant from some planet far
15 A child may watch us and exclaim:
    "See the pretty shooting star!"

Earth

John Hall Wheelock

"A planet doesn't explode of itself," said drily
The Martian astronomer, gazing off into the air—
"That they were able to do it is proof that highly
Intelligent beings must have been living there."

Oliver Herford

A Man of Many Talents

The author, illustrator, cartoonist, comedian, and poet **Oliver Herford** (1863–1935) was born and raised in England and eventually settled in New York City. There his home was down the street from a theater group called the Player's Club. Herford became a member and often participated in comedy sketches.

Herford was a master of illustration, especially drawings of children and animals. He illustrated many of his own numerous volumes of light verse and is known for his series of illustrations for Rudyard Kipling's *Just So Stories,* which

originally appeared in the children's magazine *St. Nicholas* in 1898.

John Hall Wheelock

A Life in Literature

John Hall Wheelock (1886–1978) enjoyed a dual career as a poet and an editor. Wheelock graduated from Harvard University in 1908 as class poet. While just freshmen in college, Wheelock and his friend and classmate Van Wyck Brooks published their first volume of poetry.

Shortly after college, Wheelock went to work for the distinguished publishing firm Charles Scribner and Sons. There he eventually rose to become a director and senior editor and worked with many acclaimed authors.

In the meantime, Wheelock continued to write, producing several volumes of poetry and receiving many awards, including the Gold Medal from the Poetry Society of America in 1972.

Writing Workshop

Assignment

Write an original short story.

Audience

Children, teenagers, or adults (you decide).

RUBRIC
Evaluation Criteria

A good story

1. centers on a conflict or problem that a character has to solve

2. includes a series of related events that keep readers in suspense and that lead to a climax

3. provides a vividly detailed setting

4. uses dialogue and action to develop the plot

5. ends with a resolution of the conflict

North Carolina Competency Goal
1.01

SKILLS FOCUS

Writing Skills
Write a short story.

NARRATIVE WRITING
Short Story

What if you found yourself in a new school, with no friends? What if your dog could talk? What if your neighbor turned out to be from outer space? A good **short story** often begins with a "what if" idea—a situation or a character that sparks a reader's desire to know what will happen next.

Prewriting

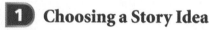

1 Choosing a Story Idea

Think about the following **prompt:**

> A short story gives you an opportunity to use your imagination, whether you write about familiar people and places or strange, fantastic worlds. Write a creative short story with the main purpose of entertaining an audience.

Ideas for stories are everywhere. Generate ideas quickly by freewriting responses to questions like these:

- Is there a personal experience that I can use as the basis for a story?

- Have I read any newspaper or magazine articles that give me ideas for a story?

- Are there characters I've met in my reading that I would like to use in an original story?

- Is there a particular problem that I'd like to explore through the characters and events of a story?

CALVIN AND HOBBES © Watterson. Reprinted with permission of UNIVERSAL PRESS SYNDICATE. All rights reserved.

2 Inventing Your Characters

Begin with **characters**. Think of people or animals that have caught your attention. What makes them interesting? What do they want? What problems do they face? What do they look like? What are they afraid of? What do they say? What do others say about them? Use your imagination to freewrite about them.

3 Building a Plot

A story's **plot**—the things that happen—will have four elements:

- a **conflict** (that is, a problem). The way characters deal with the problem is the basis of the story.

- a **series of events** that the problem sets in motion

- a **climax,** or high point, when the problem is settled

- a **resolution** that shows how things work out

Traditionally writers have used the following diagram to help them visualize the "shape" of their short stories.

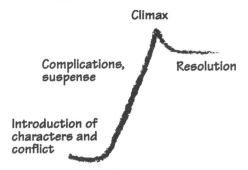

Climax

Complications, suspense

Resolution

Introduction of characters and conflict

4 Planning Your Setting

The following questions will help your plan your setting:

- Where does the story take place, and why is this location important?

- When does the story take place, and how much time does it cover?

- How does the setting affect the conflict?

- What details will establish the setting in the reader's mind?

Generating Story Ideas

Begin by thinking of familiar people, places, and situations. Then, ask yourself, "What if one thing changed?" For example:

- What if our family moved?

- What if my friends and I were stuck in an elevator?

- What if summer lasted all year long?

- What if I were trapped in a giant computer?

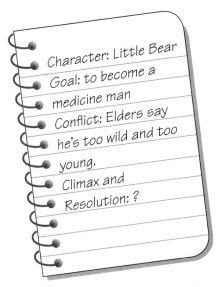

Character: Little Bear
Goal: to become a medicine man
Conflict: Elders say he's too wild and too young.
Climax and Resolution: ?

Strategies For Elaboration

Listening can help you write realistic **dialogue**—words spoken by characters in a story. Listen closely to people talking. Notice the following elements:

- use of contractions and slang
- use of half-finished sentences and phrases
- interruptions—how, when, and why speakers interrupt one another

Read your dialogue aloud, or ask a classmate to do so. Keep changing it until your characters sound like real people talking.

Language Handbook
H E L P

Problems with verbs: See Agreement, 2, and Using Verbs, 3.

Drafting

No matter how much planning you do, you won't know the whole story until you actually write it. Even if you don't feel ready to begin, just start anyway—you'll be amazed to find that ideas will come to you when you need them! If your writing takes you in a direction you didn't expect, see where it leads.

1 Telling the Story

All short stories have a narrator who tells the story. The narrator tells the story from a certain angle called the **point of view.** When the narrator is a character in the story who refers to himself or herself with first-person pronouns (*I, me, my, mine*), the story is told from the **first-person point of view.** When the narrator is not a character in the story but tells what is going on, the story has a **third-person point of view** and uses third-person pronouns (*he, she, they, them*). Be consistent in your story's point of view.

2 Drafting the Story's Beginning

Your first few sentences should pull your readers into the story and make them want to know what happens next. Try to create suspense and to show your characters in action. If you find it difficult to write the opening, that's all right—write the rest of the story first, and then come back and write the beginning last.

3 Concluding the Story

A good story has a satisfying ending. Whether you leave your reader happy or sad, angry or inspired, the ending should feel complete. Show how your characters have been affected by the problem and by the way it was settled. Have they changed or learned a lesson? How will their future be different now than it might have been without the problem?

Student Model

Apples in the Snow

Snow Child used to be called Little Bear. He was as free as the wind with his Cherokee family and was very happy. The only thing he longed for was to become the sacred medicine man of the tribe.

The elders, though, thought it unwise for him to become the medicine man. They said that he was too wild and young. But Little Bear persisted. Finally, the elders said, "Go out into the hills. If you can find apples in the snow, it will be a sign that the Great Spirit wills you to become our medicine man."

Little Bear fasted all day. Then he set out into the hills. He climbed and searched to no avail for that day and the next. He stopped often to pray to Mon-o-La, the earth, and to the Great Spirit.

Then, on the third night, Little Bear had a dream. He dreamed that he was standing by a golden apple tree. Around it the snow was melted. Then from inside the tree came a musical voice. "Come pick my apples. I grow them for you, for you, for you. . . ." Little Bear awoke. He tried to think what the dream meant. While he thought, he walked up the hill.

Thinking and walking, he soon reached the top. There he began to pray. When he opened his eyes, there was the golden apple tree of his dream. He waited for the voice to come, but when it did not, he decided that it had spoken in his dream and that was enough. So he picked the apples and started down the mountain, thanking the goodness of the spirits. When he turned to look at the tree, it was gone.

When he reached his village, there was great feasting. The elders told him that the golden tree was the tree of Mon-o-La. So Little Bear became Snow Child and would soon become the tribe's sacred medicine man.

—Jane Caflisch
Kensington, Maryland

The first paragraph introduces the **main character** *and tells us what he wants.*

This **dialogue** *establishes Little Bear's main* **conflict:** *The elders think he is too young to be a medicine man.*

The writer narrates a **series of events.**

Sensory details paint a picture of the dream's **setting.**

This is the high point, or **climax.** *Little Bear has met his challenge.*

The conflict is resolved.

INTERNET

More Writer's Models

Keyword: LE5 6-1

Evaluating and Revising

Use the following chart to evaluate and revise your short story.

Short Story: Content and Organization Guidelines		
Evaluation Questions	▶ **Tips**	▶ **Revision Techniques**
❶ **Does your introduction establish the setting?**	▶ **Put a check mark** next to details about the setting.	▶ **Add** details about time and place, if needed.
❷ **Are the characters convincing?**	▶ **Highlight** character details, description, and dialogue.	▶ **Elaborate** as needed by adding sensory details, concrete language, and dialogue.
❸ **Is the problem, or conflict, of the story clear?**	▶ **Underline** the conflict.	▶ If necessary, **add** sentences that describe the problem.
❹ **Are events arranged in order and clearly connected? Does the plot keep readers in suspense?**	▶ **Number** each event. Check that events are in correct order. **Bracket** words or sentences that help create suspense.	▶ **Rearrange** events in order, if necessary. **Add** details to tie events together and to heighten suspense. **Cut** or **rearrange** details that reveal plot developments too soon.
❺ **Is the point of view clear and consistent?**	▶ **Circle** pronouns that establish the point of view in opening paragraphs.	▶ **Cut** pronouns or details that shift point of view.
❻ **Is the conflict resolved? Does the story outcome make sense?**	▶ **Underline in color** the story's climax and outcome.	▶ **Add** a climax, or high point, if necessary. **Add** details to show how the conflict is resolved.

On the next page you'll find the opening paragraphs of a short story. Following the model are questions to help you evaluate the writer's revisions.

Revision Model

Axdotel had ignored his mother's instruction to return

by the hour of first stellar watch. Now, as he ∧ watched   *tearfully*

the family ~~ship~~ lifting off, he realized that he was being   *spaceship*

left behind on a strange planet. Would they come back

for him, he wondered, or would they leave him to his

fate? His parents might not miss him for hours.

Wiping away his tears∧, Axdotel adjusted his   *with his anterior fins*

eyepiece to view his ∧ surroundings. Coming toward   *unfamiliar*

him was a tall creature moving on two long extensions

totally unlike Axdotel's posterior fins. Axdotel

attempted to run, but his fins, so nimble for swimming

and flying ∧ were unable to move over the ground.   *through the regions of his homeland, Mugatuk,*

~~Axdotel~~ heard the creature shriek. Axdotel had been   *Then he*

discovered!

Evaluating the Revision

1. Which details have been added to elaborate on setting and character?

2. How have words or sentences been rearranged?

PROOFREADING

 TIPS

Ask a classmate to proofread your story for mistakes. Find and correct any errors in spelling, punctuation, capitalization, and grammar before you create your final draft. Use the spellchecker on your computer if you have one.

Communications Handbook
H E L P

See Proofreaders' Marks.

PUBLISHING

TIPS

Illustrations can help readers visualize the characters, setting, or events in your short story. To include pictures in your story, draw your own illustrations or use clip art from computer software.

Test Practice

DIRECTIONS: Read the story. Then, answer each question.

The Path Through the Cemetery

Leonard Q. Ross

Ivan was a timid little man—so timid that the villagers called him "Pigeon" or mocked him with the title "Ivan the Terrible." Every night Ivan stopped in at the saloon which was on the edge of the village cemetery. Ivan never crossed the cemetery to get to his lonely shack on the other side. That path would save many minutes, but he had never taken it—not even in the full light of noon.

Late one winter's night, when bitter wind and snow beat against the saloon, the customers took up the familiar mockery. "Ivan's mother was scared by a canary when she carried him." "Ivan the Terrible—Ivan the Terribly Timid One."

Ivan's sickly protest only fed their taunts, and they jeered cruelly when the young Cossack lieutenant flung his horrid challenge at their quarry.

"You are a pigeon, Ivan. You'll walk all around the cemetery in this cold—but you dare not cross it."

Ivan murmured, "The cemetery is nothing to cross, Lieutenant. It is nothing but earth, like all the other earth."

The lieutenant cried, "A challenge, then! Cross the cemetery tonight, Ivan, and I'll give you five rubles—five gold rubles!"

Perhaps it was the vodka. Perhaps it was the temptation of the five gold rubles. No one ever knew why Ivan, moistening his lips, said suddenly: "Yes, Lieutenant, I'll cross the cemetery!"

The saloon echoed with their disbelief. The lieutenant winked to the men and unbuckled his saber. "Here, Ivan. When you get to the center of the cemetery, in front of the biggest tomb, stick the saber into the ground. In the morning we shall go there. And if the saber is in the ground—five gold rubles to you!"

Ivan took the saber. The men drank a toast: "To Ivan the Terrible!" They roared with laughter.

The wind howled around Ivan as he closed the door of the saloon behind him. The cold was knife-sharp. He buttoned his long coat and crossed the dirt road. He could hear the lieutenant's voice, louder than the rest, yelling after him, "Five rubles, pigeon! If you live!"

Ivan pushed the cemetery gate open. He walked fast. "Earth, just earth . . .

like any other earth." But the darkness was a massive dread. "Five gold rubles . . ." The wind was cruel and the saber was like ice in his hands. Ivan shivered under the long, thick coat and broke into a limping run.

He recognized the large tomb. He must have sobbed—that was the sound that was drowned in the wind. And he knelt, cold and terrified, and drove the saber through the crust into the hard ground. With all his strength, he pushed it down to the hilt. It was done. The cemetery . . . the challenge . . . five gold rubles.

Ivan started to rise from his knees. But he could not move. Something held him. Something gripped him in an unyielding and implacable hold. Ivan tugged and lurched and pulled— gasping in his panic, shaken by a monstrous fear. But something held Ivan. He cried out in terror, then made senseless gurgling noises.

They found Ivan, next morning, on the ground in front of the tomb that was in the center of the cemetery. He was frozen to death. The look on his face was not that of a frozen man, but of a man killed by some nameless horror. And the lieutenant's saber was in the ground where Ivan had pounded it—through the dragging folds of his long coat.

---

1. Ivan can best be described as —
   A brave
   B proud
   C fearful
   D sickly

2. Ivan's main **problem** is that he must —
   F carry the heavy saber
   G conquer his terror of the cemetery
   H fight the lieutenant
   J find the biggest tomb

3. When Ivan drives the saber into the frozen ground —
   A his heart gives out
   B he overcomes his fear
   C he sees a ghost
   D he pins his coat to the ground

4. By the **resolution** of the story, Ivan has —
   F claimed his five gold rubles
   G frozen to death
   H disappeared
   J been killed by the saber

Constructed Response

5. What overall feeling does the **setting** of this story create? Explain your answer, using details from the story.

Collection 1: Skills Review

Informational Reading Skills

Test Practice

DIRECTIONS: Read the Web page. Then, answer each question.

FEATURES | HOME | SEARCH | FEEDBACK | SITE MAP | NASA

WELCOME! Solar System Exploration is one of four space science themes for the Office of Space Science at the National Aeronautics and Space Administration (NASA). This Web site is your launching pad to find out more about the programs and people in them.

FEATURES

WHY EXPLORE OUR SOLAR SYSTEM? | THE **PLANETS**

A **HISTORY** OF EXPLORATION | THE **PEOPLE**

WHAT'S NEW? **EXTRA!** Mars 2001 Odyssey is on its way to Mars!

SCIENCE GOALS –
NEWS –
MISSIONS –
TECHNOLOGY –
RESEARCH –
EDUCATION –

LATE BREAKING

Perseid Dawn
The best time to see this year's Perseid meteor shower is just before dawn on August 12, 2000.

New Asteroid Target Chosen for Japanese-U.S. Mission
The MUSES-C project has announced that the asteroid target of the project and the launch date have been changed.

Hubble Discovers Missing Pieces of Comet Linear
The Hubble telescope discovered a small armada of "minicomets" left behind from what some scientists had prematurely thought was a total disintegration of the explosive comet LINEAR.

More News . . .

LATEST IMAGES

The Color of Regolith

On June 14, 2000, NEAR Shoemaker trained its camera on Eros' large-diameter crater for a series of color pictures intended to measure the properties of regolith inside the asteroid's craters.

RESEARCH ANNC.

CLICK HERE to find out about upcoming research opportunities in the NASA Office of Space Science.

RECENT ADDITIONS

17 MAY 2000
SSE main page has a new look!

17 MAY 2000
The history timeline has been updated.

| Internal | NASA Office of Space Science |

Curator: A. M. Sohus
Webmaster: J. Tenisci
Last Updated: 9 August 2000

North Carolina Competency Goal 2.01

Reading Skills
Understand the structural features of popular media.

1. The source of this home page is —
   A NASA (the National Aeronautics and Space Administration)
   B a group of amateur astronomers
   C the MUSES-C project
   D Solar System Exploration

2. This page was last updated on —
   F June 14, 2000
   G May 17, 2000
   H August 12, 2000
   J August 9, 2000

3. If you wanted to find out about the scientists who work at NASA, which feature would you go to?
   A A History of Exploration
   B The Planets
   C The People
   D Education

4. If you wanted to find out about research opportunities at NASA, what would you click on?
   F Recent Additions
   G Research Announcements
   H Latest Images
   J Late Breaking

5. If you wanted to find out about water on Mars, what would you click on?
   A The Planets
   B Latest Images
   C Recent Additions
   D A History of Exploration

6. Suppose you've read "Hubble Discovers Missing Pieces of Comet Linear." To read more about the Hubble telescope, you should click on —
   F "The Color of Regolith"
   G "The People"
   H "Recent Additions"
   J "More News"

7. Which of the following topics are listed in the contents of this Web page?
   A "Missions" and "Education"
   B "Feedback" and "Site Map"
   C "The Planets" and "The People"
   D "Welcome!" and "Features"

Constructed Response

8. Briefly explain the overall purpose of this home page.

Collection 1: Skills Review

Vocabulary Skills

Multiple-Meaning Words

DIRECTIONS: Each of the sentences below is from "All Summer in a Day." Read the sentence. Then, choose the answer in which the underlined word is used in the same way.

1. "And once, a month ago, she had refused to shower in the school shower rooms. . . ."
   A The baby shower is next Thursday.
   B The children were caught in a shower and came home drenched.
   C The singer smiled modestly as her admirers poured out a shower of praise.
   D The players dashed off to shower after football practice.

2. "She . . . had clutched her hands to her ears and over her head, screaming the water mustn't touch her head."
   F The movie didn't touch me at all.
   G The bow tie added a jaunty touch to his outfit.
   H We were glad to hear from you. Please keep in touch.
   J Don't blame it on me. I didn't touch him.

3. "She glanced at her watch."
   A Watch for Grandma; she should be here soon.
   B As they worked, Jane kept watch over the door.
   C Watch out! That foul ball almost hit you.
   D What time is it by your watch?

4. "The world ground to a standstill."
   F After the rain the ground was soaked.
   G Slowly the train ground to a halt.
   H The parade ground was deserted.
   J Stand your ground or they will make you do it.

5. "The sky darkened into midnight in a flash."
   A Flash your light over here.
   B The boy saw his parents flash a glance at each other.
   C He'll be with you in a flash.
   D We saw a flash of purple light.

North Carolina Competency Goal
6.01

SKILLS FOCUS

Vocabulary Skills
Use multiple-meaning words.

Collection 1: Skills Review

Writing Skills

Test Practice

DIRECTIONS: Read this paragraph from a short story. Then, answer each question.

Flat Out of Luck

Mrs. Fiona McNulty was late. She smashed her wig onto her head, pulled up the suspenders on her overalls, crammed her feet into the openings of her oversized shoes, grabbed her bag of tricks, and raced out the door to her small car. "Oops," she thought to herself, "I should have had that tire checked. It looks low. I don't have time to check it now. I'll do it on the way home from the birthday party." Fifteen minutes later, in the middle of the five o'clock rush-hour traffic jam, Mrs. McNulty felt the tire go flat. She braced herself and moved as quickly as she could to the side of the road. She turned off the motor and climbed out of her car. "Great! What do I do now?" she thought. Mrs. McNulty was already late for her appearance at a child's birthday party as JoJo the Juggling Clown.

1. What words did the writer use to establish the setting?

   A "crammed her feet into the openings of her oversized shoes"

   B "in the middle of the five o'clock rush-hour traffic jam"

   C "braced herself and moved as quickly as she could"

   D "should have had that tire checked"

2. If the writer wanted to add sensory details to the story, which of the following sentences would be appropriate?

   F The birthday party was at a house across town.

   G She had to hurry if she wanted to be on time.

   H She couldn't call anyone because she had left her cell phone at home.

   J Passers-by stared at the clown in a red wig, baggy overalls, and oversized shoes.

3. Why did the student put the sentence "Great! What do I do now?" in quotation marks?

   A Because the sentence is dialogue

   B Because it is the title of the story

   C Because it is the story conflict

   D Because it creates suspense

4. Why did the student identify her character first as Mrs. Fiona McNulty and later as JoJo the Juggling Clown?

   F To reveal that Mrs. McNulty is not a real person

   G To clarify that the character changed her clothing in the car

   H To create suspense by describing Mrs. McNulty's strange clothing before revealing that it is a clown's costume

   J To make the reader to feel sympathy for Mrs. McNulty's predicament

North Carolina Competency Goal 5.01

Writing Skills
Write a short story.

Fiction

Facing Your Fear

In *Jungle Dogs* by Graham Salisbury, Boy Regis, a sixth-grader, is scared of the wild dogs he sees in his Hawaiian village. Even worse, his older brother, Damon, always fights off the bullies who pick on him. As the confrontations become more violent, Boy needs to prove to Damon, and himself, that fighting is not the answer to his problems. Can he do it before somebody gets badly hurt?

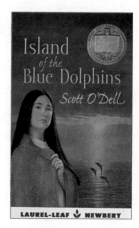

Left Behind

What would you do if you were left totally on your own? In Scott O'Dell's *Island of the Blue Dolphins,* a twelve-year-old Native American girl named Karana is stranded on an island off the coast of California during the nineteenth century. She learns to build shelter and find food and wins an animal friend in this gripping tale of survival and self-discovery.

Shipwrecked

Phillip is traveling to Virginia when his ship is hit by a torpedo. Left blind in the middle of the ocean, he is rescued by Timothy, a West Indian man who leads Phillip onto a life raft. As they work together to survive on a deserted island, their friendship blossoms in *The Cay* by Theodore Taylor. If you like this story, you may also enjoy the prequel, *Timothy of the Cay.*

This title is available in the HRW Library.

The Shaking Earth

In *Earthquake at Dawn,* Kristiana Gregory looks back at the earthquake that devastated San Francisco in 1906. Fifteen-year-old Daisy and her friend Edith search for Daisy's father and try to help others amid the rubble and confusion. This historical novel is based on a letter written by a survivor of the earthquake and on photographs taken at the scene of the disaster.

Nonfiction

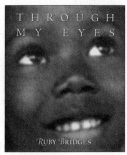

Battling Prejudice

In *Through My Eyes,* Ruby Bridges tells what it was like to be the first African American student in an all-white elementary school. In this moving memoir, we see her confronting abuse and isolation with remarkable courage. Newspaper articles, photographs, and quotations from the time provide a deeper understanding of her struggle.

Ancient Scientists

How did the ancient Egyptians build the pyramids? How did they mummify their dead? How did they use mathematics? Were there dentists? Find the answers to questions like these in *Science in Ancient Egypt* by Geraldine Woods. In this book you'll learn how the early Egyptians pioneered some of the key technologies of today.

Another Land, Another Time

Have you ever wondered what it would be like to live in the past? Fiona MacDonald shows you in *How Would You Survive as an Ancient Greek?* This interactive book, packed with useful information and colorful illustrations, tells you how you would eat, work, and travel in ancient Greece.

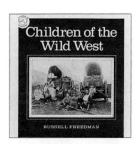

Children of Experience

In *Children of the Wild West,* Russell Freedman documents the lives of children in the American West during the nineteenth century. The book includes firsthand accounts by the sons and daughters of the pioneers. Unforgettable photographs present a moving portrait of family life and convey the special hardships faced by Native American and immigrant children.

Silver Horizons by Nelson Tsosie.

Characters: The People You'll Meet

Literary Focus:
Analyzing Characters

Informational Focus:
Taking Notes and Outlining

INTERNET
Collection
Resources
Keyword: LE5 6-2

Elements of Literature

Characters *by* Madeline Travers Hovland

THE ACTORS IN A STORY

Characters are the people or animals in a story. Characters are sometimes so lifelike that they seem to jump off the page at you. Like real people, characters in stories have qualities such as courage, laziness, or ambition. The character's qualities influence the events in a story—the way your qualities influence what happens to you in real life.

Who's Who?

Remember "The Three Little Pigs"? The characters in that story are three pigs, all members of the same family. Two of the pigs have similar qualities (sadly for them!). They're happy, good-natured fellows who mean well, but they're also timid, lazy, careless, and not very smart.

The third pig has more than his share of admirable qualities. He's hardworking, brave, intelligent, and determined to succeed.

The villain of the story, the wolf, has qualities that make him easy to dislike. He thinks he's a lot smarter than he is. He's mean and tricky, and he takes advantage of the weak and helpless (and the plump and delicious). He also likes to eat pigs for breakfast, lunch, and dinner.

Losers and Winners

The three pigs are the good guys. Even though two of them are losers, we feel sympathy for them—they're so foolish

and scared. In fact, we might feel sympathy for these two pigs because they are a lot like us.

Even if you didn't know the **plot,** the series of related events that make up the story, you could probably predict what will happen. In this plot the characters' qualities set them on a collision course.

Characters in Conflict

The basic situation is set when the three pigs build their houses. The **conflict** starts when the wolf strolls by and decides to make the pigs his dinner. The character traits of the first two pigs create **complications** in the plot. The two happy-go-lucky pigs have thrown together houses of straw and sticks, which are not very sturdy. The third pig has taken the time and trouble to build a strong house of bricks.

The enemy easily blows down the houses of the two good-natured pigs. Whether he wolfs down those pigs or whether they get away to their brother's house depends on who is telling the story. But in every version of the tale, the wolf doesn't stop after he ruins the pigs' houses. His appetite for pork drives him on to the house of the third little pig.

This clever pig gets a pot of water boiling in the fireplace. At this point the wolf has given up trying to blow the brick

North Carolina Competency Goal
5.01

INTERNET
More About Characters
Keyword: LE5 6-2

Literary Skills
Analyze characters and the way they affect plot.

"Listen out there! We're George and Harriet Miller! We just dropped in on the pigs for coffee! We're coming out! ... We don't want trouble!"

house down and is squeezing himself down the chimney. The plot is now about to reach its **climax.** This is the moment when the tension in the story is greatest and when we learn how the conflict will be resolved. The wolf falls into the pot of boiling water, and the third little pig becomes the winner, not dinner.

Character Counts

A Greek philosopher, or thinker, named Heraclitus (her′ə·klīt′əs) once wrote, "Character is destiny." (Destiny is a person's fate or lot in life.) When Heraclitus wrote that 2,500 years ago, he was thinking about real people, not characters in a story. But you'll discover that what's true about life is often true about literature. Character *counts*. The qualities of characters in a story have a major influence on the plot.

Practice

Think about a story you've read in a book or seen on TV or at the movies. Try to pick a story that involves a **conflict** between two strong **characters** and that has a clear winner and loser (many stories don't). On a piece of paper, draw an outline of two heads like the ones below. These represent the two main characters in the story or movie. In each of the outlined heads, list three or four important traits of each character, just as in the model. Then, complete the sentence below the heads. Name the character who won the conflict, and explain how qualities of character affected the way the plot came out.

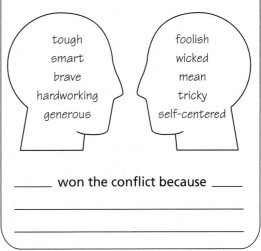

tough
smart
brave
hardworking
generous

foolish
wicked
mean
tricky
self-centered

_____ won the conflict because _____
_____
_____

Reading Skills and Strategies

Making Inferences

by Kylene Beers

While looking down at the floor of your room, which is covered with clothes, old homework, dirty towels, and bits of stale pizza crusts, your mom says, "You cleaned this just for me?" Though she didn't say it, you know your mom doesn't really think your room is clean. Her tone of voice and the frown on her face hint that her words don't carry the full message. You **infer** that she isn't pleased as you combine what she said (the external message) with what you know (frowns aren't good). Your **inference** lets you know how best to respond.

When you take the information that an author puts on a page (the external knowledge) and combine it with what you already know (your internal knowledge), you are making an **inference.**

For instance, if you read "The girl gulped down the food, barely chewing it before taking another bite," the external knowledge tells you that the girl is eating quickly. Then if you read "She could hear the school bus heading toward her house," you can infer that she is eating fast not because she is hungry, but because she needs to hurry to catch the bus. What else can you infer from these two sentences? Did you infer that the "she" in the second sentence refers to "the girl" mentioned in the first? Could you figure out which meal of the day she is eating?

North Carolina Competency Goal 5.01

SKILLS FOCUS

Reading Skills Make inferences.

Hints for Making Inferences

To make an **inference** about a character or event in a story, combine the information the author gives you with what you already know. If you aren't sure when to make an inference as you read, keep these questions in mind:

- What does the writer tell you about how the character acts or thinks or dresses? What do you know—or think you know—about people who act or think or dress that way?

- What does the writer tell you about problems the character faces? What do you know about that situation or similar situations?

- What does the writer tell you about the way people respond to the character. What do these responses usually tell you about a person?

As you read the next selection, from a novel about a boy called Bud, keep these questions in mind.

from Bud, Not Buddy

Christopher Paul Curtis

Using the
Strategy

ERE WE GO AGAIN. We were all standing in line waiting for breakfast when one of the caseworkers came in and *tap-tap-tap*ped down the line. Uh-oh, this meant bad news, either they'd found a foster home for somebody or somebody was about to get paddled. All the kids watched the woman as she moved along the line, her high-heeled shoes sounding like little firecrackers going off on the wooden floor. ❶ 📖📖

As you read this selection, think about the information that the author gives you and the information you must supply on your own. When you combine what's in the text with what you already know, you are making an **inference**.

MAKE AN INFERENCE

❶ Look at the first sentence of the story: *"HERE WE GO AGAIN."* Is it possible to know who the "we" is just by reading that sentence? Sometimes when you are confused by something, you need to read on to figure out what's confusing you. By the end of this paragraph, you should be able to infer who the "we" is in that first sentence.

Brothers (1934) by Malvin Gray Johnson.
Smithsonian American Art Museum, Washington, D.C.

MAKE AN INFERENCE

❷ Does this case-worker know Bud or Jerry well? What information in the text helps you make your inference?

MAKE AN INFERENCE

❸ Are Bud and Jerry happy to have new homes? What does the author, Christopher Paul Curtis, write that tells you how they feel? Did he actually write "The boys are not happy" or "The boys are very happy"? Without a specific sentence like that, how did you decide how the boys feel?

MAKE AN INFERENCE

❹ Why do you think Jerry and Bud know how to finish the case-worker's sentence?

Shoot! She stopped at me and said, "Are you Buddy Caldwell?"

I said, "It's Bud, not Buddy, ma'am."

She put her hand on my shoulder and took me out of line. Then she pulled Jerry, one of the littler boys, over. "Aren't you Jerry Clark?" He nodded. ❷

"Boys, good news! Now that the school year has ended, you both have been accepted in new temporary-care homes starting this afternoon!"

Jerry asked the same thing I was thinking. "Together?"

She said, "Why, no. Jerry, you'll be in a family with three little girls . . ."

Jerry looked like he'd just found out they were going to dip him in a pot of boiling milk.

" . . . and Bud . . ." She looked at some papers she was holding. "Oh, yes, the Amoses, you'll be with Mr. and Mrs. Amos and their son, who's twelve years old, that makes him just two years older than you, doesn't it, Bud?"

"Yes, ma'am."

She said, "I'm sure you'll both be very happy."

Me and Jerry looked at each other. ❸

The woman said, "Now, now, boys, no need to look so glum. I know you don't understand what it means, but there's a depression going on all over this country. People can't find jobs and these are very, very difficult times for everybody. We've been lucky enough to find two wonderful families who've opened their doors for you. I think it's best that we show our new foster families that we're very . . ."

She dragged out the word very, waiting for us to finish her sentence for her.

Jerry said, "Cheerful, helpful and grateful." I moved my lips and mumbled. ❹

She smiled and said, "Unfortunately, you won't have time for breakfast. I'll have a couple of pieces of fruit put in a bag. In the meantime go to the sleep room and strip your beds and gather all of your things."

Here we go again. I felt like I was walking in my sleep as I followed Jerry back to the room where all the boys' beds were jim-jammed together. This was the third foster home I was going to and I'm used to packing up and leaving, but it still surprises me that there are always a few seconds, right after they tell you you've got to go, when my nose gets all runny and my throat gets all choky and my eyes get all stingy.

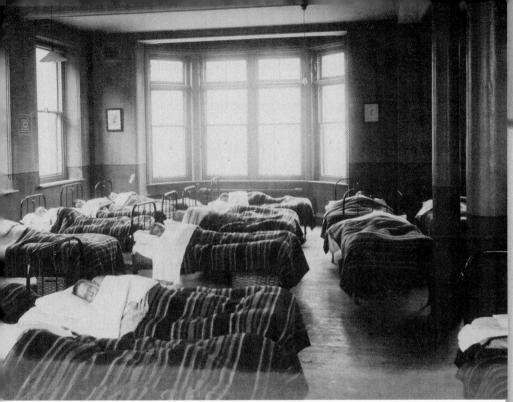

But the tears coming out doesn't happen to me anymore, I don't know when it first happened, but it seems like my eyes don't cry no more. ❺ 📖

Jerry sat on his bed and I could tell that he was losing the fight not to cry. Tears were popping out of his eyes and slipping down his cheeks.

I sat down next to him and said, "I know being in a house with three girls sounds terrible, Jerry, but it's a lot better than being with a boy who's a couple of years older than you. I'm the one who's going to have problems. A older boy is going to want to fight, but those little girls are going to treat you real good. They're going to treat you like some kind of special pet or something."

Jerry said, "You really think so?"

I said, "I'd trade you in a minute. The worst thing that's going to happen to you is that they're going to make you play house a lot. They'll probably make you be the baby and will hug you and do this kind of junk to you." I tickled Jerry under his chin and said, "Ga-ga goo-goo, baby-waby."

Jerry couldn't help but smile. I said, "You're going to be great."

Jerry looked like he wasn't so scared anymore so I went over to my bed and started getting ready. ❻ 📖

MAKE AN INFERENCE

❺ Was there ever a time when Bud would cry tears? Which specific sentence in this paragraph gives you the answer? At the end of the paragraph, Curtis tells readers that Bud's "eyes don't cry no more." Why might that be important information for you to know?

MAKE AN INFERENCE

❻ Do you think Bud really would trade places with Jerry? What can you tell about Bud's personality from his conversation with Jerry? The author doesn't tell you that Bud is or is not a nice guy. Instead, he shows what Bud is like through Bud's words and actions, then lets you infer what kind of guy Bud is. What could Bud have done differently with Jerry that would have led you to think differently about Bud?

MAKE AN INFERENCE

❼ What did the first foster home teach Bud? Curtis doesn't directly state what Bud learned—he lets you infer it. How could Curtis have told you directly what Bud learned? Would that have been as interesting to read? Why or why not?

MAKE AN INFERENCE

❽ Bud spends a lot of time describing an ordinary experience—losing baby teeth. What else do you learn about Bud as you read this section? Do you think he has a good sense of humor? Do you think he remembers what it feels like to be six? Explain.

MAKE AN INFERENCE

❾ Why was six a tough age for Bud? List the reasons he gives. Which reason does he say the least about? What does this help you to infer about him?

Even though it was me who was in a lot of trouble I couldn't help but feel sorry for Jerry. Not only because he was going to have to live around three girls, but also because being six is a real rough age to be at. Most folks think you start to be a real adult when you're fifteen or sixteen years old, but that's not true, it really starts when you're around six.

It's at six that grown folks don't think you're a cute little kid anymore, they talk to you and expect that you understand everything they mean. And you'd best understand too, if you aren't looking for some real trouble, 'cause it's around six that grown folks stop giving you little swats and taps and jump clean up to giving you slugs that'll knock you right down and have you seeing stars in the middle of the day. The first foster home I was in taught me that real quick. ❼

Six is a bad time too 'cause that's when some real scary things start to happen to your body, it's around then that your teeth start coming a-loose in your mouth.

You wake up one morning and it seems like your tongue is the first one to notice that something strange is going on, 'cause as soon as you get up there it is pushing and rubbing up against one of your front teeth and I'll be doggoned if that tooth isn't the littlest bit wiggly.

At first you think it's kind of funny, but the tooth keeps getting looser and looser and one day, in the middle of pushing the tooth back and forth and squinching your eyes shut, you pull it clean out. It's the scariest thing you can think of 'cause you lose control of your tongue at the same time and no matter how hard you try to stop it, it won't leave the new hole in your mouth alone, it keeps digging around in the spot where that tooth used to be.

You tell some adult about what's happening but all they do is say it's normal. You can't be too sure, though, 'cause it shakes you up a whole lot more than grown folks think it does when perfectly good parts of your body commence to loosening up and falling off of you.

Unless you're as stupid as a lamppost you've got to wonder what's coming off next, your arm? Your leg? Your neck? Every morning when you wake up it seems a lot of your parts aren't stuck on as good as they used to be. ❽

Six is real tough. That's how old I was when I came to live here in the Home. That's how old I was when Momma died. ❾

Meet the Writer

Christopher Paul Curtis

From Factory to Fiction

Christopher Paul Curtis (1953–) is the author of *The Watsons Go to Birmingham—1963,* a highly acclaimed novel for young readers. Narrated by nine-year-old Kenny Watson, the novel tells the story of the Watson family's summer trip from Detroit, Michigan, to Birmingham, Alabama, at the height of the civil rights movement. Part of the story, in which a Birmingham church is bombed, is based on an actual historical event. The novel was singled out for many awards.

Curtis's follow-up novel, *Bud, Not Buddy*, was published to even greater fanfare, capturing both the Coretta Scott King Medal and the Newbery Medal. The novel tells the story of ten-year-old orphan Bud Caldwell, who runs away from a bad foster home and sets out in search of his father during the Great Depression of the 1930s.

According to Curtis, he never set out to be a young adult author. "When I wrote *Bud, Not Buddy,*" he says, "I just had a story to tell and wanted to tell it. I didn't think of it as a children's book, per se."

Curtis grew up in Flint, Michigan. After high school, he began working on the assembly line at Fisher Body, a historic automotive factory, while attending the University of Michigan. Curtis worked at Fisher Body for thirteen years in all, and there he began writing:

66 When I was in the factory, I was keeping a journal. Writing took my mind off the line. I hated being in the factory. When I was writing, I forgot I was there.

I'd tried fiction, but I knew it was terrible. When kids say they don't like what they've written, I tell them: 'Be patient. Fiction takes a long time.' I didn't really feel comfortable with fiction until my late thirties, early forties. I'd tried it, but I wasn't happy with the results. 99

For Independent Reading

If you enjoyed the excerpt from *Bud, Not Buddy*, you may wish to read the entire novel.

Making Inferences

PRACTICE 1

1. In the excerpt from *Bud, Not Buddy,* you met Bud and Jerry. The author tells you some things about Bud and wants you to make inferences about other things. Read each statement, and explain which ones are inferences:

   • Bud wants Jerry to be happy.

   • Bud and Jerry would rather be together than go to two separate foster homes.

   • Bud thinks it's tough to be six.

2. Look at the first five paragraphs, and decide which pronouns go with which nouns. Why is it important to connect pronouns to the correct nouns?

3. Re-read what Bud tells Jerry about living with three girls. Do you know someone who would help a friend or a younger person feel better about a bad situation? What does that tell you about Bud?

4. Re-read the part where Bud talks about losing baby teeth. Can you remember losing your first tooth? Does that memory help you understand Bud? Do you think Bud's memories of being six help him understand Jerry? Explain.

PRACTICE 2

You can use a strategy called It Says, I Say, and So to help you keep track of what's in the text (the external information) and what's in your mind (the internal information). Use this strategy by making a chart that looks like this:

It Says	I Say	And So

SKILLS FOCUS

Reading Skills
Make inferences.

North Carolina Competency Goal
5.01; 5.02

As you read a question or think about the questions listed under "Hints for Making Inferences" on page 126, ask yourself first what the text tells you. List that information under "It Says." That's the external information—facts you can check in the text. Then, ask yourself what information you have. That's your internal information—information that's in your head. List that information under the "I Say" column. Finally, think about what conclusions you can reach from combining what's in the text with what's in your head. Put that under the "And So" column. Here's one example and one question for you to try:

	It Says	I Say	And So
1. How does Jerry feel when he's told he's going to live with a new family?	The text says Jerry "looked like he'd found out they were going to dip him in a pot of boiling milk."	That look on his face must be awful.	I think Jerry must feel terrible.
2. Have the tough times he's been through made Bud a tough guy?			

You can use this strategy with the stories in this collection. If you want to make inferences about any piece of literature, try It Says, I Say, and So.

Before You Read The Short Story

Ta-Na-E-Ka

Make the Connection
Quickwrite 🖉

Imagine that your family expects you to keep up a tradition they think is important but you're not sure you want to. Write a few sentences telling how you might deal with this conflict.

Literary Focus
Character and Conflict

A **character** is a person or an animal in a story. Characters in stories have qualities—courage or cruelty, for instance—just as people do in real life. What happens in a story depends on the way the characters respond to a **conflict.** There are two basic kinds of conflict. **External conflict** is a struggle between a character and an outside force, such as a rival or an earthquake. **Internal conflict** is a struggle in a character's mind or heart. A character might struggle with shyness, for example, or fear or jealousy.

Reading Skills 📖
Comparison and Contrast

As you read this story, you'll see little open-book signs and questions alongside the text. Some of these questions will help you **compare and contrast** the characters and the ways they deal with their conflicts. When you **compare,** you look for ways in which things are alike. When you **contrast,** you look for ways in which things are different.

North Carolina Competency Goal
1.04; 4.01; 5.01; 5.02

INTERNET
Vocabulary Activity
Keyword: LE5 6-2

> ### Vocabulary Development
>
> You'll be learning these words as you read "Ta-Na-E-Ka":
>
> **loftiest** (lôf′tē·əst) *adj.:* noblest; highest. *Grandfather described endurance as the loftiest virtue.*
>
> **shrewdest** (shrōod′əst) *adj.* used as *n.:* sharpest; most clever. *Only the shrewdest could survive Ta-Na-E-Ka.*
>
> **grimaced** (grim′ist) *v.:* twisted the face to express pain, anger, or disgust. *Roger grimaced at the thought of eating grasshoppers.*
>
> **gorging** (gôrj′iŋ) *v.:* filling up; stuffing. *During his Ta-Na-E-Ka, the boy dreamed he was gorging himself on hamburgers.*
>
> **audacity** (ô·das′ə·tē) *n.:* boldness; daring. *Mary's parents were shocked at her audacity.*

SKILLS FOCUS

Literary Skills
Understand character and conflict.

Reading Skills
Use comparison and contrast.

Background
Literature and Social Studies

This story has to do with the traditions of the Native Americans known as the Kaw or Kansa. Both names are forms of a word that means "People of the South Wind." The Kaw originally lived along the Kansas River.

TA·NA·E·KA

MARY WHITEBIRD

As my birthday drew closer, I had awful nightmares about it. I was reaching the age at which all Kaw Indians had to participate in Ta-Na-E-Ka. Well, not all Kaws. Many of the younger families on the reservation were beginning to give up the old customs. But my grandfather, Amos Deer Leg, was devoted to tradition. He still wore handmade beaded moccasins instead of shoes and kept his iron-gray hair in tight braids. He could speak English, but he spoke it only with white men. With his family he used a Sioux dialect.[1]

Grandfather was one of the last living Indians (he died in 1953, when he was eighty-one) who actually fought against the U.S. Cavalry. Not only did he fight, he was wounded in a skirmish at Rose Creek—a famous encounter in which the celebrated Kaw chief Flat Nose lost his life. At the time, my grandfather was only eleven years old. ❶

> **COMPARE/ CONTRAST**
> ❶ How is Mary's grandfather different from many younger Kaw Indians?

---

1. **Sioux** (sōō) **dialect:** one of the languages spoken by the Plains Indians, including the Kaw.

Eleven was a magic word among the Kaws. It was the time of Ta-Na-E-Ka, the "flowering of adulthood." It was the age, my grandfather informed us hundreds of times, "when a boy could prove himself to be a warrior and a girl took the first steps to womanhood."

"I don't want to be a warrior," my cousin, Roger Deer Leg, confided to me. "I'm going to become an accountant."

"None of the other tribes make girls go through the endurance ritual," I complained to my mother.

"It won't be as bad as you think, Mary," my mother said, ignoring my protests. "Once you've gone through it, you'll certainly never forget it. You'll be proud."

I even complained to my teacher, Mrs. Richardson, feeling that, as a white woman, she would side with me.

She didn't. "All of us have rituals of one kind or another," Mrs. Richardson said. "And look at it this way: How many girls have the opportunity to compete on equal terms with boys? Don't look down on your heritage."

Heritage, indeed! I had no intention of living on a reservation for the rest of my life. I was a good student. I loved school. My fantasies were about knights in armor and fair ladies in flowing gowns being saved from dragons. It never once occurred to me that being an Indian was exciting.

But I've always thought that the Kaw were the originators of the women's liberation movement. No other Indian tribe—and I've spent half a lifetime researching the subject—treated women more "equally" than the Kaw. Unlike most of the subtribes of the Sioux Nation, the Kaw allowed men and women to eat together. And hundreds of years before we were "acculturated,"[2] a Kaw woman had the right to refuse a prospective husband even if her father arranged the match.

The wisest women (generally wisdom was equated with age) often sat in tribal councils. Furthermore, most Kaw legends revolve around "Good Woman," a kind of super-squaw, a Joan of Arc[3] of the high plains. Good Woman led Kaw warriors into battle after battle, from which they always seemed to emerge victorious.

And girls as well as boys were required to undergo Ta-Na-E-Ka.

The actual ceremony varied from tribe to tribe, but since the Indians' life on the plains was dedicated to survival, Ta-Na-E-Ka was a test of survival.

"Endurance is the loftiest virtue of the Indian," my grandfather explained. "To survive, we must endure. When I was a boy, Ta-Na-E-Ka was more than the mere symbol it is now. We were painted white with the juice of a sacred herb and sent naked into the wilderness without so much as a knife. We couldn't return until the white had worn off. It wouldn't wash off. It took almost eighteen days, and during that time we had to stay alive, trapping food, eating insects and roots and berries, and watching out for ene-

---

2. **acculturated** (ə·kul′chər·āt′id) *v.* used as *adj.*: adapted to a new or different culture.
3. **Joan of Arc** (1412–1431): French heroine who led her country's army to victory over the English in 1429.

Vocabulary
loftiest (lôf′tē·əst) *adj.*: noblest; highest.

mies. And we did have enemies—both the white soldiers and the Omaha warriors, who were always trying to capture Kaw boys and girls undergoing their endurance test. It was an exciting time."

"What happened if you couldn't make it?" Roger asked. He was born only three days after I was, and we were being trained for Ta-Na-E-Ka together. I was happy to know he was frightened, too.

"Many didn't return," Grandfather said. "Only the strongest and shrewdest. Mothers were not allowed to weep over those who didn't return. If a Kaw couldn't survive, he or she wasn't worth weeping over. It was our way."

"What a lot of hooey," Roger whispered. "I'd give anything to get out of it."

"I don't see how we have any choice," I replied.

Roger gave my arm a little squeeze. "Well, it's only five days."

Five days! Maybe it was better than being painted white and sent out naked for eighteen days. But not much better.

We were to be sent, barefoot and in bathing suits, into the woods. Even our very traditional parents put their foot down when Grandfather suggested we go naked. For five days we'd have to live off the land, keeping warm as best we could, getting food where we could. It was May, but on the northernmost reaches of the Missouri River, the days were still chilly and the nights were fiercely cold.

Grandfather was in charge of the month's training for Ta-Na-E-Ka. One day he caught a grasshopper and demonstrated how to pull its legs and wings off in one flick of the fingers and how to swallow it.

I felt sick, and Roger turned green. "It's a darn good thing it's 1947," I told Roger teasingly. "You'd make a terrible warrior." Roger just grimaced. ❷

📖 **COMPARE/ CONTRAST**
❷ What feelings do Roger and Mary share about Ta-Na-E-Ka?

I knew one thing. This particular Kaw Indian girl wasn't going to swallow a grasshopper no matter how hungry she got. And then I had an idea. Why hadn't I thought of it before? It would have saved nights of bad dreams about squooshy grasshoppers.

I headed straight for my teacher's house. "Mrs. Richardson," I said, "would you lend me five dollars?"

"Five dollars!" she exclaimed. "What for?"

Vocabulary

shrewdest (shrōōd′əst) *adj.* used as *n.:* sharpest; most clever.

grimaced (grim′ist) *v.:* twisted the face to express pain, anger, or disgust.

"You remember the ceremony I talked about?"

"Ta-Na-E-Ka. Of course. Your parents have written me and asked me to excuse you from school so you can participate in it."

"Well, I need some things for the ceremony," I replied, in a half-truth. "I don't want to ask my parents for the money."

"It's not a crime to borrow money, Mary. But how can you pay it back?"

"I'll baby-sit for you ten times."

"That's more than fair," she said, going to her purse and handing me a crisp, new five-dollar bill. I'd never had that much money at once.

"I'm happy to know the money's going to be put to a good use," Mrs. Richardson said.

A few days later the ritual began with a long speech from my grandfather about how we had reached the age of decision, how we now had to fend for ourselves and prove that we could survive the most horrendous of ordeals. All the friends and relatives who had gathered at our house for dinner made jokes about their own Ta-Na-E-Ka experiences. They all advised us to fill up now, since for the next five days we'd be gorging ourselves on crickets. Neither Roger nor I was very hungry. "I'll probably laugh about this when I'm an accountant," Roger said, trembling.

"Are you trembling?" I asked.

"What do you think?"

"I'm happy to know boys tremble, too," I said.

At six the next morning, we kissed our parents and went off to the woods. "Which side do you want?" Roger asked. According to the rules, Roger and I would stake out "territories" in separate areas of the woods, and we weren't to communicate during the entire ordeal.

"I'll go toward the river, if it's OK with you," I said.

"Sure," Roger answered. "What difference does it make?"

To me, it made a lot of difference. There was a marina a few miles up the river, and there were boats moored there. At least, I hoped so. I figured that a boat was a better place to sleep than under a pile of leaves.

"Why do you keep holding your head?" Roger asked.

"Oh, nothing. Just nervous," I told him. Actually, I was afraid I'd lose the five-dollar bill, which I had tucked into my hair with a bobby pin. As we came to a fork in the trail, Roger shook my hand. "Good luck, Mary."

"N'ko-n'ta," I said. It was the Kaw word for "courage."

The sun was shining and it was warm, but my bare feet began to hurt immediately. I

Vocabulary
gorging (gôrj'iŋ) *v.:* filling up; stuffing.

spied one of the berry bushes Grandfather had told us about. "You're lucky," he had said. "The berries are ripe in the spring, and they are delicious and nourishing." They were orange and fat, and I popped one into my mouth.

Argh! I spat it out. It was awful and bitter, and even grasshoppers were probably better tasting, although I never intended to find out.

I sat down to rest my feet. A rabbit hopped out from under the berry bush. He nuzzled the berry I'd spat out and ate it. He picked another one and ate that, too. He liked them. He looked at me, twitching his nose. I watched a redheaded woodpecker bore into an elm tree, and I caught a glimpse of a civet cat[4] waddling through some twigs. All of a sudden I realized I was no longer frightened. Ta-Na-E-Ka might be more fun than I'd anticipated. I got up and headed toward the marina. ❸

> 📖 **PREDICT**
> ❸ How do you predict Mary will handle her conflict with nature?

"Not one boat," I said to myself dejectedly. But the restaurant on the shore, Ernie's Riverside, was open. I walked in, feeling silly in my bathing suit. The man at the counter was big and tough-looking. He wore a sweat shirt with the words "Fort Sheridan, 1944," and he had only three fingers on one of his hands. He asked me what I wanted.

"A hamburger and a milkshake," I said, holding the five-dollar bill in my hand so he'd know I had money.

"That's a pretty heavy breakfast, honey," he murmured.

_____
4. **civet** (siv′it) **cat** *n.*: furry spotted skunk.

"That's what I always have for breakfast," I lied.

"Forty-five cents," he said, bringing me the food. (Back in 1947, hamburgers were twenty-five cents and milkshakes were twenty cents.)

"Delicious," I thought. "Better 'n grasshoppers—and Grandfather never once mentioned that I couldn't eat hamburgers."

While I was eating, I had a grand idea. Why not sleep in the restaurant? I went to the ladies' room and made sure the window was unlocked. Then I went back outside and played along the riverbank, watching the water birds and trying to identify each one. I planned to look for a beaver dam the next day.

The restaurant closed at sunset, and I watched the three-fingered man drive away. Then I climbed in the unlocked window. There was a night light on, so I didn't turn on any lights. But there was a radio on the counter. I turned it on to a music program. It was warm in the restaurant, and I was hungry. I helped myself to a glass of milk and a piece of pie, intending to keep a list of what I'd eaten so I could leave money. I also planned to get up early, sneak out through the window, and head for the woods before the three-fingered man returned. I turned off the radio, wrapped myself in the man's apron, and in spite of the hardness of the floor, fell asleep.

"What the heck are you doing here, kid?"

It was the man's voice.

It was morning. I'd overslept. I was scared.

"Hold it, kid. I just wanna know what you're doing here. You lost? You must be from the reservation. Your folks must be worried sick about you. Do they have a phone?"

"Yes, yes," I answered. "But don't call them."

I was shivering. The man, who told me his name was Ernie, made me a cup of hot chocolate while I explained about Ta-Na-E-Ka.

"Darnedest thing I ever heard," he said, when I was through. "Lived next to the reservation all my life and this is the first I've heard of Ta-Na-whatever-you-call-it." He looked at me, all goose bumps in my bathing suit. "Pretty silly thing to do to a kid," he muttered.

That was just what I'd been thinking for months, but when Ernie said it, I became angry. "No, it isn't silly. It's a custom of the Kaw. We've been doing this for hundreds of years. My mother and my grandfather and everybody in my family went through this ceremony. It's why the Kaw are great warriors." ❹

📖 **COMPARE/ CONTRAST**
❹ How has Mary's attitude toward Ta-Na-E-Ka changed?

"OK, great warrior," Ernie chuckled, "suit yourself. And, if you want to stick around, it's OK with me." Ernie went to the broom closet and tossed me a bundle. "That's the lost-and-found closet," he said. "Stuff people left on boats. Maybe there's something to keep you warm."

The sweater fitted loosely, but it felt good. I felt good. And I'd found a new friend. Most important, I was surviving Ta-Na-E-Ka.

My grandfather had said the experience would be filled with adventure, and I was having my fill. And Grandfather had never said we couldn't accept hospitality.

I stayed at Ernie's Riverside for the entire period. In the mornings I went into the woods and watched the animals and picked flowers for each of the tables in Ernie's. I had never felt better. I was up early enough to watch the sun rise on the Missouri, and I went to bed after it set. I ate everything I wanted—insisting that Ernie take all my money for the food. "I'll keep this in trust for you, Mary," Ernie promised, "in case you are ever desperate for five dollars." (He did, too, but that's another story.)

I was sorry when the five days were over. I'd enjoyed every minute with Ernie. He taught me how to make western omelets and to make Chili Ernie Style (still one of my favorite dishes). And I told Ernie all about the legends of the Kaw. I hadn't realized I knew so much about my people.

But Ta-Na-E-Ka was over, and as I approached my house at about nine-thirty in the evening, I became nervous all over again. What if Grandfather asked me about the berries and the grasshoppers? And my feet were hardly cut. I hadn't lost a pound and my hair was combed.

"They'll be so happy to see me," I told myself hopefully, "that they won't ask too many questions."

I opened the door. My grandfather was in the front room. He was wearing the ceremonial beaded deerskin shirt which had belonged to *his* grandfather. "N'g'da'ma," he said. "Welcome back."

I embraced my parents warmly, letting go only when I saw my cousin Roger sprawled on the couch. His eyes were red and swollen. He'd lost weight. His feet were an unsightly mass of blood and blisters, and he was moaning: "I made it, see. I made it. I'm a warrior. A warrior."

My grandfather looked at me strangely. I was clean, obviously well fed, and radiantly healthy. My parents got the message. My uncle and aunt gazed at me with hostility. ❺

INFER
❺ What "message" is Mary sending to her family?

Finally my grandfather asked, "What did you eat to keep you so well?"

I sucked in my breath and blurted out the truth: "Hamburgers and milkshakes."

"Hamburgers!" my grandfather growled.

"Milkshakes!" Roger moaned.

"You didn't say we had to eat grasshoppers," I said sheepishly.

"Tell us all about your Ta-Na-E-Ka," my grandfather commanded.

I told them everything, from borrowing the five dollars, to Ernie's kindness, to observing the beaver.

"That's not what I trained you for," my grandfather said sadly.

I stood up. "Grandfather, I learned that Ta-Na-E-Ka is important. I didn't think so during training. I was scared stiff of it. I handled it my way. And I learned I had nothing to be afraid of. There's no reason in 1947 to eat grasshoppers when you can eat a hamburger."

I was inwardly shocked at my own audacity. But I liked it. "Grandfather, I'll bet you never ate one of those rotten berries yourself."

Grandfather laughed! He laughed aloud! My mother and father and aunt and uncle were all dumbfounded. Grandfather never laughed. Never.

"Those berries—they are terrible," Grandfather admitted. "I could never swallow them. I found a dead deer on the first day of my Ta-Na-E-Ka—shot by a soldier, probably—and he kept my belly full for the entire period of the test!"

Grandfather stopped laughing. "We should send you out again," he said.

I looked at Roger. "You're pretty smart, Mary," Roger groaned. "I'd never have thought of what you did."

"Accountants just have to be good at arithmetic," I said comfortingly. "I'm terrible at arithmetic."

Roger tried to smile but couldn't. My grandfather called me to him. "You should have done what your cousin did. But I think you are more alert to what is happening to our people today than we are. I think you would have passed the test under any circumstances, in any time. Somehow, you know how to exist in a world that wasn't made for Indians. I don't think you're going to have any trouble surviving."

Grandfather wasn't entirely right. But I'll tell about that another time. ❻

RETELL
❻ How is Mary's conflict with the older generation resolved?

Vocabulary
audacity (ô·das′ə·tē) *n.*: boldness; daring.

First Thoughts

1. Is the way Mary survives Ta-Na-E-Ka fair, or should she be sent out again? Explain. You may to want to refer to your Quickwrite notes.

Thinking Critically

2. Mary and Roger face an **external conflict** with the older generation. What arguments do Mary's mother, grandfather, and teacher give in support of Ta-Na-E-Ka? What arguments do Mary and Roger give against it? **Compare** and **contrast** their arguments, using a chart like the one below. Whose side are you on?

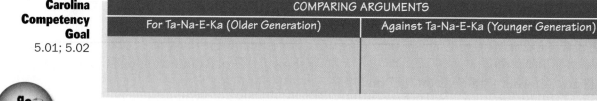

COMPARING ARGUMENTS	
For Ta-Na-E-Ka (Older Generation)	Against Ta-Na-E-Ka (Younger Generation)

3. What **internal conflict** does Mary experience when Ernie says that Ta-Na-E-Ka is silly?

4. What **character** traits does Mary have that affect the **resolution** of the **conflicts** in the story? Explain.

Extending Interpretations

5. Does this story teach a lesson about the role of tradition in today's society? What do you think that lesson might be?

6. Mary's teacher says to her, "Don't look down on your heritage." Why do people sometimes look down on their heritage? What parts of your heritage do you value most?

WRITING

Writing a Letter

Roger suffers during his Ta-Na-E-Ka while Mary has a good time. How do you think Roger feels about that? Write a letter from Roger to a friend, telling about the two Ta-Na-E-Kas. Describe Mary's character, and tell what you (Roger) think of her.

Reading Check

Imagine that you are Mary. Write three diary entries in which you describe your experiences and feelings (1) before Ta-Na-E-Ka, (2) during your time in the woods, and (3) after the ritual is over. What does Ta-Na-E-Ka teach Mary?

North Carolina Competency Goal
5.01; 5.02

INTERNET
Projects and Activities
Keyword: LE5 6-2

SKILLS FOCUS

Literary Skills
Analyze character and conflict.

Reading Skills
Use comparison and contrast.

Writing Skills
Write a letter.

Developing Fluency in Word Usage

PRACTICE

We discover new words by reading; we develop **fluency,** or ease of use, by using those words as often as we can. How fluent are you with the Word Bank words? See if you can answer these questions.

1. In your opinion, what is the loftiest quality a person can have? What is the opposite of a lofty quality?
2. What is the shrewdest way to deal with a conflict? What adjective is the opposite of shrewd?
3. What would you do if someone grimaced at you? How is a grimace different from a smile?
4. Is gorging yourself acceptable or rude? Explain.
5. Name three deeds that require audacity to carry out.

> **Word Bank**
> loftiest
> shrewdest
> grimaced
> gorging
> audacity

Grammar Link

Subjects and Verbs—in Perfect Agreement

To find the right verb when a sentence has a **compound subject**—that is, two subjects joined by *and, or,* or *nor*—follow these rules:

- Subjects joined by the word *and* take a plural verb.

  Mary and Roger were afraid.

- Singular subjects joined by *or* or *nor* take a singular verb.

  Either Roger or Mary reaches the river.

- When a singular subject and a plural subject are joined by *or* or *nor*, the verb agrees with the subject nearer the verb.

  Neither Mary's parents nor her *grandfather* is able to predict how Mary will survive.

  Neither Mary's grandfather nor her *parents* are able to predict how Mary will survive.

PRACTICE

Choose the right verb for each sentence below.

1. Either Mary's teacher or her grandfather explains/explain that Kaw girls and boys compete on equal terms.
2. Both her mother and her teacher says/say that tradition is important.
3. Neither Mary's parents nor her grandfather knows/know that she has five dollars.

For more help, see Problems in Agreement, 2c–j, in the Language Handbook.

North Carolina Competency Goal
5.01; 5.02; 6.01

Vocabulary Skills
Develop fluency in word usage.

Grammar Skills
Practice subject-verb agreement.

Outlining

Reading Focus

Creating an Outline

While the Kaw live on through stories like "Ta-Na-E-Ka," the last real-life member of the Kaw nation died in 2000. Learn more about the history and unfortunate demise of the Kaw in the following nonfiction article. Then, use the information from the article to practice taking notes and outlining.

Outlining is a good way to organize and record information in factual writing. **Outlining** usually involves three steps:

1. getting the main ideas

2. taking notes

3. putting the notes into outline form

Before you start, get a stack of three-by-five-inch index cards.

1. Getting the main ideas. You'll probably have to read the article more than once to identify the main ideas. Note that the article has four **subheads.** You should look for a main idea and supporting details for each of these four sections of the article. As you read, ask **clarifying questions**—like these: Who? What? When? Where? How? Why? What happened then? What caused this to happen? What were the effects of this event?

■ Now, read "The Wind People." Look for these four main ideas as you read the article:

- the Kaw creation story
- encounters with European explorers

- winds of change
- the end of the Kaw

2. Taking notes. Write down each idea at the top of a note card; then, read the article again. When you find an important detail supporting one of the main ideas, stop and add it to the card for that idea. Try to write it in your own words. If you do use the author's exact words, put quotation marks around them.

3. Putting the notes into outline form. Now that you have your notes, it is time to organize them in an outline. An outline is set up this way:

I.   Main idea
   A. Detail supporting point I
      1. Detail supporting point A
        a. Detail supporting point 1

Make sure that there are at least two headings at each level.

■ You have four main ideas from the Kaw article. Now, finish outlining the content of the article by filling in supporting details. The first main idea has been outlined for you:

I.   The Kaw creation story
   A. The Kaw nation lived on an island that was too small for them.
   B. Because of this, Kaw mothers prayed to the Great Spirit.
   C. As a result, beavers, muskrats, turtles were sent to make the island bigger.
   D. In time the earth became large, and plants and animals thrived.

North Carolina Competency Goal
2.01; 5.01; 5.02

INTERNET
Interactive Reading Model
Keyword: LE5 6-2

SKILLS FOCUS

Reading Skills
Make an outline; take notes.

The Wind People

FACTS ABOUT THE KAW

by Flo Ota De Lange

William Mehojah.

On April 23, 2000, a sad story appeared in many American newspapers. William Mehojah, eighty-two years old, had died. Mr. Mehojah was the last member of the Sovereign Nation° of the Kaw. With his death, the Kaw people were gone forever.

The Kaw Creation Myth

According to a Kaw creation story, the Kaw originally lived on an island that was too small for their numbers. Because there were so many Kaw people in those days, the Kaw mothers offered prayers to the Great Spirit begging for more living space. The Great Spirit responded to their pleas. He sent beavers, muskrats, and turtles to enlarge the Kaw's island, using materials from the bottom of the great waters. In time the earth took shape. Plants and animals thrived. The world became spacious and vibrant. The Kaw population problem was resolved.

Encounters with European Explorers

By the early 1800s, the Kaw nation was prospering. Their land stretched over twenty million acres, from what is now Kansas east into Missouri and Iowa and north into

---

° **Sovereign Nation:** Native American nations govern themselves and are not subject to the laws of the U.S. government except through treaty or agreement.

Nebraska. The first Europeans who came in contact with the Kaw were French explorers. The French were interested in commerce, and that required a working knowledge of the geography of the Great Southern Plains and Mississippi Valley, as well as knowledge of the people who lived there and of the languages they spoke. To obtain this knowledge, the French (just like the English and Spanish explorers in other parts of the country) would ask for the names of the new animals, trees, rivers, and mountains they saw and of the new people they met. "What do you call this?" the French would ask. "And this? And this?" Then the French would eagerly record the answers in their ledgers and on their maps. But though the names they wrote down might have sounded roughly like the original names, they were spelled the way the French would spell them. Furthermore, many of the sounds the European explorers heard had no equivalents in their own languages, so the new words usually bore little

Kaw sisters in the early 1900s.

A Kaw dwelling from about 1900.

resemblance to the native words. This is how *U-Moln-Holn* became *Omaha* and *Wi-Tsi-Ta* became *Wichita*. The Kaw (or Kansa) called themselves Koln-Za or Kanza; the names we know them by are the French and English versions of those names.

Winds of Change

The Kaw are also known as the Wind People or the People of the South Wind. They believed that since they could not control the wind, they should try to form a relationship with it. But when the winds of change hit the Kaw, with the westward push of European immigrants, the Kaw were helpless. They saw their lands and their population shrink. The European settlers brought deadly diseases with them—diseases such as influenza and smallpox, to which the Kaw had no immunity. Battles with other Native American peoples further reduced the Kaw's numbers.

The End of the Kaw

The most devastating blow to the Kaw was struck by the U.S. government. Beginning in 1825, other peoples were permitted to occupy Kaw land; the Kaw themselves were confined to two million acres in what is now the Kansas, or Kaw, River valley. In 1872, the federal government moved the nation from the valley to a 100,000-acre reservation in Oklahoma. After the Kaw were removed from their native land, struggles over leadership broke out, dividing and fatally weakening the nation.

By 1995, only four Kaw were left: Mr. Mehojah, his brother, and two nephews. Mr. Mehojah's last surviving nephew died in 1998. By the year 2000, the Kaw were gone.

Creating an Outline

The Wind People

Test Practice

1. The writer probably tells the Kaw creation myth because —
   - **A** it contrasts with what eventually happened to the Kaw
   - **B** it explains why the Kaw died out
   - **C** it predicts what happened to the Kaw
   - **D** it explains how they got the name Kaw

2. Suppose an **outline** of this article lists these main ideas:
   - I. The Kaw creation story
   - II.
   - III. Winds of change
   - IV. The end of the Kaw

   Which **main idea** should be Roman numeral II?
   - **F** Last Kaw dies on April 23, 2000
   - **G** Encounters with European explorers
   - **H** Europeans bring disease
   - **J** Other people allowed to occupy Kaw land

3. French explorers learned Kaw names for local peoples and places by —
   - **A** studying a textbook
   - **B** talking to the Kaw
   - **C** taking part in Kaw rituals
   - **D** looking at maps of the Mississippi Valley

4. Suppose an **outline** of this article has a main heading that reads "Winds of Change." Which of these details do *not* support that main idea?
   - **F** With European immigration, Kaw lands and population shrink.
   - **G** Deadly diseases spread among Kaw.
   - **H** Kaw fight with other Native Americans and reduce population further.
   - **J** French explorers change Kaw names.

North Carolina Competency Goal
1.04; 2.01; 4.01; 4.02; 5.01

Constructed Response

1. Review the notes you took as you read this article. Then, use your notes to create an **outline.** For a start, see page 144.

2. List three Kaw names that were modified by the French and English.

3. Where were the Kaw moved to in 1872?

Reading Skills
Create an outline.

Vocabulary Development

Words from Native American Languages

Many rivers, mountains, and other geographical features in the United States were given English versions of Indian names, from the Appalachian Mountains in the East to the Willamette River in the West.

PRACTICE 1

1. The names of more than twenty states come from Native American languages. Can you name five? Use a dictionary to check your guesses and to learn about the origins of the names. Write down the names' original meanings and spellings.

2. If you look at a map or an atlas of the United States, you'll find a variety of place names that come from Native American languages. Choose three, and look up their original meanings in a dictionary.

PRACTICE 2

Many English words come from other languages. The words in the list below come from Native American languages. Use the words to answer the questions that follow. Then, write sentences using the words, or draw pictures to create an illustrated dictionary.

hickory	opossum or possum	squash
hominy	pecan	succotash
mackinaw	persimmon	toboggan
moccasins	raccoon	woodchuck
moose	sequoia	
muskrat	skunk	

North Carolina Competency Goal
2.01; 6.01

Which of the items on the list

1. would you be most likely to put on your feet?
2. are animals?
3. are foods?
4. are types of trees?
5. will carry you down a hill?
6. will carry you across a river or keep you warm?

Vocabulary Skills
Understand word origins.

The Bracelet

Make the Connection
Quickwrite ✏️

What stories or movies or TV shows can you think of in which painful events are used to teach us never to repeat mistakes? Give at least two examples, and describe the lessons you learned.

Literary Focus
Character and Point of View
This story lets you into the mind of its main character, Ruri, who is also the narrator. Ruri uses the **first-person point of view,** speaking as "I." As she tells her story, Ruri reveals the qualities of her character, as well as her thoughts and feelings. Because Ruri is telling the story herself, you won't know for sure what other people are thinking and feeling. You'll know only what Ruri tells you.

Reading Skills
Making Predictions

As you read stories, you make **predictions.** That means you guess what will happen next. You base your guesses on clues the writer gives you and on what you know from your own experience. Making predictions is part of the fun of reading stories. We match wits with the writer, to see if we can guess how all the puzzles and problems will be worked out. Probably we are pleased when we guess correctly, but most of us also love to be surprised.

Vocabulary Development

Look for these words as you read the story. Notice how **context,** the words near each Vocabulary word, helps you guess its meaning.

evacuated (ē · vak′yōō · āt′id) *v.*: removed from an area. *During the war, Japanese Americans were evacuated from the West Coast. Their removal had tragic consequences.*

interned (in · turnd′) *v.*: imprisoned or confined. *Ruri's father was interned in a prisoner-of-war camp.*

aliens (āl′yənz) *n.*: foreigners. *The U.S. government treated Japanese Americans as if they were enemy aliens.*

forsaken (fôr · sā′kən) *adj.*: abandoned; deserted. *The garden looked as forsaken as Ruri felt when she had to leave home.*

North Carolina Competency Goal
1.04; 4.01; 5.01; 5.02

INTERNET
Vocabulary Activity
•
More About Uchida
Keyword: LE5 6-2

Background

Literature and Social Studies   Shortly after the United States entered World War II against Japan, more than 110,000 people of Japanese ancestry who were living in the United States were forced to move to guarded camps. Most were American citizens who had been born here and had done nothing wrong. But the U.S. government feared that they might give support to Japan. When they were finally allowed to leave the camps, after the war, many Japanese Americans found that other people had taken over their homes and businesses. In 1989, the U.S. government issued a formal apology to Japanese Americans for the injustice that had been done to them.

SKILLS FOCUS

Literary Skills
Understand character and point of view.

Reading Skills
Make predictions.

149

The Bracelet

YOSHIKO UCHIDA

"Mama, is it time to go?" I hadn't planned to cry, but the tears came suddenly, and I wiped them away with the back of my hand. I didn't want my older sister to see me crying.

"It's almost time, Ruri," my mother said gently. Her face was filled with a kind of sadness I had never seen before.

I looked around at my empty room. The clothes that Mama always told me to hang up in the closet, the junk piled on my dresser, the old rag doll I could never bear to part with—they were all gone. There was nothing left in my room, and there was nothing left in the rest of the house. The rugs and furniture were gone, the pictures and drapes were down, and the closets and cupboards were empty. The house was like a gift box after the nice thing inside was gone; just a lot of nothingness.

It was almost time to leave our home, but we weren't moving to a nicer house or to a new town. It was April 21, 1942. The United States and Japan were at war, and every Japanese person on the West Coast was being evacuated by the government to a concentration camp. Mama, my sister Keiko, and I were being sent from our home, and out of Berkeley, and eventually out of California.

Vocabulary

evacuated (ē·vak′yo͞o·āt′id) *v.*: removed from an area.

The doorbell rang, and I ran to answer it before my sister could. I thought maybe by some miracle a messenger from the government might be standing there, tall and proper and buttoned into a uniform, come to tell us it was all a terrible mistake, that we wouldn't have to leave after all. Or maybe the messenger would have a telegram from Papa, who was <u>interned</u> in a prisoner-of-war camp in Montana because he had worked for a Japanese business firm.

The FBI had come to pick up Papa and hundreds of other Japanese community leaders on the very day that Japanese planes had bombed Pearl Harbor. The government thought they were dangerous enemy <u>aliens</u>. If it weren't so sad, it would have been funny. Papa could no more be dangerous than the mayor of our city, and he was every bit as loyal to the United States. He had lived here since 1917.

When I opened the door, it wasn't a messenger from anywhere. It was my best friend, Laurie Madison, from next door. She was holding a package wrapped up like a birthday present, but she wasn't wearing her party dress, and her face drooped like a wilted tulip.

"Hi," she said. "I came to say goodbye."

She thrust the present at me and told me it was something to take to camp. "It's a bracelet," she said before I could open the package. "Put it on so you won't have to pack it." She knew I didn't have one inch of space left in my suitcase. We had been instructed to take only what we could carry into camp, and Mama had told us that we could each take only two suitcases.

"Then how are we ever going to pack the dishes and blankets and sheets they've told us to bring with us?" Keiko worried.

"I don't really know," Mama said, and she simply began packing those big impossible things into an enormous duffel bag—along with umbrellas, boots, a kettle, hot plate, and flashlight.

"Who's going to carry that huge sack?" I asked.

But Mama didn't worry about things like that. "Someone will help us," she said. "Don't worry." So I didn't.

Laurie wanted me to open her package and put on the bracelet before she left. It was a thin gold chain with a heart dangling on it. She helped me put it on, and I told her I'd never take it off, ever.

"Well, goodbye then," Laurie said awkwardly. "Come home soon."

"I will," I said, although I didn't know if I would ever get back to Berkeley again.

I watched Laurie go down the block, her long blond pigtails bouncing as she walked. I wondered who would be sitting in my desk at Lincoln Junior High now that I was gone. Laurie kept turning and waving, even walking backward for a while, until she got to the corner. I didn't want to watch anymore, and I slammed the door shut.

The next time the doorbell rang, it was Mrs. Simpson, our other neighbor. She was going to drive us to the Congregational Church, which was the Civil Control

Vocabulary
interned (in·turnd′) *v.:* imprisoned or confined, especially during a war.
aliens (āl′yənz) *n.:* foreigners.

Station where all the Japanese of Berkeley were supposed to report.

It was time to go. "Come on, Ruri. Get your things," my sister called to me.

It was a warm day, but I put on a sweater and my coat so I wouldn't have to carry them, and I picked up my two suitcases. Each one had a tag with my name and our family number on it. Every Japanese family had to register and get a number. We were Family Number 13453.

Mama was taking one last look around our house. She was going from room to room, as though she were trying to take a mental picture of the house she had lived in for fifteen years, so she would never forget it.

I saw her take a long last look at the garden that Papa loved. The irises beside the fish pond were just beginning to bloom. If Papa had been home, he would have cut the first iris blossom and brought it inside to Mama. "This one is for you," he would have said. And Mama would have smiled and said, "Thank you, Papa San"° and put it in her favorite cut-glass vase.

But the garden looked shabby and forsaken now that Papa was gone and Mama was too busy to take care of it. It looked the way I felt, sort of empty and lonely and abandoned.

When Mrs. Simpson took us to the Civil Control Station, I felt even worse. I was scared, and for a minute I thought I was going to lose my breakfast right in front of everybody. There must have been over a thousand Japanese people gathered at the church. Some were old and some were

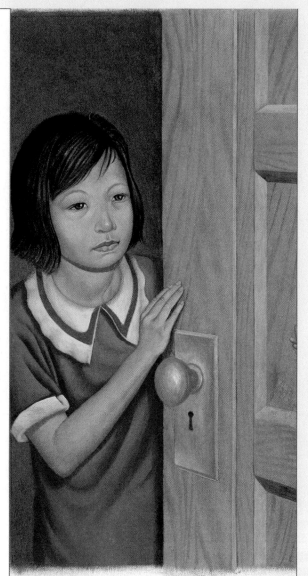

young. Some were talking and laughing, and some were crying. I guess everybody else was scared too. No one knew exactly what was going to happen to us. We just knew we were being taken to the Tanforan Race-tracks, which the army had turned into a camp for the Japanese. There were fourteen other camps like ours along the West Coast.

° **San:** Japanese term added to names to indicate respect.

Vocabulary
forsaken (fôr·sā′kən) *adj.:* abandoned; deserted.

there to help us load our duffel bag. When it was time to board the buses, I sat with Keiko, and Mama sat behind us. The bus went down Grove Street and passed the small Japanese food store where Mama used to order her bean-curd cakes and pickled radish. The windows were all boarded up, but there was a sign still hanging on the door that read, "We are loyal Americans."

The crazy thing about the whole evacuation was that we were all loyal Americans. Most of us were citizens because we had been born here. But our parents, who had come from Japan, couldn't become citizens because there was a law that prevented any Asian from becoming a citizen. Now everybody with a Japanese face was being shipped off to concentration camps.

"It's stupid," Keiko muttered as we saw the racetrack looming up beside the highway. "If there were any Japanese spies around, they'd have gone back to Japan long ago."

"I'll say," I agreed. My sister was in high school and she ought to know, I thought.

When the bus turned into Tanforan, there were more armed guards at the gate, and I saw barbed wire strung around the entire grounds. I felt as though I were going into a prison, but I hadn't done anything wrong.

We streamed off the buses and poured into a huge room, where doctors looked down our throats and peeled back our eyelids to see if we had any diseases. Then we were given our housing assignments. The man in charge gave Mama a slip of paper. We were in Barrack 16, Apartment 40.

"Mama!" I said. "We're going to live in

What scared me most were the soldiers standing at the doorway of the church hall. They were carrying guns with mounted bayonets. I wondered if they thought we would try to run away and whether they'd shoot us or come after us with their bayonets if we did.

A long line of buses waited to take us to camp. There were trucks, too, for our baggage. And Mama was right; some men were an apartment!" The only apartment I had ever seen was the one my piano teacher lived in. It was in an enormous building in San Francisco, with an elevator and thick-carpeted hallways. I thought how wonderful it would be to have our own elevator. A house was all right, but an apartment seemed elegant and special.

We walked down the racetrack, looking for Barrack 16. Mr. Noma, a friend of Papa's, helped us carry our bags. I was so busy looking around I slipped and almost fell on the muddy track. Army barracks had been built everywhere, all around the racetrack and even in the center oval.

Mr. Noma pointed beyond the track toward the horse stables. "I think your barrack is out there."

He was right. We came to a long stable that had once housed the horses of Tanforan, and we climbed up the wide ramp. Each stall had a number painted on it, and when we got to 40, Mr. Noma pushed open the door.

"Well, here it is," he said, "Apartment 40."

The stall was narrow and empty and dark. There were two small windows on each side of the door. Three folded army cots were on the dust-covered floor, and one light bulb dangled from the ceiling. That was all. This was our apartment, and it still smelled of horses.

Mama looked at my sister and then at me. "It won't be so bad when we fix it up," she began. "I'll ask Mrs. Simpson to send me some material for curtains. I could make some cushions too, and . . . well . . ." She stopped. She couldn't think of anything more to say.

Mr. Noma said he'd go get some mattresses for us. "I'd better hurry before they're all gone." He rushed off. I think he wanted to leave so that he wouldn't have to see Mama cry. But he needn't have run off, because Mama didn't cry. She just went out to borrow a broom and began sweeping out the dust and dirt. "Will you girls set up the cots?" she asked.

It was only after we'd put up the last cot that I noticed my bracelet was gone. "I've lost Laurie's bracelet!" I screamed. "My bracelet's gone!"

We looked all over the stall and even down the ramp. I wanted to run back down the track and go over every inch of ground we'd walked on, but it was getting dark and Mama wouldn't let me.

I thought of what I'd promised Laurie. I wasn't ever going to take the bracelet off, not even when I went to take a shower. And now I had lost it on my very first day in camp. I wanted to cry.

I kept looking for it all the time we were in Tanforan. I didn't stop looking until the day we were sent to another camp, called Topaz, in the middle of a desert in Utah. And then I gave up.

But Mama told me never mind. She said I didn't need a bracelet to remember Laurie, just as I didn't need anything to remember Papa or our home in Berkeley or all the people and things we loved and had left behind.

"Those are things we can carry in our hearts and take with us no matter where we are sent," she said.

And I guess she was right. I've never forgotten Laurie, even now.

Meet the Writer

Yoshiko Uchida

So It Won't Happen Again

Yoshiko Uchida (1921–1992) was in her last year of college when the United States entered World War II. Like most other people of Japanese descent on the West Coast, Uchida and her family were uprooted by the government and forced to go to an internment camp. She and her family lived at Tanforan Racetrack in horse stall 40, answering to Family Number 13453 instead of their own name. Uchida later gave the same family number and "address" to the fictional family in her short story "The Bracelet." Uchida said that in writing about the internment camps, she tried to give readers a sense of the courage and strength that enabled most Japanese Americans to endure this tragedy.

There was another reason that she wrote about the camps:

> **❝**I always ask the children why they think I wrote *Journey to Topaz* and *Journey Home*, in which I tell of the wartime experiences of the Japanese Americans. . . . 'To tell how you felt? To tell what happened to the Japanese people?'
>
> 'Yes,' I answer, but I continue the discussion until finally one of them will say, 'You wrote those books so it won't ever happen again.'
>
> And that is why I wrote this book. I wrote it for the young Japanese Americans who seek a sense of continuity with their past. But I wrote it as well for all Americans, with the hope that through knowledge of the past, they will never allow another group of people in America to be sent into desert exile ever again.**❞**

For Independent Reading

Uchida's many novels for young people include *Journey to Topaz* and its sequel, *Journey Home*. She also wrote a trilogy about a Japanese American girl called Rinko: *The Jar of Dreams, The Best Bad Thing,* and *The Happiest Ending*.

First Thoughts

1. As you read the story, what passages or scenes touched you the most? On a chart like the one below, copy the passages from the text, and note your thoughts.

Passage	My Response
"I was scared and . . . thought I was going to lose my breakfast. . . ."	She helps me to see how terrified she was.

Reading Check

Imagine you're Ruri writing a letter from Tanforan Racetrack to your friend Laurie. Tell her three things: Let her know what happened to your family after you left Berkeley; describe what the camp is like; and tell her what happened to the bracelet she gave you.

North Carolina Competency Goal
1.02; 1.04; 4.01; 4.02; 5.01; 5.02

Thinking Critically

2. When you began reading this story, how did you **predict** it would end? How accurate was your prediction?

3. List three of Ruri's character traits that are revealed in this story. How do Ruri's qualities affect the story's **resolution** (the way it ends)?

4. The plot centers on a **conflict,** or problem, that goes far beyond the characters in the story. Ruri and her family are on one side of this conflict. Who or what is on the other side of it?

5. Tell why you think the writer chose to tell this story from the first-person point of view. What can Ruri tell you that no other character can tell? What things does Ruri not know?

INTERNET

Projects and Activities

Keyword: LE5 6-2

Extending Interpretations

6. Does the author succeed in teaching a lesson in this story? Does she do this as well as the authors of the stories and the directors of the movies you listed for the Quickwrite on page 149? Explain.

SKILLS FOCUS

Literary Skills
Analyze character and conflict; analyze point of view.

Reading Skills
Make and verify predictions.

Writing Skills
Retell a story.

WRITING

Retelling the Story from Another Point of View

Suppose that Ruri's mother told this story. What might she say about the events that Ruri describes? How might Laurie tell the story? Retell the story using a different first-person narrator. Be sure to keep events in time order.

After You Read | Vocabulary Development

The Roots of English
Many of the words we use today can be traced to Latin or to Old English, the language used in England between the 400s and about 1056.

PRACTICE 1

From the Word Bank, choose the word that correctly completes each of the sentences below. Then, use each word in a sentence that shows you know its meaning.

1. The Old English word *forascan,* meaning "to oppose," is related to the word _____.
2. The Latin word *alienus,* meaning "other," is related to the word _____.
3. The Latin word *internus,* meaning "inward," is related to the word _____.
4. The Latin verb *vacuare,* meaning "to make empty," is the basis of the word _____.

> **Word Bank**
>
> evacuated
> interned
> aliens
> forsaken

PRACTICE 2

In the twentieth century, a number of words came into English from Japanese, including the words listed below. Use a dictionary to find out what each word means. Then, fill in the blanks in the sentences that follow the word list. Use context clues to find the words that fit best. Can you think of other words from Japanese that have entered the English language?

kimono (kə·mō′nə)   sayonara (sä′yô·nä′rä)
futon (foō′tän′)   origami (ôr′ə·gä′mē)
karaoke (kar′ē·o′kē)

1. I bought my friend a beautiful silk _____ for her birthday.
2. My cousin enjoyed sleeping on a _____ so much that she said "_____" to her inner-spring mattress.
3. Flocks of _____ cranes cut from red paper decorated each table.
4. My grandfather sang _____ at the party celebrating his ninetieth birthday.

North Carolina Competency Goal
5.01; 5.02; 6.01

Vocabulary Skills
Understand word origins.

Taking Notes

Reading Focus
Taking Logical Notes

"The Bracelet" is fiction, but the events the story is based on really happened. In the following article, you'll learn the facts about Executive Order 9066 and how it affected one Japanese-American woman. As you read, you'll take notes on the information in the article.

■ Get a stack of index cards, and follow these steps:

1. Read through the selection once to find the main ideas.

2. Make a card for each main idea.

3. Take notes about each main idea in your own words, or use quotation marks around the author's words.

■ As you read "Wartime Mistakes, Peacetime Apologies," look for the blanks on the model cards that appear with the selection, and write down the missing word or words on a piece of paper. Take it one idea at a time.

Government officials registering Japanese Americans at a reception center in Los Angeles, California, 1942.

North Carolina Competency Goal
5.01; 5.02

SKILLS FOCUS

Reading Skills
Take notes.

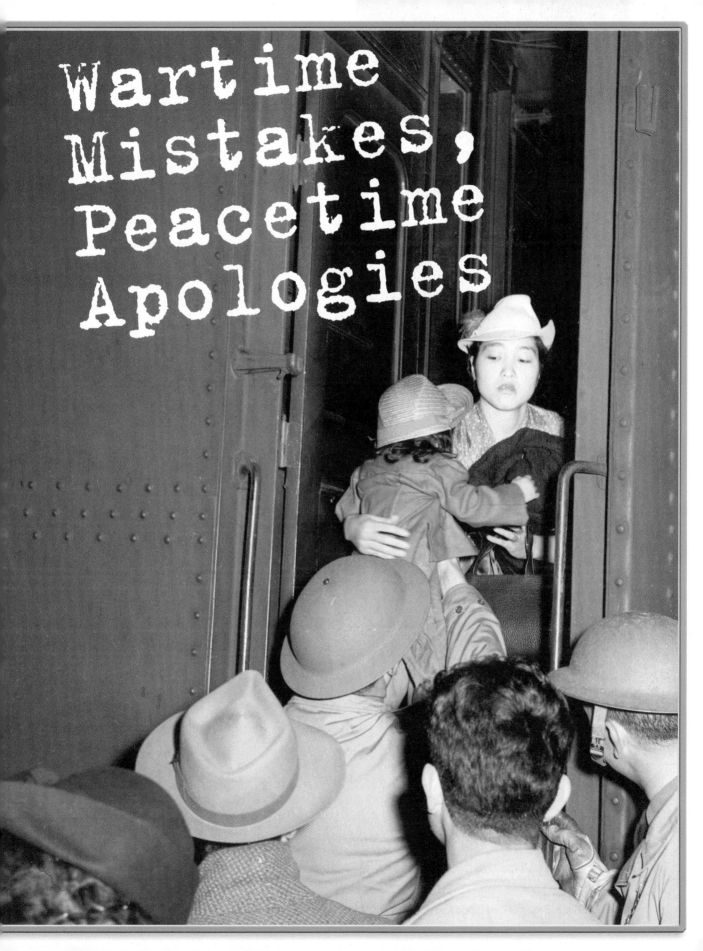

Wartime Mistakes, Peacetime Apologies

On March 13, 1942, Yoshiko Imamoto opened her door to face three FBI agents. They let her pack a nightgown and a Bible, then took her to jail while they "checked into a few things." Imamoto had lived in America for twenty-four years. She was a teacher and had done nothing wrong. But a month earlier, President Franklin D. Roosevelt had issued Executive Order 9066, which drastically changed the lives of Imamoto and more than 120,000 other people of Japanese ancestry living in the United States.

When Japan bombed Pearl Harbor on December 7, 1941, Japanese Americans were caught in the middle. They felt like Americans but looked like the enemy. Neighbors and co-workers eyed them suspiciously. Then Executive Order 9066, issued on February 19, 1942, authorized the exclusion of "any or all persons" from any areas the military chose. The word "Japanese" was never used, but the order was designed to allow the military to force Japanese Americans living near the coast to leave their homes for the duration of the war. Some were allowed to move inland, but most, like Yoshiko Imamoto, were herded into prisonlike camps.

Yoshiko Imamoto

- On _____ (when?), FBI arrested her with no warning.
- 24-year U.S. resident
- teacher
- had broken no laws

Pearl Harbor

- 12/7/1941
- Japan attacked U.S.
- Japanese Americans felt _____ (how?).
- They were treated _____ (how? by whom?).

Executive Order 9066

- issued by President Franklin D. Roosevelt
- affected _____ (how many?) people
- issued _____ (when?)
- allowed _____ (what?)
- never used _____ (what word?)
- Only _____ (who?) were moved.
- Most were moved _____ (where?).

Japanese American children wait for a train to take them to an internment camp.

I hereby authorize and direct the Secretary of War, and the Military Commanders whom he may from time to time designate, whenever he or any designated Commander deems such action necessary or desirable, to prescribe[1] military areas in such places and of such extent as he or the appropriate Military Commander may determine, from which any or all persons may be excluded, and with respect to which, the right of any person to enter, remain in, or leave shall be subject to whatever restrictions the Secretary of War or the appropriate Military Commander may impose in his discretion.[2]

—*President Franklin D. Roosevelt,*
excerpt from Executive Order 9066, 1942

After the war, Japanese Americans tried to start over. They had lost their jobs, their property, and their pride. Some used the Japanese American Evacuation Claims Act of 1948 to get compensation[3] for property they had lost. But it was not until the late 1960s that cries for redress—compensation for all they had suffered—began to emerge.

In 1976, Executive Order 9066 was officially ended by President Gerald Ford. Four years later, President Jimmy Carter signed a bill that created the Commission on Wartime Relocation and Internment of Civilians (CWRIC) to investigate the relocation of Japanese Americans. The CWRIC concluded that Executive Order 9066 was "not justified by military necessity" but was the result of "race prejudice, war hysteria,

---

After the War
- Japanese Americans had lost _____ (what?).
- _____ (what?) was used by some Japanese Americans to claim payment for lost property.
- _____ (what?) began in the late 1960s.

9066 Ended—Investigation Begun
- _____ (who?) ended 9066 in _____ (when?).
- _____ (who?) authorized CWRIC _____ (to do what?).
- CWRIC recommended _____ (what?).

---

1. **prescribe** (prē·skrīb′) *v.*: define officially.
2. **in his discretion** (di·skresh′ən): according to his wishes or judgment.
3. **compensation** *n.*: payment given to make up for a loss or injury.

and a failure of political leadership." In 1983, the commission recommended to Congress that each surviving Japanese American evacuee be given a payment of twenty thousand dollars and an apology.

A bill to authorize the payments was introduced in the House of Representatives in 1983 but met resistance. Intensive lobbying[4] by Japanese Americans was met by arguments that the government had acted legally and appropriately at the time.

Meanwhile, three men who had long since served their jail sentences for refusing to comply with curfew[5] or relocation orders filed suit[6] to challenge the government's actions. The court ruled that the government had had no legal basis for detaining Japanese Americans.

---

4. **lobbying** *v.* used as *n.*: activity aimed at influencing public officials.
5. **curfew** (kur'fyoo') *n.*: Shortly before the relocation began, the head of the Western Defense Command, Lt. Gen. John DeWitt, set a curfew. Between 8:00 P.M. and 6:00 A.M. each day, "all persons of Japanese ancestry" had to remain indoors, off the streets.
6. **filed suit:** went to court in an attempt to recover something.

Repayment
- Bill introduced in House of Representatives in 1983.
- supported by Japanese Americans
- Opponents argued that _____ (what?).

Court Ruling
- _____ (who?) took the government to court.
- The court decided _____ (what?).
- This ruling helped build support for _____ (what?).

The rulings increased pressure to provide redress. In 1988, Congress approved the final version of the redress bill, which became known as the Civil Liberties Act. It was signed by President Ronald Reagan on August 10, 1988. Two years later, Congress funded the payments.

In 1990, at the age of ninety-three, Yoshiko Imamoto opened her door not to FBI agents, but to a small brown envelope containing a check for twenty thousand dollars and an apology from President George Bush. It had taken almost fifty years and the actions of four presidents, but the government had made redress and apologized for its mistakes.

—Nancy Day,
from *Cobblestone Magazine*

Add to Repayment card:
- Congress approved repayment bill in 1988.
- called Civil Liberties Act
- signed by _____ (whom?) _____ (when?)
- Payments were sent _____ (when?).

Add to Yoshiko Imamoto card:
- in 1990, received _____ (what?)
- She was 93 years old.
- It had taken _____ (how long?).
- It had taken the work of four presidents.

A monetary sum and words alone cannot restore lost years or erase painful memories; neither can they fully convey our Nation's resolve to rectify[7] injustice and to uphold the rights of individuals. We can never fully right the wrongs of the past. But we can take a clear stand for justice and recognize that serious injustices were done to Japanese Americans during World War II.

—President George Bush,
excerpt from letter accompanying
redress checks, 1990

7. **rectify** *v.:* correct.

Taking Notes

Wartime Mistakes, Peacetime Apologies

Test Practice

1. From information in the article, you can conclude that Yoshiko Imamoto came to the United States when she was —

   A a young woman

   B a mother with a young child

   C a baby

   D a child

2. What is the **tone** of the letter the government sent with the payments?

   F Friendly

   G Angry

   H Worried

   J Apologetic

3. Discussion of a redress bill caused **conflict** between —

   A Japanese Americans and people who felt that the government had done nothing wrong

   B Japanese American members of Congress and other elected officials

   C people who had been evacuated and veterans of World War II

   D Congress and the Supreme Court

4. Which of the following is a **main idea** that could be a heading on a note card?

   F Yoshiko Imamoto arrested

   G Japan attacked United States

   H Compensation ordered

   J Pearl Harbor

5. Which sentence best **summarizes** Executive Order 9066?

   A Military commanders must follow the instructions given by the secretary of war.

   B When an area of any size is put under military control, all civilians in that area must be evacuated.

   C The military may set aside certain areas and decide who enters, stays, or leaves those areas.

   D Japanese Americans must leave California.

North Carolina Competency Goal
1.04; 2.01; 3.02; 4.01; 4.02; 5.01

Reading Skills
Analyze a text by taking logical notes.

Constructed Response

Use your note cards to answer these questions. Revise your note cards if they don't include enough information to answer the questions.

1. What powers did Executive Order 9066 give the military?

2. Which presidents helped bring about the U.S. government's "peacetime apologies" to Japanese Americans?

3. What were the results of the CWRIC's investigation?

4. What did the government finally do for interned Japanese Americans?

Vocabulary Development

Excluded People, Excluded Words

Japanese Americans were not the only group to face hostility during World War II. Germany, like Japan, was at war with the United States, and German Americans also experienced prejudice.

Some German Americans responded by changing their names—from Stein to Stone, for example, or from Knoebel to Noble. Some German-sounding street names were changed too. Even everyday words that had German origins or were connected in some way to Germany were replaced in the name of patriotism. Here are some examples:

Original		Replacement
dachshund	→	liberty pup
frankfurter	→	hot dog
German measles	→	liberty measles
German shepherd	→	Alsatian
hamburger	→	Salisbury steak

North Carolina Competency Goal
2.01; 3.02; 6.01

PRACTICE

With the class, study the words listed above. Which of the replacements are still in use today? Which of the original words have returned to everyday use? Using a good dictionary, try to find the origin of both the original words and the replacements. Which words come from the names of German cities? Why does *ham* appear in a word for ground *beef*?

SKILLS FOCUS

Vocabulary Skills
Understand word origins.

Blanca Flor

Make the Connection

The play you're about to read, *Blanca Flor*, is based on an old European story. The story's bare-bones plot could be summed up as "boy meets girl, boy loses girl, boy wins girl (or girl wins boy)." What movies and TV shows have you seen recently that can be summed up that way? Do most of these boy-meets-girl or girl-meets-boy plots turn out happily?

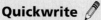

Quickwrite

Think of stories you know—children's stories, novels, stories on TV and in the movies. Work with a partner, and see if you can find examples of these popular character types:

- the strong hero or heroine
- the evil villain
- the innocent child
- the person with special powers
- the lovers in danger
- the helpful animal character
- the liar

Literary Focus
Characterization

Making characters come alive is one of the writer's most important and most difficult tasks. How do writers build characters out of words? They

- tell us directly what the character is like (good, evil, kind, sneaky)
- let the character talk
- describe the character's appearance
- show the character in action

- tell us what the character thinks
- show us how others respond to the character

In *Blanca Flor,* for example, the writer tells us directly that Don Ricardo is evil. He also tells us directly about the Duende (dwen'de). To find out what he says, check the list of characters at the beginning of the play.

Reading Skills
Making Inferences About Characters

You can use a graphic organizer like the one below to analyze the characters you meet in stories. Fill out a chart like the one below as you read *Blanca Flor* or when you review the play after your first reading. Once you have gathered your clues, look over your chart carefully. Then, write down a word or two naming the most important qualities of each character you have met.

Character [Name]:
Writer's direct comments:
Character's words:
Character's looks:
Character's actions:
Character's thoughts:
Responses of others:

North Carolina Competency Goal
1.04; 4.01; 5.01

INTERNET
Vocabulary Activity
•
Cross-curricular Connection
Keyword: LE5 6-2

SKILLS FOCUS

Literary Skills
Understand characterization.

Reading Skills
Make inferences about a character.

Characters

(in order of appearance)

The Narrator

Juanito, a young man

The Duende, a gnomelike, mischievous creature who lives in the forest

---

Blanca Flor, a young woman

Don[1] Ricardo, an evil man

Don Ramon, the father of Juanito

Doña[2] Arlette, the mother of Juanito

Two Doves, actors in costume

Scene 1.
IN THE FOREST.

The Narrator. *Blanca Flor,* "White Flower." There never was a story with such a beautiful name as this story of Blanca Flor. At the beginning of our story, a young man named Juanito has left home to seek his fortune in the world. With the blessing of his parents to aid and protect him, he has begun what will be a fantastic adventure. At the beginning of his journey, he wanders into a forest and stops by a stream to rest and eat some of the tortillas his mother had packed for his journey.

[JUANITO *enters and walks around the stage as if looking for a comfortable place to rest. He finally decides upon a spot and sits down. He takes out a tortilla from his traveling bag and he begins to talk to himself.*]

---

1. **Don** (dän): Spanish for "Sir" or "Mr."
2. **Doña** (dô′nyä): Spanish for "Lady" or "Madam."

Juanito. Whew! I'm hot. This river looks like a good spot to rest for a while. I'm so tired. Maybe this journey wasn't such a good idea. Right now I could be home with *la familia* eating a good supper that *mamacita* cooked for us. But no, I'm out in the world seeking my fortune. So far I haven't found very much, and all I have to show for my efforts are two worn-out feet and a tired body . . . oh, and don't forget (*holding up a dried tortilla*) a dried-out tortilla . . . (*He quickly looks around as if startled.*) What was that? (*He listens intently and hears a sound again.*) There it is again. I know I heard something . . .

[*As* JUANITO *is talking,* THE DUENDE *enters, sneaking up behind him.*]

Juanito. Must be my imagination. I've been out in the woods too long. You know, if you're alone too long, your mind starts to play tricks on you. Just look at me. I'm talking to my tortilla and hearing things . . .

The Duende (*in a crackly voice*). Hello.

Juanito. Yikes! Who said that! (*He turns around quickly and is startled to see* THE DUENDE *behind him.*) Who are you?

The Duende (*with a mischievous twinkle in his eye*). Hello.

Juanito. Hello . . . who, who are you? And where did you come from?

[THE DUENDE *grabs the tortilla out of* JUANITO's *hand and begins to eat it. During the rest of the scene* THE DUENDE *continues to eat tortillas.*]

Juanito. Hey, that's my tortilla.

The Duende (*in a playful manner*). Thank you very much. Thank you very much.

Juanito (*to the audience*). He must be a forest Duende. I've heard of them. They're spirits who live in the wood and play tricks on humans. I better go along with him or he might hurt me. (*He offers* THE DUENDE *another tortilla.* THE DUENDE *takes the tortilla and begins to eat it, too.*) I hope he's not too hungry. If he eats all my tortillas, I won't have any left, and it'll be days before I get food again. I'll have to eat wild berries like an animal. (*He reaches for the tortilla and* THE DUENDE *hits his hand.*) Ouch, that hurt!

The Duende. Looking for work, eh?

Juanito. Now I know he's a Duende. He can read minds.

The Duende. No work here. Lost in the forest. No work here.

Juanito. I know that. We're in the middle of the forest. But I know there'll be work in the next town.

The Duende. Maybe work right here. Maybe.

Juanito. Really. Where?

[THE DUENDE *points to a path in the forest.* JUANITO *stands up and looks down the path.*]

Juanito. There's nothing down that path. I've been down that path and there is nothing there.

The Duende. Look again. Look again. Be careful. Be careful. (*He begins to walk off, carrying the bag of tortillas with him.*)

Juanito. Hey, don't leave yet. What type of work? And where? Who do I see? Hey, don't leave yet!

The Duende (THE DUENDE *stops and turns*). Be careful. Danger. Danger. (*He exits.*)

Juanito. Hey! That's my bag of tortillas. Oh, this is great. This is really going to sound good when I get back home. My tortillas? . . . Oh, they were stolen by a forest Duende. Not to worry . . . (*He yells in the direction of the departed* DUENDE.) And I'm not lost! . . . This is great. Lost and hungry and no work. I guess I'm never going to find my fortune in the world. But what did he mean about work . . . and be careful . . . and danger. I've been down that path and there was nothing there . . . I don't think there was anything there. Oh well, there is only one way to find out. It certainly can't get much worse than things are now, and maybe there is work there.

[JUANITO *exits, in the direction of the path* THE DUENDE *indicated.*]

Scene 2.
FARTHER IN THE FOREST.

The Narrator. In spite of the Duende's warning, Juanito continued on the path of danger. As he came into a clearing, he came to a house and saw a young woman coming out of it.

[JUANITO *enters,* BLANCA FLOR *enters from the opposite side of the stage and stops, remaining at the opposite side of the stage.*]

Juanito. Where did this house come from? I was here just yesterday and there was no house here. I must really be lost and turned around. (*He sees the young woman and waves to her.*) Hey! Come here. Over here!

[BLANCA FLOR *runs to* JUANITO.]

Blanca Flor (*with fear in her voice*). How did you find this place? You must leave right away. The owner of this place is gone, but he will return soon. He leaves to do his work in the world, but he will return unexpectedly. If he finds you here, you'll never be able to leave. You must leave right away.

Juanito. Why? I haven't done anything.

Blanca Flor. Please, just leave. And hurry!

Juanito. Who are you? And why are you here?

Blanca Flor. I am Blanca Flor. My parents died long ago, and I am kept by this man to pay off their debts to him. I have to work day and night on his farm until I can be free. But he is mean, and he has kept prisoner others who have tried to free me. He makes them work until they die from exhaustion.

Juanito. Who would be so mean?

Blanca Flor. His name is Don Ricardo.

[DON RICARDO *enters, suddenly and with great force.*]

Don Ricardo (*addressing* JUANITO). Why are you here! Didn't she tell you to leave!

Blanca Flor (*scared*). Don't hurt him. He is lost in the forest and got here by mistake. He was just leaving.

Don Ricardo. Let him answer for himself. Then I will decide what to do with him.

Juanito (*gathering all his courage*). Yes, she did tell me to leave. But . . . but I am in the world seeking my fortune and I am looking for work. Is there any work for me to do here?

Don Ricardo. Seeking your fortune! They always say that, don't they, Blanca Flor. Well, I will give you the same chance I have given others. For each of three days, I will give you a job. If in three days you have completed the jobs, then you may leave. If not, then you will work here with me until you are dead. What do you say, fortune-seeker?

Blanca Flor (*pulling* JUANITO *aside*). Do not say yes. You will never leave here alive. Run and try to escape.

Juanito. But what about you? You are more trapped than anybody.

Blanca Flor. That is not your worry. Just run and try to escape.

Juanito (*suddenly turning back to* DON RICARDO). I will do the work you ask.

Don Ricardo (*laughing*). Blanca Flor, it is always your fault they stay. They all think they will be able to set you free. Well, let's give this one his "fair" chance. (*To* JUANITO) Here is your first job. See that lake over there? Take this thimble (*he gives a thimble to* JUANITO) and use it to carry all the water in the lake to that field over there.

Juanito. You want me to move a lake with a thimble?!

Don Ricardo. You wanted work, fortune-seeker. Well, this is your job. Have it finished by morning or your fate will be the same as all the others who tried to save poor Blanca Flor. (*He exits.*)

Juanito. What type of man is he? I have heard legends of evil men who keep people captive, and in my travels I heard many stories of young men seeking their fortunes who were never seen again, but I always thought they were just stories.

Blanca Flor. You have had the misfortune to get lost in a terrible part of the forest. Didn't anyone warn you to stay away from here?

Juanito. Yes . . . one person did. But I thought he was a forest Duende, and I didn't really believe him.

Blanca Flor. It was a forest Duende. In this part of the forest there are many creatures with magic. But my keeper, his magic is stronger than any of ours.

Juanito. Ours? . . . What do you mean, ours? Are you part of the magic of this forest?

Blanca Flor. Do not ask so many questions. The day is passing by, and soon it will be morning.

Juanito. Morning. I'm supposed to have moved the lake by then. I know this job is impossible, but while God is in his heaven there is a way. I will do this job. And when I am done, I will help you escape from here.

[JUANITO *and* BLANCA FLOR *exit.*]

Scene 3.
THE NEXT MORNING.

JUANITO *and* BLANCA FLOR *enter. As* THE NARRATOR *speaks,* JUANITO *and* BLANCA FLOR *act out the scene as it is described.*

The Narrator. Juanito took the thimble and started to carry the water from the lake. He worked as hard as he could, but soon he began to realize that the job really was an impossible one, and he knew he was doomed. He sat down and began to cry because his luck had abandoned him and because his parents' blessings offered no protection in that evil place. Blanca Flor watched Juanito's valiant effort to move the water. As she watched him crying, her heart was touched, and she decided to use her powers to help him. She knew that it was very dangerous to use her powers to help Juanito and to cross Don Ricardo, but she felt it was finally time to end her own torment. As Juanito cried, Blanca Flor took out her brush and began to brush his hair. She cradled Juanito in her arms and her soothing comfort soon put him to sleep . . .

[*As soon as* JUANITO *is asleep,* BLANCA FLOR *gently puts his head down and leaves, taking the thimble with her.*]

The Narrator. When Juanito awoke, he frantically looked for the thimble and, not finding it, ran to the lake. When he reached the lake, he stood at its banks in amazement.

All the water was gone. He looked over to the other part of the field, and there stood a lake where before there was nothing. He turned to look for Blanca Flor, but instead there was Don Ricardo.

[DON RICARDO *enters.*]

Don Ricardo (*in full force and very angry*). This must be the work of Blanca Flor, or else you have more power than I thought. I know Blanca Flor is too scared to ever use her powers against me, so as a test of your powers, tomorrow your next job will not be so easy. See that barren[3] ground over on the side of the mountain? You are to clear that ground, plant seeds, grow wheat, harvest it, grind it, cook it, and have bread for me to eat before I return. You still have your life now, but I better have bread tomorrow. (*He exits, with a flourish.*)[4]

[JUANITO *exits.*]

Scene 4.
THE NEXT MORNING.

As THE NARRATOR *speaks,* JUANITO *and* BLANCA FLOR *enter and act out the scene as it is described.*

The Narrator. Immediately upon waking the next morning, Juanito tried to move the rocks in the field, but they were impossible to move because of their great size. Once again, Juanito knew that his efforts were useless. He went over to the new lake and fell down in exhaustion. As he lay in the grass by the lake, Blanca Flor came to him once more and began to brush his hair. Soon, Juanito was asleep.

[BLANCA FLOR *exits.*]

---

3. **barren** *adj.:* not producing crops or fruit.
4. **flourish** *n.:* sweeping movement.

The Narrator. As before, when he awoke, Juanito dashed to the field to make one last attempt to do his work. When he got there, he again stopped in amazement. The field was clear of rocks, and the land had been planted and harvested. As he turned around, there stood Blanca Flor.

[BLANCA FLOR *enters.*]

Blanca Flor (*she hands a loaf of bread to* JUANITO). Give this to Don Ricardo.
Juanito. How did you do this?

[DON RICARDO *enters, quickly.*]

Don Ricardo. What do you have?
Juanito (*shaking with fear*). Just . . . just this loaf of bread. (*Giving the bread to* DON RICARDO) Here is the bread you asked for.
Don Ricardo (*very angry*). This is the work of Blanca Flor. This will not happen again. Tomorrow, your third job will be your final job, and even the powers of Blanca Flor will not help you this time! (*He exits.*)
Blanca Flor. Believe me, the third job will be impossible to do. It will be too difficult even for my powers. We must run from here if there is to be any chance of escaping his anger. He will kill you because I have helped you. Tonight I will come for you. Be ready to leave quickly as soon as I call for you.

[JUANITO *and* BLANCA FLOR *exit.*]

Scene 5.
LATER THAT NIGHT.

On one side of the stage, JUANITO *sits waiting. On the other side,* BLANCA FLOR *is in her room grabbing her traveling bag. As she leaves her room, she turns and mimes spitting three times as* THE NARRATOR *describes the action.*

The Narrator. Late that night, as Juanito waited for her, Blanca Flor packed her belongings into a bag. Before she left the house, she went to the fireplace and spat three times into it.

[BLANCA FLOR *joins* JUANITO.]

Blanca Flor (*quietly calling*). Juanito . . . Juanito.

Juanito. Blanca Flor, is it time?

Blanca Flor. Yes. We must leave quickly, before he finds out I am gone, or it will be too late.

Juanito. Won't he know you are gone as soon as he calls for you?

Blanca Flor. Not right away. I've used my powers to fool him. But it won't last long. Let's go!

[JUANITO *and* BLANCA FLOR *exit.*]

The Narrator. When Don Ricardo heard the noise of Juanito and Blanca Flor leaving, he called out . . .

Don Ricardo (*from offstage*). Blanca Flor, are you there?

The Narrator. The spit she had left in the fireplace answered.

Blanca Flor (*from offstage*). Yes, I am here.

The Narrator. Later, Don Ricardo called out again.

Don Ricardo (*from offstage*). Blanca Flor, are you there?

The Narrator. For a second time, the spit she had left in the fireplace answered.

Blanca Flor (*from offstage*). Yes, I am here.

The Narrator. Still later, Don Ricardo called out again, a third time.

Don Ricardo (*from offstage*). Blanca Flor, are you there?

The Narrator. By this time, the fire had evaporated Blanca Flor's spit, and there was no answer. Don Ricardo knew that Blanca Flor was gone, and that she had run away with Juanito. He saddled his horse and galloped up the path to catch them before they escaped from his land.

First Thoughts

1. Do you think Blanca Flor and Juanito will escape from Don Ricardo? Why or why not?

Thinking Critically

2. How would you quickly summarize what has happened so far in *Blanca Flor*? (Look back at the bare-bones plot summary on page 166.)

3. The narrator says that Juanito goes down the path "in spite of the Duende's warning." Did you hear the Duende's words as a warning, as encouragement, or as something else? Explain.

4. Why do you think Blanca Flor decides to help Juanito even though she hasn't helped any of the young men before? (Does the text hint at more than one reason?)

Reading Check

Match each **cause** in the left-hand column with its **effect** in the right-hand column.

Cause	Effect
1. The Duende points to a path in the forest.	a. Juanito decides to try to rescue Blanca Flor.
2. Juanito hears Blanca Flor's story	b. Don Ricardo catches Juanito on his land.
3. Juanito ignores Blanca Flor's warning and refuses to leave.	c. Juanito meets Blanca Flor.
4. Blanca Flor moves the lake for Juanito.	d. Don Ricardo gives Juanito a harder task.

North Carolina Competency Goal
6.01

Vocabulary Development

Foreign Words Frequently Used in English: Eat Your Words

Have you ever eaten a *tortilla,* as the Duende does? How about a *croissant* or a *bagel*? The names of these foods come from Spanish, French, and Yiddish. When English speakers began eating these foods, the names of the foods came into the English language. After all, *bread* is a good word, but it doesn't capture the specific—and delicious—qualities of tortillas, croissants, and bagels.

SKILLS FOCUS

Reading Skills
Analyze cause and effect.

Vocabulary Skills
Understand foreign words used in English.

PRACTICE

With a partner, create a menu of five or six foods with foreign names. Use a dictionary or the Internet to find out where the name of the food comes from.

Some Words for Your Menu

pasta
pizza
sushi
lo mein
enchilada
taco
scone

Scene 6.
IN THE FOREST.

JUANITO and BLANCA FLOR enter, running and out of breath.

Juanito. Blanca Flor, we can rest now. We are free.

Blanca Flor. No, Juanito, we will not be free until we are beyond the borders of Don Ricardo's land. As long as we are on his land, his powers will work on us.

Juanito. How much farther?

Blanca Flor. Remember the river where you met the Duende? That river is the border. Across it we are free.

Juanito. That river is still really far. Let's rest here for a while.

Blanca Flor. No, he is already after us. We must keep going. I can hear the hooves of his horse.

Juanito (*he looks around desperately*). Where? How can that be?

Blanca Flor. He is really close. Juanito, come stand by me. Quickly!

Juanito (*still looking around*). I don't hear anything.

Blanca Flor (*grabbing him and pulling him to her*). Juanito! Now!

[*As* THE NARRATOR *describes the action,* JUANITO *and* BLANCA FLOR *act out the scene.* BLANCA FLOR *does not actually throw a brush. She mimes throwing the brush and the action.*]

The Narrator. Blanca Flor looked behind them and saw that Don Ricardo was getting closer. She reached into her bag, took her brush, and threw it behind her. The brush turned into a church by the side of the road. She then cast a spell on Juanito and turned him into a little old bell ringer. She turned herself into a statue outside the church.

[DON RICARDO *enters, as if riding a horse.*]

Don Ricardo (*addressing the bell ringer* [JUANITO]). Bell ringer, have you seen two young people come this way recently? They would have been in a great hurry and out of breath.

Juanito (*in an old man's voice*). No . . . I don't think so. But maybe last week, two young boys came by. They stopped to pray in the church . . . Or was it two girls. I don't know. I am just an old bell ringer. Not many people actually come by this way at all. You're the first in a long time.

Don Ricardo. Bell ringer, if you are lying to me you will be sorry. (*He goes over to the statue* [BLANCA FLOR], *who is standing very still, as a statue. He examines the statue very closely and then addresses the bell ringer* [JUANITO].) Bell ringer, what saint is this a statue of? The face looks very familiar.

Juanito. I am an old bell ringer. I don't remember the names of all the saints. But I do know that the statue is very old and has been here a long time. Maybe Saint Theresa or Saint Bernadette.

Don Ricardo. Bell ringer, if you are lying, I will be back! (*He exits.*)

Juanito. Adiós, Señor!

[BLANCA FLOR *breaks her pose as a statue and goes to* JUANITO.]

Blanca Flor. Juanito, Juanito. The spell is over.

Juanito. What happened? I did hear the angry hooves of a horse being ridden hard.

Blanca Flor. We are safe for a while. But he will not give up, and we are not free yet.

[JUANITO *and* BLANCA FLOR *exit.*]

Scene 7. FARTHER INTO THE FOREST.

The Narrator. Blanca Flor and Juanito desperately continued their escape. As they finally stopped for a rest, they had their closest call yet.

[BLANCA FLOR *and* JUANITO *enter.*]

Juanito. Blanca Flor, please, let's rest just for a minute.

Blanca Flor. OK. We can rest here. I have not heard the hooves of his horse for a while now.

Juanito. What will he do if he catches us?

Blanca Flor. He will take us back. I will be watched more closely than ever, and you will—

Juanito (*sadly*). I know. Was there ever a time when you were free? Do you even remember your parents?

Blanca Flor. Yes. I have the most beautiful memories of my mother, our house, and our animals. Every day, my father would saddle the horses and together we would—

Juanito. Blanca Flor . . . I hear something.

Blanca Flor (*alarmed*). He's close. Very close.

[*As* THE NARRATOR *describes the action,* JUANITO *and* BLANCA FLOR *act out the scene.* BLANCA FLOR *does not actually throw a comb. She mimes throwing the comb and the action.*]

The Narrator. Blanca Flor quickly opened her bag and threw her comb behind her. Immediately the comb turned into a field of corn. This time she turned Juanito into a scarecrow, and she turned herself into a stalk of corn beside him.

[DON RICARDO *enters, as if riding a horse.*]

Don Ricardo. Where did they go? I still think that the bell ringer knew more than he was saying. They were just here. I could hear their scared little voices. Juanito will pay for this, and Blanca Flor will never have the chance to escape again . . . Now where did they go? Perhaps they are in this field of corn. It is strange to see a stalk of corn grow so close to a scarecrow. But this is a day for strange things. (*He exits.*)

Blanca Flor. Juanito, it is over again. Let's go. The river is not far. We are almost free.

[JUANITO *breaks his pose as a scarecrow and stretches and rubs his legs as* BLANCA FLOR *looks around apprehensively.*][5]

Juanito. Blanca Flor, that was close. We have to hurry now. The river is just through these trees. We can make it now for sure if we hurry.

The Narrator. But they spoke too soon. Don Ricardo had gotten suspicious about the field of corn and returned to it. When he saw Juanito and Blanca Flor he raced to catch them.

[DON RICARDO *enters suddenly and sees them.*]

Don Ricardo. There you are. I knew something was wrong with that field of corn. Now you are mine.

[*As* THE NARRATOR *describes the action,* JUANITO *and* BLANCA FLOR *act out the scene.* BLANCA FLOR *does not actually throw a mirror. She mimes throwing the mirror and the action.*]

The Narrator. When Blanca Flor saw Don Ricardo, she reached into her bag and took out a mirror, the final object in the bag. She threw the mirror into the middle of the road.

---

5. **apprehensively** *adv.*: fearfully; uneasily.

Instantly, the mirror became a large lake, its waters so smooth and still that it looked like a mirror as it reflected the sky and clouds. When Don Ricardo got to the lake, all he saw was two ducks, a male and a female, swimming peacefully in the middle of the lake. Suddenly, the ducks lifted off the lake and flew away. As they flew away, Don Ricardo knew that the ducks were Juanito and Blanca Flor, and that they were beyond his grasp. As they disappeared, he shouted one last curse.

[JUANITO *and* BLANCA FLOR *exit.*]

Don Ricardo. You may have escaped, Blanca Flor, but you will never have his love. I place a curse on both of you. The first person to embrace him will cause him to forget you forever! (*He exits.*)

Scene 8.
NEAR JUANITO'S HOME.

BLANCA FLOR *and* JUANITO *enter.*

The Narrator. Disguised as ducks, Blanca Flor and Juanito flew safely away from that evil land and escaped from Don Ricardo. They finally arrived at Juanito's home, and using Blanca Flor's magical powers, they returned to their human selves.

Juanito. Blanca Flor, we are close to my home. Soon we will be finally safe forever. I will introduce you to my family, and we will begin our new life together . . . Blanca Flor, why do you look so sad? We have escaped the evil Don Ricardo, and soon we will be happy forever.

Blanca Flor. We have not escaped. His final curse will forever be over us.

Juanito. Remember, that curse will work only in his own land. You yourself told me

that once we were beyond the borders of his land, his powers would have no hold on us.

Blanca Flor. His powers are very great, Juanito.

Juanito. Blanca Flor, you have never explained to me the source of your own powers. Are your powers also gone?

Blanca Flor. The powers have always been in the women of my family. That is why Don Ricardo would not let me leave. He was afraid that I would use my powers against him. I have never been away from that land, so I do not know about my powers in this new land.

Juanito. You will have no need for your powers here. Soon we will be with my family. Wait outside while I go and tell my family that I have returned from seeking my fortune, safe at last. Then I will tell them that the fortune I found was you.

Blanca Flor. Juanito, remember the curse.

Juanito. I am not afraid of any curse. Not with you here with me. All my dreams have come true. Come, let's go meet my family.

[JUANITO *and* BLANCA FLOR *exit.*]

Scene 9.
AT JUANITO'S HOME.

DON RAMON *and* DOÑA ARLETTE *are sitting at home passing the time with idle talk.*

The Narrator. Juanito's parents had waited patiently for their son to return from seeking his fortune in the world. They did not know that his return home was only the beginning of another chapter of his great adventure.

Doña Arlette. Do you ever think we will hear from Juanito? It has been months since he left to seek his fortune in the world.

Don Ramon. We will hear word soon. I remember when I left home to seek my fortune in the world. Eventually, I found that the best thing to do was return home and make my fortune right here, with my *familia* at my side. Soon he will discover the same thing and you will have your son back.

Doña Arlette. It is easier for a father to know those things. A mother will never stop worrying about her children.

Don Ramon. I worry about the children just as much as you do. But there is no stopping children who want to grow up. He has our blessing and permission to go, and that will be what brings him back safe to us. Soon. You just wait.

[JUANITO *enters. His parents are overjoyed to see him.*]

Juanito. Mama! Papa! I am home.

Doña Arlette. *¡Mi 'jito!*[6]

Don Ramon. Juanito!

[*Overjoyed with seeing* JUANITO, *his parents rush and embrace him.*]

Doña Arlette. God has answered my prayers. *Mi 'jito* has returned home safe.

Don Ramon. Juanito, come sit close to us and tell us all about your adventures in the world. What great adventures did you have?

Juanito. I had the greatest adventures. For the longest time I was unlucky and unable to find work but finally I . . . I . . .

Doña Arlette. What is it? Are you OK? Do you need some food?

Juanito. No, I'm OK. It's just that I was going to say something and I forgot what I was going to say.

Don Ramon. Don't worry. If it is truly important, it'll come back.

Juanito. No, I've definitely forgotten what I was going to say. Oh well, it probably wasn't important anyway.

Doña Arlette. Did you meet someone special? Did you bring a young woman back for us to meet?

Juanito. No, I didn't have those kind of adventures. Pretty much nothing happened, and then I finally decided that it was just best to come home.

Don Ramon (*to* DOÑA ARLETTE). See what I told you? That is exactly what I said would happen.

Doña Arlette. Now that you are home, it is time to settle down and start your own family. You know our neighbor Don Emilio has a younger daughter who would make a

---

6. **mi 'jito** (mē hē′tô): contraction of *mi hijito*, Spanish for "my little son."

very good wife. Perhaps we should go visit her family this Sunday.

Juanito. You know, that would probably be a good idea. I must admit that I was hoping I would find love on my adventures, but I have come home with no memories of love at all. Perhaps it is best to make my fortune right here, close to home.

Don Ramon (*to* DOÑA ARLETTE). See? That is exactly what I said would happen.

[*All exit.*]

Scene 10. MONTHS LATER AT JUANITO'S HOME.

The Narrator. Blanca Flor had seen the embrace and knew that the evil curse had been fulfilled. Brokenhearted, she traveled to a nearby village and lived there in hopes that one day the curse could be broken.

The people of the village soon got to know Blanca Flor and came to respect her for the good person she was. One day, Blanca Flor heard news that a celebration was being held in honor of Juanito's return home. She immediately knew that this might be her one chance to break the curse. From the times when she had brushed Juanito's hair, she had kept a lock of his hair. She took one strand of his hair and made it into a dove. She then took one strand of her own hair and turned it into another dove. She took these two doves to Juanito's celebration as a present.

[JUANITO *and* DON RAMON *are sitting talking.*]

Don Ramon. Juanito, what was the most fantastic thing that happened on your adventures?

Juanito. Really, Father, nothing much at all happened. Sometimes I begin to have a

memory of something, but it never becomes really clear. At night I have these dreams, but when I awake in the morning I cannot remember them. It must be some dream I keep trying to remember . . . or forget.

Don Ramon. I remember when I went into the world to seek my fortune. I was a young man like you . . .

[DOÑA ARLETTE *enters.*]

Doña Arlette. Juanito, there's a young woman here with a present for you.

Juanito. Who is it?

Doña Arlette. I don't really know her. She is the new young woman who just recently came to the village. The women of the church say she is constantly doing good works for the church and that she is a very good person. She has brought you a present to help celebrate your coming home safe.

Juanito. Sure. Let her come in.

[BLANCA FLOR *enters with the* TWO DOVES. *The* DOVES *are actors in costume.*]

Blanca Flor (*speaking to* JUANITO). Thank you for giving me the honor of presenting these doves as gifts to you.

Juanito. No. No. The honor is mine. Thank you. They are very beautiful.

Blanca Flor. They are special doves. They are singing doves.

Doña Arlette. I have never heard of singing doves before. Where did you get them?

Blanca Flor. They came from a special place. A place where all things have a magic power. There are no other doves like these in the world.

Don Ramon. Juanito, what a gift! Let's hear them sing!

Doña Arlette. Yes, let's hear them sing.

Blanca Flor (*to* JUANITO). May they sing to you?

Juanito. Yes, of course. Let's hear their song.

[*Everyone sits to listen to the* DOVES' *song. As the* DOVES *begin to chant, their words begin to have a powerful effect on* JUANITO. *His memory of* BLANCA FLOR *returns to him.*]

Doves. Once there was a faraway land
A land of both good and evil powers.
A river flowed at the edge like a steady
   hand
And it was guarded by a Duende for all the
   hours.
Of all the beautiful things the land
   did hold

The most beautiful with the purest power
Was a young maiden, true and bold
Named Blanca Flor, the White Flower.

Juanito. I remember! The doves' song has made me remember. (*Going to* BLANCA FLOR) Blanca Flor, your love has broken the curse. Now I remember all that was struggling to come out. Mama, Papa, here is Blanca Flor, the love I found when I was seeking my fortune.

[JUANITO *and* BLANCA FLOR *embrace.*]

Don Ramon. This is going to be a really good story!

[*All exit, with* JUANITO *stopping to give* BLANCA FLOR *a big hug.*]

Meet the Writer

Angel Vigil

The Oral Tradition

Angel Vigil (1947–   ) was born in New Mexico and was raised "in a large, traditional Hispanic extended family, with loving grandparents and plenty of aunts and cousins."

   Although *Blanca Flor* is based on a traditional European tale, the play also draws on Hispanic folklore. The mischievous little tricksters called *duendes* make trouble for people in stories told throughout the Hispanic Southwest.

For Independent Reading

You can find other plays based on Hispanic stories in Vigil's *¡Teatro! Plays from the Hispanic Culture for Young People.* You might also enjoy reading *The Corn Woman: Stories and Legends of the Hispanic Southwest* and *The Eagle on the Cactus: Traditional Stories from Mexico.*

First Thoughts

1. Did you like the way the play ended? Why or why not?

Thinking Critically

2. Choose two main characters in the play, and list two or three of each **character's qualities.** (If you choose Blanca Flor, for example, you might list courage and kindness.) Look back at your character chart for ideas. Then, give examples of actions that illustrate the qualities you listed.

3. Decide which character has the greatest effect on the **plot** and the **resolution** of the **conflict.** Explain your thinking by citing examples from the play.

4. The number three is a common **motif,** an element that appears again and again in literature. Where do things happen in threes in *Blanca Flor*?

Extending Interpretations

5. How would the outcome of this play have been different if Blanca Flor had been less forceful, shyer, and more accepting of her fate?

6. If you were Blanca Flor, would you have just walked away when Juanito's mother came to embrace him? What else could you have done?

WRITING
Retell the Story in a Different Setting

Retell the story of Blanca Flor, setting it in another time and place. (You might want to set it in your neighborhood today.) Before you start writing, give the characters new names. Think of three impossible tasks for the hero, and decide what items the heroine will throw and what those items will turn into. You might want to use the character types listed in the Quickwrite as characters in your retelling.

> **Reading Check**
>
> Using the events in Scenes 6–10, make a cause-and-effect matching game like the one on page 174. Trade papers with a partner and play the game he or she has made.

North Carolina Competency Goal
1.02; 1.04;
4.01; 4.02;
5.01; 5.02

INTERNET
Projects and Activities
Keyword: LE5 6-2

SKILLS FOCUS

Literary Skills
Analyze characterization.

Reading Skills
Make inferences about a character.

Writing Skills
Retell the story in a different setting.

After You Read Vocabulary Development

Using Spanish Words in English

American English has been borrowing words from Spanish for centuries, especially in the western United States. More Spanish words come into English all the time. Even if you are not a Spanish speaker, you may know the Spanish way to say goodbye to friends: *Adios, amigos.*

You can sometimes figure out the meaning of an unfamiliar Spanish word by thinking of English words that resemble it. (If Spanish is your first language, you can figure out the meanings of some English words in a similar way.)

SKILLS FOCUS

Vocabulary Skills Understand origins and meanings of foreign words used in English.

PRACTICE

Find an English dictionary that tells you the origins of words, including the language they come from. Look up each of the words listed in the first column. In the second column, write down the word's Spanish meaning or the Spanish word it's derived from. (The Spanish word itself may have come from another language.) In the third column, write the English meaning (look in a dictionary, or draw on your own knowledge). In the fourth column, write a sentence that uses the word.

North Carolina Competency Goal 6.01

TEN WORDS FROM SPANISH			
Word	Spanish Meaning or Original Spanish	English Meaning	Sentence
tornado	tornar, "to turn"	whirlwind; rapidly rotating column of air	The tornado ripped the roof off.
alligator			
armadillo			
bonanza			
cafeteria			
canyon			
chocolate			
mascara			
patio			
sombrero			
stampede			

Comparing Literature

Literary Focus
Character Traits

Just like people in real life, characters in literature possess certain traits. A **character trait** is a quality we find in a person, such as honesty, shyness, cruelty, dishonesty, generosity, or stubbornness. Some characters are famous for their traits: Scrooge from Charles Dickens's *A Christmas Carol* is famous for his stinginess. Hamlet, in Shakespeare's play, is famous for being unable to make up his mind. Dr. Seuss's Grinch, who stole Christmas, is famous for meanness.

We discover the traits of characters in stories in the same way we discover the traits of people in life: We notice how they look and dress, we watch them in action, we listen to what they say, and we watch the way they affect other people.

Character Traits
• bold/shy
• brave/cowardly
• careful/careless
• generous/selfish
• cruel/kind
• hardworking/lazy
• determined/ easy-going
• happy/sad
• confident/unsure
• powerful/weak
• wise/foolish
• honest/dishonest
• reliable/unreliable

Reading Skills
Comparing and Contrasting

As you read each selection that follows, use a Venn diagram (as shown below) to record the traits of each character—Janet, who is fictional, and Toni, who is a real teenager. The open-book signs indicate questions in the margins that will help you identify each girl's traits. Remember, when you compare two characters—real or fictional—you look for ways they are similar. When you contrast characters, you look for ways they are different.

If you need a reminder of all the thousands of traits a character can reveal, check the list in the box at the top for a few examples.

North Carolina Competency Goal
1.02; 5.01

SKILLS FOCUS

Literary Skills
Understand characterization.

Reading Skills
Compare and contrast texts.

Janet's traits — Traits in common — Toni's traits

Before You Read

Today this correspondence between two friends—or former friends— might take the form of e-mails. Instead, Janet and Richard communicate through handwritten notes on little pieces of paper. The subject of their correspondence is a baseball team that Richard plays for and manages. Janet thinks Richard should allow girls to play on the team, but he disagrees. As you read, see if you side with Janet or with her (former) friend Richard.

The Southpaw

Judith Viorst

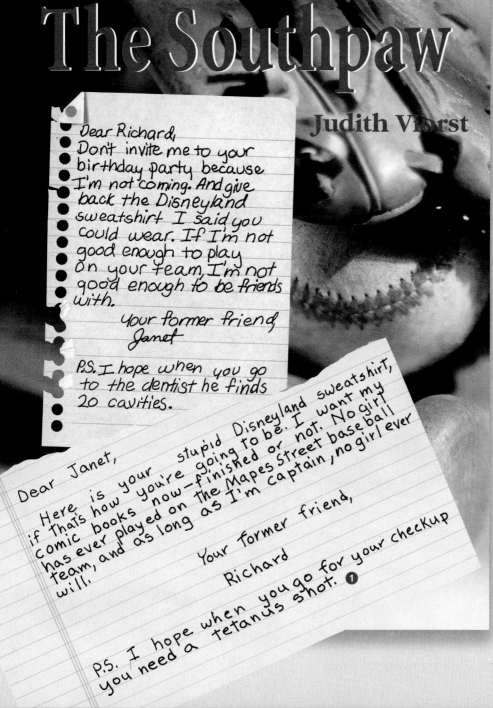

Dear Richard,
Don't invite me to your birthday party because I'm not coming. And give back the Disneyland sweatshirt I said you could wear. If I'm not good enough to play on your team, I'm not good enough to be friends with.

Your former friend,
Janet

P.S. I hope when you go to the dentist he finds 20 cavities.

Dear Janet,
Here is your stupid Disneyland sweatshirt, if that's how you're going to be. I want my comic books now—finished or not. No girl has ever played on the Mapes Street baseball team, and as long as I'm captain, no girl ever will.

Your former friend,
Richard

P.S. I hope when you go for your checkup you need a tetanus shot.

IDENTIFY

❶ What does Janet want? What is standing in her way?

The Southpaw **185**

Dear Richard,
I'm changing my goldfish's
name from Richard to
Stanley. Don't count on
my vote for class
president next year.
Just because I'm a
member of the ballet
club doesn't mean I'm
not a terrific ballplayer.
Your former friend,
Janet

P.S. I see you lost
your first game 28-0

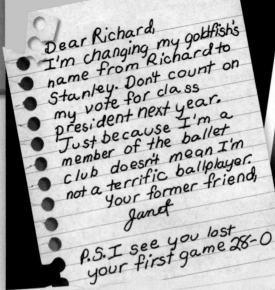

Dear Janet,

I'm not saving anymore seats for you on
the bus. For all I care you can stand the
whole way to school. Why don't you just
forget about baseball and learn something
nice like knitting?
                  your former friend,

                        Richard

P.S. Wait until Wednesday

Dear Richard,
My father said I could
call someone to go
with us for a ride
and hot-fudge sundaes.
In case you didn't
notice, I didn't call
you
      Your former friend,
      Janet

P.S. I see you lost your
second game, 34-0.

Dear Janet,
Remember when I took the laces out of my
blue-and-white sneakers and gave them
to you? I want them back.
      Your former friend,
            Richard

P.S. Wait until Friday. ❷

INFER

❷ What do you learn
about Janet from the
letters on this page?

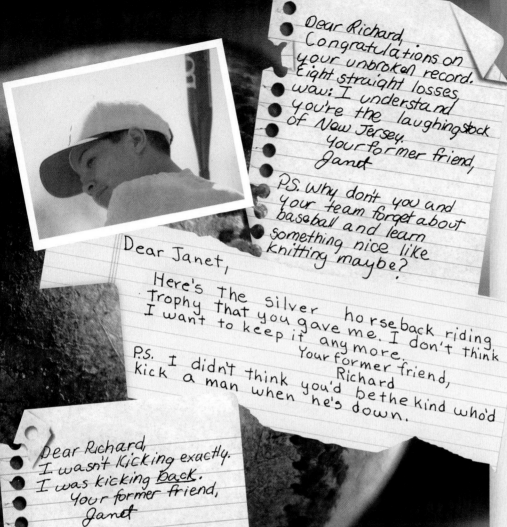

Dear Richard,
Congratulations on your unbroken record. Eight straight losses wow! I understand you're the laughingstock of New Jersey.
Your former friend,
Janet

P.S. Why don't you and your team forget about baseball and learn something nice like knitting maybe?

Dear Janet,
Here's the silver horseback riding trophy that you gave me. I don't think I want to keep it anymore.
Your former friend,
Richard
P.S. I didn't think you'd be the kind who'd kick a man when he's down.

Dear Richard,
I wasn't kicking exactly. I was kicking <u>back</u>.
Your former friend,
Janet

P.S. In case you were wondering, my batting average is .315.

Dear Janet,
Alfie is having his tonsils out tomorrow. We might be able to let you catch next week.
Richard ❸

INFER

❸ What details in these letters show that Janet can be sarcastic, saying the opposite of what she means in order to make fun of Richard or get a point across?

Dear Richard,
I pitch.
        Janet

Dear Janet,
    Joel is moving to Kansas and Danny sprained his wrist. How about a permanent place in the outfield?
        Richard

Dear Richard,
I pitch.
        Janet

Dear Janet,
    Ronnie caught the chicken pox and Leo broke his toe and Elwood has these stupid violin lessons. I'll give you first base, and that's my final offer.
        Richard ❹

INFER

❹ Which letters show that Janet is very stubborn?

Comparing Literature

Dear Richard,
Susan Reilly plays
first base, Marilyn Jackson
catches, Ethel Kahn
plays center field, I
pitch. It's a package
deal.
Janet

P.S. Sorry about your
12-game losing streak.

Dear Janet,
Please! Not Marilyn Jackson.
Richard

Dear Richard,
Nobody ever said that I
was unreasonable. How
about Lizzie Martindale
instead?
Janet

Dear Janet,
At least could you call your
goldfish Richard
again?
Your friend,
Richard ❺

INFER

❺ Which details show
that Janet is a clever
negotiator?

The Southpaw   189

Meet the Writer

Judith Viorst

Laughing at Everyday Life

Judith Viorst (1931–   ) decided when she was only seven years old that she wanted to be a writer. She sent out "terrible poems about dead dogs, mostly" to magazines in hopes of getting them published. In those days she liked to write about "deadly serious things," but she later found success in writing books that help people of all ages laugh at the ups and downs of everyday life.

Viorst has based many of her books on the experiences of her own family. When her oldest son, Anthony, started giving his younger brothers a hard time, for example, she wrote a children's book called *I'll Fix Anthony* (1969) to cheer up the younger ones. When her son Alexander was having lots of bad days, she wrote *Alexander and the Terrible, Horrible, No Good, Very Bad Day* (1972) to help him cope.

For Independent Reading

In addition to the books mentioned above, you might also enjoy *The Tenth Good Thing About Barney and Rosie and Michael.*

First Thoughts

1. Respond to "The Southpaw" by completing one or both of the following statements:
   - I think Janet is . . .
   - If I were Richard, I would . . .

Thinking Critically

2. What was the relationship between Janet and Richard before he said she couldn't play on his team? How do you know?

3. Where do Janet and Richard use sarcasm to make their points? Give some examples from the notes where they say the opposite of what they mean in order to tease and annoy each other.

4. What would you say is the main message of this story? How do you feel about the story's message?

5. Do you like the use of the letter form to tell a story? Why or why not?

Reading Check

Use the diagram below to chart the main events of this story's plot. Keep your notes for the assignment on page 197.

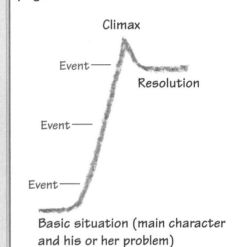

Comparing Literature

6. After you've read the next selection, you'll write an essay comparing and contrasting Janet with the girl who wrote the essay, "Summer Diamond Girl." Begin to gather details for your essay now by listing some of Janet's character traits on the Venn diagram below.

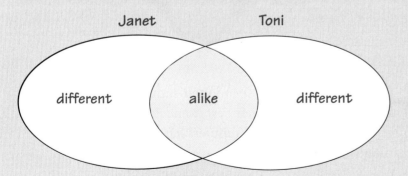

North Carolina Competency Goal
1.02; 1.04; 4.01; 4.02; 5.01; 5.02

SKILLS FOCUS

Literary Skills
Analyze characterization.

Reading Skills
Compare and contrast texts.

Before You Read

Janet's personality comes through loud and clear in her notes in "Southpaw." Here is another girl who loves to play ball. As you read, think about what kind of a person Toni is. Does she remind you of Janet? How would she have handled Janet's problem?

Summer Diamond Girl

TONI JANIK

IDENTIFY

❶ What details explain the title of this essay?

How many people can spend their summers getting down and dirty with some of their best friends? I do, and I love every minute of it! For years, my summers have been spent on softball diamonds around the United States. ❶

When I was ten years old and just four feet tall, my mother put a glove in my hand and sent me off to play with the big girls. My life hasn't been the same since. I've spent hours at catching clinics,[1] pitching clinics, and hitting clinics. I've broken two fingers on the same hand in two summers. I've been hit by pitches, line drives, and bats. I've had the sun glaring in my eyes, dust swirling in my mouth, rain pelting my head, and water pooling around my feet. And I wouldn't trade it for anything. ❷

I am a summer diamond girl. I play the game because I love it. I give up the beach, the mall, the movies, or just hanging out. l play against girls who are in college to help me improve. I sleep in dilapidated[2] motels with funky-smelling rooms in the middle of nowhere because that's where the tournament is. I travel two hundred miles to play a Saturday game at eight in the morning because that's the schedule. I have a 9 P.M. curfew because that's my coach's rule. I do everything I can to improve because I don't want to ride the bench. I live for softball. ❸

Summer diamond girls are a breed apart. You know us when you see us—we're stronger than most girls and have more fight in us. We never give up, and we never give in. We hold our heads high, as well as our bats. We keep our gloves down, and our butts too. We cheer each other on because there is no "I" in "team." We excel at what we do because we work harder than other people. We are summer diamond girls.

Most of us don't have a steady boyfriend; we don't have time. How does a boy understand that I would rather play softball than hang out with him? Or that the most important man in my life is my coach? Or just as I would never ask him to miss a game to spend time with me, neither should he ask me to do the same? Because I am a summer diamond girl. ❹

We don't sing "Take me out to the ballgame." But sing we do: "Hit it for me, baby, hit it, hit, hit, hit it." In our repertoire[3] are twenty cheers. One of the joys of traveling around the country is hearing a new cheer, bringing it home and adapting it to our team. Also high on the list is meeting new friends and visiting interesting places. ❺

When I was twelve, my team traveled to Orlando, Florida, where we won the Walt Disney World Wide World of Sports

---

1. **clinics** *n.:* classes or workshops that provide instruction in a specific skill.
2. **dilapidated** (də·lap**'**ə·dāt′ id) *adj.:* falling to pieces; shabby.
3. **repertoire** (rep**'**ər·twär′) *n.:* the collection of songs and cheers someone knows and can perform.

Comparing Literature

INFER

❷ What details show that the writer is dedicated and disciplined?

IDENTIFY

❸ How does the writer feel about softball?

INFER

❹ Find details in the two paragraphs you've just read that reveal at least three character traits of the writer.

INFER

❺ What details in these last two paragraphs show that the writer is outgoing?

Toni Janik rushes around the bases.

Thanksgivingfest Tournament. We competed against teams that practiced year-round, while our glorious New England weather limits us to six months of outside ball, at best.

Last year, my team went to Virginia in the middle of July to compete in the PONY Nationals. Although we suffered some injuries and had a very disappointing tournament, we grew as a team. We also had the experience of pintrading for the first time.

The kids liked it, but for some of the parents (including my mother), it became an obsession. The pins I collected are attached to a souvenir towel and have a prominent[4] place in my room. A special smile crosses my face when I see them. They remind me that I am a summer diamond girl. **6**

---

4. **prominent** *adj.:* important; easy to notice.

INFER

6 What details show that winning isn't everything to this writer?

First Thoughts

1. Respond to "Summer Diamond Girl" by completing one of the following sentences:
   - If I could ask Toni one question, it would be . . .
   - Toni reminds me of . . .

North Carolina Competency Goal
1.02; 5.01

Thinking Critically

2. Which lines in this essay could have been written by Janet, the letter writer in "The Southpaw"? Choose one sentence and explain your choice.

3. In your opinion, which sentence in this essay best reveals what Toni is like? Why do you think so?

4. Why do you think Toni wrote this essay? How would you state the main point of the essay in your own words?

Reading Check

a. What is a summer diamond girl?

b. How does this writer feel about softball? Give some examples from the text that show how she feels.

c. According to Toni, how are summer diamond girls different from most girls?

SKILLS FOCUS

Literary Skills
Analyze characterization.

Reading Skills
Compare and contrast texts.

Comparing Literature

5. Return to the Venn diagram on page 191 that you began after you read "The Southpaw." Complete the diagram by listing Toni's traits in the empty circle. Write the traits that Toni and Janet share in the overlapping section of the diagram. (You may have to move some of the traits you listed in Janet's circle to the overlapping section.)

Surrounded by her coaches and teammates, Toni Janik (center, front) holds her team's first-place trophy from a Thanksgiving softball tournament.

Assignment

1. Writing a Comparison-Contrast Essay

Write an essay comparing Janet in "The Southpaw" with Toni, the real-life writer of "Summer Diamond Girl." To help gather details for your essay, review your Venn diagram. What traits have you listed for each girl? Which traits do the girls have in common, and in what ways are they different? In your essay, be sure to cite details from the selections that support your character descriptions.

You may want to organize your essay like this:

In your second paragraph, discuss the character traits that Janet reveals in "Southpaw." In your third paragraph, discuss the traits that Toni reveals in "Summer Diamond Girl." If you organize by character, your second and third paragraphs might be outlined something like this:

> **Paragraph 2:** Janet's character traits
> > A. Trait 1
> > > 1. Supporting detail
> > B. Trait 2
> > > 1. Supporting detail
>
> **Paragraph 3:** Toni's character traits
> > A. Trait 1
> > > 1. Supporting detail
> > B. Trait 2
> > > 1. Supporting detail

Assignments

2. Write a Story in Letter Form

Write a story in the form of messages being passed back and forth between two characters who are having an argument. You can use notes, the way that Janet and Richard did, or you can use e-mail messages.

3. Write a Personal Essay

Write a short essay like the one written by Toni Janik, in which you describe something you love as much as she loves softball. You could imitate Toni and repeat several times for emphasis "I am . . ."

Use the workshop on writing a **comparison-contrast essay,** pages 404–409, for help with this assignment.

North Carolina Competency Goal
1.01; 1.02; 1.04; 4.01; 4.02; 5.01

SKILLS FOCUS

Writing Skills
Write a comparison-contrast essay; write a story in letter form; write a personal essay.

NO QUESTIONS ASKED

One of the most famous personalities in all of American literature is a boy named Tom Sawyer. Tom is the hero of a novel by Mark Twain that takes place in a very small Mississippi River town called St. Petersburg. Tom Sawyer lives with his Aunt Polly, his half brother Sid, and his cousin Mary. Sid is always good; Tom is always in trouble. Aunt Polly is an unmarried lady who loves Tom dearly, but she often has difficulty understanding him. Tom's friend Huckleberry Finn is also a famous personality. He doesn't have to go to school or obey anyone. He is the envy of every boy in town.

from The Adventures of Tom Sawyer   Mark Twain

Dentistry

Monday morning found Tom Sawyer miserable. Monday morning always found him so—because it began another week's slow suffering in school. He generally began that day with wishing he had had no intervening holiday, it made the going into captivity and fetters again so much more odious.[1]

Tom lay thinking. Presently it occurred to him that he wished he was sick; then he could stay home from school. Here was a vague possibility. He canvassed his system. No ailment was found, and he investigated again. This time he thought he could detect colicky symptoms,[2] and he began to encourage them with considerable hope. But they soon grew feeble, and presently died wholly away.

---

1. **odious** (ō′dē·əs) *adj.:* hateful, disgusting.
2. **colicky symptoms:** pains in the stomach.

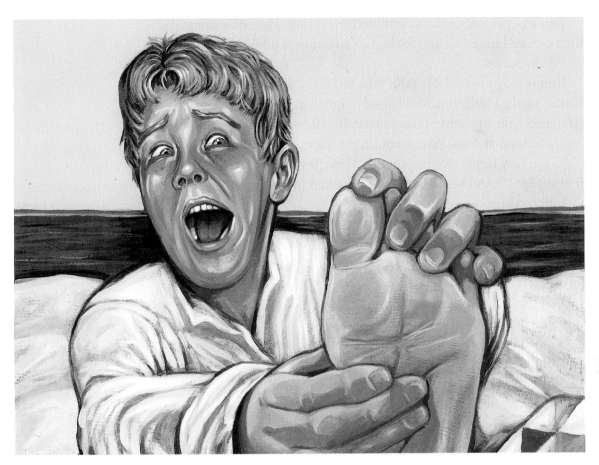

He reflected further. Suddenly he discovered something. One of his upper front teeth was loose. This was lucky; he was about to begin to groan, as a "starter," as he called it, when it occurred to him that if he came into court[3] with that argument, his aunt would pull it out, and that would hurt. So he thought he would hold the tooth in reserve for the present, and seek further. Nothing offered for some little time, and then he remembered hearing the doctor tell about a certain thing that laid up a patient for two or three weeks and threatened to make him lose a finger. So the boy eagerly drew his sore toe from under the sheet and held it up for inspection. But now he did not know the necessary symptoms. However, it seemed well worthwhile to chance it, so he fell to groaning with considerable spirit.

But Sid slept on unconscious.

Tom groaned louder and fancied that he began to feel pain in the toe.

No result from Sid.

---

3. **if he ... court:** if he came before his aunt. (Twain is comparing Tom's aunt to a judge in court.)

Tom was panting with his exertions by this time. He took a rest and then swelled himself up and fetched a succession of admirable groans.

Sid snored on.

Tom was aggravated. He said, "Sid, Sid!" and shook him. This course worked well, and Tom began to groan again. Sid yawned, stretched, then brought himself up on his elbow with a snort, and began to stare at Tom. Tom went on groaning. Sid said:

"Tom! Say, Tom!" (No response.) "Here, Tom! *Tom!* What is the matter, Tom?" And he shook him and looked in his face anxiously.

Tom moaned out:

"Oh don't, Sid. Don't joggle me."

"Why, what's the matter, Tom? I must call Auntie."

"No—never mind. It'll be over by and by, maybe. Don't call anybody."

"But I must! *Don't* groan so, Tom, it's awful. How long you been this way?"

"Hours. Ouch! Oh, don't stir so, Sid, you'll kill me."

"Tom, why didn't you wake me sooner? Oh, Tom, *don't!* It makes my flesh crawl to hear you. Tom, what *is* the matter?"

"I forgive you everything, Sid. (Groan.) Everything you've ever done to me. When I'm gone—"

"Oh, Tom, you ain't dying, are you? Don't, Tom. Oh, don't. Maybe—"

"I forgive everybody, Sid. (Groan.) Tell 'em so, Sid. And Sid, you give my window sash and my cat with one eye to that new girl that's come to town, and tell her—"

But Sid had snatched his clothes and gone. Tom was suffering in reality, now, so handsomely was his imagination working, and so his groans had gathered quite a genuine tone.

Sid flew downstairs and said:

"Oh, Aunt Polly, come! Tom's dying!"

"Dying!"

"Yes'm. Don't wait—come quick!"

"Rubbage! I don't believe it!"

But she fled upstairs, nevertheless, with Sid and Mary at her heels. And her face grew white, too, and her lip trembled. When she reached the bedside she gasped out:

"You, Tom! Tom, what's the matter with you?"

"Oh, Auntie, I'm—"

"What's the matter with you—what is the matter with you, child?"

"Oh, Auntie, my sore toe's mortified!"

The old lady sank down into a chair and laughed a little, then cried a little, then did both together. This restored her and she said:

"Tom, what a turn you did give me. Now you shut up that nonsense and climb out of this."

The groans ceased and the pain vanished from the toe. The boy felt a little foolish, and he said:

"Aunt Polly, it *seemed* mortified, and it hurt so I never minded my tooth at all."

"Your tooth indeed! What's the matter with your tooth?"

"One of them's loose, and it aches perfectly awful."

"There, there, now, don't begin that groaning again. Open your mouth. Well—your tooth *is* loose, but you're not going to die about that. Mary, get me a silk thread and a chunk of fire out of the kitchen."

Tom said:

"Oh, please, Auntie, don't pull it out. It don't hurt any more. I wish I may never stir if it does. Please don't, Auntie. *I* don't want to stay home from school."

"Oh, you don't, don't you? So all this row[4] was because you thought you'd get to stay home from school and go a-fishing? Tom, Tom, I love you so, and you seem to try every way you can to break my old heart with your outrageousness."

By this time the dental instruments were ready. The old lady made one end of the silk thread fast to Tom's tooth with a loop and tied the other to the bedpost. Then she seized the chunk of fire and suddenly thrust it almost into the boy's face. The tooth hung dangling by the bedpost now.

But all trials bring their compensations. As Tom wended[5] to school after breakfast, he was the envy of every boy he met because the gap in his upper row of teeth enabled him to expectorate[6] in a new and admirable way. He gathered quite a following of lads interested in the exhibition; and one that had cut his finger, and had been a center of fascination and homage up to this time, now found himself suddenly without an adherent,[7] and shorn of his glory. His heart was heavy, and he said with a disdain which he did not feel, that it wasn't anything to spit like Tom Sawyer. But another boy said, "Sour grapes!" and he wandered away a dismantled hero.

Huck Finn

Shortly, Tom came upon the juvenile pariah[8] of the village, Huckleberry Finn, son of the town drunkard. Huckleberry was cordially hated and dreaded by all the mothers of the town, because he was idle and lawless and vulgar and bad—and because all their children admired him so, and delighted in his forbidden society, and wished they dared to be like him. Tom was like the rest of the respectable boys in that he envied Huckleberry his gaudy[9] outcast condition, and was under strict orders not to play with him. So he played with him every time he got a chance. Huckleberry was always dressed in the castoff clothes of full-grown men, and they

---

4. **row** (rou) *n.:* noise and quarreling.
5. **wended** *v.* used as *adj.:* traveled.
6. **expectorate** (ek·spek′tə·rāt′) *v.:* spit.
7. **adherent** (ad·hir′ənt) *n.:* follower.
8. **pariah** (pə·rī′ə) *n.:* outcast.
9. **gaudy** (gô′dē) *adj.:* flashy; showy and in poor taste.

NO QUESTIONS ASKED

One of the most famous personalities in all of American literature is a boy named Tom Sawyer. Tom is the hero of a novel by Mark Twain that takes place in a very small Mississippi River town called St. Petersburg. Tom Sawyer lives with his Aunt Polly, his half brother Sid, and his cousin Mary. Sid is always good; Tom is always in trouble. Aunt Polly is an unmarried lady who loves Tom dearly, but she often has difficulty understanding him. Tom's friend Huckleberry Finn is also a famous personality. He doesn't have to go to school or obey anyone. He is the envy of every boy in town.

from The Adventures of Tom Sawyer Mark Twain

Dentistry

Monday morning found Tom Sawyer miserable. Monday morning always found him so—because it began another week's slow suffering in school. He generally began that day with wishing he had had no intervening holiday, it made the going into captivity and fetters again so much more odious.[1]

Tom lay thinking. Presently it occurred to him that he wished he was sick; then he could stay home from school. Here was a vague possibility. He canvassed his system. No ailment was found, and he investigated again. This time he thought he could detect colicky symptoms,[2] and he began to encourage them with considerable hope. But they soon grew feeble, and presently died wholly away.

---

1. **odious** (ōʹdē·əs) *adj.*: hateful, disgusting.
2. **colicky symptoms:** pains in the stomach.

Assignment

1. Writing a Comparison-Contrast Essay

Write an essay comparing Janet in "The Southpaw" with Toni, the real-life writer of "Summer Diamond Girl." To help gather details for your essay, review your Venn diagram. What traits have you listed for each girl? Which traits do the girls have in common, and in what ways are they different? In your essay, be sure to cite details from the selections that support your character descriptions.

You may want to organize your essay like this:

In your second paragraph, discuss the character traits that Janet reveals in "Southpaw." In your third paragraph, discuss the traits that Toni reveals in "Summer Diamond Girl." If you organize by character, your second and third paragraphs might be outlined something like this:

> **Paragraph 2:** Janet's character traits
> 　　A. Trait 1
> 　　　　1. Supporting detail
> 　　B. Trait 2
> 　　　　1. Supporting detail
> **Paragraph 3:** Toni's character traits
> 　　A. Trait 1
> 　　　　1. Supporting detail
> 　　B. Trait 2
> 　　　　1. Supporting detail

Use the workshop on writing a **comparison-contrast essay,** pages 404–409, for help with this assignment.

North Carolina Competency Goal
1.01; 1.02; 1.04; 4.01; 4.02; 5.01

Assignments

2. Write a Story in Letter Form

Write a story in the form of messages being passed back and forth between two characters who are having an argument. You can use notes, the way that Janet and Richard did, or you can use e-mail messages.

3. Write a Personal Essay

Write a short essay like the one written by Toni Janik, in which you describe something you love as much as she loves softball. You could imitate Toni and repeat several times for emphasis "I am . . ."

SKILLS FOCUS

Writing Skills
Write a comparison-contrast essay; write a story in letter form; write a personal essay.

Pinch Bug in Church by Norman Rockwell, an illustration of one of Tom Sawyer's adventures.

were in perennial bloom and fluttering with rags. His hat was a vast ruin with a wide crescent lopped out of its brim; his coat, when he wore one, hung nearly to his heels and had the rearward buttons far down the back; but one suspender supported his trousers; the seat of the trousers bagged low and contained nothing; the fringed legs dragged in the dirt when not rolled up.

Huckleberry came and went at his own free will. He slept on doorsteps in fine weather and in empty hogsheads[10] in wet; he did not have to go to school or to church, or call any being master or obey anybody; he could go fishing or swimming when and where he chose, and stay as long as it suited him; nobody forbade him to fight; he could sit up as late as he pleased; he was always the first boy that went barefoot in the spring and the last to resume leather in the fall; he never had to wash, nor put on clean clothes; he could swear wonderfully. In a word, everything that goes to make life precious, that boy had. So thought every harassed, hampered, respectable boy in St. Petersburg.

Tom hailed the romantic outcast: "Hello, Huckleberry! . . . Say—what's that?"

"Nothing but a tick."

"Where'd you get him?"

"Out in the woods."

"What'll you take for him?"

"I don't know. I don't want to sell him."

"All right. It's a mighty small tick, anyway."

"Oh, anybody can run a tick down that don't belong to them. I'm satisfied with it. It's a good enough tick for me."

"Sho, there's ticks a-plenty. I could have a thousand of 'em if I wanted to."

"Well, why don't you? Becuz you know mighty well you can't. This is a pretty early tick, I reckon. It's the first one I've seen this year."

"Say, Huck—I'll give you my tooth for him."

"Less see it."

Tom got out a bit of paper and carefully unrolled it. Huckleberry viewed it wistfully. The temptation was very strong. At last he said, "Is it genuwyne?"

Tom lifted his lip and showed the vacancy.

---

10. **hogsheads** *n.:* very large barrels.

"Well, all right," said Huckleberry, "it's a trade."

Tom enclosed the tick in the percussion-cap box that had lately been the pinch bug's prison,[11] and the boys separated, each feeling wealthier than before.

---

11. Tom collects all sorts of things, including bugs and dead cats and teeth.

Meet the Writer

Mark Twain

The Great Humorist

Mark Twain (1835–1910) is America's greatest comic writer and the author of two famous novels about growing up:

The Granger Collection, New York.

The Adventures of Tom Sawyer (1876) and *The Adventures of Huckleberry Finn* (1884).

Twain was born Samuel Langhorne Clemens on the Missouri frontier, and he grew up in a town on the Mississippi River. As a boy he thrived on the teeming river traffic. As an adult he took his famous pen name from the cry the boatmen made when the water reached the safe depth of two fathoms: "Mark twain!" He later wrote *Life on the Mississippi,* a book about his experiences as a cub pilot on a Mississippi River steamboat.

For Independent Reading

To better know Tom Sawyer and his friends Jim, Becky, and Huck Finn, read *The Adventures of Tom Sawyer.* (This title is available in the HRW Library.)

Writing Workshop

PERSUASIVE WRITING
Problem-Solution Essay

Most of us would avoid tough problems if we could—but eventually we have to solve them. Luckily we can often call on our creativity to come up with solutions. In this Writing Workshop you'll identify a **problem** important to you, big or small, and try to figure out how to solve it.

Prewriting

1 Choosing a Topic

Consider the following prompt:

> Problem solving is a critical-thinking skill that has many uses in our daily lives. In order to solve a problem, we must first identify it and then provide a satisfactory solution that is both practical and reasonable. Find a problem that is important to people in your school, your neighborhood, or your community. Then write an essay in which you present the problem and persuade readers to accept your solution or solutions.

With a partner or group, take a few minutes to make a list of problems that concern you. Think about problems involving

- your family or friends
- your school or community
- our global community
- an event in the news
- a situation you noticed today

PEANUTS reprinted by permission of United Feature Syndicate, Inc.

North Carolina Competency Goal
3.02; 4.03

2 Finding Solutions

List two or three problems that concern you most. Then, brainstorm to come up with possible solutions for each one. Fill in a chart like the one shown below.

Problem	Possible Solution
Destruction of used books and magazines	Create a book and magazine exchange in school.
	Donate materials to hospitals and senior centers.

You can also explore solutions to the problems in a cluster diagram like the one shown to the right. Finally, choose the problem for which you have the most workable solution.

3 Identifying and Reaching Your Audience

Decide who your readers will be. For example, consider who would be helped most by reading about the problem you've identified. Whom do you want to persuade to try out your solutions?

Remember, it's easy to persuade readers who will probably agree with your ideas from the beginning. (This is called "preaching to the choir.") The real challenge in solving a problem is to change the minds of readers who may not agree with you at first. To consider the **point of view** of your audience, imagine yourself in your readers' shoes. How might they respond to your ideas? What details might help them see the problem clearly? How might they argue with your ideas, and how might you answer their argument? A flowchart like the one on the right can help you.

Drafting

1 Starting Strong by Defining the Problem

What makes the problem important to you? Can you think of an event or an example that serves as a good beginning? Perhaps you can spark your readers' interest with a startling fact, a vivid anecdote, or a good quotation.

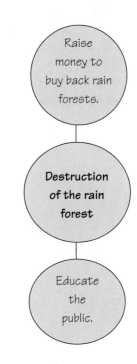

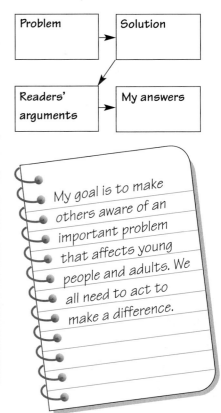

My goal is to make others aware of an important problem that affects young people and adults. We all need to act to make a difference.

Framework for a Problem-Solution Essay

Introduction (a strong example or statement):

_____

_____

Problem: _____

_____

Details (the problem's causes, seriousness, and effects): _____

_____

Solution: _____

_____

Details: _____

_____

Benefits: _____

_____

Possible objections: _____

_____

Your responses: _____

_____

Conclusion (a strong argument, a summary, or a call to action):

_____

You have to find a way to make the importance of the problem clear to the reader. Try one of the following techniques:

- Tell an anecdote that puts the problem on a personal level.
- Discuss the causes of the problem.
- Tell what will happen if the problem is unsolved.

2 Working out a Solution

The solution is the heart of the matter, your reason for writing the essay. And there's no one way to tell you how to go about it. If you're an orderly problem solver, you might begin by analyzing the ideas you came up with by brainstorming. Another type of person might write freely about the problem. The act of putting words on paper may lead to new ideas. If you take this approach, you might think of yourself writing a letter to a friend about the problem.

Whatever approach you take to work out your solution, be sure you clearly explain your solution to your readers. You might stress how practical your solution is, how easy it is to accomplish, or the consequences of taking no action. You might list steps that readers themselves can take.

3 Anticipating Objections

Be sure you can answer possible objections to your solution. Think of the arguments that might be raised against your ideas so that you can anticipate and respond to any resistance. Can you persuade readers by countering their arguments?

Look for weak points in your proposed solution and see if you can strengthen them. Deal with objections by stressing the benefits of your approach.

4 Drafting a Strong Ending

In problem-solution writing it is particularly important to end in a convincing way. You might end with your strongest argument or with a summary of your proposals. State what you want your readers to do. Do you want to change their thinking? Do you want them to take action?

Student Model

Predictions vary as to how long the rain forests will survive, or how long we can survive once they are gone. We don't have much time left. Some say that rain forests will soon disappear. Other experts say that the rain forests will be gone by the year 2056. . . .

   Although it looks like saving our rain forests is an overwhelming problem, many groups . . . raise money to buy rain forests back from those who would destroy them. Schools are helping out, too, by holding raffles, bake sales, and other fundraisers that enable them to purchase rain forest property. Wildlife federations organize fundraisers and TV marathons, which bring in monies to promote rain forest preservation. Such groups strive to educate people and make them aware of this most pressing global issue.

   So you see, our rain forests can be saved, but it will take the help of everyone. Together, we are a force to be reckoned with, standing up to those who would tear down our precious rain forests, those who would bring suffocation to plants, animals, and eventually, humans as well. Together, we can make a difference. Won't you please become involved? Your life may depend on it.

—Todd Lehne
James Williams Jr. High School
Rhinelander, Wisconsin

This model first appeared in *Merlyn's Pen: the National Magazines of Student Writing.*

*The writer defines the **problem.***

*A **statistic** shows how serious the problem is.*

*The writer addresses a possible **objection.***

*The writer's solution includes several **specific suggestions.***

*The last paragraph makes a strong **call to action.***

Strategies For Elaboration

To support your problem-solution essay, you can use

- facts (including statistics) and other evidence from research
- anecdotes and other examples from personal experience
- opinions from experts
- discussions of solutions' practicality, in terms of money, time, and difficulty
- comparisons of solutions

Language Handbook
H E L P

End marks, 12a–d; Commas in a series, 12f; Apostrophes, 14a–e.

Problem–Solution Clue Words

- as a result
- nevertheless
- therefore
- this led to
- thus

Evaluating and Revising

Use the following chart to evaluate and revise your problem-solution essay.

Problem–Solution Essay: Content and Organization Guidelines		
Evaluation Questions	▶ **Tips**	▶ **Revision Techniques**
❶ Do you catch the reader's attention with a strong beginning? Does your introduction state the problem clearly?	▶ **Underline** the attention-getting opening. **Highlight** the statement of the problem.	▶ **Add** a strong statement, a statistic, or a vivid example of the problem, if necessary.
❷ Do you provide details that describe the problem?	▶ **Put stars** next to the details that show the causes and effects of the problem.	▶ **Add** evidence that reveals the seriousness of the problem.
❸ Does your essay propose a solution to the problem? Does it examine the pros and cons of the solution?	▶ **Circle** the statements that suggest a solution. **Check** the descriptions of benefits and objections.	▶ **Summarize** your solution, and elaborate with details as needed.
❹ Does your essay target your audience?	▶ **Check** phrases or sentences that identify your audience.	▶ **Adjust tone,** if necessary, to reach audience.
❺ Are paragraphs arranged in order of importance?	▶ **Number** each paragraph according to importance of ideas.	▶ **Rearrange** paragraphs to build toward your most important idea.
❻ Does the conclusion include a convincing call to action?	▶ **Draw a wavy line** under the call to action.	▶ **Add** a call to action, or **revise** your statement to make it more specific and reasonable.

On the next page you'll find the opening paragraphs of a problem-solution essay that has been revised. After the Revision Model you'll find questions to help you evaluate the writer's revisions.

Revision Model

Many libraries and households have books and magazines they no longer need or want.

∧ "A library, like a garden, sometimes requires weeding," as Colette Brooks points out in a <u>New York Times</u> article. Public

discard

libraries are forced to ~~get rid of~~ books because they have limited shelf space. Books that aren't read very often or that

However,

have aged badly are thrown away. ∧ Unwanted books and

in a number of different ways

magazines don't have to be destroyed. They can be recycled ∧ so that they continue to provide hours of reading pleasure.

One way to do this is through a book and magazine exchange, where readers trade reading materials. A second way to deal

to hospitals, nursing homes, and community centers

with the problem is through donations ∧. As a third solution, books and magazines can be offered free of charge to readers who wish to have them for their personal libraries.

PROOFREADING
TIPS

After you've revised your paper, go back and look for mistakes in grammar, usage, spelling, and punctuation. Work with a partner and double-check each other's work.

PUBLISHING
TIPS

If you wrote about a problem affecting your school, you might read your paper aloud to your class, put it up on your class or school bulletin board, or publish it in a school newspaper. If the problem affects your neighborhood or the larger community, you might send your essay to a local newspaper.

Evaluating the Revision

1. Why do you think the writer added a sentence at the beginning of the essay?

2. What specific details have been added to clarify the causes or effects of the problem?

3. How has the writer improved transitions?

Test Practice

DIRECTIONS: Read the following article. Then, answer each question that follows.

Celebrating the Quinceañera
Mara Rockliff

You stand at the back of the church between your parents and godparents, your knees shaking. You feel special, and a bit awkward, in your first formal dress and your tiara. Your honor court has walked up the aisle ahead of you: fourteen girls in pastel dresses, fourteen boys in tuxedos. With you and your escort there are fifteen couples—one for each year of your life. The long months of planning and preparation have finally ended. Your quinceañera has begun.

The quinceañera (kēn'sā·ä·nye'rə, from the Spanish words *quince,* "fifteen," and *años,* "years") is a rite of passage celebrated by Mexicans and Mexican Americans. People believe that the tradition can be traced back to the Aztec culture, in which girls commonly married at the age of fifteen. Today a girl's quinceañera marks her coming-of-age. It means that she is ready to take on adult privileges and responsibilities.

The most important part of your quinceañera is the *misa de acción de gracias,* the thanksgiving Mass. You slowly walk up the aisle to the front of the church. You kneel, placing a bouquet of fifteen roses on the altar to thank the Virgin Mary for bringing you to this important day. A birthstone ring glitters on your finger, and a religious medal hangs from your neck, inscribed with your name and today's date—special gifts from adult relatives or friends of the family. The priest will bless your medal during the Mass.

Next comes a sermon, followed by prayers and readings from the Bible. You recite your speech, and the service ends. Then the photographer rushes over, and you pose for an endless series of photographs with your family and friends.

But the quinceañera celebration has just begun, for the fiesta is still to come. You enter to the sound of music, a traditional mariachi band or a DJ playing current hits. You dance in turn with your father, your grandfathers, your escort. You and your honor court perform a group dance that you have rehearsed. Then everyone joins in the dancing.

North Carolina Competency Goal
2.01

Reading Skills
Create an outline.

You're almost too excited to eat, but the food is wonderful. There's your favorite—chicken in mole sauce, made from chilies and unsweetened chocolate. The tables are covered with everything from tamales and corn soup to an elaborately decorated cake.

Later, as everyone watches, your father removes the flat shoes you have worn all day and replaces them with a pair of high heels. In your parents' eyes you are no longer a child. They'll treat you differently from now on, and they'll expect you to act more like an adult as well.

Among your many gifts, one stands out: the last doll. It's not a toy for you to play with, of course; it's a symbol of the childhood you're leaving behind. If you have a younger sister, you might present it to her. You look around at the people who have watched you grow up. You see tears in many eyes. The quinceañera is a tradition many centuries old, but for you it will happen only once.

1. In an **outline** of this article, all of these might be details under a main heading *except* —
   A girl dances with father and grandfather
   B honor court performs dance
   C DJ or mariachi band plays music
   D what happens at the party

2. If you quoted a phrase or sentence from this article on a note card, you would put the writer's words —
   F in quotation marks
   G in capital letters
   H in parentheses
   J in a footnote

3. Which sentence best states the **main idea** of this article?
   A The food is the best part of the quinceañera.
   B The quinceañera happens only once in a girl's lifetime.
   C The quinceañera is a girl's rite of passage into adulthood.
   D Girls who celebrate their quinceañera usually do not appreciate what it represents.

Constructed Response

4. Suppose you were taking notes on this article. Re-read the second and third paragraphs. Then, list four events from the quinceañera ceremony that you would include in your notes. List the events in the order they take place.

Collection 2: Skills Review

Vocabulary Skills

Test Practice

Synonyms

DIRECTIONS: Choose the word that is closest in meaning to the underlined word.

1. A lofty idea is —
   A weak
   B old
   C noble
   D stuffed

2. A shrewd person is —
   F clever
   G nice
   H angry
   J hungry

3. To gorge on food is to —
   A overeat
   B buy
   C diet
   D investigate

4. If you have audacity, you have —
   F appetite
   G boldness
   H discomfort
   J anxiety

5. Evacuate means —
   A mistreat
   B remove
   C desert
   D value

6. If people are interned, they are —
   F drafted
   G confronted
   H confined
   J reprimanded

7. An alien is —
   A a foreigner
   B an aircraft
   C a politician
   D a warrior

8. If you are forsaken, you are —
   F bored
   G abandoned
   H dirty
   J satisfied

SKILLS FOCUS

Vocabulary Skills
Identify synonyms.

Collection 2: Skills Review

Writing Skills

Test Practice

DIRECTIONS: Read the following paragraph from a problem-solution essay. Then answer each question that follows.

(1) Our nation is facing a growing problem with the number of overweight young people. (2) Studies show that an increasing number of children are carrying around an excessive amount of weight. (3) Being overweight creates medical problems, and it can even lead to serious diseases. (4) Most people care about the way they look. (5) The major causes of the problem have been identified. (6) Many children eat lots of food high in calories and they don't get enough exercise. (7) To attack this problem we need widespread public education about good eating habits. (8) What everyone can do immediately is to pay close attention to the foods they eat and to adopt a sensible program of physical exercise.

1. This paragraph would be strengthened—
   - A by a discussion of hereditary illnesses
   - B by comparison of various methods of dieting
   - C by a definition for the term obesity
   - D by reference to the number of overweight adults

2. Which sentence is beside the point and could be deleted?
   - F Sentence 2
   - G Sentence 3
   - H Sentence 4
   - J Sentence 6

3. The problem this essay will deal with is identified in—
   - A Sentence 1
   - B Sentence 4
   - C Sentence 5
   - D Sentence 6

4. Sentence 2 could be improved—
   - F by adding statistics showing the number of overweight children
   - G by naming the specific scientific studies
   - H by identifying precisely the age groups of affected youth
   - J by all of the above

5. Which sentence could be improved by adding specific illnesses such as diabetes and heart disease?
   - A Sentence 2
   - B Sentence 3
   - C Sentence 5
   - D Sentence 6

6. The audience for this essay would most likely be—
   - F children and teenagers
   - G healthcare workers
   - H parents
   - J all of the above

North Carolina Competency Goal
2.01; 3.02

SKILLS FOCUS

Writing Skills
Analyze a problem-solution essay.

Fiction

Happy Together

When ten-year-old Opal Buloni moves to a small town in Florida, her life changes for the better. The title of Kate DiCamillo's novel explains why: *Because of Winn-Dixie.* Winn-Dixie is the eccentric but lovable dog Opal adopts upon her arrival. Winn-Dixie helps Opal make some wonderful friends, including a pet-store clerk who plays a mean guitar and a librarian who makes delicious candy. Winn-Dixie also brings Opal closer to her quiet preacher father.

A Mysterious Stranger

In David Almond's *Skellig*, Michael is dealing with a messy new house and an ill baby sister when he comes across Skellig, a strange, decrepit creature residing in Michael's filthy garage. Initially Michael is frightened by Skellig, until he and his new friend Mina order Chinese food for the creature and help lead him out of the darkness. From this relationship Michael discovers the value of compassion and the magic in his own life.

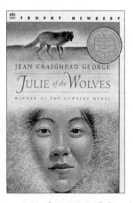

A Member of the Pack

A thirteen-year-old Inuit girl named Miyax runs away from home and gets lost on the Alaskan tundra—a vast, treeless wilderness region—in Jean Craighead George's Newbery Medal–winning novel *Julie of the Wolves.* Miyax is menaced by a host of dangers until a pack of wolves gradually accepts her as one of their own.

A Lack of Communication

Philip Molloy is suspended when he defies school policy by humming along to the national anthem. He *says* he is humming to be patriotic. But that's only part of the story: He really wants to irritate his English teacher, who gave him a D and kept him off the track team. Philip's deception turns a minor infraction into a media circus in Avi's popular novel *Nothing but the Truth.*

This title is available in the HRW Library.

Nonfiction

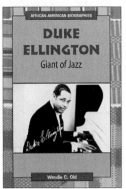

The Duke

If you're interested in music or African American history, you'll enjoy Wendie C. Old's *Duke Ellington: Giant of Jazz*. Ellington's compositions and performances helped bring jazz into the American mainstream. Old introduces you to Ellington's music and to the members of his band. If you'd like to hear one of Ellington's best albums, try *Ellington at Newport 1956*.

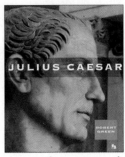

The Leader of an Empire

In this biography, called *Julius Caesar*, Robert Green gives an overview of the Roman dictator's life and career. You'll find out about Caesar's ambition to be Rome's dictator and his brilliance as a military strategist. Green's text includes maps, time lines, and illustrations to help you feel you are there in ancient Rome.

Creative Minds

In *Black Stars: African American Inventors*, Otha Richard Sullivan tells the stories of twenty-five African Americans who overcame prejudice to become important inventors. Their inventions range from a gas mask to a lighting system used in theaters. If you like these stories, you may want to try other books in the *Black Stars* series.

True Stories

Homelessness in America is a problem that can't be ignored. Margie Chalofsky, Glen Finland, and Judy Wallace give eight homeless children a voice in *Changing Places: A Kid's View of Shelter Living*. Some of the children, like twelve-year-old Molly, are hopeful that they will soon find a home of their own. Others, like eight-year-old Anthony, are troubled by self-doubt. All tell stories you will not soon forget.

Illustration of the "Fairy Tale of the Golden Rooster" (1934) by I. Bakanov. Painted box. Russian Folk Art. State Museum, Palech, Russia.

Theme: The Heart of the Matter

Literary Focus:
Analyzing Theme

Informational Focus:
Evaluating Evidence

INTERNET
Collection Resources
Keyword: LE5 6-3

219

Elements of Literature

Theme *by* Madeline Travers Hovland

THE POWER OF A STORY

There's a big question we often ask about stories. That big question is "What does it all mean?" When we ask that question, we're asking about theme.

The **theme** of a story is the truth that it reveals about life. Theme gives a story its power.

Writers don't usually state themes directly. They want us to infer themes based on what the characters discover or how they change in the course of a story.

Theme can be supported by the language of a story. For example, writers often include details of violent weather to support a theme having to do with great passion.

"The Golden Touch" is a retelling of an ancient Greek myth about King Midas, a man who could turn everything into gold. What is its theme?

North Carolina Competency Goal
5.01

INTERNET
More About Theme
Keyword: LE5 6-3

Literary Skills
Understand theme.

The Golden Touch

Midas was king of a country in Asia Minor. He lived in a beautiful palace surrounded by lush and fragrant gardens. Midas had a little daughter whom he loved dearly. But Midas wasn't a happy king. He never looked out upon his gardens and saw the crocuses come up through the rich soil in spring. He ignored the perfume of the roses in the warm summer. He never saw the snow sparkle on the mountains.

What Midas loved most was his treasure room, deep down in a chilly stone chamber. He spent whole days amid the cobwebs in the dimly lighted room, counting his gold. He loved letting the shiny gold coins slip through his hands. But no matter how much gold he had, Midas always wanted more.

In the next part of the story, Midas makes some bad decisions. Since we know his character flaws, we are not surprised at the king's selfish actions.

One day, while Midas was sitting counting his gold, he suddenly heard a whizzing sound. Out of nowhere the god Dionysus° appeared before him. Midas was afraid and hid his face.

"Midas," the god said, "you need not fear me. I remember your kindness toward my old servant some months ago. Therefore, I have decided to grant you one wish. What do you want most of all in the world?"

Midas laughed with glee. "Gold!" he roared. "Let everything I touch turn into gold!"

Dionysus shook his head sadly. "That is unwise," the god warned. But Midas was firm. "Your wish is granted," the god said, and he took off as quickly as he had arrived.

°**Dionysus** (dī′ə·nī′səs).

Now we wonder what will happen next. What will Midas do with his golden touch? Here are the **complications** in Midas's story. Notice the words the storyteller uses to describe gold. Also notice the words used to describe nature and the king's little daughter.

Just then Midas heard a bell signaling that lunch was ready. As he walked back to the palace, he picked a dewy, fragrant pink rose for his little daughter. Imagine how startled he was when the green stem changed to hard yellow metal—gold! The soft petals hardened and turned bright yellow. The rigid gold flower was so heavy that he dropped it on the ground.

Midas ran into the dining hall, shouting with delight. Everything he touched on the way turned into gold. His robe became gleaming gold. The door became gold. The table changed into gold. Midas's gold frenzy made him very hungry, and he grabbed a loaf of soft bread. But as he bit into it, the smell and taste of metal sickened him. His teeth broke on the hard gold, and his mouth filled with blood. He quickly grabbed a glass of water and tried to drink, but choked and spit out liquid gold.

Then the little princess came running in. Before Midas could stop her, she jumped up for a hug. Even as they embraced, Midas realized that something horrible was happening. He felt his beautiful, warm child stiffening and becoming as cold as death. She too had been transformed into gold.

All night long, Midas wept tears of gold. Holding the rigid gold statue that had been his daughter, he prayed to the gods. With the morning sun, Dionysus appeared. "Please, please, please," Midas begged, "take away this terrible gift, and give me back my daughter."

Dionysus said, "So be it. From now on may you be a better person." Even as the god disappeared, Midas felt a rush of joy and love. He covered his little daughter's face with kisses as she became soft and warm, a flesh-and-blood child again.

From that time on, Midas devoted himself to enjoying the woodlands and meadows of his kingdom.

Practice

1. The lesson a character learns can often be stated as a **theme.** Always state a theme as a complete sentence. Which of these themes do you think is revealed in the Midas story? (A story may have several themes.)
   - Gold isn't everything.
   - Nothing is as important as love.
   - Do not ignore wise advice.
   - Be careful what you wish for.

2. Find at least three words that describe nature and human beings as full of life and beauty. Then, find other words that describe gold as hard and lifeless. How does this use of language help support one of the story's themes?

Finding the Theme

by Kylene Beers

The Message You Remember

Can you remember a favorite story from childhood? Even if you don't remember the name of the story or the characters' names, you probably remember what it was about. ("There was this monkey who got into trouble, and he lived with a man who wore a big yellow hat.") Most likely you also remember a message you learned from the story. (Being curious is good, but it can also get you into trouble!) That message is the story's **theme.**

Understanding Theme

A teacher asked three students to state the theme of "The Three Little Pigs." One student said, "Well, there are these pigs and they each build a house and a wolf tries to blow the houses down." Another said, "There are three pigs. The first one is really lazy, the second one is only a little lazy, and the third one isn't lazy at all." The third student said, "Doing things the easy way often isn't the best way."

Which response explains the theme? The first one tells about the plot. The second tells about the characters. It's the third response that tells the theme. **Theme** is the message that holds a story together. Theme is a truth about people, society, or the human condition. Theme is what a story tells us about our lives.

North Carolina Competency Goal
1.02; 5.01

SKILLS FOCUS

Reading Skills
Understand theme.

Hints for Figuring Out the Theme

1. Look for clues in what the narrator says.

Sometimes writers include a sentence or two in a story that give you a clue to the story's theme. No, they don't write, "The theme is . . ." Instead, they may have a character make a remark that you realize you should remember. The narrator may state something that you, the reader, recognize as significant.

2. Interpret the clues.

Here's a good example of a clue from Pam Munoz Ryan's book *Esperanza Rising:* After Esperanza faces difficult times, the narrator says, "Miguel had been right about never giving up, and she [Esperanza] had been right, too, about rising above those who held them down." It's easy to see the message about never giving up that Ryan hopes you'll remember. Often, writers are less direct about the theme, however, and you must decide for yourself the truth about life conveyed in a story.

A vat is a very large container. Milk vats are often filled with milk that has just come from the cow, so the milk contains a lot of fat. When the milk is churned up, the fat turns to butter. This story was told to the writer, Claude Brown, by a teacher who was trying to encourage him to stay out of trouble.

Two Frogs and the Milk Vat

Claude Brown

There were two frogs sitting on a milk vat one time. The frogs fell into the milk vat. It was very deep. They kept swimming and swimming around, and they couldn't get out. They couldn't climb out because they were too far down. One frog said, "Oh, I can't make it, and I'm going to give up." ❶

Like Summer Tempests Came His Tears (detail) by James Lynch, illustration for *The Wind in the Willows*.

Using the Strategy

As you read, you'll find this open-book sign at certain points in the story: ☐. Stop at these points, and think about what you've just read. Do what the prompt asks you to do.

ANALYZE THEME

❶ Where are these frogs? Why is falling into the vat dangerous for them? What will happen to the frog who stops swimming? Does this frog handle the problem well? Would you want a friend who acted like this frog? Do you know people who give up as soon as things get tough? Is that a good way to act?

❷ What happens to the second frog? How does he handle the situation? Would you want a friend who acts like this frog? What do this frog's actions show you about not giving up even when the situation looks hopeless?

Look back at the note that introduces the story. Does knowing why the teacher told this story to Claude Brown help you find the story's theme? Explain.

And the other frog kept swimming and swimming. His arms became more and more tired, and it was harder and harder and harder for him to swim. Then he couldn't do another stroke. He couldn't throw one more arm into the milk. He kept trying and trying; it seemed as if the milk was getting hard and heavy. He kept trying; he knows that he's going to die, but as long as he's got this little bit of life in him, he's going to keep on swimming. On his last stroke, it seemed as though he had to pull a whole ocean back, but he did it and found himself sitting on top of a vat of butter. ❷

Meet the Writer

Claude Brown

Claude Brown (1937–2002) survived a troubled childhood on the streets of Harlem, in New York City, to become a bestselling author. Brown's family was poor, and his father was a violent alcoholic. Brown was just eight years old when he first found himself in trouble with the law. By the time he reached his teens, he had been arrested many times and had spent several years in juvenile homes and detention centers.

At age seventeen, with the encouragement of adults he met during his detentions, Brown decided to turn his life around. He moved away from his old neighborhood and gang, began working at odd jobs, and went to night school to earn a high school diploma.

Brown eventually worked his way through Howard University in Washington, D.C., where he began writing short stories and articles. A publisher asked Brown to write a book about Harlem. Brown was stumped at first, but he finally decided to write about his own life. The result—an autobiography called *Manchild in the Promised Land*—has sold four million copies and has been translated into fourteen languages.

Practice the Strategy

Analyzing Theme

If you are asked, "What's the theme?" and you aren't sure, back up. Ask yourself other questions that will help you move from the subject of the story to the plot and on to the theme. Remember:

- Don't try to state an entire theme in one word. If you do that, you're probably confusing theme with subject.
- If you find yourself describing what happened in the story and saying, "and then this happened," you've confused theme with plot.
- A **theme** must be stated in at least one sentence that tells a truth about life, not just about the story.

Strategy Tip

Remember that there is no one correct way to state a theme. Every reader of a story will state the theme differently. Which of the possible themes in the graphic at the left do you think fits the story better? Why?

Not a theme

frogs   milk   swimming

Also not a theme

one frog who gives up; one who doesn't

Certainly not a theme

Two frogs fall in a vat of milk.   One frog gives up and drowns.

Possible themes

Often when you think there's no hope, you discover the worst is over.   A positive attitude can help you turn your troubles into triumphs.

PRACTICE

Answer these questions about "Two Frogs and the Milk Vat."

1. Where is the story set?
2. What problem do the frogs face?
3. Why do you think one frog keeps swimming while the other gives up?
4. What did you learn about humans and human nature (yes, from frogs!) that's worth remembering?

As you answered questions 1 and 2, you focused on **setting** and **plot.** Question 3 moved you toward **characterization.** Question 4 asked you to think about **theme.**

Look back at the questions that you answered while reading the story. See if you can identify the questions that asked you about each of the following elements: setting, characters, problem, and theme.

SKILLS FOCUS

Reading Skills
Analyze theme.

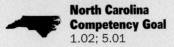

North Carolina Competency Goal
1.02; 5.01

The All-American Slurp

Make the Connection
Quickwrite ✏️

Have you ever been embarrassed because you didn't know how you were supposed to behave in a new situation—at a party, at a new friend's house, in a foreign country? Write a few lines about your experience.

Literary Focus
Subject Versus Theme

A story's theme is different from its subject. The **subject** is what the story is about. You can usually name a subject in a word or two. **Theme** is what the story means. Theme is an idea about life that the story's characters, actions, and images bring home to you.

The chart below illustrates the difference between a subject and a theme:

Subject	Theme
growing up	Growing up means taking responsibility.
nature	Nature can be beautiful but deadly.
love	People sometimes express love through actions, not words.

Always try to connect a story's theme to your own life. Also remember that no two readers will state a theme in exactly the same way.

Reading Skills 📖
Summarizing

When you **summarize** a story, you tell about its main events in your own words. Summarizing is a useful skill because it helps you recall what happens in a story. It also helps you peel a story down to its core, to the events that advance the plot and reveal the theme.

This story is divided into six parts. (Each part is numbered, as you'll see when you start reading.) After you read each part, try to summarize in two or three sentences what happened in that section.

Vocabulary Development

Here are some words that are important to Namioka's story:

lavishly (lav′ish · lē) *adv.:* generously; plentifully. *The table was heaped lavishly with food.*

mortified (môrt′ə · fīd′) *v.* used as *adj.:* ashamed; deeply embarrassed. *Mortified by her family's behavior, she fled to the ladies' room.*

spectacle (spek′tə · kəl) *n.:* remarkable sight. *The narrator fears that her noisy brother is making a spectacle of himself.*

etiquette (et′i · kit) *n.:* acceptable manners and behavior. *Slurping is not proper etiquette in a fancy restaurant.*

North Carolina Competency Goal
1.04; 4.01; 5.01; 5.02

INTERNET
Vocabulary Activity
Keyword: LE5 6-3

SKILLS FOCUS

Literary Skills
Recognize the difference between subject and theme.

Reading Skills
Summarize plot.

THE ALL-AMERICAN SLURP

Lensey Namioka

❶ The first time our family was invited out to dinner in America, we disgraced ourselves while eating celery. We had immigrated to this country from China, and during our early days here we had a hard time with American table manners.

In China we never ate celery raw, or any other kind of vegetable raw. We always had to disinfect the vegetables in boiling water first. When we were presented with our first relish tray, the raw celery caught us unprepared.

We had been invited to dinner by our neighbors, the Gleasons. After arriving at the house, we shook hands with our hosts and packed ourselves into a sofa. As our family of four sat stiffly in a row, my younger brother and I stole glances at our parents for a clue as to what to do next.

Mrs. Gleason offered the relish tray to Mother. The tray looked pretty, with its tiny red radishes, curly sticks of carrots, and long, slender stalks of pale-green celery. "Do try some of the celery, Mrs. Lin," she said. "It's from a local farmer, and it's sweet."

Mother picked up one of the green stalks, and Father followed suit. Then I picked up a stalk, and my brother did too. So there we sat, each with a stalk of celery in our right hand.

Mrs. Gleason kept smiling. "Would you like to try some of the dip, Mrs. Lin? It's my own recipe: sour cream and onion flakes, with a dash of Tabasco sauce."

Most Chinese don't care for dairy products, and in those days I wasn't even ready to drink fresh milk. Sour cream

sounded perfectly revolting. Our family shook our heads in unison.

Mrs. Gleason went off with the relish tray to the other guests, and we carefully watched to see what they did. Everyone seemed to eat the raw vegetables quite happily.

Mother took a bite of her celery. *Crunch.* "It's not bad!" she whispered.

Father took a bite of his celery. *Crunch.* "Yes, it is good," he said, looking surprised.

I took a bite, and then my brother. *Crunch, crunch.* It was more than good; it was delicious. Raw celery has a slight sparkle, a zingy taste that you don't get in cooked celery. When Mrs. Gleason came around with the relish tray, we each took another stalk of celery, except my brother. He took two.

There was only one problem: Long strings ran through the length of the stalk, and they got caught in my teeth. When I help my mother in the kitchen, I always pull the strings out before slicing celery.

I pulled the strings out of my stalk. *Z-z-zip, z-z-zip.* My brother followed suit. *Z-z-zip, z-z-zip, z-z-zip.* To my left, my parents were taking care of their own stalks. *Z-z-zip, z-z-zip, z-z-zip.*

Suddenly I realized that there was dead silence except for our zipping. Looking up, I saw that the eyes of everyone in the room were on our family. Mr. and Mrs. Gleason, their daughter Meg, who was my friend, and their neighbors the Badels—they were all staring at us as we busily pulled the strings of our celery.

That wasn't the end of it. Mrs. Gleason announced that dinner was served and invited us to the dining table. It was lavishly covered with platters of food, but we couldn't see any chairs around the table. So we helpfully carried over some dining chairs and sat down. All the other guests just stood there.

Mrs. Gleason bent down and whispered to us, "This is a buffet dinner. You help yourselves to some food and eat it in the living room."

Our family beat a retreat back to the sofa as if chased by enemy soldiers. For the rest of the evening, too mortified to go back to the dining table, I nursed a bit of potato salad on my plate.

Next day, Meg and I got on the school bus together. I wasn't sure how she would feel about me after the spectacle our family made at the party. But she was just the same as usual, and the only reference she made to the party

was, "Hope you and your folks got enough to eat last night. You certainly didn't take very much. Mom never tries to figure out how much food to prepare. She just puts everything on the table and hopes for the best."

I began to relax. The Gleasons' dinner party wasn't so different from a Chinese meal after all. My mother also puts everything on the table and hopes for the best.

2 Meg was the first friend I had made after we came to America. I eventually got acquainted with a few other kids in school, but Meg was still the only real friend I had. My brother didn't have any problems making friends. He spent all his time with some boys who were teaching him baseball, and in no time he could speak English much faster than I could—not better, but faster.

"Z-z-zip"

I worried more about making mistakes, and I spoke carefully, making sure I could say everything right before opening my mouth. At least I had a better accent than my parents, who never really got rid of their Chinese accent, even years later. My parents had both studied English in school before coming to America, but what they had studied was mostly written English, not spoken.

Father's approach to English was a scientific one. Since Chinese verbs have no tense, he was fascinated by the way English verbs

Vocabulary
lavishly (lav′ish·lē) *adv.:* generously; plentifully.
mortified (môrt′ə·fīd′) *v.* used as *adj.:* ashamed; deeply embarrassed.
spectacle (spek′tə·kəl) *n.:* strange or remarkable sight.

changed form according to whether they were in the present, past, perfect, pluperfect, future, or future perfect tense. He was always making diagrams of verbs and their inflections, and he looked for opportunities to show off his mastery of the pluperfect and future perfect tenses, his two favorites. "I shall have finished my project by Monday," he would say smugly.

Mother's approach was to memorize lists of polite phrases that would cover all possible social situations. She was constantly muttering things like "I'm fine, thank you. And you?" Once she accidentally stepped on someone's foot and hurriedly blurted, "Oh, that's quite all right!" Embarrassed by her slip, she resolved to do better next time. So when someone stepped on *her* foot, she cried, "You're welcome!"

In our own different ways, we made progress in learning English. But I had another worry, and that was my appearance. My brother didn't have to worry, since Mother bought him blue jeans for school, and he dressed like all the other boys. But she insisted that girls had to wear skirts. By the time she saw that Meg and the other girls were wearing jeans, it was too late. My school clothes were bought already, and we didn't have money left to buy new outfits for me. We had too many other things to buy first, like furniture, pots, and pans.

The first time I visited Meg's house, she took me upstairs to her room, and I wound up trying on her clothes. We were pretty much the same size since Meg was shorter and thinner than average. Maybe that's how we became friends in the first place. Wearing

"shloop"

Meg's jeans and T-shirt, I looked at myself in the mirror. I could almost pass for an American—from the back, anyway. At least the kids in school wouldn't stop and stare at me in the hallways, which was what they did when they saw me in my white blouse and navy-blue skirt that went a couple of inches below the knees.

When Meg came to my house, I invited her to try on my Chinese dresses, the ones with a high collar and slits up the sides. Meg's eyes were bright as she looked at herself in the mirror. She struck several sultry poses, and we nearly fell over laughing.

❸ The dinner party at the Gleasons' didn't stop my growing friendship with Meg. Things were getting better for me in other ways too. Mother finally bought me some jeans at the end of the month, when Father got his paycheck. She wasn't in any hurry about buying them at first, until I worked on her. This is what I did. Since we didn't have a car in those days, I often ran down to the neighborhood store to pick up things for her. The groceries cost less at a big supermarket, but the closest one was many blocks away. One day, when she ran out of flour, I offered to borrow a bike from our neighbor's son and buy a ten-pound bag of flour at the big supermarket. I mounted the boy's bike and waved to Mother. "I'll be back in five minutes!"

Before I started pedaling, I heard her voice behind me. "You can't go out in public like that! People can see all the way up to your thighs!"

"I'm sorry," I said innocently. "I thought you were in a hurry to get the flour." For dinner we were going to have pot stickers (fried Chinese dumplings), and we needed a lot of flour.

"Couldn't you borrow a girl's bicycle?" complained Mother. "That way your skirt won't be pushed up."

"There aren't too many of those around," I said. "Almost all the girls wear jeans while riding a bike, so they don't see any point buying a girl's bike."

We didn't eat pot stickers that evening, and Mother was thoughtful. Next day we took the bus downtown and she bought me a pair of jeans. In the same week, my brother made the baseball team of his junior high school, Father started taking driving lessons, and Mother discovered rummage sales. We soon got all the furniture we needed, plus a dartboard and a 1,000-piece jigsaw puzzle. (Fourteen hours later, we discovered that it was a 999-piece jigsaw puzzle.) There was hope that the Lins might become a normal American family after all.

❹ Then came our dinner at the Lakeview restaurant. The Lakeview was an expensive restaurant, one of those places where a head-waiter dressed in tails conducted you to your seat, and the only light came from candles and flaming desserts. In one corner of the room a lady harpist played tinkling melodies.

Father wanted to celebrate because he had just been promoted. He worked for an

electronics company, and after his English started improving, his superiors decided to appoint him to a position more suited to his training. The promotion not only brought a higher salary but was also a tremendous boost to his pride.

Up to then we had eaten only in Chinese restaurants. Although my brother and I were becoming fond of hamburgers, my parents didn't care much for Western food, other than chow mein.

But this was a special occasion, and Father asked his co-workers to recommend a really elegant restaurant. So there we were at the Lakeview, stumbling after the headwaiter in the murky dining room.

At our table we were handed our menus, and they were so big that to read mine, I almost had to stand up again. But why bother? It was mostly in French, anyway.

Father, being an engineer, was always systematic. He took out a pocket French dictionary. "They told me that most of the items would be in French, so I came prepared." He even had a pocket flashlight the size of a marking pen. While Mother held the flashlight over the menu, he looked up the items that were in French.

"*Pâté en croûte,*" he muttered. "Let's see . . . *pâté* is paste . . . *croûte* is crust . . . hmmm . . . a paste in crust."

The waiter stood looking patient. I squirmed and died at least fifty times.

At long last Father gave up. "Why don't we just order four complete dinners at random?" he suggested.

"Isn't that risky?" asked Mother. "The French eat some rather peculiar things, I've heard."

"A Chinese can eat anything a Frenchman can eat," Father declared.

The soup arrived in a plate. How do you get soup up from a plate? I glanced at the other diners, but the ones at the nearby tables were not on their soup course, while the more distant ones were invisible in the darkness.

Fortunately my parents had studied books on Western etiquette before they came to America. "Tilt your plate," whispered my mother. "It's easier to spoon the soup up that way."

She was right. Tilting the plate did the trick. But the etiquette book didn't say anything about what you did after the soup reached your lips. As any respectable Chinese knows, the correct way to eat your soup is to slurp. This helps to cool the liquid and prevent you from burning your lips. It also shows your appreciation.

We showed our appreciation. *Shloop,* went my father. *Shloop,* went my mother. *Shloop, shloop,* went my brother, who was the hungriest.

The lady harpist stopped playing to take a rest. And in the silence, our family's consumption of soup suddenly seemed unnaturally loud. You know how it sounds on a rocky beach when the tide goes out and the water drains from all those little pools? They go *shloop, shloop, shloop.* That was the Lin family eating soup.

At the next table a waiter was pouring wine. When a large *shloop* reached him, he froze. The bottle continued to pour, and red wine flooded the table top and into the lap of a customer. Even the customer didn't notice anything at first, being also hypnotized by the *shloop, shloop, shloop.*

Vocabulary
etiquette (et′i·kit) *n.:* acceptable manners and behavior.

It was too much. "I need to go to the toilet," I mumbled, jumping to my feet. A waiter, sensing my urgency, quickly directed me to the ladies' room.

I splashed cold water on my burning face, and as I dried myself with a paper towel, I stared into the mirror. In this perfumed ladies' room, with its pink-and-silver wallpaper and marbled sinks, I looked completely out of place. What was I doing here? What was our family doing in the Lakeview restaurant? In America?

The door to the ladies' room opened. A woman came in and glanced curiously at me. I retreated into one of the toilet cubicles and latched the door.

Time passed—maybe half an hour, maybe an hour. Then I heard the door open again, and my mother's voice. "Are you in there? You're not sick, are you?"

There was real concern in her voice. A girl can't leave her family just because they slurp their soup. Besides, the toilet cubicle had a few drawbacks as a permanent residence. "I'm all right," I said, undoing the latch.

Mother didn't tell me how the rest of the dinner went, and I didn't want to know. In the weeks following, I managed to push the whole thing into the back of my mind, where it jumped out at me only a few times a day. Even now, I turn hot all over when I think of the Lakeview restaurant.

❺ But by the time we had been in this country for three months, our family was definitely making progress toward becoming Americanized. I remember my parents' first PTA meeting. Father wore a neat suit and tie, and Mother put on her first pair of high heels. She stumbled only once. They met my homeroom teacher and beamed as she told

them that I would make honor roll soon at the rate I was going. Of course Chinese etiquette forced Father to say that I was a very stupid girl and Mother to protest that the teacher was showing favoritism toward me. But I could tell they were both very proud.

❻ The day came when my parents announced that they wanted to give a dinner party. We had invited Chinese friends to eat with us before, but this dinner was going to be different. In addition to a Chinese American family, we were going to invite the Gleasons.

"Gee, I can hardly wait to have dinner at your house," Meg said to me. "I just *love* Chinese food."

That was a relief. Mother was a good cook, but I wasn't sure if people who ate sour cream would also eat chicken gizzards stewed in soy sauce.

Mother decided not to take a chance with chicken gizzards. Since we had Western guests, she set the table with large dinner plates, which we never used in Chinese meals. In fact we didn't use individual plates at all, but picked up food from the platters in the middle of the table and brought it directly to our rice bowls. Following the practice of Chinese American restaurants, Mother also placed large serving spoons on the platters.

The dinner started well. Mrs. Gleason exclaimed at the beautifully arranged dishes of food: the colorful candied fruit in the sweet-and-sour pork dish, the noodle-thin shreds of chicken meat stir-fried with tiny peas, and the glistening pink prawns° in a ginger sauce.

At first I was too busy enjoying my food to notice how the guests were doing. But soon I remembered my duties. Sometimes

—————————————————

°**prawns** *n.:* large shrimps.

guests were too polite to help themselves and you had to serve them with more food.

I glanced at Meg to see if she needed more food, and my eyes nearly popped out at the sight of her plate. It was piled with food: The sweet-and-sour meat pushed right against the chicken shreds, and the chicken sauce ran into the prawns. She had been taking food from a second dish before she finished eating her helping from the first!

Horrified, I turned to look at Mrs. Gleason. She was dumping rice out of her bowl and putting it on her dinner plate. Then she ladled prawns and gravy on top of the rice and mixed everything together, the way you mix sand, gravel, and cement to make concrete.

I couldn't bear to look any longer, and I turned to Mr. Gleason. He was chasing a pea around his plate. Several times he got it to the edge, but when he tried to pick it

"slurp"

up with his chopsticks, it rolled back toward the center of the plate again. Finally he put down his chopsticks and picked up the pea with his fingers. He really did! A grown man!

All of us, our family and the Chinese guests, stopped eating to watch the activities of the Gleasons. I wanted to giggle. Then I caught my mother's eyes on me. She frowned and shook her head slightly, and I understood the message: The Gleasons were not used to Chinese ways, and they were just coping the best they could. For some reason I thought of celery strings.

When the main courses were finished, Mother brought out a platter of fruit. "I hope you weren't expecting a sweet dessert," she said. "Since the Chinese don't eat dessert, I didn't think to prepare any."

"Oh, I couldn't possibly eat dessert!" cried Mrs. Gleason. "I'm simply stuffed!"

Meg had different ideas. When the table was cleared, she announced that she and I were going for a walk. "I don't know about you, but I feel like dessert," she told me, when we were outside. "Come on, there's a Dairy Queen down the street. I could use a big chocolate milkshake!"

Although I didn't really want anything more to eat, I insisted on paying for the milkshakes. After all, I was still hostess.

Meg got her large chocolate milkshake and I had a small one. Even so, she was finishing hers while I was only half done. Toward the end she pulled hard on her straws and went *shloop, shloop*.

"Do you always slurp when you eat a milkshake?" I asked, before I could stop myself.

Meg grinned. "Sure. All Americans slurp."

Meet the Writer

Lensey Namioka

Moving Between Cultures

It's only natural for **Lensey Namioka** (1929–   ) to write about young people trying to cope with the strange ways of a new culture. She has spent much of her own life adjusting to new people and places. Namioka was born in China, where her family moved around a lot when she was young. "Being on the move meant that I grew up with almost no toys," she says. "To amuse ourselves, my sister and I made up stories." When she was a teenager, her family immigrated to the United States.

Before she began writing for young people, Namioka worked as a mathematics teacher. Her realistic novels about teenagers today draw on her Chinese heritage. Her adventure novels set in long-ago Japan draw on her husband's Japanese heritage.

For Independent Reading

If you liked "The All-American Slurp," you might "shloop" up Namioka's novels about a musical family of Chinese immigrants living in Seattle, including *Yang the Eldest and His Odd Jobs*. For a more challenging novel written for teenagers, try Namioka's *Ties That Bind, Ties That Break*. Set in China and San Francisco, it tells of a girl who rebels against the age-old Chinese tradition of binding girls' feet.

First Thoughts

1. What scene in this story do you remember most clearly? Why?

Thinking Critically

2. What American customs confuse the Lins when they eat at the Gleasons'? What mistakes do the Gleasons make when they eat at the Lins'?

3. List some of the steps the Lins take to adapt to their new surroundings. Then, make a **prediction** about how they will eventually fit into American life.

4. Meg's comment that "all Americans slurp" hints at the story's **theme.** What do you think that theme is?

North Carolina Competency Goal
1.02; 1.04;
4.01; 4.02;
5.01; 5.02;
6.01; 6.02

Reading Check

Copy the chart below, and use it to sum up what happens in each of the story's six episodes. (The first episode is summarized for you.)

a. The Lins eat at the Gleasons' and pull strings out of celery, which they've never eaten raw. They aren't sure how to act at a buffet.
b.
c.

and so on.

Extending Interpretations

5. You may know people who have come to the United States from another country. Does the author make the immigrant experience sound too easy, or is she on target? Did the story remind you of your own experiences in a new situation? Refer to your Quickwrite notes before answering.

6. Did Namioka's story make you see any of your own customs in a new light? Do you think some of your family's or culture's customs might seem odd or confusing to an outsider? Explain.

SPEAKING AND LISTENING

Performing a Dramatic Reading

Work with a few classmates to prepare a dramatic reading of one or more scenes in this story. Prepare a script for each scene. How many readers will you need? You may want to split up the narrator's part and have more than one reader handle it. Consider using props in your performance. Rehearse your reading; then, perform it in front of an audience. Ask the audience members to provide feedback on the performance.

INTERNET

Projects and Activities
Keyword: LE5 6-3

SKILLS FOCUS

Literary Skills
Analyze theme.

Reading Skills
Summarize plot.

Speaking and Listening Skills
Perform a dramatic reading.

Using Context Clues to Clarify Meaning

PRACTICE 1

Write four sentences about the story, using the words in the Word Bank. You can use another form of a word if you wish—for example, *lavish* instead of *lavishly*. Use **context clues** that will help someone figure out the words' meanings. Here is an example of the use of context clues in the story (page 229): "'This is a buffet dinner. You help yourselves to some food and eat it in the living room.'" What clues tell you what a *buffet* is?

> **Word Bank**
>
> lavishly
> mortified
> spectacle
> etiquette

Interpreting Figurative Language

Figurative language, which is not literally true, compares one thing to something very different. Three common figures of speech are metaphor, simile, and personification.

PRACTICE 2

1. A **metaphor** directly compares two very different things. What is a red face compared to in this sentence?

   Her face blazed with embarrassment.

2. A **simile** compares two very different things but uses a word of comparison, such as *like, as, as if, resembles,* or *seems.*

   Her face was like a blazing fire.

   Make up another simile to describe a red face. Begin with "Her face was like . . ."

3. **Personification** gives human or living characteristics to something that is not human or is not alive. What are these appetizers compared to? (What does this statement make you *see?*)

   Strange appetizers stared up from the tray.

North Carolina Competency Goal
5.01; 5.02; 6.01

Vocabulary Skills
Use context clues; interpret figurative language.

Evaluating Conclusions

Reading Focus
Evaluating a Writer's Conclusions

Some informative texts are written to present certain conclusions. The writer presents evidence and then draws a conclusion based on that evidence. For example, a writer might present facts and statistics about changing weather conditions and end with the conclusion that we are experiencing the effects of global warming. Your job, as a reader, is to evaluate the conclusion.

Summarizing Evidence

When you read informational texts, you expect the writer's evidence to add up to a conclusion that makes sense. But don't be fooled—writers aren't perfect. The fact that something looks nice and neat on a printed page doesn't mean it's well thought out. One way to see if a writer's evidence supports a conclusion is to **summarize** the important information—that is, sum up in your own words the writer's evidence. Then, review your summary. Does all the evidence clearly support the writer's conclusion?

■ "The All-American Slurp" is a fictional account of an immigrant family's experience in the United States. In the selection that follows, an immigrant girl from Iran talks about coming to America. Her main points are summarized next to the selection. Do you think they support her conclusion? You'll have a chance to explain at the end of "Everybody Is Different, but the Same Too."

North Carolina Competency Goal
2.01; 5.01; 5.02

INTERNET
Interactive
Reading Model
Keyword: LE5 6-3

SKILLS FOCUS

Reading Skills
Evaluate a
writer's
conclusions.

In the following responses to an interviewer, Nilou, an Iranian American girl, talks about fitting into American life. As a Jewish girl living in Iran, Nilou felt out of place. After the monarchy in Iran was overthrown, in 1979, religious freedom was suppressed. Nilou had to go to school on Saturday, the Jewish day of rest and worship. Her family had few freedoms, and they feared for their future. When Nilou was eight years old, her parents decided that the family had to leave the country. They secretly began selling their possessions, even though they worried about being caught and punished—perhaps even killed—for trying to leave. In 1985, Nilou and her family finally managed to leave Iran. They flew to New York and eventually settled in Maryland.

Everybody Is Different, but the Same Too

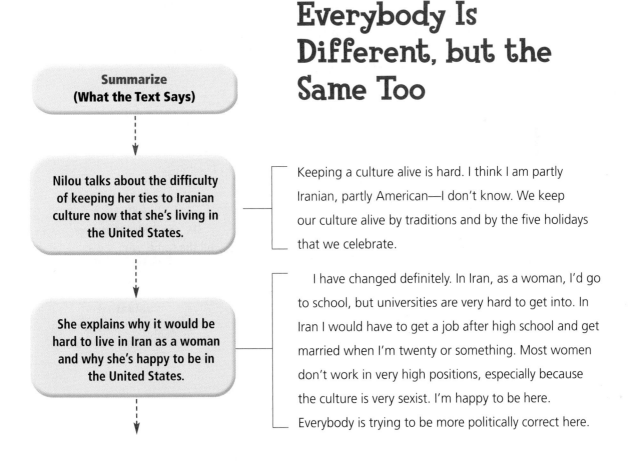

Summarize (What the Text Says)

Nilou talks about the difficulty of keeping her ties to Iranian culture now that she's living in the United States.

Keeping a culture alive is hard. I think I am partly Iranian, partly American—I don't know. We keep our culture alive by traditions and by the five holidays that we celebrate.

She explains why it would be hard to live in Iran as a woman and why she's happy to be in the United States.

I have changed definitely. In Iran, as a woman, I'd go to school, but universities are very hard to get into. In Iran I would have to get a job after high school and get married when I'm twenty or something. Most women don't work in very high positions, especially because the culture is very sexist. I'm happy to be here. Everybody is trying to be more politically correct here.

In schools there is a Spanish club, a Chinese club, but I don't know if there is an Iranian club. We are trying to make an Iranian club but I don't know if it will work—there are [only] about eleven or twelve kids.

I think a club is a way of trying to keep the culture alive. In the Hispanic club, every Thursday, they get together and they dance, and on Tuesdays, they have meetings. We also have an international concert that we can go to. [You can] sing if you like, dance, bring food, you know, just whatever you want to do, whatever you want to present of your culture.

About fitting into American life: When I came to public school, I saw that America is really a melting pot; it borrows things from other cultures—schools, building, furniture, everything from different cultures—and so there is no American way. You can't look at people and say they look like Americans, because America is really borrowing from everything else and everybody is American. And that was when I realized I am American—because all Americans are different.

We should teach that people are people and everybody is the same. They just have different ways of handling their problems and different lifestyles. But we probably have the same goals.

My friends are from all different parts of the world. My American friends are different, my Iranian friends are different, everybody is different, but the same too.

—Nilou, from *Newcomers to America*

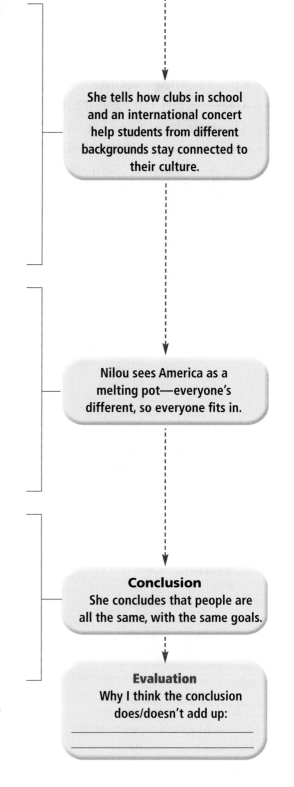

She tells how clubs in school and an international concert help students from different backgrounds stay connected to their culture.

Nilou sees America as a melting pot—everyone's different, so everyone fits in.

Conclusion
She concludes that people are all the same, with the same goals.

Evaluation
Why I think the conclusion does/doesn't add up:
_____
_____

Evaluating Conclusions

Everybody Is Different, but the Same Too

Test Practice

1. According to Nilou, a major difference between the United States and Iran is that in the United States —

   A women have more opportunities

   B there is more prejudice

   C most people do not appreciate what it means to be free

   D anyone who wants to can go to college

2. Nilou suggests all of these ways of keeping a culture alive *except* —

   F celebrating the holidays of that culture

   G having a club for students of that cultural background

   H following the traditions of that culture

   J refusing to mix with people of different cultures

3. When Nilou says, "America is a melting pot," she is using a **metaphor** that compares America to —

   A a pot of rice

   B a pot in which all kinds of ingredients are melted together

   C a bucket of melted steel, which will harden and become strong

   D different kinds of foods

4. Which statement best expresses Nilou's **conclusion**?

   F The differences between people will always cause trouble.

   G People change a great deal when they move to a new country.

   H We have small differences, but people are all just about the same.

   J You have to work very hard if you want to keep your culture alive.

Constructed Response

1. What does Nilou think would have happened to her after high school if she had stayed in Iran?

2. What did Nilou learn about fitting into American life when she started public school?

3. What ideas about people would Nilou like to see taught?

SKILLS FOCUS

Reading Skills
Evaluate a writer's conclusions.

North Carolina Competency Goal
1.04; 2.01; 4.01; 4.02; 5.01

Figurative Language

Figurative language is language based on unusual comparisons, and it is not literally true. People who study these things say that there are more than three hundred kinds of figures of speech. Two popular kinds of figurative language are similes and metaphors.

- A **simile** compares two unlike things, using a word of comparison, such as *like, as, than,* or *resembles.*

    America is <u>like</u> a melting pot.

- A **metaphor** compares two unlike things directly, without using a word of comparison.

    America <u>is</u> a melting pot.

PRACTICE

1. In his autobiography, *Barrio Boy,* the writer Ernesto Galarza describes America not as a melting pot but as a griddle, on which his teachers warmed knowledge into their students and roasted racial hatreds out of them. Make up three metaphors or similes that compare America to something else. Be ready to explain your comparisons. (Remember that similes and metaphors must be based on some similarities between the two things being compared; otherwise, they don't make sense.) Open with "America is . . ."

2. Make up at least three metaphors and three similes, each of which compares one of the items listed below to another very different thing (it must be a noun). The first one has been done for you.

    My cat . . .
    My cat Honey is a steam shovel at mealtime.

A smile . . .	Happiness . . .
My brain . . .	A computer . . .
Home . . .	Love . . .

3. Use three similes or metaphors to describe your favorite place or a place you don't like at all.

North Carolina Competency Goal
2.01; 6.01

SKILLS FOCUS

Vocabulary Skills
Identify and interpret figurative language.

Before You Read | The Fairy Tale

The Emperor's New Clothes

Make the Connection
Quickwrite

The emperor in this story loves clothes. Think about how you would describe your fashion style. Is it classic? wild? preppy? grunge? hip-hop? Why do you love to wear certain clothes—and dislike wearing others? Jot down words that describe the clothes you most like to wear.

Literary Focus
Theme: Getting the Message

Writers of stories send messages. A story's message is its **theme**, what it reveals to us about people or life. Theme is different from plot. The **plot** of "The Emperor's New Clothes" is the sequence of events in the story. Theme is what the story means. You infer a theme from what happens in a story, but a theme goes far beyond the story to state a truth about real life. As you read, see what message you get from this story.

Reading Skills
Making Generalizations: Putting It All Together

A **generalization** is a broad, general conclusion drawn from several examples or pieces of evidence. A statement of a story's theme is a kind of generalization. From specific evidence in the story, you make a universal statement about life. To make a statement about the theme of "The Emperor's New Clothes," you have to

- think about the main events and conflicts in the story
- decide what the characters have learned by the end of the story
- state the idea in a general way, so that it applies not just to the story but to real life

North Carolina Competency Goal
1.04; 4.01; 4.02; 5.01

go.
hrw
.com

INTERNET
More About Andersen
Keyword: LE5 6-3

SKILLS FOCUS

Literary Skills
Recognize the difference between theme and plot.

Reading Skills
Make generalizations.

THE EMPEROR'S NEW CLOTHES

Hans Christian Andersen

Many years ago there lived an Emperor who was so fond of new clothes that he spent all his money on them. He did not care for his soldiers, or for the theater, or for driving in the woods, except to show off his new clothes. He had an outfit for every hour of the day, and just as they say of a king, "He is in the council chamber," so they always said of him, "The Emperor is in his dressing room."

The great city where he lived was very lively, and every day many strangers came there. One day two swindlers came. They claimed that they were weavers and said they could weave the finest cloth imaginable. Their colors and patterns, they said, were not only exceptionally beautiful, but the clothes made of this material possessed the wonderful quality of being invisible to any man who was unfit for his office, or who was hopelessly stupid.

"Those must be wonderful clothes," thought the Emperor. "If I wore them, I should be able to find out which men in my empire were unfit for their posts, and I could tell the clever from the stupid. Yes, I must have this cloth woven for me without delay." So he gave a lot of money to the two swindlers in advance, so that they could set to work at once.

They set up two looms[1] and pretended to be very hard at work, but they had nothing on the looms. They asked for the finest silk and the most precious gold, all of which they put into their own bags, and worked at the empty looms till late into the night.

"I should very much like to know how they are getting on with the cloth," thought the Emperor. But he felt rather uneasy when he remembered that whoever was not fit for his office could not see it. He believed, of course, that he had nothing to fear for himself, yet he thought he would send somebody else first to see how things were progressing.

Everybody in the town knew what a wonderful property the cloth possessed, and all were anxious to see how bad or stupid their neighbors were.

"I will send my honest old minister to the weavers," thought the Emperor. "He can judge best how the cloth looks, for he is intelligent, and nobody is better fitted for his office than he."

So the good old minister went into the room where the two swindlers sat working at the empty looms. "Heaven help us!" he thought, and opened his eyes wide. "Why, I cannot see anything at all," but he was careful not to say so.

Both swindlers bade him be so good as to step closer and asked him if he did not admire the exquisite pattern and the beautiful colors. They pointed to the empty looms, and the poor old minister opened his eyes even wider, but he could see nothing, for there was nothing to be seen. "Good Lord!" he thought, "can I be so stupid? I should never have thought so, and nobody must know it! Is it possible that I am not fit for my office? No, no, I must not tell anyone that I couldn't see the cloth."

"Well, have you got nothing to say?" said one, as he wove.

"Oh, it is very pretty—quite enchanting!" said the old minister, peering through his glasses. "What a pattern, and what colors! I shall tell the Emperor that I am very much pleased with it."

"Well, we are glad of that," said both the weavers, and they described the colors to him and explained the curious pattern. The old minister listened carefully, so that he might tell the Emperor what they said.

Now the swindlers asked for more money, more silk, and more gold, which they required for weaving. They kept it all for themselves, and not a thread came near the looms, but they continued, as before, working at the empty looms.

Soon afterward the Emperor sent another honest official to the weavers to see how they were getting on and if the cloth was nearly finished. Like the old minister, he looked and looked but could see nothing, as there was nothing to be seen.

"Is it not a beautiful piece of cloth?" said the two swindlers, showing and explaining the magnificent pattern, which, however, was not there at all.

"I am not stupid," thought the man, "so it must be that I am unfit for my high post. It

_____

1. **looms** _n._: machines used for weaving thread into cloth.

is ludicrous,[2] but I must not let anyone know it." So he praised the cloth, which he did not see, and expressed his pleasure at the beautiful colors and the fine pattern. "Yes, it is quite enchanting," he said to the Emperor.

Everybody in the whole town was talking about the beautiful cloth. At last the Emperor wished to see it himself while it was still on the loom. With a whole company of chosen courtiers, including the two honest councilors who had already been there, he went to the two clever swindlers, who were now weaving away as hard as they could but without using any thread.

"Is it not magnificent?" said both the honest statesmen. "Look, Your Majesty, what a pattern! What colors!" And they pointed to the empty looms, for they imagined the others could see the cloth.

"What is this?" thought the Emperor. "I do not see anything at all. This is terrible! Am I stupid? Am I unfit to be Emperor? That would indeed be the most dreadful thing that could happen to me!"

"Yes, it is very beautiful," said the Emperor. "It has our highest approval," and nodding contentedly, he gazed at the empty loom, for he did not want to say that he could see nothing. All the attendants who were with him looked and looked, and, although they could not see anything more than the others, they said, just like the Emperor, "Yes, it is very fine." They all advised him to wear the new magnificent clothes at a great procession that was soon to take place. "It is magnificent! beautiful, excellent!" went from mouth to mouth, and everybody seemed delighted. The Emperor awarded each of the swindlers the cross of the order of knighthood to be worn in their buttonholes, and the title of Imperial Court Weavers.

Throughout the night preceding the procession, the swindlers were up working, and they had more than sixteen candles burning. People could see how busy they were, getting the Emperor's new clothes ready. They pretended to take the cloth from the loom, they snipped the air with big scissors, they sewed with needles without any thread, and at last said: "Now the Emperor's new clothes are ready!"

---

2. **ludicrous** (lo͞o′di·krəs) *adj.:* ridiculous; laughable.

The Emperor, followed by all his noblest courtiers, then came in. Both the swindlers held up one arm as if they held something, and said: "See, here are the trousers! Here is the coat! Here is the cloak!" and so on. "They are all as light as a cobweb! They make one feel as if one had nothing on at all, but that is just the beauty of it."

"Yes!" said all the courtiers, but they could not see anything, for there was nothing to see.

"Will it please Your Majesty graciously to take off your clothes?" said the swindlers. "Then we may help Your Majesty into the new clothes before the large mirror!"

The Emperor took off all his clothes, and the swindlers pretended to put on the new clothes, one piece after another. Then the Emperor looked at himself in the glass from every angle.

"Oh, how well they look! How well they fit!" said all. "What a pattern! What colors! Magnificent indeed!"

"They are waiting outside with the canopy which is to be borne over Your Majesty in the procession," announced the master of ceremonies.

"Well, I am quite ready," said the Emperor. "Doesn't my suit fit me beautifully?" And he turned once more to the mirror so that people would think he was admiring his garments.

The chamberlains, who were to carry the train, fumbled with their hands on the ground as if they were lifting up a train. Then they pretended to hold something up in their hands. They didn't dare let people know that they could not see anything.

And so the Emperor marched in the procession under the beautiful canopy, and all who saw him in the street and out of the windows exclaimed: "How marvelous the Emperor's new suit is! What a long train he has! How well it fits him!" Nobody would let the others know that he saw nothing, for then he would have been shown to be unfit for his office or too stupid. None of the Emperor's clothes had ever been such a success.

"But he has nothing on at all," said a little child.

"Good heavens! Hear what the innocent child says!" said the father, and then each whispered to the other what the child said: "He has nothing on—a little child says he has nothing on at all!" "He has nothing on at all," cried all the people at last. And the Emperor too was feeling very worried, for it seemed to him that they were right, but he thought to himself, "All the same, I must go through with the procession." And he held himself stiffer than ever, and the chamberlains walked on, holding up the train which was not there at all.

Hans Christian Andersen

A Fairy Tale Life

Once upon a time, **Hans Christian Andersen** (1805–1875), the son of a poor shoemaker, lived in a small town in Denmark called Odense. As a boy, Hans loved the theater, but he couldn't pay for tickets. So he made friends with an usher and got a copy of each program.

> 66 With this I seated myself in a corner and imagined an entire play, according to the name of the piece and the characters in it. That was my first unconscious poetizing. 99

A fortuneteller predicted a great future for Hans and said his hometown would someday be lighted up in his honor. Hans was only fourteen when he went to Copenhagen to seek his fortune. By age twenty-eight he had failed as a singer, actor, and dancer, though he had had some success as a writer. That year he began writing the fairy tales that soon made him known around the world. Ideas for these tales came from his life, he said.

> 66 [They] lay in my mind like seeds and only needed a gentle touch— the kiss of a sunbeam or drop of malice—to flower. 99

Portrait of Hans Christian Andersen (1852) by Frederik Ludwig Storch. Oil on canvas.
Hans Christian Andersen Museum, Odense, Denmark.

Almost every year around Christmas until he was sixty-eight, Andersen published new fairy tales. Late in his life his hometown of Odense held a festival for him, and the whole city was lighted up in his honor. It's no wonder that Andersen called his autobiography *The Fairy Tale of My Life*!

For Independent Reading

You can find more tales by Hans Christian Andersen in his collected works. If you haven't read his stories yet, you might want to read them now. Andersen's stories can be read both for entertainment and for their deeper meaning. Here are some favorites: "Thumbelina," "The Ugly Duckling," "The Little Mermaid," "The Steadfast Tin Soldier," "The Snow Queen," and "The Nightingale."

First Thoughts

1. If you were watching the emperor's procession, how would you react?

Thinking Critically

2. A character's **motives** are the reasons for his or her actions. What motives do the emperor's officials have for not telling the emperor the truth?

3. The emperor continues to march even though everyone knows he's wearing no clothes. What **character traits** does the emperor reveal through his actions?

4. Readers often find different **themes** in the same story. From the following **generalizations,** choose the one that you think best states the main theme of "The Emperor's New Clothes," or come up with your own statement of the theme. Explain why you chose the theme you did. Be sure to give examples from the story to support your theme.

   a. We should not trust people who use flattery.

   b. People often do not speak the truth to the powerful because they're afraid of looking foolish.

   c. Children always tell the truth.

Extending Interpretations

5. Why do you suppose the only person who dares to tell the emperor the truth is a child? What seems to be the storyteller's opinion of children as opposed to his opinion of adults? Explain why you agree or disagree with his opinions.

WRITING

Writing and Supporting a Topic Statement

In your Quickwrite you jotted down notes on the clothes you like to wear and what they say about you. Refer to your notes, and write a paragraph about yourself and your favorite clothes. You might even include an illustration. Be sure to include a topic statement that sums up the main point you are making about your clothes.

> ### Reading Check
>
> Imagine that you are the emperor. The procession is over. Night has fallen. Take out your diary to write about your day. Describe the events that led up to the procession, what happened during the procession, and the way you feel about the outcome.

North Carolina Competency Goal
1.02; 1.04;
4.01; 4.02;
5.01

INTERNET

Projects and Activities
Keyword: LE5 6-3

Literary Skills
Analyze theme.

Reading Skills
Make generalizations.

Writing Skills
Write and support a statement.

Identifying Hyperbole

Hyperbole (hī·pʉr'bə·lē) is exaggerated or overstated language. Hyperbole is a type of figurative language and so is not to be taken literally. If you say, "I ate a mountain of food," you're using hyperbole. You want to make a point about how hungry you were.

PRACTICE 1

Find three examples of hyperbole in the sentences below:

> "If I've told you once, I've told you a thousand times," the emperor shouted at his officials, so loudly that he could be heard miles away. "Don't tell me about the poor people in this kingdom. Such talk bores me to death. Now help me get ready for my procession."

Interpreting Idioms

An **idiom** (id'ē·əm) is an expression unique to a language. (*Idiom* comes from the Greek word *idios,* meaning "one's own" or "personal.") *Head over heels in love* and *raining cats and dogs* are English idioms. Idioms are difficult because they mean something different from what the words actually say. People who grow up with a language understand its idioms without even thinking about them. If you're learning a new language, however, idioms may give you trouble.

PRACTICE 2

Find at least five idioms in the following paragraph. Working with a partner, see if you can explain what each idiom means.

> The weavers pretended to be working their fingers to the bone, but they were pulling the wool over everybody's eyes. The emperor's servants weren't willing to stick their necks out. Things came to a head during the procession. The emperor thought he was dressed to kill. Then a child spilled the beans. "That man has no clothes on," she said. The weavers had made a monkey out of the emperor.

North Carolina Competency Goal
6.01

Vocabulary Skills
Identify hyperbole; interpret idioms.

Recognizing and Evaluating Evidence

Reading Focus

Recognizing Evidence

The emperor in "The Emperor's New Clothes" isn't the only one who worries about his clothes. To wear—or not to wear—school uniforms is a hotly debated issue in many school districts today. In the article that follows, the writer presents arguments and evidence from both sides of the debate, then draws her own conclusion.

Writers often cite many kinds of **evidence** to support a conclusion. When writers deal with emotionally charged issues—like requiring students to wear school uniforms—they usually bring out the heavy artillery: quotations, statistics, case studies.

1. **Quotations** are likely to be comments from people who have something significant to say about the topic. **Direct quotations**—people's exact words—are easy to spot. They're always enclosed in quotation marks.

> According to a sixth-grader at Valley Academy, "Kids are proud of who they are instead of worrying about what they're wearing."

2. **Statistics** are information expressed as numbers (such as percentages or measurements). Sometimes statistics are presented in charts or graphs.

> One principal says that test scores went up 20 percent the first year kids wore uniforms.

3. **Case studies** are specific examples. Case studies may illustrate the point made in the conclusion.

> A recent study conducted in more than thirty public schools where uniforms are required shows that social and economic conflicts were greatly reduced.

Evaluating Evidence

When you read informational materials intended to persuade you to take a certain action or to think in a certain way, be sure to examine the kinds of support the writer has used. Ask yourself,

- Does the evidence support the conclusion?

- Would other kinds of support have worked better?

- Should the writer have presented *more* evidence—has the conclusion been supported only partially?

When you consider questions like these, you're evaluating the adequacy and appropriateness of the writer's evidence.

■ Look for evidence, such as quotations and statistics, in the following article on school uniforms. Does this evidence support the writer's conclusion?

North Carolina Competency Goal 2.01; 5.02

SKILLS FOCUS

Reading Skills
Recognize and evaluate evidence.

Uniform Style

Some claim that they make students harder working, less violent, and better behaved. Others protest that they take away students' freedom to think for themselves.

Is this debate about a fiendish plot to control students through brain implants? No—it's about rules requiring public school students to wear uniforms.

Why are more and more public schools in the United States considering uniforms? "It's the whole issue of setting a tone for the day," says Mary Marquez, an elementary school principal in Long Beach, California, the first school district in the nation to make uniforms mandatory.[1] "When students are in their uniforms, they know they are going to school to learn, not going outside to play."

If sporting the latest fashions makes kids feel hip and cool, does wearing a school uniform make them feel more like serious students? Many teachers and principals say yes. They believe that uniforms motivate[2] their students to live up to higher standards and that they promote school spirit, discipline, and academic excellence.

---

1. **mandatory** (man′də·tôr′ē) *adj.:* required.
2. **motivate** (mōt′ə·vāt′) *v.:* cause someone to do something or act in a certain way; push or drive.

But what about the right to individuality, creativity, self-expression? That's what civil liberties experts are concerned about, and many students and parents agree. Some have even gone so far as to bring lawsuits against schools that won't let students wear what they like.

Still, many parents, tired of shelling out money month after month to buy trendy clothing for their children, are only too pleased to have uniforms settle the question once and for all. Many students also welcome an end to clothing competition. "I don't worry about what I wear in the morning," says twelve-year-old uniform wearer Hortencia Llanas. "I just slip on the clothes." Students from wealthy families no longer show off their expensive clothes at school, and students who can't afford them no longer face ridicule for the way they dress. (Of course, buying school uniforms can be hard on the pocketbook as well. A number of schools have started programs to help parents pay for them.)

Some of the statements made by supporters of uniforms may seem exaggerated—for example, how could requiring students to dress alike make public schools safer? But there are logical arguments to back up this claim. Fights are less likely to break out over a leather jacket or a $150 pair of sneakers if no one is wearing such items to school. Those who don't belong on school grounds stand out among students wearing school uniforms.

In Long Beach, statistics tell the story: School crime went down 36 percent after students began wearing uniforms. Fighting dropped 51 percent and vandalism 18 percent. Other districts that began requiring uniforms report similar improvements.

In public school districts across the country, the jury is still out on the question of school uniforms. But with so many possible benefits, many ask: Why not give uniforms a try?

—Mara Rockliff

Recognizing and Evaluating Evidence

Uniform Style

Test Practice

1. Which statement best expresses the writer's **conclusion**?

   A   Requiring students to wear uniforms solves all of their schools' problems.

   B   Since uniforms offer many benefits, schools should give them a try.

   C   School uniforms keep students from being creative.

   D   School uniforms have proved to be a bad idea.

2. Why does the writer mention the concerns of civil liberties experts?

   F   To prove that students who wear uniforms are less violent than students who wear street clothes to school

   G   To remind readers that everyone should be concerned about students' test scores

   H   To show that some people oppose school uniforms

   J   To show how expensive kids' clothes are

3. Which of the following **conclusions** is supported in the article?

   A   Students' ability to focus on their schoolwork improves when they aren't thinking about being fashionable.

   B   Wearing uniforms makes kids feel hip and cool.

   C   A family has no right to bring a lawsuit against a public school.

   D   Schools that require students to wear uniforms should pay for them.

4. What **support** does the writer give for the idea that requiring students to wear uniforms instead of street clothes can prevent violence?

   F   Statements by civil liberties experts

   G   Statistics from Long Beach

   H   A quotation from a school superintendent

   J   A quotation from Hortencia Llanas

Constructed Response

1. What people are **quoted** in this article? What point does each person make?

2. Give three **statistics** cited by the writer in support of school uniforms.

3. What is civil liberties experts' concern about school uniforms?

4. Do you believe the writer has provided strong **support** for her final statement? Explain why or why not.

North Carolina Competency Goal 2.01

Reading Skills Recognize and evaluate evidence.

Interpreting Idioms

When your friend says she's going to hit the books, you don't expect her to start punching her math book. *Hitting the books* is an **idiom,** an expression whose meaning differs from the literal meaning of the words. An idiom's meaning is unique to a particular language, so it may be hard for someone learning the language to understand.

PRACTICE

How would you explain the following idioms from "Uniform Style" to someone? Use each idiom in a sentence, and then write a definition of it.

1. live up to

2. shell out

3. hard on the pocketbook

4. jury is still out

Grammar Link

Clear Pronoun References

North Carolina Competency Goal
1.04; 2.01; 4.01; 4.02; 5.01; 6.01

Pronouns always refer to a noun or to another pronoun. The word the pronoun refers to is called its **antecedent** (an′tə·sēd′′nt). To avoid confusion, make sure each pronoun you use clearly refers to its antecedent.

CONFUSING **Ralph talked to Miguel about the dress code. He did not agree with it.**

Who did not agree with the dress code, Ralph or Miguel? It is not clear because *He* could refer to either boy. Replace *He* with the correct name.

CLEAR **Ralph talked to Miguel about the dress code. Miguel did not agree with it.**

SKILLS FOCUS

Vocabulary Skills
Interpret idioms.

Grammar Skills
Use clear pronoun references.

PRACTICE

Rewrite each sentence so that the antecedent of each pronoun is clear.

1. When Tracy and her mother saw the uniform, she said she didn't like it.

2. Kim called Norma when she was choosing a uniform.

3. Roberto talked to Henry and then called Trong. He would not change his mind.

For more help, see the Pronoun, 1b, in the Language Handbook.

Baucis and Philemon

Make the Connection

Quickwrite ✏️

Suppose you were traveling centuries ago, long before the days of motels and campgrounds. Hungry and tired, you would have to find shelter as night approached. If you stopped at a house, you could be fairly certain that you'd be welcomed and given a meal and a bed for the night. Hospitality, or generosity to guests, was a sacred duty in many parts of the ancient world, especially ancient Greece. People were expected to share what they had, even with strangers. Freewrite about the way we treat strangers today.

Literary Focus

Universal Themes: Ties That Bind

Whenever you read literature—whether it's an African folk tale first told hundreds of years ago or a novel set in New York City today—you're likely to run into familiar character types, plots, and themes. Why are there so many similarities between stories from different places and periods? No one knows for sure. But the similarities suggest that people who lived long ago had many of the same fears and wishes that we have today. The similarities also suggest that people from different parts of the world can agree on what is important in life.

As you read the ancient Greek myth "Baucis and Philemon," look for similarities between this story from long ago and real life today. In particular, think about **theme,** the message of the myth. Does that message still apply today?

Metamorphosis: Shifting Shapes

A **metamorphosis** (met′ə·môr′fə·sis) is a total change in shape or form. A larva's transformation into a butterfly is a metamorphosis. The wormlike larva undergoes a dramatic change in form to become a beautiful butterfly. A tadpole goes through a metamorphosis to become a frog. Metamorphosis is important in mythology. "Baucis and Philemon" begins with a metamorphosis in which the gods Zeus and Hermes change into humans. In myths, gods can transform anyone or anything into any form they choose. As you read this myth, look for another amazing metamorphosis.

Reading Skills 📖

Recognizing Connections

Myths speak in a universal language—that's why you still see so many references to them today, on television and in newspapers as well as in stories. As you read "Baucis and Philemon," be on the lookout for **connections** wherever you encounter the little open-book sign.

- What kind of behavior does the story encourage? What qualities in people are rewarded? Are qualities like these rewarded today?
- How are people today tested for the depth of their concern for others?
- Is the **theme** of this old story still important to us today?

North Carolina Competency Goal
1.04; 4.01; 5.01

SKILLS FOCUS

Literary Skills
Understand universal themes; understand metamorphosis.

Reading Skills
Recognize connections.

Baucis AND Philemon

GREEK MYTH,
RETOLD BY
OLIVIA COOLIDGE

Fruit Basket by Caravaggio
(1573–1610).
Pinocoteca Ambrosiana, Milan, Italy.
© Scala/Art Resource, NY.

One time Zeus[1] and Hermes[2] came down to earth in human form and traveled through a certain district, asking for food and shelter as they went. For a long time they found nothing but refusals from both rich and poor until at last they came to a little, one-room cottage rudely thatched with reeds from the nearby marsh, where dwelled a poor old couple, Baucis[3] and Philemon.[4]

1. **Zeus** (zōōs): chief god in Greek mythology.
2. **Hermes** (hʉrʹmēzʹ): god who serves as messenger of the other gods.
3. **Baucis** (bôʹsis).
4. **Philemon** (fi·lēʹmən).

The two had little to offer, since they lived entirely from the produce of their plot of land and a few goats, fowl, and pigs. Nevertheless, they were prompt to ask the strangers in and to set their best before them. The couch that they pulled forward for their guests was roughly put together from willow boughs, and the cushions on it were stuffed with straw. One table leg had to be propped up with a piece of broken pot, but Baucis scrubbed the top with fragrant mint and set some water on the fire. Meanwhile Philemon ran out into the garden to fetch a cabbage and then lifted down a piece of home-cured bacon from the blackened beam where it hung. While these were cooking, Baucis set out her best delicacies on the table. There were ripe olives, sour cherries pickled in wine, fresh onions and radishes, cream cheese, and eggs baked in the ashes of the fire. There was a big earthenware bowl in the midst of the table to mix their crude, homemade wine with water. **❶**

The second course had to be fruit, but there were nuts, figs, dried dates, plums, grapes, and apples, for this was their best season of the year. Philemon had even had it in mind to kill their only goose for dinner, and there was a great squawking and cackling that went on for a long time. Poor old Philemon wore himself out trying to catch

> **MAKE CONNECTIONS**
> **❶** Do Baucis and Philemon act like people you know?

that goose, but somehow the animal always got away from him until the guests bade him let it be, for they were well served as it was. It was a good meal, and the old couple kept pressing their guests to eat and drink, caring nothing that they were now consuming in one day what would ordinarily last them a week.

At last the wine sank low in the mixing bowl, and Philemon rose to fetch some more. But to his astonishment as he lifted the wine-skin to pour, he found the bowl was full again as though it had not been touched at all. Then he knew the two strangers must be gods, and he and Baucis were awed and afraid. But the gods smiled kindly at them, and the younger, who seemed to do most of the talking, said, "Philemon, you have welcomed us beneath your roof this day when richer men refused us shelter. Be sure those shall be punished who would not help the wandering stranger, but you shall have whatever reward you choose. Tell us what you will have."

The old man thought for a little with his eyes bent on the ground, and then he said: "We have lived together here for many years, happy even though the times have been hard. But never yet did we see fit to turn a stranger from our gate or to seek a reward for entertaining him. To have spoken with the immortals[5] face to face is a thing few

---

5. **immortals** *n.:* ancient Greek gods.

men can boast of. In this small cottage, humble though it is, the gods have sat at meat. It is as unworthy of the honor as we are. If, therefore, you will do something for us, turn this cottage into a temple where the gods may always be served and where we may live out the remainder of our days in worship of them."

"You have spoken well," said Hermes, "and you shall have your wish. Yet is there not anything that you would desire for yourselves?"

Philemon thought again at this, stroking his straggly beard, and he glanced over at old Baucis with her thin, gray hair and her rough hands as she served at the table, her feet bare on the floor of trodden earth. "We have lived together for many years," he said again, "and in all that time there has never been a word of anger between us. Now, at last, we are growing old and our long companionship is coming to an end. It is the only thing that has helped us in the bad times and the source of our joy in the good. Grant us this one request, that when we come to die, we may perish in the same hour and neither of us be left without the other." ❷

He looked at Baucis and she nodded in approval, so the old couple turned their eyes on the gods.

"It shall be as you desire," said Hermes. "Few men would have made such a good and moderate request." ❸

Thereafter the house became a temple, and the neighbors, amazed at the change, came often to worship and left offerings for the support of the aged priest and priestess there. For many years Baucis and Philemon lived in peace, passing from old to extreme old age. At last, they were so old and bowed that it seemed they could only walk at all if they clutched one another. But still every evening they would shuffle a little way down the path that they might turn and look together at the beautiful little temple and praise the gods for the honor bestowed on them. One evening it took them longer than ever to reach the usual spot, and there they turned arm in arm to look back, thinking perhaps that it was the last time their limbs would support them so far. There as they stood, each one felt the other stiffen and change and only had time to turn and say once, "Farewell," before they disappeared. In their place stood two tall trees growing closely side by side with branches interlaced. They seemed to nod and whisper to each other in the passing breeze.

MAKE CONNECTIONS
❷ What does Philemon's request show about the things he and his wife value? Do you know anyone with the same values?

MAKE CONNECTIONS
❸ What requests of the gods might more selfish people make?

Meet the Writer

Olivia Coolidge

A Twist of Fate

Olivia Coolidge (1908–   ) was enjoying a perfectly normal childhood in London with a perfectly normal dislike for Greek literature (which her father was urging her to read) when she twisted her ankle. For three months the cruel sprain kept her from going outside to play, and so she read—and read. Pretty soon she was even reading Greek poetry, and she made a shocking discovery. She loved it!

As happens sometimes in Greek myths, the young woman gladly accepted her fate: a lifelong love of the classics. (The word *classics* refers to Greek myths and other timeless works.) Her interest led her to Oxford University, where she continued her studies in the classics. Later, reflecting on why her own stories often spring from the classics, Olivia Coolidge noted:

> "I write about history, biography, and ancient legends for teens because I am more interested in values that always have been of concern to people than I am in the form we express them in at this moment. Distant places and past ages show that these values are not expressed better in the United States in the twentieth century, but merely differently. My general purpose therefore is to give a picture of life."

For Independent Reading

If you'd like to read other myths retold by Olivia Coolidge, look for *Greek Myths*. To learn more about the ancient world from which these myths come, see Coolidge's book *The Golden Days of Greece*.

Response and Analysis

First Thoughts

1. Finish one or both of these sentences.
   - If I were Philemon, I would have wished for . . .
   - This myth made me realize that . . .

Thinking Critically

2. In a myth a **metamorphosis** can be a reward, a punishment, or just a disguise. Which types of metamorphoses occur in this myth? What purpose does each transformation serve? You might organize your ideas in a chart like this one:

Metamorphosis	Type and Purpose
Zeus and Hermes become humans.	The gods disguise themselves. Their purpose is . . .

3. The ancient myths were meant to teach lessons about how to behave. What lessons do you think the Greeks learned from this story? Are those lessons still important today? Why or why not?

Extending Interpretations

4. Look at your notes for the Quickwrite on page 257. How do we treat strangers today? Why? (How do you think Zeus and Hermes would be treated if they arrived in your neighborhood today?)

WRITING

Writing About Theme

A **theme** is an idea about life that is revealed in a work of literature. These are some of the themes of "Baucis and Philemon":

- Generous people are rewarded.
- You do not need to be wealthy to be generous.
- Always be kind to strangers, as there's no telling who they are.

Choose one of these themes to write about in a paragraph or two. Use details from the myth to show how the story expresses this theme.

Reading Check

a. Why do the two gods come down to earth?

b. When do Baucis and Philemon realize that the strangers are gods?

c. How do the old couple please the gods?

d. What reward does Hermes offer?

e. What are Philemon's two wishes? In what ways do they come true?

INTERNET

Projects and Activities

Keyword: LE5 6-3

SKILLS FOCUS

Literary Skills
Analyze universal themes; analyze metamorphosis.

Reading Skills
Make connections.

Writing Skills
Write about theme.

North Carolina Competency Goal
1.02; 1.04; 4.01; 4.02; 5.01; 5.02

After You Read — Vocabulary Development

Words from Mythology

The Greek and Roman names for the gods are still used in modern life. For instance, Pluto, the name of the god of the underworld, is now the name of a planet and a cartoon character.

PRACTICE

How have these mythological names been used in the modern world? Are some of the names used for more than one thing?

Mars	Saturn	Mercury	Vulcan
Venus	Apollo	Jupiter	Poseidon

Grammar Link

Pronouns as Objects of Prepositions

A **prepositional phrase** begins with a preposition and ends with a noun or pronoun, which is called the **object of the preposition.**

to Baucis	about Philemon
without her	for him
after her	between him and her

When a pronoun is the object of the preposition, it must be in the objective form. Choosing the correct form of the pronoun isn't difficult when the object of a preposition is a single pronoun. The trouble comes when a preposition has two objects:

The myth appealed to Lila and I/me.

To figure out the correct choice, try out the sentence with just one pronoun at a time. (You wouldn't say, "The myth appealed to I.")

CORRECT The myth appealed to Lila and me.

North Carolina Competency Goal
6.01

SKILLS FOCUS

Vocabulary Skills
Identify word origins.

Grammar Skills
Use pronouns correctly.

PRACTICE

For each sentence, decide which of the underlined pronouns is correct.

1. Baucis was in the kitchen when the gods decided to test Philemon and she/her.

2. The gods gave he/him and she/her a choice.

3. Between you and I/me, I would not have passed that test.

4. Was turning into trees a happy ending for Philemon and she/her?

For more help, see The Object Form, 4c–e, in the Language Handbook.

Evaluating Evidence

"Baucis and Philemon" teaches a lesson about being a good neighbor and showing concern for others. The article on page 266 tells about a modern-day young man who has obviously taken this age-old lesson to heart.

Reading Focus
Evaluating Evidence: A Case Study

"Hey, our new coach is great!" exclaims Tam.

"How do you know?" you ask.

"I just know. Take my word for it."

Tam has drawn a conclusion (our new coach is great!), and you want to know how he has reached his conclusion. By asking your question, you're trying to decide two things: First, does Tam have enough information to form a reliable conclusion? Second, does Tam have evidence to support his conclusion? Here's Tam's evidence: "I just know." This reply gives no evidence at all. Tam just says, "Take my word for it."

Since Tam's evidence doesn't convince you, you keep digging. "Not good enough, Tam. Tell me more."

"She looks like this other really cool coach I used to know."

Looking like someone else does not make a "great" coach! Dig on. "So what? What else do you know?"

"Her teams have won almost all of their games for the last five years."

That is certainly adequate and appropriate evidence for deciding whether a coach is good. But does a winning average automatically make a great coach?

"She showed me how to fix a problem I've been having with my jump shot. I've been struggling with that shot for a year, but she knew what I was doing wrong just from watching me play once."

This is certainly reliable evidence. It shows that the coach is knowledgeable.

■ Judging evidence is easy. **Inappropriate evidence** makes you think, "What does that have to do with anything?" If you have to trust the person instead of relying on facts, it's **inadequate evidence.** Evidence is adequate when you've been given enough information to draw your own conclusion. So what do you think? Is she a great coach or not?

Distinguishing Between Fact and Opinion

Appropriate evidence is based on facts. **Facts** are pieces of information that can be proved true. In the discussion about the coach, Tam cites facts about the coach's winning average. In contrast, **opinions** are personal beliefs or attitudes. Tam states a few of those, such as "I just know" (definitely inappropriate evidence). A **valid opinion** is a belief or judgment supported by facts. Valid opinions can provide strong support for a conclusion.

■ Be on the lookout for facts and valid opinions in "One Child's Labor of Love."

North Carolina Competency Goal
2.01; 3.01; 3.03; 4.03

SKILLS FOCUS

Reading Skills
Evaluate evidence; distinguish between fact and opinion.

One Child's Labor of Love

CBS, NEW YORK—Tuesday, October 5, 1999, 6:14 P.M.—When *60 Minutes* correspondent Ed Bradley first met Craig Kielburger three years ago, the 13-year-old possessed a passionate intolerance for child labor and slavery.

Craig Kielburger with children in Manila, Philippines, in 1998.

Now 16, Craig has met with some of the most important political and religious leaders of his time. And last year, he joined the ranks of John F. Kennedy, Harry Truman, Elie Wiesel, and Desmond Tutu as he took home the prestigious[1] Franklin and Eleanor Roosevelt Medal of Freedom. Bradley recently revisited Craig to track his progress.

To understand how a teenager from Toronto became the inspiration for a 5,000-member organization called Free the Children, with chapters in 25 countries, consider what Craig had to say at age 13: "Basically, we're told slavery [was] abolished," Craig explained. "But it was really shocking, because . . . I was just reading through the different research that I got, and you find the worst type of slavery still exists today—slavery of children."

When Craig was age 12, he read a newspaper article about a boy his age in Pakistan, Iqbal Masih. Iqbal's parents, like so many others, had offered their son's labor at age 4 in exchange for a small loan. Iqbal spent the next six years chained to a rug loom, working 12-hour days for pennies, until he finally escaped and joined a crusade against child labor. But after Iqbal won worldwide recognition, his life was cut short when, at age 12, he was shot dead in the streets of his village. No one has been convicted of the murder, and Craig vowed to keep his cause alive. . . .

Craig started a group called Free the Children. The board of directors meet Saturdays in Craig's den, which has become the command center. They are in daily contact, by phone or fax, with a host of international human rights groups.

Having always done his homework to keep up on the issue, Craig soon felt that homework isn't enough. He had to meet the children he was trying to help. . . . This prompted him to take a trip to Asia—a trip his parents were wholeheartedly against. . . . Craig's parents eventually found his cause so convincing that they . . . bought his plane ticket to travel halfway around the world. Chaperoned at each stop by local human rights advocates[2] and armed with a video camera, Craig went from Bangladesh to Thailand, and then to India, Nepal, and Pakistan.

---

1. **prestigious** (pres·tij′əs) *adj.*: much admired and sought after.
2. **advocates** (ad′və·kits) *n.*: supporters; defenders.

"The perception that I had was that child labor is all in the deep, dark back alleys, [where] no one can see it, beyond public scrutiny.[3] But the truth is, it's practiced in the open," Craig says. . . .

"One shop that I went into, I met one 8-year-old girl . . . [who] was just pulling apart syringes and needles, piece by piece, and putting them in buckets for their plastics. She wore no gloves, literally had no shoes. . . . All she was doing was squatting on the ground, surrounded by a pile of needles. They were from hospitals, from the street, from the garbage. We asked her, 'Don't you worry about AIDS and other diseases like that?' We got no response. She didn't know what they were." . . .

Craig spends a great deal of his time on the road, often alone. He is part of an individualized program that allows him to travel and keep up with his class work. . . . "I plan on going all the way through my Ph.D., so I'm going to be in school till I'm

40 or something," Craig says. "I hope to . . . study international conflict mediation.[4] I've had the chance to travel to Bosnia quite a bit . . . and areas of armed conflict . . . to see what war does. I want to be involved in helping stop wars before they begin." . . .

Craig has met his share of political leaders. . . . "It's great meeting with them. . . . They're all incredibly interesting people. I enjoyed meeting all of them, but they're still not the people who impress me the most." . . .

So who does impress this teenager?

"In Thailand, there was a young street girl, [to whom] I handed an orange. And she automatically took the orange, and she peeled it, and she broke it, and she shared it with her friends," Craig says. "Or a child I saw in India. He was crippled, so his friends were carrying him from place to place so he wouldn't be left behind. And to this day I'm convinced that if you took these children and put them in those positions of power, we would see this world truly be a different place."

—from *60 Minutes*

(Top) Craig Kielburger with the Dalai Lama in Stockholm, Sweden, in 2000.
(Above) Students at a school in Nicaragua that is sponsored by Free the Children.

3. **scrutiny** (skro͞ot′'n·ē) *n.:* close examination or study.
4. **mediation** (mē′·dē·ā′shən) *n.:* attempt to settle disputes by stepping in and trying to help.

Evaluating Evidence

One Child's Labor of Love

Test Practice

1. What **theme** is addressed in both "Baucis and Philemon" and "One Child's Labor of Love"?
   - **A** Generous people are rewarded.
   - **B** Slavery must be abolished worldwide.
   - **C** Good always triumphs over evil.
   - **D** People should try to help those in need.

2. Which of the following statements is an **opinion**?
   - **F** "I've had the chance to travel to Bosnia quite a bit . . . to see what war does."
   - **G** "He was crippled, so his friends were carrying him from place to place so he wouldn't be left behind."
   - **H** "I'm convinced that if you took these children and put them in those positions of power, we would see this world truly be a different place."
   - **J** "I plan on going all the way through my Ph.D. . . . ."

3. There is **adequate evidence** for the reader to conclude that Craig meets with political leaders to —
   - **A** talk with the people who have impressed or inspired him most
   - **B** complete an assignment for school
   - **C** bring the issue of children's rights to their attention
   - **D** have his picture taken with them

4. The author provides **adequate evidence** to support all of the following conclusions *except* —
   - **F** Craig Kielburger cares deeply about the rights of children
   - **G** Craig Kielburger is intolerant of child labor and slavery
   - **H** one teenager's actions can make a big difference in the world
   - **J** Craig Kielburger hopes to become famous and win awards

North Carolina Competency Goal
2.01; 3.01; 3.03; 5.01

Reading Skills
Evaluate evidence; distinguish between fact and opinion.

Constructed Response

1. The writer concludes that Craig Kielburger is intolerant of child labor and slavery, that he refuses to allow these wrongs to exist unchallenged. Find three examples of **appropriate evidence** that support this conclusion.

2. The author concludes that Craig Kielburger is "passionate" about his beliefs. Find three examples of **evidence** that support this conclusion about Craig's strong feelings.

The Homophones *Their, There,* and *They're*

Are you confused about when to use *their, there,* and *they're*? There are good reasons for mixing these words up. They're homophones (häm′ə·fōnz′)—words that are pronounced the same although their meanings are different.

their	there	they're
a pronoun—the possessive form of *they*	an adverb that means "in that place"	a contraction of *they are*
At first the directors held their meetings in Craig's den.	There in Bosnia he saw what war does.	"They're all incredibly interesting people."
	or	
	a word used with forms of the verb *to be,* usually at the beginning of a sentence	
	"In Thailand, there was a young street girl. . . ."	

PRACTICE

Copy the following sentences, and write the correct word—*their, there,* or *they're*—in each blank. If you have trouble, see if the words *they are* (for *they're*) fit. If they don't make sense, you know that *they're* is incorrect.

Then, ask yourself if the word is a possessive: Does it signify ownership? If it doesn't, you know that *their* is incorrect.

1. I enjoyed meeting all of them _____, but _____ not the ones who impress me the most.

2. I thought it was _____ in the dark back alleys.

3. _____ were several kids having _____ pictures taken with Craig.

For more help, see Glossary of Usage, Part 16, in the Language Handbook.

SKILLS FOCUS

Grammar Skills Understand homophones.

North Carolina Competency Goal 1.04; 2.01; 4.01; 4.02; 5.01

Comparing Literature

Literary Focus
Fairy Tales

When something wonderful happens, people sometimes describe it as "a fairy tale come true." Yet fairy tales are more than pleasant stories with happy endings. The events that lead up to the "happily ever after" endings are often filled with danger, violence, and cruelty.

Fairy tales are a form of folk literature—stories originally told by ordinary people and passed along orally (by word of mouth) from one generation to the next. Writers like the Grimm brothers collected such stories and wrote them down, but most fairy tales and other folk tales were around for centuries before anyone put them into writing.

Fairy tales are both entertaining and meaningful; they're the kinds of stories told to children at bedtime. Traditionally, they were often meant to teach children how to behave and to warn them about the dangers of the world in a way that would get their attention and amuse them. Most fairy tales contain a clear moral message or lesson about life.

Reading Skills and Strategies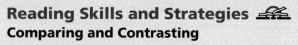
Comparing and Contrasting

You are about to compare and contrast two German fairy tales, "Rapunzel" and "Rumpelstiltskin." Both were first recorded by the Grimms in the 1800s. Read the stories once just for fun. Then, read them again, this time looking for similarities and differences between the two. Keep an eye out for familiar fairy tale character types.

> ### Elements of Fairy Tales
> - a happy ending
> - charms, spells, and other kinds of magic
> - disguises
> - seemingly impossible tasks
> - elements that occur in threes, such as wishes
> - an only child or the youngest child in a family as hero
> - the triumph of goodness and innocence over unfairness and evil
> - rooms with doors that can't be opened
> - difficult riddles
> - character types such as the beautiful princess, the handsome prince, the wicked witch, elves, and trolls

North Carolina Competency Goal
1.02

Literary Skills
Understand fairy tales.

Reading Skills
Compare and contrast fairy tales.

Before You Read

Think of some familiar fairy tale characters: the beautiful young girl, the handsome prince, the wicked witch. Unlike people in real life, these characters are either all good or all bad. They don't grow and change the way real people do. A character in a fairy tale may be a **symbol**—something that stands for both itself and something else. Often, a character stands for a quality such as love, patience, or greed. As you read "Rapunzel," notice which **character types** appear.

Rapunzel

retold by Neil Philip

There was once a man and a woman who longed in vain for a child. But at last it seemed as if God would answer their prayer.

From the window at the back of their house they could see a wonderful garden full of beautiful flowers and herbs. It was surrounded by a high wall, and no one dared go into it because it belonged to a powerful witch, and everyone was afraid of her. ❶

One day the wife was standing by this window and looking down into the garden, when she caught sight of a lovely bed of rapunzel, which is a kind of lettuce. It looked so fresh and green it made her mouth water. Her craving for the rapunzel grew every day. It was so frustrating to be able to see it but never to eat it that she began to waste away. When her husband saw her so pale and wan,[1] he asked, "What's wrong, darling?"

"Oh," she answered, "if I can't eat some of that rapunzel I shall die."

Her husband loved her, and he thought, *Sooner than let my wife die, I shall get her some of that rapunzel, whatever the cost.*

---

1. **wan** *adj.:* sickly; weak.

PREDICT

❶ Which common **character type** will play a role in the story? Do you think she will be good or bad? Explain.

PREDICT

❷ What price do you think the husband and wife will pay for taking the witch's rapunzel?

As dusk fell, he climbed over the wall into the witch's garden, snatched a handful of rapunzel, and took it to his wife. She made it into a salad straightaway and ate it greedily. It tasted good to her— so very good. The next day her craving was three times as great. It wouldn't let her rest. ❷

There was nothing for it. The husband had to go back to the witch's garden. At dusk, he climbed the wall again. But when he came down on the other side, he nearly jumped out of his skin. There stood the witch, right in front of him!

She glared at him. "How dare you sneak into my garden and steal my rapunzel! I'll make you wish you hadn't."

"Have mercy," he pleaded. "I had to do it. My wife saw the rapunzel from our window, and she felt such a craving for it that she would have died if she hadn't got some to eat."

The witch's face softened. "If that's the case, I will let you pick as much rapunzel as you like, on one condition. When your wife's baby is born, you must give it to me. I will look after it and love it like a mother."

The man was so frightened he would have agreed to anything. ❸

So when the baby was born, the witch came and took it away. It was a baby girl, and the witch called her Rapunzel.

Rapunzel grew into the most beautiful child under the sun. When she was twelve years old, the witch took her into the forest and shut her up in a tower that had neither stairs nor door, but only a little window right at the top. When the witch wanted to come in, she stood beneath it and called,

> *Rapunzel, Rapunzel,*
> *Let down your hair.*

Rapunzel had wonderful long hair, as fine as spun gold. When she heard the witch calling, she undid her braided tresses[2] and let them tumble all the way to the ground so that the witch could climb up them. ❹

A few years later, it happened that a prince was passing through the forest and rode by the tower. From it, he heard someone singing. It was Rapunzel, who often sang to herself. Her voice was so lovely and haunting that the prince stopped to listen. He wanted to climb up to her, but when he looked for the door to the tower, he could not find one. He rode away, but the singing had moved him so much that he came back every day to listen to it.

Once, when the prince was standing listening to Rapunzel's singing, the witch came. He heard her call,

> *Rapunzel, Rapunzel,*
> *Let down your hair.*

Then Rapunzel let down her tresses, and the witch climbed up to her.

Aha! he thought. *If that is the ladder by which I can climb up to her, then I will try my luck.* Next day, as dark fell, he went to the tower and called,

> *Rapunzel, Rapunzel,*
> *Let down your hair.*

---

2. **tresses** *n.:* long locks of hair.

Comparing Literature

EVALUATE

❸ Has the husband made a good bargain? Explain.

ANALYZE

❹ The witch seems to view Rapunzel as a possession. Think about the witch's attitude toward her garden and now toward Rapunzel. What quality might the witch stand for?

EVALUATE

❺ Why does Rapunzel agree to marry the prince, even though she has just met him? Do you think he is a good or a bad character? Explain.

ANALYZE

❻ In fairy tales, places and objects, as well as characters, can be **symbols**. What might the desert symbolize in "Rapunzel"?

The hair fell down, and he climbed up.

At first Rapunzel was terrified. She had never seen a man before. But the prince spoke so gently to her that she lost her fear. He said, "My heart was so moved by your singing that I could not rest. Please marry me."

He was so young and handsome, and Rapunzel thought he would love her more truly than the old witch. "Yes," she said. "I will marry you." And she gave him her hand. ❺

Then Rapunzel said, "But how will I ever get down? . . . I know. Every time you come, you must bring a skein³ of silk, and then I can make a ladder with it. When it's finished, I will climb down, and you can carry me off on your horse." They agreed that until that time, he should visit her every evening, for the old witch always came in the day.

The old witch suspected nothing, until one day Rapunzel wondered aloud, "Why are you so much heavier to pull up than the prince? He is up in a moment."

"You wicked child!" screeched the witch. "What did you say? I thought I had shut you away from the world, but you have tricked me!" She was so angry that she took a pair of scissors and cut off all Rapunzel's beautiful hair. *Snip-snap* went the scissors, and the lovely tresses fell to the floor. Then the pitiless witch sent Rapunzel into the desert to live in grief and want. ❻

That evening, the witch fastened the severed tresses to the window latch, and when the prince called,

> *Rapunzel, Rapunzel,*
> *Let down your hair,*

she let the hair down. The prince climbed up, but instead of his dear Rapunzel he found the witch, who fixed him with her evil eyes.

"Ah!" she said. "Your lovebird has flown. She is no longer singing in her nest. And she won't be singing anymore. The cat has taken her, and she'll scratch your eyes out too. You've lost Rapunzel. You'll never see her again."

The prince was in an agony of grief. In despair he leaped from the tower. His fall was broken by brambles,⁴ but the thorns scratched his eyes and left him blind.

---

3. **skein** (skān) *n.:* length of loosely wound thread or yarn.
4. **brambles** *n.:* prickly shrubs or vines.

7 Even though Rapunzel has been banished and the prince has been blinded, they still manage to find each other. What message about love does this story convey? What does it suggest about greed and cruelty?

The prince wandered blindly through the forest, living on roots and berries, and weeping and wailing over the loss of his dear wife.

He wandered in misery like this for several years, until at last he came to the desert where Rapunzel was living a wretched existence. He heard a voice that seemed familiar, and approached it. Rapunzel recognized him at once and flung herself weeping around his neck.

Two of Rapunzel's tears fell on his eyes, and gave him back his sight.

He took her back to his kingdom. They were welcomed with great rejoicing and lived happily together for many years to come. **7**

First Thoughts

1. Finish these sentences:

- This story made me feel . . .
- The most frightening part of this story is . . .

Thinking Critically

2. Why do you think the witch locks Rapunzel up in the tower?

3. The wife's craving for rapunzel is a kind of greed. What occurs as a result of her greed?

4. Fairy tales were often told to teach children lessons about life. Explain the lesson that this story presents.

5. Look back at the list of elements of fairy tales on page 270. Which elements can you find in "Rapunzel"? List two or three.

Reading Check

Check your comprehension by **retelling** "Rapunzel" to a partner. Start with the title, main characters, and setting. Next, state what the conflict or problem is. Then, sum up the main events in the order in which they occur. Be sure to describe the climax (the most suspenseful moment in the story). Finally, explain how the conflict is resolved. Have your partner use a Retelling Checklist (see page 17) to give you feedback on your retelling.

Comparing Literature

6. Comparing "Rapunzel" with "Rumpelstiltskin" will help you understand the elements of fairy tales. Use a chart like the one below to organize your thoughts. You can fill in the second column of this chart on page 281, after you read "Rumpelstiltskin."

Comparing Fairy Tales		
	"Rapunzel"	"Rumpelstiltskin"
Characters		
Plot		
Ending		
Theme		

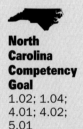

North Carolina Competency Goal
1.02; 1.04; 4.01; 4.02; 5.01

SKILLS FOCUS

Literary Skills
Analyze fairy tales.

Reading Skills
Compare and contrast fairy tales.

Before You Read

If you were to rewrite your favorite fairy tale, would you give it a different ending? In this version of "Rumpelstiltskin," the writer gives the story a modern ending. Do you know the traditional version of this fairy tale? If not, try to guess how it ends. If you do know the story, look for differences between this version and the original.

Rumpelstiltskin

Rosemarie Künzler, *translated by Jack Zipes*

After the miller had boasted that his daughter could spin straw into gold, the king led the girl into a room filled with straw and said, "If you don't spin this straw into gold by tomorrow morning, you must die." ❶

Then he locked the door behind him. The poor miller's daughter was scared and began to cry. Suddenly a little man appeared and asked, "What will you give me if I spin the straw into gold for you?"

After the girl gave him her necklace, the little man sat down at the spinning wheel, and *whiz, whiz, whiz,* three times the wheel went round, and soon the spool was full and had to be replaced. And so it went until morning. By then all the straw had been spun into gold. ❷

When the king saw this, he was pleased. He immediately brought the miller's daughter to a larger room, also filled with straw, and ordered her again to spin the straw into gold by morning if she valued her life. And again the miller's daughter cried until the little man appeared. This time she gave him the ring from her finger. The little man began to make the wheel whiz, and by morning all the straw was spun into gold. ❸

ANALYZE

❶ What problem does the girl face? Is it the kind of problem you might find in a realistic story? Why or why not?

ANALYZE

❷ How does the little man help the miller's daughter? Look back at the list on page 270. Which typical elements of a fairy tale can you identify in this part of the story?

COMPARE AND CONTRAST

❸ How is the king similar to the witch in "Rapunzel"?

PREDICT

❹ The little man makes the same demand as the witch in "Rapunzel," but he gets a very different response. What do you think he will do?

COMPARE AND CONTRAST

❺ In the original tale the miller's daughter marries the king after promising her first-born child to the little man. When she has her baby, the little man comes to claim it, and the miller's daughter must guess his name in order to keep her child. Which version of "Rumpelstiltskin" is more similar to "Rapunzel"? Explain.

When the king saw the gold, he was overjoyed. But he was still not satisfied. He led the miller's daughter into an even larger room and said, "If you spin this straw into gold by tomorrow, you shall become my wife."

When the girl was alone, the little man appeared for the third time and asked, "What will you give me if I help you?"

But the miller's daughter had nothing to give away.

"Then promise to give me your first child when you become queen."

These words jolted her and finally made her open her eyes.

"You're crazy!" the miller's daughter yelled. "I'll never marry this horrible king. I'd never give my child away." ❹

"I'm not going to spin. I'll never spin again!" the little man screamed in rage. "I've spun in vain!"

The little man stamped with his right foot so ferociously that it went deep into the ground and jarred the door to the room open. Then the miller's daughter ran out into the great wide world and was saved. ❺

First Thoughts

1. Respond to "Rumpelstiltskin" by completing one or both of the following sentences:
   - The strangest part of this fairy tale was . . .
   - I thought the ending of this fairy tale was . . .

Thinking Critically

2. Which people in this fairy tale represent the **character types** listed below?
   - the beautiful princess
   - the elf or troll

   Is there a traditional handsome young prince in this tale? Explain.

3. In a traditional fairy tale the maiden and the prince are married at the end and live happily ever after. Why do you think the author of this version of "Rumpelstiltskin" has ended the story differently? Would you call this new ending a happy ending? Explain.

4. How would you state the **theme** or message of this fairy tale?

Comparing Literature

5. Comparing "Rapunzel" with "Rumpelstiltskin" will help you understand fairy tales. Use the chart below to organize your thoughts. Now that you have read "Rumpelstiltskin," you can fill in the second column of the chart.

Reading Check

To check your comprehension, fill in a story map like the one below for "Rumpelstiltskin."

Title:	
Author:	
Characters:	
Conflict:	
Resolution:	
Setting:	

North Carolina Competency Goal
1.02; 5.01; 5.02

Literary Skills
Analyze fairy tales.

Reading Skills
Compare and contrast fairy tales.

Comparing Fairy Tales		
	"Rapunzel"	"Rumpelstiltskin"
Characters		
Plot		
Ending		
Theme		

Assignment

1. Write a Comparison-Contrast Essay

Write a short essay comparing "Rapunzel" and "Rumpelstiltskin." Before you begin planning your essay, review the chart you filled in after you read the stories. In your essay, focus on one or two elements that interest you and that are very similar or different in the stories. For example, you might want to compare the heroines of the stories, Rapunzel and the miller's daughter, or the lessons each story teaches about life.

Make sure your essay has an introduction, a body, and a conclusion. In your conclusion, state which story you prefer and explain why. Which story did you enjoy more? Which story challenged you more? Use examples from the stories to support your responses.

Use the workshop on writing a **comparison-contrast essay,** pages 404–409, for help with this assignment.

Assignment

2. Write a Modern Fairy Tale

Write a modern version of an old fairy tale— "Cinderella," "Snow White," "Rapunzel," or another fairy tale you know. Consider the theme, or message, of this fairy tale. How would you update the message for a modern audience? As necessary, change elements of the story, including the ending, to convey this message. Share your updated fairy tale with a group or the entire class in an oral presentation. Ask for feedback on the ending, and use any helpful comments to revise your tale.

Assignment

3. Present an Oral Report

Do some research on fairy tales from a non-European culture or tradition. Here are some ideas:

- "Yeh-shen" or "Mulan" (China)
- "The Crane Wife" (Japan)
- "Sinbad the Sailor" from *The Arabian Nights* (India and Persia)

Using your research, prepare an oral report for the class. Make sure to discuss what you see as the story's theme in your report. As part of your presentation, retell one of the tales. Use your voice to give life to the different characters.

North Carolina Competency Goal
1.02; 1.04; 4.01; 4.02; 5.01

SKILLS FOCUS

Writing Skills
Write a comparison-contrast essay; write a modern fairy tale.

Speaking and Listening Skills
Present an oral report.

KING Long Shanks

Jane Yolen

King Long Shanks had very good legs and was a nice shade of green. Everyone said so. So it had to be true.

The cook said it.
The gardener said it.
The butler, maid, and doorman said it.
The lords-in-waiting said it.
And the two visiting tailors said it, too. Not once but many times.
"Fine legs," said the small tailor.
"Fine long legs," said the tall tailor.
"Fine long strong legs," they said together. "And a very nice shade of green."

So when the two tailors added, "We have just the thing to show off those fine long strong legs, Your Majesty," King Long Shanks ordered: "Tell me."

So they did. The small tailor stretched very high (to make himself taller). And the tall tailor squatted very low (to make himself smaller). Then they whispered simultaneously and at the same time in King Long Shanks' ears.

> The cloth is green,
> The cloth is blue,

The very shade
That's right for you.

The cloth is blue,
The cloth is red,
To match the jewel
Inside your head.

The cloth is red,
The cloth is gold,
And only the true
     and good
     and honest
     and smart
     and loyal
Can it behold.

"What do you mean?" roared King Long Shanks. He was not fond
of poetry, especially poetry that bumped in the wrong places and
pretended to mean much more than it did. It made him go all
cranky. "How can there be a cloth that is green and blue and red and
gold? How can it match my head and the jewel inside it? How did
you know about that jewel, anyway? It's a family secret."

He had many questions.

The tailors had many answers.

"It's a plaid cloth, sire," they said.

"It's a magic plaid cloth, sire," they said.

"It's a mysterious magic plaid cloth, sire," they said.

"And besides," they said, "it's very expensive."

Now, King Long Shanks did not know a lot about fashion, but he
did know that expense was a good part of it.

"Show me," he ordered.

So the two tailors held their hands out, first wide apart, then
close together. "What do you think?" they asked.

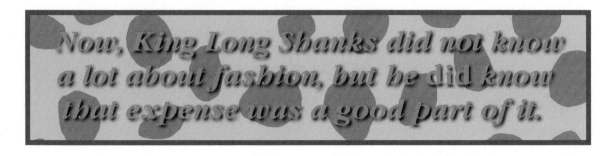

Now, King Long Shanks did not know a lot about fashion, but he did know that expense was a good part of it.

Since there appeared to be nothing between their hands but air, King Long Shanks did not know *what* to think. So he did what he always did when he wanted to pretend he understood something and didn't. He looked at the ceiling, hummed his favorite pond tune, and waited for a passing fly.

KA–ZAAAACK! He caught the fly with his tongue, then looked back at the tailors with a seriously informed expression.

"It's an *invisible* plaid cloth," said the tall tailor.

"Only someone who is true, good, honest, and smart can see the cloth," added the small tailor.

"And loyal," reminded the tall tailor.

"No one can question *my* loyalty," said King Long Shanks, "since it is loyalty to me."

"No one does," the tailors said quickly. "But the cloth is a sure way to check on the rest of the kingdom."

King Long Shanks swallowed the fly. "Then I will want a complete outfit," he said. He touched the air between the tailors, as if feeling a piece of cloth. "Lovely color." Then he turned on his fine long strong legs and leaped away.

The tailors spent many hours sewing their invisible cloth. The small tailor sewed large stitches. The tall tailor sewed tiny stitches. They cut and shaped and measured and cut again.

"Mother," said the princess one day as she watched them work, "there is nothing there. No cloth, no coat, no . . ."

"Hush," said the queen, "or your father will think you disloyal. Eat your flies."

"Mother," said the prince, "there really *is* nothing there. No pants, no socks, no . . ."

"Double hush," said the queen. "Loyalty begins at home. Your bugs are getting cold."

And because the queen and the princess and the prince said nothing, no one else said anything at all. Not the cook. Not the gardener. Not the butler, maid, or doorman. Not the lords-in-waiting.

And certainly not the tailors, who were, after all, being paid for their work.

Since no one said anything, King Long Shanks believed what he wanted to believe. Or needed to believe. Or thought he believed. Except for once, when he asked, "Are you *sure* that cloth is . . . well . . . right for me?"

The small tailor stretched himself very high (to make himself taller). And the tall tailor squatted very low (to make himself smaller). Then they whispered simultaneously and at the same time in King Long Shanks' ears.

> The cloth is short,
> The cloth is long,
> For you it's right,
> Another—wrong.
>
> The cloth is narrow,
> The cloth is wide,
> So you can wear
> Your clothes with pride.
>
> The cloth is thick,
> The cloth is thin,
> And only the true
> > and good
> > and honest
> > and smart
> > and loyal—

"I know, I know," interrupted King Long Shanks because he hated their poetry, and besides he didn't want them to suspect he couldn't see anything. KA–ZAAAACK! He ate another fly hastily and felt exceedingly cranky.

"You know everything, sire," said the small tailor.

"That's why you get the big bucks, Your Majesty," said the tall tailor.

And then they smiled simultaneously and at the same time. It was not a pretty sight.

And so the tailors continued to sew on an invisible cloth that no one dared say was not there for fear of being thought a ninny, a nonny, a numbskull, or a nincompoop. And disloyal besides.

Days went by. Weeks even. And at last it was time for the Summer Parade, when lily pads opened their big broad petals and the air fair hummed with insects.

King Long Shanks called the tailors to his throne room. "Will my new outfit be ready for the big parade?" he asked.

"That is exactly what we have been aiming for, sire," said the small tailor.

"We will sew you into it ourselves," the tall tailor added.

"For all your loyal subjects to see," they said together.

And on the morning of the parade, the two tailors, their hands full of the invisible cloth, dressed the king themselves.

First they put on his invisible shirt.

Then his invisible shorts.

Then his invisible jacket and cloak and socks and shoes.

"We have a hat as well, Your Majesty," they said.

"I will wear my crown," King Long Shanks said. "So my loyal subjects will know me."

They brought him the royal mirror.

King Long Shanks stared and stared.

"Toadally majestic," said the tall tailor.

"Ribeting," said the small tailor.

And they laughed secretly behind their hands simultaneously and at the same time.

King Long Shanks did not notice them laugh. He was too busy staring.

"The mirror cannot, of course, show you how wonderful the outfit is," said the small tailor.

"After all," added the tall tailor, "a mirror is not true or good or honest or smart."

"Or loyal," they said together.

"Well, at least you are right about one thing," said King Long Shanks, glancing at his reflection one last time.

"We are?" they asked.

"This outfit certainly shows off my fine long strong legs." He turned, went down the hall and

out into the courtyard, where the Summer Parade was about to begin.

The queen and prince and princess were waiting there, dressed in their finery. The cook and the gardener were there as well. And so were the butler, maid, and doorman, and all the lords-in-waiting. And round them were the guards from the guardhouse, the soldiers from the armory, the townsfolk and farmfolk and the folk who tended the woods. In fact, everyone from the entire kingdom was there, waiting to walk in the parade that wound down from the palace to the pond, where the king would declare the opening of Summer.

Only the two tailors were missing. They had already collected their pay and were well on their way to the next kingdom.

There was a murmur when King Long Shanks appeared, dressed in his invisible clothes. But the queen had warned them all. And since they were all really terribly loyal to their king, the parade started with not one comment.

The parade was halfway to the pond when a little tad spoke up. "Mama," she said. "Papa—look at the king. He has no . . ."

"Hush!" her mama and papa said.

They were three-fourths of the way to the pond when the tad spoke up again. "But Mama, but Papa, really, King Long Shanks has no . . ."

"Hush!" said her mama and papa and her brothers and sisters and cousins. "Hush! We are loyal to our king."

They were all the way down to the pond when the tad spoke again, in a voice the waters carried. "Mama, Papa, brothers and sisters and cousins—King Long Shanks is bare! His fine long strong legs and—*everything*!"

Just then a breeze rippled the pond and it looked like all the lily pads were laughing. That set the child and her brothers and sisters and cousins and mama and papa—and finally the woodfolk and farmfolk and townsfolk—to grinning. And *that* set the soldiers from the armory, the guards from the guardhouse, the

butler and maid and doorman to giggling. And *that* set the cook and gardener to guffawing. And *that* made the prince and princess collapse in the green grass in hysterics.

Only the queen was somber. Silently she tore off a piece of her own beautiful gown and covered King Long Shanks with it, for she was the most loyal one of them all.

As to the tailors, they never entered *that* particular kingdom again with their magic cloth. But they played their same trick on one hundred and one other kings and emperors around the world. You may have heard of them.

However, none of those one hundred and one other kings and emperors had legs nearly as good or fine or long or strong—or green—as King Long Shanks. Of that I am sure.

MORAL
True loyalty cannot be measured as simply as cloth. But it covers a lot more than legs.

Meet the Writer

Jane Yolen

Jane Yolen (1939–   ) was born and raised in New York City and now resides in Massachusetts. A poet, songwriter, and professional storyteller, Yolen has written more than two hundred books for children, young adults, and adults.

Like *King Long Shanks,* many of Yolen's books were inspired by the traditional tales that she loved to read as a child. *Newsweek* magazine has called Yolen "the Hans Christian Andersen of America"; the *New York Times* has described her as a modern Aesop.

Yolen's work has been translated into fourteen languages. She has won dozens of awards for her writing, including the Regina Medal, the Christopher Medal, and the Daedalus award. According to Yolen, however, "awards just sit on the shelf gathering dust. The best awards are when children love my books."

Writing Workshop

Assignment

Write a narrative about an experience you've had.

Audience

Your teacher, classmates, friends, or family.

RUBRIC
Evaluation Criteria

A good personal narrative

1. concerns a single incident

2. has an opening that grabs the reader's attention

3. relates events in a clear order

4. includes sensory details

5. includes all necessary background information

6. explains what the incident means to the writer

NARRATIVE WRITING
Personal Narrative

In a **personal narrative** you bring an experience or memory to life by sharing a true story about yourself. A personal narrative often deals with an important experience that taught you something about yourself or others. Like a short story, a personal narrative includes a setting, a plot, a point of view, and characters. It may also contain dialogue.

Prewriting

1 Choosing a Subject

Read and think about the following **prompt:**

> Life is often compared to a stage and people to the actors in a drama. Think about the different "scenes" in the drama of your life. Try to remember one important episode that still has special meaning for you. Tell the story of what happened. Include your thoughts and feelings, and explain why this experience is meaningful to you.

To spark memories, make cluster maps for words that name feelings, such as *anger, joy, pride, fear,* and *surprise.* Around each word, jot down notes about personal experiences that gave you that feeling. See the example on the next page.

A time line of your life may also help you find a topic. Draw a line, and label the left end *Birth* and the right end *Now.* Above the line, write down the major events in your

PEANUTS reprinted by permission of United Feature Syndicate, Inc.

North Carolina Competency Goal
1.01

life, such as the birth of a sibling or a move to a new home. One of these may become your topic.

Birth ⟶ Now

From your ideas, choose a topic that meets these criteria:

- I'm willing to share this experience with others.
- I remember a lot about this incident.
- This incident means something important to me.

2 Explaining the Importance of the Experience

Jot down a few notes on why this incident is important to you. This kind of explanation usually comes near the end of a personal narrative. For example, look at the conclusion of the student model on page 295.

File your notes away, and pull them out after you write about the incident. You might want to change your explanation at that point.

Drafting

1 Writing Your First Draft

You'll recall details of your experience as you write your draft. To get started, jot down answers to the *5W-How?* questions: *who? what? when? where? why?* and *how?* To be sure that you remember details clearly, you might create a time line showing events in order.

2 Organizing the Details

Fill in a framework like the one on the next page to guide you in organizing your details. A writer's framework usually includes an **introduction,** a **body,** and a **conclusion.** Grab your audience's attention with an interesting opening. In your conclusion, state what the experience meant to you.

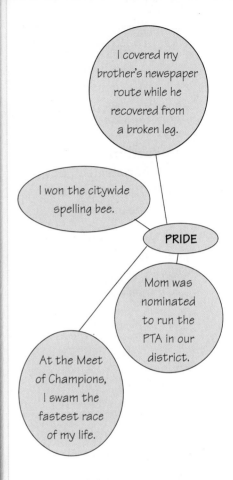

I covered my brother's newspaper route while he recovered from a broken leg.

I won the citywide spelling bee.

PRIDE

Mom was nominated to run the PTA in our district.

At the Meet of Champions, I swam the fastest race of my life.

Brainstorming for Ideas

- Examine souvenirs, photographs, and letters.
- Ask your family and friends to recall stories about you.
- Think about holidays, birthdays, and other special celebrations.
- Remember the first time you did something.

Framework for a Personal Narrative

What the experience means to me: _____
_____

Introduction (dialogue, question, statement, or description that grabs the reader's attention): _____
_____

Body (description of events in the order in which they happened):

1. _____
2. _____
3. _____
4. _____

Conclusion (statement explaining the importance of the experience): _____
_____

Writing Tips

The events in a personal narrative are usually told in **chronological (time) order.** You can also start with the most important moment and tell the rest in **flashback.** Another option is to **compare and contrast** aspects of your experience, such as the good and bad parts.

3 **Elaborating**

Use the strategies shown on page 295 to find vivid details to add to your essay. Replay the incident in your mind. Recall the names of people and places as well as bits of dialogue (spoken words). Try to remember how people—including you—looked, sounded, and moved. Record these actions and sensory details.

How did you feel during the incident? You might try acting it out.

If possible, talk to others who were involved in the incident. Their memories may help you recall more details.

4 **Using Dialogue**

If you use dialogue, it should sound the way people really talk. Here are some lines of dialogue from "The All-American Slurp" (page 234).

> **"Do you always slurp when you eat a milkshake?" I asked, before I could stop myself.**
>
> **Meg grinned. "Sure. All Americans slurp."**

Even though you avoid slang and sentence fragments in formal writing, you may want to use them in your personal narrative to make your writing sound more natural. See Quotation Marks, 13b–j, in the Language Handbook to review the rules for punctuating dialogue.

5 **Keeping a Consistent Point of View**

Use the first-person pronouns, such as *I, me,* and *my,* when talking about yourself. Use your natural voice—the words and phrases you would use when telling the story to your friends.

Student Model

The Swim of My Life

It was a typical Houston day in the summer, hot and humid. The insects kept buzzing in my ears, and sweat dripped down

Sensory details grab our attention.

my forehead like ice cream melting and running down a cone. I got to splash into the water, but, although it felt good, I couldn't swim for fun. This was the Meet of Champions, and I had to show my opponents what I was made of. I had six chances to place and swim for a medal. Every time I jumped into the water, I had to swim to my fullest extent. Stroke after stroke was stronger and stronger. It was a race against the clock.

The writer gives background information about the incident.

After a swim I would jump out of the water soaking wet, look around, and check with my coach to see if I had placed. Two out of six times I had placed. I was so excited I could barely hold it all in.

She presents details in time order.

I was sitting on the ready bench waiting nervously to swim. I would be swimming the stroke that was my natural stroke, breast stroke. I had so many butterflies in my stomach I thought they were having a family reunion!

She describes her feelings of excitement and nervousness.

"All thirteen–fourteen girl breast-strokers to the edge of the pool!" the monotonous voice of the intercom spoke out. I was shaking from nervousness.

"Down and ready," the gunsman yelled, and then the shot was fired. In I jumped. I swam the fastest swim of my life. I was a dolphin, and the water was my home. I touched the wall third and had broken my record!

Details of the incident, including actual words spoken, make us feel as if we were at the scene.

Victory at last!

The writer reveals the importance of the incident.

—Lacey Clayton
West Memorial Junior High School
Katy, Texas

Strategies for Elaboration

Help your readers share your experience by including sensory details in your narrative. To find details, complete these statements:

- I saw . . .
- I heard . . .
- I smelled . . .
- I tasted . . .
- I felt . . .

Writing Tip

Transitional Expressions

To show the order of events clearly, use transitional words and phrases, such as *first*, *afterward*, *next*, *finally*, and *at last*.

INTERNET

More Writer's Models
Keyword: LE5 6-3

Evaluating and Revising

Use the following chart to evaluate and revise your personal narrative.

Personal Narrative: Content and Organization Guidelines		
Evaluation Questions	▶ **Tips**	▶ **Revision Techniques**
❶ Does your introduction grab the reader's attention and set the scene?	▶ **Put stars** next to interesting or surprising details. **Circle** details that reveal the setting.	▶ **Add** a catchy quotation or statement to the introduction. **Add** details that reveal when and where the event took place.
❷ Have you arranged events in a clear order?	▶ **Number** the events as they appear in the essay. Make sure that this sequence matches the actual order of events.	▶ **Rearrange** events to put them in the correct order, if necessary. **Add** transitional words to link events.
❸ Is the point of view consistent throughout your narrative?	▶ **Draw a box** around third-person pronouns, such as *he*, *she*, and *themselves*. Make sure that these pronouns do not refer to you.	▶ **Use** first-person pronouns, such as *I*, *we*, and *my*, to talk about yourself.
❹ Have you included details that make people, places, and events come to life?	▶ **Highlight** details that appeal to the senses. In the margin, **note** which of the senses are involved.	▶ **Elaborate** with dialogue or sensory details. **Delete** any irrelevant details.
❺ Have you included your thoughts and feelings?	▶ **Put a check mark** next to statements of your feelings or thoughts.	▶ **Add** any other thoughts and feelings you have about what happened.
❻ Does your conclusion explain why the experience is important?	▶ **Underline** the statement that reveals the importance of the experience.	▶ If necessary, **add** a clear statement explaining why the experience was important.

A revised portion of a personal narrative appears on the next page.
Read the passage; then, answer the questions that follow.

Revision Model

I stood at the doorway of the band-rehearsal room. ̂, ~~I kept~~

~~looking at the empty chairs and instrument cases.~~ ~~I~~

~~wondered what the band would be playing at the parade next~~

~~month.~~ I was waiting to be interviewed by the head of the

school
̂ music department for a place in the band. ^*Soon* Mrs. Allen,

beaming at me, appeared and motioned me into the room.

nervously
I sat down and ̂ waited for the questions to begin.

Are/sure you
"So," Mrs. Allen said kindly, " ^ you ^ want to join the band

as a snare drummer? We don't have any girls in the

percussion section." ̂

"I'd like to be the first," I responded. ⟨She looked at me

quizzically.⟩

Evaluating the Revision

1. Where has the writer added modifiers? Do they improve the narrative? Explain.

2. Do you agree with the writer's deletions? Explain why or why not.

3. Where has the writer rearranged text? Has she made her writing clearer? Explain.

PROOFREADING

TIPS

Proofread carefully, marking errors in spelling, punctuation, and grammar. Then, exchange papers with another student. If you're working on a computer, use the spellchecker and grammar checker.

**Communications
Handbook
H E L P**

See Proofreaders' Marks.

PUBLISHING

TIPS

- *Create a bulletin board display. Include photos, drawings, souvenirs, and other related items with your writing.*

- *Arrange for a story hour in the school library, and read your narrative to other students.*

- *Send your work to a magazine that publishes student writing, such as Merlyn's Pen or Stone Soup. Directions for submitting work can be found in the front of the magazine.*

Test Practice

DIRECTIONS: Read the following folk tale. Then, answer each question that follows.

Little Mangy One

Lebanese folk tale, retold by Inea Bushnaq

Once upon a time three little goats were grazing on the side of a stony hill. Their names were Siksik, Mikmik, and Jureybon, the Little Mangy One. Soon a hyena scented them and loped up. "Siksik!" called the hyena. "Yes sir!" answered the goat. "What are those points sticking out of your head?" "Those are my little horns, sir," said the goat. "What is that patch on your back?" continued the hyena. "That is my hair, sir," replied the goat. "Why are you shivering?" roared the hyena. "Because I am afraid of you, sir," said the goat. At this the hyena sprang and gobbled him right up. Next the hyena turned to Mikmik, who answered like his brother, and he too was quickly devoured.

Then the hyena approached Jureybon, the Little Mangy One. Before the hyena came within earshot, Jureybon began to snort. As the hyena drew nearer, Jureybon bellowed, "May a plague lay low your back, O cursed one! What have you come for?" "I wish to know what the two points on your head are," said the hyena. "Those? Why, those are my trusty sabers!" said the goat. "And the patch on your back, what is that?" said the hyena. "My sturdy shield, of course!" sneered the goat. "Then why are you shivering?" asked the hyena. "Shivering? I'm trembling with rage! I'm shaking with impatience, for I cannot wait to throttle you and squeeze your very soul till it starts out of your eye sockets!" snarled the goat, and began to advance on the hyena.

The hyena's heart stopped beating for an instant; then he turned and ran for his life. But Jureybon sprang after him over the rocks and gored him with his sharp little horns, slitting open his belly and freeing his two little brothers inside.

North Carolina Competency Goal 1.02; 5.01

Literary Skills Identify and analyze theme.

1. Unlike Siksik and Mikmik, Jureybon responds to the hyena by —

   A running away

   B refusing to talk to him

   C attacking him

   D answering all of his questions

2. The words Jureybon uses to describe his horns and the patch on his back suggest images of —

   F strength

   G anger

   H hunger

   J fear

3. What is the **conflict** in this story?

   A A hyena tries to eat three goats.

   B Three goats are arguing among themselves.

   C Three goats try to kill a hyena.

   D A hyena is trying to find his way home.

4. The first paragraph contains a context clue you can use to figure out the meaning of devoured. Which group of words helps you understand *devoured*?

   F "gobbled him right up"

   G "the hyena sprang"

   H "I am afraid of you"

   J "turned to Mikmik"

Constructed Response

5. In your opinion, what is the **theme** of "Little Mangy One"? What does the story have to say about cleverness versus size and strength?

Test Practice

DIRECTIONS: Read the article. Then, answer each question that follows.

Too Much TV Can Equal Too Much Weight

by Jamie Rodgers, 12 years old

Children's Express

In 1970, only 10 percent of kids in America were overweight. In the 1980s, it was 30 percent, and in the 1990s, it was 60 percent. Studies show that obesity is linked to watching TV and using the Internet.

Children's Express interviewed two professors from Johns Hopkins University School of Medicine about the link. Ross Andersen, M.D., is with the weight management center, and Carlos Crespo, M.D., is an assistant professor of health and fitness.

"Dr. Crespo and I have published a study that appeared in the *Journal of the American Medical Association*. We looked at how fat kids were in relation to the number of hours of television they watch per day," said Andersen. "We found that kids who are low TV watchers were much leaner. The kids who were the fattest were those who watched a lot of TV. We defined a lot as four or more hours per day. Roughly, one in three kids in America is watching four or more hours per day. I would estimate sitting in front of a computer would be just as great a risk factor for being overweight."

Andersen and Crespo say the blame is not just on the parents. Sometimes it's a lack of places to play.

"[It's a] lack of facilities, services for the children to be able to go out and play basketball or go to a swimming pool. The community should have open spaces and safe spaces for girls and boys to be active," said Crespo.

"The thing is not that it's bad to watch TV; it's just that you need to have a balance. There [is] a certain number of hours in the day you're supposed to sleep, do your homework, . . . [and] go to school, and then there is a certain

North Carolina Competency Goal
2.01

Reading Skills
Evaluate a writer's conclusions.

[number] of hours that you're free to do whatever you want. If you spend that time watching TV, then you spend less time doing physical activity.". . .

"Kids and parents need to look for opportunities to remain physically active. So instead of sitting down to watch *Who Wants to Be a Millionaire,* it may be that the whole family could get up and go for a walk.". . .

1. What percentage of American children were overweight during the 1990s?
   A   10
   B   20
   C   40
   D   60

2. Studies show that obesity is linked to watching TV and —
   F   going for walks
   G   doing homework
   H   using the Internet
   J   taking long naps

3. Which of the following statements is *not* true?
   A   The author uses quotations to support her conclusions.
   B   The author uses statistics to support her conclusions.
   C   The author uses experts' opinions to support her conclusions.
   D   The author does not provide adequate support for her conclusions.

4. The doctors define "a lot of TV" as —
   F   one or more hours per day
   G   two or more hours per day
   H   three or more hours per day
   J   four or more hours per day

5. Andersen and Crespo place part of the blame for overweight in children on —
   A   lack of playgrounds
   B   poor health education
   C   lack of medical attention
   D   fast foods

6. The doctors believe that children and parents should —
   F   prepare meals together
   G   remain physically active
   H   watch TV together
   J   surf the Internet

Constructed Response
7. What **conclusion** does the author draw about children and obesity? How does she think obesity can be prevented?

Collection 3: Skills Review
Vocabulary Skills

Test Practice

Context Clues

DIRECTIONS: Use **context clues** to determine the meaning of the underlined words in each of the following sentences.

1. I can't believe you have the audacity to show up fifteen minutes late when I asked you to be on time. And you're eating an ice-cream cone! *Audacity* means —
   A decency
   B boldness
   C willpower
   D intelligence

2. Joe was mortified when his pants split as he sat down. *Mortified* means —
   F pleased
   G offended
   H embarrassed
   J frightened

3. I've seen earthquakes cause quite a bit of damage, but this one was truly devastating. *Devastating* means —
   A destructive
   B interesting
   C fulfilling
   D disappointing

4. Jack claims he can't pay his rent, yet he spends money lavishly on expensive gifts for his friends. *Lavishly* means —
   F generously
   G unhappily
   H foolishly
   J intelligently

5. Since he was wearing his velvet cape and neon jumpsuit, I assumed James wished to make a spectacle of himself. *Spectacle* means —
   A warrior
   B display
   C mockery
   D mannequin

6. Our school doesn't win state championships too often, so I'm really going to savor the victory parade. *Savor* means —
   F ruin
   G ignore
   H remember
   J enjoy

7. The fact that he started eating before everyone had been served shows that he's not concerned about etiquette. *Etiquette* means —
   A clothing
   B criticism
   C manners
   D regulations

8. After the fire alarm sounded, the residents were evacuated from the building. *Evacuated* means —
   F cared for
   G forgotten
   H removed
   J misplaced

North Carolina Competency Goal
6.01

SKILLS FOCUS

Vocabulary Skills
Use context clues.

Collection 3: Skills Review

Writing Skills

DIRECTIONS: Read the following paragraph from a personal narrative. Then, answer each question that follows.

(1) I nearly drowned at the age of five when some wise guy pushed me into the deep end of a pool. (2) Luckily, a lifeguard fished me out before I had inhaled too much water. Because of that incident, I grew up terrified of the water. (3) The technical name for this fear is hydrophobia. (4) While my friends ducked one another in the deep end of the pool, I'd splash around in the shallow end with the toddlers. (5) Pretty soon, I refused to go to the beach, the lake, or the pool because I was ashamed to be called a "scaredy cat." (6) Finally, in fifth grade, I signed up for swimming lessons. (7) I went to a pool in a neighboring town so that no one I knew would see me. (8) To my great relief, I discovered that I wasn't alone. (9) In my class were several adults, two teenage girls, and a boy my own age. (10) I felt a glimmer of hope that I might succeed.

1. The body of this personal narrative will probably deal with —
   A the narrator's friendship with other students in the class
   B a description of swimming strokes
   C the narrator's struggle to overcome the fear of water
   D the narrator's achievements as a champion swimmer

2. The writer uses informal language, or slang, in —
   F sentence 1
   G sentence 2
   H sentence 5
   J all of the above

3. Which sentence is not needed and should be deleted?
   A sentence 3
   B sentence 5
   C sentence 6
   D sentence 9

4. The writer uses transitional expressions in all of the following *except* —
   F sentence 2
   G sentence 5
   H sentence 6
   J sentence 10

5. If you were listening to an oral narrative of this story, you would expect the tone to be —
   A funny
   B serious
   C light and breezy
   D hopelessly sad

6. All of the following titles might be appropriate for the narrative *except* —
   F Getting In over My Head
   G Facing My Fear
   H Swim Team Captain
   J Learning to Swim

North Carolina Competency Goal
1.01

SKILLS FOCUS

Writing Skills
Analyze a personal narrative.

Fiction

Windows of Opportunity

Have you ever wondered what your first job will be like? Maybe you've had a few odd jobs already. If so, you may see yourself in *Help Wanted,* a collection of twelve quirky short stories about young people at work. In this anthology, compiled by Anita Silvey, you'll meet a former child actress who finds truth in the La Brea Tar Pits, a young secretary whose typewriter has a mind of its own, and a teen who gets a little help in the fast-food business from her aunt Edna.

"How Glad I Am to Be Alive!"

In Paul Zindel's novel *The Pigman,* John and Lorraine befriend Mr. Pignati, a lonely widower with a weakness for bad jokes and miniature pigs and a passion for life. This unlikely hero becomes a model of joy, freedom, and courage for John and Lorraine. Then tragedy tears the Pigman away. In the sequel, *The Pigman's Legacy,* John and Lorraine are drawn back to the Pigman's abandoned house and are shaken when they discover another lonely older man living there. For the true story of the year the teenage Zindel met his own "pigman," try *The Pigman and Me.*

This title is available in the HRW Library.

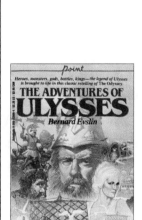

Fight to the Finish

After conquering Troy, Ulysses angers the gods, who determine that his voyage home will last ten years. On his odyssey he meets the one-eyed Cyclops; the sorceress Circe, who turns men into pigs; and the monsters Scylla and Charybdis. *The Adventures of Ulysses,* retold by Bernard Evslin, recounts the story of a hero's struggle to return and reclaim his home.

The Open Road

When her father, the legendary Kit Carson, goes searching for adventure, Adaline Falling Star is left with her mother's relatives in St. Louis. They are offended by her bold personality, so she decides to leave and head into the wilderness. In Mary Pope Osborne's novel *Adaline Falling Star,* Adaline searches for her father and discovers herself along the way.

Nonfiction

Glory Days

Did you know that the ancient Romans were skilled city planners? David Macaulay goes back to 26 B.C. in *City: A Story of Roman Planning and Construction* to describe the way the Romans built their cities. Drawing on his knowledge of hundreds of ancient Roman cities, he shows how planners might have created an imaginary city called Verbonia. Macaulay's illustrations show aqueducts, a forum, a house, a central market, and storehouses. He also draws a comparison between ancient cities and cities of today.

Larger Than Life

American outlaws like Jesse James and Belle Starr capture our imaginations. But are the stories about their lives fact or fiction? In *Bad Guys*, Andrew Glass looks at eight of these mysterious figures and uncovers the truth behind the legends. You'll find that many of these desperadoes preferred the stories told about them to the facts.

Walking with the Dinosaurs

Using stunning photographs and imaginative design, *Prehistoric Life* by William Lindsay transports you to the distant past, where you'll step into some pretty big footprints. You can watch the past unfold in the accompanying *Eyewitness Video* series.

Twinkle, Twinkle

When you gaze at the night sky, what do you see? You'll know what you're looking at after you read *The Stars* by H. A. Rey. Using clear graphics and easy-to-read text, Rey shows you a fun, exciting new way of looking at the constellations. You'll never get lost in the dark again!

Untitled (1985) by Romare Bearden.
© Romare Bearden Foundation/Licensed by VAGA, New York, NY.

Forms of Fiction

Literary Focus:
Identifying and Analyzing Forms of Fiction

Informational Focus:
Analyzing Comparison and Contrast

INTERNET

Collection Resources

Keyword: LE5 6-4

307

Elements of Literature

Forms of Fiction *by* Mara Rockliff

IT'S ALL A STORY

Why do we love to read stories we know are pure products of the imagination? Maybe it's because a good story seems as if it *could* have happened. Maybe we feel that it *should* have happened. Whether it's the latest in Bruce Coville's Alien Adventures series or J.R.R. Tolkien's *The Lord of the Rings* trilogy, we just can't get enough of **fiction,** the made-up stories that fill our lives.

Good fiction shows us something important about life. It may not be factual, but we know that what it reveals is *true.*

Myths: Our First Stories?

Probably the first stories people ever told were **myths**—stories about gods and heroes that people told to give human shape to the world around them. Myths often address very basic questions: Where does fire come from? What makes the seasons change? Why do people die? Although myths differ greatly in their details, most were connected at some time with a culture's religious beliefs. These stories were passed on orally from generation to generation long before they were written down.

Myths are central to human experience. In the Western world the best-known myths are from ancient Greece and Rome. (*Myth* comes from the Greek word *mythos,* meaning "story.") These myths have been written down for more than two thousand years. But the myths of Greece and Rome are only a small part of the body of myths. There are thousands of cultures, and myths are central to every one of them.

Some people believe that scientific explanations have taken the place of myths. But myths also answer questions well beyond the scope of science: Who are we? Where are we going? How should we live? What is courage? What is love? Who are our heroes? What is the difference between right and wrong?

Fables: Teaching Stories

Another very old type of story is the short teaching story called the **fable.** Fables are told by people all over the world—from Africa to India to America. The most famous fables in the Western world were told by Aesop (ē′səp), a man held in slavery in ancient Greece. The boy who cried wolf, the goose that laid the golden eggs, the slow but steady tortoise who outraced the speedy hare—references to Aesop's fables, with their practical morals, can still be heard in everyday conversation today, 2,600 years later. (You'll find two of Aesop's fables, retold as reader's theater, on pages 371–373.)

North Carolina Competency Goal
5.02

INTERNET
More About Forms of Fiction
Keyword: LE5 6-4

SKILLS FOCUS

Literary Skills
Identify forms of fiction.

Legends: Stories Based on History

People tell stories about historical events too. As these stories are told and retold, they often become less and less accurate. Heroes become superhuman, enemies become more villainous, victories become more fantastic. These exaggerated stories about historic events are called **legends.** We still read legends about the Trojan War, for instance. These legends are partly true (there really was a war in Troy around 1200 B.C.) and partly imaginary (a serpent probably did *not* rise out of the sea and strangle one of the Trojans). American history has also been the source of legends, such as the ones about the frontiersman Davy Crockett. Crockett did fight at the Alamo, but he probably did *not* wade across the Mississippi or ride a streak of lightning.

Folk Tales: Traveling Stories

A **folk tale** is a story that has been passed down over the years by word of mouth. Generations of storytellers have passed on tales of genies and flying carpets, giants and elves and princesses, talking animals and magical wishes that come in threes.

Folk tales tend to travel from one culture to another. Folk tales with similar story lines often turn up in cultures thousands of miles apart. Whose evil stepmother makes her do all the work and won't let her go to the big party? Who goes anyway and loses her slipper? In Europe the answer is Cinderella; in China it's Yeh-Shen. West Africans, Egyptians, Koreans, Americans from the Appalachian Mountains—all have their own versions of this folk tale.

Fiction: Stories Today

The word **fiction** usually refers to short stories and novels. Fiction can be an adventure, a mystery, or a romance. Fiction can be fantasy, science fiction, or historical fiction. "Formula fiction" satisfies us by following a formula—"boy meets girl" or "the good guy wins" or "crime doesn't pay." Today most writers of good fiction try to be original. They move beyond the old plot formulas to bring us new, surprising forms of stories (like a murder mystery written by forty-five people and published on the Internet). That's the magic of fiction: In stories as in life, you never know what will happen next.

Practice

Copy this cluster diagram, showing types of fiction popular today. Then, think of an example of each type of fiction, and write the title in the bubble. Add a sentence or two defining that type of fiction. You might work with a group on this project and create a large display for the class bulletin board.

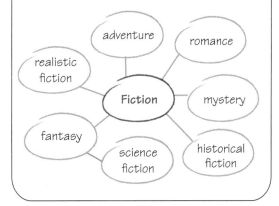

Reading Skills and Strategies

When the Words Are Tough

by Kylene Beers

A sixth grader told me that reading was tough only when the words were hard. I started to laugh, but then I realized how right the student was. As long as the words are easy, getting through the text probably will be easy. But what do you do when the words in the text are words you don't know? Being a skilled reader means having the skills to get through texts, even when the words are tough.

Steps to Reading Success

You can use a strategy called **SBT** (**S**ay-**B**reak-**T**hink) to figure out the meaning of an unfamiliar word when a dictionary isn't near. Let's try SBT with the word *gurney* from this sentence: *The patient was lying on a* gurney, *waiting to be wheeled into surgery.*

1. First, **SAY the word aloud.** Once you hear it, you may recognize it. If you aren't sure how to pronounce the whole word, look for smaller parts that you know or that look like other words you know. The *gurn* in *gurney* looks like *turn*. Use that to help you pronounce *gurney*.

2. If you need more help, try to **BREAK the word apart** to see whether it has a prefix, suffix, or root word you recognize. (See page 315 for a list of prefixes and suffixes and their meanings.) *Gurney* has no parts that help with its meaning, so move on to the third step.

3. Finally, **THINK what fits** in the context in which you encountered the tough word. In other words, what makes sense with the surrounding words and sentences? In the sentence we're working with, the context tells you that a patient lies on a gurney and the gurney has wheels. So we can figure out that a gurney must be a type of bed for moving people who are sick or hurt.

North Carolina Competency Goal
6.01

Reading Skills
Use semantic and context clues to clarify word meanings.

I Was Not Alone

An interview with Rosa Parks by Brian Lanker
from *I Dream a World*

When Rosa Parks refused to give up her seat on a Montgomery, Alabama, bus in 1955, her silent defiance spoke for a whole people. Her arrest sparked a 381-day bus boycott,[1] which ignited the civil rights movement and changed America. Fired from her tailoring job, she moved to Detroit, Michigan, where she was a special assistant to Congressman John Conyers for twenty-five years. She is the founder and president of the Rosa and Raymond Parks Institute for Self-Development, inaugurated[2] in 1988.

As far back as I can remember, being black in Montgomery we were well aware of the inequality of our way of life. I hated it all the time. I didn't feel that, in order to have some freedom, I should have to leave one part of the United States and go to another part of the same country just because one was South and one was North. ❶ ⬒

My mother believed in freedom and equality even though we didn't know it for reality during our life in Alabama.

In some stores, if a woman wanted to go in to try a hat, they wouldn't be permitted to try it on unless they knew they were going to buy it, or they put a bag on the inside of it. In the shoe stores they had this long row of seats, and all of those in the front could be vacant, but if one of us would go in to buy, they'd always take you to the last one, to the back of the store. There were no black salespersons.

---

1. **boycott:** act of joining together and refusing to deal with a company for political reasons.
2. **inaugurated:** formally begun.

CLARIFY WORD MEANINGS

❶ Look at the word *inequality* in the first sentence. Try the SBT strategy. First, **say** *inequality* aloud.

If you need to, **break** the word apart. Think about what the prefix *in–* means.

Finally, **think** what would fit in that paragraph. Parks hated the way black people were treated in Montgomery. So *inequality* must mean something like "unfairness."

Using the Strategy

At the Montgomery Fair [a department store] I did men's alterations. Beginning in December coming up to the Christmas holiday, the work was a bit heavy. When I left the store that evening, I was tired, but I was tired every day. I had planned to get an electric heating pad so I could put some heat to my shoulder and my back and neck. After I stepped up on the bus, I noticed this driver as the same one who had evicted me from another bus way back in 1943.

Just back of the whites there was a black man next to one vacant seat. So I sat down with him. A few white people boarded the bus and they found seats except this one man. That is when the bus driver looked at us and asked us to let him have those seats. After he saw we weren't moving immediately, he said, "Y'all make it light on yourselves and let me have those seats."

When he saw that I was still remaining in the seat, the driver said, "If you don't stand up, I'm going to call the police and have you arrested." I said, "You may do that."

Two policemen came and wanted to know what was the trouble. One said, "Why don't you stand up?" I said, "I don't think I should have to." At that point I asked the policemen, "Why do you push us around?" He said, "I don't know, but the law is the law and you're under arrest."

The decision was made by the three of us, my husband, my mother, and me, that I would go on and use my case as a test case, challenging segregation on the buses. ❷

When I woke up the next morning and realized I had to go to work and it was pouring down rain, the first thing I thought about was the fact that I never would ride a segregated bus again. That was my decision for me and not necessarily for anybody else.

People just stayed off the buses because I was arrested, not because I asked them. If everybody else had been happy and doing well, my arrest wouldn't have made any difference at all.

The one thing I appreciated was the fact that when so many others, by the hundreds and by the thousands, joined in, there was a kind of lifting of a burden from me individually. I could feel that whatever my individual desires were to be free, I was not alone. There were many others who felt the same way.

The first thing that happened after the people stayed off was the black cab companies were willing to just charge bus fare instead of charging cab fare. Others who had any kind of car at all would give

CLARIFY WORD MEANINGS

❷ This paragraph includes a difficult phrase, "challenging segregation on the buses." Look at the words *challenging* and *segregation* one at a time. Try saying each word aloud. Look for word parts that you can break apart from the rest of each word.

Now think about context. Parks has chosen to break a law that says blacks must give up their bus seats to whites. She thinks the law is wrong. So when Parks says she will be "challenging segregation on the buses," she probably means she will be fighting that law.

Mrs. Rosa Parks, forty-three, sits in the front of a city bus as a Supreme Court ruling that banned segregation on the city's public transit system takes effect.

people rides. They had quite a transportation system set up. Mass meetings were keeping the morale up. They were singing and praying and raising money in the collection to buy gasoline or tires. ❸ 📖

There was a lot of humor in it, too. Somebody told a story about a [white] husband who had fired the family cook because she refused to ride the bus to work. When his wife came home, she said, "If you don't go get her, you better be on your way." Some white people who were not wanting to be deprived of their domestic help[3] would just go themselves

3. **domestic help:** household servants: cooks, maids, or drivers.

CLARIFY WORD MEANINGS

❸ Use your SBT strategy to break down *transportation*. (Hint: It comes from the Latin root word *portare*, meaning "to carry.") Check page 315 for a list of prefixes and suffixes and what they mean.

and pick up the people who were working for them.

The officials really became furious when they saw that the rain and bad weather or distance or any other problem didn't matter.

Many whites, even white Southerners, told me that even though it may have seemed like the blacks were being freed, they felt more free and at ease themselves. They thought that my action didn't just free blacks but them also.

Some have suffered much more than I did. Some have even lost their lives. I just escaped some of the physical—maybe not all—but some of the physical pain. And the pain still remains. From back as far as I can remember.

Rosa Parks at the annual NAACP Image Awards, Pasadena, California, 1997.

When people made up their minds that they wanted to be free and took action, then there was a change. But they couldn't rest on just that change. It was to continue.

It just doesn't seem that an older person like I am should still have to be in the struggle, but if I have to be in it then I have no choice but to keep on.

I've been dreaming, looking, for as far back as I had any thought, of what it should be like to be a human being. My desires were to be free as soon as I had learned that there had been slavery of human beings and that I was a descendant from them. If there was a proclamation[4] setting those who were slaves free, I thought they should be indeed free and not have any type of slavery put upon us. ❹

---

4. **proclamation:** official announcement.

CLARIFY WORD MEANINGS

❹ Look at the word *descendant*. Do you recognize the base word *descend* inside it? It means "to come down." Now check the meaning of the suffix *–ant* on page 315. Think about what Parks says about people held as slaves. She seems to feel that she is related to them in some way. Use all that information to decide what *descendant* means.

Practice the Strategy

Important Prefixes to Know

Prefix	Meaning	Examples
auto-	self	autobiography, automatic
co-	together	cocaptain, coexist, cooperate, co-worker
de-	opposite	deactivate, decontaminate, defrost
dis-	opposite	disengage, dislike, disrespect
in-	not	inactive, inedible, insane
re-	again	redo, remake, re-read, rewrite
trans-	across	transatlantic, transfer, transportation

Strategy Tip

Use the SBT strategy to figure out unknown words when a dictionary is not close.

S = Say it aloud
B = Break it apart
T = Think about what fits

Important Suffixes to Know

Suffix	Meaning	Examples
-al	state or result of	arrival, denial, refusal
-ant	one who	attendant, descendant, servant
-ation	action or process	emancipation, narration, transportation
-ism	state or quality of	heroism, racism
-less	without	careless, joyless, penniless
-ment	action or process	development, government
-ment	action or quality of	amusement, bewilderment, punishment

North Carolina Competency Goal
6.01

PRACTICE

Read each sentence below. Then use the **SBT** strategy to figure out the meaning of each underlined word. Look up unfamiliar prefixes and suffixes on the charts above.

1. The driver showed <u>disrespect</u> for Parks when he ordered her to give up her seat.

2. Rosa Parks says she was just tired, but most people say that her <u>refusal</u> to give up her seat was an act of <u>heroism</u>.

3. Almost all of the black citizens of Montgomery <u>cooperated</u> in the bus boycott.

4. The boycott was a way to force the city of Montgomery to <u>rewrite</u> racist laws.

SKILLS FOCUS

Reading Skills
Use semantic and context clues to clarify word meanings.

The Gold Cadillac

Make the Connection

Did you know that at one time there were

- separate drinking fountains and restrooms for whites and African Americans?
- restaurants in which African Americans were not allowed to eat?

These things used to be a reality, right here in the United States. The civil rights movement of the 1950s and 1960s ended most forms of segregation, but this story takes place earlier.

Quickwrite ✏️

Write down your thoughts on the conditions described above. What can people do to prevent this kind of injustice today?

Literary Focus
The Novella

A novel, a novella, and a short story are all members of the family of fiction. They resemble each other too. They have plot, characters, setting, and theme—all the elements you studied in Collections 1–3. If they were lined up by size for a family photo, the novel would be the tall one at one end. The short story would, of course, be the short one at the other end, and the novella would be in the middle. In other words, a **novella** is a story that's shorter than a novel but longer than a short story.

A novella is small enough to be published with other stories yet long enough to be published by itself. *The*

Gold Cadillac is a novella; it was first published as a short book.

Reading Skills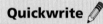
Making and Adjusting Predictions

When we read, we make **predictions** by combining new information with our prior knowledge. When we get more information, we often **adjust** these predictions.

As you read this story, you'll notice open-book signs. When you see a sign, make a prediction in response to the question next to it.

Vocabulary Development

You'll learn these words as you read the story:

evident (ev′ə·dənt) *adj.:* obvious. *It's evident to everyone that Dee is angry.*

rural (rσσr′əl) *adj.:* having to do with country life. *The narrator's grandparents live in a rural area, on a big farm.*

heedful (hēd′fəl) *adj.:* attentive; keeping in mind. *Heedful of her parents' warnings, she watches carefully.*

ignorance (ig′nə·rəns) *n.:* lack of knowledge. *Her father says that people sometimes pass unfair laws out of ignorance.*

North Carolina Competency Goal
1.04; 4.01; 5.01; 5.02

INTERNET
Vocabulary Activity
•
More About Taylor
•
Cross-curricular Connections
Keyword: LE5 6-4

SKILLS FOCUS

Literary Skills
Understand forms of fiction: the novella.

Reading Skills
Make and adjust predictions.

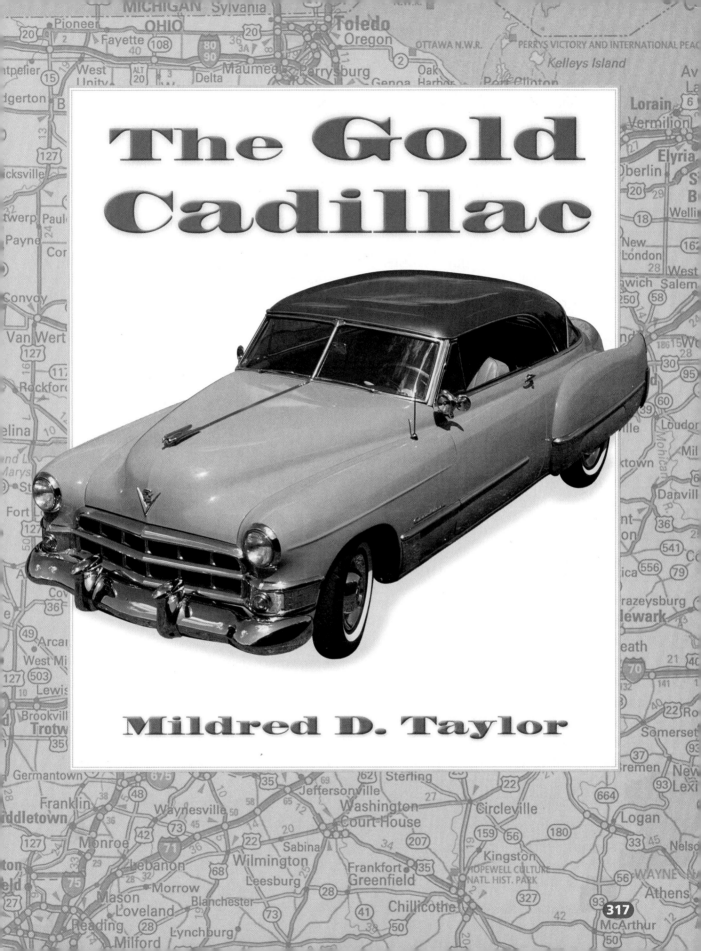

The Gold Cadillac

Mildred D. Taylor

My sister and I were playing out on the front lawn when the gold Cadillac rolled up and my father stepped from behind the wheel. We ran to him, our eyes filled with wonder. "Daddy, whose Cadillac?" I asked.

And Wilma demanded, "Where's our Mercury?"

My father grinned. "Go get your mother and I'll tell you all about it."

"Is it ours?" I cried. "Daddy, is it ours?"

"Get your mother!" he laughed. "And tell her to hurry!"

Wilma and I ran off to obey, as Mr. Pondexter next door came from his house to see what this new Cadillac was all about. We threw open the front door, ran through the downstairs front parlor and straight through the house to the kitchen, where my mother was cooking and one of my aunts was helping her. "Come on, Mother-Dear!" we cried together. "Daddy say come on out and see this new car!"

"What?" said my mother, her face showing her surprise. "What're you talking about?" ❶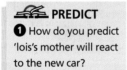

"A Cadillac!" I cried.

"He said hurry up!" relayed Wilma.

And then we took off again, up the back stairs to the second floor of the duplex. Running down the hall, we banged on all the apartment doors. My uncles and their wives stepped to the doors. It was good it was a Saturday morning. Everybody was home.

"We got us a Cadillac! We got us a Cadillac!" Wilma and I proclaimed in unison.[1]

🛶 **PREDICT**

❶ How do you predict 'lois's mother will react to the new car?

---

1. **in unison:** in chorus; in the same words, spoken at the same time.

We had decided that the Cadillac had to be ours if our father was driving it and holding on to the keys. "Come on see!" Then we raced on, through the upstairs sunroom, down the front steps, through the downstairs sunroom, and out to the Cadillac. Mr. Pondexter was still there. Mr. LeRoy and Mr. Courtland from down the street were there too, and all were admiring the Cadillac as my father stood proudly by, pointing out the various features.

"Brand-new 1950 Coupe deVille!" I heard one of the men saying.

"Just off the showroom floor!" my father said. "I just couldn't resist it."

My sister and I eased up to the car and peeked in. It was all gold inside. Gold leather seats. Gold carpeting. Gold dashboard. It was like no car we had owned before. It looked like a car for rich folks.

"Daddy, are we rich?" I asked. My father laughed.

"Daddy, it's ours, isn't it?" asked Wilma, who was older and more practical than I. She didn't intend to give her heart too quickly to something that wasn't hers.

"You like it?"

"Oh, Daddy, yes!"

He looked at me. "What 'bout you, 'lois?"

"Yes, sir!"

My father laughed again. "Then I expect I can't much disappoint my girls, can I? It's ours, all right!"

Wilma and I hugged our father with our joy. My uncles came from the house, and my aunts, carrying their babies, came out too. Everybody surrounded the car and owwed and ahhed. Nobody could believe it.

Then my mother came out.

Everybody stood back grinning as she approached the car. There was no smile on her face. We all waited for her to speak. She stared at the car, then looked at my father, standing there as proud as he could be. Finally she said, "You didn't buy this car, did you, Wilbert?"

"Gotta admit I did. Couldn't resist it."

"But . . . but what about our Mercury? It was perfectly good!"

"Don't you like the Cadillac, Dee?"

"That Mercury wasn't even a year old!"

My father nodded. "And I'm sure whoever buys it is going to get themselves a good car. But we've got ourselves a better one. Now stop frowning, honey, and let's take ourselves a ride in our brand-new Cadillac!"

My mother shook her head. "I've got food on the stove," she said and, turning away, walked back to the house.

There was an awkward silence, and then my father said, "You know Dee never did much like surprises. Guess this here Cadillac was a bit too much for her. I best go smooth things out with her."

Everybody watched as he went after my mother. But when he came back, he was alone.

"Well, what she say?" asked one of my uncles.

My father shrugged and smiled. "Told me I bought this Cadillac alone, I could just ride in it alone."

Another uncle laughed. "Uh-oh! Guess she told you!"

"Oh, she'll come around," said one of my aunts. "Any woman would be proud to ride in this car."

"That's what I'm banking on," said my father as he went around to the street side of the car and opened the door. "All right! Who's for a ride?"

"We are!" Wilma and I cried.

All three of my uncles and one of my aunts,

Harlem Girl 1 (1925) by Fritz Winold Reiss.
Museum of Art and Archaeology, University of Missouri-Columbia. Gift of Mr. W. Tjark Reiss.

still holding her baby, and Mr. Pondexter climbed in with us, and we took off for the first ride in the gold Cadillac. It was a glorious ride, and we drove all through the city of Toledo. We rode past the church and past the school. We rode through Ottawa Hills, where the rich folks lived, and on into Walbridge Park and past the zoo, then along the Maumee River. But none of us had had enough of the car, so my father put the car on the road and we drove all the way to Detroit. We had plenty of family there, and everybody was just as pleased as could be about the Cadillac. My father told our Detroit relatives that he was in the doghouse with my mother about buying the Cadillac. My uncles told them she wouldn't ride in the car. All the Detroit family thought that was funny, and everybody, including my father, laughed about it and said my mother would come around.

It was early evening by the time we got back home, and I could see from my mother's face she had not come around.

She was angry now not only about the car, but that we had been gone so long. I didn't understand that, since my father had called her as soon as we reached Detroit to let her know where we were. I had heard him myself. I didn't understand either why she did not like that fine Cadillac and thought she was being terribly disagreeable with my father. That night, as she tucked Wilma and me in bed, I told her that too.

"Is this your business?" she asked.

"Well, I just think you ought to be nice to Daddy. I think you ought to ride in that car with him! It'd sure make him happy."

"I think you ought to go to sleep," she said and turned out the light.

Later I heard her arguing with my father. "We're supposed to be saving for a house!" she said.

"We've already got a house!" said my father.

"But you said you wanted a house in a better neighborhood. I thought that's what we both said!"

"I haven't changed my mind."

"Well, you have a mighty funny way of saving for it, then. Your brothers are saving for houses of their own, and you don't see them out buying new cars every year!"

"We'll still get the house, Dee. That's a promise!"

"Not with new Cadillacs we won't!" said my mother, and then she said a very loud good night, and all was quiet.

The next day was Sunday, and everybody figured that my mother would be sure to give in and ride in the Cadillac. After all, the family always went to church together on Sunday. But she didn't give in. What was worse, she wouldn't let Wilma and me ride in the Cadillac either. She took us each by the hand, walked past the Cadillac where my father stood waiting, and headed on toward the church three blocks away. I was really mad at her now. I had been looking forward to driving up to the church in that gold Cadillac and having everybody see.

On most Sunday afternoons during the summertime, my mother, my father, Wilma, and I would go for a ride. Sometimes we just rode around the city and visited friends and family. Sometimes we made short trips over to Chicago or Peoria or Detroit to see relatives there or to Cleveland, where we had relatives too, but we could also see the Cleveland Indians play. Sometimes we joined our aunts and uncles and drove in a caravan[2] out to the park or to the beach. At the park or the beach, Wilma and I would run and play. My mother and my aunts would spread a picnic, and my father and my uncles would shine their cars.

But on this Sunday afternoon, my mother refused to ride anywhere. She told Wilma and me that we could go. So we left her alone in the big, empty house, and the family cars, led by the gold Cadillac, headed for the park. For a while I played and had a good time, but then I stopped playing and went to sit with my father. Despite his laughter he seemed sad to me. I think he was missing my mother as much as I was.

That evening, my father took my mother to dinner down at the corner cafe. They walked. Wilma and I stayed at the house, chasing fireflies in the backyard. My aunts and uncles sat in the yard and on the porch, talking and laughing about the day and watching us. It was a soft summer's evening, the kind that came every day and was expected. The smell of charcoal and of

---

2. **caravan** *n.:* group of cars traveling together.

Family No. 9 (1968) by Charles Alston.

barbecue drifting from up the block, the sound of laughter and music and talk drifting from yard to yard were all a part of it. Soon one of my uncles joined Wilma and me in our chase of fireflies, and when my mother and father came home, we were at it still. My mother and father watched us for a while, while everybody else watched them to see if my father would take out the Cadillac and if my mother would slide in beside him to take a ride. But it soon became evident that the dinner had not changed my mother's mind. She still refused to ride in the Cadillac. I just couldn't understand her objection to it.

Though my mother didn't like the Cadillac, everybody else in the neighborhood certainly did. That meant quite a few folks too, since we lived on a very busy block. On one corner was a grocery store, a cleaner's, and a gas station. Across the street was a beauty shop and a fish market, and down the street was a bar, another grocery store, the Dixie Theater, the cafe, and a drugstore. There were always people strolling to or from one of these places, and because our house was right in the middle of the block, just about everybody had to pass our house and the gold Cadillac. Sometimes people took in the Cadillac as they walked, their heads turning for a longer look as they passed. Then there were people who just outright stopped and took a good look before continuing on their way. I was proud to say that car belonged to my family. I felt mighty important as people called to me as I ran down the street. "'Ey, 'lois! How's that Cadillac, girl? Riding fine?" I told my mother how much everybody liked that car. She was not impressed and made no comment.

Since just about everybody on the block knew everybody else, most folks knew that my mother wouldn't ride in the Cadillac. Because of that, my father took a lot of good-natured kidding from the men. My mother got kidded too, as the women said if she didn't ride in that car, maybe some other woman would. And everybody laughed about it and began to bet on who would give in first, my mother or my father. But then my father said he was going to drive the car south into Mississippi to visit my grandparents, and everybody stopped laughing.

My uncles stopped.

So did my aunts.

Everybody.

"Look here, Wilbert," said one of my uncles, "it's too dangerous. It's like putting a loaded gun to your head."

"I paid good money for that car," said my father. "That gives me a right to drive it where I please. Even down to Mississippi."

My uncles argued with him and tried to talk him out of driving the car south. So did my aunts, and so did the neighbors, Mr. LeRoy, Mr. Courtland, and Mr. Pondexter. They said it was a dangerous thing, a mighty dangerous thing, for a black man to drive an expensive car into the rural South.

"Not much those folks hate more'n to see a northern Negro coming down there in a fine car," said Mr. Pondexter. "They see those Ohio license plates, they'll figure you coming down uppity, trying to lord your fine car over them!"

I listened, but I didn't understand. I didn't understand why they didn't want my father to drive that car south. It was his.

Vocabulary

evident (ev'ə·dənt) *adj.:* easily seen or understood; obvious.

rural (roor'əl) *adj.:* having to do with the country or country life.

"Listen to Pondexter, Wilbert!" cried another uncle. "We might've fought a war to free people overseas, but we're not free here! Man, those white folks down south'll lynch[3] you soon's look at you. You know that!" ❷

Wilma and I looked at each other. Neither one of us knew what *lynch*[3] meant, but the word sent a shiver through us. We held each other's hand.

My father was silent, then he said: "All my life I've had to be heedful of what white folks thought. Well, I'm tired of that. I worked hard for everything I got. Got it honest, too. Now I got that Cadillac because I liked it and because it meant something to me that somebody like me from Mississippi could go and buy it. It's my car, I paid for it, and I'm driving it south."

My mother, who had said nothing through all this, now stood. "Then the girls and I'll be going too," she said.

"No!" said my father.

My mother only looked at him and went off to the kitchen.

My father shook his head. It seemed he didn't want us to go. My uncles looked at

---

3. **lynch** *v.:* kill a person without legal authority, usually by hanging. Lynchings are committed by violent mobs that have taken the law into their own hands.

each other, then at my father. "You set on doing this, we'll all go," they said. "That way we can watch out for each other." My father took a moment and nodded. Then my aunts got up and went off to their kitchens too.

All the next day, my aunts and my mother cooked and the house was filled with delicious smells. They fried chicken and baked hams and cakes and sweet potato pies and mixed potato salad. They filled jugs with water and punch and coffee. Then they packed everything in huge picnic baskets, along with bread and boiled eggs, oranges and apples, plates and napkins, spoons and forks and cups. They placed all that food on the back seats of the cars. It was like a grand, grand picnic we were going on, and Wilma and I were mighty excited. We could hardly wait to start.

My father, my mother, Wilma, and I got into the Cadillac. My uncles, my aunts, my cousins got into the Ford, the Buick, and the Chevrolet, and we rolled off in our caravan headed south. Though my mother was finally riding in the Cadillac, she had no praise for it. In fact, she said nothing about it at all. She still seemed upset, and since she still seemed to feel the same about the car, I wondered why she had insisted upon making this trip with my father.

We left the city of Toledo behind, drove through Bowling Green and down through the Ohio countryside of farms and small towns, through Dayton and Cincinnati, and across the Ohio River into Kentucky. On the other side of the river, my father stopped the car and looked back at Wilma and me and said, "Now from here on, whenever we stop

Vocabulary
heedful (hēd′fəl) *adj.:* attentive; keeping in mind.

and there're white people around, I don't want either one of you to say a word. *Not one word!* Your mother and I'll do the talking. That understood?"

"Yes, sir," Wilma and I both said, though we didn't truly understand why.

My father nodded, looked at my mother, and started the car again. We rolled on, down Highway 25 and through the bluegrass hills of Kentucky. Soon we began to see signs. Signs that read: "White Only, Colored Not Allowed." Hours later, we left the Bluegrass State and crossed into Tennessee. Now we saw even more of the signs saying: "White Only, Colored Not Allowed." We saw the signs above water fountains and in restaurant windows. We saw them in ice cream parlors and at hamburger stands. We saw them in front of hotels and motels, and on the restroom doors of filling stations. I didn't like the signs. I felt as if I were in a foreign land.

I couldn't understand why the signs were there, and I asked my father what the signs meant. He said they meant we couldn't drink from the water fountains. He said they meant we couldn't stop to sleep in the motels. He said they meant we couldn't stop to eat in the restaurants. I looked at the grand picnic basket I had been enjoying so much. Now I understood why my mother had packed it. Suddenly the picnic did not seem so grand.

Finally we reached Memphis. We got there at a bad time. Traffic was heavy and we got separated from the rest of the family. We tried to find them but it was no use. We had to go on alone. We reached the Mississippi state line, and soon after, we heard a police siren. A police car came up behind us. My father slowed the Cadillac, then stopped. Two white policemen got out of their car.

They eyeballed the Cadillac and told my father to get out. ❸ 🏊

🏊 **PREDICT**
❸ What do you think the police will do to 'lois's father?

"Whose car is this, boy?" they asked.

I saw anger in my father's eyes. "It's mine," he said.

"You're a liar," said one of the policemen. "You stole this car."

"Turn around, put your hands on top of that car, and spread-eagle," said the other policeman.

My father did as he was told. They searched him and I didn't understand why. I didn't understand either why they had called my father a liar and didn't believe that the Cadillac was his. I wanted to ask, but I remembered my father's warning not to say a word, and I obeyed that warning.

The policemen told my father to get in the back of the police car. My father did. One policeman got back into the police car. The other policeman slid behind the wheel of our Cadillac. The police car started off. The Cadillac followed. Wilma and I looked at each other and at our mother. We didn't know what to think. We were scared.

The Cadillac followed the police car into a small town and stopped in front of the police station. The policeman stepped out of our Cadillac and took the keys. The other policeman took my father into the police station.

"Mother-Dear!" Wilma and I cried. "What're they going to do to our daddy? They going to hurt him?"

"He'll be all right," said my mother. "He'll be all right." But she didn't sound so sure of that. She seemed worried.

We waited. More than three hours we waited. Finally my father came out of the police station. We had lots of questions to

Open Road, from the series *Landscape of the Apocalypse* (1972) by Martin Hoffman.
Acrylic on canvas (60″ × 80″).

ask him. He said the police had given him a ticket for speeding and locked him up. But then the judge had come. My father had paid the ticket and they had let him go.

He started the Cadillac and drove slowly out of the town, below the speed limit. The police car followed us. People standing on steps and sitting on porches and in front of stores stared at us as we passed. Finally we were out of the town. The police car still followed. Dusk was falling. The night grew black, and finally the police car turned around and left us.

We drove and drove. But my father was tired now and my grandparents' farm was still far away. My father said he had to get some sleep, and since my mother didn't

drive, he pulled into a grove of trees at the side of the road and stopped.

"I'll keep watch," said my mother.

"Wake me if you see anybody," said my father.

"Just rest," said my mother.

So my father slept. But that bothered me. I needed him awake. I was afraid of the dark and of the woods and of whatever lurked there. My father was the one who kept us safe, he and my uncles. But already the police had taken my father away from us once today, and my uncles were lost.

"Go to sleep, baby," said my mother. "Go to sleep."

But I was afraid to sleep until my father

woke. I had to help my mother keep watch. I figured I had to help protect us too, in case the police came back and tried to take my father away again. There was a long, sharp knife in the picnic basket, and I took hold of it, clutching it tightly in my hand. Ready to strike, I sat there in the back of the car, eyes wide, searching the blackness outside the Cadillac. Wilma, for a while, searched the night too, then she fell asleep. I didn't want to sleep, but soon I found I couldn't help myself as an unwelcome drowsiness came over me. I had an uneasy sleep, and when I woke, it was dawn and my father was gently shaking me. I woke with a start and my hand went up, but the knife wasn't there. My mother had it.

My father took my hand. "Why were you holding the knife, 'lois?" he asked.

I looked at him and at my mother. "I— I was scared," I said.

My father was thoughtful. "No need to be scared now, sugar," he said. "Daddy's here and so is Mother-Dear." ❹

🏞 **PREDICT**
❹ Will the family keep going south, or will they turn back?

Then after a glance at my mother, he got out of the car, walked to the road, looked down it one way, then the other. When he came back and started the motor, he turned the Cadillac north, not south.

"What're you doing?" asked my mother.

"Heading back to Memphis," said my father. "Cousin Halton's there. We'll leave the Cadillac and get his car. Driving this car any farther south with you and the girls in the car, it's just not worth the risk."

And so that's what we did. Instead of driving through Mississippi in golden splendor, we traveled its streets and roads and highways in Cousin Halton's solid, yet not so splendid, four-year-old Chevy. When we reached my grandparents' farm, my uncles and aunts were already there. Everybody was glad to see us. They had been worried. They asked about the Cadillac. My father told them what had happened, and they nodded and said he had done the best thing.

We stayed one week in Mississippi. During that week I often saw my father, looking deep in thought, walk off alone across the family land. I saw my mother watching him. One day I ran after my father, took his hand, and walked the land with him. I asked him all the questions that were on my mind. I asked him why the policemen had treated him the way they had and why people didn't want us to eat in the restaurants or drink from the water fountains or sleep in the hotels. I told him I just didn't understand all that.

My father looked at me and said that it all was a difficult thing to understand and he didn't really understand it himself. He said it all had to do with the fact that black people had once been forced to be slaves. He said it had to do with our skins being colored. He said it had to do with stupidity and ignorance. He said it had to do with the law, the law that said we could be treated like this here in the South. And for that matter, he added, any other place in these United States where folks thought the same as so many folks did here in the South. But he also said, "I'm hoping one day though we can drive that long road down here and there won't be any signs. I'm hoping one day the police won't stop us just because of the color of our skins

Vocabulary
ignorance (ig′nə·rəns) n.: lack of knowledge.

and we're riding in a gold Cadillac with northern plates."

When the week ended, we said a sad good-bye to my grandparents and all the Mississippi family and headed in a caravan back toward Memphis. In Memphis, we returned Cousin Halton's car and got our Cadillac. Once we were home, my father put the Cadillac in the garage and didn't drive it. I didn't hear my mother say any more about the Cadillac. I didn't hear my father speak of it either. ❺

📖 **PREDICT**

❺ What do you predict the family will do with the Cadillac?

Some days passed, and then on a bright Saturday afternoon while Wilma and I were playing in the backyard, I saw my father go into the garage. He opened the garage doors wide so the sunshine streamed in and began to shine the Cadillac. I saw my mother at the kitchen window staring out across the yard at my father. For a long time, she stood there watching my father shine his car. Then she came out and crossed the yard to the garage, and I heard her say, "Wilbert, you keep the car."

He looked at her as if he had not heard.

"You keep it," she repeated and turned and walked back to the house.

My father watched her until the back door had shut behind her. Then he went on shining the car and soon began to sing. About an hour later he got into the car and drove away. That evening when he came back, he was walking. The Cadillac was nowhere in sight.

"Daddy, where's our new Cadillac?" I demanded to know. So did Wilma.

He smiled and put his hand on my head. "Sold it," he said as my mother came into the room.

"But how come?" I asked. "We poor now?"

"No, sugar. We've got more money towards our new house now, and we're all together. I figure that makes us about the richest folks in the world." He smiled at my mother, and she smiled too and came into his arms.

After that, we drove around in an old 1930s Model A Ford my father had. He said he'd factory-ordered us another Mercury, this time with my mother's approval. Despite that, most folks on the block figured we had fallen on hard times after such a splashy showing of good times, and some folks even laughed at us as the Ford rattled around the city. I must admit that at first I was pretty much embarrassed to be riding around in that old Ford after the splendor of the Cadillac. But my father said to hold my head high. We and the family knew the truth. As fine as the Cadillac had been, he said, it had pulled us apart for a while. Now, as ragged and noisy as that old Ford was, we all rode in it together, and we were a family again. So I held my head high.

Still, though, I thought often of that Cadillac. We had had the Cadillac only a little more than a month, but I wouldn't soon forget its splendor or how I'd felt riding around inside it. I wouldn't soon forget either the ride we had taken south in it. I wouldn't soon forget the signs, the policemen, or my fear. I would remember that ride and the gold Cadillac all my life.

Meet the Writer

Mildred D. Taylor

Weaving Memories into Fiction

Mildred D. Taylor (1943–   ) tells about the memories behind *The Gold Cadillac:*

❝ For a few years when I was a child, I lived in a big house on a busy street with my mother, my father, my sister, and many aunts and uncles and cousins. We were originally a Mississippi family who had migrated to the industrial North during and after World War II. My father was the first of the family to go to the North and that was when I was only three weeks old. When I was three months old, my mother, my older sister, and I followed. A year after our arrival, my parents bought the big house on the busy street. During the next nine years, aunts and uncles and cousins from both sides of the family arrived yearly from Mississippi and stayed in that big house with us until they had earned enough to rent another place or buy houses of their own.

I loved those years. There were always cousins to play with. There was always an aunt or uncle to talk to when my parents were busy, and there seemed always to be fun things to do and plenty of people to do them with. On the weekends the whole houseful of family often did things together. Because my father, my uncles, and my older male cousins all loved cars, we often rode in caravan out to the park, where the men would park their cars in a long, impressive row and shine them in the shade of the trees while the women spread a picnic and chatted, and my sister, younger cousins, and I ran and played. Sometimes we traveled to nearby cities to watch a baseball game. And sometimes we took even longer trips, down country highways into the land called the South.

I have many good memories of those years, including the year my father brought home a brand-new Cadillac. I also have memories of those years that long troubled me. I have woven some of those memories into this story of fiction called *The Gold Cadillac.* ❞

For Independent Reading

If you'd like to read more fiction woven from Taylor's memories, check out *Song of the Trees* and *Roll of Thunder, Hear My Cry,* winner of the Newbery Medal for distinguished American literature for children. *Let the Circle Be Unbroken* is the sequel to *Roll of Thunder, Hear My Cry.*

First Thoughts

1. If you were 'lois's father, would you sell the car? Why or why not?

Thinking Critically

2. What do you think the gold Cadillac stands for in the eyes of Wilbert and his neighbors?

3. How can you tell that 'lois's parents love each other even though they disagree about the car?

4. How do you think the journey south changes 'lois? How does her father change?

5. Go back to the **predictions** you made as you read. At which points did you adjust your predictions?

6. 'Lois wonders if her family is poor. What does her father mean when he says they may be "the richest folks in the world"?

7. In one or two words, state what you think the subject of this story is. Then, in a complete sentence, state what you see as the story's **theme.** Find at least one passage in the story that supports the theme.

Extending Interpretations

8. In the 1950s, a Cadillac was a sign of wealth and status. What qualifies as a status symbol today? Why?

9. Do you think what happened to 'lois's father in the 1950s could happen in the United States today? Why or why not?

WRITING

Narrating an Experience

Have you ever met with an injustice that changed your view of the world? Describe your experience in a short narrative, referring to your notes from the Quickwrite on page 316. Organize your details in a chart like this one:

Place:
What happened:
How it ended:
My feelings:

Reading Check

a. Why doesn't 'lois's mother like the new Cadillac?

b. How does the rest of the family feel about the car?

c. Why do the uncles think that driving the Cadillac to the South is a bad idea?

d. What do the police accuse 'lois's father of?

e. At the end of the story, why does 'lois's father sell the Cadillac?

INTERNET
Projects and Activities
Keyword: LE5 6-4

SKILLS FOCUS

Literary Skills
Analyze a novella.

Reading Skills
Adjust predictions.

Writing Skills
Describe an experience.

North Carolina Competency Goal
1.01; 1.02; 1.04; 4.01; 4.02; 5.01

After You Read   Vocabulary Development

Synonyms and Antonyms

PRACTICE 1

Semantic mapping can help you clarify a word's meaning. Using the cluster opposite as a model, map the three other words listed in the Word Bank. At the center of the map, write a Word Bank word. Then, write down a synonym and an antonym, and write a sentence using the word.

Remember that **synonyms** are words with similar meanings. **Antonyms** are words that are opposite or nearly opposite in meaning.

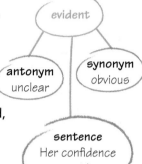

Words with Multiple Meanings

A **multiple-meaning word** is like a fork in the road: Each road, and each definition, will take you in a different direction. To make things even more complicated, many multiple-meaning words can function as different parts of speech.

> **Dad came back to the car.** [Here, *back* is an adverb meaning "toward an earlier position."]
> **Mother decided to back Dad's plan.** [Here, *back* is a verb meaning "support."]

To decide on the correct meaning of a multiple-meaning word, decide what part of speech it is and look at its context, the words and sentences around it. Then, check your definition against the original sentence to see if it makes sense.

North Carolina Competency Goal 6.01

PRACTICE 2

Define the underlined multiple-meaning word in each set of sentences, and tell what part of speech it is.

1. Tired of arguing, he decided to <u>smooth</u> things out with his wife.

   I kept slipping on the <u>smooth</u> floor.

2. I finally asked the question that had been on my <u>mind</u>.

   <u>Mind</u> your little sister while I go to the store.

   Would you <u>mind</u> closing that door?

Vocabulary Skills
Use semantic mapping; identify multiple-meaning words.

Understanding Comparison and Contrast

Reading Focus
Comparison and Contrast

"Sue's party was like a rock concert."
"Brenda's party was ten times better."

People make sense of the world by noting ways in which people, places, and ideas are similar (**comparing**) and different (**contrasting**). The next time you're with your friends, notice how often they use a comparison or a contrast.

The article that follows is about segregation in the United States before 1954. Until then, segregation was legal as long as "separate but equal" facilities were provided for whites and African Americans. In some parts of the country, it was not unusual to encounter signs such as the WHITE ONLY, COLORED NOT ALLOWED signs that confused and upset, 'lois in "The Gold Cadillac." To help us understand what segregation was like, the writer of this article compares life for blacks and for whites under segregation.

Every American should know about the two cases mentioned in this article: *Plessy* v. *Ferguson* and *Brown* v. *Board of Education of Topeka, Kansas.*

■ As you read about the cases, note the differences between schools and other facilities for whites and for blacks.

Background
Informational Text and Social Studies

Legal cases are given names that usually indicate who is arguing against whom. *Plessy* v. *Ferguson* is a case that involved someone named Plessy arguing against someone named Ferguson. The *v.* stands for *versus,* from the Latin for "against."

Plessy was an African American man who, in 1892, was forced to leave a train car that was reserved for whites. In a Louisiana court he challenged the state law requiring separate train cars for blacks and whites. Judge John H. Ferguson decided against Plessy. The case eventually reached the U.S. Supreme Court. There Plessy argued that the law violated the U.S. Constitution.

Plessy lost his case. The majority held that requiring "separate but equal" facilities was lawful.

Brown v. *Board of Education of Topeka, Kansas* is the name of a suit brought in 1951 by Oliver Brown on behalf of his daughter Linda. The Browns lived in Topeka, Kansas, where Linda attended a blacks-only elementary school. Brown sued the Topeka Board of Education and lost the case.

Some months later Brown and the NAACP (National Association for the Advancement of Colored People) appealed to the U.S. Supreme Court, which combined their case with several other school segregation cases. In 1954, the Court ruled in favor of Brown. *Brown* v. *Board of Education* was one of the most important cases brought before the Supreme Court in the twentieth century.

North Carolina Competency Goal
2.01

INTERNET
Interactive Reading Model
Keyword: LE5 6-4

Reading Skills
Understand comparison and contrast.

Separate but Never Equal

When I was a boy, I would go downtown . . . , and I'd see the signs saying "White" and "Colored" on the water fountains. There'd be a beautiful, shining water fountain in one corner of the store marked "White," and in another corner was just a little spigot marked "Colored." I saw the signs saying "White Men," "Colored Men," and "White Women," "Colored Women." And at the theater we had to go upstairs to go to a movie. You bought your ticket at the same window that the white people did, but they could sit downstairs, and you had to go upstairs.

—U.S. Congressman and civil rights leader John Lewis

Lunch-counter segregation protest in 1960.

❶ In 1896, in a famous case known as *Plessy* v. *Ferguson*, the U.S. Supreme Court ruled that states could enact laws separating people by skin color as long as the facilities for African Americans were equivalent to those for whites. This "separate but equal" decision stood for more than half a century, supporting a system of racial segregation in states throughout the South.

❷ In reality, separate was never equal. Take buses, for example. The fare was the same for all passengers, regardless of race. But if the "white section" at the front of the bus filled up, the invisible line separating it from the "colored section" simply moved back. Black people had to stand up so that white people could sit.

❸ Consider shopping. An African American woman could buy the same dress as a white woman, but she wasn't allowed to try it on in the store—and if she found that it didn't fit, she couldn't return it. Or restaurants. Some white-owned restaurants filled orders for blacks only at their takeout window. Others wouldn't serve them at all.

❹ Perhaps most separate, and most unequal, were the public schools. If you attended a "colored school," you might walk eight miles to school every morning, while buses full of white children drove past on their way to schools closer by. The schools attended by white children would be modern and well

Students attending a segregated school in the 1890s.

maintained, while yours would be old and run-down. White students would have up-to-date books and materials, while you might be forced to share a twenty-year-old textbook with three other students.

5 In 1949, several African American parents sued their school district over the inequalities between the local white elementary school and the school their children were forced to attend. Two years earlier the district had built a brand-new school for white students while leaving the black students' school in disrepair. Unlike the all-black school, the all-white school had an auditorium, a kindergarten, a part-time music teacher, a well-equipped playground, and a lunch program. The all-white school had a teacher and a separate room for each grade; the all-black school had only two teachers and two classrooms for all eight grades.

6 Finally, in 1954, the U.S. Supreme Court ruled in *Brown* v. *Board of Education* that segregated schools were by their very nature unequal. No longer would the highest court in the land support the myth of *Plessy* v. *Ferguson*. Separate could never be equal.

—Mara Rockliff

Analyzing a Comparison–Contrast Article

Separate but Never Equal

1. In *Brown* v. *Board of Education* the Supreme Court ruled that segregated schools are —
   - A similar
   - B legal
   - C unequal
   - D illegal

2. "Separate but Never Equal" works as a **title** for this article because the article —
   - F shows why the *Plessy* v. *Ferguson* ruling was unfair
   - G examines the conditions in public schools
   - H shows that things change over time
   - J justifies segregation

3. To learn more about the conditions described in this essay, you should —
   - A ask your principal
   - B talk to your history teacher
   - C read about conditions in northern schools
   - D study a map of the South

4. In which of these situations would reading a **compare-and-contrast** article be most helpful?
   - F You need to find out how life in China today differs from life in the United States.
   - G You need to do research on *Brown* v. *Board of Education*.
   - H You need to find out how many books Mildred Taylor has written.
   - J You want to learn how the Supreme Court works.

North Carolina Competency Goal
2.01

SKILLS FOCUS

Reading Skills
Analyze a comparison-contrast article.

Constructed Response

1. In the opening quotation, John Lewis makes three **comparisons.** What are they?
2. What is *Plessy* v. *Ferguson*?
3. Why did some African American parents sue their school district in 1949?
4. How long after that did it take for the Supreme Court to rule that separate schools were unequal?

5. In paragraph 5, the writer **contrasts** the schools attended by black children with those attended by white children. Draw an outline of two school buildings. Label one *All-White School* and one *All-Black School*. In each, list the contrasting points made in the essay.

La Bamba

Make the Connection
Quickwrite ✏️

Jot down some notes about a time when you had to perform in front of an audience. What do you remember about the experience? Did your mouth go dry? Did your voice shake? Did you forget your lines?

Literary Focus
The Short Story

Some forms of fiction have existed for centuries, but the short story is a newcomer. It became popular in the United States during the nineteenth century. At that time, magazines were beginning to be published, and new stories appeared in each issue. People gobbled them up, and a new form of fiction was born.

A **short story** is a fictional prose narrative that generally runs from five to twenty pages. A fictional narrative is one that's made up, invented by the writer.

Story and Structure

From the time they first appeared, short stories have been built the same way. You can use a chart like this one to map the structure of most stories:

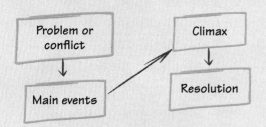

These building blocks are also found in novels and novellas, but the short story is, well, short. A short story usually has just one or two main characters and one conflict. It usually has no subplots.

Most short stories can be read in about an hour, in one sitting. Good short stories deliver an emotional punch, and they deliver fast. Maybe that's why the short story is so popular in our fast-paced age.

Reading Skills
Sequencing: What Happened When?

Most narratives are written in **chronological** order—the writer relates events in the **sequence** in which they happen. As you read a story, you'll find **time clues,** such as *later, next morning, three days earlier.* These clues tell you when events occur.

When you review a story, ask yourself these questions:

- What are the story's key events?
- When did each event happen?
- What happened before that event?
- What happened afterward?
- Did one event cause another event to happen?

As you read "La Bamba," look for a **flashback** to an earlier time—to an incident involving a flashlight.

North Carolina Competency Goal
1.04; 4.01; 5.01; 5.02

INTERNET
More About Soto
Keyword: LE5 6-4

SKILLS FOCUS

Literary Skills
Understand forms of fiction: the short story.

Reading Skills
Understand sequence.

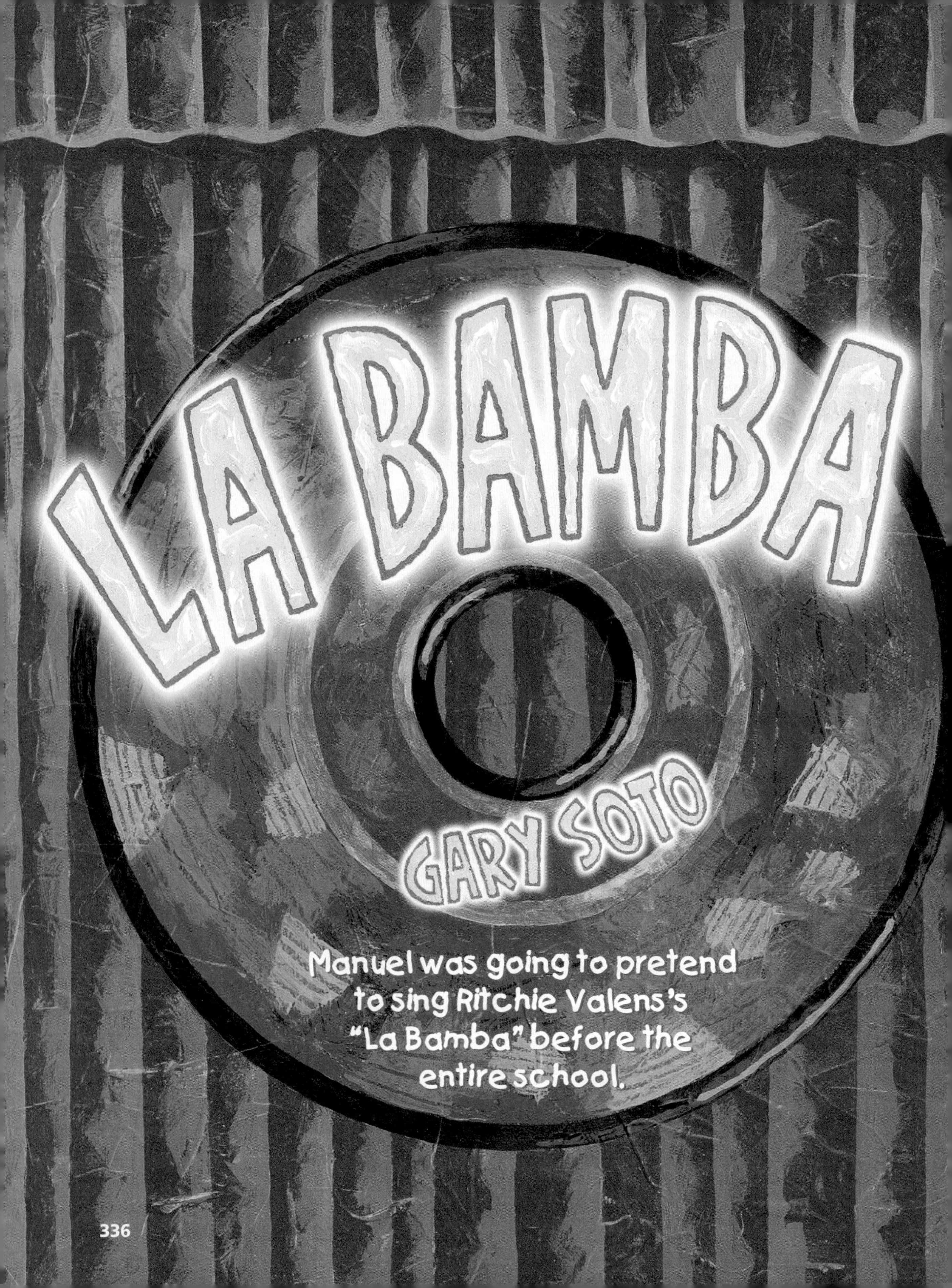

LA BAMBA

GARY SOTO

Manuel was going to pretend
to sing Ritchie Valens's
"La Bamba" before the
entire school.

Manuel was the fourth of seven children and looked like a lot of kids in his neighborhood: black hair, brown face, and skinny legs scuffed from summer play. But summer was giving way to fall: The trees were turning red, the lawns brown, and the pomegranate trees were heavy with fruit. Manuel walked to school in the frosty morning, kicking leaves and thinking of tomorrow's talent show. He was still amazed that he had volunteered. He was going to pretend to sing Ritchie Valens's[1] "La Bamba" before the entire school.

Why did I raise my hand? he asked himself, but in his heart he knew the answer. He yearned for the limelight. He wanted applause as loud as a thunderstorm and to hear his friends say, "Man, that was bad!" And he wanted to impress the girls, especially Petra Lopez, the second-prettiest girl in his class. The prettiest was already taken by his friend Ernie. Manuel knew he should be reasonable since he himself was not great-looking, just average.

Manuel kicked through the fresh-fallen leaves. When he got to school, he realized he had forgotten his math workbook. If the teacher found out, he would have to stay after school and miss practice for the talent show. But fortunately for him, they did drills that morning.

During lunch Manuel hung around with Benny, who was also in the talent show. Benny was going to play the trumpet in spite of the fat lip he had gotten playing football.

"How do I look?" Manuel asked. He cleared his throat and started moving his lips in pantomime. No words came out, just a hiss that sounded like a snake. Manuel tried to look emotional, flailing his arms on the high notes and opening his eyes and mouth as wide as he could when he came to "Para bailar la baaaaammmba."[2]

After Manuel finished, Benny said it looked all right but suggested Manuel dance while he sang. Manuel thought for a moment and decided it was a good idea.

"Yeah, just think you're like Michael Jackson or someone like that," Benny suggested. "But don't get carried away."

During rehearsal, Mr. Roybal, nervous about his debut as the school's talent co-ordinator, cursed under his breath when the lever that controlled the speed on the record player jammed.

"Darn," he growled, trying to force the lever. "What's wrong with you?"

"Is it broken?" Manuel asked, bending over for a closer look. It looked all right to him.

Mr. Roybal assured Manuel that he would have a good record player at the talent show, even if it meant bringing his own stereo from home.

---

1. **Ritchie Valens** (1941–1959), the professional singer mentioned in the story, was the first Mexican American rock star. In 1959, when he was only seventeen, Valens was killed in a plane crash.

2. **para bailar la bamba** (pä′rä bī′lär lä bäm′bä): Spanish for "to dance the bamba."

Manuel sat in a folding chair, twirling his record on his thumb. He watched a skit about personal hygiene, a mother-and-daughter violin duo, five first-grade girls jumping rope, a karate kid breaking boards, three girls singing "Like a Virgin," and a skit about the pilgrims. If the record player hadn't been broken, he would have gone after the karate kid, an easy act to follow, he told himself.

As he twirled his forty-five record, Manuel thought they had a great talent show. The entire school would be amazed. His mother and father would be proud, and his brothers and sisters would be jealous and pout. It would be a night to remember.

Benny walked onto the stage, raised his trumpet to his mouth, and waited for his cue. Mr. Roybal raised his hand like a symphony conductor and let it fall dramatically. Benny inhaled and blew so loud that Manuel dropped his record, which rolled across the cafeteria floor until it hit a wall.

Manuel raced after it, picked it up, and wiped it clean.

"Boy, I'm glad it didn't break," he said with a sigh.

That night Manuel had to do the dishes and a lot of homework, so he could only practice in the shower. In bed he prayed that he wouldn't mess up. He prayed that it wouldn't be like when he was a first-grader. For Science Week he had wired together a C battery and a bulb and told everyone he had discovered how a flashlight worked. He was so pleased with himself that he practiced for hours pressing the wire to the battery, making the bulb wink a dim, orangish light. He showed it to so many kids in his neighborhood that when it was time to show his class how a flashlight worked, the battery was dead. He pressed the wire to the battery, but the bulb didn't respond. He pressed until his thumb hurt and some kids in the back started snickering.

But Manuel fell asleep confident that nothing would go wrong this time.

The next morning his father and mother beamed at him. They were proud that he was going to be in the talent show.

"I wish you would tell us what you're doing," his mother said. His father, a pharmacist who wore a blue smock with his name on a plastic rectangle, looked up from the newspaper and sided with his wife. "Yes, what are you doing in the talent show?"

"You'll see," Manuel said, with his mouth full of Cheerios.

The day whizzed by, and so did his afternoon chores and dinner. Suddenly he was dressed in his best clothes and standing next to Benny backstage, listening to the commotion as the cafeteria filled with school kids and parents. The lights dimmed, and Mr. Roybal, sweaty in a tight suit and a necktie with a large knot, wet his lips and parted the stage curtains.

"Good evening, everyone," the kids behind the curtain heard him say. "Good evening to you," some of the smart-alecky kids said back to him.

"Tonight we bring you the best John Burroughs Elementary has to offer, and I'm sure that you'll be both pleased and amazed that our little school houses so much talent. And now, without further ado, let's get on with the show." He turned and, with a swish of his hand, commanded, "Part the curtain." The curtains parted in jerks. A girl dressed as a toothbrush and a boy dressed as a dirty gray tooth walked onto the stage and sang:

Brush, brush, brush
Floss, floss, floss
Gargle the germs away—hey! hey! hey!
After they finished singing, they turned to Mr. Roybal, who dropped his hand. The toothbrush dashed around the stage after the dirty tooth, which was laughing and having a great time until it slipped and nearly rolled off the stage.

Mr. Roybal jumped out and caught it just in time. "Are you OK?"

The dirty tooth answered, "Ask my dentist," which drew laughter and applause from the audience.

The violin duo played next, and except for one time when the girl got lost, they sounded fine. People applauded, and some even stood up. Then the first-grade girls maneuvered onto the stage while jumping rope. They were all smiles and bouncing ponytails as a hundred cameras flashed at once. Mothers "awhed" and fathers sat up proudly.

The karate kid was next. He did a few kicks, yells, and chops, and finally, when his father held up a board, punched it in two. The audience clapped and looked at each other, wide-eyed with respect. The boy bowed to the audience, and father and son ran off the stage.

Manuel remained behind the stage, shivering with fear. He mouthed the words to "La Bamba" and swayed left to right. Why did he raise his hand and volunteer? Why couldn't he have just sat there like the rest of the kids and not said anything? While the karate kid was onstage, Mr. Roybal, more sweaty than before, took Manuel's forty-five record and placed it on a new record player.

"You ready?" Mr. Roybal asked.

"Yeah . . ."

Mr. Roybal walked back on stage and announced that Manuel Gomez, a fifth-grader in Mrs. Knight's class, was going to pantomime Ritchie Valens's classic hit "La Bamba."

The cafeteria roared with applause. Manuel was nervous but loved the noisy crowd. He pictured his mother and father applauding loudly and his brothers and sister also clapping, though not as energetically.

Manuel walked on stage and the song started immediately. Glassy-eyed from the shock of being in front of so many people, Manuel moved his lips and swayed in a made-up dance step. He couldn't see his parents, but he could see his brother Mario, who was a year younger, thumb-wrestling with a friend. Mario was wearing Manuel's favorite shirt; he would deal with Mario later. He saw some other kids get up and head for the drinking fountain, and a baby sitting in the middle of an aisle sucking her thumb and watching him intently.

What am I doing here? thought Manuel. This is no fun at all. Everyone was just sitting there. Some people were moving to the beat, but most were just watching him, like they would a monkey at the zoo.

But when Manuel did a fancy dance step, there was a burst of applause and some girls screamed. Manuel tried another dance step. He heard more applause and screams and started getting into the groove as he shivered and snaked like Michael Jackson around the stage. But the record got stuck, and he had to sing

Para bailar la bamba
Para bailar la bamba
Para bailar la bamba
Para bailar la bamba

again and again.

Manuel couldn't believe his bad luck. The audience began to laugh and stand up in their chairs. Manuel remembered how the forty-five record had dropped from his hand and rolled across the cafeteria floor. It probably got scratched, he thought, and now it was stuck, and he was stuck dancing and moving his lips to the same words over and over. He had never been so embarrassed. He would have to ask his parents to move the family out of town.

After Mr. Roybal ripped the needle across the record, Manuel slowed his dance steps to a halt. He didn't know what to do except bow to the audience, which applauded wildly, and scoot off the stage, on the verge of tears. This was worse than the homemade flashlight. At least no one laughed then; they just snickered.

Manuel stood alone, trying hard to hold back the tears as Benny, center stage, played his trumpet. Manuel was jealous because he sounded great, then mad as he recalled that it was Benny's loud trumpet playing that made the forty-five record fly out of his hands. But when the entire cast lined up for a curtain call, Manuel received a burst of applause that was so loud it shook the walls of the cafeteria. Later, as he min-gled with the kids and parents, everyone

patted him on the shoulder and told him, "Way to go. You were really funny."

Funny? Manuel thought. Did he do something funny?

Funny. Crazy. Hilarious. These were the words people said to him. He was confused but beyond caring. All he knew was that people were paying attention to him, and his brother and sisters looked at him with a mixture of jealousy and awe. He was going to pull Mario aside and punch him in the arm for wearing his shirt, but he cooled it. He was enjoying the limelight. A teacher brought him cookies and punch, and the popular kids who had never before given him the time of day now clustered around him. Ricardo, the editor of the school bulletin, asked him how he made the needle stick.

"It just happened," Manuel said, crunching on a star-shaped cookie.

At home that night his father, eager to undo the buttons on his shirt and ease into his La-Z-Boy recliner, asked Manuel the same thing, how he managed to make the song stick on the words "Para bailar la bamba."

Manuel thought quickly and reached for scientific jargon he had read in magazines. "Easy, Dad. I used laser tracking with high optics and low functional decibels per channel." His proud but confused father told him to be quiet and go to bed.

"Ah, que niños tan truchas,"[3] he said as he walked to the kitchen for a glass of milk. "I don't know how you kids nowadays get so smart."

Manuel, feeling happy, went to his bedroom, undressed, and slipped into his pajamas. He looked in the mirror and began to pantomime "La Bamba," but stopped because he was tired of the song. He crawled into bed. The sheets were as cold as the moon that stood over the peach tree in their backyard.

He was relieved that the day was over. Next year, when they asked for volunteers for the talent show, he wouldn't raise his hand. Probably.

---

3. **que niños tan truchas** (kā nēn′yōs tän trōō′chäs): Spanish for "what smart kids."

Meet the Writer

Gary Soto

"My Friends . . . Jump Up and Down on the Page"

Like Manuel in "La Bamba," **Gary Soto** (1952–   ) grew up in a Mexican American family in California's San Joaquin Valley. He remembers being competitive:

> 66 I was a playground kid. I jumped at every chance to play. The game didn't matter. It could be kickball or baseball, or chess or Chinese checkers—anything that allowed me to compete. 99

He also says that he was not a very good student until he went to college and discovered poetry. Soon he yearned to be a writer himself—to win recognition by recapturing the world of his childhood in words. Of his early days as a writer, Soto remembers this:

> 66 I was a poet before I was a prose writer. As a poet, I needed only a sheaf of paper, a pen, a table, some quiet, and, of course, a narrative and spurts of image. I liked those years because the writing life was tidy. When I first started writing recollections and short stories, however, I needed more. I needed full-fledged stories and the patience of a monk. I needed to recall the narrative, characters, small moments, dates, places, etc. I was responsible for my writing, and, thus, it was tremendous work to keep it all in order. When I was writing *Living up the Street,* I clacked away on my typewriter with a bottle of white-out within view. I wrote, rewrote, and rewrote the rewrite, so that my friends would jump up and down on the page. 99

For Independent Reading

To meet more of Gary Soto's lively friends, check out *Baseball in April* and *Local News.*

First Thoughts

1. Complete one or both of these sentences:
   - If I were Manuel I would not . . .
   - "La Bamba" is realistic/unrealistic because . . .

Thinking Critically

2. Manuel remembers his attempt to show how a flashlight works. What does this memory tell you about Manuel's **character**?

3. A **simile** is a comparison between two unlike things, using a word such as *like, as,* or *resembles.* While he's onstage, what simile does Manuel use to describe the audience members watching him? Find two other similes in the story.

4. How are Manuel's moments onstage different from what he imagined they would be? Does the audience agree with Manuel that his performance is a disaster? Explain why, in your opinion, Manuel will or won't volunteer for the talent show next year.

Extending Interpretations

5. Do you think "La Bamba" is a funny story? If so, tell which moments or descriptions you found humorous. If not, explain why you didn't laugh.

6. How believable are Manuel's experiences and feelings? Review your Quickwrite notes, and compare Manuel's stage debut with your own experiences in front of an audience.

WRITING

Creating an Advice Manual

How would you help someone handle stage fright? Compile a list of tips called "How to Deal with Stage Fright." You can find advice in an article or book about stage acting or public speaking. You might even interview a performer or someone who often gives speeches (maybe a soloist in a choir or the PTA president). Collect as many tips as you can.

Reading Check

Make a sequence chart like the one below, showing the order of the main events in "La Bamba."

Sequence
Manuel volunteers for the talent show.
↓
During rehearsal he almost breaks his record.
↓
Event 3
↓
Event 4

[and so on]

go.hrw.com

INTERNET
Projects and Activities
Keyword: LE5 6-4

SKILLS FOCUS

Literary Skills
Analyze a short story.

Reading Skills
Analyze sequence.

Writing Skills
Write a "how-to" explanation.

North Carolina
Competency Goal
1.02; 1.04; 4.01; 4.02; 5.01; 5.02

Words with Multiple Meanings

Multiple-meaning words are words with more than one meaning. When you look up a multiple-meaning word in a dictionary, you'll find a numbered list of definitions, as in this example:

> **shower** (shou'ər) *n.* **1.** a brief rainfall   **2.** a party at which someone is honored and given gifts   **3.** a bath in which water pours down on the body   —*v.* **1.** to spray   **2.** to pour forth like a shower   **3.** to take a shower

If you come across a multiple-meaning word and you're not sure which meaning is the one intended, figure out what part of speech it is. Then, look at its **context,** the words around it. If you're still confused, look at the definitions listed in a dictionary. Then, choose the one that fits best in the sentence.

Here is a sentence from "La Bamba." Which definition of *shower* fits best in the context?

> **"That night Manuel had to do the dishes and a lot of homework, so he could only practice in the shower."**

PRACTICE

The following multiple-meaning words are from "La Bamba." Think about the different meanings of each word. Then, choose four of the words. For each of your words, write *two* sentences that show *two* distinct meanings. If you can't think of more than one meaning for a word, look in a dictionary.

cast   fall   wire   sign   battery   stage   time

Choose one of the pairs of sentences you've written, and illustrate them with pictures that show the difference in meaning.

North Carolina Competency Goal
5.01; 5.02; 6.01

SKILLS FOCUS

Vocabulary Skills
Identify and interpret multiple-meaning words.

Analyzing Text Structures: Comparison and Contrast

Reading Focus
Point-by-Point and Block Patterns

Writers who want to present two sides of an issue often organize their material in a comparison-and-contrast pattern. This is a good way to show how two or more things are different and also how they're alike. When writers **compare** things, they look for similarities. When they **contrast** things, they look for differences.

When writers compare and contrast, they generally arrange their ideas according to one of two organizational patterns: the **point-by-point pattern** and the **block pattern.**

A writer using the point-by-point pattern moves back and forth between the subjects being compared, discussing one feature at a time. (See the chart below on the left.)

A writer using the block pattern covers all the points of comparison for the first subject, then for the second subject, and so on. (See the chart below on the right.)

■ The following article explains how audio technology has evolved from vinyl records—such as the one Manuel plays—to compact discs. Which organizational pattern does the writer use?

North Carolina Competency Goal
2.01; 5.01; 5.02

Comparing Records and CDs: Point-by-Point Pattern	
Point of comparison 1: how they're made	• **records:** vibrations produced by sound waves cut a groove on a disc • **CDs:** computers translate sound waves into electronic information
Point of comparison 2: how they sound	• **records:** somewhat inaccurate • **CDs:** nearly perfect

Comparing Records and CDs: Block Pattern	
Subject 1: records	• **Feature 1:** how they're made • **Feature 2:** how they sound
Subject 2: CDs	• **Feature 1:** how they're made • **Feature 2:** how they sound

SKILLS FOCUS

Reading Skills
Analyze a comparison-contrast article.

GOOD BYE RECORDS, Hello CDs

Twenty years ago every music lover in America had a turntable for playing vinyl records. Then, in 1983, the CD player arrived on the scene. It quickly became the fastest-selling machine in home-electronics history. Record stores couldn't order the new CDs fast enough to keep up with demand. Soon CDs were everywhere, and record players had gone the way of the dinosaurs. What happened?

THE FIRST "RECORD"

It all goes way back to 1877, when the inventor Thomas Edison made the first sound recording ever. The "record" was a cylinder covered with tinfoil, and the recorder was a hand-cranked machine with a metal **stylus,** or needle. "Mary had a little lamb," Edison said into the machine, and as he turned the crank, the vibrations of his voice made the stylus wiggle, carving grooves and dents in the foil.

Edison called his new machine a **phonograph.** The word comes from the Greek roots –*phono*–, meaning "sound," and –*graph*–, meaning "write." The stylus had "written" the sounds of his words on the foil, and it could "read" them back over and over. The dents made the stylus vibrate, and the vibrations came out through a horn as a scratchy, croaking version of Edison's voice—at least until the foil wore out, as it did after about five playings.

A century later, sound recording had come a long way. Edison's tinfoil cylinders and hand-cranked phonograph were ancient history, replaced by long-playing vinyl records that were played on high-fidelity electronic stereo systems. Country music, disco, rock—whatever you liked, you could slide a record album out of its cardboard cover, drop it on your turntable, set the needle in the groove, and settle back to listen to some pretty good sounds.

What had *not* changed was the basic technology. It was still **analog,** meaning that each squiggly groove cut in the surface of a record corresponded to the sound wave it captured. And analog technology had certain problems. In a live performance the volume of the music can range from extremely soft to extremely loud. But to fit in a groove that a stylus could follow, the range of volume in any one recording had to be narrowed. Then there were playback problems, such as "wow" and "flutter" (changes in pitch caused by slight variations in the turntable's speed) and "rumble" (noise picked up from the turntable's motor).

The writer describes problems with records and record players.

Even records that sounded good at first could eventually warp or wear out. Records also got scratched easily—often by a slip of the same stylus that read the grooves—and a scratch could ruin a record, making the same bit of music play over and over and over: "*Para bailar la bamba, para bailar la bamba, para bailar la bamba . . .*"

She explains how records can be damaged.

THE CD REVOLUTION

Enter the compact disc, or CD. Sound is recorded on a CD not by a needle cutting a groove on a disk but by a computer translating sound waves into electronic information. The computer divides each second of sound into 44,100 units, each of which gets its own digital code. The code represents one of 65,536 possible sound values. This wide range of sound values allows tiny variations in sound to be captured with amazing accuracy. That's why the sound of a CD is true to life. Imagine that you're trying to match a particular shade of paint to a color in a picture. If you have 65,536 shades to choose from, you have a good chance of finding one that's almost exactly like the color you're looking for.

Subject 2: CDs
The writer explains how CDs work.

At first the CD sometimes sounded *too* perfect. Early CDs reproduced even the squeak of a violinist's fingers on an instrument's string, something a live concert audience would probably never hear—or want to. Some music lovers found the sound of CDs cold and artificial in its computerized perfection.

Then listeners came to appreciate the benefits of CDs. Not only is their sound better than that of records, but they're more durable, thanks to the new technology. Sound is recorded on the surface of a CD in the form of tiny pits and smooth areas. The surface is then covered with layers of aluminum and acrylic. Thus, the laser in a CD player never actually touches the surface on which the music is recorded. Unlike a phonograph needle, which can scratch or wear out a record, the laser will not damage or wear out a CD.

She describes some of the advantages of CDs.

Best of all, unlike record players, which cost more the better the sound quality, all CD systems use lasers and digital technology. So even the cheapest CD player offers music lovers excellent sound. Edison would be amazed.

The writer ends with a final point of contrast.

—Mara Rockliff

Analyzing a Comparison–Contrast Article

GOODBYE RECORDS, Hello CDs

Test Practice

1. Which of the following statements is true of CDs?
   A They do not wear out easily.
   B They're made by cutting a groove on a disc.
   C They're played on a turntable.
   D Their sound is not true to life.

2. This article was written mainly to —
   F persuade people to buy records
   G explain the differences between CDs and records
   H prove that live music is best
   J describe the life of Thomas Edison

3. In the word telegraph the Greek root –graph– means —
   A write
   B draw
   C speak
   D picture

4. In the first paragraph of the essay, the writer says that "record players had gone the way of the dinosaurs." She uses the expression "gone the way of the dinosaurs" to show that record players —
   F take up too much room
   G are disliked by consumers
   H are easier to operate than CD players
   J are no longer in use

5. According to the article, another word for stylus is —
   A flutter
   B needle
   C groove
   D turntable

North Carolina Competency Goal
1.04; 2.01;
4.01; 4.02;
5.01

Reading Skills
Analyze a comparison-contrast article.

Constructed Response

1. What overall pattern of organization does the writer use: **point by point** or **block**? To check your answer, make a chart showing how the essay is organized. (You can use the charts on page 345 as models.)

2. How is **analog** technology defined?

3. What are some of the problems with analog technology? How are these problems avoided with the technology used to make CDs?

4. **Compare** and **contrast** records and CDs by naming two ways in which they're similar and two ways in which they're different.

After You Read | Vocabulary Development

Words with Multiple Meanings

PRACTICE

The quotations below are taken from "Goodbye Records, Hello CDs." Write a sentence about each of the subjects listed below each quotation, using the underlined word. You may be able to think of several meanings for some of the words. Use any form of the words you like.

1. "Every music lover in America had a turntable for playing vinyl records." Use the word *records* in sentences about a —
   - trial
   - dance contest

2. "The vibrations came out through a horn as a scratchy, croaking version of Edison's voice. . . ." Use the word *horn* in sentences about a —
   - zoo
   - concert

3. "Country music, disco, rock—whatever you liked, you could . . . settle back to listen to some pretty good sounds." Use the word *rock* in sentences about a —
   - forest
   - fishing trip

4. "Changes in pitch caused by slight variations in the turntable's speed . . ." Use the word *pitch* in sentences about a —
   - song
   - baseball game

5. "Sound is recorded . . . by a computer translating sound waves into electronic information." Use the word *waves* in sentences about —
   - the ocean
   - a farewell party

SKILLS FOCUS

Vocabulary Skills
Identify and interpret multiple-meaning words.

North Carolina Competency Goal
2.01, 6.01

Goodbye Records, Hello CDs   **349**

Medusa's Head *and*
Perseus and the Gorgon's Head

Make the Connection
Talk It Over

The idea of fate is important in this Greek myth. *Fate* refers to a power that is believed to decide the future no matter what we do. You learn right away in this story that a king has received bad news from an oracle (ôr′ə·kəl)—a priest or priestess who can foretell the future. He has learned that one day he will be killed by his own grandson.

Think about this situation for a few minutes. Then, with several classmates, discuss what it would be like to know what will happen in the future.

Literary Focus
Mythic Heroes

What characters can fly, become invisible, and call on other magical powers in the fight against evil? You'll probably think of modern comic-book characters, such as Batman or Superman. In "Medusa's Head" you'll meet an ancient mythic hero, Perseus, who can do all these things—and more.

In the world of **myth,** heroes do things we wish we could do and things we're glad we don't have to do. Heroes in myths represent the hopes and fears of the people who created them.

Heroes in myths are often helped by gods. Sometimes they are gods themselves. These superheroes usually have magical powers, and they always face great difficulties and challenges

(like slaying a monster). Often a mythic hero saves a whole society from ruin.

Reading Skills
Dialogue with the Text

As you read this story, jot down your responses to it. Ask questions about unfamiliar words, and try to predict what will happen next.

Vocabulary Development

These are the words you'll learn as you read "Medusa's Head":

descended (dē·send′id) *v.:* moved to a lower place; came down. *Out of pity, Zeus, king of the Greek gods, descended to the imprisoned girl.*

perplexity (pər·plek′sə·tē) *n.:* bewilderment; confusion. *In his perplexity, Perseus turned to Athene.*

perpetual (pər·pech′ōō·əl) *adj.:* permanent; constant. *Medusa's sisters live in a place of perpetual twilight, where there is neither day nor night.*

recesses (rē′ses·əz) *n.:* inner places. *The sisters scrambled to the recesses of the cave after Perseus stole their sight.*

hovered (huv′ərd) *v.:* remained suspended in the air. *Wearing the winged sandals, Perseus hovered high above the rocks.*

North Carolina Competency Goal
1.04; 4.01; 5.01

go.hrw.com

INTERNET
Vocabulary Activity
Keyword: LE5 6-4

SKILLS FOCUS

Literary Skills
Identify forms of fiction: myths.

Reading Skills
Dialogue with the text.

Characters and Places

King Acrisios (ə·crē′sē·ōs′) **of Argos** (är′gäs′):
Argos was an ancient city and kingdom in
southern Greece. Also spelled Acrisius.

Proitos (prō·ē′tōs): brother of King Acrisios.

Danae (dan′ā·ē′): daughter of King Acrisios.
She bears Zeus's son Perseus.

Apollo: Greek god of light, medicine, poetry,
and prophecy. The oracle of Apollo was a
priest or priestess through whom the god
was believed to speak.

Zeus (zoōs): king of the Greek gods.

Dictys (dic′tis): fisherman, brother of Polydectes. He and Polydectes live on the
island of Seriphos. Also spelled Seriphus.

Polydectes (päl′ē·dek′tēz): king of Seriphos.

Perseus (pʉr′sē·əs): son of Danae and Zeus.

Gorgons: three fearsome sisters with brass
hands, gold wings, and serpentlike scales.

Medusa, the youngest Gorgon, has
snakes for hair and a face so terrible that
it turns to stone anyone who looks at it.

Athene (ə·thē′nē): Greek goddess of crafts,
war, and wisdom. Her name is also
spelled *Athena*.

Phorcides (fôr′sə·dēz): three sisters who live
in a cave and have only one eye and one
tooth between them.

Hermes (hʉr′mēz′): messenger of the gods.

Cepheus (sē′fē·əs): king of Ethiopia.

Cassiopeia (kas′ē·ō·pē′ə): queen of Ethiopia.

Andromeda (an·dräm′ə·də): daughter of
King Cepheus and Queen Cassiopeia. She
has been chained to a rock near the sea
to calm the anger of the god Poseidon.

Nereus (nir′ē·əs): a minor sea god.

Poseidon (pō·sī′dən): god of the sea.

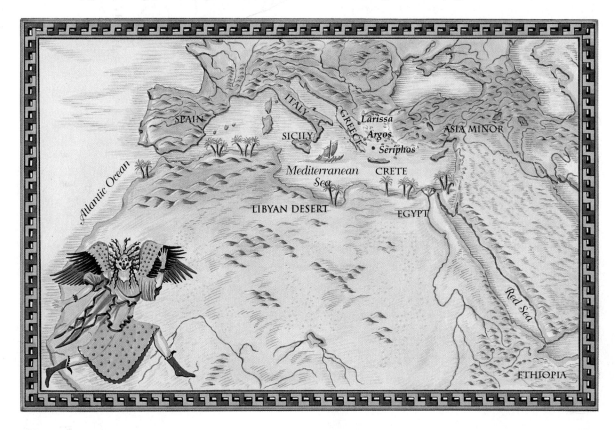

The Head of Medusa by Peter Paul Rubens (1577–1640). Oil on canvas.
Kunsthistorisches Museum, Gemaeldegalerie, Vienna, Austria.

Medusa's Head

Greek myth, retold by
Olivia Coolidge

King Acrisios of Argos was a hard, selfish man. He hated his brother, Proitos, who later drove him from his kingdom, and he cared nothing for his daughter, Danae. His whole heart was set on having a son who should succeed him, but since many years went by and still he had only the one daughter, he sent a message to the oracle of Apollo to ask whether he should have more children of his own. The answer of the oracle was terrible. Acrisios should have no son, but his daughter, Danae, would bear him a grandchild who should grow up to kill him. At these words Acrisios was beside himself with fear and rage. Swearing that Danae should never have a child to murder him, he had a room built underground and lined all through with brass. Thither he conducted Danae and shut her up, bidding her spend the rest of her life alone.

It is possible to thwart the plans of mortal men, but never those of the gods. Zeus himself looked with pity on the unfortunate girl, and it is said he <u>descended</u> to her through the tiny hole that gave light and air to her chamber, pouring himself down into her lap in the form of a shower of gold.

When word came to the king from those who brought food and drink to his daughter that the girl was with child, Acrisios was angry and afraid. He would have liked best to murder both Danae and her infant son, Perseus, but he did not dare for fear of the gods' anger at so hideous a crime. He made, therefore, a great chest of wood with bands of brass about it. Shutting up the girl and her baby inside, he cast them into the sea, thinking that they would either drown or starve.

Again the gods came to the help of Danae, for they caused the planks of the chest to swell until they fitted tightly and let no water in.

The chest floated for some days and was cast up at last on an island. There Dictys, a fisherman, found it and took Danae to his brother, Polydectes, who was king of the island. Danae was made a servant in the palace, yet before many years had passed, both Dictys and Polydectes had fallen in love with the silent, golden-haired girl. She in her heart preferred Dictys, yet since his brother was king, she did not dare to make her choice. Therefore she hung always over Perseus, pretending that mother love left her no room for any other, and year after year a silent frown would cross Polydectes' face as he saw her caress the child.

At last, Perseus became a young man, handsome and strong beyond the common and a leader among the youths of the island, though he was but the son of a poor servant. Then it seemed to Polydectes that if he could once get rid of Perseus, he could force Danae to become his wife, whether she would or not. Meanwhile, in order to lull the young man's suspicions, he pretended that he intended to marry a certain noble maiden and would collect a wedding gift for her. Now the custom was that this gift of the bridegroom to the bride was in part his own and in part put together from the marriage presents of his friends and relatives. All the young men, therefore, brought Polydectes a present, excepting Perseus, who was his servant's son and possessed nothing to bring. Then Polydectes said to the others, "This young man owes me more than any of you, since I took him in and brought him

Vocabulary

descended (dē·send′id) v.: moved to a lower place; came down.

Medusa by Michelangelo Caravaggio (1573–1610).
Uffizi, Florence, Italy. © Scala/Art Resource, NY.

up in my own house, and yet he gives me nothing."

Perseus answered in anger at the injustice of the charge, "I have nothing of my own, Polydectes, yet ask me what you will, and I will fetch it, for I owe you my life."

At this Polydectes smiled, for it was what he had intended, and he answered, "Fetch me, if this is your boast, the Gorgon's head."

Now the Gorgons, who lived far off on the shores of the ocean, were three fearful sisters with hands of brass, wings of gold, and scales like a serpent. Two of them had scaly heads and tusks like the wild boar, but the third, Medusa, had the face of a beautiful woman with hair of writhing serpents, and so terrible was her expression that all who looked on it were immediately turned to stone. This much Perseus knew of the Gorgons, but of how to find or kill them, he had no idea. Nevertheless, he had given his promise, and though he saw now the satisfaction of King Polydectes, he was bound to keep his word. In his perplexity, he prayed to the wise goddess Athene, who came to him in a vision and promised him her aid.

"First, you must go," she said, "to the sisters Phorcides, who will tell you the way to the nymphs who guard the hat of darkness, the winged sandals, and the knapsack which can hold the Gorgon's head. Then I will give you a shield, and my brother Hermes will give you a sword, which shall be made of adamant, the hardest rock. For nothing else can kill the Gorgon, since so venomous is her blood that a mortal sword, when plunged in it, is eaten away. But when you come to the Gorgons, invisible in your hat of darkness, turn your eyes away from them and look only on their reflection in your gleaming shield. Thus you may kill the monster without yourself being turned to stone. Pass her sisters by, for they are immortal, but smite off the head of Medusa with the hair of writhing snakes. Then put it in your knapsack and return, and I will be with you."

The vision ended, and with the aid of Athene, Perseus set out on the long journey to seek the Phorcides. These live in a dim cavern in the far north, where nights and days are one and where the whole earth is overspread with perpetual twilight. There sat the three old women mumbling to one another, crouched in a dim heap together, for they had but one eye and one tooth between them, which they passed from hand to hand. Perseus came quietly behind them, and as they fumbled for the eye, he put his strong, brown hand next to one of the long,

---

Vocabulary

perplexity (pər·plek′sə·tē) *n.:* bewilderment; confusion.

perpetual (pər·pech′oo·əl) *adj.:* permanent; constant.

yellow ones, so that the old crone thought that it was her sister's and put the eye into it. There was a high scream of anger when they discovered the theft, and much clawing and groping in the dim recesses of the cavern. But they were helpless in their blindness and Perseus could laugh at them. At length, for the price of their eye, they told him how to reach the nymphs, and Perseus, laying the eye quickly in the hand of the nearest sister, fled as fast as he could before she could use it.

Again it was a far journey to the garden of the nymphs, where it is always sunshine and the trees bear golden apples. But the nymphs are friends of the wise gods and hate the monsters of darkness and the spirits of anger and despair. Therefore, they received Perseus with rejoicing and put the hat of darkness on his head, while on his feet they bound the golden, winged sandals, which are those Hermes wears when he runs down the slanting sunbeams or races along the pathways of the wind. Next, Perseus put on his back the silver sack with the gleaming tassels of gold, and flung across his shoulder the black-sheathed sword that was the gift of Hermes. On his left arm he fitted the shield that Athene gave, a gleaming silver shield like a mirror, plain without any marking. Then he sprang into the air and ran, invisible like the rushing wind, far out over the white-capped sea, across the yellow sands of the eastern desert, over strange streams and towering mountains, until at last he came to the shores of the distant ocean which flowed round all the world.

There was a gray gorge of stone by the ocean's edge, where lay Medusa and her

Medusa. Mosaic.   The Athens Museum.

Vocabulary
recesses (rē′ses·əz) *n.:* inner places.

Perseus beheading the Gorgon Medusa, from a temple in Selinunte, an ancient Greek colony in Sicily.

Galleria Nationale, Palermo, Italy. © Scala/Art Resource, NY.

sisters sleeping in the dim depths of the rock. All up and down the cleft, the stones took fantastic shapes of trees, beasts, birds, or serpents. Here and there, a man who had looked on the terrible Medusa stood forever with horror on his face. Far over the twilit gorge Perseus <u>hovered</u> invisible, while he loosened the pale, strange sword from its black sheath. Then, with his face turned away and eyes on the silver shield, he dropped, slow and silent as a falling leaf, down through the rocky cleft, twisting and

turning past countless strange gray shapes, down from the bright sunlight into a chill, dim shadow echoing and reechoing with the dashing of waves on the tumbled rocks beneath. There on the heaped stones lay the Gorgons sleeping together in the dimness, and even as he looked on them in the shield, Perseus felt stiff with horror at the sight.

Two of the Gorgons lay sprawled together,

Vocabulary
hovered (huv′ərd) *v.*: remained suspended in the air.

356   Collection 4 / Forms of Fiction

shaped like women, yet scaled from head to foot as serpents are. Instead of hands they had gleaming claws like eagles, and their feet were dragons' feet. Skinny metallic wings like bats' wings hung from their shoulders. Their faces were neither snake nor woman, but part both, like faces in a nightmare. These two lay arm in arm and never stirred. Only the blue snakes still hissed and writhed round the pale, set face of Medusa, as though even in sleep she were troubled by an evil dream. She lay by herself, arms outstretched, face upwards, more beautiful and terrible than living man may bear. All the crimes and madnesses of the world rushed into Perseus' mind as he gazed at her image in the shield. Horror stiffened his arm as he hovered over her with his sword uplifted. Then he shut his eyes to the vision and in the darkness struck.

There was a great cry and a hissing. Perseus groped for the head and seized it by the limp and snaky hair. Somehow he put it in his knapsack and was up and off, for at the dreadful scream the sister Gorgons had awakened. Now they were after him, their sharp claws grating against his silver shield. Perseus strained forward on the pathway of the wind like a runner, and behind him the two sisters came, smelling out the prey they could not see. Snakes darted from their girdles,° foam flew from their tusks, and the great wings beat the air. Yet the winged sandals were even swifter than they, and Perseus fled like the hunted deer with the speed of desperation. Presently the horrible noise grew faint behind him, the hissing of snakes and the sound of the bat wings died away. At last the Gorgons could smell him no longer and returned home unavenged.

° **girdles** *n*.: belts or sashes.

By now, Perseus was over the Libyan desert, and as the blood from the horrible head touched the sand, it changed to serpents, from which the snakes of Africa are descended.

The storms of the Libyan desert blew against Perseus in clouds of eddying sand, until not even the divine sandals could hold him on his course. Far out to sea he was blown, and then north. Finally, whirled around the heavens like a cloud of mist, he alighted in the distant west, where the giant Atlas held up on his shoulders the heavens from the earth. There the weary giant, crushed under the load of centuries, begged Perseus to show him Medusa's head. Perseus uncovered for him the dreadful thing, and Atlas was changed to the mighty mountain whose rocks rear up to reach the sky near the gateway to the Atlantic. Perseus himself, returning eastwards and still battling with the wind, was driven south to the land of Ethiopia, where King Cepheus reigned with his wife, Cassiopeia.

As Perseus came wheeling in like a gull from the ocean, he saw a strange sight. Far out to sea the water was troubled, seething and boiling as though stirred by a great force moving in its depths. Huge, sullen waves were starting far out and washing inland over sunken trees and flooded houses. Many miles of land were under water, and as he sped over them, he saw the muddy sea lapping around the foot of a black, upstanding rock. Here on a ledge above the water's edge stood a young girl chained by the arms, lips parted, eyes open and staring, face white as her linen garment. She might have been a statue, so still she stood, while the light breeze fluttered her dress and stirred her loosened hair. As Perseus looked at her and

Gorgon (6th century B.C.).

looked at the sea, the water began to boil again, and miles out a long gray scaly back of vast length lifted itself above the flood. At that, there was a shriek from a distant knoll where he could dimly see the forms of people, but the girl shrank a little and said nothing. Then Perseus, taking off the hat of darkness, alighted near the maiden to talk to her, and she, though nearly mad with terror, found words at last to tell him her tale.

Her name was Andromeda, and she was the only child of the king and of his wife, Cassiopeia. Queen Cassiopeia was exceedingly beautiful, so that all people marveled at her. She herself was proud of her dark eyes, her white, slender fingers, and her long black hair, so proud that she had been heard to boast that she was fairer even than the sea nymphs, who are daughters of Nereus. At this, Nereus in wrath stirred up Poseidon, who came flooding in over the land, covering it far and wide. Not content with this, he sent a vast monster from the dark depths of the bottomless sea to ravage the whole coast of Ethiopia. When the unfortunate king and queen had sought the advice of the oracle on how to appease the god, they had been ordered to sacrifice their only daughter to the sea monster Poseidon had sent. Not daring for their people's sake to disobey, they had chained her to this rock, where she now awaited the beast who should devour her.

Perseus comforted Andromeda as he stood by her on the rock, and she shrank closer against him while the great gray back writhed its half-mile length slowly towards the land. Then, bidding Andromeda hide her face, Perseus sprang once more into the air, unveiling the dreadful head of dead Medusa to the monster, which reared its dripping jaws yards high into the air. The mighty tail stiffened all of a sudden, the boiling of the water ceased, and only the gentle waves of the receding ocean lapped around a long, gray ridge of stone. Then Perseus freed Andromeda and restored her to her father and beautiful mother. Thereafter, with their consent, he married her amid scenes of tremendous rejoicing, and with his bride set sail at last for the kingdom of Polydectes.

Polydectes had lost no time on the departure of Perseus. First he had begged Danae to become his wife, and then he had threatened her. Undoubtedly, he would have got his way by force if Danae had not fled in terror to Dictys. The two took refuge at the altar of a temple whence Polydectes did not dare drag them away. So matters stood when Perseus returned. Polydectes was enraged to see him, for he had hoped at least that Danae's most powerful protector would never return. But now, seeing him famous and with a king's daughter to wife, he could not contain himself. Openly he laughed at the tale of Perseus, saying that the hero had never killed the Gorgon, only pretended to, and that now he was claiming an honor he did not deserve. At this, Perseus, enraged by the insult and by reports of his mother's persecution, said to him, "You asked me for the Gorgon's head. Behold it!" And with that he lifted it high, and Polydectes became stone.

Then Perseus left Dictys to be king of that island, but he himself went back to the Grecian mainland to seek out his grandfather, Acrisios, who was once again king of Argos.

First, however, he gave back to the gods the gifts they had given him. Hermes took back the golden sandals and the hat of darkness, for both are his. But Athene took Medusa's head, and she hung it on a fleece around her neck as part of her battle equipment, where it may be seen in statues and portraits of the warlike goddess.

Perseus took ship for Greece, but his fame had gone before him, and King Acrisios fled secretly from Argos in terror, since he remembered the prophecy and feared that Perseus had come to avenge the wrongs of Danae. The trembling old Acrisios took refuge in Larissa, where it happened the king was holding a great athletic contest in honor of his dead father.

Heroes from all over Greece, among whom was Perseus, came to the games. As Perseus was competing at the discus throwing, he threw high into the air and far beyond the rest. A strong wind caught the discus as it spun, so that it left the course marked out for it and was carried into the stands. People scrambled away to right and left. Only Acrisios was not nimble enough. The heavy weight fell full on his foot and crushed his toes, and at that, the feeble old man, already weakened by his terrors, died from the shock. Thus the prophecy of Apollo was fulfilled at last; Acrisios was killed by his grandson. Then Perseus came into his kingdom, where he reigned with Andromeda long and happily.

To read about Olivia Coolidge, see Meet the Writer on page 262.

Perseus and the Gorgon's Head

retold by Marcia Williams

King Acrisius of Argos was a worried man.

He had been warned that his daughter, Danaë, would have a son who would kill him.

So when Danaë bore a baby boy, named Perseus,

Acrisius put them both in a wooden chest

and pushed it out to sea.

For days the chest tossed on the waves.

Finally, it washed up on the shores of Seriphus

where Dictys, the brother of King Polydectes, found it.

He was amazed to see Danaë and Perseus inside.

The grumpy king allowed them to stay in the palace.

Perseus grew up strong and handsome.

Meanwhile, the king fell in love with Danaë.

He proposed to her at every opportunity.

And at every opportunity, Danaë refused him.

Polydectes plotted to get rid of Perseus by sending him on a deadly mission.

Still Danaë refused to marry the king.

So Polydectes sent Perseus to fetch the head of the Gorgon Medusa.

Medusa was one of three monstrous sisters, with brass hands and golden wings, whose glance could turn men and beasts to stone.

But Perseus was not afraid.

He traveled for many days

but found no sign of Medusa.

Wearily, he lay down to rest.

As he slept, the goddess Athena came to him, bringing him a shield

in which he could look at Medusa's reflection, so that he would not be turned to stone.

The next day he set off again, but there was still no sign of Medusa.

That night, the god Hermes visited Perseus.

He gave him a sickle with which to cut off Medusa's snake-covered head.

Then Hermes told Perseus to go to the Gray Ones.

These three sisters had only one eye and one tooth between them.

Perseus went to Mount Atlas, where the Gray Ones lived.

Creeping up behind them, he snatched their single eye and tooth.

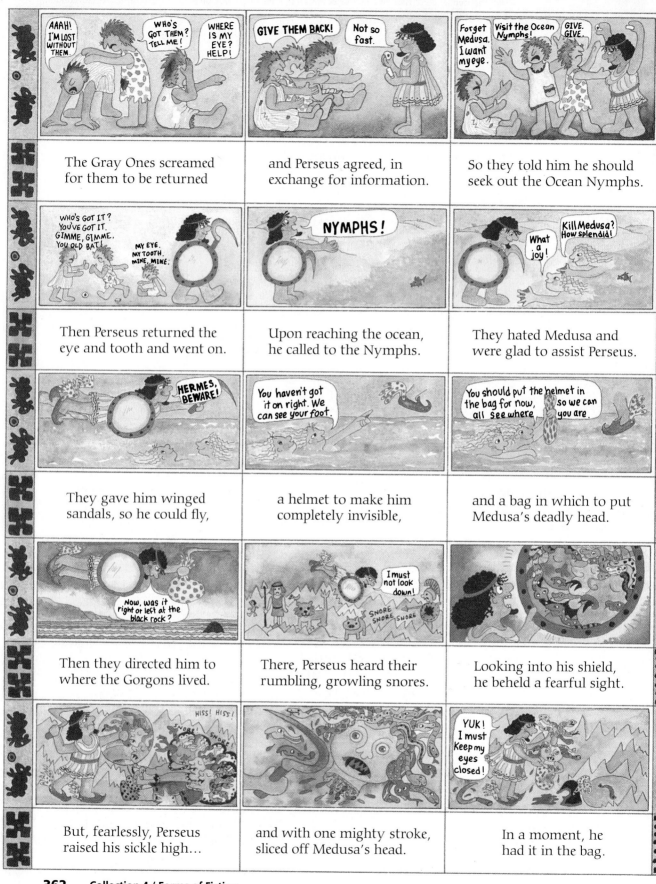

The Gray Ones screamed for them to be returned

and Perseus agreed, in exchange for information.

So they told him he should seek out the Ocean Nymphs.

Then Perseus returned the eye and tooth and went on.

Upon reaching the ocean, he called to the Nymphs.

They hated Medusa and were glad to assist Perseus.

They gave him winged sandals, so he could fly,

a helmet to make him completely invisible,

and a bag in which to put Medusa's deadly head.

Then they directed him to where the Gorgons lived.

There, Perseus heard their rumbling, growling snores.

Looking into his shield, he beheld a fearful sight.

But, fearlessly, Perseus raised his sickle high…

and with one mighty stroke, sliced off Medusa's head.

In a moment, he had it in the bag.

As he leapt into the air, Medusa's sisters woke.

Quickly, Perseus donned the helmet and instantly vanished from their sight.

His journey home was not an easy one.

But, after a year, he arrived at Seriphus.

Perseus found his mother hiding from King Polydectes in the temple.

So he went on to the palace.

Polydectes was convinced that Perseus had long since been turned to stone.

The king was horrified to see him alive.

But before he could speak, Perseus pulled out Medusa's head.

Its gaze immediately turned the king to stone.

Perseus then rescued his mother and, before leaving the island, crowned Dictys the new King of Seriphus.

They sailed for Argos where, later, Perseus accidentally killed King Acrisius, as the oracle had predicted.

First Thoughts

1. What do you think of Perseus? Do we have heroes like him today? Refer to your reading notes for your responses to the story.

Thinking Critically

2. Why is Perseus a good example of a mythic hero? (Think about how he handles challenges and how the gods help him.)

3. How does this myth illustrate the idea that no one can escape fate? What do you think of the ancient Greek belief that everything that happens is decided in advance by fate?

Extending Interpretations

4. Modern stories of action heroes often resemble ancient myths. What movies or TV shows remind you of the story of Perseus? Think about these elements in the myth:

a. the hero threatened at birth

b. the beautiful woman in danger

c. the awful monster

d. the role played by magic

e. the perils faced by the hero

f. the people who help the hero

g. the triumph of good over evil

WRITING

Writing a Story

Make up a story about a character who can become invisible. Jot down some ideas about the way the character becomes invisible, the things he or she can do that visible characters can't do, and the dangers that an invisible person would face. If you wish, tell your story in the form of a cartoon.

North Carolina Competency Goal
1.01; 1.02; 1.04; 4.01; 4.02; 5.01

go.hrw.com

INTERNET
Projects and Activities
Keyword: LE5 6-4

SKILLS FOCUS

Literary Skills
Analyze a myth.

Reading Skills
Dialogue with the text.

Writing Skills
Write a short story.

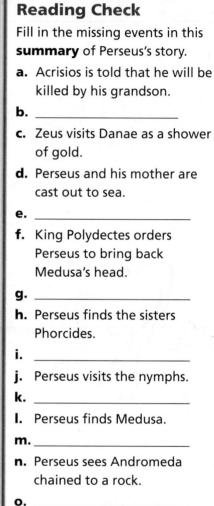

Reading Check

Fill in the missing events in this **summary** of Perseus's story.

a. Acrisios is told that he will be killed by his grandson.

b. _____

c. Zeus visits Danae as a shower of gold.

d. Perseus and his mother are cast out to sea.

e. _____

f. King Polydectes orders Perseus to bring back Medusa's head.

g. _____

h. Perseus finds the sisters Phorcides.

i. _____

j. Perseus visits the nymphs.

k. _____

l. Perseus finds Medusa.

m. _____

n. Perseus sees Andromeda chained to a rock.

o. _____

p. Perseus turns Polydectes to stone.

q. _____

r. Perseus kills Acrisios with a discus.

Clarifying Word Meanings

PRACTICE

1. Use the words *descended* and *hovered* to explain how Perseus captures Medusa's head.

2. Use the word *perplexity* to explain how Perseus feels when he's told to fetch the Gorgon's head.

3. Use the word *perpetual* to explain what Atlas's job is.

4. Use the word *recesses* to describe the den of the Gorgons.

Word Bank

descended
perplexity
perpetual
recesses
hovered

Grammar Link

Pronoun and Contraction Mix-ups

Contraction	Possessive Pronoun
it's (it is/has)	its
they're (they are)	their
you're (you are)	your
who's (who is/has)	whose

1. Use an apostrophe to show where letters are missing in a **contraction** (a shortened form of a word or group of words):

   <u>Who's</u> [Who is] the man holding the Gorgon's head?

2. Don't use an apostrophe with a **possessive personal pronoun.**

   <u>They're</u> [They are] sleeping on the rocks near <u>their</u> sister, Medusa.

   Andromeda, <u>you're</u> [you are] free, and <u>your</u> future looks bright.

   <u>Whose</u> head is that? <u>Who's</u> [Who is] asking?

   <u>It's</u> [It is] a hat of darkness that protects <u>its</u> owner.

PRACTICE

Write a short dialogue between Perseus and Andromeda in which Perseus explains how he killed Medusa. Use *it's* and *its*, *your* and *you're*, *their* and *they're*, and *whose* and *who's* in your dialogue.

For more help, see The Forms of Personal Pronouns, part 4, in the Language Handbook.

SKILLS FOCUS

Vocabulary Skills
Clarify word meanings.

Grammar Skills
Use personal pronouns and contractions correctly.

North Carolina Competency Goal
6.01

He Lion, Bruh Bear, and Bruh Rabbit *and*
The Fox and the Crow *and*
The Wolf and the House Dog

Make the Connection
Quickwrite ✏

Would you choose to be the strongest person in the world, the smartest, or the most self-confident? Would you choose freedom over safety and comfort? Write two or three sentences explaining your choices.

Literary Focus
Folk Tales and Fables

Folk tales and fables have been around for thousands of years, much, much longer than novels, novellas, and short stories. Both folk tales and fables are stories that were told aloud for hundreds of years before they were written down.

The first folk tale that follows comes from Africa. On the surface, stories like this one seem to be entertaining tales about big, mean animals and small, crafty ones. But if you read between the lines, you often find that the point the storyteller is making has to do with people, not animals.

The Trickster Hero

The heroes of many folk tales are **tricksters.** They're underdogs, like the cartoon characters Mighty Mouse, Tweety the Canary, and Roadrunner. Their enemies may be big and powerful, but tricksters win every time because they're so clever—though they sometimes seem silly, even stupid.

What's more, their tricks often teach important lessons. Don Coyote, Anansi the Spider, Raven—tricksters like these show up time and again in folk tales from all over the world. Brer Rabbit, who is called Bruh (Brother) Rabbit in this story, is one of the trickiest.

Reading Skills 📖
Cause and Effect

A story's **plot** is made up of a series of related events. One event in a plot **causes** something else to happen, which is called an **effect.** The effect in turn becomes the cause of other events.

In each of the next three selections, a plot moves through a simple chain of causes and effects to its conclusion. Use a graphic organizer, such as a flowchart, to record the chain of events.

Event 1
↓
Event 2
↓
and so on

He Lion, Bruh Bear, and Bruh Rabbit

African American folk tale, retold by **Virginia Hamilton**

Say that he Lion would get up each and every mornin. Stretch and walk around. He'd roar, "ME AND MYSELF. ME AND MYSELF," like that. Scare all the little animals so they were afraid to come outside in the sunshine. Afraid to go huntin or fishin or whatever the little animals wanted to do.

"What we gone do about it?" they asked one another. Squirrel leapin from branch to branch, just scared. Possum playin dead, couldn't hardly move him.

He Lion just went on, stickin out his chest and roarin, "ME AND MYSELF. ME AND MYSELF."

The little animals held a sit-down talk, and one by one and two by two and all by all, they decide to go see Bruh Bear and Bruh Rabbit. For they know that Bruh Bear been around. And Bruh Rabbit say he has, too.

So they went to Bruh Bear and Bruh Rabbit. Said, "We have some trouble. Old he Lion, him scarin everybody, roarin every mornin and all day, 'ME AND MYSELF. ME AND MYSELF,' like that."

"Why he Lion want to do that?" Bruh Bear said.

"Is that all he Lion have to say?" Bruh Rabbit asked.

"We don't know why, but that's all he Lion can tell us and we didn't ask him to tell us that," said the little animals. "And him scarin the children with it. And we wish him to stop it."

"Well, I'll go see him, talk to him. I've known he Lion a long kind of time," Bruh Bear said.

"I'll go with you," said Bruh Rabbit. "I've known he Lion most long as you."

That bear and that rabbit went off through the forest. They kept hearin somethin. Mumble, mumble. Couldn't make it out. They got farther in the forest. They heard it plain now. "ME AND MYSELF. ME AND MYSELF."

"Well, well, well," said Bruh Bear. He wasn't scared. He'd been around the whole forest, seen a lot.

"My, my, my," said Bruh Rabbit. He'd seen enough to know not to be afraid of an old he lion. Now old he lions could be dangerous, but you had to know how to handle them.

The bear and the rabbit climbed up and up the cliff where he Lion had his lair.[1] They found him. Kept their distance. He watchin them and they watchin him. Everybody actin cordial.[2]

"Hear tell you are scarin everybody, all the little animals, with your roarin all the time," Bruh Rabbit said.

"I roars when I pleases," he Lion said.

"Well, might could you leave off the noise first thing in the mornin, so the little animals can get what they want to eat and drink?" asked Bruh Bear.

"Listen," said he Lion, and then he roared: "ME AND MYSELF. ME AND MYSELF. Nobody tell me what not to do," he said. "I'm the king of the forest, *me and myself.*"

"Better had let me tell you somethin," Bruh Rabbit said, "for I've seen Man, and I know him the real king of the forest."

He Lion was quiet awhile. He looked straight through that scrawny lil Rabbit like he was nothin atall. He looked at Bruh Bear and figured he'd talk to him.

"You, Bear, you been around," he Lion said.

"That's true," said old Bruh Bear. "I been about everywhere. I've been around the whole forest."

"Then you must know somethin," he Lion said.

"I know lots," said Bruh Bear, slow and quiet-like.

"Tell me what you know about Man," he Lion said. "He think him the king of the forest?"

"Well, now, I'll tell you," said Bruh Bear, "I been around, but I haven't ever come across Man that I know of. Couldn't tell you nothin about him."

So he Lion had to turn back to Bruh Rabbit. He didn't want to but he had to. "So what?" he said to that lil scrawny hare.

"Well, you got to come down from there if you want to see Man," Bruh Rabbit said. "Come down from there and I'll show you him."

He Lion thought a minute, an hour, and a whole day. Then, the next day, he came on down.

He roared just once, "ME AND MYSELF. ME AND MYSELF. Now," he said, "come show me Man."

---

1. **lair** *n.*: home of a wild animal; den.
2. **cordial** (kôr′jəl) *adj.*: warm and friendly.

So they set out. He Lion, Bruh Bear, and Bruh Rabbit. They go along and they go along, rangin the forest. Pretty soon, they come to a clearin. And playin in it is a little fellow about nine years old.

"Is that there Man?" asked he Lion.

"Why no, that one is called Will Be, but it sure is not Man," said Bruh Rabbit.

So they went along and they went along. Pretty soon, they come upon a shade tree. And sleepin under it is an old, olden fellow, about ninety years olden.

"There must lie Man," spoke he Lion. "I knew him wasn't gone be much."

"That's not Man," said Bruh Rabbit. "That fellow is Was Once. You'll know it when you see Man."

So they went on along. He Lion is gettin tired of strollin. So he roars, "ME AND MY-SELF. ME AND MYSELF." Upsets Bear so that Bear doubles over and runs and climbs a tree.

"Come down from there," Bruh Rabbit tellin him. So after a while Bear comes down. He keepin his distance from he Lion, anyhow. And they set out some more. Goin along quiet and slow.

In a little while they come to a road. And comin on way down the road, Bruh Rabbit sees Man comin. Man about twenty-one years old. Big and strong, with a big gun over his shoulder.

"There!" Bruh Rabbit says. "See there, he Lion? There's Man. You better go meet him."

"I will," says he Lion. And he sticks out his chest and he roars, "ME AND MYSELF. ME AND MYSELF." All the way to Man he's roarin proud, "ME AND MYSELF, ME AND MYSELF!"

"Come on, Bruh Bear, let's go!" Bruh Rabbit says.

"What for?" Bruh Bear wants to know.

"You better come on!" And Bruh Rabbit takes ahold of Bruh Bear and half drags him to a thicket. And there he makin the Bear hide with him.

For here comes Man. He sees old he Lion real good now. He drops to one knee and he takes aim with his big gun.

Old he Lion is roarin his head off: "ME AND MYSELF! ME AND MYSELF!"

The big gun goes off: PA-LOOOM!

He Lion falls back hard on his tail.
The gun goes off again. PA-LOOOM!

He Lion is flyin through the air. He lands in the thicket.

"Well, did you see Man?" asked Bruh Bear.

"I seen him," said he Lion. "Man spoken to me unkind, and got a great long stick him keepin on his shoulder. Then Man taken that stick down and him speakin real mean. Thunderin at me and lightnin comin from that stick, awful bad. Made me sick. I had to turn around. And Man pointin that stick again and thunderin at me some more. So I come in here, cause it seem like him throwed some stickers at me each time it thunder, too."

"So you've met Man, and you know zactly what that kind of him is," says Bruh Rabbit.

"I surely do know that," he Lion said back.

Awhile after he Lion met Man, things were some better in the forest. Bruh Bear knew what Man looked like so he could keep out of his way. That rabbit always did know to keep out of Man's way. The little animals could go out in the mornin because he Lion was more peaceable. He didn't walk around roarin at the top of his voice all the time. And when he Lion did lift that voice of his, it was like, "Me and Myself and Man. Me and Myself and Man." Like that.

Wasn't too loud at all.

Meet the Writer

Virginia Hamilton

Telling Tales

For most of her life, **Virginia Hamilton** (1936–2002) lived in the place where she was born and raised: Yellow Springs, Ohio. It's where her grandfather settled after he escaped from slavery in pre–Civil War days. Virginia was named for the state where he lived before his escape.

About her family and Yellow Springs, the place she called home, Hamilton said:

❝ My mother's 'people' were warm-hearted, tight with money, generous to the sick and landless, close-mouthed, and fond of telling tales and gossip about one another and even their ancestors. They were a part of me from the time I understood that I belonged to all of them. My uncle King told the best tall tales; my aunt Leanna sang the finest sorrowful songs. My own mother could take a slice of fiction floating around the family and polish it into a saga. ❞

For Independent Reading

You'll find more folk tales in Hamilton's collection *The People Could Fly.* If you like animal tales, check out her collection *A Ring of Tricksters.*

The Fox and the Crow

Aesop

Greek fable, dramatized by **Mara Rockliff**

Narrator. One fine morning a Fox was wandering through the woods, enjoying the lovely spring weather.

Fox. Lovely spring weather is all very well, but a fox can't live on sunshine and fresh air. I could use some breakfast right about now.

Narrator. Suddenly he noticed a Crow sitting on the branch of a tree above him. The Fox didn't think much of crows as a rule, but this particular Crow had something very interesting in her beak.

Fox. Cheese. Mmm. A nice big yellow chunk of cheese. I would love that cheese. I deserve that cheese. But how can I get that cheese?

Narrator. The Fox thought awhile, and then he called up to the Crow.

Fox. Good morning, you fabulous bird.

Narrator. The Crow looked at him suspiciously. But she kept her beak closed tightly on the cheese and said nothing.

Fox. What beautiful beady eyes you have! And you certainly look great in black feathers. I've seen a lot of birds in my time, but you outbird them all. A bird with your good looks must have a voice to match. Oh, if only I could hear you sing just one song. Then I would know you were truly the Greatest Bird on Earth.

Narrator. Listening to all this flattery, the Crow forgot her suspicion of the Fox. She forgot her cheese, too. All she could think of was impressing the Fox with a song. So she opened her beak wide and let out a loud "Caw!" Down fell the cheese, right into the Fox's open mouth.

Fox. Thanks! That tasted every bit as good as it looked. Well, now I know you have a voice—and I hope I never have to hear it again. But where are your brains?

All Together. If you let flattery go to your head, you'll pay the price.

The Wolf and the House Dog

Aesop

Greek fable, dramatized by **Mara Rockliff**

Narrator. Once there was a Wolf who never got enough to eat. Her mouth watered when she looked at the fat geese and chickens kept by the people of the village. But every time she tried to steal one, the watchful village dogs would bark and warn their owners.

Wolf. Really, I'm nothing but skin and bones. It makes me sad just thinking about it.

Narrator. One night the Wolf met up with a House Dog who had wandered a little too far from home. The Wolf would gladly have eaten him right then and there.

Wolf. Dog stew . . . cold dog pie . . . or maybe just dog on a bun, with plenty of mustard and ketchup . . .

Narrator. But the House Dog looked too big and strong for the Wolf, who was weak from hunger. So the Wolf spoke to him very humbly and politely.

Wolf. How handsome you are! You look so healthy and well fed and delicious—I mean, uh, terrific. You look terrific. Really.

House Dog. Well, you look terrible. I don't know why you live out here in these miserable woods, where you have to fight so hard for every crummy little scrap of food. You should come live in the village like me. You could eat like a king there.

Wolf. What do I have to do?

House Dog. Hardly anything. Chase kids on bicycles. Bark at the mailman every now and then. Lie around the house letting people pet you. Just for that they'll feed you till you burst—enormous steak bones with fat hanging off them, pizza crusts, bits of chicken, leftovers like you wouldn't believe.

Narrator. The Wolf nearly cried with happiness as she imagined how wonderful her new life was going to be. But then she noticed a strange ring around the Dog's neck where the hair had been rubbed off.

Wolf. What happened to your neck?

House Dog. Oh . . . ah . . . nothing. It's nothing, really.

Wolf. I've never seen anything like it. Is it a disease?

House Dog. Don't be silly. It's just the mark of the collar that they fasten my chain to.

Wolf. A chain! You mean you can't go wherever you like?

House Dog. Well, not always. But what's the difference?

Wolf. What's the difference? Are you kidding? I wouldn't give up my freedom for the biggest, juiciest steak in the world. Never mind a few lousy bones.

Narrator. The Wolf ran away, back to the woods. She never went near the village again, no matter how hungry she got.

All Together. Nothing is worth more than freedom.

Meet the Writer

Aesop

Fables for Freedom

Not much is known about **Aesop** (sixth century B.C.). According to the ancient Greek historian Herodotus, he came from Africa and was held in slavery in Greece. The fables credited to Aesop may have originally come from ancient India. Aesop's fables were used to make points about politics. Aesop eventually won his freedom, but he met a violent death, perhaps because his fables offended someone powerful.

Aesop, with figures from his fables. Printed in Augsburg, Bavaria, in 1498 by Johann Schonsperger.

First Thoughts

1. Does he Lion get what he deserves, or is Bruh Rabbit too mean to him? Explain.

Thinking Critically

2. What qualities do rabbits and foxes have that make people think they'd be good **tricksters**?

3. What does he Lion mean when he roars "ME AND MYSELF. ME AND MYSELF"?

4. At the end of the story, he Lion roars less loudly and less often. Why?

5. Unlike short stories, folk tales and fables teach **morals,** or practical lessons about how to behave and get along in the world. What lesson is taught in each of these stories? What do you think about each lesson? Refer to your Quickwrite notes as you explain your responses. 🖊

Extending Interpretations

6. The animals in folk tales and fables often talk and act like people. Do you know people who remind you of the lion and the crow? Explain.

North Carolina Competency Goal
6.01; 6.02

INTERNET

Projects and Activities
Keyword: LE5 6-4

SKILLS FOCUS

Literary Skills
Analyze folk tales and fables.

Reading Skills
Analyze causes and effects.

Speaking and Listening Skills
Script and present an oral narrative.

Reading Check

a. Review and compare the flowcharts you made to track the events of each selection. Did you include all the **causes** and **effects**? 🔖

b. Who is the trickster in each story?

c. In "He Lion, Bruh Bear, and Bruh Rabbit," which animal thinks he's the strongest? Which animal turns out to be the strongest?

d. In "The Fox and the Crow," why does the crow open her beak? What does the fox get from the crow?

e. In "The Wolf and the House Dog," what does the house dog encourage the wolf to do? What does the wolf value above everything else?

SPEAKING AND LISTENING

Performing a Fable

Get together with a group of classmates interested in presenting "He Lion . . ." or one of the fables by Aesop. You can either do a live performance with props and costumes or tape your reading. If you decide on "He Lion . . . ," break the story into scenes. Decide whether you need a narrator to provide details not supplied in the dialogue. Write out each character's lines. You may want to get together with groups who have prepared the two other stories and present them to the class in the order in which they appear in the book. Assign other students to act as your critics.

Vocabulary Development

Words with Multiple Meanings

Multiple-meaning words can be confusing. A multiple-meaning word is always spelled the same way, but it means different things in different **contexts.** To find the correct meaning, figure out what part of speech the word is; then, examine its context. Finally, decide which meaning best fits the sentence.

SKILLS FOCUS

Vocabulary Skills
Use multiple-meaning words.

Grammar Skills
Understand homophones.

PRACTICE

Choose the correct meaning of each underlined word.

1. Does a fox know the difference between <u>right</u> and wrong?

   a. opposite of left   **b.** what is just and proper

2. He broke every <u>rule</u> in the forest.

   a. law   **b.** line

3. He Lion went flying through the <u>air</u>.

   a. tune   **b.** sky

4. "I surely do know that," he Lion answered <u>back</u>.

   a. in return   **b.** part of a chair

Grammar Link

Understanding Homophones:
To, Too, and *Two*

To, too, and *two* are **homophones** (häm′ə·fōnz′)—words that sound alike but are spelled differently and have different meanings. Don't let trickster words like *to, too,* and *two* fool you. Remembering what each word means will help you use it correctly.

- **to:** toward; in the direction of (*to* is also part of the infinitive form of a verb)

- **too:** also; more than enough

- **two:** a number—one plus one

PRACTICE

Choose the correct word in the underlined pair in each sentence.

The little animals go <u>to/two</u> see Bruh Bear and Bruh Rabbit because he Lion is making <u>too/to</u> much noise. He Lion doesn't like talking <u>too/to</u> Bruh Rabbit. He Lion's roar is <u>too/to</u> loud for Bruh Bear. He Lion wants <u>two/to</u> see Man. After seeing Man, he Lion is no longer <u>two/too</u> loud.

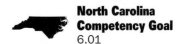

North Carolina Competency Goal
6.01

Author Study Zora Neale Hurston

Literary Focus: Folklore

Storytelling is an important part of every culture and as natural as life itself. Long before there was writing, stories were passed on orally from one storyteller to another. The term **folklore** is used for the traditional songs, stories, proverbs, and riddles passed down from generation to generation.

Zora Neale Hurston was one of the shining lights of the Harlem Renaissance—an explosion of black art and literature that took place in New York City in the 1920s and 1930s. Hurston wrote novels and an **autobiography** (the story of one's own life), but she is best known for her lively retellings of African American folk tales. The stories she collected were published in *Mules and Men,* the first book of African American folklore published by a black person.

North Carolina Competency Goal
4.02; 5.02

> ### Hurston's folk tales often
>
> - include animals from the American South as characters
> - explain something
> - are told in dialect
> - contain sly humor
> - feature characters that use tricks or bargaining to get what they want
> - feature small, weak characters that outsmart larger, more powerful characters

Literary Skills
Understand folklore.

Reading Skills
Draw conclusions.

Reading Skills
Drawing Conclusions

When you read several works by one writer, you draw **conclusions** about the writer's work. For example, you might conclude that a writer's stories often have similar plots or that the characters are always underdogs. After you read each folk tale that follows, use the chart provided to note features you find interesting. (See the list in the box above for ideas.)

Photograph and signature courtesy of the Yale Collection of American Literature, Beinecke Rare Book and Manuscript Library.

Before You Read

People from different regions and social groups speak different varieties of English, each with its own vocabulary, pronunciations, and grammar. These forms of English are called **dialects.**

This folk tale was recorded by Hurston, who made field trips to collect oral narratives in her native state of Florida. As you will see, Hurston was careful to preserve the dialect spoken by the storytellers. Here are a few examples of dialect you'll find as you read the three folk tales in this feature: *de* (the), *Ah* (I), *lak* (like), *dis* (this). You'll be able to figure out the meanings of most of the words in dialect by using context clues.

Remember that folk tales were passed on orally for many years before they were written down, so they are meant to be spoken aloud. As you read this tale, think of the storyteller face to face with the audience. Read this tale aloud to hear how Hurston captured the speech of the storytellers.

Crawling Snake (1988) by Sultan Rogers.
Courtesy of the University Museum, University of Mississippi Cultural Center.

"You got to have some kind of a protection."

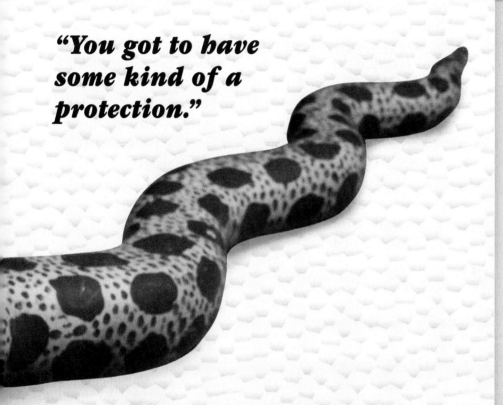

HOW THE SNAKE GOT POISON

an African American folk tale, retold by
Zora Neale Hurston

Well, when God made de snake he put him in de bushes to ornament de ground. But things didn't suit de snake so one day he got on de ladder and went up to see God.

"Good mawnin', God."

"How do you do, Snake?"

"Ah ain't so many, God, you put me down there on my belly in de dust and everything trods upon me and kills off my generations. Ah ain't got no kind of protection at all."

God looked off towards immensity and thought about de subject for awhile, then he said, "Ah didn't mean for nothin' to be stompin' you snakes lak dat. You got to have some kind of a protection. Here, take dis poison and put it in yo' mouf and when they tromps on you, protect yo' self."

So de snake took de poison in his mouf and went on back.

So after awhile all de other varmints went up to God.

"Good evenin', God."

"How you makin' it, varmints?"

"God, please do somethin' 'bout dat snake. He' layin' in de bushes there wid poison in his mouf and he's strikin' everything dat shakes de bush. He's killin' up our generation. Wese skeered to walk de earth." ❶

So God sent for de snake and tole him:

"Snake, when Ah give you dat poson, Ah didn't mean for you to be hittin' and killin' everything dat shake de bush. I give you dat poson and tole you to protect yo' self when they tromples on you. But you killin' everything dat moves. Ah didn't mean for you to do dat."

Den snake say, "Lawd, you know Ah'm down here in de dust. Ah ain't got no claws to fight wid,

COMPARE AND CONTRAST

❶ Most stories about creation are very serious. God is a faraway figure who inspires awe in His creatures. Where does God seem to live in this story? How do these creatures deal with God?

Rooster.
© Shelburne Museum, Shelburne, Vermont.
Photography by Ken Burris.

and Ah ain't got no feets to git me out de way. All Ah kin see is feets comin' to tromple me. Ah can't tell who my enemy is and who is my friend. You gimme dis protection in my mouf and Ah uses it."

God thought it over for a while then he says:

"Well, snake, I don't want yo' generations all stomped out and I don't want you killin' everything else dat moves. Here take dis bell and tie it to yo' tail. When you hear feets comin' you ring yo' bell and if it's yo' friend, he'll be keerful. If it's yo' enemy, it's you and him." ❷

So dat's how de snake got his poison and dat's how come he got rattles.

Biddy, Biddy, bend my story is end.

Turn loose de rooster and hold de hen.

Pair of folk art parrots.

© Shelburne Museum, Shelburne, Vermont. Photography by Ken Burris.

Before You Read

The storyteller has just told a story about Noah's ark. He says that a whole lot went on "in dat ole Ark. Dat's where de possum lost de hair off his tail." A listener doubts this. "Now don't you tell me no possum ever had no hair on dat slick tail of his'n . . . 'cause Ah know better." So the next story begins.

How the Possum Lost the Hair on Its Tail

Zora Neale Hurston

Yes, he did have hair on his tail one time. Yes, indeed. De possum had a bushy tail wid long silk hair on it. Why, it useter be one of de prettiest sights you ever seen. De possum struttin' 'round wid his great big ole plumey tail. Dat was 'way back in de olden times before de big flood.

But de possum was lazy—jus' like he is today. He sleep too much. You see Ole Nora[1] had a son named Ham and he loved to be playin' music all de time. He had a banjo and a fiddle and maybe a guitar too. But de rain come up so sudden he didn't have time to put 'em on de ark. So when rain kept comin' down he fretted a lot 'cause he didn't have nothin' to play. So he found a ole cigar box and made hisself a banjo, but he didn't have no strings for it. ❶ So he seen de possum stretched out sleeping wid his tail all spread 'round. So Ham slipped up and shaved de possum's tail and made de strings for his banjo out de hairs. When dat possum woke up from his nap, Ham was playin' his tail hairs down to de bricks and dat's why de possum ain't got no hair on his tail today. Losin' his pretty tail sorta broke de possum's spirit too. He ain't never been de same since. Dat's how come he always actin' shame-faced. He know his tail ain't whut it useter be; and de possum feel mighty bad about it. ❷

1. **Ole Nora:** Noah was ordered to build an ark so that he and his family might survive the flood (Genesis 6:9).

PREDICT

❶ Knowing that the possum sleeps a lot (and is proud of his tail) and that Ham is looking for banjo strings, what do you think will happen?

INTERPRET

❷ Why was the possum's spirit broken?

Before You Read

Many African American folk tales feature the clever Brer (brother) Rabbit. The rabbit is very small, but he is sharp and can outwit bigger animals, who are usually stupid and full of themselves. Brer Rabbit is known as a trickster—he uses tricks to get what he wants. Watch him at work.

Why the 'Gator Is Black

Zora Neale Hurston

INTERPRET

❶ Stories of exaggeration are sometimes called "lies." They often give humorous explanations about how and why certain things came to be. What is the 'gator like at the beginning of the story?

Ah'm tellin' dis lie on de 'gator. Well, de 'gator was a pretty white varmint wid coal black eyes. He useter swim in de water, but he never did bog up in de mud lak he do now. When he come out de water he useter lay up on de clean grass so he wouldn't dirty hisself all up. **❶**

So one day he was layin' up on de grass in a marsh sunnin' hisself and sleepin' when Brer Rabbit come bustin' cross de marsh and run right over Brer 'Gator before he stopped. Brer 'Gator woke up and seen who it was trompin' all over him and trackin' up his pretty

white hide. So he seen Brer Rabbit, so he ast him, "Brer Rabbit, what you mean by runnin' all cross me and messin' up my clothes lak dis?"

Brer Rabbit was up behind a clump of bushes peerin' out to see what was after him. So he tole de 'gator, says: "Ah ain't got time to see what Ah'm runnin' over nor under. Ah got trouble behind me."

'Gator ast, "Whut is trouble? Ah ain't never heard tell of dat befo'."

Brer Rabbit says, "You ain't never heard tell of trouble?"

Brer 'Gator tole him, "No."

Rabbit says: "All right, you jus' stay right where you at, and Ah'll show you whut trouble is." ❷

He peered 'round to see if de coast was clear and loped off, and Brer 'Gator washed Brer Rabbit's foot tracks off his hide and went on back to sleep agin.

Brer Rabbit went on off and lit him a li'dard knot[1] and come on back. He set dat marsh afire on every side. All around Brer 'Gator de fire was burnin' in flames of fire. De 'gator woke up and pitched out to run, but every which a way he run de fire met him.

He seen Brer Rabbit sittin' up on de high ground jus' killin hisself laughin'. So he hollered and ast him:

"Brer Rabbit, whut's all dis goin' on?"

"Dat's trouble, Brer 'Gator, dat's trouble youse in."

De 'gator run from side to side, round and round. Way after while he broke thru and hit de water "ker ploogum!" He got all cooled off but he had done got smoked all up befo' he got to de water, and his eyes is all red from de smoke. And dat's how come a 'gator is black today—cause de rabbit took advantage of him lak dat. ❸

---

1. **li'dard knot:** a kind of wood used in torches.

INFER

❷ Why do you think Brer Rabbit wants to show Brer 'Gator what trouble is?

INTERPRET

❸ How does Brer Rabbit fool Brer 'Gator? Why do you think Brer Rabbit's behavior made him a popular hero?

First Thoughts

1. Read the three stories aloud. Which details in the stories do you find especially humorous?

Thinking Critically

2. What does each story explain?

3. Which characters use tricks or make clever deals with a more powerful character to get what they want?

> ### Reading Check
>
> Retell the events of each tale by writing sentences that start with these words:
>
> First _____
>
> So _____
>
> But _____
>
> Then _____
>
> Finally _____

4. Some people criticize Hurston for using the African American dialect of the rural South to tell these tales. What do you think of the way the stories are told? Would your response to the stories have been different if they were told in more formal language? Explain.

Comparing an Author's Works

5. Fill in a chart like the one below with details from the three tales. You'll use the chart to draw **conclusions** and write an essay about Hurston's work on page 397.

Features to discuss	Snake	Possum	'Gator
Animal characters			
Use of dialect			
Explanations of how and why			
Use of humor			
Characters' tricks or clever deals			

North Carolina Competency Goal
4.02; 5.01; 5.02

SKILLS FOCUS

Literary Skills
Analyze folk tales.

Reading Skills
Draw conclusions.

Zora Neale Hurston with children in Eatonville, Florida, 1935.

Before You Read

This incident is from the beginning of Hurston's autobiography. She is living in Eatonville, Florida, and, she says, she is always asking questions.

I Kept on Probing to Know

from Dust Tracks on a Road

Zora Neale Hurston

Zora Neale Hurston smiling, waving, sitting in chair. This photograph was originally taken by Baxter Snark a.k.a Prentiss Taylor.
Yale Collection of American Literature, Beinecke Rare Book and Manuscript Library.

No matter whether my probings made me happier or sadder, I kept on probing to know. For instance, I had a stifled longing. I used to climb to the top of one of the huge chinaberry trees which guarded our front gate, and look out over the world. The most interesting thing that I saw was the horizon. Every way I turned, it was there, and the same distance away. Our house then, was in the center of the world. It grew upon me that I ought to walk out to the horizon and see what the end of the world

A Hurston Time Line

Events in History

1920
Harlem Renaissance begins in New York City.

1920
Nineteenth Amendment grants American women right to vote.

1890s
Under Jim Crow laws, southern states have racially segregated schools and public transportation.

1929
Stock market crash leads to Great Depression; Harlem especially hard hit.

1890–1910	1920	1930

Events in Hurston's Life

1891
Hurston is born in Notasulga, Alabama.

1892
Hurston family moves to Eatonville, Florida.

1924
Hurston earns degree from Howard University in Washington, D.C.

1925
Hurston enters Barnard College in New York on scholarship.

1927
Hurston goes to Florida to collect African American folklore.

1928
Hurston receives degree from Barnard.

1935
Mules and Men (book on black culture and folklore) is published.

1937
Their Eyes Were Watching God (novel) is published.

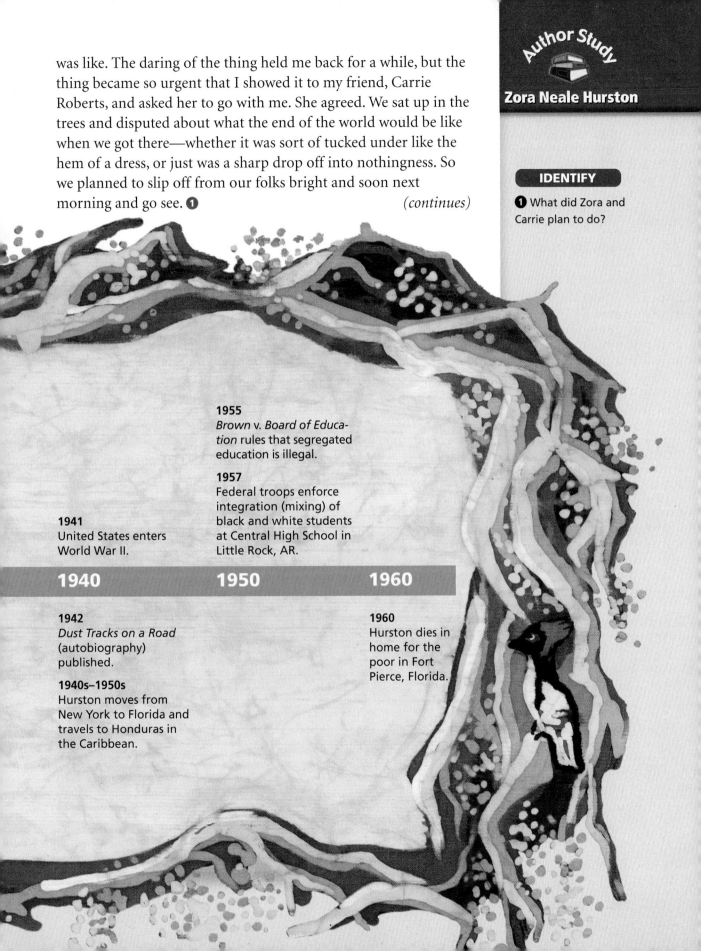

was like. The daring of the thing held me back for a while, but the thing became so urgent that I showed it to my friend, Carrie Roberts, and asked her to go with me. She agreed. We sat up in the trees and disputed about what the end of the world would be like when we got there—whether it was sort of tucked under like the hem of a dress, or just was a sharp drop off into nothingness. So we planned to slip off from our folks bright and soon next morning and go see. ❶   *(continues)*

IDENTIFY

❶ What did Zora and Carrie plan to do?

1955
Brown v. *Board of Education* rules that segregated education is illegal.

1957
Federal troops enforce integration (mixing) of black and white students at Central High School in Little Rock, AR.

1941
United States enters World War II.

1940   1950   1960

1942
Dust Tracks on a Road (autobiography) published.

1940s–1950s
Hurston moves from New York to Florida and travels to Honduras in the Caribbean.

1960
Hurston dies in home for the poor in Fort Pierce, Florida.

INTERPRET

❷ What do you think Hurston meant by wanting to find out about the "end of things"? Do you think this curiosity may be part of what leads her to collect folk tales? Explain.

I could hardly sleep that night from the excitement of the thing. I had been yearning for so many months to find out about the end of things. I had no doubts about the beginnings. They were somewhere in the five acres that was home to me. Most likely in Mama's room. Now, I was going to see the end, and then I would be satisfied. ❷

As soon as breakfast was over, I sneaked off to the meeting place in the scrub palmettoes, a short way from our house and waited. Carrie didn't come right away. I was on my way to her house by a round-about way when I met her. She was coming to tell me that she couldn't go. It looked so far that maybe we wouldn't get back by sundown, and then we would both get a whipping. When we got big enough to wear long dresses, we could go and stay as long as we wanted to. Nobody couldn't whip us then. No matter how hard I begged, she wouldn't go. The thing was too bold and brazen to her thinking. We had a fight, then. I had to hit Carrie to keep my heart from stifling me. Then I was sorry I had struck my friend, and went on home and hid under the house with my heartbreak. But I did not give up the idea of my journey. I was merely lonesome for someone brave enough to undertake it with me. I wanted it to be Carrie. She was a lot of fun, and always did what I told her. Well, most of the time, she did. This time it was too much for even her loyalty to surmount. She even tried to talk me out

School Bell Time by Romare Bearden.
Courtesy of Kingsborough Community College, a college of The City University of New York.

© Romare Bearden Foundation/Licensed by VAGA, New York, NY.

of my trip. I couldn't give up. It meant too much to me. I decided to put it off until I had something to ride on, then I could go by myself.

So for weeks I saw myself sitting astride of a fine horse. My shoes had sky-blue bottoms to them, and I was riding off to look at the belly-band of the world.

It was summer time, and the mockingbirds sang all night long in the orange trees. Alligators trumpeted from their stronghold in Lake Belle. So fall passed and then it was Christmas time.

Papa did something different a few days before Christmas. He sort of shoved back from the table after dinner and asked us all what we wanted Santa Claus to bring us. My big brothers wanted a baseball outfit. Ben and Joel wanted air rifles. My sister wanted patent leather pumps and a belt. Then it was my turn. Suddenly a beautiful vision came before me. Two things could work together. My Christmas present could take me to the end of the world.

"I want a fine black riding horse with white leather saddle and bridles," I told Papa happily.

"You, what?" Papa gasped. "What was dat you said?"

"I said, I want a black saddle horse with . . ."

"A saddle horse!" Papa exploded. "It's a sin and a shame! Lemme tell you something right now, my young lady; you ain't white. Riding horse! Always trying to wear de big hat! I don't know how you got in this family nohow. You ain't like none of de rest of my young 'uns." ❸

"If I can't have no riding horse, I don't want nothing at all," I said stubbornly with my mouth, but inside I was sucking sorrow. My longed-for journey looked impossible.

"I'll riding-horse you, Madam!" Papa shouted and jumped to his feet. But being down at the end of the table big enough for all ten members of the family together, I was near the kitchen door, and I beat Papa to it by a safe margin. He chased me as far as the side gate and turned back. So I did not get my horse to ride off to the edge of the world. I got a doll for Christmas.

Since Papa would not buy me a saddle horse, I made me one up. No one around me knew how often I rode my prancing horse, nor the things I saw in far places. Jake, my puppy, always went along and we made great admiration together over the things we saw and ate. We both agreed that it was nice to be always eating things. ❹

INFER

❸ How does Hurston's father block her wish to see the end of the world? What do you think he means when he says that she's always "trying to wear de big hat"?

INFER

❹ What details in this essay show that Hurston was very imaginative even as a child?

Before You Read

At Columbia University, Zora Neale Hurston studied under Dr. Franz Boas. Boas was a highly respected anthropologist—a scientist who studies human cultures and societies. At Boas's suggestion, Hurston went south from New York City to collect African American folklore. She boarded a train bound for Florida in 1927. That trip ended in failure—Hurston was unable to collect many tales. Early the following year, she tried again, and this time her work was successful. Here is the beginning of the book she published about her adventures.

Searching for Stories

from Mules and Men

Zora Neale Hurston

I was glad when somebody told me, "You may go and collect Negro folklore."

In a way it would not be a new experience for me. When I pitched headforemost into the world I landed in the crib of negroism.[1] From the earliest rocking of my cradle, I had known about the capers Brer Rabbit is apt to cut and what the Squinch Owl says from the house top. But it was fitting me like a tight chemise.[2] I couldn't see it for wearing it. It was only when I was off in college, away from my native surroundings, that I could see myself like somebody else and stand off and look at my garment. Then I had to have the spy-glass of Anthropology to look through at that.❶

Dr. Boas asked me where I wanted to work and I said, "Florida," and gave, as my big reason, that "Florida is a place that draws people—white people from all over the world, and Negroes from every

INFER

❶ What does Hurston mean when she says she couldn't see herself until she got away from home?

---

1. **negroism:** here, African American society and culture.
2. **chemise** (shə·mēz′): a type of women's slip or dress.

African Americans gather outside a restaurant in the old South.

Southern state surely and some from the North and West." So I knew that it was possible for me to get a cross section of the Negro South in the one state. And then I realized that I was new myself, so it looked sensible for me to choose familiar ground.

First place I aimed to stop to collect material was Eatonville, Florida. . . .

An African American family in Southern Pines, North Carolina, in 1914.

I hurried back to Eatonville because I knew that the town was full of material and that I could get it without hurt, harm, or danger. As early as I could remember it was the habit of the men folks particularly to gather on the store porch of evenings and swap stories. Even the women folks would stop and break a breath with them at times. As a child when I was sent down to Joe Clarke's store, I'd drag out my leaving as long as possible in order to hear more.... **2**

I thought about the tales I had heard as a child. How even the Bible was made over to suit our vivid imagination. How the devil always outsmarted God and how that over-noble hero Jack or John—not *John Henry*,[3] who occupies the same place in Negro folklore that Casey Jones[4] does in white lore and if anything is more recent—outsmarted the devil. Brer Fox, Brer Deer, Brer 'Gator, Brer Dawg, Brer Rabbit, Ole Massa and his wife were walking the earth like natural men way back in the days when God himself was on the ground and men could talk with him.... **3**

So I rounded Park Lake and came speeding down the straight stretch into Eatonville, the city of five lakes, three croquet courts, three hundred brown skins, three hundred good swimmers, plenty guavas, two schools, and no jail-house. **4**

---

3. **John Henry:** a hero of African American folk tales, known for his incredible strength. For more about John Henry, see the poem on page 651.
4. **Casey Jones:** a famous train engineer and folk hero.

IDENTIFY

2 Why does Hurston go to her hometown of Eatonville?

INTERPRET

3 What details here connect with the stories you have just read about the snake, opossum, and alligator?

INTERPRET

4 How do these remarks show Hurston's sense of humor?

Meet the Writer

Zora Neale Hurston

An American Original

Zora Neale Hurston (1891–1960) grew up in the village of Eatonville, Florida, the first incorporated African American town in the United States. From her birth, she heard stories.

Zora's father was the mayor of Eatonville, and her mother taught school from time to time. Zora's mother recognized her daughter's talent early. "Jump at the sun," she would say, encouraging Zora to try for the best.

Hurston was more or less on her own after age thirteen, when her mother died. She had to work hard and quit school so often that she was twenty-seven by the time she started college at Howard University in Washington, D.C. She arrived in New York in 1925, when the Harlem Renaissance was in high gear.

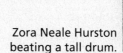

Zora Neale Hurston beating a tall drum.

Hurston soon became friends with many of the great writers and artists of the Renaissance, including the poet Langston Hughes. But Zora refused to write stories about the way black people were mistreated by white society. This turned many people against her.

Hurston always went her own way. She loved parties and big hats and dancing; she also loved shocking people and celebrating her own unique blackness.

In the last years of her life, Hurston went downhill. Book publishers no longer wanted to publish her work. She took odd jobs to support herself and died in poverty in Florida. Her gravesite might have been forgotten if it weren't for the writer Alice Walker, who placed a marker there.

Critics have a way of changing their minds. Today Hurston is again seen as a great original voice in American literature. Around 1930, Hurston and Langston Hughes worked together on a musical comedy called *Mule Bone*. They argued, and the work was not produced in their lifetime. In 1991, *Mule Bone* was produced in New York City. Actress Vanessa Williams played a part, and the music was composed by Taj Mahal.

"I Kept on Probing to Know" and "Searching for Stories"

First Thoughts

1. If you could ask Hurston three questions, what would you ask?

Thinking Critically

2. "I Kept on Probing to Know" is full of humorous touches. Which did you like the best?

3. Hurston says in "Searching for Stories" that in the stories she heard as a child, clever characters outwitted powerful characters. Where does that happen in the stories you have read in this author study?

4. Do you know anyone—perhaps a family member or someone from your community—who tells stories you feel should be written down? Discuss the storytellers you know of and why their stories are important. If you don't know any storytellers, think about some of your favorite traditional tales. Give a few reasons why you think these tales are worth collecting.

Reading Check

a. What does Hurston mean by "I kept on probing to know"?

b. What does the title "Searching for Stories" mean?

Comparing Literature

5. In 1927, when Hurston went to the South to collect her stories, racial bias and segregation (laws separating black people from whites) still existed in this country. (For more information, see the time line on pages 388–389 and the article "Separate but Never Equal" on page 332.) The storytellers Hurston interviewed knew what it was like to be oppressed—treated unfairly and unjustly—by powerful white people. Knowing this, can you draw any **conclusions** about why so many rural African American folk tales tell of small characters who cleverly outsmart larger, more powerful characters?

Poster for the 1991 production of *Mule Bone* at Lincoln Center in New York City.

North Carolina Competency Goal 4.02

SKILLS FOCUS

Reading Skills
Draw conclusions.

After You Read | Selections by Zora Neale Hurston

Assignment

1. Writing an Essay About a Writer's Work

Write an essay in which you discuss at least one **conclusion** you have reached about Zora Neale Hurston's folk tales. Base your essay on the folk tales and the autobiographical selections (stories about Hurston's life) that you have just read. You should find ideas for your essay in the chart you filled out on page 386 after you read the folk tales. Remember to support your conclusions with specific details from the texts. Here are some possible conclusions:

- Hurston's folk tales are written in dialect that creates humor and makes the tellers come alive. [Give examples.]
- Hurston's folk tales feature animal characters who often use tricks to get what they want from more powerful characters. [Give examples.]
- Hurston's folk tales explain how certain animals came to be the way they are. [Give examples.]
- Hurston was a successful folk tale collector because she gathered the stories from people who lived in the place where she grew up. [Add specific supporting details.]

Assignment

2. Presenting a Reading

With some of your classmates, present a read-aloud of at least one of Hurston's tales. Assign someone to take the role of narrator, and a different person to read each of the animal roles. Practice reading your parts smoothly, in conversational voices, so that the dialect sounds natural.

Assignment

3. Creating a Graphic Story

Draw and write a **graphic story** of one of these tales. Like comic strips, graphic stories are told in panels. The characters' dialogue—the words they speak—is put in bubbles, like the dialogue in comic strips. Before you start, choose the most important events of each story. Then, figure out how much dialogue you can pick up from the story.

North Carolina Competency Goal
6.01; 6.02

SKILLS FOCUS

Writing Skills
Write an essay about a writer's work.

Speaking and Listening Skills
Present a reading.

Writing and Art Skills
Create a graphic story.

Why Dogs Chase Cats

an African American folk tale, retold by Julius Lester

398

Long before this time we call today, and before that time called yesterday, and even before "What time is it?" the world wasn't like it is now.

Long before time wound its watch and started ticking and chasing after tomorrow, which it can never catch up to, well, that was the time when Dog and Cat were friends. There weren't two creatures in creation who were better friends than Dog and Cat. From sunup to sundown, from moonup to moondown, Dog and Cat did everything together and never a cross word passed between them.

That's how matters stood until hard times came to visit and decided to stay awhile. Hard times are what you have when you look in your dinner plate and all you see is your face looking back at you.

After a few days of not finding anything to eat, Dog and Cat knew they had to do something. But what?

They scratched their fleas and thought. They thought and scratched each other's fleas. They stopped thinking and stopped scratching. That was when Dog got an idea.

"There's only one thing we can do."

"What's that?" Cat wanted to know.

"We must go our separate ways. It's easier for one to find food than it is for two."

Cat agreed.

"I know where you can find food," Dog continued.

"Where?" Cat asked eagerly.

"Go to Adam's house."

"What will you do?"

"Don't worry about me," Dog said. "I'll find something somewhere."

"But what if you don't?" Cat wondered.

"Well, maybe I'll have to come to Adam's house."

That was what Cat was afraid of. "You eat more than I do. If you come where I am, you'll eat everything and there won't be enough for me. We have to promise that we will never look for food in the place where the other one is."

Dog promised and Cat promised and the two friends went their separate ways.

Cat went to Adam's house. When Eve saw Cat sitting on the back porch, she thought he was the cutest thing she'd ever seen. She picked him up, put him on her lap, and started stroking him. When night came, Eve brought Cat to bed with her. Adam didn't like the idea of sleeping in the same bed with an animal, but he didn't want to get into an argument with Eve about it.

In the middle of the night, Adam was awakened suddenly by a noise. He sat up. By the light of the moon, he saw Cat catching a mouse. Seeing how useful Cat was going to be, Adam treated him very kindly from that day on, and Cat was never hungry because there were many mice to catch.

Dog was not as lucky. The first night after he and Cat separated, Dog went to the cave of Wolf and asked for shelter.

Wolf said he was welcome to stay but not to ask for any food. Wolf scarcely had enough for himself.

Dog found a spot near the front of the cave, settled down and went to sleep. Everybody knows that Dog has the best hearing of almost any animal in the world. Dog could hear a raindrop fall on cotton.

In the darkest part of the night, the time of night that's so scary even Moon wishes she had someplace to hide, Dog woke up suddenly.

He listened. He heard trees and bushes being torn out of the ground, and footsteps in the distance. He ran to the back of the cave, where Wolf was sleeping.

"Something is coming!"

"If you run it away, I'll give you some of my food."

Dog ran back to the front of the cave and waited. The footsteps got louder and louder until out of the forest, holding a tree in each hand, came Gorilla.

Dog growled his growliest growl. He rushed at Gorilla and barked his barkiest bark. Gorilla looked down, picked Dog up, and threw him over his shoulder. It was three days and five nights before Dog came down to earth.

Poor Dog didn't know what to do. He wandered and he wandered, but no one had more than a few scraps of food to share with him. He was so hungry there was nothing to do but go to Adam's house.

When Adam saw Dog in the backyard, he immediately liked him. He gave Dog something to eat. After he'd filled his stomach, Dog crawled underneath the porch and went to sleep.

In the middle of the night, Dog woke up suddenly. He heard something! He started barking. Adam awoke, grabbed his bow and arrow, and hurried outside. There, in the darkness, he saw a rhinocehorse. Adam shot arrows at it and drove the rhinocehorse away.

Adam patted Dog on the head and told him he could stay forever. His barking had saved Adam's and Eve's lives.

The next morning when Eve put Cat outside, the first thing Cat saw was Dog lying beneath a shade tree.

"What're you doing here?" Cat asked angrily.

Dog started explaining about what a hard time he'd had and how there was more than enough food at Adam's for the two of them.

Cat didn't want to hear a word. "We made a promise and you broke it."

"Let's go to Adam and maybe he can solve our problem," Dog suggested.

Adam listened while Cat said his say. Then he listened to Dog say his say. When each had finished saying their say, it was Adam's turn to say.

"Dog, let there be no mistake. You and Cat made a promise and you broke it. However, Cat, you must understand that I am the one who told Dog he could stay here. There is more than enough food for both of you. I need both of you. Cat, you are useful for catching mice. Dog, you warn me when danger is around. I want you both to stay."

"No!" said Cat. "No, no, no!"

"Why?" Adam asked.

"Because," said Cat, "a promise is a promise."

Dog pleaded with Cat. He reminded Cat that they had been best friends since water was wet. Nothing Dog said could change Cat's mind.

Finally Adam said to Dog, "I'm sorry, but you're going to have to go."

"Where can I go?" Dog wanted to know.

"My son, Seth, lives down the road and around the curve."

So Dog went to live with Seth and he was very happy there.

But from that time to this, whenever a dog sees a cat, he chases after it because he still wants the cat to be his friend.

Meet the Writer

Julius Lester

Folk Tales: "More Fun Than Television"

Julius Lester (1939–   ) grew up in Missouri, Tennessee, and Arkansas. During his childhood he absorbed the rich traditions, stories, and music of African Americans in the rural South.

After college, Lester did many things. He was active in the civil rights movement in the 1960s. He played the banjo and performed with popular folk singers like Judy Collins. For a while he had his own radio and TV shows in New York City. However, writing became his lifework.

Lester explains why he retells folk tales:

66 They're more fun than television. There is also the sense that there are people behind these tales as opposed to an author behind the stories. For me folk tales are . . . creations, and we'll never know who the creators are. That's wonderful and mysterious to me. They're a distillation of an entire people's learning and knowledge and wisdom into a very brief tale. Implied are values of the worth of ordinary people, and that's a value that I consider very important. I want to communicate to children that you don't have to be somebody to have worth. And here are all these tales that you love, and the same things are inside you. 99

For Independent Reading

You'll find more of Lester's entertaining folk tales in *The Tales of Uncle Remus: The Adventures of Brer Rabbit* (Dial), *How Many Spots Does a Leopard Have? and Other Tales* (Scholastic), and *The Knee-High Man and Other Tales* (Dial).

Writing Workshop

Writing Skill
Write a comparison-contrast essay.

EXPOSITORY WRITING
Comparison-Contrast Essay

Have you ever met someone who reminded you of someone else, or seen a scary movie that was a lot like another scary movie? You probably compare and contrast the people and things in your life every day. When you **compare,** you look for similarities. When you **contrast,** you look for differences. Comparison and contrast is also a good way to analyze two stories, poems, or other texts that have something in common. In this workshop, you'll write an essay comparing and contrasting two literary works or two characters.

Prewriting

1 Choosing a Topic

Read and respond to this **prompt:**

> You can compare and contrast any two stories, poems, novels, or characters that have at least one important feature in common. One myth may remind you of another you have read; two characters faced with the same type of problem may handle it in different ways; a short story and poem may have similar themes. Choose two works, or two characters from works, that you have read in this book or on your own. Then, write an essay comparing and contrasting the characters or works.

How will you approach this assignment? You might begin by looking through this book for selections with similar topics, themes, or characters. The works you choose don't have to be in the same form as long as they share at least one important feature. For example, Collection Four includes a folk tale ("He Lion . . .") and a fable ("The Fox and the Crow") that feature **tricksters** (Bruh Rabbit and Fox). These two

North Carolina Competency Goal
1.02; 4.03

characters have many differences, but they also have one major similarity—they are good at outwitting others. Here are several essay topics that might work:

- two **characters,** in the same work or in different works, who face similar conflicts or problems
- **theme** in two works
- the importance of **setting** in two works
- two **Greek myths** or two **fables** or **folk tales** from different cultures

Identify a pair of selections for your essay. Then, freewrite about them, jotting down similarities and differences.

2 Finding Points of Comparison

Which features will you compare and contrast? You should compare like with like. If you choose to compare and contrast two short stories, discuss the same aspects of both works: plot elements, characters, or themes, for example. If you choose two characters, focus on each character's physical traits, actions, thoughts, and feelings.

A **Venn diagram** can help you brainstorm ideas about how your subjects are alike and different. Here is a Venn diagram based on the Student Model on page 407. Similarities between the two poems are listed where the two circles overlap; differences are listed where they don't overlap.

Oliver Herford's poem "Earth" (See page 106.)
John H. Wheelock's poem "Earth" (See page 106.)

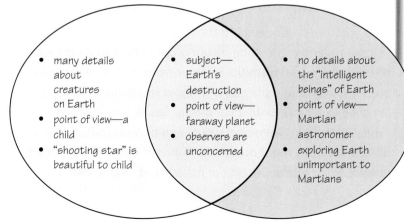

Writing Tip

Sometimes the word *compare* is used to mean both "compare" and "contrast." Whenever you see the word *compare* on a test or essay assignment, find out whether you're expected to look for similarities only or for similarities *and* differences.

Framework for a Comparison–Contrast Essay

Introduction (clear statement of the subjects and your main idea about how they relate to each other): _____

_____

Body (organized by either the block method or the point-by-point method): _____

_____

Conclusion (summary of your main idea, noting its importance or usefulness):

_____

_____

Block Method

Subject 1: Oliver Herford's poem "Earth"

Feature 1: Topic of poem

Feature 2: Point of view

Feature 3: Author's tone

Subject 2: John Hall Wheelock's poem "Earth"

Feature 1: Topic of poem

Feature 2: Point of view

Feature 3: Theme

Point–by–Point Method

Feature 1: Topic of poems

Subject 1: Herford's poem

Subject 2: Wheelock's poem

Feature 2: Point of view

Subject 1: Herford's poem

Subject 2: Wheelock's poem

Feature 3: Theme

Subject 1: Herford's poem

Subject 2: Wheelock's poem

INTERNET

More Writer's Models

Keyword: LE5 6-4

3 Organizing Your Information

When writing a comparison-contrast essay, the writer usually organizes the details using one of these patterns: the **block method** or the **point-by-point method.** With the block method the writer discusses all the points of comparison for the first subject and then discusses them in the same order for the second subject. Using the point-by-point method, the writer explains each point for both subjects before moving onto the next point. See the column to the left for examples.

Drafting

1 Developing Your Draft

Your essay should be developed in three parts:

- **Introduction:** Identify the topic of your paper, giving titles and authors' names. In one or two sentences, state your main idea about how your subjects are alike and different. Include any necessary background information.

- **Body:** Present the two or three most important similarities and differences. Use either the block or the point-by-point method.

- **Conclusion:** Restate your main idea. Summarize the points you have made in the body of your paper. You may add a personal response to the subjects.

2 Guiding Your Reader

Help your reader understand the ideas that you are comparing and contrasting by using **clue words**—words and phrases that signal transitions from one idea to another. Here are some words and phrases that show similarities: *also, another, as well as, both, in addition, just as, like, neither, similarly,* and *too.* Transition words and phrases that show differences include *although, but, however, in contrast, instead, in spite of, nevertheless, on the other hand,* and *unlike.*

Student Model

Oh no! The Earth is exploding!

"Earth" by Oliver Herford and "Earth" by John Hall Wheelock are two poems about the same subject. Each poem describes the destruction of Earth as viewed by a creature on another planet. In Herford's poem, the Earth exploding is a beautiful sight to a child. In Wheelock's poem, on the other hand, a Martian astronomer believes it was bound to happen and means little to Martians.

The writer names the two poems to be compared, cites the authors, and identifies the common **topic.**

Herford describes in great detail how a child from a planet far away witnesses the explosion. In Herford's poem, the child sees a beautiful shooting star rushing through the sky. Lines 6–12 paint a picture of what happens to the planet's creatures as Earth falls through space.

The first **subject** *is discussed.*

The writer provides an **example.**

The poem by Wheelock has no real description at all. In this poem, an astronomer on Mars is watching the Earth explode. The Martian astronomer dryly says the explosion proves that highly intelligent beings had been living there. He thinks that they are responsible for destroying their own planet.

The second **subject** *is discussed point by point to show the differences from the first subject.*

Neither the child nor the astronomer believes the Earth's destruction is such a bad thing. However, readers here on Earth are forced to consider that the Earth is fragile. It must be protected and cared for if it is to survive.

In **conclusion,** *the writer notes that the poems have the same* **theme** *and extends her* **main point.**

—Erica Graham
Owasso Sixth Grade Center
Owasso, Oklahoma

Strategies For Elaboration

- Use **specific details** and **examples** to back up your statements. Search for passages to quote that support or elaborate on the statements you make.
- Show your understanding of the subject matter by using literary terms accurately. Be sure to check the definitions of any literary elements you refer to in your essay.
- Choose relevant details and examples to support your points of comparison.

Writing Tip

A good **conclusion** should be more than just a summary. Elaborate on the **main idea** you stated in your **introduction.** You might draw a connection between the works you are discussing and your own experiences. You might extend the conclusion to cover related works or topics.

Evaluating and Revising

Use the following chart to evaluate and revise your comparison-contrast essay.

Comparison–Contrast Essay: Content and Organization Guidelines		
Evaluation Questions	▶ **Tips**	▶ **Revision Techniques**
❶ Does your introduction state your main idea? Do you identify works by title and author?	▶ **Underline** the main idea statement. **Circle** titles and authors.	▶ **Add** a main idea statement if one is missing. Add titles of works and authors' names.
❷ Do you discuss two or more similarities and differences?	▶ **Put a star** next to each example of comparison or contrast.	▶ If necessary, **add** examples of comparison and contrast. **Delete** any irrelevant statements.
❸ Is your essay organized by either the block method or the point-by-point method?	▶ **Label** the method of organization in the margin. **Put the letter A** above each point about the first subject. **Put the letter B** above each point about the second subject.	▶ **Rearrange** statements into either block order or point-by-point order.
❹ Do you use transitional expressions to show comparison or contrast?	▶ **Highlight** transitional words and phrases.	▶ **Add** transitional words that signal similarities or differences.
❺ Do you provide relevant details and examples to support points of comparison?	▶ **Put a check mark** next to supporting details and examples.	▶ **Elaborate** with details and examples, if necessary.
❻ Does your conclusion restate and expand on the main idea stated in the introduction?	▶ **Bracket** the main idea. **Underline** statements that expand your main idea.	▶ **Summarize** the main idea. **Elaborate** on statements that expand the main idea.

The following paragraphs are from an essay comparing two heroes in classical mythology. Use the questions following the model to evaluate the writer's revisions.

Revision Model

Perseus and Theseus ∧ undertook dangerous
, two great heroes of classical mythology,

adventures and defeated fearsome monsters. ∧
While

Perseus received help from the gods and goddesses

of Olympus∧
to kill Medusa,

Theseus depended on his own wits and on the help of

~~mortals~~ to overcome ~~a monster~~.
a mortal woman   *the Minotaur*

In his quest ~~to kill Medusa~~, Perseus was

assisted by Hermes and Pallas Athena. Hermes gave

him a magical sword, and Athena gave him a shield of

bronze∧. Theseus ∧ had the help of a lovestruck
to protect him from Medusa's glare *, by contrast*

princess. Ariadne showed Theseus how to escape

from the Labyrinth by using a ball of thread.

Evaluating the Revision

1. What details has the writer added? Do they provide important background information? Explain.

2. Where has the writer added transitional words or phrases? Do they help you understand what is being compared or contrasted?

3. Where has the writer reorganized the text? Do you agree with the changes? Why or why not?

PROOFREADING
TIPS

- Check the spelling of all titles and of all authors' names.

- Use quotation marks around the titles of short poems and other short works. Underline the titles of novels and other longer works. For conventions of punctuation, see the Language Handbook.

- After you proofread your essay, enlist the help of a partner to check for errors in spelling, grammar, or mechanics.

**Communications
Handbook
H E L P**

See Proofreaders' Marks.

PUBLISHING
TIPS
Create a bulletin board for student essays. The class can choose the essays to be displayed.

Test Practice

DIRECTIONS: Read the essay. Then, answer each question that follows.

from All I Really Need to Know I Learned in Kindergarten
Robert Fulghum

This is my neighbor. Nice lady. Coming out her front door, on her way to work and in her "looking good" mode. She's locking the door now and picking up her daily luggage: purse, lunch bag, gym bag for aerobics, and the garbage bucket to take out. She turns, sees me, gives me the big, smiling Hello, and takes three steps across her front porch. And goes "AAAAAAAAGGGGGGGGG-HHHHHHHHH!!!!" *(That's a direct quote.)* At about the level of a fire engine at full cry. Spider web! She has walked full force into a spider web. And the pressing question, of course: Just where is the spider *now*?

She flings her baggage in all directions. And at the same time does a high-kick, jitter-bug sort of dance—like a mating stork in crazed heat. Clutches at her face and hair and goes "AAAAAAAGG-GGGGGHHHHHHHHHH!!!!!" at a new level of intensity. Tries opening the front door without unlocking it. Tries again. Breaks key in the lock. Runs around the house headed for the back door. Doppler effect° of "AAAAAGGGHHHHaaggh . . ."

Now a different view of this scene. Here is the spider. Rather ordinary, medium gray, middle-aged lady spider. She's been up since before dawn working on her web, and all is well. Nice day, no wind, dew point just right to keep things sticky. She's out checking the moorings and thinking about the little gnats she'd like for breakfast. Feeling good. Ready for action. All of a sudden everything breaks loose—earthquake, tornado, volcano. The web is torn loose and is wrapped around a frenzied moving haystack, and a huge piece of raw-but-painted meat is making a sound the spider never heard before: "AAAAAAAGGGGGGGGHHHHH-HHHH!!!!!!" It's too big to wrap up and eat later, and it's moving too much to hold down. Jump for it? Hang on and hope? Dig in?

°**Doppler effect:** change in the pitch of a sound, produced when the source of the sound moves toward or away from the listener.

North Carolina Competency Goal
2.01

SKILLS FOCUS

Reading Skills
Analyze a comparison-contrast essay.

Human being. She has caught a human being. And the pressing question is, of course: Where is it going, and what will it do when it gets there?

The neighbor lady thinks the spider is about the size of a lobster and has big rubber lips and poisonous fangs. The neighbor lady will probably strip to the skin and take a full shower and sham-poo just to make sure it's gone—and then put on a whole new outfit to make certain she is not inhabited.

The spider? Well, if she survives all this, she will really have something to talk about—the one that got away that was THIS BIG. "And you should have seen the JAWS on the thing!"

---

1. What does the writer **compare** and **contrast** in this essay?
    A   A jitterbug and a stork
    B   People and spiders
    C   A spider web and a front porch
    D   Breakfast foods

2. What **pattern** does the writer use to organize his essay?
    F   Block method
    G   Point-by-point method
    H   Chronological order
    J   Cause-and-effect pattern

3. Both the human and the spider start out feeling —
    A   scared
    B   hungry
    C   good
    D   sleepy

4. The human and the spider are both —
    F   very old
    G   male
    H   very young
    J   female

5. The spider —
    A   thinks of the human as a piece of raw but painted meat
    B   thinks of the human as a friend
    C   wants to go in and shower
    D   bites the human

6. The human —
    F   thinks of the spider as a piece of raw but painted meat
    G   thinks of the spider as having rubber lips and poisonous fangs
    H   doesn't think anything of the spider at all
    J   thinks the spider is cute

Constructed Response

7. According to the writer, what will the human do after the encounter with the spider? What will the spider do?

Vocabulary Skills

Test Practice

Synonyms

DIRECTIONS: Choose the word or group of words that is closest in meaning to the underlined word.

1. Someone who is awkward is —
   A quiet
   B silly
   C clumsy
   D shocking

2. To savor is to —
   F enjoy
   G forget
   H save
   J serve

3. Something that is evident is —
   A sad
   B clear
   C possible
   D strange

4. To be tolerant is to be —
   F angry
   G frightened
   H accepting
   J content

5. A rural place is —
   A warm
   B mountainous
   C agricultural
   D crowded

6. To be heedful is to be —
   F helpful
   G angry
   H aware
   J courageous

7. Audacity is —
   A loyalty
   B humor
   C boldness
   D kindness

8. To ponder something is to —
   F predict it
   G consider it
   H ignore it
   J celebrate it

9. Ignorance is —
   A lack of knowledge
   B lack of wealth
   C lack of opportunity
   D lack of ability

10. Something that is devastated is —
    F robbed
    G painted
    H occupied
    J destroyed

SKILLS FOCUS

Vocabulary Skills
Understand synonyms.

Collection 4: Skills Review

Writing Skills

Test Practice

DIRECTIONS: Read the following paragraphs from a comparison-contrast essay. Then, answer each question that follows.

(1) In Greek mythology the gods and goddesses live on Mount Olympus; in Norse mythology the deities live in Asgard. (2) Olympus and Asgard are very much alike.

(3) On Olympus the family of gods enter and leave through a gate of clouds. (4) The palace of Zeus is a great hall where the gods and goddesses feast each day on ambrosia and nectar. (5) As they eat, Apollo plays his lyre. (6) When the sun sets, the gods return to their own homes to sleep.

(7) Asgard is entered by crossing a rainbow bridge. (8) The great palace of Odin is Valhalla. (9) In Valhalla, Odin feasts with the heroes who have fallen in battle. (10) The Norse gods drink mead. (11) The flesh of the boar Schrimnir is cooked every day and then becomes whole again. (12) When not feasting, the heroes fight. (13) They all recover from their wounds by mealtime, when they return to Valhalla for the feast.

1. Which of the following statements should follow Sentence 2?
   A The gods and goddesses work very hard.
   B Warriors are important in Norse mythology.
   C They are different, though, in that Olympus bans mortals while the Norse gods welcome mortal heroes.
   D The gods and goddesses lived in splendid palaces.

2. What would be the best way to combine Sentences 8 and 9?
   F The great palace of Odin is Valhalla, and in Valhalla Odin feasts with the heroes who have fallen in battle.
   G The great palace of Odin, Valhalla, is where Odin and the heroes who have fallen in battle feast.

   H In his great palace of Valhalla, Odin feasts with the heroes who have fallen in battle.
   J Valhalla is the great palace of Odin, where the heroes who have fallen in battle are feasted.

3. All of the following points of comparison are noted except —
   A how the homes of the gods and goddesses are entered
   B the names of the homes
   C the food that is eaten
   D the appearance of the palaces

4. This passage could be improved by —
   F identifying Zeus, Apollo, and Odin
   G explaining what ambrosia and nectar are
   H defining mead
   J all of the above

North Carolina Competency Goal
5.01

Writing Skill
Analyze a comparison-contrast essay.

Fiction

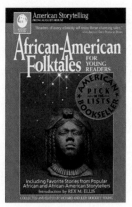

A Gold Mine of Stories

Richard and Judy Dockrey Young introduce readers to a rich tradition of storytelling in *African-American Folktales for Young Readers*. You'll meet larger-than-life characters like Annie Christmas and the mysterious Fling-a-Mile and learn about the origins of these timeless stories, described by people who still tell them today.

Expect the Unexpected

Linda Fang has collected her favorite ancient Chinese stories in *The Ch'i-Lin Purse*. Some of the stories come from Chinese novels and operas; others are inspired by actual historical events. All include twists and turns that will keep you on your toes. The stories are accompanied by lively illustrations.

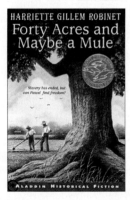

Not Quite Free

At the end of the Civil War, Pascal's brother Gideon tells Pascal and his friend Nelly that families once held in slavery have a chance to claim forty acres of land. What the young friends don't know is that finding this land will be difficult and keeping it nearly impossible. Harriette Gillem Robinet tells a tale of tragedy and injustice in *Forty Acres and Maybe a Mule*.

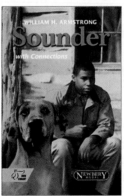

Family Ties

In his novel *Sounder,* William H. Armstrong tells the story of an African American share-cropper who is arrested for stealing food for his starving family. His son spends years searching for him; then one day the young man and Sounder, the family's hunting dog, hear footsteps approaching the house.

This title is available in the HRW Library.

Nonfiction

Hardship and Achievement

In *The Mexican American Family Album*, Dorothy and Thomas Hoobler tell about some of the historical events that have shaped the lives of Mexican Americans. The book contains photographs and firsthand accounts of generations of Mexicans who immigrated to the United States.

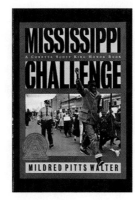

People Power

Mildred Pitts Walter chronicles the African American struggle for equal rights in Mississippi in *Mississippi Challenge*, a Coretta Scott King Honor book. The state's explosive political climate during the 1960s forms the backdrop for the protests held by people determined to end racial discrimination. Their courageous actions eventually broke down the walls of segregation.

Just a Fable?

In *Making Sense: Animal Perception and Communication*, Bruce Brooks explores the ways animals communi-cate. Brooks explains how animals "talk" to one an-other in ways you've probably never noticed.

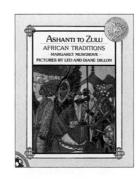

From A to Z

Margaret Musgrove introduces you to the cultures of twenty-six African peoples in *Ashanti to Zulu: African Traditions.* Accompanying the text are Leo and Diane Dillon's illustrations depicting life among these peoples.

Crowd (1996) by Judy Byford.

Biography and Autobiography: Unforgettable Personalities

Literary Focus:
Analyzing First- and Third-Person Narration

Informational Focus:
Connecting and Clarifying Main Ideas

INTERNET
Collection Resources
Keyword: LE5 6-5

Elements of Literature

First- and Third-Person Narration *by* Madeline Travers Hovland

LOOK WHO'S TALKING

"How'd It Go Today?"

If you were a middle-school student named Michael, you might answer this way:

"Well, I missed the bus and had to walk to school. So I got there late and had to check in at the principal's office. After that bad scene, I went to first-period math. Just my luck—the kids were already taking a test, so I was sent to the library. I had to give up study period to make up the test. But the rest of my day was great! Guess what? I made the soccer team!"

When you tell someone about your day, you're telling a true story. You're the narrator, so you tell the story in the **first person.** That means you use first-person pronouns—*I, me, us, our, my, mine.* You look at things one way—your way. You reveal only your own thoughts and feelings. After all, only you can know what's going on inside your own head.

Autobiography: "Self-Written Life"

Nonfiction is "not fiction"—it is writing based on fact. The subjects of nonfiction can vary as much as the world itself. The most personal kind of nonfiction is autobiographical writing. When you describe something that happened to you, you're telling an autobiographical story. An **autobiography** is a writer's account of his or her own life, written from the first-person point of view.

The word *autobiography* is made up of three parts. The prefix *auto–* means "self," the word root *–bio–* means "life," and the suffix *–graphy* means "writing." So an autobiography is a person's written account of his or her own life. Gary Paulsen's *Woodsong* (page 427) is a good example of autobiographical writing.

Biography: "Written Life"

A **biography** is the story of a person's life written by another person. Biographers write from the **third-person point of view.** They do not write from the "I" point of view because they are not the subject of the life story. Instead, they write about their subject using third-person pronouns—*his, her, their, he, she, they, them.*

A biographer writing an account of Michael's school day might begin this way:

North Carolina Competency Goal 5.02

INTERNET

More About Point of View

Keyword: LE5 6-5

Literary Skills
Understand first- and third-person narration.

Michael missed the bus, so he had to walk to school. He wasn't surprised—and neither was the vice-principal—when he got there late, again.

Biographers spend a lot of time—sometimes many years—finding out as much as they can about their subject. They interview people who knew the person. They read firsthand accounts, such as letters and journals. They dig up newspaper and magazine articles that mention the person. If they're writing about a person who lived long ago, they read historical accounts of the time so that they understand the world the subject lived in.

What a biographer chooses to leave out of a biography is as important as what he or she puts in. According to Russell Freedman, author of "The Mysterious Mr. Lincoln":

"The most difficult part of writing, whether it's biography or fiction, is deciding what to leave out. You want the reader to bring his or her own imagination to the piece. In biography, you are leaving out most things. Lincoln lived twenty-four hours a day for his whole life. It's the biographer's job to pick out the most significant details, the ones that tell something about the man or woman."

Practice

Draw a time line of your life. Label the left end "Birth" and the right end "Now." Above the line, write two or three major events that have happened in your life. Then, pick one of the events on your time line. (It's OK to choose "Birth" or "Now.") Write a paragraph about the event from the first-person point of view, as if you were writing an autobiography. Then, write about the same event from the third-person point of view, as if you were writing a biography.

Birth — We move to California. — My sister is born. — I start school. — Now

WHATCHA DOIN'?

I'M WRITING MY AUTOBIOGRAPHY.

BUT YOU'RE JUST SIX YEARS OLD.

I'VE ONLY GOT ONE SHEET OF PAPER.

Reading Skills and Strategies

Finding the Main Idea

by Kylene Beers

From Topic to Main Idea

Imagine that you're standing at your locker and you hear two friends say your name. You know they're talking about you—in other words, you are the topic. What you don't know is what they are saying about you. You want to know the main idea, or main point, of their conversation.

Finding the main idea is also important when you read. As you've seen, topic and main idea are not the same. The **topic** is what the text is all about. The **main idea** is the most important thing said about that topic. *Main idea* is a term you use when discussing nonfiction. It is not a term you use when talking about fiction, like *plot* or *theme*.

Read Between the Lines

In most texts the main idea is not stated directly. It's up to you to figure it out. As you read a text, think about its topic. Decide which details in the text are most important. Finally, ask yourself, "What do these details say about the topic?" As you read the following biographical sketch, list the details you learn about Hans Christian Andersen. On page 425, you'll use your list to find the main idea.

North Carolina Competency Goal
1.02

Reading Skills
Find the main idea.

A Model for Finding the Main Idea

Read the following paragraph. The **topic** is skateboarding. What is the **main idea**? State the main idea in a sentence.

> Many teenagers ride skateboards to school, in skateboard parks, or just around the neighborhood. But not all riders wear helmets, pads, and gloves. When skateboarders fall without protective gear, they may wind up with head injuries or broken bones. Though it's a popular sport among teens, skateboarding can be very dangerous.

The main idea *isn't* that many teenagers like to ride skateboards, since that's not what the whole paragraph is about.

By the third sentence, you are learning about some of the pitfalls of skateboarding.

The final sentence reveals the main idea.

UGLY DUCKLING OR LITTLE MERMAID?

Hans Christian Andersen

Kathleen Krull

BORN IN ODENSE, DENMARK, 1805
DIED IN ROLIGHED, DENMARK, 1875

Danish writer of fairy tales, including
"The Emperor's New Clothes," "The Steadfast Tin Soldier,"
"Thumbelina," and "The Ugly Duckling"

As you read, you'll find this open-book sign at certain points in the story: Stop at these points, and think about what you've just read. Do what the prompt asks you to do.

At last—crack—and "peep, peep," chirped the little one, and out he crept. "He is big and ugly," thought Mrs. Duck. "I fear he's a turkey after all, but we'll soon see about that."

Illustration (1894) by T. van Hoijtema for "The Ugly Duckling."
The Granger Collection, New York.

FIND THE MAIN IDEA

❶ By now you know that the topic of this biographical sketch is Hans Christian Andersen. What you don't know yet is what main idea the author wants to convey about him.

FIND THE MAIN IDEA

❷ In these first paragraphs, the author provides interesting details about Andersen's sad childhood. If the whole selection is about Andersen's childhood, then the main idea might be about how it was sad. Read on to find out.

"My life is a fairy tale," Hans Christian Andersen once wrote, and most people would have agreed: he *was* the ugly duckling. **❶**

Awkward and unattractive, Andersen came from the humblest possible background—his family history included crime, illiteracy,[1] insanity, and alcoholism. He spent his lonely childhood playing with puppets and a toy theater. On winter nights (when darkness lasts as long as seventeen hours in Denmark), he heated coins and pressed them against the windows to melt the frost so he could peer at the snowy scenes outside. **❷**

---

1. **illiteracy** (il·lit′ər·ə·sē) *n.*: inability to read or write.

The house on the right is the birthplace of Hans Christian Andersen in Odense, Denmark.

He went to work in a tobacco factory at age eleven and then, dreading a lifetime of this, took the money he'd been saving up in a clay pig and left home for Copenhagen.[2] Although he received almost no encouragement, he was convinced that he excelled at singing, dancing, acting, and drawing. "First one has to endure terrible adversity,"[3] he assured his mother, "then you become famous."

All his life, the word even his friends used most often to describe Andersen was *childlike*. A nature-lover, he was known to hug trees. He was too anxious to please, too easily intimidated,[4] and a bumbler. Once he got so nervous during an exam that he sprayed the professor's face with ink by mistake. Talkative and eager, he would collar people to read his work to them. Amazingly, people were charmed by Andersen and gave him scholarships and opportunities.

He even dressed like a child. Always frugal, he wore clothes and shoes long after he had outgrown them. If someone gave him a coat that was too big, he would stuff it with newspapers to make it fit. He liked to read books while lying on a sofa, wearing brightly colored slippers and a dressing gown. ❸

He had one hobby that appealed to adults and children alike. His huge hands were skilled with a pair of scissors, and he would cut delicate creations from paper as he talked—animals, castles, goblins, and fairies.

Andersen knew he was an ugly duckling ("His nose as mighty as a cannon, / His eyes are tiny, like green peas" was how he put it), but he was vain, too, and he loved to be photographed. ❹

Andersen never settled into a home of his own. When in Denmark he stayed in hotels or with friends—he was often designated the family "candle snuffer" because he was so tall. He preferred wandering, and whenever he had enough money he went off traveling. His first train ride (at age thirty-five) was magical; he loved to watch the landscape fly by.

He desperately wanted to get married but never did. The women he chose were either long dead (his first true love was a portrait of the ancestor of a friend) or did not return his affection. The women who chose *him* repelled[5] him.

---

2. **Copenhagen:** capital of Denmark.
3. **adversity** (ad·vur′sə·tē) *n.*: bad luck; trouble.
4. **intimidated** (in·tim′ə·dāt′id) *v.* used as *adj.*: scared; made timid.
5. **repelled** *v.*: disgusted; drove away.

Using the Strategy

FIND THE MAIN IDEA

❸ By now you can see that this sketch is about more than just Andersen's childhood. You've learned some details about his adult life, too. What kind of main idea might these details support? As you read on, think about what the author wants you to understand about Andersen.

FIND THE MAIN IDEA

❹ Here you find out that even though Andersen thought he was ugly, he liked to be photographed. That's sort of odd—but would you say it's the main idea of this selection? Why or why not?

When he was feeling especially melancholy,[6] Andersen would get bad toothaches (even—after he lost all his teeth—in his false teeth). He feared death—from a splinter, food poisoning, murder, or being buried alive. He sometimes put a sign next to his bed that read I AM NOT REALLY DEAD, so that people would know he was just asleep. Most of all he feared dying young, insane, and alone.

He was, in fact, seventy when he died—probably of liver cancer—and by that time he was a much-loved figure around the world. **5**

---

6. **melancholy** (mel′ən·käl′ē) *adj.*: sad; gloomy.

FIND THE MAIN IDEA

5 Think back through the entire selection. The author provides many details about Andersen's personality quirks, likes and dislikes, and unusual habits. What big idea about Andersen do all of these details support or add up to? Try to state the main idea in your own words. Then, list three or four details that support it.

BOOKMARKS

☞ Andersen wrote plays, operas, novels, poetry, and travel books but today is known best for his 168 fairy tales. "The Little Mermaid" was his favorite, and he saw himself in the heroine. He too had come from the sea (the islands of Denmark), and all his life he felt like a "fish out of water," longing to be accepted.

☞ Andersen wrote "The Nightingale" while in love with Jenny Lind, whose nickname was the Swedish Nightingale. Andersen showered Lind—the most famous singer of the day—with flowers, poems, and gifts, but his love was not returned.

☞ A magazine once sent Andersen three woodcuts as the basis for a story. He chose one of a ragged little girl with her apron full of matches and wrote "The Little Match Girl." The woodcut reminded him of his mother, who as a child had been forced to beg.

Illustration (1932) by John Hassall for "The Ugly Duckling."
The Granger Collection, New York.

Practice the Strategy

Finding the Main Idea

PRACTICE 1

The **topic** is what a text is about. The **main idea** is the main point the author wants to make about the topic. Authors use **details** to support the main idea. Read the following sentences about Hans Christian Andersen, and decide which states a topic, which are supporting details, and which expresses the main idea. Explain your decisions.

1. Andersen had a fear of being buried alive.
2. Andersen was a talented writer who had a difficult childhood and strange adulthood.
3. This is about the life of Hans Christian Andersen.
4. Hans Christian Andersen always acted like a child.
5. Andersen left home at age eleven to go to Copenhagen.

PRACTICE 2

In "Ugly Duckling or Little Mermaid?" the topic is clearly the life of Hans Christian Andersen. What point does the author make about Andersen's life? Here's an easy way to figure it out. Look at the list of details you made as you read, and state a possible main idea. Then test your main idea by asking yourself, "Is the whole text about this idea? Do most of the details support this idea?"

Put this strategy to work by responding to each of the following statements. Explain each of your responses. The one you can answer yes to is the main idea.

Is the whole text about how . . .

a. Andersen's friends described him as childlike?
b. he left home at age eleven?
c. he enjoyed making paper cuttings?
d. he wanted to get married?
e. he lived an unusual life from childhood through adulthood?

Statue of Hans Christian Andersen in Copenhagen, Denmark.

Strategy Tip

Remember to identify the topic first. Then, ask yourself what the author wants to tell you about that topic. Check your main idea by asking yourself, "Is the whole text about this idea? Do the details in the text support this idea?" If the answer is no, then keep looking for the main idea.

SKILLS FOCUS

North Carolina Competency Goal 1.02

Reading Skills Analyze the main idea.

425

Storm

Make the Connection
Quickwrite ✏️

What can you learn about a pet or a wild animal from your own observations?

Make a two-column chart like the one below. In one column, list examples of behavior you have noticed in different animals. In the other column, write what you think each action shows about the animal.

The Animal's Actions	What They Tell Me
A big dog lies down when my dog gets near.	The big dog is showing that he's friendly.
Blue jays divebomb my cat Fern.	They want to scare her.

Literary Focus
First-Person Point of View

Everything you read is told from a particular point of view. In a story told from the **first-person point of view,** a character in the story is speaking to you. This person is called the **narrator,** which means "storyteller." It's easy to recognize a first-person narration because throughout the story the storyteller speaks of himself or herself using first-person pronouns—*I, me, we,* us, mine, ours. In this episode from a true adventure story, Gary Paulsen, the narrator, speaks as "I."

Reading Skills 📖
Finding the Main Idea

The **main idea** is the most important idea in a nonfiction piece. To figure out the main idea, follow these steps:

- Look at the **key details** or **events.** What ideas do they support?

- Look for a major idea stated several times in slightly different words.

- Look for **key passages** near the end of the selection. Is the writer summing up a main idea?

Answering the questions near the little open-book logos will help you identify Paulsen's main idea.

Vocabulary Development

Don't get snowed under! Learn these new words before you read the story.

disengage (dis'in·gāj') *v.:* unfasten. *Before I disengage the leash, I tell the dog to sit.*

regain (ri·gān') *v.:* recover. *I stopped to let the dog rest and regain her strength.*

emit (ē·mit') *v.:* give out; send forth. *Dogs emit quick breaths when they pant.*

North Carolina Competency Goal
1.04; 4.01; 5.01

go. hrw .com

INTERNET

Vocabulary Activity
•
More About Paulsen
•
Cross-curricular Connections

Keyword: LE5 6-5

SKILLS FOCUS

Literary Skills
Understand first-person point of view.

Reading Skills
Find the main idea.

Background
Literature and Social Studies

"Storm" is taken from *Woodsong,* Gary Paulsen's account of his adventures in northern Minnesota. There he ran a team of sled dogs. Paulsen later ran the Iditarod (i·dit'ə·räd), a dog-sled race across Alaska.

© Scott Kennedy

STORM

from *Woodsong* Gary Paulsen

It is always possible to learn from dogs, and in fact the longer I'm with them, the more I understand how little I know. But there was one dog who taught me the most. Just one dog. Storm. First dog. . . . **❶** 📖

Joy, loyalty, toughness, peacefulness—all of these were part of Storm. Lessons about life and, finally, lessons about death came from him.

📖 **FIND THE MAIN IDEA**
❶ What important idea does Paulsen express in this paragraph?

Eager to Run by Scott Kennedy.

He had a bear's ears. He was brindle colored[1] and built like a truck, and his ears were rounded when we got him, so that they looked like bear cub ears. They gave him a comical look when he was young that somehow hung on to him even when he grew old. He had a sense of humor to match his ears, and when he grew truly old, he somehow resembled George Burns.[2]

At peak, he was a mighty dog. He pulled like a machine. Until we retired him and used him only for training puppies, until we let him loose to enjoy his age, he pulled, his back over in the power curve, so that nothing could stop the sled.

In his fourth or fifth year as a puller, he started doing tricks. First he would play jokes on the dog pulling next to him. On long runs he would become bored, and when we least expected it, he would reach across the gang line and snort wind into the ear of the dog next to him. I ran him with many different dogs and he did it to all of them—chuckling when the dog jumped and shook his or her head—but I never saw a single dog get mad at him for it. Oh, there was once a dog named Fonzie who nearly took his head off, but Fonzie wasn't really mad at him so much as surprised. Fonzie once nailed me through the wrist for waking him up too suddenly when he was sleeping. I'd reached down and touched him before whispering his name.

Small jokes. Gentle jokes, Storm played. He took to hiding things from me. At first I couldn't understand where things were going. I would put a bootie down while working on a dog, and it would disappear. I lost a small ladle[3] I used for watering each dog, a cloth glove liner I took off while working on a dog's feet, a roll of tape, and finally, a hat.

He was so clever.

When I lost the hat, it was a hot day and I had taken the hat off while I worked on a dog's harness. The dog was just ahead of Storm, and when I knelt to work on the

---

1. **brindle colored:** gray or brown and streaked or spotted with a dark color.
2. **George Burns** (1896–1996): American comedian and actor with large ears.
3. **ladle** *n.:* cup-shaped spoon with a long handle for dipping out liquids.

© Scott Kennedy

harness—he'd chewed almost through the side of it while running—I put the hat down on the snow near Storm.

Or thought I had. When I had changed the dog's harness, I turned and the hat was gone. I looked around, moved the dogs, looked under them, then shrugged. At first I was sure I'd put the hat down; then, when I couldn't find it, I became less sure, and at last I thought perhaps I had left it at home or dropped it somewhere on the run.

Storm sat quietly, looking ahead down the trail, not showing anything at all.

I went back to the sled, reached down to disengage the hook, and when I did, the dogs exploded forward. I was not quite on the sled when they took off, so I was knocked slightly off balance. I leaned over to the right to regain myself, and when I did, I accidentally dragged the hook through the snow.

And pulled up my hat.

It had been buried off to the side of the trail in the snow, buried neatly with the snow smoothed over the top, so that it was completely hidden. Had the snow hook not scraped down four or five inches, I never would have found it.

I stopped the sled and set the hook once more. While knocking the snow out of the hat and putting it back on my head, I studied where it had happened.

Right next to Storm.

He had taken the hat, quickly dug a hole, buried the hat and smoothed the snow over it, then gone back to sitting, staring ahead, looking completely innocent.

When I stopped the sled and picked up the hat, he looked back, saw me put the hat on my head, and— I swear—smiled. Then he shook his head once and went back to work pulling. ❷

Along with the jokes, Storm had scale eyes. He watched as the sled was loaded, carefully calculated the weight of each item, and let his disapproval be known if it went too far.

One winter a friend gave us a parlor stove with nickel trim. It was not an enormous stove, but it had some weight to it and some

> ### FIND THE MAIN IDEA
> ❷ What lesson does Paulsen learn from Storm's tricks?

Vocabulary
disengage (dis′in·gāj′) *v.:* unfasten.
regain (ri·gān′) *v.:* recover.

Never Alone (detail) by Scott Kennedy.

bulk. This friend lived twelve miles away—twelve miles over two fair hills followed by about eight miles on an old, abandoned railroad grade.[4] We needed the stove badly (our old barrel stove had started to burn through), so I took off with the team to pick it up. I left early in the morning because I wanted to get back that same day. It had snowed four or five inches, so the dogs would have to break trail. By the time we had done the hills and the railroad grade, pushing in new snow all the time, they were ready for a rest. I ran them the last two miles to where the stove was and unhooked their tugs so they could rest while I had coffee.

We stopped for an hour at least, the dogs sleeping quietly. When it was time to go, my friend and I carried the stove outside and put it in the sled. The dogs didn't move.

Except for Storm.

He raised his head, opened one eye, did a perfect double take—both eyes opening wide—and sat up. He had been facing the front. Now he turned around to face the sled—so he was facing away from the direction we had to travel when we left—and watched us load the sled.

It took some time, as the stove barely fit on the sled and had to be jiggled and shuffled around to get it down between the side rails.

Through it all, Storm sat and watched us, his face a study in interest. He did not get up but sat on his back end, and when I was done and ready to go, I hooked all the dogs back in harness—which involved hooking the tugs to the rear ties on their harnesses. The dogs knew this meant we were going to head home, so they got up and started slamming against the tugs, trying to get the sled to move.

---

4. **railroad grade:** rise or elevation in a railroad track.

© Scott Kennedy

All of them, that is, but Storm.

Storm sat backward, the tug hooked up but hanging down. The other dogs were screaming to run, but Storm sat and stared at the stove.

Not at me, not at the sled, but at the stove itself. Then he raised his lips, bared his teeth, and growled at the stove.

When he was finished growling, he snorted twice, stood, turned away from the stove, and started to pull. But each time we stopped at the tops of the hills to let the dogs catch their breath after pulling the sled and stove up the steep incline, Storm turned and growled at the stove.

The enemy.

The weight on the sled.

I do not know how many miles Storm and I ran together. Eight, ten, perhaps twelve thousand miles. He was one of the first dogs and taught me the most, and as we worked together, he came to know me better than perhaps even my own family. He could look once at my shoulders and tell how I was feeling, tell how far we were to run, how fast we had to run— knew it all. ❸ 🏊

🏊 **FIND THE MAIN IDEA**
❸ What important idea does Paulsen repeat in this paragraph?

When I started to run long, moved from running a work team, a trap line team, to training for the Iditarod, Storm took it in stride, changed the pace down to the long trot, matched what was needed, and settled in for the long haul.

He did get bored, however, and one day while we were running a long run, he started doing a thing that would stay with him— with us—until the end. We had gone forty or fifty miles on a calm, even day with no bad wind. The temperature was a perfect ten below zero. The sun was bright, everything was moving well, and the dogs had settled into the rhythm that could take them a hundred or a thousand miles.

And Storm got bored.

At a curve in the trail, a small branch came out over the path we were running, and as Storm passed beneath the limb, he jumped up and grabbed it, broke a short piece off—about a foot long—and kept it in his mouth.

All day.

And into the night. He ran, carrying the stick like a toy, and when we stopped to feed or rest, he would put the stick down, eat, then pick it up again. He would put the stick down carefully in front of him, or across his paws, and sleep, and when he awakened, he would pick up the stick, and it soon became a thing between us, the stick.

He would show it to me, making a contact, a connection between us, each time

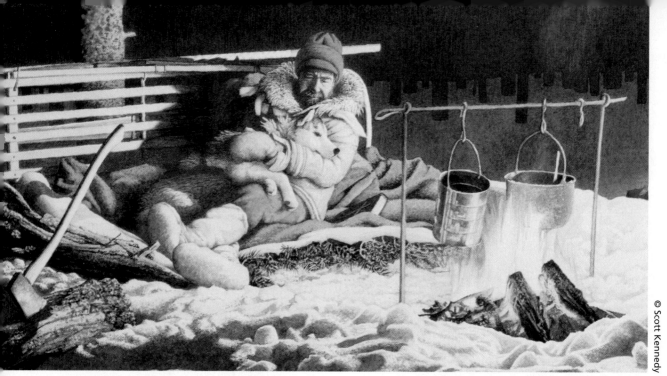

Never Alone (detail) by Scott Kennedy.

we stopped. I would pet him on top of the head and take the stick from him—he would emit a low, gentle growl when I took the stick. I'd "examine" it closely, nod and seem to approve of it, and hand it back to him.

Each day we ran, he would pick a different stick. And each time I would have to approve of it, and after a time, after weeks and months, I realized that he was using the sticks as a way to communicate with me, to tell me that everything was all right, that I was doing the right thing.

Once, when I pushed them too hard during a pre-Iditarod race—when I thought it was important to compete and win (a feeling that didn't last long)—I walked up to Storm, and as I came close to him, he pointedly dropped the stick. I picked it up and held it out, but he wouldn't take it. He turned his face away. I put the stick against his lips and tried to make him take it, but he let it fall to the ground. When I realized what he was

doing, I stopped and fed and rested the team, sat on the sled, and thought about what I was doing wrong. After four hours or so of sitting—watching other teams pass me—I fed them another snack, got ready to go, and was gratified to see Storm pick up the stick. From that time forward I looked for the stick always, knew when I saw it out to the sides of his head that I was doing the right thing. And it was always there.

Through storms and cold weather, on the long runs, the long, long runs where there isn't an end to it, where only the sled and the winter around the sled and the wind are there, Storm had the stick to tell me it was right, all things were right. ❹

FIND THE MAIN IDEA ❹ What does Storm's behavior with the stick teach Paulsen?

Vocabulary

emit (ē·mit′) *v.*: give out; send forth.

Gary Paulsen

Good Cooking

The son of an army officer who moved his family with each new assignment, **Gary Paulsen** (1939–   ) lived all over the United States when he was a boy. Because he was always moving, Paulsen had no real friends when he was growing up. One winter day he wandered into a public library to keep warm, and the librarian offered him a library card. He remembers:

> 66 When she handed me the card, she handed me the world. . . . It was as though I had been dying of thirst and the librarian had handed me a five-gallon bucket of water. I drank and drank. 99

This passion for reading eventually led to an interest in writing. Paulsen left his engineering job and became editor of a magazine, an experience he has called "the best of all possible ways to learn about writing." His first book was a collection of interviews with Vietnam War veterans. Since then he has written more than forty books, along with hundreds of magazine articles and short stories. Writing means the world to him:

> 66 I have not done anything else in my life that gives me the personal satisfaction that writing does. It pleases me to write—in the very literal sense of the word. When I have done well with it, and 'cooked' for a day so that it felt good when I put it down—it flowed and worked right. When all that is right, I go to sleep with an immense feeling of personal satisfaction. 99

For Independent Reading

Paulsen has cooked up a feast of adventure stories for young adults. If you're interested in wilderness-survival tales, try the novels *Dogsong* and *Hatchet*. Both were named Newbery Honor Books by the American Library Association.

First Thoughts

1. Complete these sentences:
   - I never realized before that dogs . . .
   - My favorite part of the story was . . .

Thinking Critically

2. In your own words, sum up what Storm teaches the narrator.

3. When Paulsen describes Storm, he also gives clues to his own character. What kind of person do you think Paulsen is?

4. Is this piece only about dogs, or is it also about something else? In one or two sentences, state what you see as Paulsen's **main idea**.

5. Paulsen describes Storm as the "dog who taught me the most." Using your Quickwrite notes, think of something you have learned from an animal. Compare what you learned with what Paulsen learns from Storm.

Extending Interpretations

6. Do you think Gary Paulsen's interpretations of Storm's jokes and tricks are accurate? To find out, what questions might you ask Paulsen? What other questions would you like to ask Paulsen about Storm?

Reading Check

a. Who is the narrator of these stories about Storm?

b. From what **point of view** is "Storm" told—first person or third person?

c. The graphic below shows how "Storm" is structured:

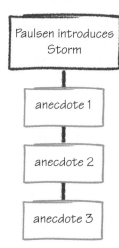

An **anecdote** (an'ik·dōt') is a brief story told to make a point. Fill in a graphic like the one above to show the structure of Paulsen's text.

WRITING

Retelling a Story from a Different Point of View

Imagine that Storm decides to tell the world a few things about Paulsen and that Storm's so smart he can write his own stories about his human pal. How would Storm tell the story of hauling the heavy stove? Use the personal pronoun *I* to retell the story from Storm's point of view.

North Carolina Competency Goal
1.02; 1.04; 4.01; 4.02; 5.01

INTERNET
Projects and Activities
Keyword: LE5 6-5

SKILLS FOCUS

Literary Skills
Analyze point of view.

Reading Skills
Analyze main idea.

Writing Skills
Write from the first-person point of view.

After You Read · Vocabulary Development

Prefixes

Each word in the Word Bank has a **prefix**—a letter or group of letters added to the beginning of a word to change its meaning. Knowing the meaning of a few prefixes can help you figure out the meaning of many unfamiliar words.

PRACTICE

Make a chart like the one below for the prefixes of the words in the Word Bank: *dis–, re–,* and *e–.*

Prefix	Meaning	Examples
anti–	against	antislavery
		antibiotic
		antifreeze

Word Bank

disengage
regain
emit

Grammar Link

Using *Good* and *Well* Correctly

The word *good* should be used to modify nouns and pronouns. The word *well* should generally be used to modify verbs.

> **Storm's funny face always looked good to Paulsen.** [*Good* modifies the noun *face.*]
> **Storm worked well with the team.** [*Well* modifies the verb *worked.*]

Do not use *good* to modify a verb.

NONSTANDARD **Storm works good even when he is tired.**

STANDARD **Storm works well even when he is tired.**

Note that *feel good* and *feel well* mean different things. *Feel good* means "feel happy or pleased." *Feel well* means "feel healthy."

> **Even if he didn't feel well** [healthy], **Paulsen felt good** [happy] **when he saw Storm.**

PRACTICE

Complete each of the following sentences by choosing the correct word from the underlined pair.

1. Storm ate good/well today.

2. The team looked good/well.

Hint: Circle the words *good* and *well* wherever they appear in your writing. Then, draw an arrow from the circled word to the word it modifies. If the arrow points to a noun or a pronoun, be sure you've used an adjective. If the arrow points to a verb, an adjective, or an adverb, be sure you've used an adverb.

For more help, see Special Problems in Using Modifiers, 5b, in the Language Handbook.

North Carolina Competency Goal 6.01

Vocabulary Skills
Understand prefixes.

Grammar Skills
Use *good* and *well* correctly.

Finding and Analyzing Main Ideas

Reading Focus
Finding the Main Idea

The topic of a piece of writing can usually be stated in just a word or two: *love, dogs, growing up.* The **main idea** is the most important thing a writer has to say *about* the topic. The main idea answers the question "What about it?"— what about love or dogs or growing up?

In "Storm," Gary Paulsen gives us a topic that's easy to identify: his dog Storm. But what does Paulsen want to say *about* Storm? By telling us about Storm, what is he saying about dogs in general?

■ Finding a main idea takes some practice. Sometimes there's more than one main idea in a piece of nonfiction, just as there can be more than one theme to a story. Copy the chart below, which shows four main ideas you might have found in "Storm."

Now, write "Storm" under each main idea that you think Paulsen's story best illustrates or supports. (You may decide to write "Storm" under all the ideas.)

The two selections that follow have animals as their topic. After you read each selection, go back to your chart. Write the selection titles ("Bringing Tang Home" and "Where the Heart Is") under the main ideas they illustrate or support. When you've finished filling in the chart, notice how some of the main ideas connect to all three selections.

North Carolina Competency Goal
1.02

INTERNET
Interactive Reading Model
Keyword: LE5 6–5

SKILLS FOCUS

Reading Skills
Find and analyze main ideas.

Possible Main Ideas	
Humans and animals have a special bond.	There are many things about animals that humans can't explain.
Animals may understand humans better than humans understand animals.	Humans can learn from their animal friends.

Vocabulary Development

These are the words you'll be learning as you read "Bringing Tang Home":

furtive (fur′tiv) *adj.:* done in a sneaky or secretive way. *The kitten made a furtive movement toward the food.*

formidable (fôr′mə·də·bəl) *adj.:* fearsome. *The cat let out a formidable yowl.*

feral (fir′əl) *adj.:* untamed; wild. *The feral cat finally let me touch her.*

lure (lŏŏr) *v.:* tempt; attract. *They used food to lure the wild cats to safety.*

controversial (kän′trə·vur′shəl) *adj.:* debatable; tending to stir up argument. *His method of rescuing wild cats is controversial.*

Bringing Tang Home

In the warm half-light at the end of a summer day, the woods near my home fall quiet as if holding their breath waiting for the wild creatures of the night. Twilight is nature's shift change: In an hour's time the day will be gone and night will be filled with the furtive rustlings of animals who'd rather their comings and goings be unnoticed by the residents of the nearby houses.

I let my own breath out slowly, quietly, for I am also waiting, as is the woman beside me. The night creatures we wait for, though, aren't meant to be wild: We are waiting for cats.

Among the Wild Things

The opossum, the raccoon, and the skunk steal food from their human neighbors on the other side of the river levee but want nothing in the way of affection. They flee from the sound of footsteps and bare formidable teeth if cornered. "Approach at your peril!" they snarl before melting into the shadows.

But the cats aren't quite so anxious to run. Perhaps this is because their kind and ours have been linked for countless generations, or perhaps it is because, among all the animals, cats alone chose the path of their own domestication and remember it still. Whatever the reason, in the heart of

---

Vocabulary

furtive (fŭr′tĭv) *adj.:* done in a sneaky or secretive way.

formidable (fôr′mə·də·bəl) *adj.:* fearsome.

these cats—of every cat gone <u>feral</u>—remains a memory of how pleasant is the company of a human, or how sweet is the feel of a hand swept warmly from just behind the ears and along the supple spine to the end of the tail.

My companion tonight is one of those people who work to return the wild ones to a life of such pleasures. The cats in these woods belong to her, as much as they belong to anyone. She traps the older ones and has them fixed and vaccinated before releasing them to these woods again, for they are too wild to be good pets. The kittens—for despite all the spaying and neutering, there are always new cats, and so, new kittens—she traps, and tames, and finds homes for.

We are after the last of the spring kittens this night, a pale orange tabby male she has named Tang (as in orange Tang). The older cats know what the trap is about, and only the most desperate starvation would <u>lure</u> them inside again. The kittens aren't so worldly-wise. The appeal of canned food is enough for them, and all but Tang have already been enticed inside for the first step on their journey back to domestication.

The Task of Taming

In the dimming light we can barely see the half-grown kitten move inside. The trap slams shut with a crack that scatters the cats—all but the young tabby, who now cannot flee. He hurls himself against the sides of his cage, yowls in fear, and hisses in anger.

The sound beside me is no less explosive. "Yes!" cries my companion. "We got him!"

Tang doesn't yet know it, but he is on his way home. After a few weeks of gentle and

gradual socialization, he'll be placed with someone who'll love him. A better fate, surely, than the one he faced as one of the ferals, whose short lives are full of desperation—and often end brutally.

Despite the dangers that claim so many, wild cats are everywhere on the edges of our lives, from the alleys of our cities and the parks of our suburbs to the wild areas and farmland that fill in the gaps between. And in many of those places are people like Tang's captor, quietly pursuing a labor of love that can be as thankless as it often is <u>controversial</u>. Some people would rather see the ferals killed, but these volunteers see another way.

One kitten, one summer evening at a time, they are making a difference. Few thoughts are as pleasant to contemplate as the summer night hugs me in a warm embrace.

—Gina Spadafori

Vocabulary
feral (fir′əl) *adj.:* untamed; wild.
lure (loor) *v.:* tempt; attract.
controversial (kän′trə·vur′shəl) *adj.:* debatable; tending to stir up argument.

Where the Heart Is

Two-year-old Bobby, partly English sheepdog but mostly collie, had become separated from Frank Brazier while on vacation in Indiana.

On a cold February evening in 1924, a gaunt dog limped up to a farmhouse in Silverton, Oregon, where he had once lived with his family as a pup. But the house was silent, the family long departed. Since August, the dog's lonely journey had taken him across Illinois and Iowa. He had swum rivers, including the dangerous and icy Missouri; he had crossed the great Rocky Mountains in the middle of winter. He had caught squirrels and rabbits for food. At times he had been helped by strangers:

He had eaten stew with hobos and Thanksgiving dinner with a family who sheltered him for several weeks. But once he had regained his strength, the dog traveled on, always heading west. The dog lay down to rest for the night at the empty farmhouse. In the morning, on paws with pads worn almost to bone, he made his way slowly into town, into the restaurant where his family now lived, and climbed upstairs to a bedroom, to lick the face of the man he had walked some three thousand miles to find. Bobby had come home.

Two-year-old Bobby, partly English sheepdog but mostly collie, had become separated from Frank Brazier while on vacation in Indiana. When word got out about Bobby's remarkable journey, the president of the Oregon Humane Society decided to document the facts and find the people who had seen or helped Bobby along the way. Bobby eventually became one of the most honored heroes in dog history, recognized with numerous medals and awards for his courage, devotion, and perseverance.

How did Bobby find his way home? Nobody knows for sure. We do know that Bobby's story is unusual but not unique. For centuries there have been reports of animals performing mystifying and wonderful feats like Bobby's. There are stories of other animals who tracked their families, sometimes over thousands of miles, to places where the animals themselves had never been, over routes the owners had never traveled. The story of Sugar may be the longest recorded trip of this kind.

Stacy Woods, a high school principal, planned to move from Anderson, California, to a farm in Gage, Oklahoma, 1,500 miles away. She couldn't take her cat Sugar, because he was terrified of riding in the car. So a neighbor agreed to adopt him. Fourteen months later, as Stacy Woods was milking a cow in her Oklahoma barn, Sugar jumped through an open window onto her shoulder. The astonished Woods family later learned that Sugar had disappeared three weeks after they had left him with the neighbor. Proving that the cat was really Sugar was easy because Sugar had an unusual hip deformity. But the main question remains unanswered today: How did Sugar find his owner? Similar questions have been raised about many other animals. How did Hugh Brady Perkins's homing pigeon find his way to Hugh's hospital window, 120 miles from his home, after the boy was rushed to the hospital in the middle of the night? How do some pets know when their favorite family members are coming home unexpectedly? How do some pets know from great distances when their family members are hurt or ill or in trouble?

In recent decades, researchers have studied questions like these. They have pondered the possibility that animals draw on information picked up in some way other

Fourteen months later, as Stacy Woods was milking a cow in her Oklahoma barn, Sugar jumped through an open window onto her shoulder.

than through the five well-known senses (sight, hearing, smell, taste, and touch).

Researchers have found that some animals have senses humans lack, like bats' ability to detect objects from echoes and certain snakes' ability to sense tiny temperature differences through special organs. Some people theorize that animals have a form of ESP (extrasensory perception). At Duke University, Joseph Banks Rhine collected more than five hundred stories of unexplainable animal feats that seem to support this theory. Rhine devoted his life to researching these events. Studies conducted at the Research Institute at Rockland State Hospital in New York also support the notion of an extrasensory connection between animals and humans, particularly humans the animals know well and trust.

Of course, whatever our theories say, we don't really know what goes on in the heart and mind of an animal. Perhaps the question of *how* they find us is not the most important one. A better question to ponder may be *why* they find us, even when faced with overwhelming difficulties. It has been said that home is where the heart is. It's clear that for Bobby and Sugar and countless others, home is where one particular heart is.

—Sheri Henderson

Analyzing and Connecting Main Ideas

Storm / Bringing Tang Home / Where the Heart Is

1. The writers of all three selections would probably agree that —
   A dogs and cats are not intelligent
   B relationships between animals and people benefit both
   C abandoned and lost animals should be left to survive on their own
   D dogs and cats stay with humans only because humans feed them

2. If you were writing an essay on close relationships between people and animals, which of the following animals would *not* be a good example to use?
   F Storm
   G Tang
   H Bobby
   J Sugar

3. In which selections are scientific **facts** as well as **anecdotes** (very brief stories told to make a point) used to support the main idea?
   A "Where the Heart Is"
   B "Storm"
   C "Bringing Tang Home"
   D All of the above

4. Which statement about the **point of view** of these selections is accurate?
   F All selections are written from the first-person point of view.
   G The stories of Tang and Storm are told from the first-person point of view.
   H The story of Tang and "Where the Heart Is" are told from the first-person point of view.
   J All three selections are told from the third-person point of view.

North Carolina Competency Goal
1.02; 1.04; 4.01; 4.02; 5.01

SKILLS FOCUS

Reading Skills
Analyze and connect main ideas.

Constructed Response

1. Go back to the chart of possible main ideas that you made before you read "Bringing Tang Home" and "Where the Heart Is" (page 436). Write the titles of these two selections under the main ideas that they best illustrate or support.

2. Which of the main ideas applies to "Storm," "Bringing Tang Home," and "Where the Heart Is"? Support your answer with examples from each selection.

Context Clues

You can often figure out the meaning of a new word by looking at its **context**—the words or sentences surrounding it. For example, in "Bringing Tang Home," Gina Spadafori writes, "In the dimming light we can barely see the half-grown kitten move inside." You may not know the meaning of *dimming,* but you do know that you need light to see. Since it is nightfall and Spadafori can barely see the kitten, you can figure out that *dimming* means "fading."

> **Word Bank**
> furtive
> formidable
> feral
> lure
> controversial

PRACTICE

Read each of the quotations below, using context to help you choose the correct meaning of the underlined word.

1. "In an hour's time the day will be gone and night will be filled with the furtive rustlings of animals who'd rather their comings and goings be unnoticed by the residents of the nearby houses."

   a. playful **b.** secretive **c.** noisy **d.** foolish

2. "They flee from the sound of footsteps and bare formidable teeth if cornered. 'Approach at your peril!' they snarl before melting into the shadows."

   a. surprising **b.** playful **c.** fearsome **d.** weak

3. "The night creatures we wait for . . . aren't meant to be wild: We are waiting for cats. . . . In the heart of these cats— of every cat gone feral—remains a memory of how pleasant is the company of a human. . . ."

   a. tame **b.** fierce **c.** insane **d.** wild

4. "The older cats know what the trap is about, and only the most desperate starvation would lure them inside again."

   a. yank **b.** want **c.** tempt **d.** shove

5. "And in many of those places are people like Tang's captor, quietly pursuing a labor of love that can be as thankless as it often is controversial. Some people would rather see the ferals killed, but these volunteers see another way."

   a. debatable **b.** fair **c.** humorous **d.** persuasive

North Carolina Competency Goal
6.01

Vocabulary Skills
Use context clues.

Before You Read   The Autobiography

Brother

Make the Connection
Quickwrite 🖉

In her autobiography, Maya Angelou says simply that her brother, Bailey, was "the greatest person in my world." Who is the greatest person in your world? Your choice could be someone you know or a public figure you admire. Write a few sentences identifying the person and explaining why he or she is "the greatest."

Literary Focus
Autobiography

When you write in a diary or journal about something that happened to you, you're writing a true story about yourself. An **autobiography** is the true story of a person's life written by that person.

Autobiographies are written from the **first-person point of view.** That means that the writer speaks in the first person, using pronouns like *I, we, me, us, mine,* and *ours.* Reading an autobiography puts us inside the writer's mind and heart. It lets us see the world through another person's eyes.

Description

Description is writing that helps us imagine someone or something, usually by appealing to our sense of sight. In this selection, Maya Angelou paints a portrait in words of her brother, Bailey, as a boy. He's "small, graceful, and smooth," with "velvet-black skin" and "black curls." As you can tell from these details, description can also help us *feel*

something (the velvet skin). It can appeal to our senses of smell, taste, and hearing as well.

Description is used in all kinds of writing—in fiction and poetry, of course, but also in historical accounts, science writing, newspaper articles, even personal letters and journals.

Reading Skills 📖
Inferring the Main Idea

Some writers state the **main idea** of a piece of writing directly. Others leave it up to you to figure out the main idea. This means that you have to use details in the text to **infer,** or guess, the larger idea the writer is getting at. Read this text twice; the second time, list key details and important passages that you think reveal Angelou's main idea.

Vocabulary Development

Here are the words you'll learn as you read Maya Angelou's description of her brother:

grating (grāt′iŋ) *adj.:* irritating. *The visitors found Maya's manner grating.*

lauded (lôd′id) *v.:* praised highly. *They lauded Bailey for his looks and insulted me.*

aghast (ə·gast′) *adj.:* shocked; horrified. *Momma was aghast at our behavior.*

precision (prē·sizh′ən) *n.:* exactness; accuracy. *Bailey moved with grace and precision.*

North Carolina Competency Goal
1.04; 4.01; 5.01; 5.02

INTERNET

Vocabulary Activity
•
More About Angelou

Keyword: LE5 6-5

Literary Skills
Understand autobiography and first-person point of view; understand description.

Reading Skills
Infer the main idea.

Brother

FROM *I Know Why the Caged Bird Sings*

MAYA ANGELOU

Boy by the Sea (1995) by Jonathan Green, Naples, Florida. Oil on canvas (18" × 17").

Photograph by Tim Stamm.

Bailey was the greatest person in my world. And the fact that he was my brother, my only brother, and I had no sisters to share him with, was such good fortune that it made me want to live a Christian life just to show God that I was grateful. Where I was big, elbowy, and grating, he was small, graceful, and smooth. . . . He was lauded for his velvet-black skin. His hair fell down in black curls, and my head was covered with black steel wool. And yet he loved me.

When our elders said unkind things about my features (my family was handsome to a point of pain for me), Bailey would wink at me from across the room, and I knew that it was a matter of time before he would take revenge. He would allow the old ladies to finish wondering how on earth I came about, then he would ask, in a voice like cooling bacon grease, "Oh Mizeriz[1] Coleman, how is your son? I saw him the other day, and he looked sick enough to die."

Aghast, the ladies would ask, "Die? From what? He ain't sick."

And in a voice oilier than the one before, he'd answer with a straight face, "From the Uglies."

I would hold my laugh, bite my tongue, grit my teeth, and very seriously erase even the touch of a smile from my face. Later, behind the house by the black-walnut tree, we'd laugh and laugh and howl.

Bailey could count on very few punishments for his consistently outrageous behavior, for he was the pride of the Henderson/Johnson family.

His movements, as he was later to describe those of an acquaintance, were activated with oiled precision. He was also able to find more hours in the day than I thought existed. He finished chores, homework, read more books than I, and played the group games on the side of the hill with the best of them. He could even pray out loud in church and was apt at stealing pickles from the barrel that sat under the fruit counter and Uncle Willie's nose.

Once when the Store was full of lunchtime customers, he dipped the strainer, which we also used to sift weevils[2] from meal and flour, into the barrel and fished for two fat pickles. He caught them and hooked the strainer onto the side of the barrel, where they dripped until he was ready for them. When the last school bell rang, he picked the nearly dry pickles out of the strainer, jammed them into his pockets, and threw the strainer behind the oranges. We ran out of the Store. It was summer and his pants were short, so the pickle juice made clean streams down his ashy legs, and he jumped with his pockets full of loot and his eyes laughing a "How about that?" He smelled like a vinegar barrel or a sour angel.

After our early chores were done, while Uncle Willie or Momma minded the Store,

___
1. **Mizeriz:** dialect term for "Mrs."

___
2. **weevils** *n.*: small beetles that feed on grains, cotton, and other crops.

___
Vocabulary
grating (grāt′iŋ) *adj.*: irritating; annoying.
lauded (lôd′id) *v.*: praised highly.
aghast (ə·gast′) *adj.*: shocked; highly horrified.
precision (prē·sizh′ən) *n.*: exactness; accuracy.

Fishing on the Trail (1990) by Jonathan Green, Naples, Florida. Oil on canvas (47″ × 79″).

we were free to play the children's games as long as we stayed within yelling distance. Playing hide-and-seek, his voice was easily identified, singing, "Last night, night before, twenty-four robbers at my door. Who all is hid? Ask me to let them in, hit 'em in the head with a rolling pin. Who all is hid?" In follow the leader, naturally he was the one who created the most daring and interesting things to do. And when he was on the tail of the pop the whip, he would twirl off the end like a top, spinning, falling, laughing, finally stopping just before my heart beat its last, and then he was back in the game, still laughing.

Of all the needs (there are none imaginary) a lonely child has, the one that must be satisfied, if there is going to be hope and a hope of wholeness, is the unshaking need for an unshakable God. My pretty black brother was my Kingdom Come.

Meet the Writer

Maya Angelou

"The Power of the Word"

Maya Angelou's remarkable career has taken her far from the time when she was Bailey's lonely, gawky sister. Angelou (1928–   ) has worked hard all her life—as a streetcar conductor, a waitress, a singer, a dancer, an actress, a civil rights worker, a college professor, a TV producer, and above all, a writer. In 1993, Maya Angelou read to the nation the poem President Clinton had asked her to compose and deliver at his inauguration.

In an interview, Angelou talks about how she has triumphed, both as a person and as a writer, over obstacles in her path:

"I believe all things are possible for a human being, and I don't think there's anything in the world I can't do. Of course, I can't be five feet four because I'm six feet tall. I can't be a man because I'm a woman. The physical gifts are given to me, just like having two arms is a gift. In my creative source, wherever that is, I don't see why I can't sculpt. Why shouldn't I? Human beings sculpt. I'm a human being. . . .

All my work, my life, everything is about survival. All my work is meant to say 'You may encounter many defeats, but you must not be defeated.' In fact, the encountering may be the very experience which creates the vitality and the power to endure."

For Independent Reading

For more of Angelou's ideas about life, read her poem "Life Doesn't Frighten Me."

First Thoughts

1. Divide a piece of paper into two columns. In the left-hand column, quote three or four descriptions from "Brother" that helped you to **visualize** Bailey. In the right-hand column, write your response to each quotation.

Thinking Critically

2. What words would *you* use to describe Bailey's personality? How did you feel about him?

3. Were you surprised by anything in the last paragraph of "Brother"? What does this paragraph tell you about Angelou?

4. Angelou says her brother was the greatest person in her world. What do you think she meant to him? Why do you think he was so nice to her?

Extending Interpretations

5. Angelou says that she was not as handsome as Bailey was. Is physical appearance important in making someone lovable? Explain.

6. The writer says that a lonely child's greatest need is "an unshakable God." Do you agree? What else do you think a lonely child might need?

WRITING

Writing a Character Sketch 🖉

Look back at your Quickwrite notes, and review what you wrote about the greatest person in your world. Now, write a character sketch describing that person. Help your readers see what the person looks like. Describe an action taken by the person that reveals his or her personality. (Now that you've read Angelou's description, you may want to write about someone other than the person you first chose.) Be sure to explain why he or she is "the greatest."

Writing About Main Idea 📖

Check your reading notes, and write a few sentences stating what you think Angelou's main idea is. Sometimes the main idea of a passage is summed up in the first or last paragraph. Which details in the first and last paragraphs help you understand what Angelou's brother means to her?

Reading Check

a. From which **point of view** is this selection written? How can you tell?

b. **Retell** the selection for a partner. Explain who Bailey is and how the writer feels about him and about herself.

North Carolina Competency Goal
1.02; 5.01

INTERNET

Projects and Activities

Keyword: LE5 6-5

SKILLS FOCUS

Literary Skills
Analyze an autobiography.

Reading Skills
Infer the main idea.

Writing Skills
Write a character sketch; write about the main idea.

Antonyms: Reversing Meaning

Antonyms (an'tə·nimz') are words that are opposite in meaning.
For example, the words *graceful* and *clumsy* are antonyms; they have
opposite meanings.

Word Bank

grating
lauded
aghast
precision

PRACTICE 1

Find a Word Bank word that is an **antonym** of the underlined
word in each sentence. Then, rewrite the sentence, using the
Word Bank word in place of the underlined word.

1. The guard's sloppiness lost the game for us.

2. That bully insulted my best friend.

3. Jack has a soothing voice.

4. Max was untroubled by the mean remarks.

Finding Synonyms: Thesaurus Rex to the Rescue

Synonyms (sin'ə·nimz) are words with the same or nearly the
same meanings. A **thesaurus** (from a Greek word meaning
"treasure") contains lists of synonyms for certain words. If you
look up *aghast* in a thesaurus, you'll find synonyms like
thunderstruck, surprised, shocked, and *astonished.*

PRACTICE 2

**North
Carolina
Competency
Goal
6.01**

In a thesaurus, look up the four words listed in the Word Bank,
and list the synonyms you find for each word. (Look up *grate,*
not *grating,* and *laud,* not *lauded.*) Then, go back to the text,
and substitute some of your synonyms for Angelou's original
choices. Do all the synonyms work?

**SKILLS
FOCUS**

**Vocabulary
Skills**
Identify and
explain
synonyms and
antonyms.

THE BORN LOSER reprinted by permission of Newspaper Enterprise Association, Inc.

Comparing Main Ideas of Related Texts

Reading Focus

Review: Finding the Main Idea

When you have to identify the **main idea** of a piece of nonfiction, ask yourself, "What's the topic?" (Remember that the topic can often be summed up in one word or phrase.) Sometimes the **title** tells you what the topic is. What was the title of the last selection? "Brother." That's your topic. Now ask yourself, "What about it?" What *about* a brother? Your answer to that question is your main idea.

On a sheet of paper, write one sentence summing up Maya Angelou's main idea about her brother. (If you think there's more than one, write a sentence for each.) Don't get caught in the details. If you find yourself starting on your second sheet of paper, you've lost your focus. Look at the big picture, and try again. Ask yourself, "What's the most important thing Angelou says about her brother?"

Review: Comparing Main Ideas

■ The next selection is called "The Brother I Never Had." (Do you see a pattern here?) After you read this selection, write a sentence stating its main idea.

Then, compare the main ideas of the two selections. In what ways are they connected? In what ways are they different from each other? (You may want to collect your main ideas in a chart like the one on page 436.)

(continued)

North Carolina Competency Goal 2.01

SKILLS FOCUS

Reading Skills
Compare main ideas of related texts.

Analyzing Related Texts

Think back to the work you did as you read "Storm" (page 427), "Bringing Tang Home" (page 437), and "Where the Heart Is" (page 439). The topic of all three selections is animals, and all three deal with the relationships between animals and people. What other connections can you find in topics related to the bond between animals and people? You might think about how pets improve your health, how animals are used in rescue work, and how to listen to your pet. You might even think about animal brains and how they are different from human brains.

Why is all of this important? It's important because ideas are inter-connected. Seeing how one idea relates to another broadens your understanding of our rich and complex world. You'll find this skill especially useful whenever you do research. Some people think that finding connections between ideas should be a lifelong quest!

■ Now, think about the subject of brothers, which is also very broad. On your paper, jot down a few topics related to the subject of brothers. Make a cluster diagram like the one below. Put the **main idea** you discovered in "Brother" in the circle under "Main idea." Put each of your related topics in other circles in a cluster.

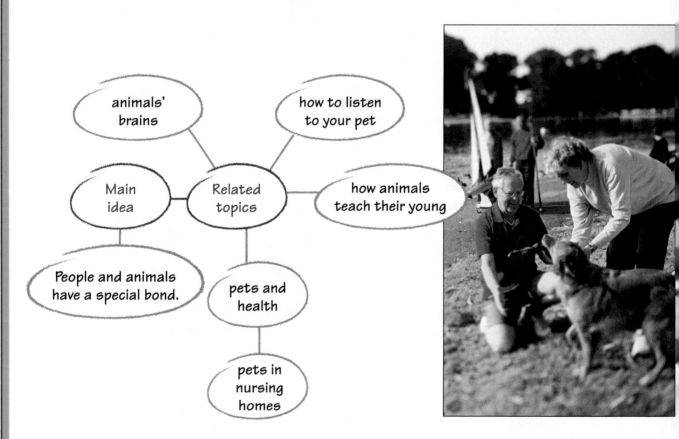

The Brother
I Never Had

That day stood clear in my mind. My cousin Joe and I were taking a stroll in the Jamaica area of New York. We had left my uncle's office at about three o'clock and walked to Mila's Diner down the street. I had always thought of Joe as my older brother, and today's experience reaffirmed it.

We walked into that neat little diner and ordered onion rings and Coke. Those onion rings were the best I had ever eaten. Joe introduced me to all the regulars at the diner, and then we sat with them for about an hour. They talked and I listened. They talked about college, work, girls, and life. My cousin kept trying to get me into the conversation, but I refused to speak.

After some time we walked over to the Jamaica Fish Market and looked at all the strange fish they had brought in that day. I tried to pick up a crab out of a basket full of crabs and got pinched. I tried to get some sympathy from Joe, but all he did was smile—not laugh, just smile.

We left the store and headed back to Mila's Diner. We hadn't talked much, just walked. I never had an older brother, and Joe was the only person that was like me and the only one I would consider as my older brother. I wanted to be just like him. He was strong, kind, and caring, and most of all, he loved me.

Now five years later I'm the older brother of two little people. I try to be the same person Joe was for me. He cared for me, as I care for my brothers. He watched out for me, as I watch out for my brothers. Joe is now in college and I guess we've gotten a bit farther apart. That's what getting older does to a person. Every once in a while, though, I think about that walk, and I always wonder if we can ever do it again.

—Gim George
Holy Spirit Regional School
Huntsville, Alabama

Analyzing the Main Ideas of Related Texts

Brother / The Brother I Never Had

These questions will test your skill at connecting and analyzing the **main ideas** in "Brother" (page 445) and "The Brother I Never Had" (page 453).

1. The reader can **infer** that without their "brothers," life for these two writers would be —
    - **A** lonelier
    - **B** easier
    - **C** calmer
    - **D** more satisfying

2. Which **main idea** is presented in *both* selections?
    - **F** Brothers and sisters can be best friends.
    - **G** Someone close to you, like a brother or cousin, can show you how to live.
    - **H** Brothers and sisters often compete.
    - **J** A person doesn't have to be your parents' child to be a brother to you.

3. Which of these **titles** could be used for *both* selections?
    - **A** "A Cousin, a Brother, a Friend"
    - **B** "A Walk to Remember"
    - **C** "The Sour Angel"
    - **D** "My Brother, My Hero"

4. All the titles below could be considered **related topics** to "Brother" and "The Brother I Never Had" *except* —
    - **F** "The Childless Household: A New Study"
    - **G** "I'm a Twin and Proud of It!"
    - **H** "Sibling Rivalry: What Happens When Brothers and Sisters Don't Get Along?"
    - **J** "Are Siblings Better Off in Life Than Only Children?"

North Carolina Competency Goal
2.01

Constructed Response

1. Identify a main idea that is presented *only* in "Brother." State it in your own words.

2. Now, identify and state a main idea that is presented *only* in "The Brother I Never Had."

Reading Skills
Analyze main ideas of related texts.

Modifiers: Comparing with Adjectives

A **comparative** is an adjective or adverb used to compare two things. A **superlative** is an adjective or adverb used to compare three or more things. Watch out for these two common mistakes:

- Don't use a superlative to compare only two people or things.

sharper

Mrs. Coleman was sharp, but Bailey was ~~sharpest~~.

more

Of the two children, Bailey was ~~most~~ daring.

- Don't use both *more* and *–er* to form a comparative. Don't use both *most* and *–est* to form a superlative.

Bailey's work was ~~more~~ better than the other children's.

Bailey is the most graceful~~est~~ person I've ever seen.

Modifiers: Don't Misplace Them

To work well, modifiers have to be in the right place. Here's an example of a **misplaced modifier:**

Maya and Bailey would play after they finished their chores with their friends.

Did Bailey and Maya do their chores with their friends? No, the phrase *with their friends* has been misplaced in the sentence. To fix the sentence, place the modifier as close as possible to the word it modifies—*play.*

Maya and Bailey would play with their friends after they finished their chores.

PRACTICE 1

Correct these comparisons:

1. I cannot imagine anyone more sweeter than Bailey.
2. Between Bailey and his sister, I liked Bailey best.
3. Sometimes I think Mrs. Coleman is the most meanest person I've ever known.
4. Bailey was the most beautifullest person in Maya's world.
5. Some of her poems are more easier than others.
6. Angelou is one of the most strongest women I know.

PRACTICE 2

Move the misplaced modifier in each sentence to the right place. If you are uncertain of the correct placement, draw an arrow from the modifier to the word it modifies. Then, place the modifier next to that word.

1. Bailey was not punished when he misbehaved by his parents.
2. In front of their relatives, Maya admired Bailey's fearlessness.
3. I almost understood every word in the story.

SKILLS FOCUS

Grammar Skills
Use modifiers correctly.

 North Carolina Competency Goal
1.02; 1.04; 4.01; 4.02; 5.01

from The Land I Lost

Make the Connection
Quickwrite ✏️

Take a good look at the crocodile on page 463. Then, make a cluster diagram showing all the things you associate with crocodiles.

Literary Focus
Narrators: First Person and Third Person

This excerpt from an **autobiography** starts with **first-person narration.** The writer, Huynh Quang Nhuong (hʊɔn kwaŋ′ nyʊɔŋ), uses the pronoun *I* to tell about his boyhood in Vietnam. This autobiography is the story of more than one person, though. As the narrative progresses, Nhuong switches to the **third person.** You'll notice that when he tells the story of Lan and Trung, "So Close," Nhuong describes the thoughts and feelings of many of the characters. He tells his story from the point of view of someone outside it.

North Carolina Competency Goal
1.02; 1.04; 4.01; 5.01; 5.02

INTERNET

Vocabulary Activity

Keyword: LE5 6-5

SKILLS FOCUS

Literary Skills
Compare first- and third-person narration.

Reading Skills
Summarize main events.

Reading Skills 📖
Summarizing

When you **summarize** a narrative, you describe the **main events** and **key details** in your own words. Summarizing is a useful skill because it helps you recall the main characters and events of a story. After you read "So Close," map out the framework of the story in an organizer like the one below:

Setting:
Main Characters:
Conflict or Problem:
Sequence of Main Events: 1. Trung and Lan get married.
2. That night, Lan goes to the river to bathe.
[Etc.]
Resolution:

Vocabulary Development

Learning these words will help you read the story:

infested (in·fest′id) *v.:* inhabited in large numbers (said of something harmful). *Crocodiles infested the river.*

wily (wī′lē) *adj.:* sly; clever in a sneaky way. *A crocodile becomes more wily with age.*

hallucination (hə·lōō′si·nā′shən) *n.:* sight or sound of something that isn't really there. *Trung's relatives think that the voice he heard was a hallucination.*

placate (plā′kāt′) *v.:* calm or soothe (someone who is angry). *Some people believe that Lan is trying to placate the crocodile.*

avenge (ə·venj′) *v.:* get revenge for; get even for. *Trung vows to avenge Lan's death.*

Background
Literature and Social Studies

One place where you're likely to meet up with a crocodile is Vietnam, a tropical country in Southeast Asia with many warm, muddy rivers and swamps. Vietnam is about the size of New Mexico, and as you can see on the map, it extends south from China in a long, narrow S-curve.

Most Americans probably still associate Vietnam with war. In this excerpt from his **autobiography,** Huynh Quang Nhuong recalls a more peaceful time in his beautiful country. He shows us a place where people visit with neighbors, fall in love, and work together to solve problems, just as people do all over the world.

from The Land I Lost

Huynh Quang Nhuong

I was born on the central highlands of Vietnam in a small hamlet on a riverbank that had a deep jungle on one side and a chain of high mountains on the other. Across the river, rice fields stretched to the slopes of another chain of mountains.

There were fifty houses in our hamlet, scattered along the river or propped against the mountainsides. The houses were made of bamboo and covered with coconut leaves, and each was surrounded by a deep trench to protect it from wild animals or thieves. The only way to enter a house was to walk across a "monkey bridge"—a single bamboo stick that spanned the trench. At night we pulled the bridges into our houses and were safe.

There were no shops or marketplaces in our hamlet. If we needed supplies—medicine, cloth, soaps, or candles—we had to cross over the mountains and travel to a town nearby. We used the river mainly for traveling to distant hamlets, but it also provided us with plenty of fish.

During the six-month rainy season, nearly all of us helped plant and cultivate fields of rice, sweet potatoes, Indian mustard, eggplant, tomatoes, hot peppers, and corn. But during the dry season, we became hunters and turned to the jungle.

Wild animals played a very large part in our lives. There were four animals we feared the most: the tiger, the lone wild hog, the crocodile, and the horse snake. Tigers were always trying to steal cattle. Sometimes, however, when a tiger became old and slow it became a man-eater. But a lone wild hog was even more dangerous than a tiger. It attacked every creature in sight, even when it had no need for food. Or it did crazy things, such as charging into the hamlet in broad daylight, ready to kill or to be killed.

The river had different dangers: crocodiles. But of all the animals, the most hated and feared was the huge horse snake. It was sneaky and attacked people and cattle just for the joy of killing. It would either crush its victim to death or poison it with a bite.

Like all farmers' children in the hamlet, I started working at the age of six. My seven sisters helped by working in the kitchen, weeding the garden, gathering eggs, or taking water to the cattle. I looked after the family herd of water buffaloes. Someone always had to be with the herd because no matter how carefully a water buffalo was trained, it always was ready to nibble young rice plants when no one was looking. Sometimes, too, I fished for the family while I guarded the herd, for

there were plenty of fish in the flooded rice fields during the rainy season.

I was twelve years old when I made my first trip to the jungle with my father. I learned how to track game, how to recognize useful roots, how to distinguish edible mushrooms from poisonous ones. I learned that if birds, raccoons, squirrels, or monkeys had eaten the fruits of certain trees, then those fruits were not poisonous. Often they were not delicious, but they could calm a man's hunger and thirst.

My father, like most of the villagers, was a farmer and a hunter, depending upon the season. But he also had a college education, so in the evenings he helped to teach other children in our hamlet, for it was too small to afford a professional schoolteacher.

My mother managed the house, but during the harvest season she could be found in the fields, helping my father get the crops home; and as the wife of a hunter, she knew how to dress and nurse a wound and took good care of her husband and his hunting dogs.

I went to the lowlands to study for a while because I wanted to follow my father as a teacher when I grew up. I always planned to return to my hamlet to live the rest of my life there. But war disrupted my dreams. The land I love was lost to me forever.

These stories are my memories. . . .

SO CLOSE

My grandmother was very fond of cookies made of banana, egg, and coconut, so my mother and I always stopped at Mrs. Hong's house to buy these cookies for her on our way back from the marketplace. My mother also liked to see Mrs. Hong because they had been very good friends since grade-school days. While my mother talked with her friend, I talked with Mrs. Hong's daughter, Lan. Most of the time Lan asked me about my older sister, who was married to a teacher and lived in a nearby town. Lan, too, was going to get married—to a young man living next door, Trung.

Trung and Lan had been inseparable playmates until the day tradition did not allow them to be alone together anymore. Besides, I think they felt a little shy with each other after realizing that they were man and woman.

Lan was a lively, pretty girl, who attracted the attention of all the young men of our hamlet. Trung was a skillful fisherman who successfully plied[1] his trade on the river in front of their houses. Whenever Lan's mother found a big fish on the kitchen windowsill, she would smile to herself. Finally, she decided that Trung was a fine young man and would make a good husband for her daughter.

Trung's mother did not like the idea of her son giving good fish away, but she liked the cookies Lan brought her from time to time. Besides, the girl was very helpful; whenever she was not busy at her house, Lan would come over in the evening and help Trung's mother repair her son's fishing net.

Trung was happiest when Lan was helping his mother. They did not talk to each other, but they could look at each other when his mother was busy with her work. Each time Lan went home, Trung looked at the chair Lan had just left and secretly wished that nobody would move it.

One day when Trung's mother heard her son call Lan's name in his sleep, she decided it was time to speak to the girl's mother about marriage. Lan's mother agreed they should be married and even waived[2] the custom whereby the bridegroom had to give the bride's family a fat hog, six chickens, six ducks, three bottles of wine, and thirty kilos[3] of fine rice, for the two families had known each other for a long time and were good neighbors.

The two widowed mothers quickly set the dates for the engagement announcement and for the wedding ceremony. Since their decision was immediately made known to relatives and friends, Trung and Lan could now see each other often. . . .

At last it was the day of their wedding. Friends and relatives arrived early in the morning to help them celebrate. They brought gifts of ducks, chickens, baskets filled with fruits, rice wine, and colorful fabrics. Even though the two houses were next to each other, the two mothers observed all the proper wedding day traditions.

First, Trung and his friends and relatives came to Lan's house. Lan and he prayed at her ancestors' altars and asked for their blessing. Then they joined everyone for a luncheon.

After lunch there was a farewell ceremony for the bride. Lan stepped out of her house and joined the greeting party that was to accompany her to Trung's home. Tradition called for her to cry and to express her sorrow at leaving her parents behind and forever becoming the daughter of her husband's family. In some villages the bride was even supposed to cling so tightly to her mother that it would take several friends to pull her away from her home. But instead of crying,

---

1. **plied** *v.*: worked at.

2. **waived** *v.*: gave up voluntarily.
3. **kilos** *n.*: kilograms, about 2.2 pounds each.

One day when Trung's mother heard her son call Lan's name in his sleep, she decided it was time to speak to the girl's mother about marriage.

Lan smiled. She asked herself, why should she cry? The two houses were separated by only a garden; she could run home and see her mother anytime she wanted to. So Lan willingly followed Trung and prayed at his ancestors' altars before joining everyone in the big welcome dinner at Trung's house that ended the day's celebrations.

Later in the evening of the wedding night, Lan went to the river to take a bath. Because crocodiles infested the river, people of our hamlet who lived along the riverbank chopped down trees and put them in the river to form barriers and protect places where they washed their clothes, did their dishes, or took a bath. This evening, a wily crocodile had avoided the barrier by crawling up the riverbank and sneaked up behind Lan. The crocodile grabbed her and went back to the river by the same route that it had come.

Trung became worried when Lan did not return. He went to the place where she was supposed to bathe, only to find that her clothes were there, but she had disappeared. Panic-stricken, he yelled for his relatives. They all rushed to the riverbank with lighted torches. In the flickering light they found traces of water and crocodile claw-prints on the wet soil. Now they knew that a crocodile had grabbed the young bride and dragged her into the river.

Since no one could do anything for the girl, all of Trung's relatives returned to the house, urging the bridegroom to do the same. But the young man refused to leave the place; he just stood there, crying and staring at the clothes of his bride.

Suddenly the wind brought him the sound of Lan calling his name. He was very frightened, for according to an old belief, a crocodile's victim must lure a new victim to his master; if not, the first victim's soul must stay with the beast forever.

Trung rushed back to the house and woke all his relatives. Nobody doubted he thought he had heard her call, but they all believed that he was the victim of a hallucination. Everyone pleaded with him and tried to convince him that nobody could survive when snapped up by a crocodile and dragged into the river to be drowned and eaten by the animal.

The young man brushed aside all their arguments and rushed back to the river. Once again, he heard the voice of his bride in the wind, calling his name. Again he rushed back and woke his relatives. Again they tried to persuade him that it was a hallucination, although some of the old folks suggested that maybe the ghost of the young girl was having to dance and sing to placate the angry crocodile because she failed to bring it a new victim.

No one could persuade Trung to stay inside. His friends wanted to go back to the river with him, but he said no. He resented them for not believing him that there were desperate cries in the wind.

Trung stood in front of the deep river alone in the darkness. He listened to the sound of the wind and clutched the clothes Lan had left behind. The wind became stronger and stronger and often changed direction as the night progressed, but he did not hear any more calls. Still he had no doubt

Vocabulary

infested (in·fest′id) *v.:* inhabited in large numbers (said of something harmful).

wily (wī′lē) *adj.:* sly; clever in a sneaky way.

hallucination (hə·lōō′si·nā′shən) *n.:* perception of something that isn't really there.

placate (plā′kāt′) *v.:* calm or soothe (someone who is angry).

He again
heard, very
clearly, Lan
call him for help.

that the voice he had heard earlier was absolutely real. Then at dawn, when the wind died down, he again heard, very clearly, Lan call him for help.

Her voice came from an island about six hundred meters away. Trung wept and prayed: "You were a good girl when you were still alive, now be a good soul. Please protect me so that I can find a way to kill the beast in order to free you from its spell and avenge your tragic death." Suddenly, while wiping away his tears, he saw a little tree moving on the island. The tree was jumping up and down. He squinted to see better. The tree had two hands that were waving at him. And it was calling his name.

Trung became hysterical and yelled for help. He woke all his relatives and they all rushed to his side again. At first they thought that Trung had become stark mad. They tried to lead him back to his house, but he fiercely resisted their attempt. He talked to them incoherently[4] and pointed his finger at the strange tree on the island. Finally his relatives saw the waving tree. They quickly put a small boat into the river, and Trung got into the boat along with two other men. They paddled to the island and discovered that the moving tree was, in fact, Lan. She had covered herself with leaves because she had no clothes on.

At first nobody knew what had really happened because Lan clung to Trung and cried and cried. Finally, when Lan could talk, they pieced together her story.

Lan had fainted when the crocodile snapped her up. Had she not fainted, the crocodile surely would have drowned her before carrying her off to the island. Lan did not know how many times the crocodile had

tossed her in the air and smashed her against the ground, but at one point, while being tossed in the air and falling back onto the crocodile's jaw, she regained consciousness. The crocodile smashed her against the ground a few more times, but Lan played dead. Luckily the crocodile became thirsty and returned to the river to drink. At that moment Lan got up and ran to a nearby tree and climbed up it. The tree was very small.

Lan stayed very still for fear that the snorting, angry crocodile, roaming around trying to catch her again, would find her and shake her out of the tree. Lan stayed in this frozen position for a long time until the crocodile gave up searching for her and went back to the river. Then she started calling Trung to come rescue her.

Lan's body was covered with bruises, for crocodiles soften up big prey before swallowing it. They will smash it against the ground or against a tree, or keep tossing it into the air. But fortunately Lan had no broken bones or serious cuts. It was possible that this crocodile was very old and had lost most of its teeth. Nevertheless, the older the crocodile, the more intelligent it usually was. That was how it knew to avoid the log barrier in the river and to snap up the girl from behind.

Trung carried his exhausted bride into the boat and paddled home. Lan slept for hours and hours. At times she would sit up with a start and cry out for help, but within three days she was almost completely recovered.

Lan's mother and Trung's mother decided to celebrate their children's wedding a second time because Lan had come back from the dead.

---

4. **incoherently** *adv.:* not clearly.

Vocabulary
avenge (ə·venj′) *v.:* get revenge for; get even for.

Meet the Writer

Huynh Quang Nhuong

To Make People Happy

Huynh Quang Nhuong (1946–   ) was born in a small village in Vietnam between a deep jungle and a chain of high mountains. At the age of six, Huynh learned to tend his family's herd of water buffaloes. His favorite, named Tank, takes part in many of the adventures described in *The Land I Lost*.

Nhuong left his village to study chemistry at the University of Saigon. When war broke out, "the land I love was lost to me forever," he recalls. Nhuong was drafted into the army of South Vietnam. One day on the battlefield he was shot and paralyzed.

In 1969, Nhuong left Vietnam to receive special medical treatment in the United States. He stayed, earned degrees in literature and French, and settled in Columbia, Missouri. His writing is a link between his two lands. He says:

> **❝I hope that my books will make people from different countries happy, regardless of their political adherences, creeds, and ages.❞**

For Independent Reading

If you'd like to learn more about Nhuong's youth in Vietnam, read *Water Buffalo Days*.

First Thoughts

1. How did you feel about what happens to Lan?

Thinking Critically

2. This selection is about a faraway land where customs are very different from those in the United States. What values and feelings do you share with Nhuong's people?

3. Where does the writer shift from **first-person narration** to **third-person narration**? How do you think the writer learned all these details of Lan's terrifying experience?

4. What have you learned about crocodiles from the story of Lan and Trung? Look at the cluster diagram you made for the Quick-write before you began reading. Now that you've read this account, what changes would you make to your diagram?

5. Think of what you learn about Lan's character before she is attacked by the crocodile. Does it surprise you that she is able to escape? Why or why not?

6. You may not have to worry about crocodiles, but every place has its dangers. Did this story make you think of any of the dangers where you live? Explain.

Extending Interpretations

7. Does this story about a crocodile seem like a tall tale? Do you think this narrative is totally factual? How could this story be proved true?

WRITING

Writing a Summary

Writing a **summary** is a way of summing up the most important events in a story. Refer to the organizer you filled in as you read "So Close," the story of Lan and Trung. Then, write a summary of the story. Use words like *then, after,* and *there* to show your readers when and where events happened. Use words and phrases like *because* and *as a result* to show **cause-and-effect** connections between events.

> ### Reading Check
>
> Huynh tells a **narrative** about a girl's ordeal with a crocodile. In many ways a narrative is just like a short story, although it can be either fictional or true. Who are the **hero** and **heroine** of the story? What is their problem or **conflict**? How do they **resolve** their problem?

North Carolina Competency Goal
1.02; 1.04; 4.01; 4.02; 5.01

INTERNET
Projects and Activities
Keyword: LE5 6-5

SKILLS FOCUS

Literary Skills
Compare first- and third-person narration.

Reading Skills
Summarize main events.

Writing Skills
Write a summary.

After You Read   Vocabulary Development

Context Clues

PRACTICE 1

Go back and locate the passage in the story where each word in
the Word Bank is used. Try to find clues in the passage that help
explain the word's meaning. Put the context clues for the Word
Bank words in a cluster diagram like this one, which contains
clues for the word *infested*:

Word Bank

infested
wily
hallucination
placate
avenge

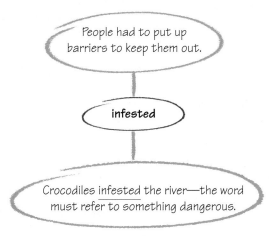

People had to put up
barriers to keep them out.

infested

Crocodiles infested the river—the word
must refer to something dangerous.

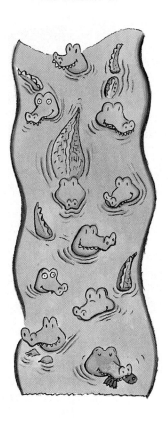

PRACTICE 2

Answer these questions about other context clues in the
selection.

1. Find the word *hamlet* in the first paragraph. Which words in
   the first three paragraphs provide clues to the meaning of
   hamlet? How would you define the word?

2. Find the term *monkey bridge* in the second paragraph.
   Where does the writer provide a definition of this term
   right in the context?

3. Find the passage where the word *edible* is used (page 459).
   What context clues tell you that this word means "fit to be
   eaten"?

4. Find the word *disrupted* at the very end of the first section
   (page 459). Use context clues to guess the meaning of
   disrupted.

SKILLS FOCUS

**Vocabulary
Skills**
Use context
clues.

**North Carolina
Competency Goal**
6.01

A Glory over Everything

Make the Connection

"A Glory over Everything" takes place during the mid-1800s, when slavery was still legal in most southern states. The horror of slavery began in the United States in 1619, when the first Africans arrived in the stinking holds of Dutch slave ships. Slavery was not abolished in the United States until 1865.

What would people feel who were held in slavery—"owned" body and soul by another person? What would they be unable to do? What sorrows would they face? What would they risk if they tried to escape?

Discussion. Share your thoughts with a small group of classmates. Then, choose a group member to summarize for the rest of the class the ideas your group discussed.

Quickwrite ✏️

Write about what you felt and learned during your group discussion. What questions do you have about slavery?

Literary Focus
Biography and Third-Person Point of View

"A Glory over Everything" is taken from a **biography,** the true story of a person's life written by another person. Ann Petry tells the story of Harriet Tubman, who escaped from slavery and led many others to freedom. Petry uses the **third-person point of view.** In other words, she writes from the standpoint of someone *outside* the story, not from the standpoint of a character in the story. Using third-person pronouns such as *he, she, they,* and *it,* Petry describes the characters' thoughts and feelings as she imagines them.

Reading Skills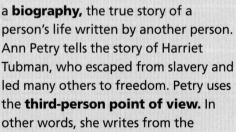
Following the Sequence

Sequence is the order of events in a story. Writers often use words like *first, then,* and *when* to indicate the order of events and the amount of time that has passed. Track Tubman's journey to freedom by completing a chart like the one below. Include six events in your chart, and use time-order words that indicate the sequence of events.

Sequence Chart
1. **That night,** Harriet prepared to leave.
2. **As** she worked, she heard John stir in his sleep.
3. **When** she was done, she headed for the woods.

Background
Literature and Social Studies

In 1849, when the following portion of Harriet Tubman's **biography** takes place, runaway slaves were free once they crossed into a free state. But after the Fugitive Slave Law was passed in 1850, runaways were not safe until they reached Canada. The Underground Railroad was an operation set up by opponents of slavery to help runaways make their way to freedom. The Underground Railroad wasn't a railroad, and it didn't run underground. It was made up of people from both the North and the South who offered food, shelter, and protection to people escaping to freedom in the North. To keep the route secret, the organization used railroad terms, such as *stations* for the houses along the way and *conductors* for the people who offered help.

Harriet Tubman, who had escaped from slavery, became one of the most famous conductors on the railroad. She helped more than three hundred men, women, and children along the perilous road to freedom.

In this excerpt from her biography, we meet Harriet Tubman when she is a field hand at the Brodas Plantation in Maryland.

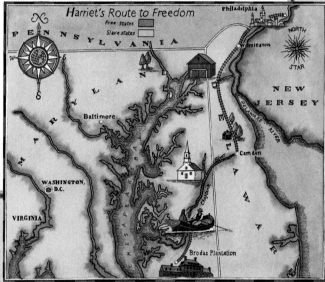

Vocabulary Development

Don't let these words elude you when you read about Harriet Tubman:

elude (ē·lōōd′) *v.:* escape the notice of; avoid detection by. *A runaway must elude the patrol.*

inexplicable (in·eks′pli·kə·bəl) *adj.:* not explainable. *Tubman's inexplicable seizures put her at risk.*

legitimate (lə·jit′ə·mət) *adj.:* here, reasonable; justified. *Runaways had a legitimate reason to fear capture.*

defiant (dē·fī′ənt) *adj.:* disobedient; openly and boldly resisting. *Harriet's defiant manner disturbed Dr. Thompson.*

sinewy (sin′yōō·ē) *adj.:* strong; firm; tough. *Her arms were sinewy from hard work.*

When Harriet heard of the sale of her sisters, she knew that the time had finally come when she must leave the plantation.

A GLORY OVER EVERYTHING

Ann Petry

from Harriet Tubman:

Conductor on the

Underground Railroad

One day in 1849, when Harriet was working in the fields near the edge of the road, a white woman wearing a faded sunbonnet went past, driving a wagon. She stopped the wagon and watched Harriet for a few minutes. Then she spoke to her, asked her what her name was, and how she had acquired the deep scar on her forehead.

Harriet told her the story of the blow she had received when she was a girl. After that, whenever the woman saw her in the fields, she stopped to talk to her. She told Harriet that she lived on a farm near Bucktown. Then one day she said, not looking at Harriet but looking instead at the overseer[1] far off at the edge of the fields, "If you ever need any help, Harriet, ever need any help, why, you let me know."

---

1. **overseer** *n.:* person who supervises workers; in this case, a slave driver.

That same year the young heir to the Brodas estate[2] died. Harriet mentioned the fact of his death to the white woman in the faded sunbonnet the next time she saw her. She told her of the panic-stricken talk in the quarter, told her that the slaves were afraid that the master, Dr. Thompson, would start selling them. She said that Doc Thompson no longer permitted any of them to hire their time.[3] The woman nodded her head, clucked to the horse, and drove off, murmuring, "If you ever need any help—"

The slaves were right about Dr. Thompson's intention. He began selling slaves almost immediately. Among the first ones sold were two of Harriet Tubman's sisters. They went south with the chain gang[4] on a Saturday.

When Harriet heard of the sale of her sisters, she knew that the time had finally come when she must leave the plantation. She was reluctant to attempt the long trip north alone, not because of John Tubman's threat to betray her[5] but because she was afraid she might fall asleep somewhere along the way and so would be caught immediately.

She persuaded three of her brothers to go with her. Having made certain that John was asleep, she left the cabin quietly and met her brothers at the edge of the plantation. They agreed that she was to lead the way, for she was more familiar with the woods than the others.

The three men followed her, crashing through the underbrush, frightening themselves, stopping constantly to say, "What was that?" or "Someone's coming."

She thought of Ben[6] and how he had said, "Any old body can go through a woods crashing and mashing things down like a cow." She said sharply, "Can't you boys go quieter? Watch where you're going!"

> "On a night like this, with all the stars out, it's not black dark."

One of them grumbled, "Can't see in the dark. Ain't got cat's eyes like you."

"You don't need cat's eyes," she retorted. "On a night like this, with all the stars out, it's not black dark. Use your own eyes."

She supposed they were doing the best they could, but they moved very slowly. She kept getting so far ahead of them that she had to stop and wait for them to catch up with her, lest they lose their way. Their progress was slow, uncertain. Their feet got tangled in every vine. They tripped over fallen logs, and once one of them fell flat on his face. They jumped, startled, at the most ordinary sounds: the murmur of the

---

2. **Brodas estate:** Edward Brodas, the previous owner of the plantation, died in 1849 and left his property to his heir, who was not yet old enough to manage it. In the meantime the plantation was placed in the hands of the boy's guardian, Dr. Thompson.

3. **hire their time:** Some slaveholders allowed the people they held in slavery to hire themselves out for pay to other plantation owners who needed extra help. In such cases the workers were permitted to keep their earnings.

4. **chain gang** *n.:* group of prisoners chained together.

5. Harriet's husband, John Tubman, was a free man who was content with his life. He violently disapproved of his wife's plan to escape and threatened to tell the master if she carried it out.

---

6. **Ben:** Harriet Tubman's father. Her mother is called Old Rit.

wind in the branches of the trees, the twittering of a bird. They kept turning around, looking back.

They had not gone more than a mile when she became aware that they had stopped. She turned and went back to them. She could hear them whispering. One of them called out, "Hat!"

"What's the matter? We haven't got time to keep stopping like this."

"We're going back."

"No," she said firmly. "We've got a good start. If we move fast and move quiet—"

Then all three spoke at once. They said the same thing, over and over, in frantic hurried whispers, all talking at once:

They told her that they had changed their minds. Running away was too dangerous. Someone would surely see them and recognize them. By morning the master would know they had "took off." Then the handbills advertising them would be posted all over Dorchester County. The patterollers[7] would search for them. Even if they were lucky enough to elude the patrol, they could not possibly hide from the bloodhounds. The hounds would be baying after them, snuffing through the swamps and the underbrush, zigzagging through the deepest woods. The bloodhounds would surely find them. And everyone knew what happened to a runaway who was caught and brought back alive.

She argued with them. Didn't they know that if they went back they would be sold, if

> **Harriet went on working but she knew a moment of panic.**

not tomorrow, then the next day, or the next? Sold south. They had seen the chain gangs. Was that what they wanted? Were they going to be slaves for the rest of their lives? Didn't freedom mean anything to them?

"You're afraid," she said, trying to shame them into action. "Go on back. I'm going north alone."

Instead of being ashamed, they became angry. They shouted at her, telling her that she was a fool and they would make her go back to the plantation with them. Suddenly they surrounded her, three men, her own brothers, jostling her, pushing her along, pinioning[8] her arms behind her. She fought against them, wasting her strength, exhausting herself in a furious struggle.

She was no match for three strong men. She said, panting, "All right. We'll go back. I'll go with you."

She led the way, moving slowly. Her thoughts were bitter. Not one of them was willing to take a small risk in order to be free. It had all seemed so perfect, so simple, to have her brothers go with her, sharing the dangers of the trip together, just as a family should. Now if she ever went north, she would have to go alone.

Two days later, a slave working beside Harriet in the fields motioned to her. She bent

---

8. pinioning (pin′yən·iŋ) v.: pinning.

Vocabulary

elude (ē·lo͞od′) v.: escape the notice of; avoid detection by.

---

7. **patterollers** n.: patrollers.

The Harriet Tubman Series (1939–1940), No. 7, by Jacob Lawrence.
Harriet Tubman worked as water girl to field hands. She also worked at plowing, carting, and hauling logs.

toward him, listening. He said the water boy had just brought news to the field hands, and it had been passed from one to the other until it reached him. The news was that Harriet and her brothers had been sold to the Georgia trader and that they were to be sent south with the chain gang that very night.

Harriet went on working but she knew a moment of panic. She would have to go north alone. She would have to start as soon as it was dark. She could not go with the chain gang. She might die on the way because of those inexplicable sleeping seizures. But then she—how could she run away? She might fall asleep in plain view along the road.

But even if she fell asleep, she thought, the Lord would take care of her. She murmured a prayer, "Lord, I'm going to hold steady on to You, and You've got to see me through."

Afterward, she explained her decision to run the risk of going north alone in these words: "I had reasoned this out in my mind; there was one of two things I had a *right* to, liberty or death; if I could not have one, I would have the other; for no man should take me alive; I should fight for my liberty as long as my strength lasted, and when the time came for me to go, the Lord would let them take me."

At dusk, when the work in the fields was over, she started toward the Big House.[9] She had to let someone know that she was going north, someone she could trust. She no longer trusted John Tubman and it gave her a lost, lonesome feeling. Her sister Mary worked in the Big House, and she planned to tell Mary that she was going to run away, so someone would know.

As she went toward the house, she saw the master, Doc Thompson, riding up the drive on his horse. She turned aside and went toward the quarter. A field hand had no legitimate reason for entering the kitchen of the Big House—and yet—there must be some way she could leave word so that afterward someone would think about it and know that she had left a message.

As she went toward the quarter, she began to sing. Dr. Thompson reined in his horse, turned around, and looked at her. It was not the beauty of her voice that made him turn and watch her, frowning; it was the words of the song that she was singing and something defiant in her manner that disturbed and puzzled him.

When that old chariot comes,
I'm going to leave you,
I'm bound for the promised land,
Friends, I'm going to leave you.

I'm sorry, friends, to leave you,
Farewell! Oh, farewell!
But I'll meet you in the morning,
Farewell! Oh, farewell!

I'll meet you in the morning,
When I reach the promised land;
On the other side of Jordan,
For I'm bound for the promised land.

That night when John Tubman was asleep and the fire had died down in the cabin, she took the ash cake that had been baked for their breakfast and a good-sized piece of salt herring and tied them together in an old bandanna. By hoarding this small stock of food, she could make it last a long time, and with the berries and edible roots she could find in the woods, she wouldn't starve.

Vocabulary

inexplicable (in·eks′pli·kə·bəl) *adj.*: not explainable.

legitimate (lə·jit′ə·mət) *adj.*: here, reasonable; justified.

defiant (dē·fī′ənt) *adj.*: disobedient; openly and boldly resisting.

---

9. **Big House:** plantation owner's house.

She decided that she would take the quilt[10] with her, too. Her hands lingered over it. It felt soft and warm to her touch. Even in the dark, she thought she could tell one color from another because she knew its pattern and design so well.

Then John stirred in his sleep, and she left the cabin quickly, carrying the quilt carefully folded under her arm.

Once she was off the plantation, she took to the woods, not following the North Star, not even looking for it, going instead toward Bucktown. She needed help. She was going to ask the white woman who had stopped to talk to her so often if she would help her. Perhaps she wouldn't. But she would soon find out.

When she came to the farmhouse where the woman lived, she approached it cautiously, circling around it. It was so quiet. There was no sound at all, not even a dog barking or the sound of voices. Nothing.

She tapped on the door, gently. A voice said, "Who's there?" She answered, "Harriet, from Dr. Thompson's place."

When the woman opened the door, she did not seem at all surprised to see her. She glanced at the little bundle that Harriet was carrying, at the quilt, and invited her in. Then she sat down at the kitchen table and wrote two names on a slip of paper and handed the paper to Harriet.

She said that those were the next places where it was safe for Harriet to stop. The first place was a farm where there was a gate with big white posts and round knobs on top of them. The people there would feed her, and when they thought it was safe for her to go on, they would tell her how to get to the next house or take her there.

For these were the first two stops on the Underground Railroad—going north, from the eastern shore of Maryland.

Thus Harriet learned that the Underground Railroad that ran straight to the North was not a railroad at all. Neither did it run underground. It was composed of a loosely organized group of people who offered food and shelter, or a place of concealment, to fugitives who had set out on the long road to the North and freedom.

Harriet wanted to pay this woman who had befriended her. But she had no money. She gave her the patchwork quilt, the only beautiful object she had ever owned.

That night she made her way through the woods, crouching in the underbrush whenever she heard the sound of horses' hoofs, staying there until the riders passed. Each time, she wondered if they were already hunting for her. It would be so easy to describe her, the deep scar on her forehead like a dent, the old scars on the back of her neck, the husky speaking voice, the lack of height, scarcely five feet tall. The master would say she was wearing rough clothes when she ran away, that she had a bandanna on her head, that she was muscular and strong.

She knew how accurately he would describe her. One of the slaves who could

> She tapped on the door, gently. A voice said, "Who's there?"

---

10. **the quilt:** Tubman had painstakingly stitched together a quilt before her wedding.

read used to tell the others what it said on those handbills that were nailed up on the trees along the edge of the roads. It was easy to recognize the handbills that advertised runaways because there was always a picture in one corner, a picture of a black man, a little running figure with a stick over his shoulder and a bundle tied on the end of the stick.

Whenever she thought of the handbills, she walked faster. Sometimes she stumbled over old grapevines, gnarled and twisted, thick as a man's wrist, or became entangled in the tough <u>sinewy</u> vine of the honeysuckle. But she kept going.

In the morning she came to the house where her friend had said she was to stop. She showed the slip of paper that she carried to the woman who answered her knock at the back door of the farmhouse. The woman fed her and then handed her a broom and told her to sweep the yard.

Harriet hesitated, suddenly suspicious. Then she decided that with a broom in her hand, working in the yard, she would look as though she belonged on the place; certainly no one would suspect that she was a runaway.

That night the woman's husband, a farmer, loaded a wagon with produce. Harriet climbed in. He threw some blankets over her, and the wagon started.

It was dark under the blankets and not exactly comfortable. But Harriet decided that riding was better than walking. She was surprised at her own lack of fear, wondered how it was that she so readily trusted these strangers who might betray her. For all she knew, the man driving the wagon might be taking her straight back to the master.

She thought of those other rides in wagons, when she was a child, the same clop-clop of the horses' feet, creak of the wagon, and the feeling of being lost because she did not know where she was going. She did not know her destination this time either, but she was not alarmed. She thought of John Tubman. By this time he must have told the master that she was gone. Then she thought of the plantation and how the land rolled gently down toward the river, thought of Ben and Old Rit, and that Old Rit would be inconsolable because her favorite daughter was missing. "Lord," she prayed, "I'm going to hold steady onto You. You've got to see me through." Then she went to sleep.

The next morning, when the stars were still visible in the sky, the farmer stopped the wagon. Harriet was instantly awake.

He told her to follow the river, to keep following it to reach the next place where people would take her in and feed her. He said that she must travel only at night and she must stay off the roads because the patrol would be hunting for her. Harriet climbed out of the wagon. "Thank you," she said simply, thinking how amazing it was that there should be white people who were willing to go to such lengths to help a slave get to the North.

When she finally arrived in Pennsylvania, she had traveled roughly ninety miles from Dorchester County. She had slept on the ground outdoors at night. She had been rowed for miles up the Choptank River by a man she had never seen before. She had been concealed in a haycock[11] and had, at one point, spent a week hidden in a potato

---

11. **haycock** *n.:* pile of hay in a field.

Vocabulary
sinewy (sin′yoo·ē) *adj.:* strong; firm; tough.

The Harriet Tubman Series (1939–1940), No. 11, by Jacob Lawrence.

"$500 Reward! Runaway from subscriber of Thursday night, the 4th inst., from the neighborhood of Cambridge, my negro girl, Harriet, sometimes called Minty. Is dark chestnut color, rather stout build, but bright and handsome. Speaks rather deep and has a scar over the left temple. She wore a brown plaid shawl. I will give the above reward captured outside the county, and $300 if captured inside the county, in either case to be lodged in the Cambridge, Maryland, jail.

(signed) George Carter,
Broadacres, near Cambridge, Maryland,
September 24th, 1849"

hole in a cabin which belonged to a family of free Negroes. She had been hidden in the attic of the home of a Quaker. She had been befriended by stout German farmers, whose guttural[12] speech surprised her and whose well-kept farms astonished her. She had never before seen barns and fences, farmhouses and outbuildings, so carefully painted. The cattle and horses were so clean they looked as though they had been scrubbed.

When she crossed the line into the free state of Pennsylvania, the sun was coming up. She said, "I looked at my hands to see if I was the same person now I was free. There was such a glory over everything, the sun came like gold through the trees and over the fields, and I felt like I was in heaven."

---

12. **guttural** *adj.:* harsh; rasping.

Meet the Writer

Ann Petry

"Remember Them"

Ann Petry (1908–1997) is best known for her biography of Harriet Tubman. In a speech at the New York Public Library, Petry told of meeting a girl who had just read the biography. The meeting made Petry think about what she wanted the book to say to her readers.

66 As I was about to leave, a little girl came in to return a book of mine, a book I wrote about Harriet Tubman. She was carrying it hugged close to her chest. She laid it down on the table, and the librarian said to her, 'You know, this is Mrs. Petry, the author of the book you are returning.'

I must confess that I was dismayed; . . . though I have had children tell me they enjoyed something I had written, I had never had a face-to-face encounter with a young reader who was actually holding one of my books. The child looked at me, and I looked at her—and she didn't say anything and neither did I. I didn't know what to say. Neither did she. Finally she reached out and touched my arm, ever so gently, and then drew her hand back as though she were embarrassed. I copied her gesture, touching her gently on the arm, because I felt it would serve to indicate that I approved her gesture.

Then I left the library, but I left it thinking to myself: What have I said to this child in this book? . . . Of course, I have been saying: Let's take a look at slavery. I said it in *Harriet Tubman* and again in *Tituba of Salem Village* [another book by Petry].

But what else was I saying? Over and over again, I have said: These are people. Look at them, listen to them, . . . remember them. Remember for what a long, long time black people have been in this country, have been a part of America: a sturdy, indestructible, wonderful part of America, woven into its heart and into its soul. 99

First Thoughts

1. Would you have tried to escape if you had been in Harriet Tubman's situation? Why or why not?

Thinking Critically

2. Think about your Quickwrite notes and about the discussion of slavery you had before you began reading. Did any of your feelings or ideas change after you read this biography? Did it raise more questions for you? Explain. ✎

3. What **inferences** can you make about the **character traits** that helped Tubman find freedom? What makes her an unforgettable person?

4. Many Africans held in slavery used songs to communicate forbidden messages. When Harriet sings about leaving on the chariot, what message is she giving to her sister?

5. Re-read the paragraph on page 474 that begins, "As she went toward the quarter, she began to sing." Explain why this paragraph could appear in a **biography** but not in an **autobiography.** Choose another paragraph of at least five lines. Using the first-person point of view, rewrite it as if it were an autobiography.

Extending Interpretations

6. Tubman says that "there was one of two things I had a *right* to, liberty or death; if I could not have one, I would have the other; for no man should take me alive." What other people, in history or living today, have risked death in order to be free?

WRITING AND ART

Writing Captions

With a few classmates, paint a mural about Tubman's escape. Choose three or four incidents that you want to illustrate. Before you start painting, make sketches, decide on the materials and colors you'll use, and discuss ways to make the painting interesting. When you're done painting, write captions identifying events depicted in your mural. You might want to use as models the captions that accompany Jacob Lawrence's *Harriet Tubman Series* (see pages 473, 477, and 489–492).

Reading Check 📖

Imagine that you're a reporter for a secret newspaper put out by the Underground Railroad. Record information for a news story on Tubman's escape. Refer to your **sequence chart** to order the events. Use details in the story to answer the questions *who? what? when? where? why?* and *how?*

INTERNET
Projects and Activities
Keyword: LE5 6-5

SKILLS FOCUS

Literary Skills
Compare and contrast autobiography with biography.

Reading Skills
Track sequence of events.

Writing and Art Skills
Paint and write captions for a mural.

North Carolina Competency Goal
1.02; 5.01; 5.02

Clarifying Word Meanings

PRACTICE

Imagine that you're a newspaper reporter writing about Harriet Tubman.

1. Explain how Tubman managed to elude her pursuers.
2. Mention an inexplicable event that happened to Tubman.
3. Explain why Tubman had a legitimate reason to be defiant.
4. To illustrate your story, draw a picture of the sinewy vines Tubman encountered on her flight.

Word Bank

elude
inexplicable
legitimate
defiant
sinewy

Grammar Link

Don't Use *Bad* and *Badly* Badly

Follow these rules when you're deciding between *bad* and *badly:*

- Use *bad* to modify a noun or a pronoun.
- Use *badly* to modify an adjective or a verb.

> **Tubman worried that she would have a bad fall.**
> [*Bad* modifies the noun *fall.*]

> **Tubman wanted her freedom badly.**
> [*Badly* modifies the verb *wanted.*]

The word *bad* should never be used to modify a verb.

NONSTANDARD	**Mr. Thompson treated runaways bad.**
STANDARD	**Mr. Thompson treated runaways badly.**

Note that the expression *feel badly* has become acceptable, though it is ungrammatical, informal English.

INFORMAL	**Tubman felt badly about leaving Old Rit.**
FORMAL	**Tubman felt bad about leaving Old Rit.**

North Carolina Competency Goal
6.01

SKILLS FOCUS

Vocabulary Skills
Clarify word meanings.

Grammar Skills
Use *bad* and *badly* correctly.

PRACTICE

Act as an editor. Decide which underlined word in each pair is grammatically correct.

1. Tubman felt bad/badly that her brothers gave up their attempt to escape.
2. The situation looked bad/badly to Tubman.
3. If Tubman were caught, she would be beaten bad/badly.
4. She wanted to escape bad/badly.

For more help, see A Glossary of Usage, 16, in the Language Handbook.

Connecting Main Ideas Across Texts: Two Readings on Harriet Tubman

Reading Focus

Connecting Main Ideas Across Texts

If you read "A Glory over Everything," you already know a lot about Harriet Tubman. Here are two more sources on Tubman:

- an article on Thomas Garrett, who sheltered more than 2,700 people fleeing slavery and was a lifelong friend of Tubman's (page 483)

- four paintings from Jacob Lawrence's *Harriet Tubman Series*, accompanied by captions telling about Tubman's life (page 489)

■ Read the materials once for pleasure. Then, read them a second time, keeping a piece of paper handy. Copy the chart of main ideas on the next page, and fill it in by writing down evidence and support from the two sources.

Look for more **main ideas** to add to the chart as you read. (Remember, there is often more than one main idea in a piece of nonfiction.) Add boxes to your chart if you need them. You don't have to fill in every idea box for each selection; some main ideas will apply to only one of the pieces.

Vocabulary Development

Here are the words you'll be learning as you read "All Aboard with Thomas Garrett":

prudent (pro͞o'dənt) *adj.:* wise; sensible. *The runaways stayed with Garrett until he felt it was prudent to send them on.*

hazardous (haz'ər·dəs) *adj.:* dangerous; risky. *The Underground Railroad helped runaways make the hazardous journey north.*

diligence (dil'ə·jəns) *n.:* steady effort. *Garrett promised to double his diligence in helping people escape from slavery.*

servitude (sʉr'və·to͞od') *n.:* condition of being under another person's control. *The Fifteenth Amendment stated that no citizen should be denied the vote simply because of previous servitude.*

jubilant (jo͞o'bə·lənt) *adj.:* joyful. *Crowds of jubilant people celebrated the passage of the amendment.*

SKILLS FOCUS

Reading Skills
Connect and clarify main ideas across texts.

North Carolina Competency Goal
2.01

Connecting Main Ideas Across Texts

Two Readings on Harriet Tubman				
Main Ideas	**Idea 1:** It was important for free people to help those who were enslaved.	**Idea 2:** People fleeing slavery were in constant danger.	**Idea 3:** Freeing people from slavery required hard work and sacrifice.	**Idea 4:**
Evidence and Support from Readings				
"All Aboard with Thomas Garrett"	No runaway was ever turned away from his door.	"Slave catchers" searched the streets of Wilmington for runaways.		
The Harriet Tubman Series	Harriet Tubman worked hard and saved all her money to help free more slaves.		She traveled at night and hid during the day. She climbed mountains and crossed rivers.	

Harriet Tubman (1951)
by Robert Savon Pious.

National Portrait Gallery, Smithsonian
Institution, Washington, D.C./Art Resource, NY.

Thomas Garrett.
The Granger Collection, New York.

All Aboard with Thomas Garrett

Alice P. Miller

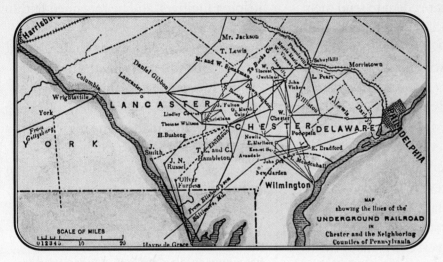

Nineteenth-century map showing the route of the Underground Railroad in southeastern Pennsylvania.

The Granger Collection, New York.

The elderly couple walked sedately down the stairs of the red brick house, every detail of their costumes proclaiming their respectability. The small lady was wearing an ankle-length gray gown, a snowy-white lawn kerchief, and a pleated gray silk bonnet, draped with a veil. The tall white-haired gentleman wore the wide-brimmed beaver hat and the long black waistcoat that was customary among Quakers.

When they reached the sidewalk, he assisted her into the four-wheeled barouche[1] that stood at the curb. Then he climbed into the barouche himself. The driver drove the horses away at a leisurely pace. Not until they were beyond the city limits did he allow the horses to prance along at a brisk pace across the few miles that separated Wilmington, Delaware, from the free state of Pennsylvania.

That tall white-haired gentleman was Thomas Garrett, a white man who

---

1. **barouche** (bə·rōōsh′) *n.:* type of horse-drawn carriage.

had for many years been breaking the law by sheltering runaway slaves. And the little lady at his side was runaway slave Harriet Tubman, clad in clothes donated by his wife. On the preceding night Harriet had slept in a small room secreted behind one wall of Garrett's shoe store, a room that never remained unoccupied for very long. It was Harriet's first visit to Garrett, but she would be returning many times in the future.

Runaway slaves remained with Garrett for one night or two or three until such time as Garrett considered it <u>prudent</u> to send them along to the next station on the Underground Railroad. He provided them with clothing and outfitted them with new shoes from his shoe store. He fed them hearty meals and dressed their wounds. He also forged passes for them so that any slave stopped by a slave catcher would have evidence that he or she was on a legitimate errand.

Some of the money he needed to cover the cost of his hospitality came out of his own pocket, but he was not a rich man. He could not have taken care of so many fugitives were it not for donations made by fellow abolitionists in the North as well as from supporters in foreign countries. There was never quite enough money, but no fugitive was ever turned away from his door. He would have gone without food himself before he would have refused food to a hungry slave.

Garrett, who was born in Upper Darby, Pennsylvania, in 1789, had been helping runaway slaves ever since 1822, when he rescued a young black woman who was trying to escape from her master. At that time he vowed to devote the rest of his life to helping fugitives, and he remained faithful to that vow.

Of all the stations on the Underground Railroad his was probably the most efficiently run and the one most frequently used. The fact that Wilmington was so close to Pennsylvania made it the most <u>hazardous</u> stop on the route. Slave catchers prowled the streets of Wilmington, on the alert for any indication that a black person might be a

Vocabulary
prudent (proo′dənt) *adj.:* wise; sensible.
hazardous (haz′ər·dəs) *adj.:* dangerous; risky.

An old building in Baltimore, Maryland, once used as a stop on the Underground Railroad.

The Underground Railroad (1893) by Charles T. Weber.

runaway. They kept a sharp eye on all roads leading north from Wilmington.

For many years Garrett managed to get away with his illegal activities because he was a clever man and knew ways to avoid detection by the slave catchers. Sometimes he disguised a slave, as he had done with Harriet. Sometimes he dressed a man in a woman's clothing or a woman in a man's clothing or showed a young person how to appear like one bent over with age. Another reason for his success was that he had many friends who admired what he was doing and who could be trusted to help him. They might, for example, conceal slaves under a wagonload of vegetables or in a secret compartment in a wagon.

The slave catchers were aware of what he was doing, but they had a hard time finding the kind of evidence that would stand up in court. At last, in 1848, he was sued by two Maryland slave owners who hoped to bring a stop to his activities by ruining him financially.

The suit was brought into the federal circuit court of New Castle under a 1793 federal law that allowed slave owners to recover penalties from any person who harbored a runaway slave. The case was heard by Willard Hall, United States District Judge, and by Roger B. Taney, Chief Justice of the United States Supreme Court. Bringing in a verdict in favor of the slave owners, the jurors decided that the slave owners were entitled to $5,400 in fines.

Garrett didn't have anywhere near that much money, but he stood up and addressed the court and the spectators in these words:

"I have assisted fourteen hundred slaves in the past twenty-five years on their way to the North. I now consider this penalty imposed upon me as a license for the remainder of my life. I am now past sixty and have not a dollar to my name, but be that as it may, if anyone knows of a poor slave who needs shelter and a breakfast, send him to me, as I now publicly pledge myself to double my diligence and never neglect an opportunity to assist a slave to obtain freedom, so help me God!"

As he continued to speak for more than an hour, some of the spectators hissed while others cheered. When he finished, one juror leaped across the benches and pumped Garrett's hand. With tears in his eyes, he said, "I beg your forgiveness, Mr. Garrett."

After the trial Garrett's furniture was auctioned off to help pay the heavy fine. But he managed to borrow money from friends and eventually repaid those loans, rebuilt his business, and became prosperous. Meanwhile he went on sheltering slaves for many more years. By the time President Lincoln issued the Emancipation Proclamation[2] in 1863, Garrett's records showed that he had sheltered more than 2,700 runaways.

During those years he had many encounters with Harriet Tubman, as she kept returning to the South and coming back north with bands of slaves. Much of what we know about Harriet today is based on letters that he sent to her or wrote about her. A portion of one of those letters reads thus:

"I may begin by saying, living as I have in a slave State, and the laws being very severe where any proof could be made of anyone aiding slaves on their way to freedom, I have not felt at liberty to keep any written word of Harriet's labors as I otherwise could, and now would be glad to do; for in truth I never met with any person, of any color, who had more confidence in the voice of God, as spoken direct to her soul. . . . She felt no more fear of being arrested by her former master, or any other person, when in his immediate neighborhood, than she did in the State of New York or Canada, for she said she ventured only where God sent her, and her faith in the Supreme Power truly was great."

In April, 1870, the black people of Wilmington held a huge celebration upon the passage of the fifteenth amendment to the Constitution of the United States. That amendment provided that the right of citizens to vote should not be denied or abridged by the United States or by any state on account of race, color, or previous condition of servitude.

Jubilant blacks drew Garrett through the streets in an open carriage on one side of which were inscribed the words "Our Moses."

---

2. **Emancipation Proclamation:** presidential order abolishing slavery in the South.

Vocabulary

diligence (dil′ə·jəns) n.: steady effort.

servitude (sur′və·tood′) n.: condition of being under another person's control.

jubilant (joo′bə·lənt) adj.: joyful.

Connecting and Clarifying Main Ideas

All Aboard with Thomas Garrett

Constructed Response

1. In what ways did Thomas Garrett help people fleeing slavery?

2. Why was Thomas Garrett brought to trial?

3. How did Garrett respond to the jury's verdict?

4. What did African Americans in Wilmington celebrate in April 1870?

5. What does Garrett's speech tell you about his devotion to his cause? What does his letter add to your knowledge of Harriet Tubman's character?

6. What is the meaning of the last line of this biographical article—that Garrett was called "Our Moses"?

Vocabulary Development

Related Words: Word Trees Increase Your Vocabulary

You can easily add to your vocabulary by checking a dictionary for words related to each new word you look up. Try it right now with *servitude*. In your dictionary you can find *serf, serve, service,* and *servile*. All these words are related: They all come from the Latin root word *servus,* meaning "slave."

The beginning of a family tree for *servus* appears on the right.

Word Bank

servitude
prudent
hazardous
diligence
jubilant

servus,
"slave"

North Carolina Competency Goal
2.01; 6.01

Vocabulary Skills
Identify related words.

PRACTICE 1

Complete the family tree for *servus* by defining each of the four words shown in the tree's branches.

PRACTICE 2

Do a dictionary search for the other Word Bank words. See how many family trees you can make with your discoveries. Share your trees in class.

Multiple-Meaning Words

PRACTICE 3

When you come across a word that means more than one thing, you can often use **context** to decide on the correct meaning. Each of the passages below contains an underlined word. Several definition choices for that word follow. All the definitions are correct in one context or another, but only one of the definitions fits in the sentence. Choose the definition that fits best. Then, identify the words in the sentence that helped you make your choice. Item 1 has been completed for you.

1. "The <u>small</u> lady was wearing an ankle-length gray gown, a snowy-white lawn kerchief, and a pleated gray silk bonnet, draped with a veil. The tall white-haired gentleman wore the wide-brimmed beaver hat and the long black waistcoat that was customary among Quakers."

   a. little

   b. selfish

   c. unimportant

   Answer: The definition that works best in this context is "little." There is no indication that the woman is selfish or unimportant, and in the next sentence the man is described as *tall*, which means the opposite of *little*. Choice **a** seems like the best answer.

2. "On the preceding night Harriet had slept in a small room secreted behind one wall of Garrett's shoe <u>store</u>, a room that never remained unoccupied for very long."

   a. shop

   b. gather or accumulate

   c. stockpile of provisions

Blocks from a quilt made by Harriet Powers after the Civil War. Powers was born into slavery in Georgia in 1837.

THE BIBLE by Harriet Powers. National Museum of American History, Smithsonian Institution.

3. "He fed them hearty meals and <u>dressed</u> their wounds."

   a. decorated

   b. applied medication to

   c. clothed

4. "At that time he vowed to devote the <u>rest</u> of his life to helping fugitives, and he remained faithful to that vow."

   a. sleep

   b. remainder

   c. relax

Background
Literature and Art

Jacob Lawrence (1917–2000) created *The Harriet Tubman Series* of thirty-one paintings between 1939 and 1940. The series is a visual biography that depicts Tubman's work with the Underground Railroad and her service in the Civil War. The series is one of Lawrence's most famous works.

Lawrence wrote long captions to go with the paintings because at the time he created the series most people knew little about Tubman's life.

from The *Harriet Tubman* Series
Jacob Lawrence

The Harriet Tubman Series (1939–1940), No. 15, by Jacob Lawrence.

In the North, Harriet Tubman worked hard. All her wages she laid away for the one purpose of liberating her people, and as soon as a sufficient amount was secured, she disappeared from her Northern home, and as mysteriously appeared one dark night at the door of one of the cabins on the plantation, where a group of trembling fugitives was waiting. Then she piloted them North, traveling by night, hiding by day, scaling the mountains, wading the rivers, threading the forests—she, carrying the babies, drugged with paregoric. So she went, nineteen times liberating over three hundred pieces of living, breathing "property."

The Harriet Tubman Series (1939–1940), No. 19, by Jacob Lawrence.

Such a terror did she become to the slave-holders that a reward of forty thousand dollars was offered for her head, she was so bold, daring, and elusive.

The Harriet Tubman Series (1939–1940), No. 22, by Jacob Lawrence.

Harriet Tubman, after a very trying trip North in which she had hidden her cargo by day and had traveled by boat, wagon, and foot at night, reached Wilmington, where she met Thomas Garrett, a Quaker who operated an Underground Railroad station. Here, she and the fugitives were fed and clothed and sent on their way.

The Harriet Tubman Series (1939–1940), No. 20, by Jacob Lawrence.

In 1850, the Fugitive Slave Law was passed, which bound the people north of the Mason and Dixon Line to return to bondage any fugitives found in their territories—forcing Harriet Tubman to lead her escaped slaves into Canada.

Connecting and Clarifying Main Ideas

All Aboard with Thomas Garrett / *from* The Harriet Tubman Series

Test Practice

1. Which **main idea** is presented in both Tubman readings?

   A Runaways were always in danger of being returned to slaveholders.

   B Thomas Garrett spent most of his money sheltering runaways.

   C African Americans celebrated the passage of the Fifteenth Amendment.

   D A large reward was offered for Harriet Tubman's capture.

2. Which of the following **main ideas** does the statement "I now consider this penalty imposed upon me as a license for the remainder of my life" connect to?

   F Thomas Garrett gave runaways large sums of money.

   G Runaways often faced harsh conditions when they headed north.

   H Thomas Garrett would not allow a fine to stop him from sheltering runaways.

   J Harriet Tubman feared being returned to a slaveholder.

3. The writers of both readings would probably agree that —

   A runaways felt no obligation toward the people they left behind

   B African Americans enjoyed a comfortable life as soon as they reached the North

   C freeing people from slavery required hard work on the part of many people

   D everyone she met was eager to help Harriet Tubman

4. From the readings you can **infer** that both writers —

   F were friendly with Harriet Tubman

   G knew Thomas Garrett

   H sympathize with the fugitives

   J grew up under harsh conditions

North Carolina Competency Goal
1.02; 1.04; 2.01; 4.01; 4.02; 5.01

Constructed Response

1. Go back to the chart you made for the readings on Harriet Tubman (see page 482). Add another **main idea** to the chart so that you have four ideas across the top.

2. Fill in the idea boxes with evidence and support from the readings on Harriet Tubman. (Remember that you don't have to fill in every idea box for each reading. Some main ideas will apply to only one of the selections.)

SKILLS FOCUS

Reading Skills
Connect and clarify main ideas across texts.

Comparing Literature

Literary Focus
Tone

Biographers and autobiographers almost always provide information about their subjects' families. The family, in fact, may be one of the most common topics in all of literature. Poets also write about family. Each of the three poems you're about to read reveals something about the speaker's relationship with a family member.

While all three poems are about family, each poem has its own unique **tone.** *Tone* refers to the speaker's *attitude*—the way the speaker is feeling about the subject of the poem. When you talk to people face to face, you can usually tell from their expressions and voices how they feel—whether they are serious, happy, worried, or angry, for instance. When you read a poem or story, however, you have to depend on words alone to learn how the speaker is feeling. As you read each poem, think about its tone. What is the speaker's attitude toward his or her family member?

North Carolina Competency Goal
1.02; 4.02

Words to Describe Tone

admiring

affectionate

angry

bitter

cold

friendly

grateful

humorous

joyful

loving

playful

resentful

respectful

sad

serious

timid

warm

Literary Skills
Understand tone.

Reading Skills
Make generalizations.

Reading Skills
Making Generalizations

After each poem you'll find a chart in which you can record what you think the poem says about family life. When you make such a statement about a text, you are making a **generalization.** You are looking at all the details in the text and making a statement that sums up what all those details say.

Before You Read

In the following poem, the speaker tells about her grandmother, a horse trainer. First, read the poem all the way through without stopping. Then, re-read it, pausing to read and respond to the notes in the margin.

Yes, It Was My Grandmother

Luci Tapahonso

Yes, it was my grandmother
who trained wild horses for pleasure and pay.
People knew of her, saying:
    She knows how to handle them.
5   Horses obey that woman. ❶

IDENTIFY

❶ What did the speaker's grandmother do? What did people know and say about her?

She worked,
skirts flying, hair tied securely in the wind and dust.
She rode those animals hard and was thrown,
time and time again.
10   She worked until they were meek
and wanting to please.
        She came home at dusk,
        tired and dusty,
        smelling of sweat and horses.

15   She couldn't cook,
my father said smiling,
your grandmother hated to cook. ❷

        Oh, Grandmother,
        who freed me from cooking.
20   Grandmother, you must have made sure
        I met a man who would not share the kitchen.

        I am small like you and
        do not protect my careless hair
        from wind or rain—it tangles often,
25   Grandma, and it is wild and untrained. ❸

INTERPRET

❷ How does the speaker's father feel about his mother? What qualities do you think he admires in her?

INTERPRET

❸ How is the speaker like her grandmother? Why do you think she mentions her "wild and untrained" hair?

Meet the Writer

Luci Tapahonso

Beautiful Talk

Luci Tapahonso (1953–   ), a member of the Navajo nation, was born and raised in Shiprock, New Mexico, within sight of a gigantic red-rock formation that early explorers thought was a fantastic ship looming over the flat desert landscape. Ever since she was a little girl, Tapahonso and her family have shared stories and songs. This family tradition has been a rich source for Tapahonso's own writing.

66 There is such a love of stories among Navajo people that it seems each time a group of more than two gathers, the dialogue eventually evolves into sharing stories and memories, laughing, and teasing.... It is true that daily conversations strengthen us, as do the old stories of our ancestors that have been told since the beginning of the Navajo time....

The combination of song, prayer, and poetry is a natural form of expression for many Navajo people. A person who is able to 'talk beautifully' is well thought of and considered wealthy. To know stories, remember stories, and to

Minnie Manygoats by Star Liana York. Courtesy of the Zaplin-Lampert Gallery, Santa Fe, New Mexico.

retell them well is to have been 'raised right'; the family of such an individual is also held in high esteem. 99

After You Read "Yes, It Was My Grandmother"

First Thoughts

1. What do you think is the most important word or phrase in this poem? Why?

Thinking Critically

2. Why do you think the speaker's father points out that her grandmother couldn't cook? How might the grandmother have been different from many women of her time?

3. What words would you use to describe the speaker's **tone,** or attitude, toward her grandmother? Do you think the speaker is glad to be like her grandmother? Explain.

4. What importance do you see in the fact that the speaker's hair is tangled, wild, and untamed? (What connection is she suggesting between her own hair and her grandmother's personality?)

Comparing Literature

5. The chart below will help you make a **generalization** about this poem. Copy the chart, and fill it out. After you've read the next two poems, you'll fill out similar charts. You'll use all your charts for the writing assignment on page 506.

Title of poem: ____________________

Most important word or phrase: ____________________

Key details:

- ____________________
- ____________________
- ____________________
- ____________________

What this poem says about a special family member:

____

____

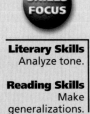

North Carolina Competency Goal
5.02

SKILLS FOCUS

Literary Skills Analyze tone.

Reading Skills Make generalizations.

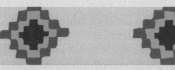

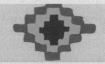

Portrait of Virginia
(1929) by Frida Kahlo.
© 2003 Banco de México
Diego Rivera & Frida Kahlo
Museums Trust. Av. Cinco
de Mayo No. 2, Col. Centro,
Del. Cuauhtémoc 06059,
México, D. F.

Before You Read

"In the Blood" appears here both in English and in Spanish (page 500). If you know Spanish, compare the two poems as you read. If you don't, look for words in the Spanish version that remind you of English words you know.

In the Blood

Pat Mora

The brown-eyed child
and the white-haired grandfather
dance in the silent afternoon.
They snap their fingers
to a rhythm only those
who love can hear.

INTERPRET

What do you think the title of the poem means? Explain how it adds to your understanding of the poem.

En la Sangre

La niña con ojos cafés
y el abuelito con pelo blanco
bailan en la tarde silenciosa.
Castañetean los dedos
a un ritmo oído solamente
por los que aman.

Meet the Writer

Pat Mora

"In Words I Save Images"

Pat Mora (1942–) is a Mexican American who grew up in El Paso, Texas, near the border between the United States and Mexico. Much of her poetry is about the blending of Hispanic culture into American society. "I write because I believe that Hispanics need to take their rightful place in American literature," she says.

In addition to several books of poetry, she has written books for children that are based on her own childhood experiences.

Using imagery is Mora's way of collecting her experiences and looking them over again. She says:

 Writing is a way of thinking about what I see and feel. In words I save images of people and scenes. Writing is not exactly like a picture album, though, because when I write I have to think about why I want to save those images, how I feel about them. 99

First Thoughts

1. Describe the scene you see when you read this poem. What do you hear?

Thinking Critically

2. How would you **paraphrase**—that is, restate using your own words—the last three lines of "In the Blood"?

3. Look at the Spanish version of the poem. Here are some details about Spanish, in case you are not a Spanish speaker:

- *Niña* means "girl."
- *Abuelito* means something like "grandpapa" (*abuelo* means "grandfather").
- *Castañetean* could mean "drumming."

  Do you think the poem is a literal (exact) translation from English into Spanish, or could it have been worded slightly differently? Would you prefer any other wording?

4. How would you describe the **tone** of this poem? How do you think the speaker feels about family relationships?

Comparing Literature

5. As you filled out a chart after reading "Yes, It Was My Grandmother," fill out the one below. You'll use the chart when you complete the writing assignment on page 506.

Title of poem: _____

Most important word or phrase: _____

Key details:

- _____

- _____

- _____

- _____

What this poem says about a special family member:

_____

_____

North Carolina Competency Goal
5.02

SKILLS FOCUS

Literary Skills
Analyze tone.

Reading Skills
Make generalizations.

Comparing Literature

Before You Read

David Kherdian was born in Wisconsin to an Armenian father. Here is a poem about how the father attempts to participate in his son's culture—and what he teaches his son about the power of love. Read the poem once without stopping, as you did with "Yes, It Was My Grandmother." Then, re-read it, pausing to read and respond to the margin notes.

THAT DAY

David Kherdian

Just once
my father stopped on the way
into the house from work
and joined in the softball game
5   we were having in the street,
and attempted to play in *our*
game that *his* country had never
known. **❶**

Just once
10   and the day stands out forever
in my memory
as a father's living gesture
to his son,
that in playing even the fool
15   or clown, he would reveal
that the lines of their lives
were sewn from a tougher fabric
than the son had previously known. **❷**

IDENTIFY

❶ Why hasn't the father ever played softball with his son before?

INTERPRET

❷ Is the boy ashamed because his father doesn't play well? Explain. What does the son discover about his relationship with his father that day?

Contemplation by Alice Kent Stoddard.
David David Gallery, Philadelphia, USA.

About "That Day"

David Kherdian

In many ways my father and I were strangers to each other. At home I was his Armenian son, but in the streets I was an American stranger. I'm putting this a little bluntly. I'm exaggerating. So far as I knew, children did not play games in the Old Country. Therefore I did not believe that he understood any of the games I was involved in. And then, one day, while walking home from work, along the street where we were playing a pick-up game of softball, he stopped and either pitched the ball, or picked up the bat and tried to give the ball a hit. He was *intentionally* participating, he was joining in, and by doing so he was sharing with me something that was of value in my life that I did not believe had any importance in his life. I was deeply touched by this, though why I was touched, or where I was touched, or even how I was touched, was beyond my understanding at the time. Which brings me to poetry and why I write: But that's another story, and has to do with why I wrote *all* of my poems, not just the one you are looking at today.

After You Read "That Day"

First Thoughts

1. What would you say is the most important word or phrase in this poem? Explain.

Thinking Critically

2. Why does the day stand out forever in the speaker's memory?

3. What does the **title** of the poem refer to?

4. The word *gesture* can mean several things. One meaning of *gesture* is "action that shows a feeling or an idea." For example, in many countries a bow is a gesture of respect. What is the father's "living gesture"?

5. Describe the **tone** of this poem. What is the speaker's attitude toward his father? What feeling does the father show the son?

6. Find the **metaphor** at the end of the poem that compares the life of the family to a fabric. How would you explain this metaphor in your own words? Does the metaphor suggest a strong family or a weak one? Explain.

7. Does Kherdian's comment about the poem help you to understand it better? Explain your response.

Comparing Literature

8. Fill out the chart that follows, using details from "That Day" to make a **generalization** about the poem.

David Kherdian as a boy.

Title of poem: _____

Most important word or phrase: _____

Key details:

. _____

. _____

. _____

. _____

What this poem says about a special family member:

_____

_____

Use the workshop on writing a **comparison-contrast essay,** pages 404–409, for help with this assignment.

Assignment

1. Writing a Comparison-Contrast Essay

Write an essay in which you compare these poems about family life and important family members. Organize your essay this way:

Paragraph 1: Present a key detail from "Yes, It Was My Grandmother," and discuss what the poem might reveal about an important family member.

Paragraph 2: Present a key detail from "In the Blood," and discuss what the poem might reveal about family love.

Paragraph 3: Present a key detail from "That Day," and discuss what the poem and the poet's comment might reveal about what is important in family life.

Paragraph 4: Tell which poem, for you, expressed the most powerful feelings about family in general or an important family member. Give one reason for your response.

Before you start to write, review the details you gathered in the charts you filled in after you read each poem.

Assignment

2. Make a Poetic Collage

Working alone or with a group of classmates, make a collage about the objects, people, and events you see in one of the poems you just read. A collage can be made up of pictures, objects, and words: photos from magazines, your own drawings, words from the Spanish version of "In the Blood," even items such as cloth, pebbles, locks of hair, and so on. What makes a collage interesting is how all the different items are put together. How does your collage compare with classmates' collages about the same poem?

SKILLS FOCUS

Writing Skills
Write a comparison-contrast essay.

Art Skills
Make a collage.

North Carolina Competency Goal
5.01

NO QUESTIONS ASKED

Background

Literature and Social Studies

In 1949, a man named Mao Tse-tung led his political party, the Communists, to power in China. Seventeen years later, Chairman Mao was still in power but afraid that his position was weakening. In 1966, he launched a movement called the Cultural Revolution. His goal was to stamp out the "Four Olds"—old ideas, old culture, old customs, and old habits—and replace them with his own ways and ideas.

Mao Tse-tung and the Cultural Revolution

During the Cultural Revolution, owning anything traditional, expensive, or fancy was frowned upon. Property owners and business-people were viewed as anti-Communist and were regarded with suspicion. Teachers and professors were looked down upon for spreading old ideas. Schools were taken over by the Communist Party, and many teachers were fired and replaced by Party representatives.

The Red Guards

To carry out the Cultural Revolution, Mao looked to the youth of China. Young people were encouraged to join groups called Red Guards. Red Guard members were expected to police their elders for signs of the Four Olds (called fourolds in this selection). Children were asked to turn in their neighbors, their teachers, and even their parents for owning traditional items and following old ways. Thousands of people were jailed, and many were killed for their supposed loyalty to tradition.

In this excerpt from her memoir, *Red Scarf Girl,* Ji-li Jiang is twelve years old and the Cultural Revolution has recently begun. Ji-li, a good student and loyal follower of Mao, is excited about the possibility of joining the Red Guards, as are her younger brother, Ji-yun, and younger sister, Ji-yong. But the older generation is not so enthusiastic. Ji-li's father, an intellectual who works for a theater, has strong doubts about the Red Guards. So do her mother and grandmother, who lives with the family. Soon enough Ji-li will learn why.

The Landlord's Granddaughter
from Red Scarf Girl

Ji-li Jiang

Dad was often kept late at the theater, and sometimes he did not come home until after we were in bed. There were a lot of meetings, he told us. Often I would wake up when I heard him come in, and as I went back to sleep, I heard him and Mom talking in low voices. They must have made their decision about the trunks at one of those late-night conferences, but the first we knew about it was on a Sunday morning when they started carrying the trunks up to the roof.

The four trunks were part of Grandma's dowry.[1] They were a rich red leather, with a pattern stamped in gold. Each trunk had two

---

1. **dowry** *n.:* money or property given by the bride's family to the wedding couple.

Chinese silk slippers.

Chinese schoolgirl in a Red Guard uniform, standing outside of school.

sets of brass locks on its front and a round brass handle on each end. When they were stacked up on their rack, they made our room shine. Now Dad was going to dye them black so that they would not be considered fourolds.

Four stools were waiting in the middle of the roof, and the first chest was placed upon them. The dark dye was already mixed. Dad set to work.

"Wait a minute," exclaimed Grandma. There was a dark stain about the size of a thumb print on one of the brass handles. She took out her handkerchief and rubbed the handle over and over until it was clean and bright. She looked at the chest with a dreamy expression and gently laid her hand on it. Against the deep red leather her skin seemed even paler.

"It won't look bad after it's painted," Dad said softly.

Grandma seemed to wake up. "Oh, I know," she said. "You go ahead." She went down to the room and did not come back.

"Her mother gave her these trunks when Grandma got married. That's why she's sad," Dad explained.

I thought of Grandma getting married so long ago, bringing the four beautiful trunks full of gifts her mother had sent from Tianjin[2] to Shanghai.[3] Grandma must have been excited and exhausted, traveling a thousand miles to marry a man she had never met.

Dad started to paint, wielding the brush awkwardly.

"Dad, it's too dry. Look how it's streaking."

Dad dipped the brush in the dye again.

"Look out! It's dripping, Dad."

Shouting advice, we ran around the trunks excitedly.

Eventually Dad's painting improved, and the first trunk was finished. But the original color could still be seen through the dye, and he had to put on a second coat. Ji-yun and I grew tired of watching and went back downstairs. Ji-yong stayed to help.

An amazing sight stopped the two of us in the doorway.

"Wow," Ji-yun said.

Glowing silks and satins spilled out of an old trunk. The whole room was alive with color.

Ji-yun grabbed a piece of silk. "Gorgeous! Are these costumes, Mom?"

They were old clothes, long gowns like the ones ancient courtiers and scholars wore in the movies. Many of them were embroidered with golden dragons or phoenixes. Some were printed with magnificent colorful patterns, and some were even crusted with pearls and gold sequins.

"These belonged to our ancestors. Grandma thought they were too nice to throw away, so we kept them in the bottom of this chest." Mom reached in and pulled out a bunch of colorful silk neckties. She threw them all on the floor.

I was worried. "Mom, aren't these all fourolds?"

"That's right. That's why Grandma and I decided to make comforter covers out of them. We can use the ties to make a mop."

"It seems terrible to just cut them all up. Why don't we just give them to the theater or to the Red Guards?" Ji-yun held a gown up in front of her. She was imagining what it would be like to wear it, I knew.

"The theater doesn't need them, and it's too late to turn them in

---

2. **Tianjin** (tyen′ jin′): city in northeastern China.
3. **Shanghai** (shaŋ′ hī′): China's largest city, located in eastern China, at the mouth of the Yangtze River.

now. The Red Guards would say that we were hiding them and waiting for New China to fall. Besides, even if we did turn them in, the Red Guards would just burn them anyway." Grandma looked at me and shook her head as she picked up her scissors. "I just couldn't bear to sell them," she said sadly. "Even when your father was in college and we needed money." She picked up a lovely gold-patterned robe and said softly, "This was a government official's uniform. I remember my grandfather wearing it."

"It *is* pretty, Grandma," I said, "but it is fourolds. Don't feel bad about it."

The long gowns were so large that the back of one was big enough for half a quilt cover. Mom and Grandma discussed the job while cutting: which parts could be used for covers and which parts for cushions. Ji-yun and I were enchanted by the pearls and gold sequins littering the floor. We pestered Grandma and Mom to let us have them, and finally Mom sighed and yielded.

Ji-yun and I were overjoyed. We sat amid the piles of silks, picking up pearls and putting them in a jar. Little White[4] was happy too. She rolled over and over among the scraps of silk and batted pearls around the floor.

While we played, Mom made two quilt covers out of the gowns, one deep purple and the other a bright gold. Then she made a pair of mops from the ties. We were delighted with them. You could not find anything like our tie mops in the stores.

Dad and Ji-yong finally finished the second coat of dye on the trunks. The gold stamping still obstinately showed through the layers, but the deep red had become a dark burgundy. The room seemed dressed up with the glowing new quilts and the

Chinese embroidered purple-patterned silk robe.

4. **Little White:** Ji-li's family's pet cat.

A simple schoolroom in China.

repainted trunks. I felt good. We had really done what Chairman Mao asked, breaking with the old and establishing the new.

"You did a nice job on the trunks," Grandma said. "I don't think the Red Guards will notice them."

Ji-yun looked up from the bed where she was lying with her face in the silky new cover. "Are the Red Guards going to come and search our house?" Everyone stood still. I stopped playing with the pearls. Even Little White stopped rolling around the floor.

"It's possible," Mom said slowly, "but you don't have to be afraid. You are just children, and a search would have nothing to do with you."

The new decor lost all its brightness. The pearls I had been playing with lost their luster, and I put them down.

As the Cultural Revolution wears on, Ji-li's father finds himself in serious trouble with the Red Guards. They have long been suspicious of him because his father was a landlord, which the Red Guards consider a fourolds occupation. Now the Guards are concerned about Mr. Jiang's past political activities. They have decided to pressure Ji-li for more information.

During Math class a few days later, Teacher Hou from the Revolutionary Committee popped his head into my classroom. He barely glanced at Teacher Li before saying curtly, "Jiang Ji-li, come to our office right away. Someone wants to talk to you."

I stood up nervously, wondering what it could be. I felt my classmates' piercing eyes as I mechanically left the classroom. Teacher Hou walked ahead of me without seeming to notice my presence. I followed silently.

I tried not to panic. Maybe it was not bad. Maybe it was about the exhibition. Maybe Chairman Jin wanted me to help the others with their presentations. At the end of the long, dark hallway Teacher Hou silently motioned me into the office and then walked away.

I wiped my hands on my trousers and slowly opened the door. The thin-faced foreman from Dad's theater was right in front of me.

My face must have shown my dismay.

"Sit down, sit down. Don't be afraid." Chairman Jin pointed to the empty chair. "These comrades from your father's work unit are just here to have a study session with you. It's nothing to worry about."

I sat down dumbly.

I had thought about their coming to my home but never imagined this. They were going to expose my family in front of my teachers and classmates. I would have no pride left. I would never be an educable child again.

Thin-Face sat opposite me, with a woman I had never seen before. Teacher Zhang was there too, his eyes encouraging me.

Thin-Face came straight to the point. "Your father's problems are very serious." His cold eyes nailed me to my seat. "You may have read the article in the *Workers' Revolt*[5] that exposed your family's filthy past." I slumped down in my chair without taking my eyes off his face. "In addition to coming from a landlord family, your father

---

5. *Workers' Revolt:* newspaper published by the Communist Party of China.

committed some serious mistakes during the Antirightist Movement[6] several years ago, but he still obstinately refuses to confess." His cold manner became a little more animated. "Of course we won't tolerate this. We have decided to make an example of him. We are going to have a struggle meeting of the entire theater system to criticize him and force him to confess." He suddenly pounded the table with his fist. The cups on the table rattled.

I tore my eyes away from him and stared at a cup instead.

"As I told you before, you are your own person. If you want to make a clean break with your family, then you can be an educable child and we will welcome you to our revolutionary ranks." He gave Chairman Jin a look, and Chairman Jin chimed in, "That's right, we welcome you."

"Jiang Ji-li has always done well at school. In addition to doing very well in her studies, she participates in educational reform," Teacher Zhang added.

"That's very good. We knew that you had more sense than to follow your father," Thin-Face said with a brief, frozen smile. "Now you can show your revolutionary determination." He paused. "We want you to testify against your father at the struggle meeting."

I closed my eyes. I saw Dad standing on a stage, his head bowed, his name written in large black letters, and then crossed out in red ink, on a sign hanging from his neck. I saw myself standing in the middle of the stage, facing thousands of people, condemning Dad for his crimes, raising my fist to lead the chant, "Down with Jiang Xi-reng." I saw Dad looking at me hopelessly, tears on his face.

"I . . . I . . ." I looked at Teacher Zhang for help. He looked away.

The woman from the theater spoke. "It's really not such a hard thing to do. The key is your class stance. The daughter of our former Party Secretary resolved to make a clean break with her mother. When she went onstage to condemn her mother, she actually slapped her face. Of course, we don't mean that you have to slap your father's face. The point is that as long as you have the correct class stance, it will be easy to testify." Her voice grated on my ears.

"There is something you can do to prove you are truly Chairman Mao's child." Thin-Face spoke again. "I am sure you can tell us some things your father said and did that show his landlord and

---

6. **Antirightist Movement:** a 1957 movement begun by Mao's Communist Party to punish intellectuals—such as Ji-li's father—whom the Communists felt had unfairly criticized the government.

Red Guard youths holding books of Chairman Mao's quotations.

rightist mentality." I stared at the table, but I could feel his eyes boring into me. "What can you tell us?"

"But I don't know anything," I whispered. "I don't know—"

"I am sure you can remember something if you think about it," Thin-Face said. "A man like him could not hide his true beliefs from a child as smart as you. He must have made comments critical of Chairman Mao and the Cultural Revolution. I am sure you are loyal to Chairman Mao and the Communist Party. Tell us!"

"But my father never said anything against Chairman Mao," I protested weakly. "I would tell you if he did." My voice grew stronger with conviction. "He never said anything against the Party."

"Now, you have to choose between two roads." Thin-Face looked straight into my eyes. "You can break with your family and follow Chairman Mao, or you can follow your father and become an

Chairman Mao with young students.

enemy of the people." His voice grew more severe. "In that case we would have many more study sessions, with your brother and sister too, and the Red Guard Committee and the school leaders. Think about it. We will come back to talk to you again."

Thin-Face and the woman left, saying they would be back to get my statement. Without knowing how I got there, I found myself in a narrow passageway between the school building and the school-yard wall. The gray concrete walls closed around me, and a slow drizzle dampened my cheeks. I could not go back to the classroom, and I could not go home. I felt like a small animal that had fallen into a trap, alone and helpless, and sure that the hunter was coming.

Meet the Writer

Ji-li Jiang

Red Scarf Girl

Ji-li Jiang (1954–   ) was born in Shanghai, the largest city in China. When the Cultural Revolution swept through the country, she was only twelve years old. The memoir *Red Scarf Girl,* from which "The Landlord's Granddaughter" is taken, vividly describes the hardships Jiang and those around her experienced during the revolution. Jiang explains:

66 I grew up and moved to the United States, but still, whatever I did, wherever I went, vivid memories of my childhood kept coming back to me. After thinking so much about that time, I wanted to do something for the little girl I had been, and for all the children who lost their [childhood] as I did. This book is the result. 99

Years after the revolution, Jiang attended Shanghai Teachers' College and Shanghai University. She decided to become a science teacher. In 1984, Jiang moved to the United States. She later started her own company, called East West Exchange, which participates in exchange programs between China and western countries. Jiang has said:

66 Helping to bridge the gap between China and western countries is something I find fascinating, challenging, and rewarding. I truly believe that better understanding among people around the world is the route to peace. 99

For Independent Reading

If you'd like to learn more about Chinese culture, take a look at Ji-li Jiang's second book, *The Magical Monkey King: Mischief in Heaven,* an adapted version of "Journey to the West," a popular Chinese tale.

Writing Workshop

RUBRIC
Evaluation Criteria

A good informative report

1. centers on a thesis, or central idea, supported by details, facts, and explanations
2. includes accurately documented information from several sources
3. presents clearly organized information
4. ends by summarizing ideas or drawing an overall conclusion

EXPOSITORY WRITING
Informative Report

An **informative report** lets you expand and share your knowledge—about anything from dinosaurs to dynamite. Research often begins with a question about a subject that interests you. The success of your report will depend on the evidence you use to support your **thesis**—your central idea or claim about your subject. In this workshop you'll be the expert, informing readers about a subject of your choice.

Prewriting

1 Choosing a Subject

Read and respond to these **prompts:**

- Why is the sky blue?
- What books did students my age read long ago?
- Is it possible to transport objects through space?
- What is being done to save the cheetah (or another endangered species)?
- How were songs used by those held in slavery to communicate forbidden messages?

Any of these questions might serve as a subject for research. For your report, decide on a subject that interests you—perhaps sports, nature, animals, or art. Then, brainstorm a list of possible questions to research about your subject. Keep your questions focused—not too broad. See the box in the margin of the next page for an example of how to narrow a topic.

North Carolina Competency Goal
4.03

For help thinking of research questions, make a list of two things you know and two things you'd like to know about your subject. Then, trade lists with a partner, and ask each other more questions about the topics.

2 Finding and Evaluating Sources

Plan to use at least three sources of information for your report. Whenever possible, use **primary sources.** A primary source is a firsthand account, such as a diary, letter, or memoir, written by someone who was there when an event happened. **Secondary sources** are reports or descriptions of events based on primary sources. They include magazine features, newspaper articles, encyclopedia entries, and TV and video documentaries. You can access both primary and secondary sources on the Internet and in the library, and you may be able to get additional information from museums, colleges, and experts in the field.

Evaluate every source before you begin taking notes. Use the following questions:

- Is the source factual (nonfiction)?
- Is the information up-to-date?
- Is the source trustworthy?

3 Taking Notes

Keep in mind the following tips:

- Write your information on notecards. Use one card for each main idea and its supporting details. On each card, include the source of the information. List the address of the Web page, or the title and page number of the print source, where you found the information.

- **Paraphrase,** or restate, information in your own words. If you copy material word for word, put quotation marks around it in your notes. You will have to give credit to the original source for each quotation you use in your report and for each idea that is not your own.

For more information about **taking notes,** see page 158.

Narrowing a Topic

Broad: cats

Less broad: wildcats

Narrow: cheetah

Narrower: What efforts are being made to save the cheetah from extinction?

Framework for an Informative Report

Introduction (hook to catch reader's interest, with a clear statement of the main idea):_____
_____

Body (facts, examples, and details presented in a logical order):

1. Subtopic:_____
   _____

   Details:_____
   _____

2. Subtopic:_____
   _____

   Details:_____
   _____

3. Subtopic:_____
   _____

   Details:_____
   _____

Conclusion (restatement of the main idea or reflection on the topic):
_____
_____

Thesis Statement
The snow leopard is a predator.

Strategies for Elaboration

Comparisons make facts interesting and clear to your readers. Imagine that you quote a fact like this: "A giraffe drinks fifty gallons of water per week." To clarify, you can add a comparison: "That's equal to about one bathtubful." Many comparisons include *like* or *as:*

- A leopard chases its prey *like* a race car heading for the finish line.

INTERNET

More Writer's Models

Keyword: LE5 6-5

4 Writing a Thesis Statement

Your **thesis statement** tells what the point of the paper will be. It usually appears in the introductory paragraph, and it may take the form of an answer to the question you researched. In the Student Model (page 521), the thesis statement appears at the beginning of the second paragraph.

5 Organizing the Report

Organize important information in an outline. Sort your notes into several major categories. Then, divide each category into subtopics, each to be developed into a full paragraph. Decide how you will organize the information in your report—by order of importance or in chronological (time) order—and make your outline.

For more information about **outlining,** see page 144.

Drafting

1 Starting Strong

Start with a bang. Open with a quotation, a vivid description, or a personal experience. If you wish, you can wait and draft the introduction after drafting the body.

2 Drafting the Body

The body of your report should contain facts that support your controlling idea. As you write, you may decide to rearrange your ideas, take out information, or add new information. Keep referring to your notes, and go back to your sources if you need more information.

Support facts with details and comparisons that create pictures in your reader's mind. Note, for example, the comparisons in the Student Model on page 521.

3 Wrapping It Up

End your report by tying your ideas together. You might sum up your main idea, draw conclusions, or discuss your thoughts about the information. Consider closing with a vivid image.

4 Listing Sources

At the end of your paper, list your sources of information. Use the Modern Language Association (MLA) style guide in the Communications Handbook or one that your teacher selects.

Communications Handbook HELP

See Listing Sources and Taking Notes.

Student Model

Snow Leopard—The Predator!

The snow leopard seems calm from far away, but a run-in with one could lead to deadly consequences. The snow leopard's fur is not sleek, but it is thick and long which makes it easier for the snow leopard to adapt to the cold climate it lives in. The tropical leopard and many big cats have large ears in proportion to the size of their heads, but the snow leopard's ears are small. Its tail is also longer than other big cats' tails. The snow leopard's tail is three feet long and is used as a blanket in its cold habitat when it is sleeping.

The snow leopard is a predator. If it weren't for its cunning cleverness and its quick speed, the snow leopard's diet would be plants, bugs, and other small animals. It attacks its prey like a race car passing the finish line. It runs and runs until it gets there and attacks the prize. The snow leopard's movement is so quick that it makes its attack like stealing candy from a baby.

—Jenny Boscamp
Frost Elementary School
Chandler, Arizona

Title suggests main idea.

First sentence grabs reader's attention and reinforces main idea.

*Paper is clearly organized. This paragraph discusses the snow leopard's physical appearance. The writer provides **facts and details** throughout.*

*Last paragraph discusses the animal's role as predator. Two colorful comparisons provide a **strong conclusion.***

Evaluating and Revising

Use the following chart to evaluate and revise your informative report.

Informative Report: Content and Organization Guidelines		
Evaluation Questions	▶ **Tips**	▶ **Revision Techniques**
❶ Does your introduction contain a thesis statement? Does this statement identify both the topic and your main point?	▶ **Underline** your statement of the report's topic and main point.	▶ **Add** a thesis statement, or **add** the main point about the topic to the statement, if necessary.
❷ Does each paragraph in the body of your paper develop one subtopic?	▶ **Label** the margin of each paragraph with the subtopic it develops.	▶ **Delete** unrelated ideas. **Rearrange** information into specific paragraphs where necessary. **Link** ideas with transitional words.
❸ Does each body paragraph contain supporting evidence, such as facts, examples, and direct quotations?	▶ **Highlight** the facts, examples, and quotations that support each subtopic.	▶ **Add** your facts and examples from notes, if necessary.
❹ Does your conclusion sum up your overall findings?	▶ **Put a check mark** next to your final statement or summary.	▶ **Summarize** your research. **Revise** your final statement for clarity, or add a personal comment.
❺ Have you included at least three sources in the *Works Cited* list?	▶ **Number** the sources listed.	▶ **Add** sources to the *Works Cited* list, if needed. **Add** information from those sources to your report.

On the next page is an excerpt from an informative report that has been revised. Use the questions that follow the Revision Model to evaluate the writer's changes.

Revision Model

(1917–2000)
Jacob Lawrence once told a reviewer, "I am the black

community." After seeing W.E.B. DuBois's play Haiti, in

the Haitian general and liberator
1936, he began to research the life of Toussaint

Lawrence
L'Ouverture. In his paintings, ~~he~~ recorded important

events in African American history and culture. He

completed forty-one paintings about Haiti's struggle for

(1938–1939)
independence. Other series followed: Frederick Douglass,

Harriet Tubman (1939–1940), and John Brown (1941).

Lawrence's most famous work ~~is~~ the Migration series

depicts
~~It tells about~~ the movement of African Americans from

at the time of World War I
the rural South to the industrial North.

Evaluating the Revision

1. What material has been added? Do these changes improve the writing? Explain.

2. How has the writer rearranged material? Does this change improve coherence? Tell why or why not.

DIRECTIONS: Read the following two selections. Then, answer each question that follows.

John Brown (1800–1859) was an abolitionist, someone working to end slavery in the United States. The first selection that follows is from Gwen Everett's biography of John Brown. Everett writes from the point of view of Brown's daughter Annie. In this selection, Annie recalls her father's fateful raid on a federal arsenal in Harpers Ferry, Virginia, in 1859. Brown had planned to march south with his "liberation army," freeing people from slavery, enlisting volunteers, and eventually bringing slavery to an end. He raided the arsenal in search of weapons.

from John Brown: One Man Against Slavery

Gwen Everett

We listened carefully to Father's reasons for wanting to end slavery. None of us questioned his sincerity, for we knew he believed God created everyone equal, regardless of skin color. He taught us as his father had taught him: To own another person as property—like furniture or cattle—is a sin. When Father was twelve years old, he witnessed the cruel treatment of black men, women, and children held in bondage and he vowed, then and there, that one day he would put an end to the inhumanity.

"I once considered starting a school where free blacks could learn to read and write, since laws in the South forbid their education," he told us. "And, when we moved to North Elba, New York, we proved that black and white people could live together in peace and brotherhood."

"One person—one family—can make a difference," he said firmly.

"Slavery won't end by itself. It is up to us to fight it."

Father called us by name: Mary, John, Jason, Owen, and Annie (me). He asked us to say a prayer and swear an oath that we, too, would work to end slavery forever. Then he told us his plan.

He would lead a small group of experienced fighting men into a state that allowed slavery. They would hide in the mountains and valleys during daylight. And, under the cover of night, members of his "liberation army" would sneak onto nearby plantations and help the slaves escape.

Freed slaves who wished to join Father's army would learn how to use rifles and pikes—spear-shaped weapons. Then, plantation by plantation, Father's liberation army would move deeper south—growing larger and stronger—eventually freeing all the slaves.

SKILLS FOCUS

Review Literary Skills
Recognize the difference between first- and third-person narration.

Father's idea sounded so simple. Yet my brothers and I knew this was a dangerous idea. It was illegal for black people to handle firearms and for whites to show them how. It was also against the law to steal someone else's property; and, in effect, Father was doing this by encouraging slaves to leave their masters.

The fateful night of Sunday, October 16, 1859, Father and eighteen of his men marched into Harpers Ferry. They succeeded in seizing the arsenal and several buildings without firing a single shot. By morning the townspeople discovered the raiders and began to fight back. Then a company of marines led by Lieutenant Colonel Robert E. Lee arrived to reinforce the local troops.

The fighting lasted almost two days. When it was over, Father was wounded and four townspeople and ten of Father's men were dead. Newspapers across the country reported every detail of the trial, which was held during the last two weeks of October in Charles Town, Virginia. On October 31, the jury took only forty-five minutes to reach its decision. They found Father guilty of treason against the Commonwealth of Virginia, conspiring with slaves to rebel, and murder.

On December 1, my mother visited him in jail, where they talked and prayed together for several hours. I wished I could have been there to tell Father how courageous I thought he was.

He was executed the next morning.

Father's raid did not end slavery. But historians said that it was one of the most important events leading to the Civil War, which began in April 1861. The war destroyed slavery forever in our country, but it also took 619,000 lives and ruined millions of dollars' worth of property. My father must have known this would come to pass, for the day he was hanged, he wrote: "I, John Brown, am now quite certain that the crimes of this guilty land will never be purged away but with Blood."

Years after Father's death, I still had sleepless nights. Sometimes I recalled our conversations. Other times I found comfort in the verse of a song that Union soldiers sang about Father when they marched into battle.

His sacrifice we share! Our sword
  will victory crown!
For freedom and the right remember
  old John Brown!
His soul is marching on.

Yes indeed, I think to myself, one man against slavery did make a difference.

Test Practice *(continued)*

In 1850, Congress passed the Fugitive Slave Law. This law required federal officials to arrest people fleeing slavery and return them to their "owners." Here, Harriet Tubman comes to the aid of a runaway who has been captured and is in danger of being returned to slavery.

from Harriet Tubman: Conductor on the Underground Railroad

Ann Petry

On April 27, 1860, [Harriet Tubman] was in Troy, New York. She had spent the night there and was going on to Boston to attend an antislavery meeting. That morning she was on her way to the railroad station. She walked along the street slowly. She never bothered to find out when a train was due; she simply sat in the station and waited until a train came which was going in the direction she desired.

It was cold in Troy even though it was the spring of the year. A northeast wind kept blowing the ruffle on her bonnet away from her face. She thought of Maryland and how green the trees would be. Here they were only lightly touched with green, not yet in full leaf. Suddenly she longed for a sight of the Eastern Shore with its coves and creeks, thought of the years that had elapsed since she first ran away from there.

She stopped walking to watch a crowd of people in front of the courthouse, a pushing, shoving, shouting crowd. She wondered what had happened. A fight? An accident? She went nearer, listened to the loud excited voices. "He got away." "He didn't." "They've got him handcuffed." Then there was an eruptive movement, people pushing forward, other people pushing back.

Harriet started working her way through the crowd, elbowing a man, nudging a woman. Now and then she asked a question. She learned that a runaway slave named Charles Nalle had been arrested and was being taken inside the courthouse to be tried.

When she finally got close enough to see the runaway's face, a handsome frightened face, his guards had forced him up the courthouse steps. They were trying to get through the door but people blocked the way.

She knew a kind of fury against the system, against the men who would force this man back into slavery when they themselves were free. The Lord did not intend that people should be slaves, she thought. Then without even thinking, she went up the steps, forced her way through the crowd, until she stood next to Nalle.

There was a small boy standing near her, mouth open, eyes wide with curiosity. She grabbed him by the collar and whispered to him fiercely, "You go out in the street and holler 'Fire, fire' as loud as you can."

The crowd kept increasing and she gave a nod of satisfaction. That little boy must have got out there in the street and must still be hollering that there's a fire. She bent over, making her shoulders droop, bending her back in the posture of an old woman. She pulled her sunbonnet way down, so that it shadowed her face. Just in time, too. One of the policemen said, "Old woman, you'll have to get out of here. You're liable to get knocked down when we take him through the door."

Harriet moved away from Nalle, mumbling to herself. She heard church bells ringing somewhere in the distance, and more and more people came running. The entire street was blocked. She edged back toward Nalle. Suddenly she shouted, "Don't let them take him! Don't let them take him!"

She attacked the nearest policeman so suddenly that she knocked him down. She wanted to laugh at the look of surprise on his face when he realized that the mumbling old woman who had stood so close to him had suddenly turned into a creature of vigor and violence. Grabbing Nalle by the arm, she pulled him along with her, forcing her way down the steps, ignoring the blows she received, not really feeling them, taking pleasure in the fact that in all these months of inactivity she had lost none of her strength.

When they reached the street, they were both knocked down. Harriet snatched off her bonnet and tied it on Nalle's head. When they stood up, it was impossible to pick him out of the crowd. People in the street cleared a path for them, helped hold back the police. As they turned off the main street, they met a man driving a horse and wagon. He reined in the horse. "What goes on here?" he asked.

Harriet, out of breath, hastily explained the situation. The man got out of the wagon. "Here," he said, "use my horse and wagon. I don't care if I ever get it back just so that man gets to safety."

Nalle was rapidly driven to Schenectady and from there he went on to the West—and safety.

Collection 5: Skills Review

(continued)

1. The account called *John Brown: One Man Against Slavery* was written —
   - **A** in the third person
   - **B** in the first person
   - **C** by Harriet Tubman
   - **D** by John Brown himself

2. Which of the following statements would John Brown and Harriet Tubman be most likely to agree with?
   - **F** One person fighting against slavery could make a difference.
   - **G** The Fugitive Slave Law was fair and just.
   - **H** Slavery could be ended without violence.
   - **J** People should not involve family members in attempts to end slavery.

3. Which of the following sentences is an example of **first-person narration**?
   - **A** "Harriet started working her way through the crowd. . . ."
   - **B** "Years after Father's death, I still had sleepless nights."
   - **C** "She knew a kind of fury against the system. . . ."
   - **D** "People in the street cleared a path for them. . . ."

4. *Harriet Tubman: Conductor on the Underground Railroad* is —
   - **F** a biography
   - **G** an autobiography
   - **H** an essay
   - **J** a short story

5. Which of these titles seems most likely to be the title of an **autobiography**?
   - **A** *The Civil War: 1861–1865*
   - **B** *How I Gained My Freedom*
   - **C** *Work Songs and Field Hollers*
   - **D** *The Story of the Underground Railroad*

Constructed Response

6. In one or two sentences, state a difference between Ann Petry's account and Gwen Everett's account. Consider the type of narration (first or third person) used in each selection, as well as its genre (biography or autobiography).

Test Practice

DIRECTIONS: Read the following passages. Then, answer each question that follows.

Pet Heroes

We got Max from a group that traps wild kittens and tames them. When Max came to us, he was scrawny and little. Now he's a broad-shouldered, sun-yellow cat, the biggest cat in the 'hood. Max is my hero because he's a gentle giant with a soft meow. Yet he's kept some of his wild ways. He runs from everybody except me and my parents. He insists on his freedom to roam outside, especially on moonlit nights. He won't eat cat food unless he's really, really hungry. He prefers the mice and rats he catches on his own. Max knows we don't want him to catch birds, so he just watches them. He's kind to other cats—as long as they show him respect. He hates being pounced on. He loves curling up next to the sweet-smelling lavender plants in our yard, jumping from high places, cuddling at night, and getting stroked and scratched while giving me a cat massage with his big paws. I used to worry when he took off for a few days, but he always comes back. Max is my golden boy. He has a little voice but a big heart.

—Lynn

Rita is a small, shaggy, sandy-brown fluff ball. She's what some people call a mix—some poodle, some terrier, and a bit of something else. Rita is my hero because she's my hearing-ear dog. A woman from a place that trains dogs for deaf people found Rita in an animal shelter. Rita had been there for weeks, and nobody had claimed her. She went through five months of training. Then I got lucky. I was chosen to be the one who got to take her home.

I get along well by using American Sign Language, but having Rita tell me when she hears sounds like the ringing of an alarm clock or a telephone makes me feel even more independent. I love Rita. She is my special friend.

—Alex and Rita

Before I got Mopsy, I didn't know a bunny could be so much fun. Mopsy likes to play jokes on our cat. She creeps up behind him and nibbles his tail. She follows me around like a hopping shadow. Sometimes, to get attention, she jumps straight up in the air. Then, when she gets tired, she flops

North Carolina Competency Goal
2.01

Reading Skills
Connect and clarify main ideas; understand related topics.

Test Practice *(continued)*

down and takes a power nap. Mopsy loves to play, and she's never mean. My mom says that Mopsy must have learned her playful ways from her mother, who was a classroom rabbit.

Once a week we take Mopsy to visit my great-grandfather at his nursing home. He and his friends love to see her. Mopsy gets to sit on their laps and on their beds. She is quiet and never bites. That's why she's my hero.

—Michael

1. Which **title** fits all three paragraphs?
   A "Giving Humans a Helping Hand"
   B "My Pet Is My Hero"
   C "Courageous Critters"
   D "Keeping Animals Safe"

2. Which of the following **main ideas** is found in all three paragraphs?
   F To be considered a hero, an animal must show great courage.
   G Animals make better use of their time than humans do.
   H Owning a pet can be very rewarding.
   J People should spend more time with their pets.

3. All of the following titles describe articles that probably deal with topics related to these readings *except* —
   A "Tips on Caring for Your Dog"
   B "Can Pets Make People Happy?"
   C "My Iguana Is a Good Friend"
   D "When Rover Made My Day"

4. What word *best* describes the **tone** of all three paragraphs?
   F sarcastic
   G critical
   H sincere
   J mocking

5. Which of the following statements about pets is *not* a **fact**?
   A Cats make better pets than dogs.
   B Dogs can be trained to help deaf people.
   C Some cats like to hunt for their own food.
   D Mopsy visits a nursing home every week.

Constructed Response

6. In what ways are the three pets in these paragraphs alike? Write a sentence or two telling what the pets have in common.

Collection 5: Skills Review
Vocabulary Skills

Test Practice

Multiple-Meaning Words

DIRECTIONS: Read each of the following sentences. Then, choose the answer in which the underlined word is used in the same way.

1. After much preparation, the men were set for their journey.
   In which sentence does the word *set* have the same meaning as in the sentence above?
   A Mom set the plates on the table.
   B The stage crew had to construct a set for the play.
   C The coach said her team was set to play.
   D I set the alarm for 6:00 A.M.

2. Thomas Garrett made a call for the end of slavery.
   In which sentence does the word *call* have the same meaning as in the sentence above?
   F Call me on the cell phone.
   G The task force considered making a call for volunteers.
   H Harry was ready to call the family for dinner.
   J The doctor was on call during the night.

3. It's obvious that Thomas Garrett felt deep sympathy for enslaved people.
   In which sentence does the word *deep* have the same meaning as in the sentence above?
   A The swimming pool is eight feet deep.
   B Mr. Jones took a deep breath.
   C Mrs. Lopez feels deep affection for her husband.
   D Harriet hid deep in the woods.

4. Harriet Tubman's heroism would fill her friends with admiration.
   In which sentence does the word *fill* have the same meaning as in the sentence above?
   F I had my fill of turkey.
   G I think she can fill the position of class president.
   H Could you fill out this form?
   J A sunny day can fill me with joy.

5. Harriet Tubman would return to the South to free more people.
   In which sentence does the word *return* have the same meaning as in the sentence above?
   A Send in your tax return by April 15.
   B Ms. Jones will be happy when she can return to work after her illness.
   C Bill will return the favor someday.
   D The return trip seemed much longer.

North Carolina Competency Goal
6.01

SKILLS FOCUS

Vocabulary Skills
Use multiple-meaning words.

Test Practice *(continued)*

6. Harriet Tubman had a scar on her face as the result of a <u>blow</u> she received as a child.
   - F Can you <u>blow</u> hard enough to inflate these balloons?
   - G I hope I don't <u>blow</u> my chance to score the winning point in the game.
   - H The boxer was knocked out by a <u>blow</u> to the head.
   - J I watched a leaf <u>blow</u> by in the wind.

7. Thomas Garrett had to pay a large <u>fine</u> for helping slaves to escape.
   - A I paid my <u>fine</u> at the library.
   - B You did a <u>fine</u> job on that project.
   - C <u>Fine</u> art increases in value over the years.
   - D The kids did <u>fine</u> on their own when the <u>coach</u> was sick.

8. One day, when her <u>work</u> in the fields was done, Harriet Tubman went to the Big House and told her sister she was going to run away.
   - F The latest <u>work</u> by this author is a novel.
   - G Farming is John's favorite kind of <u>work</u>.
   - H On Sunday, I will <u>work</u> on my report all afternoon.
   - J This radio does not <u>work</u> anymore.

9. In her slave days, Harriet Tubman was a field <u>hand</u> on a plantation.
   - A Lisa hurt her <u>hand</u> in the basketball game.
   - B Can you lend me a <u>hand</u> moving these boxes?
   - C Please <u>hand</u> me that book.
   - D Last summer, Marco worked as a hired <u>hand</u> on a farm.

Harriet Tubman.

Collection 5: Skills Review

Writing Skills

Test Practice

DIRECTIONS: Read the following paragraph from a research report. Then, answer each question that follows.

(1) One of the North American Indian groups who built mounds was the Adena. (2) They built the mounds as burial places in what is now southern Ohio. (3) Mounds made by other groups are found in Indiana, Michigan, Illinois, Wisconsin, Iowa, Missouri, and Canada. (4) The Adena buried most of their dead in simple graves within the mounds, covering the bodies with dirt and stone. (5) Leaders and other important people from the village were buried in log tombs before being covered with dirt and stones. (6) Gifts were often placed in the tombs. (7) A pipe made of clay or stone was a usual gift placed in the tombs. (8) Grave Creek Mound is one of the largest mounds built by the Adena. (9) At about seventy feet high, it is a mysteriously beautiful monument.

1. Which of the following research questions does the information in this paragraph best answer?
   A   Why did the Adena build mounds?
   B   How were the Adena leaders chosen?
   C   When did the Adena build mounds?
   D   Who are the other mound builders?

2. If the student wanted to add a fact to develop this paragraph, which of the following sentences would be most appropriate for a research report?
   F   I saw a burial mound in Hillsboro, Ohio.
   G   The mounds should be protected.
   H   The Adena began to build mounds around 700 B.C.
   J   It is amazing to think how the mounds were built.

3. If you were revising this paragraph to improve the coherence, which sentence might you delete?

   A   1
   B   3
   C   5
   D   8

4. Which transitional words could be added to the beginning of sentence 5 to show how it relates to sentence 4?
   F   Therefore,
   G   Finally,
   H   Next,
   J   However,

5. If you were to use the information above in a presentation, which visual display would best support sentence 9?
   A   a drawing of a clay or stone pipe
   B   maps of the United States and Canada
   C   a time line showing when mounds were built
   D   a photograph of Grave Creek Mound

North Carolina Competency Goal
2.02

Writing Skills
Analyze a research report.

Fiction

Not Your Average Family

The adventures of the family in William Sleator's *Oddballs* are simply hilarious. Wild ideas flow nonstop out of such kooky characters as Jack, the budding hypnotist; Vicky, who likes to dye herself purple; and Bill, mastermind of the odd "pituh-plays." Mischievous and witty, the characters in this collection of stories set a style of their own as they cope with growing up.

A Modern-Day Myth

In Jerry Spinelli's Newbery Award–winning novel *Maniac Magee,* twelve-year-old Lionel Magee captures the imagination of the residents of Two Mills, Pennsylvania. His athletic feats surprise and impress his classmates—you won't believe how many touchdowns he scores! His most amazing accomplishment is something that anyone with a kind heart is capable of.

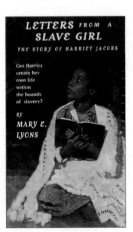

A Life Imagined

Harriet Jacobs's life story is truly inspirational. Jacobs escaped from slavery and an abusive owner by hiding in her grandmother's attic for seven years and then making her way north to freedom. Mary E. Lyons's *Letters from a Slave Girl* is a fictionalized account of Jacobs's ordeal told in the form of letters.

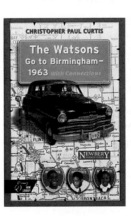

Traveling On

In Christopher Paul Curtis's novel *The Watsons Go to Birmingham—1963,* ten-year-old Kenny's brother Byron keeps getting into trouble. Kenny's parents decide to head south from their home in Flint, Michigan, to visit Grandma Sands in Alabama, hoping she'll bring Byron into line. The trip takes a terrifying turn when racial tensions explode.

This title is available in the HRW Library.

Nonfiction

She Gave All She Had

Sarah Bradford's biography *Harriet Tubman: The Moses of Her People* is a firsthand account of the woman who did so much to free African Americans from slavery. Bradford tells of Tubman's many sacrifices and heroic acts during the Civil War period.

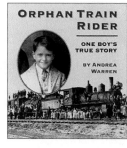

A Long Ride

For many reasons, hundreds of American children were sent west by train to new homes and families during the late nineteenth and early twentieth century. Lee Nailling was one such child. Andrea Warren recounts Nailling's early experiences and eventual happiness in *Orphan Train Rider*. Warren also presents an overview of the history of these trains and describes the problems the children faced with their new families.

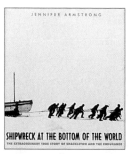

Endurance

Jennifer Armstrong's *Shipwreck at the Bottom of the World* tells the story of Ernest Shackleton, who tried to cross Antarctica with his crew of twenty-seven explorers. On the journey his ship broke up in icebound waters. Shackleton and five of his men lived for several months on ice floes and eventually had to navigate a tiny boat through the perilous South Atlantic Ocean to search for help. (We won't tell you how the story ends!)

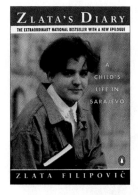

Surrounded by Horror

Zlata Filipović began keeping a diary in September 1991. Soon after, war broke out in her home country, Bosnia and Herzegovina. In *Zlata's Diary* she describes her family's struggle to survive amid the violence and tells how the war came between her and many of her friends. In the end, Zlata remains hopeful that her life will change for the better.

Dutch Interior I by Joan Miro.
The Museum of Modern Art, New York, NY, U.S.A., ©2005 Successió Miró/Artists Rights Society (ARS), New York/ADAGP, Paris.

The Writer's Craft: Metaphors, Symbols, and Images

Literary Focus:
Analyzing
Literary Devices

Informational Focus:
Making Assertions
About a Text

Elements of Literature
Literary Devices *by* John Leggett

USING YOUR IMAGINATION

Fiction is a way we communicate our feelings. In fact, some people say that fiction works only when it does just that. If your feelings are asleep when you read a story, the story is probably a failure. Here are some of the ways writers use words to awaken our feelings as well as our imaginations.

Making Us Feel

Let's say that Charlie is on his way to an important job interview when he finds that he's coming down with a cold. (Maybe that sounds pretty unimportant to you, but it makes a conflict, and it increases our interest in Charlie. Most of us know what it feels like to have a cold coming on.)

Rather than just saying Charlie is coming down with a cold, a good writer will make us *feel* the way Charlie feels, which isn't very good:

Charlie saw how the rain was spattering the high shine on his shoes and turned up his coat collar against the cold. Then he felt a little prickling at the back of his throat, the place where he believed two holes led upward into his nose. A tingling within these channels announced a sneeze. Out it came. *Kachooo!* Charlie's ears now felt too warm, his spine felt chilly, and ice water seemed to be seeping through his toes. He recognized these as sure signs of a cold.

The worst of it, though, was the misery. It didn't matter anymore if he found a nice girlfriend, or lived to a splendid old age, or ever had a better job. Nothing mattered at all—except whether the stupid bus would ever come and deliver him from this miserable street corner.

If you shared Charlie's misery—if you thought, "I know exactly how he feels"—then the writer was successful. Here are three of the many ways writers use words to affect our feelings and appeal to our imagination.

Imagery: Words That Create Pictures

Imagery is language that creates pictures. Imagery can also reach our other senses. It can help us not only to see something but also to smell or taste it, hear it, and feel its textures and temperatures.

The first stroke of the young violinist's bow produced a piercing whine, so unintended that the artist's eyes rolled in sympathy with his audience.

This image helps you picture a concert scene, hear a piercing sound, and then see the artist roll his eyes. (The image might make you laugh as well.)

North Carolina Competency Goal
5.01

INTERNET
More About Imagery
•
More About Simile/Metaphor
Keyword: LE5 6-6

SKILLS FOCUS

Literary Skills
Understand the use of imagery, figurative language, and symbolism in fiction and nonfiction.

Simile and Metaphor: Making Comparisons

In a **simile** a writer describes something by comparing it to something else—something very different. A simile makes its comparison with words such as *like, as, than,* and *resembles.*

By the time we took the meatloaf out of the oven, it resembled a chunk of coal.

The sea was as smooth as glass.

In a **metaphor** a writer compares two different things directly, without using words such as *like, as, than,* or *resembles.*

The sea was a sheet of glass.

By the time we took it out of the oven, the meatloaf was a chunk of coal.

Personification: Making the World Human

In **personification** something non-human is spoken of as if it were human. Personification can also occur when something that is not living is spoken of as if it were alive.

The sea sang a song of peace.

The meatloaf looked at me sadly.

Symbolism: Ripples of Meaning

Some symbols are public; we all agree on what they stand for. A blindfolded woman holding a scale symbolizes justice. A red rose symbolizes love. In literature a **symbol** is a person, place, or thing that stands for itself and for something beyond itself as well.

In the Genesis account in the Bible, the apple that Eve hands to Adam is an apple, but it also symbolizes many things to many people. That apple could stand for temptation, knowledge, even sin.

Practice

1. **Images.** Choose an object in the room, and describe it in a way that makes it seem appealing. Now, describe the same object in a way that makes us want to get out of the room. Use words that help us see the object—perhaps smell it, hear it, taste it, feel it.

2. **Figurative language.** The general term for similes, metaphors, personification, and symbols is *figurative language.* (The word *figurative* suggests that these uses of language are not meant to be taken literally. That meatloaf did not literally stare at you. It has no eyes.) Use these starters to create your own figures of speech:

Love is . . .	The world is . . .
Happiness is . . .	Ice is . . .
Security is . . .	Fire is . . .

3. **Symbol.** Draw an animal that could symbolize a human quality (courage, greed, laziness). Underneath your picture, identify the quality your creature represents.

Reading Skills and Strategies

Improving Fluency and Reading Rate

by Kylene Beers

Did you know that people sometimes get tickets for driving too *slowly*? It's also possible to read too slowly. If people read too quickly, they may miss important information; if they read too slowly, they may have trouble making sense of what they're reading.

How Can I Improve?

Reading fluency (how easily and well you read) and **reading rate** (how fast you read) are related. If you are a fluent reader, you

- read with expression
- know when to pause
- read by phrases or thought groups instead of word by word
- know when you don't understand what you've read
- know how to adjust your rate to what you are reading

If you want to improve your fluency, practice reading aloud, either alone (use a tape recorder so that you can listen to yourself) or with a buddy.

Choose a passage or paragraph that's about 150 to 200 words long. Read it to yourself silently a few times: then, read it aloud. Afterward, fill out the checklist at the right.

North Carolina Competency Goal 5.01

SKILLS FOCUS

Reading Skills Improve fluency and reading rate.

Oral Fluency	Often 5 points	Some-times 3 points	Never 0 points
Reads word by word			
Stops and starts			
Re-reads words or sentences			
Ignores			
• periods			
• commas			
• question marks			
• quotation marks			
Reads too fast			
Reads too slowly			
Slurs words			
Reads too loudly			
Reads too softly			
Guesses at pronunciations			
Seems nervous			
Loses place in text			
Final Score:			

Evaluate Your Fluency

Check your oral fluency by reading aloud the following passage from "What Do Fish Have to Do with Anything?" (you'll find the entire story, beginning on page 557.) Then, fill out the oral fluency chart on page 540. Keep practicing; you'll soon see that your score is going down—which means that your fluency is going up.

● ● ●

Every day, Mrs. Markham waited for her son, Willie, to come out of school when it was over. They walked home together. If asked why, Mrs. Markham would say, "Parents need to protect their children."

One Monday afternoon as they approached their apartment building, she suddenly tugged at Willie. "Don't look that way," she said.

"Where?"

"At that man over there."

As they walked, Willie stole a look back over his shoulder. A man Willie had never seen before was sitting on a red plastic milk crate near the curb. His matted, streaky gray hair hung like a ragged curtain over a dirty face. His shoes were torn. Rough hands lay upon his knees. One hand was palm up.

"What's the matter with him?" Willie asked.

Keeping her eyes straight ahead, Mrs. Markham said, "He's sick." She pulled Willie around. "Don't stare. It's rude."

"What kind of sick?"

Mrs. Markham searched for an answer. "He's unhappy," she said.

"What's he doing?"

"Come on, Willie; you know. He's begging."

"Did anyone give him anything?"

"I don't know. Now come on, don't look."

"Why don't you give him anything?"

"We have nothing to spare."

● ● ●

(continues)

(continued)

What's My Reading Rate?

If fluency is tied to reading rate, then what rate is right? Remember that different rates are right for different kinds of texts. You might zip through a comic book, but you need to move more slowly through your social studies textbook. In other words, your reading rate depends on what you're reading and why you're reading it.

If you think you read too slowly all the time, you can improve your reading rate. Follow these steps:

1. Choose something you want to read. (Don't choose something that's too easy.)
2. Ask a friend to time you as you read aloud for one minute.
3. Count the words you read in that one minute.
4. Repeat this process two more times, with different passages.
5. Add the three numbers, and divide the total by three. That number is your oral reading rate.

The chart at the right shows average reading rates for students in grades 3–6.

If you think your rate is too low, practice reading aloud every week or so. Have someone time you as you read for one minute. Use new passages each time you check your reading rate.

Grade Level	Average Words per Minute
3	110
4	140
5	160
6	180

Evaluate Your Reading Rate

Use the following passage from a science textbook to practice improving your reading rate. Follow the instructions on page 542 to calculate your rate. If your reading rate isn't satisfactory, keep practicing with new passages.

Fishes

Find a body of water, and you'll probably find fish. Fishes live in almost every water environment, from shallow ponds and streams to the depths of the oceans. You can find fishes in cold arctic waters and in warm tropical seas. Fishes can be found in rivers, lakes, marshes, and even in water-filled caves.

Fish were the first vertebrates on Earth. Fossil evidence indicates that fish appeared about 500 million years ago. Today Earth's marine and freshwater fishes make up more species than all other vertebrates combined. There are more than 25,000 species of fishes, and more are being discovered.

Fish Characteristics

Although different kinds of fishes can look very different from each other, they share many characteristics that help them live in water.

Many fishes are predators of other animals. Others are herbivores. Because they must actively search for food, they need a strong body, well-developed senses, and a brain.

Born to Swim. Fishes have many body parts that help them swim. Strong muscles attached to the backbone allow fishes to swim vigorously after their prey. Fishes swim through the water by moving their fins. Fins are fanlike structures that help fish move, steer, stop, and balance. Many fishes have bodies covered by scales, which protect the body and reduce friction as they swim through the water. The diagram below shows some of the external features of a typical fish.

Comprehension Tips

If you don't understand what you read, you aren't reading fluently. As you read, pause from time to time to follow these guidelines:

- Ask yourself if what you're reading makes sense.
- If you feel confused, re-read.
- Sum up the main events or ideas.
- Be sure you understand what causes events to happen.
- Compare what actually happens with what you expected to happen.

If you still don't understand what you're reading, try reading more slowly.

North Carolina Competency Goal 5.01

SKILLS FOCUS

Reading Skills
Improve fluency and reading rate.

Eye

Dorsal fin

Tail fin

Gill cover

Gills

Pectoral fin

Lateral line

Fishes come in a variety of shapes and sizes, but all have gills, fins, and a tail.

Anal fin

Pelvic fin

The Mysterious Mr. Lincoln

North Carolina Competency Goal
1.04; 4.01; 5.01

go.hrw.com

INTERNET

Vocabulary Activity
•
More About Freedman

Keyword: LE5 6-6

SKILLS FOCUS

Literary Skills
Understand the use of metaphor in nonfiction.

Reading Skills
Use prior knowledge.

Make the Connection
Quickwrite ✏

What does it take to be a good leader? List the qualities, and describe the background, experience, and education you think a president should have.

Literary Focus
Metaphor

When you say, "My cell phone is my lifeline," you're using a metaphor. A **metaphor** is an imaginative comparison between two things that seem to have little in common. A metaphor says that something *is* something else: not "His hand is *like* a wet fish" but "His hand *is* a wet fish."

Metaphors are often used in poetry. You could even call metaphor *the soul of poetry* (that's a metaphor). Writers use metaphors to stir our imagination, to help us see ordinary things in new and fresh ways. A metaphor can sometimes make a point as well as hundreds of words can.

Reading Skills
Using Prior Knowledge

Preview "The Mysterious Mr. Lincoln" by surveying the text and the photographs and captions. This process will help you recall what you already know about Lincoln and will suggest questions to you. Afterward, record facts you know and questions about the man who, in 1861, became our sixteenth president. Use the K and W columns of the KWL chart below.

K What I Know	W What I Want to Know	L What I Learned
Lincoln was president during the Civil War.	Why is Lincoln "mysterious"?	

Statue of Lincoln at the Lincoln Memorial in Washington, D.C.

The Mysterious Mr. Lincoln

Russell Freedman

Abraham Lincoln wasn't the sort of man who could lose himself in a crowd. After all, he stood six feet four inches tall, and to top it off, he wore a high silk hat.

His height was mostly in his long, bony legs. When he sat in a chair, he seemed no taller than anyone else. It was only when he stood up that he towered above other men.

At first glance most people thought he was homely. Lincoln thought so too, referring once to his "poor, lean, lank face." As a young man he was sensitive about his gawky looks, but in time, he learned to laugh at himself. When a rival called him "two-faced" during a political debate, Lincoln replied: "I leave it to my audience. If I had another face, do you think I'd wear this one?"

According to those who knew him, Lincoln was a man of many faces. In repose he often seemed sad and gloomy. But when he began to speak, his expression changed.

Vocabulary
gawky (gô′kē) *adj.:* clumsy; awkward.
repose (ri·pōz′) *n.:* state of rest or inactivity.

(Log cabin) The Granger Collection, New York.

President Lincoln's first Home in Illinois.

"The dull, listless features dropped like a mask," said a Chicago newspaperman. "The eyes began to sparkle, the mouth to smile; the whole countenance[1] was wreathed in animation, so that a stranger would have said, 'Why, this man, so angular and solemn a moment ago, is really handsome!'"

Lincoln was the most photographed man of his time, but his friends insisted that no photo ever did him justice. It's no wonder. Back then, cameras required long exposures. The person being photographed had to "freeze" as the seconds ticked by. If he blinked an eye, the picture would be blurred. That's why Lincoln looks so stiff and formal in his photos. We never see him laughing or joking.

Artists and writers tried to capture the "real"

Lincoln that the camera missed, but something about the man always escaped them. His changeable features, his tones, gestures, and expressions, seemed to defy description.

Today it's hard to imagine Lincoln as he really was. And he never cared to reveal much about himself. In company he was witty and talkative, but he rarely betrayed his inner feelings. According to William Herndon, his law partner, he was "the most secretive—reticent—shut-mouthed man that ever lived."

In his own time, Lincoln was never fully

Vocabulary

listless (list'lis) *adj.*: lifeless; lacking in interest or energy.

animation (an'i·mā'shən) *n.*: liveliness; life.

defy (dē·fī') *v.*: resist; oppose.

reticent (ret'ə·sənt) *adj.*: reserved; tending to speak little.

1. **countenance** (koun'tə·nəns) *n.*: face.

understood even by his closest friends. Since then, his life story has been told and retold so many times he has become as much a legend as a flesh-and-blood human being. While the legend is based on truth, it is only partly true. And it hides the man behind it like a disguise.

The legendary Lincoln is known as Honest Abe, a humble man of the people who rose from a log cabin to the White House. There's no doubt that Lincoln was a poor boy who made good. And it's true that he carried his folksy manners and homespun speech to the White House with him. He said "howdy" to visitors and invited them to "stay a spell." He greeted diplomats while wearing carpet slippers, called his wife "mother" at receptions, and told bawdy[2] jokes at cabinet meetings.

Lincoln may have seemed like a common man, but he wasn't. His friends agreed that he was one of the most ambitious people they had ever known. Lincoln struggled hard to rise above his log-cabin origins, and he was proud of his achievements. By the time he ran for president he was a wealthy man, earning a large income from his law practice and his many investments. As for the nickname Abe, he hated it. No one who knew him well ever called him Abe to his face. They addressed him as Lincoln or Mr. Lincoln.

Lincoln is often described as a sloppy dresser, careless about his appearance. In fact, he patronized the best tailor in Springfield, Illinois, buying two suits a year. That was at a time when many men lived, died, and were buried in the same suit.

It's true that Lincoln had little formal

Abraham Lincoln and his son Tad (1865).

"eddication," as he would have pronounced it. Almost everything he "larned" he taught himself. All his life he said "thar" for *there,* "git" for *get,* "kin" for *can.* Even so, he became an eloquent public speaker who could hold a vast audience spellbound and a great writer whose finest phrases still ring in our ears. He was known to sit up late into the night, discussing Shakespeare's plays with White House visitors.

He was certainly a humorous man, famous for his rollicking stories. But he was also moody and <u>melancholy</u>, tormented by long and frequent bouts of depression. Humor was his therapy. He relied on his yarns,[3] a friend observed, to "whistle down sadness."

---

2. **bawdy** *adj.:* humorous but crude.

3. **yarns** *n.:* entertaining stories filled with exaggeration. Storytellers like Lincoln could be said to "spin" yarns.

Vocabulary
melancholy (mel′ən·käl′ē) *adj.:* mournful; gloomy.

He had a cool, logical mind, trained in the courtroom, and a practical, commonsense approach to problems. Yet he was deeply superstitious, a believer in dreams, omens, and visions.

We admire Lincoln today as an American folk hero. During the Civil War, however, he was the most unpopular president the nation had ever known. His critics called him a tyrant, a hick,[4] a stupid baboon who was unfit for his office. As commander in chief of the armed forces, he was denounced as a bungling amateur who meddled in military affairs he knew nothing about. But he also had his supporters. They praised him as a farsighted statesman, a military mastermind who engineered the Union victory.

Lincoln is best known as the Great Emancipator, the man who freed the slaves. Yet he did not enter the war with that idea in mind. "My paramount object in this struggle *is* to save the Union," he said in 1862, "and is *not* either to save or destroy slavery." As the war continued, Lincoln's attitude changed. Eventually he came to regard the conflict as a moral crusade to wipe out the sin of slavery.

No black leader was more critical of Lincoln than the fiery abolitionist[5] writer and editor Frederick Douglass. Douglass had grown up as a slave. He had won his freedom by escaping to the North. Early in the war, impatient with Lincoln's cautious leadership, Douglass called him "preeminently the white man's president, entirely devoted to the welfare of white men." Later, Douglass changed his mind and came to admire Lincoln. Several years after the war, he said this about the sixteenth president:

"His greatest mission was to accomplish two things: first, to save his country from dismemberment[6] and ruin; and second, to free his country from the great crime of slavery. . . . Taking him for all in all, measuring the tremendous magnitude of the work before him, considering the necessary means to ends, and surveying the end from the beginning, infinite wisdom has seldom sent any man into the world better fitted for his mission than Abraham Lincoln."

---

4. **hick** *n.:* awkward, inexperienced person from the country.

5. **abolitionist** *n.:* person who supported abolishing, or ending, slavery in the United States.
6. **dismemberment** *n.:* separation into parts; division.

Vocabulary

omens (ō'mənz) *n.:* things believed to be signs of future events.

paramount (par'ə·mount') *adj.:* main; most important.

crusade (krōō·sād') *n.:* struggle for a cause or belief.

Meet the Writer

Russell Freedman

"I Know Lincoln Better Than I Know Some of My Friends"

Russell Freedman (1929–   ) has written more than thirty nonfiction books for children and young adults. His book *Lincoln: A Photobiography*, which includes "The Mysterious Mr. Lincoln," won the Newbery Medal for the most distinguished contribution to children's literature in 1988. Freedman had this to say about writing a biography of the famous sixteenth president:

❝The Lincoln I grew up with was a cardboard figure, too good to believe. As an adult, I read a couple of books that indicated he was just like everyone else—someone subject to depression, someone who had trouble making up his mind—and that intrigued me. When I had some inkling he was a complicated person in his own right, I decided I wanted to know more about him.

I got to know Lincoln the way I'd try to know anyone in real life. How do you understand people? You observe them, discover their memories, find out their thoughts, their ideas of right and wrong. Once you do that, they become somebody's you know. I'd say I know Lincoln better than I know some of my friends because I've studied him more closely.❞

For Independent Reading

You may enjoy Freedman's books about other personalities he's studied closely. His biographies include *Eleanor Roosevelt: A Life of Discovery; Babe Didrikson Zaharias: The Making of a Champion; Teenagers Who Made History; The Life and Death of Crazy Horse;* and *The Wright Brothers: How They Invented the Airplane.*

First Thoughts

1. If you could ask Lincoln one question, what would you ask him?

Thinking Critically

2. Why does the writer call Lincoln "mysterious"?

3. How do you think Lincoln would have responded to this first chapter of his biography?

4. Freedman uses **metaphor** when he says that Lincoln "towered above other men." Explain this comparison—what does it tell you about Lincoln?

5. Using another **metaphor,** Frederick Douglass said that Lincoln's first great mission was to "save his country from dismemberment." What does *dismemberment* mean? What is Douglass comparing the country to when he uses this term?

North Carolina Competency Goal
1.02; 1.04; 4.01; 4.02; 5.01

INTERNET

Projects and Activities
Keyword: LE5 6-6

SKILLS FOCUS

Literary Skills
Analyze the use of metaphor in nonfiction.

Reading Skills
Use prior knowledge.

Speaking and Listening Skills
Write and present a book review.

> ## Reading Check
> Go back to the KWL chart you made before you started reading. Correct any inaccurate statements in the K column. Then, in the L column, list six facts you learned about Lincoln. What was the most surprising thing you learned about Lincoln? Why did it surprise you?

Extending Interpretations

6. Review your Quickwrite notes. Does Lincoln have the qualifications for president that you listed? Do you think he would win if he ran for president in our next election? Explain why or why not.

7. If Lincoln could send a message to the American people today, what do you think he would say?

SPEAKING AND LISTENING

Reviewing Books

Read Russell Freedman's *Lincoln: A Photobiography* and another book or article on Lincoln. Team up with a classmate who has read the same two books, and discuss the strengths and weaknesses of each. Then, present the books to the class as if you were a pair of reviewers on TV. Rate each book on a scale of one to ten, with ten being excellent and one being really bad. Explain why you would—or wouldn't—recommend each book to readers your age.

Finding Synonyms

A **thesaurus** (from the Greek for "treasure") is a reference book containing lists of synonyms. (You can find a thesaurus online or in a library.) **Synonyms** (sin′ə·nimz) are words that are similar in meaning. If you look up *gawky* in a thesaurus, you'll find synonyms like *awkward, ungainly, clumsy, graceless,* and *inelegant.*

The meanings of synonyms are related but slightly different. Try replacing a word in a sentence with one of its synonyms. You'll find that the meaning may change slightly.

PRACTICE

Below the Word Bank is another list of words. Go through the list, and find one or two synonyms for each Word Bank word. Next, go back to the text, and replace each Word Bank word with its synonym. Then, read each sentence. Has the meaning remained the same, or has it changed slightly? Set up your sentences this way:

> **"As a young man he was sensitive about his gawky/clumsy looks."**

Clumsy is not the same as *gawky.* It refers to the way someone moves rather than the way someone looks.

Word Bank
gawky
repose
listless
animation
defy
reticent
melancholy
omens
paramount
crusade

Synonyms
campaign
clumsy
disobey
gloomy
inactivity
lifeless
liveliness
main
principal
reserved
resist
rest
sad
signs
silent

ROGET'S BRONTOSAURUS

From *The New Yorker Cartoon Album 1975–1985.*

North Carolina Competency Goal 6.01

SKILLS FOCUS

Vocabulary Skills
Understand shades of meaning.

Making and Supporting Assertions

Reading Focus
Assertions and Evidence

An **assertion** is a statement or claim. In his biography of Abraham Lincoln, Russell Freedman makes several assertions about Lincoln. For example, he claims that Lincoln was "mysterious." Freedman is careful to back up his statements about Lincoln with **evidence.** Evidence gives weight to an assertion and helps make it believable.

Look at the following chart to see how Freedman supported some of his assertions. What evidence does Freedman offer for the third assertion? Flip back through "The Mysterious Mr. Lincoln" to find out.

■ Read the next article, and see if the writer supports his assertions about Lincoln's sense of humor.

The Granger Collection, New York.

| "The Mysterious Mr. Lincoln" ||
Assertion (Claim)	Evidence (Support)
1. "Lincoln was a man of many faces."	• He was sad and gloomy in repose. • He was smiling and animated when speaking.
2. People think of Lincoln as a "man of the people," but in many ways he wasn't.	• He was highly ambitious. • Although he had little formal education, he was an accomplished speaker and writer. • He was wealthy.
3. Lincoln is sometimes thought of as a careless dresser, but he actually cared a great deal about his appearance.	[You find the evidence.]

Long Abraham Lincoln a Little Longer.

North Carolina Competency Goal
3.01; 3.03; 4.01; 4.03; 5.02

Reading Skills
Make and support assertions.

Lincoln's Humor

It is puzzling how Lincoln could laugh, joke, and tell stories, despite his terrible burdens as president during the Civil War. Lincoln was the first and the best humorist ever to occupy the White House. A friend said, "He could make a cat laugh."

Lincoln called laughter "the joyous, beautiful, universal evergreen of life." For Lincoln laughter relieved life's pressures and soothed its disappointments. Both as a lawyer and as a politician, he used amusing stories to make important points clear to his listeners. Storytelling put people at ease or nudged them from an unwanted topic or point of view. It also pleasantly brought an interview to a close and a visitor's welcome departure from the president's office.

Political opponents feared Lincoln's humorous jabs, which often destroyed their best arguments. Stephen A. Douglas, Lincoln's opponent in a Senate race, said, "Every one of his stories seems like a whack upon my back. . . . When he begins to tell a story, I feel that I am to be overmatched."

Lincoln's words got extra force from his facial expressions and gestures—a shrug of his shoulders, raised eyebrows, a turned-down mouth, a comically twisted face—which made his audiences roar with laughter.

Here is a sampling of Lincoln's humor and the uses he made of it:

- As a young lawyer, Lincoln once defended a farmer who had been attacked by his neighbor's dog. To fend off the dog, the farmer had poked it with a pitchfork, wounding it. The dog's owner then took the case to court to recover damages. His lawyer argued that the farmer should have struck the dog with the handle end of the pitchfork to avoid causing it serious harm. In the farmer's defense, Lincoln exclaimed that the dog should have avoided frightening the farmer by approaching him with *its* other end.

- As president, Lincoln was besieged with visitors seeking jobs and favors. One day while a visitor was pressing his demands, Lincoln's doctor entered the room. Lincoln, holding out his hands, asked him, "Doctor, what are those blotches?" "They're a mild smallpox," the doctor replied. "They're all over me," said Lincoln. "It's contagious, I believe." "Very contagious," said the doctor as the visitor hastily departed. "There is one good thing about this," said Lincoln to his doctor after the caller had left. "I now have something I can give to everybody."

- Impatient with his Civil War generals, who were slow to engage their forces in battle, Lincoln began requiring frequent reports of their progress. An irritated general sent this telegram to the White House: "We have just captured six cows. What shall we do with them?" Lincoln replied, "Milk them."

—Louis W. Koenig

Analyzing Assertions and Support

LINCOLN'S HUMOR

Test Practice

1. The information in this article supports the **assertion** that —
   A   Lincoln used humor to cope with the difficulties of being president
   B   Lincoln should have appeared more serious to the public
   C   Lincoln was the most popular president ever
   D   Lincoln worried about his health

2. What **evidence** from the article suggests that Lincoln would do well in a debate if he were a candidate today?
   F   Lincoln was handsome, so he would look good on television.
   G   Lincoln always seemed more intelligent than his opponents.
   H   The quotation by Stephen A. Douglas shows that Lincoln used humor effectively to defeat debating opponents.
   J   Lincoln's plain speaking appealed to people all over the country.

3. We can reasonably **assert** that this essay was written mainly to —
   A   persuade people to like Lincoln
   B   persuade people to laugh more
   C   describe Lincoln's sense of humor
   D   criticize Lincoln's character

4. The information in this essay supports the **assertion** that —
   F   Lincoln disliked the military
   G   Lincoln used humor and amusing stories throughout his career
   H   Lincoln did not get impatient during the Civil War
   J   Lincoln told funny stories only when he was a lawyer

5. The three samples of Lincoln's humor at the end of this article support the **assertion** that —
   A   Lincoln told jokes for no reason at all
   B   Lincoln used humor to cope with problems
   C   Lincoln used humor to hurt people
   D   Lincoln's humor went over the heads of most people

North Carolina Competency Goal
1.04; 2.01; 4.01; 4.02; 5.01

Constructed Response

1. What **assertion** about Lincoln does the writer make in the first paragraph?

2. How does the writer **support** his assertion that Lincoln's sense of humor helped him?

SKILLS FOCUS

Reading Skills
Analyze assertions and support.

Antonyms

An **antonym** (an′tə·nim′) is a word that is opposite or nearly opposite in meaning to another word. In the selection you just read, you learned that Lincoln's opponents feared his humor. Some antonyms for *opponents* are *colleagues, allies,* and *companions.* Learning antonyms of unfamiliar words can broaden your vocabulary. (You can sometimes find antonyms in dictionary and thesaurus entries.)

PRACTICE

Read each of the sentences below. Then, choose the **antonym,** or opposite, of the underlined word.

1. Lincoln called laughter "the joyous, beautiful, universal evergreen of life." An antonym of *joyous* is —

   a. sad   **b.** ugly   **c.** peaceful   **d.** happy

2. Lincoln used humorous stories to ease visitors' departure from his office. An antonym of *departure* is —

   a. rush   **b.** leaving   **c.** arrival   **d.** exit

3. Lincoln felt that laughter soothed life's disappointments. An antonym of *soothed* is —

   a. worsened   **b.** smoothed   **c.** corrected   **d.** helped

4. Lincoln grew impatient with generals who were slow to engage their forces in battle. An antonym of *engage* is —

   a. marry   **b.** rally   **c.** withdraw   **d.** employ

5. As a young lawyer, Lincoln once defended a farmer who had been threatened by a dog. An antonym of *defended* is —

   a. attacked   **b.** freed   **c.** supported   **d.** protected

North Carolina Competency Goal
2.01; 6.01

Vocabulary Skills
Identify and understand antonyms.

What Do Fish Have to Do with Anything?

Make the Connection
What's Your Opinion?

Rate the following ideas about life, all of which are expressed in the story. Use this scale to rate the statements:
1 = disagree, 2 = no opinion, 3 = agree.

1. "Parents need to protect their children."
2. "Questions that have no answers shouldn't be asked."
3. "Money will cure a lot of unhappiness."
4. "People are ashamed of being unhappy."

Quickwrite ✏️

From the list, choose a statement that you agree or disagree with. Explain why you feel the way you do.

Literary Focus
Symbolism

A **symbol** is a person, place, thing, or action that has meaning in itself and that stands for something else as well. Many symbols are traditional. They're easily understood because people have agreed on their meaning. A dove, for example, often symbolizes peace. Uncle Sam is a symbol of the United States. Peter Pan is a symbol of everlasting childhood.

Symbolism, the use of symbols, adds another layer of meaning to all kinds of texts, from poetry to fiction and nonfiction. In this story the writer uses

things, like cave-dwelling fish and a poundcake, to mean what they are—and much more.

Reading Skills
Making Inferences

Writers rarely come right out and explain what their symbols mean. You have to find the symbols and figure out their meaning on your own. You do this by **making inferences.** You use details to **infer,** or guess at, the larger ideas the writer is trying to convey.

As you read, you'll see little open-book signs at certain points in the story. Stop at those points, and answer the questions.

North Carolina Competency Goal
1.04; 3.01; 3.03; 4.01; 5.01; 5.02

INTERNET

Vocabulary Activity

Keyword: LE5 6-6

SKILLS FOCUS

Literary Skills
Understand the use of symbolism in fiction.

Reading Skills
Make inferences.

Vocabulary Development

Look for and learn these words as you read the story:

vaguely (vāg′lē) *adv.*: not clearly or definitely; in a general way. *She answered vaguely because she felt uncomfortable telling the whole story.*

urgency (ʉr′jən·sē) *n.*: pressure; insistence. *Hearing the urgency in her voice, Willie quickly turned around.*

contemplated (kän′təm·plāt′id) *v.*: studied carefully. *Willie contemplated his food before eating it.*

intently (in·tent′lē) *adv.*: with close attention. *Willie gazed intently at the man.*

What Do Fish Have to Do with Anything?

Avi

E very day Mrs. Markham waited for her son, Willie, to come out of school when it was over. They walked home together. If asked why, Mrs. Markham would say, "Parents need to protect their children."

One Monday afternoon as they approached their apartment building, she suddenly tugged at Willie. "Don't look that way," she said.

"Where?"

"At that man over there."

As they walked, Willie stole a look back over his shoulder. A man Willie had never seen before was sitting on a red plastic milk crate near the curb. His matted, streaky gray hair hung like a ragged curtain over a dirty face. His shoes were torn. Rough hands lay upon his knees. One hand was palm up.

"What's the matter with him?" Willie asked.

Keeping her eyes straight ahead, Mrs. Markham said, "He's sick." She pulled Willie around. "Don't stare. It's rude."

"What kind of sick?"

Mrs. Markham searched for an answer. "He's unhappy," she said.

"What's he doing?"

"Come on, Willie; you know. He's begging."

"Did anyone give him anything?"

"I don't know. Now come on, don't look."

"Why don't you give him anything?"

"We have nothing to spare."

When they got home, Mrs. Markham removed a white cardboard box from the refrigerator. It contained poundcake. Using her thumb as a measure, she carefully cut a half-inch-thick piece of cake and gave it to Willie on a clean plate. The plate lay on a plastic mat decorated by images of roses with diamondlike dewdrops. She also gave him a glass of milk and a folded napkin.

Willie said, "Can I have a bigger piece of cake?"

Mrs. Markham picked up the cake box and ran a manicured pink fingernail along the nutrition information panel. "A half-inch piece is a portion, and a portion contains the following nutrients. Do you want to hear them?"

"No."

"It's on the box, so you can accept what it says. Scientists study people and then write these things. If you're smart enough, you could become a scientist. Like this." Mrs. Markham tapped the box. "It pays well."

Willie ate his cake and drank the milk. When he was done, he took care to wipe the crumbs off his face as well as to blot the milk moustache with the napkin.

His mother said, "Now go on and do your homework. You're in fifth grade. It's important."

Willie gathered up his books that lay on the empty third chair. At the kitchen entrance he paused. "What *kind* of unhappiness does he have?"

"Who's that?"

"That man."

Mrs. Markham looked puzzled.

"The begging man. The one on the street."

"Could be anything," his mother said, vaguely. "A person can be unhappy for many reasons."

"Like what?"

"Willie . . ."

"Is it a doctor kind of sickness? A sickness you can cure?"

"I wish you wouldn't ask such questions."

"Why?"

"Questions that have no answers shouldn't be asked."

"Can I go out?"

"Homework first."

Willie turned to go.

"Money," Mrs. Markham suddenly said. "Money will cure a lot of unhappiness. That's why that man was begging.

A salesperson once said to me, 'Maybe you can't buy happiness, but you can rent a lot of it.' You should remember that." ❶

📖 **INFER**

❶ Why do you think Mrs. Markham is so concerned about money?

The apartment had three rooms. The walls were painted mint green. Willie walked down the hallway to his room, which was at the front of the building. By climbing up on the windowsill and pressing against the glass, he could see the sidewalk five stories below. The man was still there.

It was almost five when he went to tell his mother he had finished his school assignments. She was not there. He found her in her bedroom, sleeping. Since she had begun working the night shift at a convenience store—two weeks now—she took naps in the late afternoon.

For a while Willie stood on the threshold,[1] hoping his mother would wake up. When she didn't, he went to the front room and looked down on the street again. The begging man had not moved.

"Questions that have no answers shouldn't be asked."

---

1. **threshold** (thresh'ōld') *n.*: entrance.

Vocabulary

vaguely (vāg'lē) *adv.*: not clearly or definitely; in a general way.

Willie returned to his mother's room.

"I'm going out," he announced softly.

Willie waited a decent interval[2] for his mother to waken. When she did not, Willie made sure his keys were in his pocket. Then he left the apartment.

Standing just outside his door, he could keep his eyes on the man. It appeared as if he had still not moved. Willie wondered how anyone could go on without moving for so long in the chilly October air. Was staying in one place part of the man's sickness?

During the twenty minutes that Willie watched, no one who passed looked in the beggar's direction. Willie wondered if they even saw the man. Certainly no one put any money into his open hand.

A lady leading a dog by a leash went by. The dog strained in the direction of the man sitting on the crate. The dog's tail wagged. The lady pulled the dog away. "Heel!" she commanded.

The dog—tail between its legs—scampered to the lady's side. Even so, the dog twisted around to look back at the beggar.

Willie grinned. The dog had done exactly what he had done when his mother told him not to stare.

Pressing deep into his pocket, Willie found a nickel. It was warm and slippery. He wondered how much happiness you could rent for a nickel.

Squeezing the nickel between his fingers, Willie walked slowly toward the man. When he came before him, he stopped, suddenly nervous. The man, who appeared to be looking at the ground, did not move his eyes. He smelled bad.

"Here." Willie stretched forward and

dropped the coin into the man's open right hand.

"Bless you," the man said hoarsely, as he folded his fingers over the coin. His eyes, like high beams on a car, flashed up at Willie, then dropped.

Willie waited for a moment, then went back up to his room. From his front room he looked down on the street. He thought he saw the coin in the man's hand but was not sure.

After supper Mrs. Markham got ready to go to work. She kissed Willie good night. Then, as she did every night, she said, "If you have regular problems, call Mrs. Murphy downstairs. What's her number?"

"274–8676," Willie said.

"Extra bad problems, call Grandma."

"369–6754."

"Super-special problems, you can call me."

"962–6743."

"Emergency, the police."

"911."

"Don't let anyone in the door."

"I won't."

"No television past nine."

"I know."

"But you can read late."

"You're the one who's going to be late," Willie said.

"I'm leaving," Mrs. Markham said.

After she went, Willie stood for a long while in the hallway. The

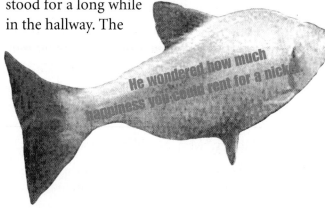

He wondered how much happiness you could rent for a nickel

---

2. **interval** *n.:* period of time between two events.

empty apartment felt like a cave that lay deep below the earth. That day in school Willie's teacher had told them about a kind of fish that lived in caves. These fish could not see. They had no eyes. The teacher had said it was living in the dark cave that made them like that.

Before he went to bed, Willie took another look out the window. In the pool of light cast by the street lamp, Willie saw the man.

On Tuesday morning when Willie went to school, the man was gone. But when he came home from school with his mother, he was there again.

"*Please* don't look at him," his mother whispered with some urgency.

During his snack Willie said, "Why shouldn't I look?"

"What are you talking about?"

"That man. On the street. Begging."

"I told you. He's sick. It's better to act as if you never saw them. When people are that way, they don't wish to be looked at."

"Why not?"

Mrs. Markham thought for a while. "People are ashamed of being unhappy."

"Are you sure he's unhappy?"

"You don't have to ask if people are unhappy. They tell you all the time."

"Is that part of the sickness?"

"Oh, Willie, I don't know. It's just the way they are."

Willie contemplated the half-inch slice of cake his mother had just given him. He said, "Ever since Dad left, you've been unhappy. Are you ashamed?"

Mrs. Markham closed her eyes. "I wish you wouldn't ask that."

Willie said, "Are you?"

"Willie . . ."

"Think he might come back?"

"It's more than likely," Mrs. Markham said, but Willie wondered if that was what she really thought. He did not think so. "Do you think Dad is unhappy?"

"Where do you get such questions?"

"They're in my mind."

"There's much in the mind that need not be paid attention to."

"Fish that live in caves have no eyes."

"What are you talking about?"

"My teacher said it's all that darkness. The fish forget to see. So they lose their eyes." ❷ 🐟

"I doubt she said that."

"She did."

"Willie, you have too much imagination."

After his mother went to work, Willie gazed down onto the street. The man was there. Willie thought of going down, but he knew he was not supposed to leave the building when his mother worked at night. He decided to speak to the man tomorrow.

Next afternoon—Wednesday—Willie said to the man, "I don't have any money. Can I still talk to you?"

The man's eyes focused on Willie. They were gray eyes with folds of dirty skin beneath them. He needed a shave.

"My mother said you were unhappy. Is that true?"

"Could be," the man said.

"What are you unhappy about?"

> **🐟 INFER**
> ❷ What might the fish stand for? What might the missing eyes and the darkness symbolize?

Vocabulary
urgency (ʉr′jən·sē) *n.:* pressure; insistence.
contemplated (kän′təm·plāt′id) *v.:* studied carefully.

The man's eyes narrowed as he studied Willie intently. He said, "How come you want to know?"

Willie shrugged.

"I think you should go home, kid."

"I am home." Willie gestured toward the apartment. "I live right here. Fifth floor. Where do you live?"

"Around."

"*Are* you unhappy?" Willie persisted.

The man ran a tongue over his lips. His Adam's apple bobbed.

Willie said, "I'm trying to learn about unhappiness."

"Why?"

"I don't think I want to say."

"A man has the right to remain silent," the man said and closed his eyes.

Willie remained standing on the pavement for a while before walking back to his apartment. Once inside his own room, he looked down from the window. The man was still there. At one moment Willie was certain he was looking at the apartment building and the floor on which Willie lived.

The next day—Thursday—after dropping a nickel in the man's palm, Willie said, "I've decided to tell you why I want to learn about unhappiness."

The man gave a grunt.

"See, I've never seen anyone look so unhappy as you do. So I figure you must know a lot about it."

The man took a deep breath. "Well, yeah, maybe."

Willie said, "And I need to find a cure for it."

"A *what*?"

"A cure for unhappiness."

The man pursed his lips and blew a silent whistle. Then he said, "Why?"

"My mother is unhappy."

"Why's that?"

"My dad left."

"How come?"

"I don't know. But she's unhappy all the time. So if I found a cure for unhappiness, it would be a good thing, wouldn't it?"

"I suppose."

Willie said, "Would you like some cake?"

"What kind?"

"I don't know. Cake."

"Depends on the cake."

On Friday Willie said to the man, "I found out what kind of cake it is."

"Yeah?"

"Poundcake. But I don't know why it's called that."

"Probably doesn't matter."

For a moment neither said anything. Then Willie said, "In school my teacher said there are fish that live in caves and the caves are dark, so the fish don't have eyes. What do you think? Do you believe that?"

"Sure."

"You do? How come?"

"Because you said so."

"You mean, just because someone *said* it you believe it?"

"Not someone. You."

Willie said, "But, well, maybe it *isn't* true."

The man grunted. "Hey, do you believe it?"

Willie nodded.

"Well, you're not just anyone. You got eyes. You see. You ain't no fish." ❸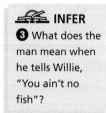

INFER

❸ What does the man mean when he tells Willie, "You ain't no fish"?

Vocabulary

intently (in·tent′lē) *adv.:* with close attention.

"Oh."

"What's your name?"

"Willie."

"That's a boy's name. What's your grown-up name?"

Willie thought for a moment. "William, I guess."

"And that means another thing." ❹

📖 **INFER**

❹ Why does the man ask Willie what his "grown-up" name is?

"What?"

"I'll take some of that cake."

Willie smiled. "You will?"

"Just said it, didn't I?"

"I'll get it."

Willie ran to the apartment. He took the box from the refrigerator as well as a knife, then hurried back down to the street. "I'll cut you a piece," he said.

As the man looked on, Willie opened the box, then held his thumb against the cake to make sure the portion was the right size. With a poke of the knife he made a small mark for the proper width.

Just as he was about to cut, the man said, "Hold it!"

Willie looked up. "What?"

"What were you doing with your thumb there?"

"I was measuring the right size. The right portion. One portion is what a person is supposed to get."

"Where'd you learn that?"

"It says so on the box. You can see for yourself." He held out the box.

The man studied the box, then handed it back to Willie. "That's just lies," he said.

"How do you know?"

"William, how can a box say how much a person needs?"

"But it does. The scientists say so. They measured, so they know. Then they put it there."

"Lies," the man repeated.

Willie studied the man. His eyes seemed bleary.[3] "Then how much should I cut?" he asked.

The man said, "You have to look at me, then at the cake, and then you're going to have to decide for yourself."

"Oh." Willie looked at the cake. The piece was about three inches wide. Willie looked up at the man. After a moment he cut the cake into two pieces, each an inch and a half wide. He gave one piece to the man and kept the other.

"Bless you," the man said, as he took the piece and laid it in his left hand. He began to break off pieces with his right hand and one by one put them into his mouth. Each piece was chewed thoughtfully. Willie watched him piece by piece.

When the man was done, he dusted his hands of crumbs.

"Now I'll give you something," the man said.

"What?" Willie said, surprised.

"The cure for unhappiness."

"You know it?" Willie asked, eyes wide.

The man nodded.

"What is it?"

"It's this: What a person needs is always more than they say."

Willie thought for a while. "Who's *they*?" he asked.

---

3. **bleary** *adj.:* dim or blurred, as from lack of rest.

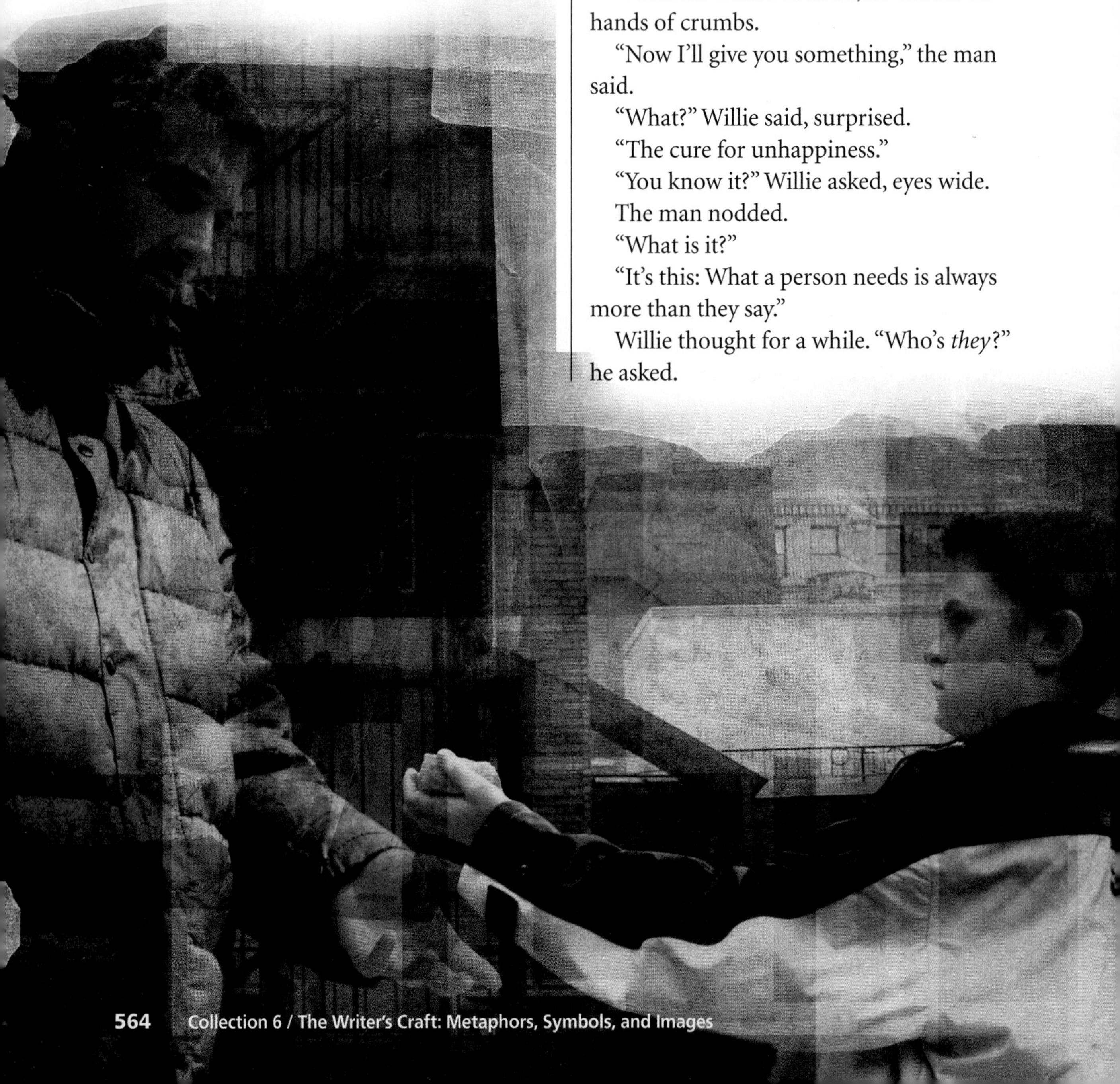

The man pointed to the cake box. "The people on the box," he said.

Willie thought for a moment; then he gave the man the other piece of cake. ❻

INFER
❺ Why does Willie give the man both pieces of cake? What might the cake symbolize?

The man took it, saying, "Good man," and then ate it.

The next day was Saturday. Willie did not go to school. All morning he kept looking down from his window for the man, but it was raining and he did not appear. Willie wondered where he was but could not imagine it.

Willie's mother woke about noon. Willie sat with her while she ate the breakfast he had made. "I found the cure for unhappiness," he announced.

"Did you?" his mother said. She was reading a memo from the convenience store's owner.

"It's, 'What a person needs is always more than they say.'"

His mother put her papers down. "That's nonsense. Where did you hear that?"

"That man."

"What man?"

"On the street. The one who was begging. You said he was unhappy. So I asked him."

"Willie, I told you I didn't want you to even look at that man."

"He's a nice man . . ."

"How do you know?"

"I've talked to him."

"When? How much?"

Willie shrank down. "I did, that's all."

"Willie, I forbid you to talk to him. Do you understand me? Do you? Answer me!"

"Yes," Willie said, but in his mind he decided he would talk to the man one more time. He needed to explain why he could not talk to him anymore.

On Sunday, however, the man was not there. Nor was he there on Monday.

"That man is gone," Willie said to his mother as they walked home from school.

"I saw. I'm not blind."

"Where do you think he went?"

"I couldn't care less. And you might as well know, I arranged for him to be gone."

Willie stopped short. "What do you mean?"

"I called the police. We don't need a nuisance like that around here. Pestering kids."

"He wasn't pestering me."

"Of course he was."

"How do you know?"

"Willie, I have eyes. I can see."

Willie stared at his mother. "No, you can't. You're a fish. You live in a cave." ❻

INFER
❻ Is Willie being fair when he tells his mother that she's a fish living in a cave? Why or why not?

"Willie, don't talk nonsense."

"My name isn't Willie. It's William." Turning, he walked back to the school playground.

Mrs. Markham watched him go. "Fish," she wondered to herself; "what do fish have to do with anything?"

Meet the Writer

Avi

"Don't Be Satisfied with Answers Others Give You"

Avi (1937–   ) says he became a writer out of sheer stubbornness. In elementary school and high school, he failed many subjects, not knowing at the time that he had a serious learning disability. Still, he was determined to prove to everyone that he could write if he just set his mind to it. First he tried to write plays, then novels for adults, but he had little success. He didn't discover his true audience until he became a father and began taking an interest in writing for children and young adults.

> " Only when my own kids came into my life did I start to write for young people. I was to find what I did best. Writing for kids has been at the center of my life ever since. "

Avi offers the following advice to young people thinking of becoming writers:

> " Listen and watch the world around you. Try to understand why things happen. Don't be satisfied with answers others give you. Don't assume that because everyone believes a thing, it is right *or* wrong. Reason things out for yourself. Work to get answers on your own. "

For Independent Reading

Avi has written many novels about strong-willed young people making tough decisions in challenging or dangerous situations. These include *Wolf Rider: A Tale of Terror; Windcatcher;* and *The True Confessions of Charlotte Doyle,* a Newbery Honor Book and the winner of the Boston Globe–Horn Book Award for fiction in 1991 (this title is available in the HRW Library).

First Thoughts

1. How did you feel when you learned that Mrs. Markham had called the police?

Thinking Critically

2. **Summarize** the conversation Willie has with the homeless man about the right amount of cake to serve a person. What do you think the man is trying to say to Willie?

3. Look back at the statements you rated on page 556. Where are they expressed in the story? How has reading the story affected the way you look at the statements? 🖊️

4. Avi mentions fish many times in this story. What do the fish **symbolize**? (Think about the **inferences** you made as you read.)

5. Who says, "What do fish have to do with anything?" Do you think the quotation makes a good title for the story? Explain. How does the title relate to the story's theme?

Extending Interpretations

6. Why do you think Willie wants to be called William at the end? What does this show about the way his **character** has grown and changed during the story?

7. On page 566, Avi says, "Don't be satisfied with answers others give you. Don't assume that because everyone believes a thing, it is right *or* wrong. Reason things out for yourself. Work to get answers on your own." Is Avi's advice good, or could it lead to trouble?

SPEAKING AND LISTENING

Debating Pros and Cons

In some cities, people can be arrested for begging on the street. Is this fair? With a few classmates, hold a debate on this question. Form two teams—one to argue that it is fair and one to argue that it's not. With your team, do research at the library or on the Internet to find evidence supporting your point of view.

Reading Check

a. What does Willie do when Mrs. Markham tells him not to look at the homeless man?

b. Why does Mrs. Markham refuse to give the man money?

c. According to Willie's teacher, why did the fish in the cave lose their eyes?

d. What does Willie give the man?

e. What happens to the man at the end of the story?

INTERNET
Projects and Activities
Keyword: LE5 6-6

SKILLS FOCUS

Literary Skills
Analyze the use of symbolism.

Reading Skills
Make inferences.

Speaking and Listening Skills
Research an issue and hold a debate.

North Carolina Competency Goal
1.02; 1.03; 1.04; 4.01; 4.02; 5.01; 5.02

What Do Fish Have to Do with Anything? 567

Identifying Antonyms

Antonyms are words with opposite meanings. *Hot* and *cold* are antonyms; so are *kind* and *cruel, generous* and *selfish, wisely* and *foolishly.* Thinking of a word's antonyms can sometimes help you pinpoint its meaning.

PRACTICE

Complete each of the following sentences with the word from the Word Bank that is the antonym of the underlined word.

1. Someone who speaks clearly is not speaking _____.
2. Someone who ignored an issue would be the opposite of someone who _____ it.
3. If you spoke carelessly or lightly about your plans, you would be the opposite of someone who spoke _____ about them.
4. The opposite of *indifference* or *unconcern* is _____.

> **Word Bank**
>
> vaguely
> urgency
> contemplated
> intently

Grammar Link

Direct and Indirect Quotations

In the story, Willie has several conversations with his mother and with the homeless man. The exact words of those talks, called **direct quotations,** are put in quotation marks.

> Willie said, "Would you like some cake?"

Sometimes, instead of quoting someone's exact words, Avi summarizes what the person said. These summaries, called **indirect quotations,** are not placed in quotation marks.

> That day in school Willie's teacher had told them about a kind of fish that lived in caves. These fish could not see. They had no eyes. The teacher had said it was living in the dark cave that made them like that.

PRACTICE

1. Find three direct quotations in the story, and rewrite them as indirect quotations.
2. Look at the indirect quotation at the left. Rewrite it as a direct quotation, using the exact words Willie's teacher might have used. Remember to put her words in quotation marks.

For more help, see Quotation Marks, 13b–k, in the Language Handbook.

Making Assertions About a Text

Reading Focus
Assertions and Citations

An **assertion** is a statement or claim. **Citations** are items of evidence from a text used to back up an assertion. Making assertions about a text is easy if you follow these steps:

- Think about the facts presented in the text.

- Put the information together, and think about what it all means.

- Use evidence from the text to make an assertion.

- Evaluate your assertion by asking yourself how well evidence from the text supports it.

In the fictional story you just read, a boy tries to help a hungry homeless man. The article you're about to read tells what a real-life Florida student named David Levitt did to fight hunger.

■ After you read the article, make a graphic organizer like the one below, showing your assertions about the text and the citations you used to support them.

"Getting Leftovers Back on the Table"

Citation
Twenty percent of the food produced in the United States goes to waste.

Citation
Millions of Americans go to sleep hungry.

Assertion
David Levitt was troubled by two big problems.

INTERNET
Interactive Reading Model
Keyword: LE5 6-6

SKILLS FOCUS

Reading Skills
Understand assertions and supporting citations.

North Carolina Competency Goal
4.01; 4.03; 5.01; 5.02

Getting Leftovers Back on the Table **569**

Getting Leftovers Back on the Table

When you're standing in line in the school cafeteria, do you ever wonder what happens to all the food that doesn't get served? Every day, giant bins behind the cafeterias—and supermarkets, restaurants, and bakeries—fill up with discarded food. As much as 20 percent of the food produced in the United States goes to waste. Yet every night millions of Americans go to sleep hungry.

Too big a problem for one kid to tackle? A sixth-grader named David Levitt didn't think so. He started small, in the halls of his own Florida middle school. By the time he was in his first year of high school, his crusade against hunger had taken him all the way to the White House.

Getting Started

David's journey began the day he noticed how much food was thrown out in his school cafeteria. He stopped the principal in the hallway and asked why the school couldn't donate leftover lunches to local homeless shelters and soup kitchens.

The principal told him that several parents had had the same idea. School rules prohibited serving the same food twice, however, so uneaten lunches had to be thrown away.

Overcoming Odds

David wasn't discouraged. He did research on a group in Kentucky that picked up leftovers from restaurants and donated them to charities. He used what he learned to draw up a plan for his own program.

Then he presented it at a meeting of the county school board. The board approved David's plan—not just for his school, but for all ninety-two schools in the county. "It just took a kid to make them see this matters," David says.

Solving New Problems

The battle wasn't over yet. Conditions set by the state department of health had to be met. For example, donated food had to be packed in special containers—which the schools didn't have the money to buy. So David wrote to manufacturers and asked for donations. Soon cases of the containers arrived at his doorstep, and David, now in seventh grade, was able to make his first delivery to a local food bank. "That," he says, "was satisfaction."

Success at Last

David went on to enlist the support of restaurants, supermarkets, and caterers. After two years his program had brought a quarter of a million pounds of food to hungry people in his area. By the time he started high school, David and his older sister were at work on a proposal to be presented to their state legislature. Under the plan similar programs would be set up to bring leftover food to hungry people all over Florida.

That spring, David went to Washington, D.C., to receive an award for his efforts. As the First Lady presented him with his medal, he asked her, "What do you do with the White House leftovers?"

—Mara Rockliff

Analyzing Assertions About an Article

Getting Leftovers Back on the Table

Test Practice

1. The information in this article supports the **assertion** that —
   A it is impossible to solve the problem of hunger
   B one person can make a big difference
   C it is difficult to persuade a school board to take action
   D researching other programs won't help you plan your own

2. Which of the following **facts** is *not* mentioned in the article?
   F Twenty percent of food produced in the United States goes to waste.
   G Millions of Americans go to sleep hungry.
   H The Florida state health department has established rules for donating food.
   J In some countries, hunger is an even bigger problem than in the United States.

3. We can reasonably **assert** that —
   A David Levitt isn't easily discouraged
   B things always go easy for David Levitt
   C David Levitt is popular at school
   D David Levitt gets good grades

4. After David's plan was approved by the school board, he did all of the following things *except* —
   F persuade manufacturers to donate containers
   G learn how to donate food in accordance with the state health department's guidelines
   H ask restaurants and supermarkets for help
   J send a proposal to Congress

Constructed Response

1. What plan did David present to the school board?

2. Describe two problems David faced in putting his plan into effect.

3. What did David ask the First Lady when she gave him his medal?

4. Make two or three **assertions** about the information in this text. Fill out a graphic organizer like the one on page 569 for each assertion. Use **citations** from the text to support your assertions.

North Carolina Competency Goal
1.04; 2.01; 4.01; 4.02; 5.01

SKILLS FOCUS

Reading Skills
Make assertions, or claims, about a text.

Connotations and Denotations: Shades of Meaning

Why do we call the president's wife the *First Lady* instead of the *First Woman*? *Woman* and *lady* have similar **denotations,** or dictionary meanings, but different connotations.

Connotations are the feelings and ideas that have become attached to certain words. Both *woman* and *lady* refer to a female adult, but *lady* suggests one who is in a high position (as in *First Lady*) or one who is refined and well-mannered.

A word's connotations can be positive or negative. A word with positive connotations calls up good associations; a word with negative connotations calls up bad associations.

"I am careful; you are thrifty; he is stingy": This old saying shows how words with related meanings can have very different connotations.

PRACTICE 1

Listed below are five words with negative connotations. For each one, think of another word with the same general meaning but with more positive connotations. You may want to use a dictionary or a thesaurus.

1. scrawny	**3.** old	**5.** cheap
2. fat	**4.** smelly	

North Carolina Competency Goal
2.01; 6.01

PRACTICE 2

Usually people agree on a word's **connotations,** but sometimes words suggest different things to different people. Look at the six words listed below. Name at least two things you associate with each word. Then, compare your list with your classmates' lists. Which do you agree on? Which do you disagree on?

1. gold	**3.** wolf	**5.** politician
2. green	**4.** lamb	**6.** volunteer

SKILLS FOCUS

Vocabulary Skills
Analyze connotations.

Eleven

Make the Connection

We all have different opinions about what is embarrassing. With a group, make a list of embarrassing situations you've faced, seen on television, or read about in a story. Then, rank each situation on a scale from 1 to 4, 1 being slightly embarrassing and 4 being "crawl under a rock" embarrassing.

Quickwrite

Jot down answers to the following questions:

- What do you do when you're embarrassed?
- Have you ever seen anybody get embarrassed in front of a group of people?

Literary Focus
Imagery:
It Appeals to Your Senses

Imagery is language that appeals to the senses: sight, hearing, smell, taste, and touch. Writers use images to create pictures of things they've experienced or imagined. They search for just the right words to create the same pictures in our minds. In "Eleven," Sandra Cisneros creates an image of a red sweater that is hard to forget.

Reading Skills
Making Inferences

An **inference** is a kind of guess. When you **make inferences** as you read, you look for clues; then you guess what will happen next and what it all means. You base your inferences on your own experiences and combine that information with clues you find in the story. See what inferences you make as you read this story. (This is one guessing game you can't lose, since you're an expert at being eleven.)

North Carolina Competency Goal
1.04; 4.01; 5.01; 5.02

INTERNET
More About Cisneros
Keyword: LE5 6-6

SKILLS FOCUS

Literary Skills
Identify imagery in fiction.

Reading Skills
Make inferences.

Eleven

Sandra Cisneros

What they don't understand about birthdays and what they never tell you is that when you're eleven, you're also ten, and nine, and eight, and seven, and six, and five, and four, and three, and two, and one. And when you wake up on your eleventh birthday you expect to feel eleven, but you don't. You open your eyes and everything's just like yesterday, only it's today. And you don't feel eleven at all. You feel like you're still ten. And you are—underneath the year that makes you eleven.

Like some days you might say something stupid, and that's the part of you that's still ten. Or maybe some days you might need to sit on your mama's lap because you're scared, and that's the part of you that's five. And maybe one day when you're all grown up maybe you will need to cry like if you're three, and that's okay. That's what I tell Mama when she's sad and needs to cry. Maybe she's feeling three.

Because the way you grow old is kind of like an onion or like the rings inside a tree trunk or like my little wooden dolls that fit one inside the other, each year inside the next one. That's how being eleven years old is.

You don't feel eleven. Not right away. It takes a few days, weeks even, sometimes even months before you say Eleven when they ask you. And you don't feel smart eleven, not until you're almost twelve. That's the way it is.

Only today I wish I didn't have only eleven years rattling inside me like pennies in a tin Band-Aid box. Today I wish I was one hundred and two instead of eleven because if I was one hundred and two I'd have known what to say when Mrs. Price put the red sweater on my desk. I would've known how to tell her it wasn't mine instead of just sitting there with that look on my face and nothing coming out of my mouth.

"Whose is this?" Mrs. Price says, and she holds the red sweater up in the air for all the class to see. "Whose? It's been sitting in the coatroom for a month."

"Not mine," says everybody. "Not me."

"It has to belong to somebody," Mrs. Price keeps saying, but nobody can remember. It's an ugly sweater with red plastic buttons and

Girl Seated at Table by Rosa Ibarra.

a collar and sleeves all stretched out like you could use it for a jump-rope. It's maybe a thousand years old and even if it belonged to me I wouldn't say so.

Maybe because I'm skinny, maybe because she doesn't like me, that stupid Sylvia Saldívar says, "I think it belongs to Rachel." An ugly sweater like that, all raggedy and old, but Mrs. Price believes her. Mrs. Price takes the sweater and puts it right on my desk, but when I open my mouth nothing comes out.

"That's not, I don't, you're not . . . Not mine," I finally say in a little voice that was maybe me when I was four.

"Of course it's yours," Mrs. Price says.

"I remember you wearing it once." Because she's older and the teacher, she's right and I'm not.

Not mine, not mine, not mine, but Mrs. Price is already turning to page thirty-two, and math problem number four. I don't know why but all of a sudden I'm feeling sick inside, like the part of me that's three wants to come out of my eyes, only I squeeze them shut tight and bite down on my teeth real hard and try to remember today I am eleven, eleven. Mama is making a cake for me for tonight, and when Papa comes home everybody will sing Happy birthday, happy birthday to you.

But when the sick feeling goes away and I open my eyes, the red sweater's still sitting there like a big red mountain. I move the red sweater to the corner of my desk with my ruler. I move my pencil and books and eraser as far from it as possible. I even move my chair a little to the right. Not mine, not mine, not mine.

In my head I'm thinking how long till lunchtime, how long till I can take the red sweater and throw it over the schoolyard fence, or leave it hanging on a parking meter, or bunch it up into a little ball and toss it in the alley. Except when math period ends Mrs. Price says loud and in front of everybody, "Now, Rachel, that's enough," because she sees I've shoved the red sweater to the tippy-tip corner of my desk and it's hanging all over the edge like a waterfall, but I don't care.

"Rachel," Mrs. Price says. She says it like she's getting mad. "You put that sweater on right now and no more nonsense."

"But it's not—"

"Now!" Mrs. Price says.

This is when I wish I wasn't eleven, because all the years inside of me—ten, nine, eight, seven, six, five, four, three, two, and one—are pushing at the back of my eyes when I put one arm through one sleeve of the sweater that smells like cottage cheese, and then the other arm through the other and stand there with my arms apart like if the sweater hurts me and it does, all itchy and full of germs that aren't even mine.

That's when everything I've been holding in since this morning, since when Mrs. Price put the sweater on my desk, finally lets go, and all of a sudden I'm crying in front of everybody. I wish I was invisible but I'm not. I'm eleven and it's my birthday today and I'm crying like I'm three in front of everybody. I put my head down on the desk and bury my face in my stupid clown-sweater arms. My face all hot and spit coming out of my mouth because I can't stop the little animal noises from coming out of me, until there aren't any more tears left in my eyes, and it's just my body shaking like when you have the hiccups and my whole head hurts like when you drink milk too fast.

But the worst part is right before the bell rings for lunch. That stupid Phyllis Lopez, who is even dumber than Sylvia Saldívar, says she remembers the red sweater is hers! I take it off right away and give it to her, only Mrs. Price pretends like everything's okay.

Today I'm eleven. There's a cake Mama's making for tonight, and when Papa comes home from work we'll eat it. There'll be candles and presents and everybody will sing Happy birthday, happy birthday to you, Rachel, only it's too late.

I'm eleven today. I'm eleven, ten, nine, eight, seven, six, five, four, three, two, and one, but I wish I was one hundred and two. I wish I was anything but eleven, because I want today to be far away already, far away like a runaway balloon, like a tiny *o* in the sky, so tiny-tiny you have to close your eyes to see it.

Meet the Writer

Sandra Cisneros

"Inside I'm Eleven"

Sandra Cisneros (1954–   ) was born in Chicago and grew up speaking Spanish and English. Although she sometimes had a hard time in school, she eventually became a teacher and a highly acclaimed writer. Her childhood experiences, her family, and her Mexican American heritage all find a place in her writing.

In much of her writing, Cisneros explores the feeling of being shy and out of place.

> **❝** What would my teachers say if they knew I was a writer? Who would've guessed it? I wasn't a very bright student. I didn't much like school because we moved so much and I was always new and funny-looking. . . . At home I was fine, but at school I never opened my mouth except when the teacher called on me, the first time I'd speak all day.
>
> When I think how I see myself, I would have to be at age eleven. I know I'm older on the outside, but inside I'm eleven. I'm the girl in the picture with skinny arms and a crumpled shirt and crooked hair. I didn't like school because all they saw was the outside of me. **❞**

For Independent Reading

Another memorable Cisneros character narrates the novel *The House on Mango Street*. Esperanza is a young girl who wishes for a lot of things in her life, including a new name: Zeze the X.

First Thoughts

1. If you were Rachel, what would you have done when Mrs. Price said, "You put that sweater on right now"? Be sure to look back at your Quickwrite notes.

Thinking Critically

2. Rachel says that "when you're eleven, you're also ten, and nine," and so on (page 574). What does she mean?

3. What assumptions does Mrs. Price seem to make about Rachel?

4. At the end of the story, Rachel says that "everybody will sing Happy birthday, . . . only it's too late" (page 576). What **inference** can you make about her from this statement?

5. List all the **images** in the story that help you see—and even smell and feel—the hated red sweater. Does Cisneros succeed in making the sweater seem real? Why or why not?

Extending Interpretations

6. How did you react to the scene in which Rachel begins to cry in class (page 576)? If you were in her class, would you have done anything? Why or why not?

7. Find the **images** and **metaphors** that Cisneros uses to describe getting older—rings in a tree trunk, layers of an onion, and so forth. Which do you think are the most interesting or accurate descriptions of growing up? Do you think any of these images are not effective? Explain.

WRITING

Writing a Short Story

"Eleven" is told from the first-person point of view, with Rachel as the narrator. She uses the words *I, me,* and *mine* as she describes her experience with the red sweater. What might Mrs. Price say about the incident? How might another student in the class describe it? Rewrite the story, using a different first-person narrator. Try to include images in your retelling. Is the red sweater as ugly as Rachel thinks it is?

Reading Check

a. How old is Rachel in this story? Why does she say she wants to be 102?

b. At the beginning of the story, Rachel says that you're acting younger than eleven when you do certain things. Make a list of the things she mentions.

c. Briefly describe what happens to Rachel after Mrs. Price asks, "Whose is this?"

North Carolina Competency Goal
1.01; 5.01; 5.02

INTERNET

Projects and Activities
Keyword: LE5 6-6

SKILLS FOCUS

Literary Skills
Analyze the use of imagery in fiction.

Reading Skills
Make inferences.

Writing Skills
Write a short story from the first-person point of view.

After You Read · Vocabulary Development

Connotations: Words Are Loaded with Feelings

A word's **connotations** are the feelings and associations that have come to be attached to the word. For example, Rachel calls the red sweater "ugly." Someone who didn't hate the sweater so much might just say it was "unattractive" or "plain." *Ugly* is a strong word with extremely negative connotations.

PRACTICE

Think about *skinny,* a word Rachel uses to describe herself. The words in the box at the right mean more or less the same thing as *skinny.* Which words have positive connotations? Which have negative connotations? Put the words in order, starting with the one whose connotations seem the most negative and ending with the one whose connotations seem the most positive.

> slim
> slender
> bony
> scrawny
> lean

Grammar Link

Punctuating Dialogue

Follow these tips when you write dialogue:

- Put quotation marks before and after a **direct quotation**— a person's exact words.

  > "Whose is this?" said Mrs. Price.

- A **speaker tag** is a phrase, such as *he said,* that identifies the speaker. If a speaker tag comes before a quotation, put a comma after the tag. If a speaker tag interrupts a sentence, put commas before and after the tag.

  > Mrs. Price said, "Put it on now."

  > "Rachel," she said, "put it on now."

- If a speaker tag follows a quotation, insert a comma, question mark, or exclamation point before the ending quotation mark. Never use a period before a speaker tag.

  > "Whose sweater is this?" she asked.

  > "Not mine," said everyone.

- Always begin a quotation with a capital letter.

  > Mrs. Price said, "Put it on now."

North Carolina Competency Goal
5.01; 5.02; 6.01

PRACTICE

Find a piece of your own writing that contains dialogue, and check the punctuation. If you've made mistakes punctuating the dialogue, copy the example sentences at the left. Refer to them when you proofread your writing.

For more help, see Quotation Marks, 13b–k, in the Language Handbook.

SKILLS FOCUS

Vocabulary Skills
Explain connotations.

Grammar Skills
Punctuate dialogue.

Comparing Literature

Literary Focus
Irony

Irony is a contrast between expectation and reality. It's the difference between what's supposed to happen and what really does happen or between what you say and what you mean.

Irony is used in literature for all kinds of effects, from humor to serious comments on the unpredictable nature of life. A humorous example of irony is found in these lines from a poem called "The Crocodile" by Lewis Carroll:

> How cheerfully he seems to grin,
>> How neatly spreads his claws,
> And welcomes little fishes in
>> With gently smiling jaws!

This speaker says one thing but really means something else. He says the crocodile "welcomes" fish into his "gently smiling jaws." He really means that the crocodile is eating the fish and that his massive, toothy jaws are anything but gentle.

More Examples of Irony

- Someone named Einstein fails a math test.
- It rains on the day some weather forecasters have scheduled a picnic.
- A firefighter's son starts a forest fire.
- Someone walks out in the middle of a hurricane and says, "Nice day."
- A famous fashion designer is seen wearing old, stained, and ripped clothes.
- An animal doctor is allergic to dogs and cats.

Reading Skills
Comparing and Contrasting

You're about to read and compare two stories that deal with the relationship between humans and machines. The stories use irony, both to create humor and to make a point about life. As you read, watch for similarities and differences between the stories.

North Carolina Competency Goal
1.02

SKILLS FOCUS

Literary Skills
Understand irony.

Reading Skills
Compare and contrast texts.

Before You Read

This science fiction story was written in 1951, before computers became common teaching tools. In "The Fun They Had," Asimov imagines life two hundred years in the future. Have any of Asimov's predictions come true so far? How do *you* predict computers will be used in the classroom by the year 2155? Will there even be classrooms?

The Fun They Had

Isaac Asimov

"Today Tommy found a real book!"

Margie even wrote about it that night in her diary. On the page headed May 17, 2155, she wrote, "Today Tommy found a real book!"

❶ What surprises Margie and Tommy about the old book? How are Margie and Tommy accustomed to reading?

❷ Use details from what you have read so far to describe a telebook.

❸ How does Margie's mechanical teacher compare with a human teacher? List some similarities and differences.

It was a very old book. Margie's grandfather once said that when he was a little boy, *his* grandfather told him that there was a time when all stories were printed on paper.

They turned the pages, which were yellow and crinkly, and it was awfully funny to read words that stood still instead of moving the way they were supposed to—on a screen, you know. And then, when they turned back to the page before, it had the same words on it that it had had when they read it the first time. ❶

"Gee," said Tommy, "what a waste. When you're through with the book, you just throw it away, I guess. Our television screen must have had a million books on it and it's good for plenty more. I wouldn't throw *it* away."

"Same with mine," said Margie. She was eleven and hadn't seen as many telebooks as Tommy had. He was thirteen. ❷

She said, "Where did you find it?"

"In my house." He pointed without looking, because he was busy reading. "In the attic."

"What's it about?"

"School."

Margie was scornful. "School? What's there to write about school? I hate school." Margie always hated school, but now she hated it more than ever. The mechanical teacher had been giving her test after test in geography, and she had been doing worse and worse until her mother had shaken her head sorrowfully and sent for the county inspector.

He was a round little man with a red face and a whole box of tools with dials and wires. He smiled at her and gave her an apple, then took the teacher apart. Margie had hoped he wouldn't know how to put it together again, but he knew how all right, and after an hour or so, there it was again, large and ugly, with a big screen on which all the lessons were shown and the questions were asked. That wasn't so bad. The part she hated most was the slot where she had to put homework and test papers. She always had to write them out in a punch code they made her learn when she was six years old, and the mechanical teacher calculated the mark in no time. ❸

The inspector had smiled after he was finished and patted her head. He said to her mother, "It's not the little girl's fault, Mrs. Jones. I think the geography sector was geared a little too quick. Those things happen sometimes. I've slowed it up to an average

ten-year level. Actually, the overall pattern of her progress is quite satisfactory." And he patted Margie's head again.

Margie was disappointed. She had been hoping they would take the teacher away altogether. They had once taken Tommy's teacher

Today's arithmetic lesson
is on the addition of
proper fractions.
Please insert yesterday's
homework in the
proper slot.

away for nearly a month because the history sector had blanked out completely.

So she said to Tommy, "Why would anyone write about school?"

Tommy looked at her with very superior eyes. "Because it's not our kind of school, stupid. This is the old kind of school that they

had hundreds and hundreds of years ago." He added loftily, pronouncing the word carefully, "*Centuries* ago."

Margie was hurt. "Well, I don't know what kind of school they had all that time ago." She read the book over his shoulder for a while, then said, "Anyway, they had a teacher."

"Sure they had a teacher, but it wasn't a *regular* teacher. It was a man."

"A man? How could a man be a teacher?"

"Well, he just told the boys and girls things and gave them homework and asked them questions."

"A man isn't smart enough." ❹

"Sure he is. My father knows as much as my teacher."

"He can't. A man can't know as much as a teacher."

"He knows almost as much I betcha."

Margie wasn't prepared to dispute that. She said, "I wouldn't want a strange man in my house to teach me."

Tommy screamed with laughter. "You don't know much, Margie. The teachers didn't live in the house. They had a special building and all the kids went there."

"And all the kids learned the same thing?"

"Sure, if they were the same age."

"But my mother says a teacher has to be adjusted to fit the mind of each boy and girl it teaches and that each kid has to be taught differently."

"Just the same, they didn't do it that way then. If you don't like it, you don't have to read the book."

"I didn't say I didn't like it," Margie said quickly. She wanted to read about those funny schools.

They weren't even half finished when Margie's mother called, "Margie! School!"

Margie looked up. "Not yet, Mamma."

"Now," said Mrs. Jones. "And it's probably time for Tommy, too."

Margie said to Tommy, "Can I read the book some more with you after school?"

"Maybe," he said, nonchalantly. He walked away whistling, the dusty old book tucked beneath his arm.

Margie went into the schoolroom. It was right next to her bedroom, and the mechanical teacher was on and waiting for her. It

ANALYZE

❹ Margie says that humans aren't smart enough to teach. What is **ironic** about this statement? Explain.

was always on at the same time every day except Saturday and Sunday, because her mother said little girls learned better if they learned at regular hours.

The screen was lit up, and it said: "Today's arithmetic lesson is on the addition of proper fractions. Please insert yesterday's homework in the proper slot."

Margie did so with a sigh. She was thinking about the old schools they had when her grandfather's grandfather was a little boy. All the kids from the whole neighborhood came, laughing and shouting in the schoolyard, sitting together in the schoolroom, going home together at the end of the day. They learned the same things so they could help one another on the homework and talk about it.

And the teachers were people. . . .

The mechanical teacher was flashing on the screen: "When we add the fractions 1/2 and 1/4 . . ."

Margie was thinking about how the kids must have loved it in the old days. She was thinking about the fun they had. **5**

ANALYZE

5 How accurate is Margie's idea about what school was like in "the old days"? Explain.

Meet the Writer

Isaac Asimov

A Writing Machine

Isaac Asimov (1920–1992) wrote or edited more than 470 books, as well as many short stories and scholarly articles. That's more books than any other American writer has turned out. Asimov also holds the unofficial record for writing about more different nonfiction subjects than any other writer in history. In fact, *The New York Times* called him a "writing machine."

Asimov was born in Russia and came to the United States with his parents when he was three years old. He submitted his first story to a science fiction magazine when he was only fourteen. The story was rejected, but the editor encouraged Asimov and helped him improve his writing.

Asimov talked about "The Fun They Had" in the first volume of his autobiography. A friend of his had asked him to write a short story for young readers. Asimov said:

> **❝ I thought about it and decided to write a little story about school. What could interest children more? It would be about a school of the future, by way of teaching machines, with children longing for the good old days when there were old-fashioned schools that children loved. I thought the kids would get a bang out of the irony. ❞**

He wrote the story at one sitting and earned ten dollars for it—"a penny a word," Asimov says.

More by the Writing Machine

You'll find short stories about robots in Asimov's book *I, Robot*. His popular series of novels, called *The Foundation Trilogy*, covers thousands of years of "future history."

First Thoughts

1. Finish this sentence:

- I think Margie's ideas about "old-fashioned" schools are . . .

Thinking Critically

2. Judging from this story, how do you think Asimov would feel about today's schools?

3. In Asimov's vison of the future, certain things have changed. Other things have stayed the same. Name three things that, according to Asimov, time and science will *not* change. Do you agree with him? Explain.

4. Is there **irony** in the last paragraph of "The Fun They Had"? Explain.

Reading Check

To check your comprehension, fill in a story map like the one below for "The Fun They Had."

Title:	
Author:	
Characters:	
Conflict:	
Resolution:	
Setting:	

Comparing Literature

5. To help you collect your observations about "The Fun They Had," fill out the first column of the chart below. Then, answer the questions below the chart. You'll add to the chart after you read "The Nightingale."

North Carolina Competency Goal
5.01; 5.02

Comparing Stories: The Power of Technology		
	"The Fun They Had"	"The Nightingale"
Details about human characters		
Details about mechanical objects		
What does the main character learn?		
What is this story's message about the power of technology? How is the message ironic?		
_____		
_____		

SKILLS FOCUS

Literary Skills
Analyze irony.

Reading Skills
Compare and contrast stories.

Before You Read

What is the difference between listening to a CD recording of your favorite band and hearing the band live? What is the difference between watching a parade on TV and being at the parade? This is a tale about how technology can mimic, or imitate, nature. In the end, which proves to be superior—the mechanical version or the real thing?

The Nightingale

Hans Christian Andersen
translated by Anthea Bell

In China, as of course you know, the Emperor is Chinese, and so are all his people. This story happened many years ago, but that makes it all the more worth hearing. Old tales should be told again before they are forgotten.

The Emperor had the most magnificent palace in the world, made all of fine porcelain,[1] so expensive and so fragile and delicate that you hardly dared touch it. Out in the garden grew wonderfully beautiful flowers, and the loveliest of all had little silver bells tied to them that rang as you went by so that you couldn't fail to notice them. Everything in the Emperor's garden was so ingeniously[2] laid out, and the garden itself stretched so far that even the gardener didn't know where it ended. If you went on beyond it you came to a very beautiful wood with tall trees and deep lakes. This wood went all the way down to the deep blue sea. Great ships could sail right in under its branches, and in the branches there lived a nightingale who sang so sweetly that even the poor fisherman, busy as he was when he came down to the sea at night to cast his nets, would stop and listen to its song. "Dear God, how beautiful it is!" he said. Then he had to get down to his work, and he forgot the bird, but when he came out next night and the nightingale sang again, he said the same: "Dear God, how beautiful it is!" ❶

Travelers from every country in the world visited the Emperor's city and marveled at the city itself and the palace and the garden, but when they heard the nightingale, every one of them said, "Ah, that's the best thing of all!"

And when the travelers were home they said what they had seen, and learned men wrote books about the city and the palace and the garden, not forgetting the nightingale: They praised that most of all. And poets wrote wonderful verses about the nightingale who lived in the wood by the deep sea.

The books went all over the world, and at last they came to the Emperor too. He sat on his golden seat and read and read, nodding his head again and again with pleasure, for he was delighted with the wonderful descriptions of his city and his palace and his garden. And then he read: "But the nightingale is best of all."

"What's all this?" said the Emperor. "Nightingale? I never heard of it. So there is such a bird in my Imperial realm, in my own garden, and I haven't heard it? Well, to think what one may learn from books!" ❷

---

1. **porcelain** (pôr′sə·lin) *n.:* fine, white china.
2. **ingeniously** (in·jēn′yəs·lē) *adv.:* skillfully or cleverly.

(Opposite) *The Chamberlain Goes in Search of the Nightingale*
(1911) by Edmund Dulac.
General Research Division, The New York Public Library. Astor, Lenox and Tilden Foundations.

DRAW CONCLUSIONS

❶ Where does this story take place? What conclusions can you draw from what you know about the palace and garden?

COMPARE AND CONTRAST

❷ In "The Fun They Had," Margie reads about the schools of the past, which she finds fascinating. What does the Emperor learn about from reading books?

And he summoned his Lord-in-Waiting, so very grand a gentleman that if anyone of lesser rank so much as spoke to him or asked him a question, he simply said, "P!" which means nothing at all.

"They say there is a remarkable bird called the nightingale here," said the Emperor, "and they say it's the finest thing in all my Empire. Why has nobody ever told me about this bird?"

"I never heard of it myself," said the Lord-in-Waiting. "It's never been presented at Court."

"I want it to come and sing for me this evening," said the Emperor. "It seems all the world knows what I have here, except me!"

"I never heard of it myself," repeated the Lord-in-Waiting. "But I'll look for it, and I'll find it."

Where was it to be found, though? The Lord-in-Waiting ran up and down all the flights of stairs, through great halls, down corridors, and no one he met had ever heard tell of the nightingale. So the Lord-in-Waiting went back to the Emperor and said it must be just a story made up by the people who wrote the books.

"Your Imperial Majesty mustn't believe everything he reads in books; they are full of invention and not to be trusted."

"But the book in which I read it," said the Emperor, "was sent to me by the high and mighty Emperor of Japan, so it must be true. I want to hear the nightingale! It is to come here this evening, and if it doesn't, I'll have the whole Court thumped in the stomach, right after they've had their supper."

"Tsing-pe!" said the Lord-in-Waiting, and he went off again and ran up and down the flights of stairs, through the halls, and down the corridors, and half the Court went with him, not wanting to be thumped in the stomach. They all asked about the remarkable nightingale, known to everyone else in the world but not to the Court. At last they found a poor little girl in the kitchen, who said "The nightingale? Oh, yes. I know the nightingale very well, and oh, how it can sing! I'm allowed to take some of the food left over from the table to my poor sick mother in the evenings, and she lives down by the shore, so when I'm on my way back, I stop for a rest in the wood and I hear the nightingale sing. It brings tears to my eyes, as if my mother were kissing me." ❸

"Little kitchenmaid," said the Lord-in-Waiting, "I will get you a steady job here in the kitchen and permission to watch the Emperor eat his dinner if you can take us to the nightingale, for it is summoned to Court this evening."

ANALYZE

❸ What knowledge does the kitchenmaid have that the people of the Court do not? Explain the **irony** in this situation.

So half the Court went out to the wood where the nightingale used to sing. And as they were going along, a cow began to moo.

"We've found the nightingale!" said the courtiers. "What a powerful voice for such a little creature! I've heard it somewhere before."

"No, those are cows," said the little kitchenmaid. "We aren't nearly there yet."

Then they heard the frogs croaking in the pond.

"Exquisite!" said the Imperial Palace Chaplain. "Now that I hear it, its song is like little church bells."

"No, those are frogs," said the little kitchenmaid. "But I think we'll soon hear the nightingale now."

And then the nightingale began to sing.

"There it is!" said the little girl. "Listen, listen! It is sitting up there." And she pointed to a small gray bird up in the branches of the trees.

"Can it be true?" said the Lord-in-Waiting. "I'd never have thought it! It looks like such an ordinary bird. All the color must have drained away from it at the sight of such grand people!" ❹

"Little nightingale," called the kitchenmaid, "our gracious Emperor wants you to sing for him."

"He's very welcome," said the nightingale, and it sang so beautifully it was a joy to hear that song.

"Like glass bells!" said the Lord-in-Waiting. "And see the way its little throat quivers! And to think we never heard it before—what a success it will be at Court!"

"Shall I sing for the Emperor again?" asked the nightingale, who thought the Emperor himself was present.

"My dear, good little nightingale," said the Lord-in-Waiting. "I am pleased and proud to invite you to a party at Court this evening, where you will delight his Imperial Majesty with your lovely song."

"It sounds best out here in the green woods," said the nightingale, but it went along with them willingly enough on hearing it was the Emperor's wish. ❺

What a cleaning and a polishing there was at the palace! The walls and floors, all made of porcelain, shone in the light of thousands of golden lamps. The loveliest of flowers, the chiming ones from the Emperor's garden, were placed along the corridor. With all the hurry and bustle there was such a draft that it made the bells ring out, and you couldn't hear yourself speak.

ANALYZE

❹ Andersen uses **irony** when he describes the Court. How does he show how important the people of the Court believe themselves to be and how silly they really are?

COMPARE AND CONTRAST

❺ In fairy tales, animals can often speak. What other fairy tales can you think of in which speaking animals play a part?

In the middle of the great hall where the Emperor sat, they placed a golden perch for the nightingale. The little girl, who now had the official title of Kitchenmaid, was allowed to stand behind the door. The entire Court was there, all dressed in their best, and they were all gazing at the little gray bird. The Emperor nodded to it.

And the nightingale sang so sweetly that tears rose to the Emperor's eyes and flowed down his cheeks, and then the nightingale sang yet more beautifully, so that its song went right to the heart. The Emperor was so delighted that he said the nightingale was to have his own golden slipper to wear around its neck. But the nightingale thanked him and said it already had its reward.

"I have seen tears in the eyes of the Emperor, and what more could I wish for? An Emperor's tears have wonderful power; God knows that's reward enough for me." And it sang again in its sweet, lovely voice.

"That's the prettiest thing I ever heard," said the ladies standing by, and they poured water into their mouths and tried to trill when they were spoken to, thinking they would be nightingales too. Even the lackeys[3] and the chambermaids expressed satisfaction, which is saying a good deal, for such folk are the very hardest to please. In short, the nightingale was a great success. ❻

And now it was to stay at Court, and have its own

The Orange Tree Egg by Fabergé.

---

3. **lackeys** *n.:* servants.

cage, and be allowed out twice by day and once by night. Twelve menservants were to go with it, each holding tight to a silken ribbon tied to the bird's leg. Of course, going out like that was no pleasure at all.

The whole city was talking of the marvelous bird, and if two friends met, one would say, "Night," and the other would say, "Gale," and they sighed, and each knew exactly what the other meant. Eleven grocers' children were named after the bird, but not one of them could sing a note.

One day a big parcel came for the Emperor, with *Nightingale* written on it.

"Here's a new book about our famous bird," said the Emperor. But it wasn't a book; it was a little mechanical toy in a box, an artificial nightingale. It was meant to look like the real one, but it was covered all over with diamonds and rubies and sapphires. As soon as you wound the bird up, it sang one of the real nightingale's songs, and its tail went up and down, all shining with silver and gold. It had a little ribbon around its neck with the words: "The Emperor of Japan's nightingale is a poor thing beside the nightingale of the Emperor of China." **7**

"How exquisite!" everyone said, and they gave the man who had brought the artificial bird the title of Lord High Nightingale Bringer.

"Now they can sing together. We'll have a duet," said the Court.

So sing together they did, but it wasn't quite right, for the real nightingale sang in its own way, and the artificial bird's song worked by means of a cylinder inside it.

"It's not the new bird's fault," said the Master of the Emperor's Music. "It keeps perfect time and performs in my very own style." So the artificial bird was to sing alone. It was just as great a success as the real bird, and then it was so much prettier to look at! It glittered like jewelry.

It sang the same song thirty-three times, and still it wasn't tired. The Court would happily have heard the song again, but the Emperor thought it was time for the real nightingale to sing. But where had it gone? No one had noticed it flying out of the open window, out and away, back to its own green wood. **8**

"What's all this?" said the Emperor, and all the courtiers said the nightingale was a most ungrateful creature. "But we still have the better bird," they said, and the mechanical nightingale had to sing the same song again, for the thirty-fourth time. It was a difficult

VISUALIZE

7 Using your own words, describe the mechanical bird. Which words and phrases in the story help you see this object?

COMPARE AND CONTRAST

8 List the similarities and differences between the mechanical nightingale and the real nightingale.

EVALUATE

❾ Why, according to the Master of the Music, is the artificial nightingale superior to the real nightingale? Do you agree with him?

song, and the Court didn't quite know it by heart yet. The Master of the Music praised the bird to the skies and actually stated that it was better than the real nightingale not just because of its plumage,[4] glittering with so many lovely diamonds, but inside too.

"For you see, my lords, and particularly your Imperial Majesty, you can never tell just what the real bird is going to sing, but with the artificial bird it's all settled. It will sing like this and it won't sing any other way. You can understand it; you can open it up and see how human minds made it, where the wheels and cylinders lie, how they work, and how they all go around." ❾

"My own opinion entirely," said everyone, and the Master of the Music got permission to show the bird to all the people next Sunday, for the Emperor said they should hear it too. And hear it they did, and they were as happy as if they had gotten tipsy on tea, for tea is what the Chinese drink; and they all said "Ooh!" and pointed their fingers in the air, and nodded. However, the poor fisherman who used to listen to the real nightingale said, "It sounds nice enough, and quite like the real bird, but there's something missing, I don't know what."

And the real nightingale was banished from the Emperor's domains.

The artificial bird had a place on a silk cushion next to the Emperor's bed. All the presents of gold and jewels it had been given lay around it, and it bore the title of Imperial Bedside-Singer-in-Chief, so it took first place on the left side: The Emperor thought the side upon which the heart lies was the better one, and even an Emperor's heart is on his left. And the Master of the Music wrote a book, in twenty-five volumes, about the mechanical bird. The book was very long and very learned and full of hard words in Chinese, so all the people at Court pretended to have read it for fear of looking stupid and being thumped in the stomach.

So it went on for a year. The Emperor, the Court, and all the other Chinese now knew every little trill of the mechanical bird's song by heart, but they liked it all the better for that. They could join in the song themselves, and they did too. Even the street urchins[5] sang, "Tweet-tweet-tweet, cluck-cluck-cluck-cluck," and the Emperor sang too. How delightful it all was!

---

4. **plumage** (plo͞om'ij) *n.*: feathers of a bird.
5. **street urchins**: mischievous youngsters from the street.

Chinese Man on Boat (1911) by Edmund Dulac.
General Research Division, The New York Public Library. Astor, Lenox and Tilden Foundations.

One evening, however, as the artificial bird was singing its very best and the Emperor lay in his bed listening, it went, "Twang!" and something broke inside it. The wheels whirred around and the music stopped.

The Emperor jumped straight out of bed and summoned his own doctor, but there was nothing the doctor could do. So they fetched the watchmaker, and after much talk and much tinkering about with it, he got the bird to work again after a fashion. However, he said it mustn't be made to sing very often, because the little pegs on the cylinders had worn out and there was no way of replacing them

INTERPRET

🔟 Think about what the Master of the Music says about the mechanical bird. Why is this a good example of **irony**?

without spoiling the tune. This was very sad indeed. They let the mechanical bird sing just once a year, and even that was a strain on it, but the Master of the Music used to make a little speech crammed with difficult words, saying the bird was still as good as ever, and so then of course it was, just as he said. 🔟

Five years passed by, and then the whole country was in great distress, for the people all loved their Emperor, and now he was sick and likely to die. A new Emperor had already been chosen, and people stood in the street and asked the Lord-in-Waiting how the old one was.

He only said, "P!" and shook his head.

The Emperor lay in his great, magnificent bed, and he was cold and pale. The whole Court thought he was dead already, and the courtiers went off to pay their respects to the new Emperor. The lackeys of the bedchamber got together for a gossip, and the maids-in-waiting were having a big coffee party. Cloth was laid down in all the halls and corridors so that you could hear no footfall, and all was quiet, very quiet. But the Emperor was not dead yet. Stiff and pale, he lay in his bed of state hung with velvet and with heavy golden tassels. There was a window open up above, and moonlight shone in on the Emperor and the mechanical nightingale.

The poor Emperor could hardly draw breath, and he felt as if something was sitting on his chest. He opened his eyes and saw that it was Death sitting there. Death was wearing his golden crown, and Death had his imperial golden saber[6] in one hand and his magnificent banner in the other. And strange faces peered out from among the folds of the great velvet hangings of the bed: Some were grim and hideous, others blessed and mild. They were the Emperor's good deeds and bad deeds all looking at him as Death sat there on his heart.

"Remember this?" they whispered, one by one. "Remember that?" And they reminded him of so many things that the sweat broke out on his forehead.

"No, no! I never knew!" said the Emperor. "Music!" he cried. "Music on the great Chinese drum to keep me from hearing what you say!"

But on they went, and Death kept nodding like a Chinese mandarin[7] at everything they said.

---

6. **saber** *n.*: heavy sword with a curved blade.
7. **Chinese mandarin:** high official.

Chinese Man in Bed with Goblin over Him (1911) by Edmund Dulac.
General Research Division, The New York Public Library. Astor, Lenox and Tilden Foundations.

"Music, music!" cried the Emperor. "Sing, my little golden bird, oh, sing! I have given you gold and treasure; I myself hung my golden slipper around your neck, so sing for me now, sing!" **⑪**

But the bird was silent, for there wasn't anyone there to wind it up, and it could not sing without being wound. And Death gazed and gazed at the Emperor through his great empty eye sockets, and all was still, all was terribly still.

And at that moment the loveliest of songs was heard coming in through the window. It was the real nightingale sitting in the branches outside. It had heard of the Emperor's sickness, and so it

INFER

⑪ Why does the Emperor want his bird to sing? What is he trying to avoid?

ANALYZE

12 Explain how the nightingale tricks Death and saves the Emperor's life.

had come to sing him a song of hope and comfort. And as it sang, the phantom shapes faded away, the blood flowed faster and faster through the Emperor's weak limbs, and Death himself listened and said, "Go on, go on, little nightingale!"

"Yes, if you give me that fine gold saber! Yes, if you give me that gorgeous banner! Yes, if you will give me the Emperor's crown!"

So Death gave all those treasures up, each for one of the nightingale's songs, and the nightingale sang on and on. It sang of the quiet churchyard where white roses grow, and the air is fragrant with elder flowers, and the fresh grass is wet with the tears of the bereaved.[8] Then Death longed for his own garden again, and he drifted away out of the window like cold white mist. **12**

"Thank you, thank you," said the Emperor. "Most blessed of little birds, I know you now! I drove you away from my domains, yet you have sung away all those evil visions from my bed and driven Death from my heart. How can I reward you?"

"You have rewarded me already," said the nightingale. "I brought tears to your eyes the first time I sang to you, and I will never forget those tears. They are the jewels that rejoice a singer's heart. But you must sleep now and be fresh and strong when you wake. Now I will sing for you."

The nightingale sang, and the Emperor fell into a sweet, gentle, and refreshing slumber.

The sun was shining in on him through the window when he woke, feeling strong and healthy. None of his servants were back, for they all thought he was dead, but the nightingale still sat there singing.

"You must stay with me forever," said the Emperor. "You need never sing unless you want to, and I will break the artificial bird into a thousand pieces."

"Don't do that," said the nightingale. "It did the best it could, after all, so you should keep it. I cannot live or nest in a palace; but let me come to you when I feel like it, and I'll sit on the branch outside your window and sing in the evening to gladden your heart and fill it with thoughts. I will sing of those who are happy and those who are sad; I will sing to the bad and the good around you. A little singing bird flies far and wide, to the poor fisherman and the peasant's hut, to people very far from you and your Court. I love your heart more than I love

---

8. **the bereaved** (bē·rēvd′): survivors of a person who recently died.

your crown, yet that crown seems to have something sacred about it. I will come and sing for you, but you must promise me one thing."

"Anything," said the Emperor, and he stood there in the imperial robes he had put on again, holding his heavy golden saber to his breast.

"All I ask is that you will not let anyone know you have a little bird who tells you everything; that will be best."

Then the nightingale flew away.

The Emperor's servants came in to look at him lying dead, and they stood there amazed.

"Good morning," said the Emperor. **13**

To read about Hans Christian Andersen, see Meet the Writer on page 249 and "Ugly Duckling or Little Mermaid?" on page 421.

INFER

13 Why do you think the nightingale wishes to remain secret? (Hint: What do you think might happen if everyone knew it had returned?)

Chinese Man with Two Women with Fans (1911) by Edmund Dulac. General Research Division, The New York Public Library. Astor, Lenox and Tilden Foundations.

After You Read "The Nightingale"

First Thoughts

1. Complete these sentences:
- I think the Emperor is . . .
- I think the nightingale is . . .

Thinking Critically

2. How does the Emperor learn about the nightingale? Is there any **irony** in this situation? Explain.

3. Why do you think the nightingale returns to sing for the Emperor on his deathbed? What do you think the nightingale means when it says, "I love your heart more than I love your crown"?

4. The Emperor and the Court grow to like the artificial nightingale better than the real nightingale. Can you think of another situation in which people have come to like an artificial or mechanical version of something better than the real thing? Explain. What might the writer be saying about human nature?

> ### Reading Check
>
> Check your comprehension by **retelling** "The Nightingale" to a partner. Start with the title, main characters, and setting. Next, tell the main events in the order in which they occur. Then, describe the **climax** (the most suspenseful moment in the story). Finally, explain the **resolution**—the way the story ends.

Comparing Literature

5. Now that you have read "The Nightingale," you can complete the second column of the chart you began on page 588. Then, answer the questions below the chart.

North Carolina Competency Goal
5.01; 5.02

SKILLS FOCUS

Literary Skills
Analyze irony.

Reading Skills
Compare and contrast stories.

Comparing Stories: The Power of Technology		
	"The Fun They Had"	"The Nightingale"
Details about human characters		
Details about mechanical objects		
What does the main character learn?		
What is this story's message about the power of technology? How is the message ironic?		
_____		
_____		

Assignment

1. Writing a Comparison-Contrast Essay

Write a short essay comparing "The Fun They Had" with "The Nightingale." To help find points of comparison, review the chart you completed after you read each story. Focus on one aspect of the stories that is very similar or very different. You should pick the element that most interests you. For example, you might want to compare the mechanical objects (the teacher and the bird). Or you might want to compare the main characters (Margie and the Emperor). Or you might want to write an essay comparing each story's message about the power of technology and what the writer's use of irony adds to the message.

Make sure your essay has an introduction, a main section in which you compare the stories, and a conclusion. In your conclusion, tell which story you prefer and why. Which story left you with more to think about? Be sure to use examples from the story to explain your responses.

Use the workshop on writing a **comparison-contrast essay**, pages 404–409, for help with this assignment.

Assignment

2. Preparing a Debate

Both "The Fun They Had" and "The Nightingale" raise questions about the relationship between humans and machines. With three other classmates (two of you representing each side), prepare a debate on the following statement:

Technology always leads to improvements in human society.

Each group of two will argue either for or against the statement above. Make sure to support your argument with evidence. You can use facts, anecdotes, quotations, or other examples. Present your arguments one side at a time. Then, allow each side a few minutes to respond to the other side's argument. Afterward, have your classmates give you feedback: Which side made the more convincing argument? Why do you think so?

North Carolina Competency Goal
1.03; 5.01

SKILLS FOCUS

Literary Skills
Analyze irony.

Reading Skills
Compare and contrast stories.

Writing Skills
Write a comparison-contrast essay.

Speaking and Listening Skills
Debate an issue.

Jimmy Jet and His TV Set

Shel Silverstein

I'll tell you the story of Jimmy Jet—
And you know what I tell you is true.
He loved to watch his TV set
Almost as much as you.

5   He watched all day, he watched all night
Till he grew pale and lean,
From *The Early Show* to *The Late Late Show*
And all the shows between.

He watched till his eyes were frozen wide,
10   And his bottom grew into his chair.
And his chin turned into a tuning dial,
And antennae grew out of his hair.

And his brains turned into TV tubes,
And his face to a TV screen.
15   And two knobs saying "VERT." and "HORIZ."
Grew where his ears had been.

And he grew a plug that looked like a tail
So we plugged in little Jim.
And now instead of him watching TV
20   We all sit around and watch him.

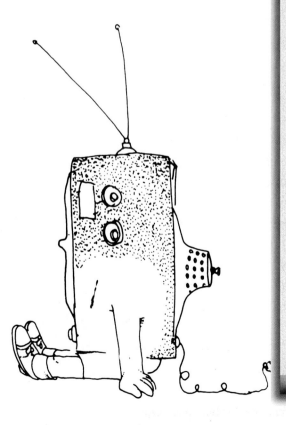

Meet the Writer

Shel Silverstein

"I Want to Go Everywhere"
Shel Silverstein (1932–1999) was always hungry for life. He wrote:

> " I want to go everywhere, look and listen to everything. You can go crazy with some of the wonderful stuff there is in life. "

Silverstein was a folksinger and songwriter who scored a hit with the song "A Boy Named Sue." He also recorded his own albums and wrote music for movies. He even acted in a movie and had stage plays produced. But he is best known for his hugely successful books of poetry.

Silverstein didn't give interviews; he communicated directly with his readers through his work. He said:

> " People who say they create only for themselves and don't care if they're published . . . I hate to hear talk like that. If it's good, it's too good not to share. "

Share Shel Silverstein
You can share more of Silverstein's humor in his bestselling collections of poems: *Where the Sidewalk Ends* and *A Light in the Attic*.

Writing Workshop

SKILLS FOCUS

Writing Skills
Write a descriptive essay.

DESCRIPTIVE WRITING
Descriptive Essay

No one else experiences the world exactly as you do. In descriptive writing you present your view of something you have observed closely. You describe all its details, especially those related to your five senses.

Prewriting

1 Choosing a Subject

Read and respond to the following prompt:

> Description occurs as an element in many different types of writing. It occurs in narratives such as short stories and novels; it is used in explaining a process; it may appear as supporting details in persuasive writing. The main purpose of a descriptive essay, however, is to evoke a mood or create a vivid impression of something through details that appeal to the senses and to the imagination. Choose a subject you would enjoy observing and describing: a place, a person, an object, an animal, or an event. Write an essay in which you bring that subject to life through detailed description.

Before choosing a subject, consider these questions:

- Can I observe this subject directly? Or, can I picture it clearly enough for a description?
- Is the subject interesting? Would a reader find it interesting?
- Will there be enough sensory details for a full description?

"All I see is more trees."
©The New Yorker Collection 1980
Barney Tobey from cartoonbank.com.
All rights reserved.

2 Finding More Ideas

Read through the following activities. Freewrite for a few minutes about one or more of the suggestions.

- Closely observe a person or object that you already know well. Do you see something you hadn't noticed before? Can you describe it?
- Remember a place where you have been happy. Describe it in detail, focusing on sounds, smells, tastes, sights, and physical feelings.
- Remember an animal you've spent time watching. Describe how the animal looks, sounds, and behaves.
- Think of the first time you rode a bike, visited a city, did a science experiment, or tasted a new food. Gather your observations of some favorite "firsts."

3 Gathering Ideas

Gather details about your subject by observing it directly or by using your memory. One writer used the chart below to record details for an essay on eating warm popcorn outdoors at night. Compare the details on the chart with those in the Student Model on page 609. Then, use a similar chart to record the details and actions you observe for your essay.

Facts	Sensory Details	Actions
• night • bowl of popcorn • tent in backyard	• popcorn—warm, lingering smell • night—dark, muggy, windy • tent light—faint, glowing	• tasting the popcorn • picking up the bowl • carrying the popcorn outside

4 Organizing

There are three common ways to organize descriptive essays:

Spatial order. When you organize details spatially, you tell where they are located—moving, for example, from left to

---

Framework for a Descriptive Essay

Introduction (identifies the subject, time, and place; gives background information): _____ _____ _____

Body (presents details in clear order; elaborates description with sensory images and figures of speech):

1. _____
Specifics: _____
2. _____
Specifics: _____
3. _____
Specifics: _____
4. _____
Specifics: _____

Conclusion (includes main impression; expresses your feelings; tells why the subject is important):

_____
_____
_____

Strategies For Elaboration

When you write a descriptive essay, use exact verbs, nouns, adjectives, and adverbs to express what you mean. Elaborate with words that appeal to the five senses. Don't describe a car simply as "yellow" when it's actually "lemon yellow" or "mustard colored." Instead of saying that a boy "is on a sofa," you might say that he "sprawls," "curls up," or "snoozes" there.

right or from near to far. Writers often use spatial order when they describe a scene.

Chronological order. When you organize chronologically, you put details in time order. This organization is best suited to describing an activity or an event. The Student Model on page 609 is organized chronologically.

Order of importance. When you organize by order of importance, you present details from most to least important or from least to most important. This type of organization helps convey your feelings about a subject.

Drafting

1 Focusing on a Main Idea

At the beginning of your essay, state your **main idea.** To state the main idea clearly, ask yourself, "What is the purpose of my essay?" or "What is my impression of my subject?"

2 Setting the Scene

Whenever you observe something, you look at it from a particular place and at a particular time. By telling readers where you are, you give them a clear viewpoint.

3 Using Transitions

Use transitional words and phrases to link ideas.

- **Words and phrases showing spatial organization:**

  across from, here, around, inside, between, near, close, next to, down, under

- **Words and phrases showing chronological order:**

  after, first, at once, now, before, then, eventually, when, finally, meanwhile

- **Words and phrases showing order of importance:**

  first, last, then, mainly, to begin with, more important

Student Model

Popcorn Nights

We entered, greeted by the warm, lingering smell of freshly popped corn. The bright blue bowl of popcorn, with ribbons of steam floating delicately off each kernel, lured us to it. I tasted a piece and let it remain there for a moment before swallowing. I picked up the bowl, and out we went into the dark and muggy night. Walking as quickly as we could without spilling the popcorn into the long grass, we hurried on our way. As we strode barefoot, with our jeans rolled to our knees, the damp grass poked and danced on our toes, and the wind became powerful hands that caressed our hair. Finally we reached our destination, a tent set up with a faint light glowing in the corner of my backyard.

—Sharon Orthey
Warren Township High School
Gurnee, Illinois

*Title identifies the **subject** and the **time** of day.*

*The writer uses lots of **details** that appeal to the senses of touch, smell, sight, and taste.*

*She uses **figurative language** to describe the grass and the wind.*

*She uses **chronological order** to describe the action.*

Writing Tip

Denotation and Connotation
Use words precisely. Let context determine the right word. For example, the words *strange* and *odd* are related in meaning. Both mean "unusual or unfamiliar." The word *odd*, however, has connotations of something that is far from ordinary, perhaps puzzling or peculiar.

Figures of Speech
Use vivid figures of speech in your writing. Here are some examples by well-known poets.

Simile
O my Luve's like a red, red rose
—Robert Burns

Metaphor
Life is a barren field
Frozen with snow.
—Langston Hughes

Personification
The Hills untied their Bonnets
—Emily Dickinson

INTERNET
More Writer's Models
Keyword: LE5 6-6

Evaluating and Revising

Use the following chart to evaluate and revise your descriptive essay.

Descriptive Essay: Content and Organization Guidelines		
Evaluation Questions	▶ **Tips**	▶ **Revision Techniques**
❶ Does your introduction catch the reader's attention? Does it identify the subject?	▶ **Bracket** interesting or surprising statements. **Circle** the subject of the essay.	▶ **Add** an attention-getting statement or a quotation. **Add** a sentence that identifies the subject of your description.
❷ Does your description include a variety of sensory details and figures of speech?	▶ **Highlight** sensory details and figures of speech. **Put an S** above sensory details. **Put an F** above figures of speech.	▶ **Elaborate** with additional details. **Delete** irrelevant details.
❸ Are the details arranged in a clear order?	▶ In the margin, **indicate** whether the order is spatial, chronological, or order of importance.	▶ **Rearrange** details if necessary. **Add** transitions for greater coherence.
❹ Does your description include your thoughts and feelings about the subject?	▶ **Put a check mark** next to any statement of your thoughts or feelings.	▶ **Add** specific details about thoughts and feelings.
❺ Does your conclusion tell why the subject is important to you? Does it convey a clear impression of the subject?	▶ **Underline** the statement that tells why the subject is important. **Bracket** statements that hint at the main impression.	▶ If necessary, **add** a statement explaining why the subject is important. **Add** a statement that conveys the main impression of the subject.

On the next page is an excerpt from a descriptive essay that has been revised. Use the questions that follow the Revision Model to evaluate the writer's changes.

Revision Model

What is the most original costume you have ever made?

For the annual school costume party, my class voted to

create a group costume based on ∧ "The Pied Piper of
Robert Browning's

Hamelin ∧." Our group costume was the hit of the party!
, a poem we had studied.

First came the Mayor and the Council members who wore
resemble

bathrobes and fake fur scarves to ~~look like~~ the official

ermine gowns. Next came the Pied Piper, whose coat and

scarf were covered with pieces of colored cloth ∧. At the
, half yellow and half red

end of his scarf ~~was hanging~~ his pipe. Groups of students
dangled

wearing dark-colored tights ~~were~~ the rats. ∧ Bringing up
took the part of   *Their long tails*

the rear were the rest of the class, who portrayed the
were made of rubber strips from an old tire.

children. They ~~came~~ into the auditorium to the strains of
were led

the piper's music. ∧

Evaluating the Revision

1. Which details appeal to the different senses?

2. What order of organization has the writer used?

3. Where has the writer replaced vague language with more precise verbs and modifiers?

4. What material has the writer rearranged? Why?

PROOFREADING
TIPS

- Read your final version at least twice to catch and correct mistakes.

- Exchange papers with a partner, and proofread each other's work.

Communications Handbook HELP

See Proofreaders' Marks.

PUBLISHING
TIPS

- Place copies of your essays in a binder to be filed in your school library for other students' reference.

- The details in your descriptive essay may lend themselves to illustration. Working alone or in a group, create a brochure, a bulletin-board display, or a multimedia presentation.

Test Practice

DIRECTIONS: Read the article. Then, answer each question that follows.

His Gift to Girls

A taxi driver funds a school in India.

Ritu Upadhyay

Hundreds of little girls in the tiny Indian village of Doobher Kishanpur wake up and go to school each day. Sure, in America girls do the same thing. But in Doobher Kishanpur (doo′ bur kish′ən·poor), it's nearly a miracle. Thanks to a generous cab driver, many of these students are the first girls in their family to read and write.

Om Dutta Sharma has spent the past 20 years driving a yellow taxicab in New York City for 80 hours a week. After saving all his extra cash, Sharma used it to open the Ram Kali School for Girls in 1997. The school is named for his mother, who—like many poor women in India—never learned to read or write.

Before the school opened, the girls in this village had no chance to learn. Their parents, who are very poor, could not afford to send them to schools in the neighboring towns where the boys study.

An Unlikely Hero

Sharma, 65, came to the U.S. 25 years ago with one goal: to make money. A trained lawyer in India, Sharma was frustrated to learn that he would not be able to practice law in the U.S. unless he went back to school. As he stood on the street, cars whizzing by, the idea of driving a taxi struck him: "I love to drive, so why not get paid?"

Sharma never wanted money for himself. He felt he had a debt to repay to the poor farming community where he grew up. "If I can help somebody be on the right path, then the purpose of living is achieved," says Sharma.

By American standards, Sharma's salary is not much. But in India, it goes a long way. Each month his dollars pay

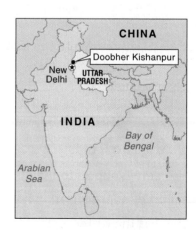

North Carolina Competency Goal
2.01

SKILLS FOCUS

Reading Skills
Analyze assertions and support.

four teachers ($58 each), a local pharmacist ($100) for medicine, and a physician ($100) to keep all the schoolchildren healthy. He also donates the earnings from a mango grove he inherited in India to the school. That pays for the students' books and school uniforms.

A Driver's Work Is Never Done
Sharma says he will retire only when he has enough money to open up four more schools, as well as free health clinics. For now, he's happy saving his money and meeting passengers. "I learn so much when they open up their hearts and minds to me."

1. Om Dutta Sharma wanted to give something back to the village where he grew up. What did he do?
   A He came to the United States and worked as a taxi driver.
   B He opened a school for boys in a neighboring town.
   C He came to the United States to study law.
   D He opened a school for girls in Doobher Kishanpur.

2. The information in the article supports the **assertion** that —
   F all children in India attend school
   G not all children in India attend school
   H all schools in India are financed by the government
   J in India, boys and girls attend classes together

3. Which statement is an **opinion**?
   A Om Dutta Sharma pays the salaries of four teachers.
   B Sharma pays for the girls' books and uniforms.
   C Sharma's mother never learned to read or write.
   D Sharma wouldn't have liked being a lawyer in the United States.

4. Which **assertion** would Sharma probably agree with?
   F Few children deserve an education.
   G Helping people gives meaning to life.
   H It's important to leave the past behind you.
   J Success is measured by the kind of job you have.

Constructed Response
5. What was the writer's **purpose** in writing this article? State the purpose of the article in your own words, and use **evidence** to support your **assertions.**

Collection 6: Skills Review

Vocabulary Skills

Test Practice

Context Clues

DIRECTIONS: Use **context clues** to determine the meaning of the underlined word in each of the following sentences.

1. For the team the new season became a <u>crusade</u> to win the state championship for their beloved coach. *Crusade* means —

   A excuse

   B cause

   C struggle

   D solution

2. Lounging on the couch, Ali enjoyed a few moments of <u>repose</u> before beginning his work. *Repose* means —

   F rest

   G anxiety

   H confusion

   J cleanliness

3. Their mysterious actions <u>defy</u> understanding. *Defy* means —

   A observe

   B resist

   C dare

   D stop

4. At the word "walk," the dog leapt up, full of <u>animation</u>. *Animation* means —

   F hostility

   G liveliness

   H anger

   J respect

5. Her <u>paramount</u> goal is to finish the project on time; everything else is secondary. *Paramount* means —

   A poor

   B hilly

   C main

   D good

6. Next to his small, graceful mother, Richard seemed <u>gawky</u> and ill at ease. *Gawky* means —

   F handsome

   G shocking

   H awkward

   J charming

7. It's hard to believe they're best friends: Lauren is outgoing and talkative, and Jane is shy and <u>reticent</u>. *Reticent* means —

   A mischievous

   B content

   C foolish

   D reserved

8. The gray, overcast sky seemed to mirror David's <u>melancholy</u> mood. *Melancholy* means —

   F gloomy

   G odd

   H angry

   J baffled

North Carolina Competency Goal
6.01

Vocabulary Skills
Use context clues.

Collection 6: Skills Review

Writing Skills

Test Practice

DIRECTIONS: Read the following paragraph from a descriptive essay. Then, answer each question that follows.

(1) My favorite time on the beach is the end of day in late summer, after the crowds have packed up and gone home. (2) I love walking along the edge of the beach to look for seashells. (3) I collect various seashells that I will put in glass vases. (4) I will use them to decorate my room. (5) The sky is streaked with rays of color from the setting sun—purple, orange, and gold. (6) Sunrise at the beach is also beautiful. (7) My toes sink into the soothing sand. (8) I enjoy wading in the water, which has absorbed the sun's rays all summer and now is warm. (9) The scent of spicy grilled food from someone's backyard barbecue comes on a light breeze. (10) In the distance there is the gentle music of wind chimes tinkling when blown by the wind.

1. Which answer correctly matches a sensory detail with the sentence in which it appears?
   - A Sentence 5: smell
   - B Sentence 9: sound
   - C Sentence 10: sight
   - D Sentence 7: touch

2. What is the best way to combine sentences 2, 3, and 4?
   - F I love walking along the edge of the beach so that I can decorate my room and put the seashells I collect in glass vases.
   - G I love walking along the edge of the beach, collecting various seashells that I will put in glass vases to decorate my room.
   - H I love collecting various seashells along the edge of the beach that I will decorate my room in glass vases.
   - J To collect various seashells to use in decorating my room, I love walking along the edge of the beach.

3. What would be the best way to revise sentence 9?
   - A A light breeze brings the scent of spicy grilled food from someone's backyard barbecue.
   - B Someone is cooking spicy grilled food, and a light breeze brings the scent in a backyard barbecue.
   - C There is a scent of spicy grilled food, which is brought on a light breeze from someone's backyard barbecue.
   - D On a light breeze from someone's backyard barbecue is brought the scent of spicy grilled food.

4. Which sentence is irrelevant and should be deleted?
   - F Sentence 5
   - G Sentence 6
   - H Sentence 9
   - J Sentence 10

North Carolina Competency Goal
3.01; 3.03

SKILLS FOCUS

Writing Skills
Analyze descriptive writing.

Fiction and Poetry

The Power of the Press

Darnell Rock, a staff writer at the *Oakdale Gazette,* doesn't think people will care about anything he writes—so why should he bother writing? Then Darnell meets Sweeby Jones, a homeless man whose troubles capture his interest. Soon, thanks to an article by Darnell, Sweeby Jones is on the minds of students, teachers, and community leaders. In Walter Dean Myers's *Darnell Rock Reporting,* a young man finds that writing about serious issues can make a difference.

A Boy and His Fawn

Have you ever seen a baby animal in the wild and wanted to bring it home and raise it? Jody Baxter does just that in *The Yearling*—but in the end he must decide his tamed fawn's fate. Marjorie Kinnan Rawlings won a Pulitzer Prize in 1939 for this novel, set near her home in rural Florida.

This title is available in the HRW Library.

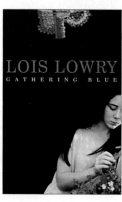

A Path to Discovery

Kira fears that her village will reject her now that she's lost her parents. She doesn't realize how much the Council of Guardians values her amazing talent for embroidery. While Kira is decorating a ceremonial robe for the annual Ruin Song Gathering, she learns about her family and her village's mysterious history. In *Gathering Blue,* Lois Lowry celebrates an artist's ability to reveal the truth.

Magic in the Arts

Is there a relationship between painting and poetry? They may be linked more closely than you think. In *Talking to the Sun,* Kenneth Koch and Kate Farrell have compiled a diverse collection of poems, each of which is accompanied by a work of art. This book will stir your imagination.

Nonfiction

A Pioneer in His Field

Frank O. Gehry's playful, imaginative designs have taken architecture in a totally new direction. Gehry's designs include a building shaped like binoculars and a pair of towers inspired by the 1930s dance team of Fred Astaire and Ginger Rogers. His pathbreaking design for the Guggenheim Museum in Bilbao, Spain, invigorated that city. In *Frank O. Gehry: Outside In,* Jan Greenberg and Sandra Jordan explore the life of the man behind these innovative ideas.

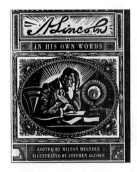

The Man Who Was the Sixteenth President

Abraham Lincoln was known as a brilliant writer and speaker. Through words he could stir people's emotions and influence their thinking. For *Lincoln: In His Own Words,* Milton Meltzer has selected speeches and writings from different periods of Lincoln's life.

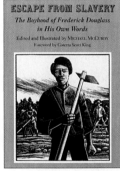

Young and Brave

In *Escape from Slavery: The Boyhood of Frederick Douglass in His Own Words,* you'll learn about one of the most important figures in America's history. Like Lincoln, Douglass was a great writer and speaker, though he never went to school. In this book, Douglass describes the struggles of his early years, which paved the way for his lifelong battle against racism. According to Coretta Scott King, Douglass's accounts provide "one of the best firsthand descriptions of slavery ever written."

Unsung Heroes

Zita Allen has long felt that an important part of the civil rights movement is underrepresented in history books: the contributions of women. In *Black Women Leaders of the Civil Rights Movement,* Allen looks at the achievements of figures like Mary McLeod Bethune and Ella Baker and explains their importance in the fight for equality.

Fine Wind, Clear Morning (1829–1833) by Hokusai.

POETRY

Literary Focus:
Analyzing Sound Effects
and Figures of Speech

go.
hrw
.com

INTERNET

Collection
Resources

Keyword: LE5 6-7

Elements of Literature

Poetry *by* John Malcolm Brinnin

SOUND EFFECTS

Rhyme: Chiming Sounds

We all love **rhyme.** Rhyme can be as simple as the pairing of *moth* with *cloth* or a bit more complicated, like *antelope* matched with *cantaloupe.* Most rhymes are made by pairing the last word in one line with the last word in another line. Rhymes formed in this way are called **end rhymes.** Sometimes the last word in a line will be echoed by a word placed at the beginning or in the middle of the following line. A rhyme formed in this way is called an **internal rhyme.**

Rhyme makes the music in poetry, and it helps you to memorize lines, or stanzas, or even whole poems. Here is a stanza by a famous poet who uses rhymes and other sound effects to make even an invasion of rats seem funny.

> And out of the houses the rats came
>   tumbling;
> Great rats, small rats, lean rats,
>   brawny rats,
> Brown rats, black rats, gray rats,
>   tawny rats,
> Grave old plodders, gay young friskers,
> Cocking tails and pricking whiskers . . .
>
>   —Robert Browning, from
>   "The Pied Piper of Hamelin"

North Carolina Competency Goal
5.02

INTERNET
More About Sounds of Poetry
Keyword: LE5 6-7

SKILLS FOCUS

Literary Skills
Understand the use of rhythm, rhyme, and repetition in poetry.

Alliteration: Repeating a Sound

Alliteration is the repetition of a single consonant sound in words that are close together (for example, *p* in "Peter Piper picked a peck of pickled peppers"). Alliteration is one of the simplest forms of repetition a poet can use. Read aloud "Cynthia in the Snow" so you can hear how the repeated faint hissing of *s* and *sh* sounds imitates the snow falling.

Cynthia in the Snow

> It SHUSHES.
> It hushes
> The loudness in the road.
> It flitter-twitters,
> And laughs away from me.
> It laughs a lovely whiteness,
> And whitely whirs away,
> To be
> Some otherwhere,
> Still white as milk or shirts.
> So beautiful it hurts.
>   —Gwendolyn Brooks

Meter: The Beat of a Poem

When poets are ready to put their ideas and feelings into words, they have to make a choice. They must ask themselves, "Should I express this idea in lines regulated by a beat that sounds like *ta-dum, ta-dum, ta-dum*? Would it be expressed better in lines that sound like ordinary conversation, such as 'Of course. You're right. I never thought of that'?" If they decide on a regular beat, all the lines they write will be more or less the same length and have the same beat. This beat is called **meter**—a regular pattern of accented and unaccented syllables. Robert Browning's lines on the rat invasion (see page 620) are written in meter. Read them aloud. You can't miss that beat.

Poets may decide to ignore meter and write in loose groupings of words and phrases, known as **free verse.** Like conversation, free verse does not have a regular beat. Free verse is simply poetry written to sound like regular conversation.

How do you decide whether to write in meter or free verse? When you write a poem, you must trust yourself. Say what comes from your heart, in the form most natural to you.

Here is a poem in free verse on what may seem like an unpoetic subject. Read the poem aloud. Use the sense of the lines to decide when to pause and when to read straight through to the next line.

Good Hot Dogs

for Kiki

Fifty cents apiece
To eat our lunch
We'd run
Straight from school
Instead of home
Two blocks
Then the store
That smelled like steam
You ordered
Because you had the money
Two hot dogs and two pops for here
Everything on the hot dogs
Except pickle lily
Dash those hot dogs
Into buns and splash on
All that good stuff
Yellow mustard and onions
And french fries piled on top all
Rolled up in a piece of wax
Paper for us to hold hot
In our hands
Quarters on the counter
Sit down
Good hot dogs
We'd eat
Fast till there was nothing left
But salt and poppy seeds even
The little burnt tips
Of french fries
We'd eat
You humming
And me swinging my legs
   —Sandra Cisneros

Reading Poetry

by Kylene Beers

How to Read a Poem

You need to go about reading a poem differently from the way you would read a novel or a note from a friend. Poetry is the shortest kind of literature, but it can be the most demanding to read. This is because poets pack a lot of meaning into just a few words.

As you read a poem, think about the **images,** or pictures, the poet creates. Poets often use **comparisons** to create images. If you're reading a poem in which snowflakes are described as if they were insects, let the comparison create a picture in your mind. What does the comparison help you see?

Poets sometimes use a kind of comparison called **personification** to give human qualities to something that is not human. ("The leaves danced in the breeze" is an example.)

Once you see the images in a poem, listen for its sounds. Words such as *boom* and *bang* are examples of **onomatopoeia** (än'ō·mat'ō·pē'ə) because their sounds imitate their meanings.

Follow the steps in the box at the right, and poetry will come alive for you.

North Carolina Competency Goal
5.01; 5.02

Reading Skills
Use specific strategies to read and understand a poem.

Six Steps to Reading a Poem

1. Look at the title and think about the image or images it creates.

2. Read the poem silently. Pay attention to **punctuation.** Pause briefly at commas and semicolons, and longer after periods. If there's no punctuation at the end of a line, don't pause.

3. Read the poem aloud. It's often easier to make sense of a poem if you hear how it sounds. Feel the poem's **rhythm** as you read. Poetry has a special rhythmic sound, like music.

4. Read the poem a third time and think about the **images** that come to mind as you read. Look for vivid verbs that help you see the action. Look for comparisons that help you see something in a new way.

5. Poets pay special attention to **word choice.** Use context clues or a dictionary to figure out the meanings of unfamiliar words. Do any of the words have more than one meaning?

6. Think about the poem's meaning. What does the poem say to you? Does it relate to your life in any way?

The Sea

James Reeves

The sea is a hungry dog,
Giant and gray.
He rolls on the beach all day.
With his clashing teeth and shaggy jaws
5 Hour upon hour he gnaws
The rumbling, tumbling stones,
And "Bones, bones, bones, bones!"
The giant sea dog moans,
Licking his greasy paws. ❷

10 And when the night wind roars
And the moon rocks in the stormy cloud,
He bounds to his feet and snuffs and sniffs,
Shaking his wet sides over the cliffs,
And howls and hollos long and loud.

15 But on quiet days in May or June,
When even the grasses on the dune
Play no more their reedy tune,
With his head between his paws
He lies on the sandy shores,
20 So quiet, so quiet, he scarcely snores. ❸

Using the Strategy

VISUALIZE

❶ Think about this title. In your mind, what pictures do you see?

ANALYZE

❷ What comparison does the poet make in line 1? Who is "he" in line 3? What does he do all day? (See lines 3–9.)

INFER

❸ If the sea is a "hungry dog" in lines 1–14, what kind of dog is it in lines 15–20?

Fleeting Shadows (1910) by Paul Dougherty.

The Sea   **623**

Meet the Writer

James Reeves

"A Continuing Craving for Poetry"

James Reeves (1909–1978) was born in a suburb of London, but he grew up in the small county of Buckinghamshire, England. As a child, Reeves loved reading, and he started writing poetry when he was only eleven years old.

Reeves attended Cambridge University and then taught for many years before becoming a writer and editor. Reeves wrote poetry and edited books for a series called the Poetry Bookshelf. Even though Reeves is known primarily for his poetry, he also had a particular interest in folk tales and myths. As a result he wrote various adaptations of traditional tales and classics.

When he was forty-one years old and already established as a respected author of books for adults, Reeves turned his attention to writing for children. He edited various prose and poetry anthologies for children that proved popular. Similarly, his original poems for children had a widespread appeal that critics praised. As Reeves once declared:

> ❝ We must always provide poetry in such a way that it creates and nourishes a continuing craving for poetry and does not kill it by making poetry seem something childish. ❞

The Giant (1923) by N. C. Wyeth.
Westtown School, Westtown, PA. Photography courtesy of the Brandywine River Museum.

Practice the Strategy

1. Read "The Sea" aloud. Pay special attention to the end punctuation. Notice that there is a comma at the end of line 1, not a period. How does that comma affect the way you read the first and second lines? Why do you think there is no punctuation at the end of line 4? As you continue reading, notice where there is and is not end punctuation. Read the poem again, pausing at the end of each line instead of where there is end punctuation. What happens to the meaning of the poem?

2. Poets often use vivid verbs to help create an image. List the verbs in lines 3, 5, 8, 9, 10, and 12 of "The Sea." How do these verbs help sustain the image of the dog and help you visualize the sea?

3. This poet wants you to see the sea as a hungry dog. How might a hungry dog behave? Why didn't the poet compare the sea to a well-fed dog? What image of the sea would that create?

4. Look carefully through the poem at all the ways the sea is compared to a dog. See if you can answer the following questions:

   a. How would the sea "roll" on the beach?

   b. What would its "clashing teeth and shaggy jaws" be?

   c. What are the "bones" the sea dog gnaws?

   d. When the sea dog is "licking its greasy paws," what is the sea doing?

   e. In line 13, what does the poet imagine the sea spray is?

   f. When the sea dog "howls and hollos," what is the sea really doing?

   g. What sound of the sea is compared to the dog's quiet snore?

5. Poets use onomatopoeia to create sound effects that echo the meaning of the poem. Three words in "The Sea" that sound like the actions they represent are *clashing, roars,* and *rumbling.* Find three more examples of onomatopoeia in "The Sea."

Strategy Tip

Always read a poem aloud. Be sure to pay attention to the end punctuation and don't pause just because you are at the end of a line. Look for comparisons that help create images.

North Carolina Competency Goal
5.02

SKILLS FOCUS

Reading Skills
Use specific strategies to read and analyze a poem.

The Sneetches

Make the Connection
Talk It Over

Like many of Dr. Seuss's poems, "The Sneetches" is meant for both children and adults. Underneath the clever wordplay and lively rhythms of the poems there's usually a serious message. As you read this poem, think about the point Dr. Seuss is making about people and the way they treat one another.

Quickwrite

Before you begin, join a small group and make a list of injustices you are aware of. Discuss events you've read about in newspapers or seen on TV. List some of the reasons people are treated unfairly. (Reasons may be as simple as the clothes people wear or as complex as their personal beliefs.)

North Carolina Competency Goal
1.04; 4.01; 5.01; 5.02

Literary Focus
Rhymes: *Sneetches* and *Eaches*

Everyone knows what a **rhyme** is: two words that have the same chiming sounds, like *nose* and *rose*. When he was asked, "What is rhyme?" Dr. Seuss replied, "A rhyme is something without which I would probably be in the dry-cleaning business." To keep his poems galloping along with catchy rhymes, Dr. Seuss often invented words to rhyme with real words. For instance, throughout "The Sneetches" he rhymes the real word *stars* with the made-up word *thars.* For that matter, who ever heard of Sneetches before Dr. Seuss invented them?

INTERNET
More About Seuss
Keyword: LE5 6-7

SKILLS FOCUS

Literary Skills
Understand rhyme and rhyme scheme.

Mark That Rhyme; Scan That Rhythm

Poets often use a pattern of rhymes, called a **rhyme scheme,** in a poem. To find a poem's rhyme scheme, mark the first line and all the lines that rhyme with it *a;* mark the second line and all the lines that rhyme with it *b;* and so on.

To find a poem's **meter,** you read the poem aloud. Mark each stressed syllable you hear with the symbol ′ and each unstressed syllable with the symbol ˘. This marking is called **scanning.**

Here are the first four lines of "The Sneetches," with the rhyme scheme and meter marked:

Now, the Star-Belly Sneetches	*a*
Had bellies with stars	*b*
The Plain-Belly Sneetches	*a*
Had none upon thars.	*b*

In poems with a strong, regular beat, variation is important. Reading a poem with an unchanging pattern of beats is as exciting as listening to the *ticktock, ticktock* of a clock. Read "The Sneetches" aloud, and notice how Dr. Seuss varies the pattern of syllables in the poem.

The SNEETCHES

Dr. Seuss (Theodor Geisel)

Now, the Star-Belly Sneetches
Had bellies with stars.
The Plain-Belly Sneetches
Had none upon thars.

5   Those stars weren't so big. They were really so small
You might think such a thing wouldn't matter at all.

But, because they had stars, all the Star-Belly Sneetches
Would brag, "We're the best kind of Sneetch on the beaches."
With their snoots in the air, they would sniff and they'd snort
10   "We'll have nothing to do with the Plain-Belly sort!"
And whenever they met some, when they were out walking,
They'd hike right on past them without even talking.

When the Star-Belly children went out to play ball,
Could a Plain Belly get in the game . . . ? Not at all.
15   You only could play if your bellies had stars
And the Plain-Belly children had none upon thars.

When the Star-Belly Sneetches had frankfurter roasts
Or picnics or parties or marshmallow toasts,
They never invited the Plain-Belly Sneetches.
20   They left them out cold, in the dark of the beaches.
They kept them away. Never let them come near.
And that's how they treated them year after year.

Then ONE day, it seems . . . while the Plain-Belly Sneetches
Were moping and doping alone on the beaches,
25 Just sitting there wishing their bellies had stars . . .
A stranger zipped up in the strangest of cars!

"My friends," he announced in a voice clear and keen,
"My name is Sylvester McMonkey McBean.
And I've heard of your troubles. I've heard you're unhappy.
30 But I can fix that. I'm the Fix-it-Up Chappie.
I've come here to help you. I have what you need.
And my prices are low. And I work at great speed.
And my work is one hundred per cent guaranteed!"

Then, quickly, Sylvester McMonkey McBean
35 Put together a very peculiar machine.
And he said, "You want stars like a Star-Belly Sneetch . . . ?
My friends, you can have them for three dollars each!"

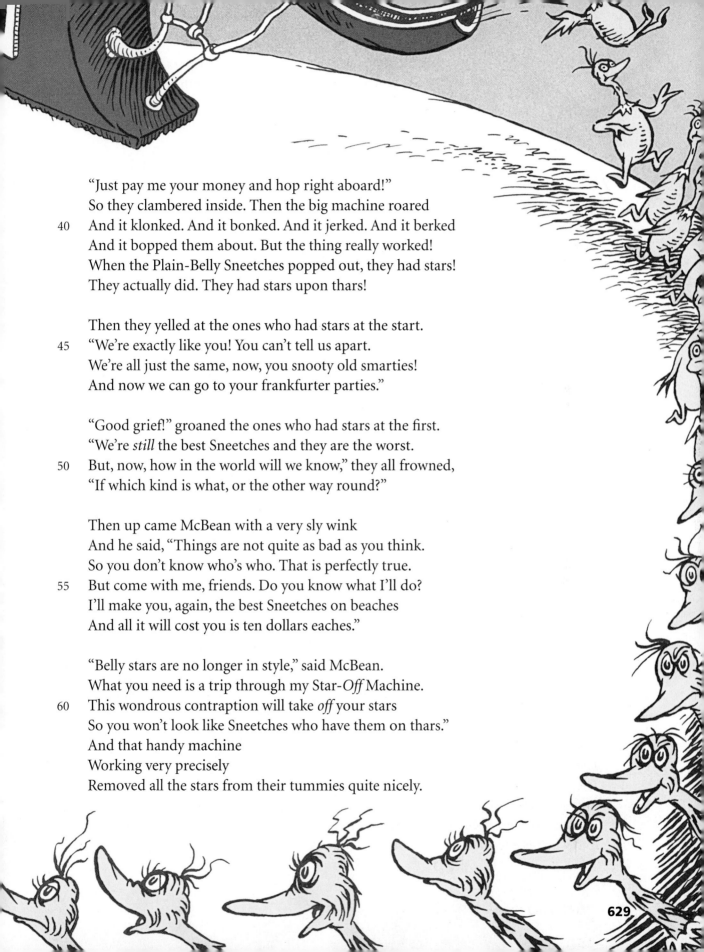

"Just pay me your money and hop right aboard!"
So they clambered inside. Then the big machine roared

40   And it klonked. And it bonked. And it jerked. And it berked
And it bopped them about. But the thing really worked!
When the Plain-Belly Sneetches popped out, they had stars!
They actually did. They had stars upon thars!

Then they yelled at the ones who had stars at the start.
45   "We're exactly like you! You can't tell us apart.
We're all just the same, now, you snooty old smarties!
And now we can go to your frankfurter parties."

"Good grief!" groaned the ones who had stars at the first.
"We're *still* the best Sneetches and they are the worst.
50   But, now, how in the world will we know," they all frowned,
"If which kind is what, or the other way round?"

Then up came McBean with a very sly wink
And he said, "Things are not quite as bad as you think.
So you don't know who's who. That is perfectly true.
55   But come with me, friends. Do you know what I'll do?
I'll make you, again, the best Sneetches on beaches
And all it will cost you is ten dollars eaches."

"Belly stars are no longer in style," said McBean.
What you need is a trip through my Star-*Off* Machine.
60   This wondrous contraption will take *off* your stars
So you won't look like Sneetches who have them on thars."
And that handy machine
Working very precisely
Removed all the stars from their tummies quite nicely.

65 Then, with snoots in the air, they paraded about
And they opened their beaks and they let out a shout,
"We know who is who! Now there isn't a doubt.
The best kind of Sneetches are Sneetches without!"

Then, of course, those with stars all got frightfully mad.
70 To be wearing a star now was frightfully bad.
Then, of course, old Sylvester McMonkey McBean
Invited *them* into his Star-Off Machine.

Then, of course from THEN on, as you probably guess,
Things really got into a horrible mess.

75 All the rest of that day, on those wild screaming beaches,
The Fix-it-Up Chappie kept fixing up Sneetches.
Off again! On again!
In again! Out again!
Through the machines they raced round and about again,
80 Changing their stars every minute or two.
They kept paying money. They kept running through
Until neither the Plain nor the Star-Bellies knew
Whether this one was that one . . . or that one was this one
Or which one was what one . . . or what one was who.

85 Then, when every last cent
Of their money was spent,
The Fix-it-Up Chappie packed up
And he went.

And he laughed as he drove
90 In his car up the beach,
"They never will learn.
No. You can't teach a Sneetch!"

But McBean was quite wrong. I'm quite happy to say
That the Sneetches got really quite smart on that day,
95 The day they decided that Sneetches are Sneetches
And no kind of Sneetch is the best on the beaches.
That day, all the Sneetches forgot about stars
And whether they had one, or not, upon thars.

Meet the Writer

Theodor Seuss Geisel

Creature Feature

Dr. Seuss is the pen name of **Theodor Seuss Geisel** (1904–1991), who began drawing fantastic animal cartoons while he was still a child. (His father ran the local zoo.) An art teacher told him that he would never learn to draw, and twenty-seven publishers rejected his first children's book, *And to Think That I Saw It on Mulberry Street* (1937). Even so, Dr. Seuss went on to write and illustrate more than forty children's classics, full of nonsense rhymes, wacky creatures, and his special brand of wisdom.

Judging by the number of books Dr. Seuss has sold—at least 200 million copies—he is one of the most popular writers in history. As he did in "The Sneetches," Dr. Seuss often used his zany characters to look at serious issues as if "through the wrong end of a telescope."

Dr. Seuss explained how he decided on his pen name:

© 2003 Bill Nelson.

> 66 The 'Dr. Seuss' name is a combination of my middle name and the fact that I had been studying for my doctorate when I decided to quit to become a cartoonist. My father had always wanted to see a Dr. in front of my name, so I attached it. I figured by doing that, I saved him about ten thousand dollars. 99

For Independent Reading

Books by Dr. Seuss that use wacky-looking creatures to convey a serious message include *The Lorax* (about protecting the environment) and *The Butter Battle Book* (about war).

First Thoughts

1. Complete the following sentence:
   - I think this poem is about . . .

Thinking Critically

2. What one word might describe the Star-Bellies? the Plain-Bellies?

3. What opinion of the Sneetches does McBean have? Do you think he is right or wrong? Why?

4. Why do the Sneetches finally change their behavior?

5. What words has Dr. Seuss made up to keep lines **rhymed**? Can you find at least one **internal rhyme**—two or more rhyming words within a line?

North Carolina Competency Goal
1.02; 1.04;
4.01; 4.02;
5.01; 5.02

6. Working with a partner, mark the **rhyme scheme** of at least three stanzas of "The Sneetches." Use the letter code you learned earlier (see page 626). Which stanzas are different? Do the differences "make a difference"? Why or why not?

7. Read a few **stanzas** of this poem aloud; then, copy two stanzas onto a sheet of paper. Scan them, marking stressed and unstressed syllables in each line (see page 626). Is the meter identical in all the lines?

Extending Interpretations

INTERNET
Projects and Activities
Keyword: LE5 6-7

8. What do you think is the **moral,** or lesson, of this poem? Can you think of anyone in real life who behaves like the characters in "The Sneetches"? (For ideas, look back at your Quickwrite notes.) 🖉

WRITING

SKILLS FOCUS

Literary Skills
Analyze rhyme and rhyme scheme.

Writing Skills
Write a rhyme.

Writing a Rhyme

To make his lines rhyme and to make the poem fun to read, Dr. Seuss sometimes changes a spelling, adds a new ending sound, or even invents a word. Find the funny words invented by Dr. Seuss in lines 4, 40, and 57. What word does each made-up word rhyme with?

Write a line of poetry to rhyme with the following line: *Eva was eating an orange.* (Since no word in English rhymes with *orange,* you'll have to invent a rhyming word.)

Reading Check

a. Why do one group of Sneetches think they're better than the other group? How do they treat that group?

b. What offer does McBean make to the Plain-Bellies? What offer does he then make to the Star-Bellies?

c. When does McBean finally leave? What happens afterward?

Elements of Literature

Poetry *by* John Malcolm Brinnin

SEEING LIKENESSES

Poetry lives and breathes because poets make especially imaginative comparisons—they have a special talent for seeing one thing in terms of something else, something very different. We call these comparisons between unlike things **figures of speech.** There are three main figures of speech: metaphors, similes, and personification.

Metaphors and Similes

"My baby sister's a doll," you might say, comparing your sister's size and sweetness to the perfection of a doll. At another time you might say, "My brother is a rat," comparing your poor brother to the nastiest little creature you can think of. In both cases you would be making a kind of comparison called a **metaphor**—a form of comparison that directly compares two unlike things. A metaphor wastes no time in getting to the point.

On the other hand, if you said, "My sister is *like* a doll," or, with a sudden change of heart, "My brother's as good as gold," you would in each case be making a **simile**—a form of comparison in which one thing is compared to another unlike thing by using specific words of comparison, such as *like, as,* and *resembles.*

Poets try to find unusual metaphors and similes. Christina Rossetti, when she was in love, used a simile and wrote, "My heart is like a singing bird." If she had made a metaphor, she would have written, "My heart *is* a singing bird." Emily Dickinson, thinking about the problems fame can bring, said, "Fame is a bee." If she had made a simile, she would have said, "Fame is *like* a bee."

Personification: Making the World Human

One of the most familiar kinds of comparison is **personification**—that is, speaking of something that is not human as if it had human abilities and human reactions.

"The sky wept buckets all day long." In this example of personification, a

(continued)

North Carolina Competency Goal 5.02

INTERNET
More About Imagery
•
More About Simile/Metaphor
Keyword: LE5 6-7

SKILLS FOCUS

Literary Skills Understand the use of figures of speech in poetry.

PEANUTS reprinted by permission of United Feature Syndicate, Inc.

natural, nonhuman thing—the sky—is spoken of as though it had human abilities and human feelings. This description is much more visual than a plain statement of fact, such as "Yesterday it rained for hours."

Any of us can turn almost anything into imaginative language. After all, each of us has "a touch of the poet." This is partly what makes us human—the ability to see connections between different parts of our world.

Your Poem, Man . . .

unless there's one thing seen
suddenly against another—a parsnip
sprouting for a President, or
hailstones melting in an ashtray—
nothing really happens. It takes
surprise and wild connections,
doesn't it? A walrus chewing
on a ballpoint pen. Two blue tail-
lights on Tyrannosaurus Rex. Green
cheese teeth. Maybe what we wanted
least. Or most. Some unexpected
pleats. Words that never knew
each other till right now. Plug us
into the wrong socket and see
what blows—or what lights up.
Try
      untried
            circuitry,
new
      fuses.
Tell it like it never really was,
man,
and maybe we can see it
like it is.

              —Edward Lueders

Ode to Mi Gato *and*
In a Neighborhood in Los Angeles *and* Hard on the Gas

Make the Connection
Quickwrite ✏️

Think about the love songs you hear on the radio. Love has also inspired thousands of poems. In two of the next three poems, the speaker lovingly recalls a relative. The speaker of the first poem celebrates a pet.

Think of someone or something special you'd like to celebrate or remember. Then, draw a gift diagram like the one below. Fill it with words, phrases, and memories telling the person or thing what he, she, or it has done for you.

To Maxwell,
You taught
me . . .

Literary Focus
Tone: The Speaker's Feelings

Tone refers to the way a speaker is feeling. When you listen to people, you can often tell from their voices and facial expressions how they feel. You can usually tell if they're serious, happy, worried, or angry. When you read a poem, however, you have to depend on words alone to learn how the speaker (the voice talking to you in the poem) is feeling.

Ode: A Poem of Praise

An **ode** is a poem written to honor someone or something of great importance to the speaker. When people hear the word *ode*, they usually think of a poem written in a grand, dignified style. Gary Soto brings the ode down to earth. He uses ordinary language and the rhythms of everyday speech as he celebrates his *gato,* or cat.

North Carolina Competency Goal
1.04; 4.01; 5.01; 5.02

SKILLS FOCUS

Literary Skills
Understand tone; understand elements of an ode.

Ode to Mi Gato Gary Soto

He's white
As spilled milk,
My cat who sleeps
With his belly
5   Turned toward
The summer sky.
He loves the sun,
Its warmth like a hand.
He loves tuna cans
10   And milk cartons
With their dribble
Of milk. He loves
Mom when she rattles
The bag of cat food,
15   The brown nuggets
Raining into his bowl.
And my cat loves
Me, because I saved
Him from a dog,
20   Because I dressed him
In a hat and a cape
For Halloween,
Because I dangled
A sock of chicken skin
25   As he stood on his
Hind legs. I love mi gato,
Porque I found
Him on the fender
Of an abandoned car.
30   He was a kitten,

With a meow
Like the rusty latch
On a gate. I carried
Him home in the loop
35   Of my arms.
I poured milk
Into him, let him
Lick chunks of
Cheese from my palms,
40   And cooked huevo
After huevo
Until his purring
Engine kicked in
And he cuddled
45   Up to my father's slippers.
That was last year.
This spring,
He's excellent at sleeping
And no good
50   At hunting. At night
All the other cats
In the neighborhood
Can see him slink
Around the corner,
55   Or jump from the tree
Like a splash of
Milk. We lap up
His love and
He laps up his welcome.

To read about Gary Soto, see
Meet the Writer on page 342.

(Opposite) *Spring Play in a T'ang Garden* (detail) (18th century). Copy of a painting attributed to Hsuan Tsung (Ming dynasty). Handscroll; colors on silk.

IN A NEIGHBORHOOD IN LOS ANGELES

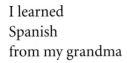

FRANCISCO X. ALARCÓN

I learned
Spanish
from my grandma

mijito°
5   don't cry
she'd tell me

on the mornings
my parents
would leave

10   to work
at the fish
canneries

my grandma
would chat
15   with chairs

sing them
old
songs

dance
20   waltzes with them
in the kitchen

when she'd say
niño barrigón°
she'd laugh

25   with my grandma
I learned
to count clouds

to point out
in flowerpots
30   mint leaves

my grandma
wore moons
on her dress

Mexico's mountains
35   deserts
ocean

in her eyes
I'd see them
in her braids

40   I'd touch them
in her voice
smell them

one day
I was told:
45   she went far away

but still
I feel her
with me

whispering
50   in my ear
mijito

—*translated by*
   Francisco X. Alarcón

---

4. *mijito* (mē·hē′tô): contraction
of *mi hijito*, Spanish for "my
little child."

23. *niño barrigón* (nēn′yô bä′rē·gôn′):
Spanish for "potbellied boy."

HARD ON THE GAS

Janet S. Wong

My grandfather taught himself to drive
rough, the way he learned to live,

push the pedal, hard on the gas,
rush up to 50,
coast a bit,

rush, rest, rush, rest—

When you clutch the bar above your right shoulder
he shoots you a look that asks,
Who said the ride would be smooth?

Meet the Writers

Francisco X. Alarcón
Janet S. Wong

"Poetry Is, in a Way, Like Shouting"

Francisco X. Alarcón (1954–   ), who grew up both in the United States and in Mexico, says that his family has been binational for four generations. Alarcón's roots are important to him; he regularly visits the Mexican village his ancestors came from.

Alarcón was brought up mainly in Los Angeles by his grandmother, the woman he celebrates in his poem "In a Neighborhood in Los Angeles." His career as a poet began when he was thirteen years old and started writing down his grandmother's songs.

Janet Wong (1962–   ) bases many of her poems on her experiences growing up Asian American. Wong decided to become a poet after working as a lawyer for several years.

> "Poetry is, in a way, like shouting. Since you can't yell at the top of your lungs for a long time, you have to decide what you really need to say, and say it quickly."

First Thoughts

1. Which speaker or character from the three poems you've just read seems like somebody you would like to meet? Why?

Thinking Critically

2. Compare these three poems by filling in a chart like the one at the bottom of this page. First, identify the subject of each poem. Next, state what he, she, or it is loved for. Then, find a word or two to describe the speaker's **tone**—the way he or she feels about the subject.

3. At the beginning of "Ode to Mi Gato," the speaker uses a **simile** comparing a cat to spilled milk. How is the cat like spilled milk? Find another simile comparing the cat to milk.

4. The grandmother in the poem "In a Neighborhood in Los Angeles" **personifies** her chairs. Which lines show her treating them as though they were people?

5. An **extended metaphor** carries a comparison through several lines or a whole poem. In "Hard on the Gas" the poet uses an extended metaphor to compare a way of driving to a way of living. What kind of life would be "hard on the gas"?

Extending Interpretations

6. Spanish words are used in Gary Soto's poem and in the translation of Alarcón's poem. What do you think of this technique? What effect does the use of Spanish words have on the poems?

WRITING

Writing an Ode

Whom or what would you like to celebrate in an ode? Look back at your Quickwrite for ideas. Before you write, list a few details about your subject to help readers understand why you feel so strongly about it. Try to include figures of speech in your ode.

North Carolina Competency Goal
5.01; 5.02

INTERNET

Projects and Activities
Keyword: LE5 6-7

SKILLS FOCUS

Literary Skills
Analyze tone; analyze elements of an ode.

Writing Skills
Write an ode.

Poem	Subject	What Subject Is Loved For	Speaker's Tone
"Ode to Mi Gato"			
"In a Neighborhood . . ."			
"Hard on the Gas"			

Haiku

Make the Connection
Quickwrite ✏️

Think of an outdoor scene you've observed. Try to picture it clearly and even hear some sounds. Freewrite for a minute or two about what you see and hear.

Literary Focus
Word Choice

In poetry every word counts, because a poet must pack a lot of meaning into just a few phrases. When choosing their words, poets consider what words mean, how they sound, and what they suggest.

Haiku

Haiku (hī′kōō′) is the most widely known form of Japanese poetry. In haiku every word must be chosen with special care because haiku have a strictly defined form. A haiku in Japanese consists of three lines and a total of

seventeen syllables: five syllables each in lines 1 and 3 and seven syllables in line 2. (The number of syllables may vary in English translations.)

Here are some of the rules that haiku poets generally follow.

1. A haiku is about a moment in daily life.
2. A haiku describes particular things, often two contrasting things.
3. A haiku records a moment of enlightenment—a sudden discovery about life.
4. A haiku is usually about a season of the year. Often a haiku contains a *kigo,* a "season" word, like *frog* for summer or *willow* for spring.

A haiku is like a painting in which the artist uses just a few brush strokes to suggest a subject, leaving the rest to your imagination.

Snow at Night by Ando Hiroshige. Japanese engraving.

The Art Archive/Oriental Art Museum, Genoa/Dagli Orti (A).

North Carolina Competency Goal
1.02; 1.04; 4.01; 4.02; 5.01; 5.02

SKILLS FOCUS

Literary Skills
Understand word choice in poetry; understand the elements of haiku.

An old silent pond . . .
A frog jumps into the pond,
splash! Silence again.

—Matsuo Bashō

Winter rain:
A farmhouse piled with firewood,
A light in the window.

—Nozawa Bonchō

Bad-tempered, I got back:
Then, in the garden,
The willow tree.

—Ōshima Ryōta

Sudden Shower at Atake (1857) by Ando Hiroshige.
Japanese woodcut.

A balmy spring wind
Reminding me of something
I cannot recall

—Richard Wright

Meet the Writers

Matsuo Bashō
Nozawa Bonchō
Ōshima Ryōta
Richard Wright

Bashō (17th century) by Ran-ku.

The True Nature of Things

Matsuo Bashō (1644–1694) is one of Japan's most famous poets. Bashō was born into a wealthy family and grew up in a village in western Japan. He began writing verses when he was nine. By the time Bashō was thirty, he was traveling around Japan and working as a professional poetry teacher. **Nozawa Bonchō** (16?? –1714) was one of his students.

Many of the haiku written by Bashō and his students were inspired by nature. Bashō urged his students to look for the "true nature of things." He insisted that haiku should be written in simple language and deal with everyday life. He took his pen name from a banana tree (*bashō* in Japanese) that he planted in his yard.

Ōshima Ryōta (1707–1787) incorporated Zen ideas into his haiku and his painting. (Zen is a form of Buddhism that emphasizes meditation.)

Modern poets in many countries have written haiku. **Richard Wright** (1908–1960), an African American writer famous for his autobiography *Black Boy*, composed more than four thousand haiku in the two years before his death. Wright called them hoku.

After You Read   Response and Analysis

First Thoughts

1. Complete this sentence:

- The picture in my mind as I read each haiku was . . .

Thinking Critically

2. Which season do you think each haiku describes? (Remember that a frog is often used to suggest summer and a willow tree to suggest spring.)

3. List three or four **images** in these haiku that help you **see** things and two **images** that help you hear sounds.

4. Which haiku present **contrasting images**?

5. In each haiku, what exactly does the speaker notice or discover? What part does nature play in each discovery?

6. Choose one haiku, and describe its **tone**—the speaker's attitude toward the subject. Which words in the haiku suggest the tone you described?

7. Choose one haiku, and state its **message** in your own words.

8. Find two haiku that contain five syllables in the first and last lines and seven syllables in the middle line.

Extending Interpretations

9. In Japan, poetry-writing contests are held every year in which judges award prizes for the best haiku. Suppose you're one of the judges, and you're considering these four haiku. Which would you award the prize for? Why?

North Carolina Competency Goal 5.02

SKILLS FOCUS

Literary Skills
Analyze word choice in poetry; analyze elements of haiku.

The Great Wave off Kanagawa (c. 1831–1833) by Katsushika Hokusai.
The Metropolitan Museum of Art, H. O. Havemeyer Collection, Bequest of Mrs. H. O. Havemeyer, 1929. (JP1847) Photograph © 1994 The Metropolitan Museum of Art.

WRITING

Writing a Haiku

Haiku are fun to write. Before you write, review the rules for writing haiku on page 641. (If you wish, you can skip the rule about the seventeen syllables.) Then, keep filling out charts like the one below until you've found images and a feeling that you think will work. You might try to open with a word naming your season. Think also about animals, plants, and other items that are associated with your season. Try to list some contrasting images in your chart. One important rule: Your poem should consist of three lines.

Haiku Ideas
Season:
Sight images:
Sound images:
Touch images:
Smell images:
Taste images:
Feeling or discovery:

North Carolina Competency Goal
5.01; 5.02

Writing Skills
Write a haiku.

Poem *and* Motto

Make the Connection
Speaking

Try this experiment with tones: With one or more partners, take turns saying these three sentences aloud. Use your voice to express the tones named in parentheses. Notice how punctuation helps suggest the different tones.

I *won!* (joy)
I won? (doubt)
I *won*? (sarcasm)

Literary Focus
Tone: An Attitude

Tone is the attitude a speaker takes toward a subject. We express tones all the time: Our words and voices can express joy, sadness, confusion, anger—and many other feelings. You might think that a poet would always express the same tone in his or her works, but that is not the case. Two poems by the same poet can express totally different tones, as in these poems by Langston Hughes.

North Carolina Competency Goal
5.02

INTERNET
More About Hughes
Keyword: LE5 6-7

Literary Skills
Understand tone.

Witness (1987) by Hughie Lee-Smith.

Courtesy, June Kelly Gallery, New York. © Estate of Hughie Lee-Smith/ Licensed by VAGA, New York, NY.

Poem
Langston Hughes

I loved my friend.
He went away from me.
There's nothing more to say.
The poem ends,
Soft as it began—
I loved my friend.

Motto
Langston Hughes

I play it cool
And dig all jive.
That's the reason
I stay alive.

My motto,
As I live and learn,
    is:
Dig And Be Dug
In Return.

Carolina Shout by Romare Bearden.

The Mint Museums, Charlotte, North Carolina. Museum Purchase: National Endowment for the Arts Matching Fund and the Charlotte Debutante Club Fund. 1975.8 © Romare Bearden Foundation/Licensed by VAGA, New York, NY.

Meet the Writer

Langston Hughes

Portrait of Langston Hughes (c. 1925) by Winold Reiss.

The Dream Keeper

Langston Hughes (1902–1967) was lonely as a child until he found a home in the world of books.

> "Books began to happen to me, and I began to believe in nothing but books and the wonderful world of books—where if people suffered they suffered in beautiful language and not in monosyllables, as we did in Kansas."

Hughes wrote his first poem in elementary school—but only *after* his classmates had elected him class poet.

> "[My class] had elected all the class officers, but there was no one in our class who looked like a poet, or had ever written a poem.... The day I was elected, I went home and wondered what I should write. Since we had eight teachers in our school, I thought there should be one verse for each teacher, with an especially good one for my favorite teacher. I felt the class should have eight, too. So my first poem was about the longest poem I ever wrote—sixteen verses, which were later cut down.

In the first half of the poem, I said that our school had the finest teachers there ever were. And in the latter half, I said our class was the greatest class ever graduated. So at graduation when I read the poem, naturally everybody applauded loudly. That was the way I began to write poetry."

Hughes later settled in New York City, where he became a leading figure in the cultural movement known as the Harlem Renaissance. His poems often echo the rhythms of blues and jazz.

For Independent Reading

Hughes is most celebrated for his poems. You can sample some of his best poems in a collection called *The Dream Keeper and Other Poems*.

After You Read   Response and Analysis

First Thoughts

1. Complete this sentence:
- My favorite line in each of these poems is . . .

Thinking Critically

2. Think about the "I" in "Poem." What do you know about this **speaker**?

3. Think about the "I" in "Motto." What do you know about this **speaker**? (What does he have to do to stay alive?)

4. Hughes used the slang of jazz musicians in many of his poems. You may know what the speaker in "Motto" means when he says, "I play it cool." What are the slang meanings of *dig* and *jive*? (Use a good dictionary if you need to.) How would you state the speaker's motto in your own words?

5. **Tone** is a speaker's feeling or attitude toward a subject. Here is a list of tones. Which would you match with "Poem"? with "Motto"? Be ready to defend your choices. (Which tones do not apply to either poem?)

sad	wistful
upbeat	sorrowful
sarcastic	defiant
bitter	boastful
desperate	joyful

Extending Interpretations

6. Try rephrasing "Motto," substituting different words for *cool, dig,* and *jive.* What happens to the tone of the poem?

7. What's your motto?

LISTENING AND SPEAKING

Preparing a Poetry Reading
Prepare the two poems for an oral presentation. Before your reading, make a script for each poem. Look carefully at the punctuation, and mark the points at which you'll pause. Decide which lines or words to emphasize (watch for short lines and long lines). Also decide what tone, or attitude, you want to convey in your readings.

Another possibility is setting the poems to music. What kind of music would suit each poem?

North Carolina Competency Goal
1.02; 1.04;
4.01; 4.02;
5.01; 5.02;
6.01; 6.02

Literary Skills
Analyze tone.

Listening and Speaking Skills
Prepare a poetry reading.

John Henry

Make the Connection

Talk It Over

"John Henry" is a ballad about a contest between a man and a machine. What can machines do better than people? What can people do better than machines? Working with a few classmates, list some answers to these questions. Then, make a chart like the one that follows, and fill it in with the best items from your list. Write down two items in each column.

North Carolina Competency Goal
1.04; 4.01; 5.01; 5.02

Contests People Would Win	Contests Machines Would Win
song writing	clothes washing

Literary Focus

Repetition

Repetition is repeating something— a word, a phrase, a stanza, a sound, a pattern. Repetition helps give poetry its music. Poets also use repetition to emphasize important ideas, to create a mood, even to build suspense.

One of the simplest kinds of repetition used in poetry, songs, and speeches is the refrain. A **refrain** is a word, phrase, line, or group of lines repeated at intervals. (The wording of a refrain may change slightly from time to time.) Most songs you hear or sing have a refrain. "The Star-Spangled Banner" includes a refrain at the end of each verse: "Oh! say, does that star-spangled banner yet wave / O'er the land of the free and the home of the brave?" Martin Luther King, Jr.'s most famous speech is built on the refrain "I have a dream."

INTERNET
Cross-curricular Connection
Keyword: LE5 6-7

SKILLS FOCUS

Literary Skills
Understand repetition and refrain.

Background

Literature and Folklore

Nobody knows whether John Henry, the hero of this song, was a real person, but people began singing about him in the early 1870s. He is said to have been an African American laborer in the crew constructing the Big Bend Tunnel of the Chesapeake and Ohio Railroad. According to the legend, someone set up a contest between John Henry and a steam drill. If you can, listen to a recording of the song "John Henry."

John Henry on the Right, Steam Drill on the Left (detail) (1944–1947) by Palmer C. Hayden.

A Gift from Miriam Hayden to The Museum of African American Art, Los Angeles, CA.

John Henry

When John Henry Was a Baby (1944–1947) by Palmer C. Hayden.

ANONYMOUS AFRICAN AMERICAN

John Henry was about three days old
Sittin' on his papa's knee.
He picked up a hammer and a little piece of steel
Said, "Hammer's gonna be the death of me, Lord, Lord!
5   Hammer's gonna be the death of me."

The captain said to John Henry,
"Gonna bring that steam drill 'round
Gonna bring that steam drill out on the job
Gonna whop that steel on down, Lord, Lord!
10 Whop that steel on down."

John Henry told his captain,
"A man ain't nothin' but a man
But before I let your steam drill beat me down
I'd die with a hammer in my hand, Lord, Lord!
15 I'd die with a hammer in my hand."

John Henry said to his shaker,°
"Shaker, why don't you sing?
I'm throwing thirty pounds from my hips on down
Just listen to that cold steel ring, Lord, Lord!
20 Listen to that cold steel ring."

John Henry said to his shaker,
"Shaker, you'd better pray
'Cause if I miss that little piece of steel
Tomorrow be your buryin' day, Lord, Lord!
25 Tomorrow be your buryin' day."

The shaker said to John Henry,
"I think this mountain's cavin' in!"
John Henry said to his shaker, "Man,
That ain't nothin' but my hammer suckin' wind,
    Lord, Lord!
30 Nothin' but my hammer suckin' wind."

---

16. shaker *n.:* worker who holds the drill.

John Henry on the Right, Steam Drill on the Left (1944–1947) by Palmer C. Hayden.

The man that invented the steam drill
Thought he was mighty fine
But John Henry made fifteen feet
The steam drill only made nine, Lord, Lord!
35   The steam drill only made nine.

John Henry hammered in the mountain
His hammer was striking fire
But he worked so hard, he broke his poor heart
He laid down his hammer and he died, Lord, Lord!
40   He laid down his hammer and he died.

John Henry had a little woman
Her name was Polly Ann
John Henry took sick and went to his bed
Polly Ann drove steel like a man, Lord, Lord!
45   Polly Ann drove steel like a man.

He Laid Down His Hammer and Cried (1944–1947)
by Palmer C. Hayden.

John Henry had a little baby
You could hold him in the palm of your hand
The last words I heard that poor boy say,
"My daddy was a steel-driving man, Lord, Lord!
50   My daddy was a steel-driving man."

They took John Henry to the graveyard
And they buried him in the sand
And every locomotive comes a-roaring by
Says, "There lies a steel-driving man, Lord, Lord!
55   There lies a steel-driving man."

Well, every Monday morning
When the bluebirds begin to sing
You can hear John Henry a mile or more
You can hear John Henry's hammer ring, Lord, Lord!
60   You can hear John Henry's hammer ring.

First Thoughts

1. What did you think of John Henry's trying to outperform a steam drill? Was this heroic or foolish? Why?

Thinking Critically

2. Who or what do you think eventually wins the contest between John Henry and the steam drill? Use lines from the song to support your answer.

3. **Folk heroes** are superheroes, people with qualities admired by those who give them lasting fame. How does John Henry show that he is a superhero, even as a baby?

4. How does Polly Ann show that she's a superhero too?

5. Who or what keeps John Henry's name alive?

Extending Interpretations

6. Which lines are repeated in each stanza? Which words are a **refrain** for the whole poem? How could the refrain be sung differently each time to suggest different feelings?

7. What is the **tone** of this song—is it mournful, defiant, proud, angry? Be ready to read John Henry's story aloud to express the tone you've named.

WRITING

Writing About a Superhero

Write a song or story for the twenty-first century about a person who challenges a machine. Where does your story take place? What is the machine? How has it challenged your hero? Who or what wins the contest—the human or the machine? For ideas, look back at the lists you made for Make the Connection on page 650.

Reading Check

Review the main events of John Henry's story; then, complete a **sequence chart** like the one below. Add as many boxes as you need.

> **a.** When John Henry was three days old, he picked up a hammer and made a prediction.

> **b.** When he grew up, he told his captain he'd rather die than be outdone by a steam drill.

> **c.**

INTERNET
Projects and Acitvities
Keyword: LE5 6-7

SKILLS FOCUS

Literary Skills
Analyze repetition and refrain.

Writing Skills
Write a story or song about a superhero.

North Carolina Competency Goal
1.02; 5.02

Identifying and Interpreting Figurative Language

Figurative language is based on comparisons; it is not meant to be understood literally. There are hundreds of types of figurative language, or figures of speech; three of the most commonly used are **similes, metaphors,** and **personification.**

PRACTICE

For each of the following quotations, identify the two things being compared, explain how they're alike, and identify the figure of speech being used: simile, metaphor, or personification.

1. "O my Love is like a red, red rose . . ."
   —Robert Burns

2. "I wandered lonely as a cloud
   That floats on high o'er vales and hills . . ."
   —William Wordsworth

3. "The Lord is my shepherd; I shall not want."
   —from Psalm 23

4. "The Lightning is a yellow Fork
   From Tables in the sky . . ."   —Emily Dickinson

5. "The sea is a hungry dog,
   Giant and gray.
   He rolls on the beach all day."   —James Reeves

6. "I hear America singing, the varied carols I hear . . ."
   —Walt Whitman

7. "My soul has grown deep like the rivers . . ."
   —Langston Hughes

8. "'Hope' is the thing with feathers—
   That perches in the soul—"
   —Emily Dickinson

9. "The wind stood up, and gave a shout;
   He whistled on his fingers, and
   Kicked the withered leaves about . . ."
   —James Stephens

10. "There is a garden in her face,
    Where roses and white lilies grow . . ."
    —Thomas Campion

North Carolina Competency Goal
5.02; 6.01

Vocabulary Skills
Identify and interpret figurative language.

A Box of Figures of Speech

simile: comparison between two unlike things in which *like, as, than, resembles,* or a similar word is used (for example, *life is like a flowing river*)

metaphor: comparison between two unlike things in which a word such as *like, as, than,* or *resembles* is not used (for example, *life is a flowing river*)

personification: figure of speech in which human traits are given to nonhuman things, such as animals or forces of nature (for example, *the river sang a song of triumph*)

End All End-Mark Errors

The punctuation at the end of a sentence is called an **end mark**. Like stop signs, end marks prevent collisions. Read the following lines aloud. Can you tell where each sentence starts and where it ends?

> **When the reporter resorted to name-calling, I realized I was reading propaganda from now on I'll read his articles carefully**

Three kinds of end marks are used in English: periods (.), question marks (?), and exclamation points (!). Read the following examples aloud to see how changing the end mark can affect the meaning of a sentence.

> **John's reasoning is faulty.**
> **John's reasoning is faulty?**
> **John's reasoning is faulty!**

The use of end marks may differ from language to language. In Spanish, for example, a question mark or exclamation point appears both before and after a question or exclamation. (Punctuation marks at the beginning of a question or exclamation are *inverted*, or set upside down.)

> **¿Qué pasa?** [What's happening?]
> **¡Qué lastima!** [What a shame!]

PRACTICE 1

Copy the paragraph below. Then, revise it by adding six end marks and capitalizing as needed.

Was Terry excited you bet the soccer match was about to begin the first game of the year is always the most exciting Terry had practiced hard for six weeks she was sure her efforts would pay off tonight

PRACTICE 2

As you proofread your own writing, highlight all your end marks. Then, check them: Ask yourself where each thought ends—really ends. Put an end mark at that point to show that the next word marks the beginning of a whole new thought.

For more help, see End Marks, 12a–e, in the Language Handbook.

North Carolina Competency Goal
5.02

PEANUTS reprinted by permission of United Feature Syndicate, Inc.

SKILLS FOCUS

Grammar Skills
Use end marks correctly.

Comparing Literature

Literary Focus
Extended Metaphor

People often talk about machines as if they were alive. Have you ever heard someone say that a car's engine "purrs" or "roars" or "hums" or "sings"? In two of the poems you're about to read, machines become fierce, roaring, snorting animals. In another poem, a skateboard and its rider become a "single engine human automobile."

The poets who wrote these poems are using one of the most powerful tools available to them—metaphor. A **metaphor** is a direct comparison between two unlike things, as in "You are my sunshine" and "He is a peach." Metaphor is a powerful literary device: After reading Charles Malam's poem, you may never look at a steam shovel again without seeing a dinosaur. An **extended metaphor** carries a comparison through several lines or an entire poem. Notice how these poets hang on to their metaphors— they extend their comparisons all the way to the ends of their poems.

Comparing and Contrasting

In this feature you will **compare** and **contrast** four poems in which metaphor is used to shed new light on a subject. When you **compare,** you point out the similarities between two or more things; when you **contrast,** you point out the differences.

North Carolina Competency Goal
1.02

Literary Skills
Understand extended metaphor.

Reading Skills
Compare and contrast poems.

Metaphors:

- The sea is a playful cat.
- My handwriting is a spider's crawl.
- The building is a laughing face.

Extended Metaphors:

- The sea is a playful cat. *It licks and paws the beach. On sunny days it lies calmly with its belly to the sun.*
- My handwriting is a spider's crawl. *It moves with many legs over the page.*
- The building is a laughing face. *The eyes blink merrily in the light. The open mouth invites all who pass to enter.*

Before You Read

Imagination enables a poet to see comparisons everywhere: The moon becomes a flower in a garden of stars. A cloud becomes a lion roaring in the sky. In the two poems you are about to read, the poets see ordinary machines in unusual ways.

The Toaster

William Jay Smith

A silver-scaled Dragon with jaws flaming red
Sits at my elbow and toasts my bread.
I hand him fat slices, and then, one by one,
He hands them back when he sees they are done. ❶

IDENTIFY

❶ Suppose this poem had no title. What clues in the poem would help you figure out what this dragon really is?

Things to Do If You Are a Subway

Bobbi Katz

Pretend you are a dragon.
Live in underground caves.
Roar about underneath the city.
Swallow piles of people.
Spit them out at the next station.
Zoom through the darkness.
Be an express.
Go fast.
Make as much noise as you please. ❶ ❷

INFER

❶ This poem is an extended metaphor. In what ways is a subway like a dragon?

COMPARE AND CONTRAST

❷ How is the subway-dragon different from the toaster-dragon described in the poem on page 659? Do you think a dragon is a better metaphor for a subway or for a toaster? Why?

"The Toaster" and "Things to Do If You Are a Subway"

First Thoughts

1. Choose your favorite poem, and read it aloud to a partner. Use your voice and movements to convey what each "dragon" is like.

Thinking Critically

2. Continue to develop the **extended metaphor** of "The Toaster": What would you say the dragon is doing when your toast burns or gets stuck in the toaster?

3. The "dragons" in these poems have personalities. What words would you use to describe each of these creatures?

4. Suppose the subway-dragon met the toaster-dragon. What do you think they might say to each other? What name might each dragon choose for himself or herself?

Comparing Literature

5. Poets often use powerful **images** to describe how something looks and sounds and acts. Compare "The Toaster" and "Things to Do If You Are a Subway" by filling in a chart like the one below. The first column is partly filled in for you. You will use this chart when you complete the assignment on page 667.

Comparing Poems		
	"The Toaster"	"Things to Do . . ."
What is the poem about?	a toaster	
What is the subject compared to?		
How does it look?	metal; red coils inside	
How does it sound?		
What does it do?		

North Carolina Competency Goal
5.02

SKILLS FOCUS

Literary Skills
Analyze extended metaphor.

Reading Skills
Compare and contrast poems.

Before You Read

What kind of machine might you compare a skateboarder to? What sort of creature might a steam shovel resemble in someone's imagination? Read on to find out how two poets have answered these questions.

The Sidewalk Racer

or

On the Skateboard

Lillian Morrison

Skimming
an asphalt sea
I swerve, I curve, I
sway; I speed to whirring
5   sound an inch above the
ground; I'm the sailor
and the sail, I'm the
driver and the wheel
I'm the one and only
10   single engine
human auto
mobile. ❶

IDENTIFY

❶ Who is the speaker ("I") in this poem? What is the speaker doing?

Steam Shovel

Charles Malam

The dinosaurs are not all dead.
I saw one raise its iron head
To watch me walking down the road
Beyond our house today.
5   Its jaws were dripping with a load
Of earth and grass that it had cropped.
It must have heard me where I stopped,
Snorted white steam my way,
And stretched its long neck out to see,
10   And chewed, and grinned quite amiably!° **❶**

10. **amiably:** in a friendly way.

IDENTIFY

❶ What is the "dinosaur"? Could you tell if the title and the photograph were covered up? List the details that reveal the dinosaur's true identity.

Meet the Writers

"Poetry Always Comes from Inside"

William Jay Smith (1918–   ) has Choctaw ancestors on his mother's side. His father was a corporal in the Sixth Infantry Band. Smith attended Washington University in St. Louis, Columbia University, Oxford University (where he was a Rhodes scholar), and the University of Florence. He has been a college teacher, a translator, and a member of the Vermont legislature.

"I've been a fashion editor, social worker, and full time mom," says **Bobbi Katz** (1933–   ). Trained as an art historian, she's also taught and run a weekly radio program called *Arts in Action*. Now she works as a writer of fiction and poetry.

❝ My poetry always comes from inside—from my deep need to express a feeling. The child in me writes picture books. My fiction is almost not mine. The characters emerge and seem to tell their own stories. Even when writing within rigid boundaries that editors sometimes set, I find the characters become very real to me. I care what happens to them. ❞

Lillian Morrison (1917–   ) was a librarian for almost fifty years. At the New York Public Library she was an expert in books and services for young adults. Besides writing poetry, she's always been interested in jazz, dancing, and sports—all kinds of sports. She has written so many poems about sports that she may hold the world record for it. In an introduction to *Sprints and Distances* (1965), one of her poetry collections, Morrison said:

> **There is an affinity between sports and poetry. Each is a form of play.... Each has the power to take us out of ourselves and at times to lift us above ourselves. They go together naturally....**

Charles Malam (1906–1981) was born in South Reygate, Vermont. He has written poems and one-act plays. His poems tend to look at everyday objects, such as steam shovels, in a light, playful way.

First Thoughts

1. Finish this sentence:

- My favorite lines in "Steam Shovel" and "The Sidewalk Racer" are . . . because . . .

Thinking Critically

2. How would you describe the personality of the dinosaur in "Steam Shovel"? How does it **compare** with the personalities of the dragons in "The Toaster" and "Things to Do If You Are a Subway"? Explain.

3. Read "The Sidewalk Racer" aloud. Let the punctuation tell you where and how long to pause. Does the poem's **rhythm** create the feeling of swooshing down the street on a skateboard?

4. What **rhymes** can you find in "The Sidewalk Racer"? How do the rhymes affect the rhythm of the poem?

Comparing Literature

5. Complete the chart below. You can use this chart and the one you filled in on page 661 as you complete the assignment on the next page. The first column is partly filled in for you.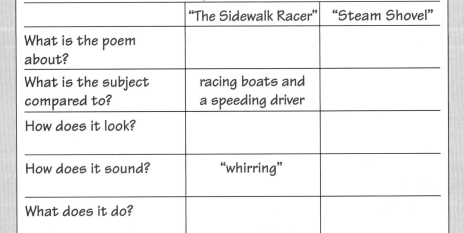

North Carolina Competency Goal
1.02; 5.02

Comparing Poems		
	"The Sidewalk Racer"	"Steam Shovel"
What is the poem about?		
What is the subject compared to?	racing boats and a speeding driver	
How does it look?		
How does it sound?	"whirring"	
What does it do?		

Literary Skills
Analyze extended metaphor.

Reading Skills
Compare and contrast poems.

Comparing "The Toaster," "Things to Do If You Are a Subway," "The Sidewalk Racer," and "Steam Shovel"

Assignment

1. Writing a Comparison-Contrast Essay

Compare and contrast two of the four poems in this feature. Choose the poems you enjoyed the most. Refer to the charts you filled in (see pages 661 and 666) for details to use in your essay. You can organize your essay according to these guidelines:

1. Identify the poems you chose, and name the extended metaphor in each poem.
2. Discuss the first poem. Decide whether the metaphor helped you see the subject in a new way, and explain why or why not. Use details from the poem in your explanation.
3. Do the same for the second poem.
4. State which poem you liked better, and explain why.

Use the workshop on writing a **comparison-contrast essay**, pages 404–409, for help with this assignment.

Assignment

2. Writing a Poem

Become a machine biologist. Write a poem in which you use **extended metaphor** to compare a machine to a living thing. Start by observing an ordinary appliance in your home or classroom or a machine you see on the street. Use your imagination. What animal or other creature does it remind you of? Think about what the machine is able to do. Try to extend your metaphor by comparing each function to a specific behavior or characteristic of the creature you chose.

Assignment

3. Illustrating a Poem

Create your own illustration—a drawing, a collage, or a sculpture—for "The Toaster," "Things to Do If You Are a Subway," or "Steam Shovel." Depict the machine displaying the behavior and personality of the creature that the poet compares it to.

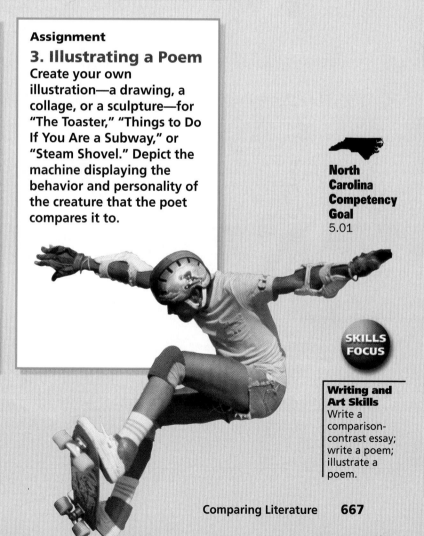

North Carolina Competency Goal
5.01

SKILLS FOCUS

Writing and Art Skills
Write a comparison-contrast essay; write a poem; illustrate a poem.

A NASH MENAGERIE

Ogden Nash

The Octopus

Tell me, O Octopus, I begs,
Is those things arms, or is they legs?
I marvel at thee, Octopus;
If I were thou, I'd call me Us.

The Panther

The panther is like a leopard,
Except it hasn't been peppered.
Should you behold a panther crouch,
Prepare to say Ouch.
Better yet, if called by a panther,
Don't anther.

The Camel

The camel has a single hump;
The dromedary, two;
Or else the other way around.
I'm never sure. Are you?

The Duck

Behold the duck
It does not cluck.
A cluck it lacks.
It quacks.
It is specially fond
Of a puddle or pond.
When it dines or sups,
It bottoms ups.

A Caution to Everybody

Consider the auk;
Becoming extinct because he forgot
    how to fly, and could only walk.
Consider man, who may well
    become extinct
Because he forgot how to walk and
    learned how to fly before he
    thinked.

Meet the Writer

Ogden Nash

The "Worsifier"

Ogden Nash (1902–1971) called himself a "worsifier" because of the "worses" he wrote. For many years, Nash has been enjoyed for his comical poetry and his clever, funny rhymes. Nash held many serious jobs before he turned to writing "silly" verse. He taught school, worked on Wall Street, wrote for an advertising agency, and labored on the editorial staff of a publishing company. Nash's first attempt at light verse was something of a doodle that ended up in a garbage can; but he fished it out and sent it to a magazine that bought it. Nash admitted having "intentionally maltreated and manhandled every known rule of grammar, prosody, and spelling." He remarked:

66 Sometimes I write from beginning to end, sometimes backward and sometimes I start in the middle. When a pun comes to me, I usually work backward on how to lead people into the trap. I keep a pad and pencil near my bed, but the poems I write when I'm half asleep aren't much good. Though I do write some fair ones sitting up on the side of the bed. Usually I do a lot of rewriting. . . . Sometimes I do get very pleased with myself and I'll show what I've done to my wife. If she doesn't laugh I become cross and go off and sulk. Later I make the revisions she suggested. 99

For Independent Reading

Ogden Nash published some twenty collections of poetry. If you liked these poems about animals, try reading his book *Custard and Company*. You also might enjoy *Parents Keep Out: Elderly Verses for Youngerly Readers*.

Nash also wrote poems to accompany classical music. Look for the Ogden Nash versions of *Carnival of the Animals* by Camille Saint-Saëns, *Peter and the Wolf* by Sergey Prokofiev, and *The Sorcerer's Apprentice* by Paul-Abraham Dukas.

Media Workshop

Assignment

Adapt a story for performance as a play.

Audience

Your classmates, teacher, and other students.

North Carolina Competency Goal
1.03; 5.01; 6.01; 6.02

Writing Skill
Adapt a story as a play.

MULTIMEDIA PRESENTATION
Staging a Performance

Although many plays have been written for a single performer, most dramatic works require the participation of several actors. A number of people also work behind the scenes: the director, costume designer, electrician, stage carpenter, choreographer, stage manager, lighting designer, and, of course, the central figure—the writer who creates the script.

In this workshop you will work with other students to create and then present an adaptation of a literary work. You can be as inventive as you like in taking your play from page to stage.

Developing a Script

1 Choosing a Story

To hold your audience's attention, choose a story that will play well. Ask yourself these questions:
- Does the story have interesting characters?
- Does the story contain suspense, action, or humor?
- Does the story include enough dialogue, or will you need to add any?
- Will the writer or writers be able to adapt the entire story or just a part of it?

Student actors perform a scene from an adaptation of "Rumpelstiltskin." (See page 278.)

- Where will the play be presented—in the classroom, the library, or an auditorium?

With your group, discuss the overall impression the story creates. Is it a funny story with a serious message? Is it a story that explores a particular event or period in history? Your interpretation of the story will affect the way you adapt it for the stage.

Here are some selections in your book that you might use:

- "Dragon, Dragon" (page 5)
- "The Stone" (page 31)
- "All Summer in a Day" (page 42)
- "La Bamba" (page 336)
- "The Fun They Had" (page 581)
- "The Nightingale" (page 589)
- "The Sneetches" (page 627)

2 Writing the Play

Once you have chosen a selection, assemble a team that will turn the story into a play. The members of this group will need to re-read the story carefully and jot down ideas for adapting the narrative to the stage. They will have to make decisions about these questions:

- How many actors will be needed?
- Will a narrator be needed to introduce the play and supply bridges between scenes?
- How many scenes will be dramatized?
- How much dialogue can be picked up? Which passages need to be rewritten as dialogue?
- What stage directions will the actors need?
- What props, costumes, and sound effects will be used?

If you plan to present several scenes, writers in the team might be assigned to work on individual scenes independently or with a partner.

Writing Dialogue

Dialogue in a play can be **formal** or **informal.** Formal language contains few contractions, no slang, and few sentence fragments or interrupted sentences.

Informal dialogue sounds more like everyday speech and sounds more natural. Formal speech may be more appropriate than informal speech for certain selections.

Remember that in a play there are no **speaker tags.** However, the writer may add stage directions to indicate how lines are to be spoken.

Writer's Tip

To see how a fable was rewritten as a short play, compare "The Fox and the Crow" (page 371) or "The Wolf and the House Dog" (page 372) with a traditional prose version of the story.

Writing Stage Directions

Stage directions give important information about a character's feelings, tone of voice, movements, and gestures. Stage directions sometimes describe props and set design, as well as sounds.

To write stage directions, imagine each scene being played on stage. How do the characters look and move? How do they react to other characters' lines?

For examples of how to write stage directions, see *In the Fog* on page 75 and *Blanca Flora* on page 167, along with the Script Model on pages 673–674.

Using Body Language

Gestures can be just as effective as words in conveying a character's feelings.

Gestures	Feelings
• shrugging	indifference
• pacing	impatience
• raising eyebrows	skepticism
• rubbing chin	puzzlement
• stamping foot	anger
• wringing hands	despair
• rolling eyes	annoyance

3 Assembling a Director's Notebook

Once your writing team has an outline for the play, the person chosen as director will need to make decisions about the following aspects of the performance:

- **Sets.** How many sets will be needed? Can a projection of an illustration or photograph be used for the background? What furniture will you need, if any?

- **Costumes.** Does the story specify information about the characters' clothing? If not, how will you decide what costumes to use?

- **Props.** Which props are mentioned in the story? List any others you will need.

- **Lighting.** Will you use lights of different colors to set the mood?

- **Sound.** What sound effects will you use? How will you produce them?

Producing the Play

1 Using Different Media

You can use recorded music, sound effects, photographs, fine art, illustrations, and even dance in a stage performance. Students will be needed to paint scenery, find or make props, create costumes, and control lighting and sound. Consider using video clips from movies or TV shows, as well as videos made with a hand-held camcorder.

2 Rehearsing the Play

Actors have to learn a great deal besides their lines. They must learn stage movements, or blocking. The director usually decides how the actors will move and how they should interpret their lines.

Actors use their bodies as well as their voices. They use facial expressions and gestures to communicate characters' feelings. In learning a part, read and re-read your lines, concentrating on their meaning. Phrase your words carefully. Try out different vocal effects, and read your lines in front of a mirror so that you can see your facial expressions and gestures. Be sure that you are pronouncing all the words correctly.

Plan on holding several rehearsals, including a dress rehearsal, before the live performance.

3 Creating Special Effects

Suppose you decide to adapt "The Nightingale" by Hans Christian Andersen (page 589). What special effects would you use?

The two nightingales—real and artificial—might be represented on stage by actors wearing costumes and masks or by hand-held puppets.

How might the birds' songs be reproduced? Students who play wind instruments might simulate the songs, using a different instrument for each bird. You might also use a recording of bird songs.

Script Model

Here is the script for a scene based on Andersen's story "The Nightingale" (page 589). The episode that has been dramatized begins on page 597.

Scene: The Emperor's bedroom. The actor portraying the mechanical bird sits on a silk cushion next to the Emperor's bed.

Narrator (*to the audience*). One night, as the mechanical bird was singing to the Emperor, there was a whirring sound and suddenly the music stopped.

Role of narrator added to play.

[The BIRD's *singing is interrupted by the sound of a spring snapping.*]

Emperor (*jumping out of his bed and calling loudly*). Doctor! Doctor!

Stage directions added.

[*The* DOCTOR *rushes in, carrying his bag of instruments.*]

Emperor (*excitedly*). There's something the matter with my mechanical bird. What's wrong?

[*The* DOCTOR *uses an old-fashioned ear trumpet to listen to the* BIRD*'s heart. He bends over the* BIRD*, turns it this way and that, and shakes it gently, but it remains silent.*]

Doctor. You had best send for the Watchmaker, Your Imperial Majesty.

Emperor (*impatiently*). Watchmaker! Watchmaker!

[*The* WATCHMAKER *rushes in. His costume is covered with clockwork symbols: geared wheels, dials, numbers. Around his neck hangs a large timepiece.*]

Actors wear humorously exaggerated costumes.

Emperor. There's something wrong with my bird.

[*The* WATCHMAKER *examines the* BIRD *and tinkers with it. Then he winds up the spring. The music begins again, feebly at first and then louder.*]

Watchmaker (*gravely*). Your Imperial Majesty, I'm afraid that the little pegs on the cylinders are worn and there is no way to replace them. The bird can still sing, but only once a year. Even that will be a strain.

Dialogue invented.

[*The* EMPEROR *looks at the* BIRD *with a mournful expression and nods his head.*]

Narrator. Sadly the Emperor agreed. From that time on, the mechanical bird sang only once a year. Each year, the Master of the Music made a speech declaring that the bird was as good as ever.

Master of the Music (*grandly*). The Imperial Bedside-Singer-in-Chief, which was presented to His Imperial Majesty by the mighty Emperor of Japan, still keeps perfect time and performs in a manner that is perfectly in tune with its wheels and cylinders.

Narrator. And so five years passed.

Evaluating Your Performance

Staging a Performance: Guidelines for Evaluation

Writers	Actors
1 Did you present a clear interpretation of the story?	**1** Did you learn all of your lines? Did you make notes on the script to guide you in speaking your lines?
2 Did your script include all the important characters in the story?	**2** Did you practice using your voice in different ways or varying the emphasis of words and phrases to convey meaning and mood?
3 Did you use dialogue from the story? Did you create new dialogue?	**3** Did you communicate with your audience through the tone of your voice, facial expressions, and gestures?
4 Did you provide stage directions, including facial expressions and gestures?	**4** Did you speak clearly? Was your voice loud enough to be heard by everyone in your audience?
5 Did you include instructions for props, costumes, scenery, and sound effects?	**5** Did you interact with the other actors on stage?
6 Did you include special effects in your scripts? What media are used?	**6** Did you stay in character throughout the performance?

Peer Evaluation

- Ask audience members to describe their overall reaction to your group's performance.

- Invite the audience to ask questions and discuss their ideas about the performance.

Test Practice

DIRECTIONS: Read the following poem. Then, read each question, and write the letter of the best response.

This poem describes a moment in the 1998 National Basketball Association Finals game between the Chicago Bulls and the Utah Jazz. The Bulls superstar Michael Jordan scored the winning shot with just 5.2 seconds left in the game. This victory brought the team their sixth NBA title. The game, which took place on June 14, 1998, in Salt Lake City, Utah, was Jordan's last with the Chicago Bulls.

Forty-one Seconds on a Sunday in June, in Salt Lake City, Utah   *for Michael Jordan*

Quincy Troupe

rising up in time, michael jordan hangs like an icon,° suspended in space,
cocks his right arm, fires a jump shot for two, the title game on the line,
his eyes two radar screens screwed like nails into the mask of his face

bore in on the basket, gaze focused, a thing of beauty, no shadow, or trace,
5   no hint of fear, in this, his showplace, his ultimate place to shine,
rising up in time michael jordan hangs like an icon, suspended in space,

after he has moved from baseline to baseline, sideline to sideline, his coal-face
shining, wagging his tongue, he dribbles through chaos, snaking serpentine,°
his eyes two radar screens screwed like nails into the mask of his face,

10   he bolts a flash up the court, takes off, floats in for two more in this race
for glory, it is his time, what he was put on earth for, he can see the headline,
rising up in time, michael jordan hangs like an icon, suspended in space,

inside his imagination, he feels the moment he will embrace, knows his place
is written here, inside this quickening pace of nerves, he will define,
15   his eyes two radar screens screwed like nails into the mask of his face,

---

1. **icon** (īʹkän′) *n.*: image; also, person or thing regarded with great respect and admiration.
8. **serpentine** (surʹpən·tīn′) *adj.* used as *adv.*: in a snakelike way.

North Carolina Competency Goal
5.02

SKILLS FOCUS

inside this moment he will rule on his own terms, quick as a cat he interfaces°
time, victory & glory, as he crosses over his dribble he is king of this shrine,°
rising up in time, michael jordan hangs like an icon, suspended in space,
his eyes two radar screens screwed like nails into the mask of his face

---

16. interfaces *v.:* brings together; joins.
17. shrine *n.:* place held in high honor because of its association with an event, a person, or a holy figure.

---

1. Which of the following phrases from the poem contains a **simile**?
   - **A** "he bolts a flash up the court"
   - **B** "fires a jump shot for two, the title game on the line"
   - **C** "he feels the moment he will embrace"
   - **D** "rising up in time, michael jordan hangs like an icon"

2. "Quick as a cat" (line 16) is an example of —
   - **F** metaphor
   - **G** simile
   - **H** personification
   - **J** refrain

3. Which of the following statements describes the poem's structure?
   - **A** The first and third lines of each stanza rhyme.
   - **B** Each stanza begins with the same line.
   - **C** Each line has the same number of words.
   - **D** The first and second lines of each stanza rhyme.

4. Which of the following phrases is repeated four times in the poem?
   - **F** "he bolts a flash up the court, floats in for two more in this race"
   - **G** "he bolts a flash up the court, takes off, floats in for two more in this race"
   - **H** "michael jordan hangs like an icon, suspended in space"
   - **J** "it is his time, what he was put on earth for, he can see the headline"

5. Which word best describes the speaker's **tone** in this poem?
   - **A** Dazed
   - **B** Admiring
   - **C** Loving
   - **D** Envious

Constructed Response

6. Find a phrase in the poem that is an example of **alliteration.** Write the phrase on your paper. Then, write a sentence explaining why the phrase is an example of alliteration.

Collection 7: Skills Review

Vocabulary Skills

Test Practice

Synonyms

DIRECTIONS: Write the letter of the word or group of words that is closest in meaning to the underlined word.

1. Someone who is <u>mortified</u> is —
   A frightened
   B ill
   C impressed
   D ashamed

2. <u>Etiquette</u> means —
   F sewing
   G manners
   H accessories
   J ideas

3. If you <u>savor</u> something, you —
   A enjoy it
   B buy it
   C dislike it
   D ignore it

4. The <u>shrewdest</u> competitor is the most —
   F talented
   G energetic
   H attentive
   J clever

5. <u>Audacity</u> means —
   A kindness
   B fear
   C daring
   D loudness

6. If a building is <u>evacuated</u>, it is —
   F damaged
   G emptied
   H decorated
   J sold

7. <u>Interned</u> means —
   A employed
   B discouraged
   C relieved
   D imprisoned

8. A <u>tolerant</u> person is —
   F eloquent
   G helpful
   H exciting
   J accepting

9. <u>Lavishly</u> means —
   A dutifully
   B cautiously
   C plentifully
   D shyly

10. A <u>spectacle</u> is a sight that is —
    F remarkable
    G frightening
    H overwhelming
    J boring

SKILLS FOCUS

Vocabulary Skills
Identify synonyms.

Collection 7: Skills Review

Writing Skills

Test Practice

DIRECTIONS: Read the following paragraph. Then, answer each question that follows.

(1) Literary works may be adapted in many ways. (2) One common way involves adapting a work into a different literary genre, such as a novel or short story made into a play. (3) Another kind of adaptation involves presenting a work in a different medium, such as a movie based on a book. (4) The film version of a literary work may be so different from the original that the two seem to have little to do with each other. (5) Another kind of adaptation involves musical interpretation, as when a literary work is made into a stage musical or an opera. (6) Another kind of adaptation involves interpreting a literary work through the medium of dance. (7) Many classic novels now appear in comic-book versions; some have become popular as animated cartoons.

1. This paragraph might be improved by—
   A deleting sentence 2
   B discussing how movies are filmed
   C discussing why books are better than movies
   D giving examples of each type of adaptation

2. The purpose of this paragraph is primarily—
   F to classify types of media
   G to identify different kinds of adaptations
   H to explain the purpose of adaptations
   J to show how easy it is to adapt literary works

3. Which sentence does *not* belong in this paragraph?
   A sentence 2
   B sentence 4
   C sentence 6
   D sentence 7

4. Which of the following words and phrases might be substituted for the word *another* in sentence 3, 5, or 6?
   F any other
   G the same
   H each
   J one more

North Carolina Competency Goal
2.01; 4.01

Writing Skills
Analyze the purpose and clarity of a paragraph.

Poetry

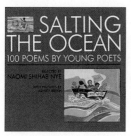

Poems by Students

During her years as a teacher, Naomi Shihab Nye assembled an enormous collection of her students' poetry. In *Salting the Ocean* she presents some of her favorites. Nye's students write with passion about subjects like a hometown, a beloved family member, even a spelling bee.

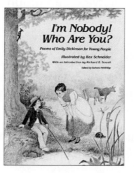

A Great American Talent

Emily Dickinson was one of the world's greatest poets. During her lifetime, however, she was anything but famous. More than seventeen hundred poems were discovered after her death in 1886, but only seven had been published while she was alive. *I'm Nobody! Who Are You?* includes poems with a special appeal for young people. Dickinson's poems are short but rich in meaning.

A Dependable Pen

Have you ever thought you'd see an *ape* on a *trapeze*? or an *elf* in a *belfry*? You never know what you'll find—or where you'll find it— in Richard Wilbur's collection *The Pig in the Spigot*. Read it to discover the magic of words within words.

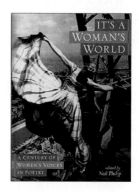

Poems by Women

During the twentieth century, women poets have become more and more visible. Neil Philip collects some of their finest work in *It's a Woman's World*. Philip includes works by poets you may recognize as well as a generous selection of works by new poets.

Nonfiction
Connections to Social Studies and Science

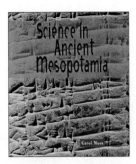

A Running Start

The people of ancient Mesopotamia (now Syria, Turkey, and Iraq), who established the first civilization in 5000 B.C., were naturally curious about how the world works. *Science in Ancient Mesopotamia* looks at their discoveries in mathematics, medicine, and astronomy. Carol Moss shows you that Mesopotamians were far ahead of their time.

Extra! Extra!

The Stone Age News is an imaginary prehistoric newspaper created by Alison Roberts and Fiona MacDonald. In it you'll find stories about hunters, advice on making a cave feel like a home, advertisements for footwear, even a weather forecast. The illustrations offer glimpses of everyday life in prehistoric times. In this book you'll also learn about the features of a newspaper.

First Steps

Have you ever wondered what city life was like long ago? In *Street Smart! Cities of the Ancient World,* you'll learn about the marble buildings of ancient Greek city-states and the grand temples built by the ancient Egyptians. You may not realize it, but most modern cities are constructed according to ideas first put into practice in ancient Rome, Mesopotamia, and other early cultures.

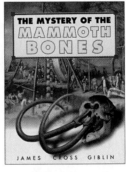

Rebuilding the Past

In 1801, Charles Willson Peale went to look at a set of huge bones that had been discovered in New York. He couldn't tell whether they had belonged to an elephant, a mammoth, or another mammal. He had to assemble a crew, risk flooding and cave-ins at digging sites, and reconstruct the creature's skeleton to find out for certain. In *The Mystery of the Mammoth Bones,* James Cross Giblin tells about Peale's quest and his scientific discovery, whose impact is still felt today.

Object (Le Dejeuner en fourrure) (1936) by Meret Oppenheim.
The Museum of Modern Art, New York, NY.
© 2005 Artists Rights Society (ARS), New York/ProLitteris, Zürich, Switzerland.

Literary Criticism: You Be the Judge

Literary Focus:
Responding Critically to Literature

Informational Focus:
Preparing Applications; Analyzing Faulty Reasoning

INTERNET

Collection Resources

Keyword: LE5 6-8

Elements of Literature
Literary Criticism *by* Kylene Beers

FINDING THE RIGHT WORDS

Your language arts teacher asks you whether you liked a story you've just read. You tell her you didn't. She asks why not. How are you most likely to respond?

1. "I don't know."
2. "It was boring."
3. "The characters were not believable; they did things real people would never do. The plot didn't seem believable either—not realistic at all."
4. "I just didn't like it."

Which response explains why you didn't like the story? It's easy to see that that would be statement 3.

You've certainly answered your teacher's question with statements 1, 2, and 4, but you haven't given specific information on what you didn't like.

Beyond "It's Boring" or "I Really Like It"

Here are some responses to Christopher Paul Curtis's novel *Bud, Not Buddy.* Which statements offer opinions that are supported with specific, detailed explanations?

1. "I liked this book a lot. It was really good. Other people will like it too."
2. "This is a great book. It is fun in parts and sad in parts, and the plot has a lot of good action."

3. "I didn't like this book too much. It wasn't good, and so I didn't like it."
4. "I didn't like this book. I didn't think it was realistic that a little kid would travel all over the country. And the ending was disappointing— he doesn't find his real dad."

If you picked statements 2 and 4, you picked the best answers. Statements 1 and 3 certainly offer opinions, but those opinions have no support.

Good literary critics know how to explain what they like or don't like about a text. They go beyond "It's really good" or "It's boring" to offer specifics. But what are those specifics? How can you discuss a text in a convincing way?

The chart on page 685 shows some of the words and phrases critics use when they talk about the characters and plot of a work of fiction. Using these words will help you move from vagueness to specifics.

Evaluating Characters: Believable or Not?

One of the most important words on these lists is *credible. Credible* means "believable." The opposite of *credible* is *incredible,* meaning "not believable." When we read fiction, we expect, above all, that the characters will be credible, that they will act the way real people

North Carolina Competency Goal
5.01

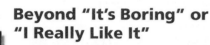

INTERNET
More About Literary Criticism
Keyword: LE5 6-8

Literary Skills
Respond critically to literature.

do. Even if we're reading science fiction with Martians as characters, we still want to believe in the characters.

To decide whether characters are credible, ask yourself these questions:

- Do the characters have weaknesses as well as strengths? Is a character too good to be true? too strong? too unselfish? too evil?

- Do the characters talk and act like real people?

- Do the characters grow and change as a result of the events in the story?

Evaluating Plot: Believable or Not?

One word critics often use in talking about plot is *contrived*.

A contrived plot includes events that are not believable. A contrived plot may contain too many coincidences, like chance meetings. In a contrived plot major obstacles are quickly overcome. If you read a story in which two lovers on a sinking ship struggle through icy water up to their waists, hack through chains holding the hero captive, kill a gunman, leap onto an ice floe, and survive, you know you're dealing with a contrived plot.

To test the credibility of a plot, ask yourself questions like these:

- Do the events in the plot grow naturally out of the decisions and actions of the characters?

- Do many of the events result from chance or luck, or are there believable causes and effects?

- Do events unfold the way they would in real life?

LITERARY CRITICISM: A GLOSSARY	
Words and Phrases Used to Describe Plot	
Positive	Negative
realistic *or* credible	unrealistic *or* not credible
well-paced	plodding
suspenseful	predictable
satisfying ending	disappointing ending
subplots tied together well	confusing subplots
Words and Phrases Used to Describe Characters	
Positive	Negative
original	stereotyped
believable *or* credible *or* convincing	unbelievable *or* unconvincing
well-rounded	flat
dynamic—*refers to characters who change and grow and make discoveries about themselves and about life*	static—*refers to characters who remain the same throughout a story*

Practice

With a partner, choose a work of fiction you've read or a movie you've seen recently. Jot down notes on the credibility of the plot and the characters. Try to come up with two comments about the characters and two comments about the plot. Give the story or movie a thumbs-up or thumbs-down rating, using the words from the lists to support your rating. Then, share your ratings in class.

Now you're talking like a real critic.

Reading Skills and Strategies

Forming Opinions

by Kylene Beers

A friend asks you about the book you're reading. "It's a book of poems by Ogden Nash," you tell him. "The poems are really hilarious." Your first statement is a **fact,** and your second statement is an **opinion.**

A Matter of Opinion

It's easy to tell facts from opinions if you remember that

- A statement of **fact** contains information that can be proved true.

  FACT "It's a book of poems by Ogden Nash."

- A statement of **opinion** expresses a personal belief or attitude.

  OPINION "The poems are really hilarious."

Valid Opinions

A **valid opinion** is a judgment or belief supported by reasons. This opinion is valid because it is supported by facts:

- Nash's poems are hilarious. They are full of funny rhymes and clever word play.

This opinion is unsupported by facts:

- I think Nash is a great poet.

  As you read the book reviews on pages 687–689, look for facts, valid opinions, and unsupported opinions. Study the opinions of the poem in the box at the right before you read the reviews.

North Carolina Competency Goal
4.03

Reading Skills
Recognize unsupported and valid opinions.

Analyzing Opinions
WEIRD!

My sister Stephanie's in love.
(I thought she hated boys.)
My brother had a yard sale and
Got rid of all his toys.
My mother started jogging, and
My dad shaved off his beard.
It's spring—and everyone but me
Is acting really weird.

—Judith Viorst

UNSUPPORTED OPINIONS
- I think Judith Viorst is a silly poet.

- I think "Weird!" is a good poem.

VALID OPINIONS
- I think Viorst is a clever poet because of the way she prints her poem upside down. She makes us realize that the speaker is weird too.

- I think Viorst's poem is good, but I like the rhymes in Nash's poems more, especially *panther/anther* and *extinct/thinked*. (See "The Panther" on page 668.)

A BOOK REVIEW

The Bad Beginning

by Lemony Snicket

When the Baudelaire children's parents die in a fire that destroys their house, the kids have to go live with their cousin, Count Olaf. He is mean and treats the children like slaves. He threatens to kill the youngest child, Sunny, if the oldest child, Violet, does not marry him. All he wants is the money their parents left Violet. Will Sunny die or will Violet marry Count Olaf? **❶**

Snicket lets you know in the first page that nothing good ever happens to the Baudelaire children. Whenever you think something good is happening, it turns bad. For example, one time Count Olaf was being nice to them, but only to persuade Violet to be in his play. When Violet refused, he almost let Sunny fall from a high tower. This seems very sad, but how they get out of their predicament turns out to be funny. **❷**

This book is great! The series goes up to book seven, so when I finish with the book I'm reading, I am going to start the next one. **❸**

—reviewed by David Avila
Mark Twain Middle School
Venice, California

IDENTIFY

❶ What facts does the reviewer use in the first paragraph to support the opinion that Count Olaf is "mean"?

IDENTIFY

❷ How does the reviewer support the statement that "Whenever you think something good is happening, it turns bad"? What opinion in this paragraph is unsupported?

ANALYZE

❸ Do you think the reviewer provides enough support for his opinion that "This book is great"? Explain.

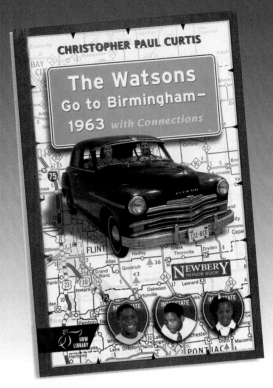

A BOOK REVIEW

The Watsons Go to Birmingham—1963

by **Christopher Paul Curtis**

This dramatic story, told by ten-year-old Kenny, takes place in the early 1960s, in Flint, Michigan. The Watson family was having trouble with their thirteen-year-old son, Byron, a juvenile delinquent. Destructive and mischievous, Byron's terrible and violent behavior got him into trouble. It got so bad, his mom and dad took Byron to Birmingham to live with his grandmother to try to find a better life for him. The family did not plan to stay that long, but their plans changed, and some drastic things happened. **❶** 📖

I advise readers who are into drama to read this book. It is also historical, because it talks about the four little girls who died in Birmingham in 1963. This happens to be one of my favorite books so far. I recommend it to anyone who loves to laugh. I loved this book so much that I think they should make a movie of it. **❷** 📖

—reviewed by Desteni Leakes
Wooddale Optional Middle School
Memphis, Tennessee

IDENTIFY

❶ What facts in this paragraph support the reviewer's opinion that this is a "dramatic story"?

IDENTIFY/ ANALYZE

❷ Find two opinions in this paragraph. Do you think that these opinions are supported? Explain.

Practice the Strategy

Analyzing Opinions

PRACTICE 1

Read the following book review. Then, read it a second time, and list examples of valid opinions.

Fever 1793

by Laurie Halse Anderson

"I woke to the sound of a mosquito whining in my left ear and my mother screeching in the right." This clever foreshadowing of the yellow fever epidemic pulls the reader into the world of 1793, where people weren't aware that mosquitoes spread yellow fever. From the first line, the reader dives right into Mathilda's fast-paced life.

Mathilda Cook thinks she is more mature than people realize, and no one listens to her great ideas for her mother's coffeehouse. Everything changes when the fever comes. As yellow fever spreads from the dock toward the coffeehouse, everyone grows increasingly frightened, and when it reaches the coffeehouse, Matilda quickly learns she is not so mature. Suddenly, fancy ideas are not important; staying alive is.

It is appalling how little people in 1793 knew about disease, and their treatment for it—bleeding—caused many people to die unnecessarily. As the church bells, which rang for each death, began to ring incessantly, they created an agonizing awareness of a desperate situation.

Fever 1793 is an entertaining and gripping history lesson. Don't miss it.

—reviewed by Gabi Meckler
Mid-Peninsula Jewish
Community Day School
San Jose, California

PRACTICE 2

1. What evidence does the reviewer cite to support her opinion that the writer uses "clever foreshadowing"?
2. The reviewer thinks that the lack of knowledge in 1793 about disease was "appalling." Do you think she supports her opinion? Explain.
3. What is your opinion of *Fever 1793* from the review you've just read? Would you like to read this book? Support your opinion with reasons from the review.

   You can distinguish fact from opinion in all the informational texts you read. Be sure your opinions are **valid opinions**—that is, supported by **facts**.

North Carolina Competency Goal
3.01

SKILLS FOCUS

Reading Skills
Analyze unsupported and valid opinions.

The Dog of Pompeii *and* Pompeii

Make the Connection
Quickwrite ✏️

Jot down any facts you know about the city of Pompeii (păm·pā′ē), in Italy, and the eruption of the volcano Vesuvius (və·sōō′vē·əs) that took place there almost two thousand years ago. If you don't know anything about the subject, look at the pictures that illustrate the story. Write down any questions that come to mind.

Literary Focus
Credible Characters: We Believe They're Real

First they spring out of a writer's mind; then they live in a reader's imagination, as if they were real. Who are they? They're **credible** (kred′ə·bəl) **characters**—people in stories who seem as real as the flesh-and-blood people we know.

Even in fantasies, where the laws of nature don't always operate, characters can be so credible, or true to life, that we find ourselves caring deeply about them.

Blanca Flor (see page 166) is a good example. The play about her is a fantasy; things happen that we know could never occur in real life. But Blanca Flor is such a credible character that we can almost picture her sitting next to us.

Reading Skills 📖
Making Inferences

As you read, you make **inferences,** or guesses. You guess what will happen

next. You guess about things the writer has deliberately left out. You base your guesses on details in the story and on your own experiences. When you make inferences as you read, you're using your imagination, just as the writer is using his or hers. You may end up supplying hundreds of details that the storyteller just couldn't fit in. In a way you become a storyteller too!

Cave Canem (Beware the Dog). Ancient Roman floor mosaic from Pompeii.

Background
Literature and Social Studies

"The Dog of Pompeii" is **historical fiction.** Louis Untermeyer combined a fictional story with facts about actual historical events. The story's setting is Pompeii, an ancient Roman city that was buried by a volcanic eruption in A.D. 79.

The volcano that destroyed the city of Pompeii also preserved it. Excavations there began in the eighteenth century. Archaeologists brought the past to life as they uncovered buildings, furniture, food, paintings, and tools. They found rock-hard loaves of bread. They also found about two thousand hollow forms of humans, dogs, and other animals that had been frozen in place by the ash that buried them. Perhaps Louis Untermeyer was inspired to write this story when he saw the forms of the dogs that had been buried by ash in Pompeii.

An Italian archaeologist named Giuseppe Fiorelli found a way to make molds of the bodies, by pumping plaster into the hollows they had left in the ashes. When the plaster within one of the hollows hardened, the ash around it was chipped off. What remained was a plaster cast in the shape of the body.

Today three quarters of old Pompeii has been unearthed. You can visit Pompeii as a tourist; no time machine is necessary. You can walk the same streets, look at the same buildings, and gaze at the same volcano, sleeping for now, that the unsuspecting residents of Pompeii saw for the last time on that day nearly two thousand years ago.

THE DOG OF POMPEII

LOUIS UNTERMEYER

Tito and his dog Bimbo lived (if you could call it living) under the wall where it joined the inner gate. They really didn't live there; they just slept there. They lived anywhere. Pompeii was one of the gayest of the old Latin towns, but although Tito was never an unhappy boy, he was not exactly a merry one. The streets were always lively with shining chariots and bright red trappings; the open-air theaters rocked with laughing crowds; sham[1] battles and athletic sports were free for the asking in the great stadium. Once a year the Caesar[2] visited the pleasure city and the fireworks lasted for days; the sacrifices[3] in the forum were better than a show.

But Tito saw none of these things. He was blind—had been blind from birth. He was known to everyone in the poorer quarters. But no one could say how old he was, no one remembered his parents, no one could tell where he came from. Bimbo was another mystery. As long as people could remember seeing Tito—about twelve or thirteen years— they had seen Bimbo. Bimbo had never left his side. He was not only dog but nurse, pillow, playmate, mother, and father to Tito.

Did I say Bimbo never left his master? (Perhaps I had better say comrade, for if anyone was the master, it was Bimbo.) I was wrong. Bimbo did trust Tito alone exactly three times a day. It was a fixed routine, a custom understood between boy and dog since the beginning of their friendship, and the way it worked was this: Early in the morning,

shortly after dawn, while Tito was still dreaming, Bimbo would disappear. When Tito awoke, Bimbo would be sitting quietly at his side, his ears cocked, his stump of a tail tapping the ground, and a fresh-baked bread— more like a large round roll—at his feet. Tito would stretch himself; Bimbo would yawn; then they would breakfast. At noon, no matter where they happened to be, Bimbo would put his paw on Tito's knee and the two of them would return to the inner gate. Tito would curl up in the corner (almost like a dog) and go to sleep, while Bimbo, looking quite important (almost like a boy), would disappear again. In half an hour he'd be back with their lunch. Sometimes it would be a piece of fruit or a scrap of meat, often it was nothing but a dry crust. But sometimes there would be one of those flat rich cakes, sprinkled with raisins and sugar, that Tito liked so much. At suppertime the same thing happened, although there was a little less of everything, for things were hard to snatch in the evening, with the streets full of people. Besides, Bimbo didn't approve of too much food before going to sleep. A heavy supper made boys too restless and dogs too stodgy[4]—and it was the business of a dog to sleep lightly with one ear open and muscles ready for action.

But, whether there was much or little, hot or cold, fresh or dry, food was always there. Tito never asked where it came from and Bimbo never told him. There was plenty of rainwater in the hollows of soft stones; the old egg woman at the corner sometimes gave him a cupful of strong goat's milk; in the grape season the fat winemaker let him have drippings of the mild juice. So there

---

1. **sham** *adj.:* make-believe.
2. **Caesar** (sē′zər) *n.:* Roman emperor. The word *Caesar* comes from the family name of Julius Caesar, a great general who ruled Rome as dictator from 49 to 44 B.C.
3. **sacrifices** *n.:* offerings (especially of slaughtered animals) to the gods.

---

4. **stodgy** (stä′jē) *adj.:* heavy and slow in movement.

was no danger of going hungry or thirsty. There was plenty of everything in Pompeii—if you knew where to find it—and if you had a dog like Bimbo.

As I said before, Tito was not the merriest boy in Pompeii. He could not romp with the other youngsters and play "hare and hounds" and "I spy" and "follow your master" and "ball against the building" and "jackstones" and "kings and robbers" with them. But that did not make him sorry for himself. If he could not see the sights that delighted the lads of Pompeii, he could hear and smell things they never noticed. He could really see more with his ears and nose than they could with their eyes. When he and Bimbo went out walking, he knew just where they were going and exactly what was happening.

"Ah," he'd sniff and say, as they passed a handsome villa,[5] "Glaucus Pansa is giving a grand dinner tonight. They're going to have three kinds of bread, and roast pigling, and stuffed goose, and a great stew—I think bear stew—and a fig pie." And Bimbo would note that this would be a good place to visit tomorrow. ❶

INFER

❶ Why would this villa be a good place to visit tomorrow?

Or, "H'm," Tito would murmur, half through his lips, half through his nostrils. "The wife of Marcus Lucretius is expecting her mother. She's shaking out every piece of goods in the house; she's going to use the best clothes—the ones she's been keeping in pine needles and camphor[6]—and there's an extra girl in the kitchen. Come, Bimbo, let's get out of the dust!"

---

5. **villa** *n.:* large house.
6. **camphor** (kam′fər) *n.:* strong-smelling substance used to keep moths away from clothing. Camphor is still used for this purpose.

Or, as they passed a small but elegant dwelling opposite the public baths, "Too bad! The tragic poet is ill again. It must be a bad fever this time, for they're trying smoke fumes instead of medicine. Whew! I'm glad I'm not a tragic poet!"

Or, as they neared the forum, "Mm-m! What good things they have in the macellum[7] today!" (It really was a sort of butcher-grocer-marketplace, but Tito didn't know any better. He called it the macellum.) "Dates from Africa, and salt oysters from sea caves, and cuttlefish, and new honey, and sweet onions, and—ugh!—water-buffalo steaks. Come, let's see what's what in the forum." And Bimbo, just as curious as his comrade, hurried on. Being a dog, he trusted his ears and nose (like Tito) more than his eyes. And so the two of them entered the center of Pompeii.

The forum was the part of the town to which everybody came at least once during the day. It was the central square, and every-thing happened here. There were no private houses; all was public—the chief temples, the gold and red bazaars, the silk shops, the town hall, the booths belonging to the weavers and jewel merchants, the wealthy woolen market, the shrine of the household gods. Everything glittered here. The buildings looked as if they were new—which, in a sense, they were. The earthquake of twelve years ago had brought down all the old structures and, since the citizens of Pompeii were <u>ambitious</u> to rival Naples and even Rome, they had seized the opportunity to rebuild the whole town. And

---

7. **macellum** (mə′sel·əm) *n.:* market, especially a meat market.

Vocabulary

ambitious (am·bish′əs) *adj.:* eager to succeed or to achieve something.

they had done it all within a dozen years. There was scarcely a building that was older than Tito.

Tito had heard a great deal about the earthquake, though being about a year old at the time, he could scarcely remember it. This particular quake had been a light one—as earthquakes go. The weaker houses had been shaken down, parts of the outworn wall had been wrecked; but there was little loss of life, and the brilliant new Pompeii had taken the place of the old. No one knew what caused these earthquakes. Records showed they had happened in the neighborhood since the beginning of time. Sailors said that it was to teach the lazy city folk a lesson and make them appreciate those who risked the dangers of the sea to bring them luxuries and protect their town from invaders. The priests said that the gods took this way of showing their anger to those who refused to worship properly and who failed to bring enough sacrifices to the altars and (though they didn't say it in so many words) presents to the priests. The tradesmen said that the foreign merchants had corrupted the ground and it was no longer safe to traffic in imported goods that came from strange places and carried a curse with them. Everyone had a different explanation and everyone's explanation was louder and sillier than his neighbor's. ❷

> **INFER**
> ❷ What didn't people at this time understand about earthquakes?

They were talking about it this afternoon as Tito and Bimbo came out of the side street into the public square. The forum was the favorite promenade[8] for rich and poor.

What with the priests arguing with the politicians, servants doing the day's shopping, tradesmen crying their wares, women displaying the latest fashions from Greece and Egypt, children playing hide-and-seek among the marble columns, knots of soldiers, sailors, peasants from the provinces[9]—to say nothing of those who merely came to lounge and look on—the square was crowded to its last inch. His ears even more than his nose guided Tito to the place where the talk was loudest. It was in front of the shrine of the household gods that, naturally enough, the householders were arguing.

"I tell you," rumbled a voice which Tito recognized as bath master Rufus's, "there won't be another earthquake in my lifetime or yours. There may be a tremble or two, but

---

8. promenade (präm′ə·nād′) *n.:* public place where people stroll.

9. provinces *n.:* places far from the capital, under Roman control.

earthquakes, like lightnings, never strike twice in the same place."

"Do they not?" asked a thin voice Tito had never heard. It had a high, sharp ring to it and Tito knew it as the accent of a stranger. "How about the two towns of Sicily that have been ruined three times within fifteen years by the eruptions of Mount Etna? And were they not warned? And does that column of smoke above Vesuvius mean nothing?"

"That?" Tito could hear the grunt with which one question answered another. "That's always there. We use it for our weather guide. When the smoke stands up straight, we know we'll have fair weather; when it flattens out, it's sure to be foggy; when it drifts to the east—"

"Yes, yes," cut in the edged voice. "I've heard about your mountain barometer.[10]

But the column of smoke seems hundreds of feet higher than usual and it's thickening and spreading like a shadowy tree. They say in Naples—"

"Oh, Naples!" Tito knew this voice by the little squeak that went with it. It was Attilio the cameo cutter.[11] "They talk while we suffer. Little help we got from them last time. Naples commits the crimes and Pompeii pays the price. It's become a <u>proverb</u> with us. Let them mind their own business."

"Yes," grumbled Rufus, "and others', too."

"Very well, my confident friends," responded the thin voice, which now sounded curiously flat. "We also have a proverb— and it is this: *Those who will not listen to*

---

10. **barometer** (bə·räm′ət·ər) *n.:* instrument for measuring atmospheric pressure. Barometers are used in forecasting changes in the weather.

11. **cameo cutter:** artist who carves small, delicate pictures on gems or shells.

Vocabulary
proverb (präv′ərb) *n.:* short traditional saying that expresses a truth.

men must be taught by the gods. I say no more. But I leave a last warning. Remember the holy ones. Look to your temples. And when the smoke tree above Vesuvius grows to the shape of an umbrella pine, look to your lives."

Tito could hear the air whistle as the speaker drew his toga about him, and the quick shuffle of feet told him the stranger had gone. ❸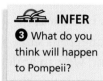

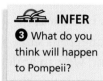**INFER**
❸ What do you think will happen to Pompeii?

"Now what," said the cameo cutter, "did he mean by that?"

"I wonder," grunted Rufus. "I wonder."

Tito wondered, too. And Bimbo, his head at a thoughtful angle, looked as if he had been doing a heavy piece of pondering. By nightfall the argument had been forgotten. If the smoke had increased, no one saw it in the dark. Besides, it was Caesar's birthday and the town was in a holiday mood. Tito and Bimbo were among the merrymakers, dodging the charioteers who shouted at them. A dozen times they almost upset baskets of sweets and jars of Vesuvian wine, said to be as fiery as the streams inside the volcano, and a dozen times they were cursed and cuffed. But Tito never missed his footing. He was thankful for his keen ears and quick instinct—most thankful of all for Bimbo.

They visited the uncovered theater, and though Tito could not see the faces of the actors, he could follow the play better than most of the audience, for their attention wandered—they were distracted by the scenery, the costumes, the byplay,[12] even by themselves—while Tito's whole attention was centered in what he heard. Then to the city walls, where the people of Pompeii watched a mock naval battle in which the city was attacked by the sea and saved after thousands of flaming arrows had been exchanged and countless colored torches had been burned. Though the thrill of flaring ships and lighted skies was lost to Tito, the shouts and cheers excited him as much as any, and he cried out with the loudest of them.

The next morning there were two of the beloved raisin-and-sugar cakes for his breakfast. Bimbo was unusually active and thumped his bit of a tail until Tito was afraid he would wear it out. The boy could not imagine whether Bimbo was urging him to some sort of game or was trying to tell him something. After a while, he ceased to notice Bimbo. He felt drowsy. Last night's late hours had tired him. Besides, there was a heavy mist in the air—no, a thick fog rather than a mist—a fog that got into his throat and scraped it and made him cough. He walked as far as the marine gate[13] to get a breath of the sea. But the blanket of haze had spread all over the bay and even the salt air seemed smoky. ❹

INFER
❹ What do you think Bimbo wants to tell Tito? What inference can you make about the smoke?

He went to bed before dusk and slept. But he did not sleep well. He had too many dreams—dreams of ships lurching in the forum, of losing his way in a screaming crowd, of armies marching across his chest, of being pulled over every rough pavement of Pompeii.

He woke early. Or, rather, he was pulled awake. Bimbo was doing the pulling. The

---

12. **byplay** *n.*: action taking place outside the main action of a play.

---

13. **marine gate:** gate in a city wall leading to the sea.

dog had dragged Tito to his feet and was urging the boy along. Somewhere. Where, Tito did not know. His feet stumbled uncertainly; he was still half asleep. For a while he noticed nothing except the fact that it was hard to breathe. The air was hot. And heavy. So heavy that he could taste it. The air, it seemed, had turned to powder—a warm powder that stung his nostrils and burned his sightless eyes.

Then he began to hear sounds. Peculiar sounds. Like animals under the earth. Hissings and groanings and muffled cries that a dying creature might make dislodging the stones of his underground cave. There was no doubt of it now. The noises came from underneath. He not only heard them—he could feel them. The earth twitched; the twitching changed to an uneven shrugging of the soil. Then, as Bimbo half pulled, half coaxed him across, the ground jerked away from his feet and he was thrown against a stone fountain.

The water—hot water—splashing in his face revived him. He got to his feet, Bimbo steadying him, helping him on again. ❺

INFER
❺ Why do you suppose the water is hot?

The noises grew louder; they came closer. The cries were even more animal-like than before, but now they came from human throats. A few people, quicker of foot and more hurried by fear, began to rush by. A family or two—then a section—then, it seemed, an army broken out of bounds. Tito, bewildered though he was, could recognize Rufus as he bellowed past him, like a water buffalo gone mad. Time was lost in a nightmare.

It was then the crashing began. First a sharp crackling, like a monstrous snapping of twigs; then a roar like the fall of a whole forest of trees; then an explosion that tore earth and sky. The heavens, though Tito could not see them, were shot through with continual flickerings of fire. Lightnings above were answered by thunders beneath. A house fell. Then another. By a miracle the two companions had escaped the dangerous side streets and were in a more open space. It was the forum. They rested here awhile—how long, he did not know. ❻

INFER
❻ Tito doesn't know what is going on. What is happening right now with the volcano?

Tito had no idea of the time of day. He could feel it was black—an unnatural blackness. Something inside—perhaps the lack of breakfast and lunch—told him it was past noon. But it didn't matter. Nothing seemed to matter. He was getting drowsy, too drowsy to walk. But walk he must. ❼ He knew it. And Bimbo knew it; the sharp tugs told him so. Nor was it a moment too soon. The sacred ground of the forum was safe no longer. It was beginning to rock, then to pitch, then to split. As they stumbled out of the square, the earth wriggled like a caught snake and all the columns of the temple of Jupiter[14] came down. It was the end of the world—or so it seemed. To walk was not enough now. They must run. Tito was too frightened to know what to do or where to go. He had lost all

INFER
❼ Why is Tito drowsy?

---

14. **Jupiter:** the supreme god in the religion of the Romans.

Vocabulary
revived (ri·vīvd′) v.: brought back to life or to a waking state.

sense of direction. He started to go back to the inner gate; but Bimbo, straining his back to the last inch, almost pulled his clothes from him. What did the creature want? Had the dog gone mad?

Then suddenly he understood. Bimbo was telling him the way out—urging him there. The sea gate, of course. The sea gate—and then the sea. Far from falling buildings, heaving ground. He turned, Bimbo guiding him across open pits and dangerous pools of bubbling mud, away from buildings that had caught fire and were dropping their burning beams. Tito could no longer tell whether the noises were made by the shrieking sky or the agonized people. He and Bimbo ran on—the only silent beings in a howling world.

New dangers threatened. All Pompeii seemed to be thronging toward the marine gate and, squeezing among the crowds, there was the chance of being trampled to death. But the chance had to be taken. It was growing harder and harder to breathe. What air there was choked him. It was all dust now—dust and pebbles, pebbles as large as beans. They fell on his head, his hands—pumice stones from the black heart of Vesuvius. The mountain was turning itself inside out. Tito remembered a phrase that the stranger had said in the forum two days ago: "Those who will not listen to men must be taught by the gods." The people of Pompeii had refused to heed the warnings; they were being taught now—if it was not too late.

Suddenly it seemed too late for Tito. The red-hot ashes blistered his skin, the stinging vapors tore his throat. He could not go on. He staggered toward a small tree at the side of the road and fell. In a moment

Bimbo was beside him. He coaxed. But there was no answer. He licked Tito's hands, his feet, his face. The boy did not stir. Then Bimbo did the last thing he could—the last thing he wanted to do. He bit his comrade, bit him deep in the arm. With a cry of pain, Tito jumped to his feet, Bimbo after him. Tito was in despair, but Bimbo was determined. He drove the boy on, snapping at his heels, worrying his way through the crowd, barking, baring his teeth, heedless of kicks or falling stones. Sick with hunger, half dead with fear and sulfur fumes, Tito pounded on, pursued by Bimbo. How long, he never knew. At last he staggered through the marine gate and felt soft sand under him. Then Tito fainted. . . .

Someone was dashing seawater over him. Someone was carrying him toward a boat.

"Bimbo," he called. And then louder, "Bimbo!" But Bimbo had disappeared.

Voices jarred against each other. "Hurry—hurry!" "To the boats!" "Can't you see the child's frightened and starving!" "He keeps calling for someone!" "Poor boy, he's out of his mind." "Here, child—take this!"

They tucked him in among them. The oarlocks creaked; the oars splashed; the boat rode over toppling waves. Tito was safe. But he wept continually.

"Bimbo!" he wailed. "Bimbo! Bimbo!"

He could not be comforted.

Eighteen hundred years passed. Scientists were restoring the ancient city; excavators[15] were working their way through the stones and trash that had buried the entire town. Much had already been brought to light—

---

15. **excavators** (eks′kə·vāt′ərz) *n*.: diggers; here, archaeologists.

statues, bronze instruments, bright mosaics,[16] household articles; even delicate paintings had been preserved by the fall of ashes that had taken over two thousand lives. Columns were dug up, and the forum was beginning to emerge.

It was at a place where the ruins lay deepest that the director paused.

"Come here," he called to his assistant. "I think we've discovered the remains of a building in good shape. Here are four huge millstones that were most likely turned by slaves or mules—and here is a whole wall standing with shelves inside it. Why! It must have been a bakery. And here's a curious thing. What do you think I found under this heap where the ashes were thickest? The skeleton of a dog!"

"Amazing!" gasped his assistant. "You'd think a dog would have had sense enough to run away at the time. And what is that flat thing he's holding between his teeth? It can't be a stone."

"No. It must have come from this bakery. You know it looks to me like some sort of cake hardened with the years. And, bless me, if those little black pebbles aren't raisins. A raisin cake almost two thousand years old! I wonder what made him want it at such a moment." ❽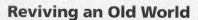

"I wonder," murmured the assistant.

---

16. **mosaics** (mō·zā′iks) *n.:* pictures or designs made by inlaying small bits of stone, glass, tile, or other materials in mortar.

> **◢◣ INFER**
> ❽ What is the answer to the director's question?

Meet the Writer

Louis Untermeyer

Reviving an Old World

Louis Untermeyer (1885–1977) may have been thinking of this story when he described the writer's job as the "struggle somehow to revive an old world, or create a new one."

As a child, Untermeyer loved to read, but he disliked school, especially math. His parents expected him to go to college, but he dropped out of high school when he was sixteen. For the next twenty-two years he worked in his family's jewelry business. He says he did not become serious about working or writing until he met the poet Robert Frost in 1915. Frost became Untermeyer's lifelong friend. It was Frost who encouraged Untermeyer to quit his day job and become a full-time writer.

Today Untermeyer is best known not for his own writing but for the very popular collections of poetry he put together, some for children and some for adults. In his autobiography *From Another World* he describes himself as a friend to three generations of poets.

Before You Read

"The Dog of Pompeii" is historical fiction, a mix of historical facts and fictional events and characters.

The historical event that is central to the story took place in A.D. 79: the eruption of Mount Vesuvius, a volcano fifteen miles south of Naples, Italy. The eruption killed about two thousand people in the seaside towns of Pompeii and Herculaneum and buried them under twenty feet of ashes and rubble.

In his nonfiction book *Lost Cities and Vanished Civilizations,* Robert Silverberg describes Pompeii in A.D. 79 and tells about the eruption of Mount Vesuvius. In writing his book, Silverberg drew on the findings of archaeologists who conducted excavations of Pompeii and Herculaneum.

■ As you read this excerpt from Silverberg's book, take notes on details that appear both there and in Untermeyer's story. Your purpose in reading this excerpt is to evaluate the accuracy of the short story. You may find it helpful to use sticky notes as you read the excerpt. When you come across a fact that's used in the short story, stick a note next to it. On the note, identify the place in the short story where the detail occurs.

Pompeii as it looks today.

POMPEII

Robert Silverberg

The people of Pompeii knew that doom was on hand, now. Their fears were doubled when an enormous rain of hot ashes began to fall on them, along with more lapilli.[1] Pelted with stones, half smothered by ashes, the Pompeiians cried to the gods for mercy. The wooden roofs of some of the houses began to catch fire as the heat of the ashes reached them. Other buildings were collapsing under the weight of the pumice stones that had fallen on them.

In those first few hours, only the quick-witted managed to escape. Vesonius Primus, the wealthy wool merchant, called his family together and piled jewelry and money into a sack. Lighting a torch, Vesonius led his little band out into the nightmare of the streets. Overlooked in the confusion was Vesonius' black watchdog, chained in the courtyard. The terrified dog barked wildly as lapilli struck and drifting

---

1. **lapilli** (lə·pil′ī′) *n.:* small pieces of hardened lava.

white ash settled around him. The animal struggled with his chain, battling fiercely to get free, but the chain held, and no one heard the dog's cries. The humans were too busy saving themselves.

Many hundreds of Pompeiians fled in those first few dark hours. Stumbling in the darkness, they made their way to the city gates, then out, down to the harbor. They boarded boats and got away, living to tell the tale of their city's destruction. Others preferred to remain within the city, huddling inside the temples, or in the public baths, or in the cellars of their homes. They still hoped that the nightmare would end—that the tranquility of a few hours ago would return. . . .

It was evening, now. And new woe was in store for Pompeii. The earth trembled and quaked! Roofs that had somehow withstood the rain of lapilli went crashing in ruin, burying hundreds who had hoped to survive the eruption. In the forum, tall columns toppled as they had in 63.[2] Those who remembered that great earthquake screamed in new terror as the entire city seemed to shake in the grip of a giant fist.

Three feet of lapilli now covered the ground. Ash floated in the air. Gusts of poisonous gas came drifting from the belching crater, though people could still breathe. Roofs were collapsing everywhere. Rushing throngs, blinded by the darkness and the smoke, hurtled madly up one street and down the next, trampling the fallen in a crazy, fruitless dash toward safety. Dozens of people plunged into dead-end streets and found themselves trapped by crashing buildings. They waited there, too frightened to run farther, expecting the end.

The rich man Diomedes was another of those who decided not to flee at the first sign of alarm. Rather than risk being crushed by the screaming mobs, Diomedes calmly led the members of his household into the solidly built basement of his villa. Sixteen people altogether, as well as his daughter's dog and her beloved little goat. They took enough food and water to last for several days.

But for all his shrewdness and foresight, Diomedes was undone anyway. Poison gas was creeping slowly into the underground shelter! He watched his daughter begin to cough and struggle for breath. Vesuvius was giving off vast quantities of deadly carbon monoxide that was now settling like a blanket over the dying city.

"We can't stay here!" Diomedes gasped. Better to risk the uncertainties outside than

---

2. There had been an earthquake in Pompeii sixteen years before Vesuvius erupted.

to remain here and suffocate. "I'll open the door," he told them. "Wait for me here."

Accompanied only by an old and faithful servant, who carried a lantern to light Diomedes' way in the inky blackness, the nobleman stumbled toward the door. He held the silver key in his hand. Another few steps and he would have been at the door, he could have opened it, they could have fled into the air—but a shroud of gas swooped down on him. He fell, still clutching the key, dying within minutes. Beneath the porch, fourteen people waited hopefully for him, their lives ticking away with each second. Diomedes did not return. At the last moment, all fourteen embraced each other, servants and masters alike, as death took them.

The poison gas thickened as the terrible night continued. It was possible to hide from the lapilli, but not from the gas, and Pompeiians died by the hundreds. Carbon monoxide gas keeps the body from absorbing oxygen. Victims of carbon monoxide poisoning get sleepier and sleepier, until they lose consciousness, never to regain it. All over Pompeii, people lay down in the beds of lapilli, overwhelmed by the gas, and death came quietly to them. Even those who had made their way outside the city now fell victim to the spreading clouds of gas. It covered the entire countryside.

In a lane near the forum, a hundred people were trapped by a blind-alley wall. Others hid in the stoutly built public bathhouses, protected against collapsing roofs but not against the deadly gas. Near the house of Diomedes, a beggar and his little goat sought shelter. The man fell dead a few feet from Diomedes' door; the faithful goat remained by his side, its silver bell tinkling, until its turn came.

Mount Vesuvius erupting in 1944.

All through the endless night, Pompeiians wandered about the streets or crouched in their ruined homes or clustered in the temples to pray. By morning, few remained alive. Not once had Vesuvius stopped hurling lapilli and ash into the air, and the streets of Pompeii were filling quickly. At midday on August 25, exactly twenty-four hours after the beginning of the holocaust,[3] a second eruption racked the volcano. A second cloud of ashes rose above Vesuvius' summit. The wind blew ash as far as Rome and Egypt. But most of the new ashes descended on Pompeii.

The deadly shower of stone and ashes went unslackening into its second day. But it no longer mattered to Pompeii whether the eruption continued another day or another year. For by midday on August 25, Pompeii was a city of the dead.

---

3. **holocaust** *n.*: great destruction of life.

First Thoughts

1. How do you think Tito feels several days after the eruption of Vesuvius? How might he feel about what Bimbo did for him?

Thinking Critically

2. Where are we taken at the end of the story? What question is answered there?

3. Review the director's question about the raisin cake on page 701. How would you answer it?

4. In this story, **setting** plays an important role; it is the setting that creates the problem for the characters. How does the setting threaten the lives of the people (and animals) of Pompeii?

5. Many people read historical fiction for its **settings,** to learn about history. What did you learn about the way people lived in Pompeii—their religious beliefs, leisure activities, diet, attitudes toward nature? If you had questions before you started reading, how were they answered?

6. Are Tito and Bimbo **credible characters**—that is, do they behave like real boys and real dogs you've met or you know of? Give one example of something you found credible or incredible in the characterization of Tito. Then, do the same for Bimbo.

Extending Interpretations

7. Why do you think stories and movies about disasters are so popular? Think of a disaster movie you've seen, and tell what you liked and didn't like about it.

SPEAKING AND LISTENING
Evaluating Texts

In class or a small group, discuss the details in "The Dog of Pompeii" that are confirmed by Silverberg's nonfiction account. You should have found at least three details that appear in both the story and the article. In your discussion, consider this question: How did Silverberg find out what happened to Vesonius Primus, his family, his dog, Diomedes, and the beggar and his goat?

Reading Check

a. Why does Tito depend on Bimbo for food?

b. What sign does the volcano give before it erupts? How do some people explain the sign?

c. Where does Bimbo take Tito during the volcano's eruption?

d. What happens to Bimbo in the end?

e. Why are scientists surprised to find a dog buried in the ruins?

North Carolina Competency Goal
1.02; 1.04;
4.01; 4.02;
5.01; 5.02

INTERNET
Projects and Activities
Keyword: LE5 6-8

SKILLS FOCUS

Literary Skills
Evaluate a character's credibility; examine the use of fact in historical fiction.

Reading Skills
Make inferences.

Speaking and Listening Skills
Compare and evaluate texts.

Clarifying Word Meanings

PRACTICE 1

Show your mastery of the words in the Word Bank by answering the following questions.

1. Do you think that an ambitious owner could make any dog a star?
2. Write a proverb that expresses a truth about animals.
3. How would you revive interest in saving an endangered species?

> **Word Bank**
>
> ambitious
> proverb
> revived

Using Word Parts to Build Meanings: Prefixes

PRACTICE 2

Sometimes you can figure out the meaning of an unfamiliar word if you analyze the meanings of its parts. The more prefixes you know, the more words you'll be able to figure out.

A **prefix** is a word part added to the beginning of a word or root. The chart below lists common prefixes.

1. Identify the **prefix** in each of the words listed just below. In the chart, find the meaning of the prefix; then, define the whole word.

   discomfort   incapable   nonstop   unhappy

2. Use each word from item 1 in a sentence or two about Bimbo and Tito.

North Carolina Competency Goal 6.01

Common Prefixes		
Prefix	**Meaning**	**Examples**
dis–	opposing; away	dishonor, dislike
in–	not	incomplete, incorrect
non–	not	nonhuman, nonprofit
un–	not	unwise

SKILLS FOCUS

Vocabulary Skills
Clarify word meanings; use prefixes.

Preparing an Application

Reading Focus
Applications: How to Fill in the Blanks

Chances are, if you want to get a part-time job or work as a volunteer, you'll be asked to fill out an application. The more carefully you prepare your application, the better your chances of getting a positive response are.

■ Imagine that you're applying to work as a volunteer guide at the Pompeii Museum. Follow these steps when you fill out your application:

1. Don't pick up your pen until you **read the application all the way through.**

2. If the application includes a question that requires more than a quick answer, **write down or type your response before you write it on the application** itself. Write in complete sentences. When you're done, ask an adult to review what you've written. Then, copy your answer, **along with any revisions,** onto the application.

3. **Answer questions truthfully.** If the application asks whether you have experience with animals, don't say yes just because you once saw a snake on a Boy Scout camping trip. You might instead point out how learning to work as part of a team in the Scouts will help you to be an effective volunteer.

4. **Print or type** information carefully, with no crossouts.

5. **Fill in** all the blanks. Write *n/a* (for "not applicable") in response to questions that don't apply to you.

6. Check your **spelling.**

7. **Sign and date** your application.

You may be asked to give references on an application. A **reference** is someone the person reviewing your application can call to get information about you. (Anyone you list as a reference should be an adult.) For example, on a job application you might be asked for references the employer could call to find out whether you're a good worker. Be sure to ask permission before you list someone as a reference. Your reference will then expect the call and will have a chance to prepare detailed and useful information about you.

North Carolina Competency Goal
1.04; 2.01

INTERNET
Interactive Reading Model
Keyword: LE5 6-8

SKILLS FOCUS

Reading Skills
Prepare an application.

Pompeii Museum
Application for Volunteer Work

Be neat and complete.

General Information

1. Name: _____

Print all information.

2. Parent's or guardian's name: _____

3. Address: _____
   Street   City   State and zip code

Make sure that any names, addresses, and telephone numbers you give are accurate.

4. Phone number: _____ E-mail address: _____

5. School name: _____ Teacher's name: _____

   School address: _____

Work Information

This volunteer work involves leading small groups of children in grades 1–3 on informative tours of the museum. Volunteers must be able to learn information about the museum and convey it in a way that interests young children. Please answer the following questions in your own handwriting.

Carefully follow all directions for filling out and returning the application.

6. What experience do you have that you think would help you work with young children? _____

   _____

Answer questions like these in complete sentences.

7. What made you interested in working as a volunteer in this museum? _____

   _____

8. What do you think are some good ways to interest children in a topic? _____

   _____

9. Do you have dependable transportation to and from the museum? _____

   _____

10. Please return this application no later than June 10. With your application, please enclose a letter of recommendation from an adult (not a family member) who is familiar with your work habits and your ability to work with children.

Signature _____ Date _____

Preparing an Application

Pompeii Museum Application for Volunteer Work

Test Practice

1. The museum director's purpose in asking questions 6–8 is to find out —
   A where you live
   B where you go to school
   C whether you have transportation to and from the museum
   D about you and your interest in the job

2. You could enclose a letter of recommendation from any of the following people *except* —
   F your teacher
   G your soccer coach
   H your aunt
   J a neighbor you've done babysitting for

3. The best time to mail your application would be —
   A as soon as possible
   B on June 10
   C on June 9
   D on June 15

4. The purpose of question 9 is to find out whether —
   F you'll be able to get to work every day
   G you like to walk
   H you live in the neighborhood
   J you own a bicycle

5. When you sign the application form, you're telling the museum that you —
   A are the best person for the position
   B have answered the questions truthfully
   C really want the job
   D are under no obligation to accept the position

Constructed Response

1. What are the volunteers' main duties?

2. Take out a sheet of paper, and number it from 1 to 10. Write down your answers to each of the application questions. Next to number 10, write down the name of the person you would choose to write the letter of recommendation.

3. Why isn't it a good idea to type your answers on the form?

4. Why shouldn't you ask your best friend, who's in the seventh grade, to write the letter of recommendation?

North Carolina Competency Goal
1.04; 2.01; 4.01; 4.02; 5.01

SKILLS FOCUS

Reading Skills
Prepare an application.

Zlateh the Goat *and* Trial by Fire

Make the Connection

Think-pair-share. What messages have animals sent you lately? Think of a time when you realized an animal was telling you something or showing you how it felt. Share your story with a classmate.

Literary Focus
Suspense: What Happens Next?

Isaac Bashevis Singer, the author of "Zlateh the Goat," liked reading stories that kept him wondering what would happen next. "From my childhood I have always loved tension in a story," he wrote. Singer is talking about **suspense**—that feeling of anxious curiosity about what will happen next in a story.

At first glance, "Zlateh the Goat" seems to be just a story about a family living in a small village and a boy who is sent to market with the family's goat. But Zlateh is an unusually appealing animal, and this account of her trip to the butcher could change your attitude toward goatdom. That's because a sudden change in the weather transforms this simple tale into a suspenseful page turner.

Reading Skills
Making Predictions

When we read a suspenseful story, we often find ourselves predicting what will happen next. If we predict correctly, we're pleased. If the writer surprises us, we're even happier. We like to be surprised by what happens in stories— just as we enjoy being surprised by things that happen in real life.

Vocabulary Development

Be sure you know these words as you read the story:

penetrated (pen′i·trāt′id) *v.:* pierced; made a way through. *Sunlight penetrated the clouds.*

cleft (kleft) *adj.:* split; divided. *Goats have cleft hooves.*

chaos (kā′äs′) *n.:* total confusion or disorder. *The storm created chaos outside Aaron's shelter.*

exuded (eg·zyō͞od′id) *v.:* gave off. *The hay exuded warmth.*

North Carolina Competency Goal
1.04; 4.01; 5.01; 5.02

go.hrw.com

INTERNET

Vocabulary Activity
•
More About Singer
Keyword: LE5 6-8

SKILLS FOCUS

Literary Skills
Understand suspense.

Reading Skills
Make predictions.

Background
Literature and Religion

"Zlateh the Goat" takes place around Hanukkah (khä′noo·kä′), a Jewish religious festival usually observed in December. Hanukkah celebrates the rededication of the Temple in Jerusalem in 165 B.C., following the victory of Jewish fighters over a huge Syrian army. The Temple, which had been taken over by Antiochus, ruler of the Syrians, had been violated and damaged. While the Jews were purifying and repairing the Temple, a miracle occurred. A tiny bit of oil for the holy lamp—barely enough for one day—lasted eight days. Do you see a miracle in Zlateh's story as well?

ISAAC BASHEVIS SINGER

Zlateh
THE GOAT

At Hanukkah time the road from the village to the town is usually covered with snow, but this year the winter had been a mild one. Hanukkah had almost come, yet little snow had fallen. The sun shone most of the time. The peasants complained that because of the dry weather there would be a poor harvest of winter grain. New grass sprouted, and the peasants sent their cattle out to pasture.

For Reuven the furrier[1] it was a bad year, and after long hesitation he decided to sell Zlateh the goat. She was old and gave little milk. Feyvel the town butcher had offered eight gulden[2] for her. Such a sum would buy Hanukkah candles, potatoes and oil for pancakes, gifts for the children, and other holiday necessaries for the house. Reuven told his oldest boy, Aaron, to take the goat to town.

Aaron understood what taking the goat to Feyvel meant, but he had to obey his father. Leah, his mother, wiped the tears from her eyes when she heard the news. Aaron's younger sisters, Anna and Miriam, cried loudly. Aaron put on his quilted jacket and a cap with earmuffs, bound a rope around Zlateh's neck, and took along two slices of bread with cheese to eat on the road. Aaron was supposed to deliver the goat by evening, spend the night at the butcher's, and return the next day with the money.

---

1. **furrier** (fur′ē·ər) *n.*: someone who makes and repairs fur garments.
2. **gulden** (gŏŏl′dən) *n.*: coins formerly used in several European countries.

When Aaron brought her out on the road to town, she seemed somewhat astonished. She'd never been led in that direction before.

While the family said goodbye to the goat, and Aaron placed the rope around her neck, Zlateh stood as patiently and good-naturedly as ever. She licked Reuven's hand. She shook her small white beard. Zlateh trusted human beings. She knew that they always fed her and never did her any harm.

When Aaron brought her out on the road to town, she seemed somewhat astonished. She'd never been led in that direction before. She looked back at him questioningly, as if to say, "Where are you taking me?" But after a while she seemed to come to the conclusion that a goat shouldn't ask questions. Still, the road was different. They passed new fields, pastures, and huts with thatched roofs. Here and there a dog barked and came running after them, but Aaron chased it away with his stick.

The sun was shining when Aaron left the village. Suddenly the weather changed. A large black cloud with a bluish center appeared in the east and spread itself rapidly over the sky. A cold wind blew in with it. The crows flew low, croaking. At first it looked as if it would rain, but instead it began to hail as in summer. It was early in the day, but it became dark as dusk. After a while the hail turned to snow.

In his twelve years Aaron had seen all kinds of weather, but he had never experienced a snow like this one. It was so dense it shut out the light of the day. In a short time their path was completely covered. The wind became as cold as ice. The road to town was narrow and winding. Aaron no longer knew where he was. He could not see through the snow. The cold soon <u>penetrated</u> his quilted jacket.

At first Zlateh didn't seem to mind the change in weather. She too was twelve years old and knew what winter meant. But when her legs sank deeper and deeper into the snow, she began to turn her head and look at Aaron in wonderment. Her mild eyes seemed

Vocabulary
penetrated (pen′i·trāt′id) *v.:* pierced; made a way
   through.

to ask, "Why are we out in such a storm?" Aaron hoped that a peasant would come along with his cart, but no one passed by.

The snow grew thicker, falling to the ground in large, whirling flakes. Beneath it Aaron's boots touched the softness of a plowed field. He realized that he was no longer on the road. He had gone astray. He could no longer figure out which was east or west, which way was the village, the town. The wind whistled, howled, whirled the snow about in eddies. It looked as if white imps were playing tag on the fields. A white dust rose above the ground. Zlateh stopped. She could walk no longer. Stubbornly she anchored her cleft hooves in the earth and bleated as if pleading to be taken home. Icicles hung from her white beard, and her horns were glazed with frost.

Aaron did not want to admit the danger, but he knew just the same that if they did not find shelter, they would freeze to death. This was no ordinary storm. It was a mighty blizzard. The snowfall had reached his knees. His hands were numb, and he could no longer feel his toes. He choked when he breathed. His nose felt like wood, and he rubbed it with snow. Zlateh's bleating began to sound like crying. Those humans in whom she had so much confidence had dragged her into a trap. Aaron began to pray to God for himself and for the innocent animal.

Suddenly he made out the shape of a hill. He wondered what it could be. Who had piled snow into such a huge heap? He moved toward it, dragging Zlateh after him. When he came near it, he realized that it was a large haystack which the snow had blanketed.

Aaron realized immediately that they were saved. With great effort he dug his way through the snow. He was a village boy and knew what to do. When he reached the hay, he hollowed out a nest for himself and the goat. No matter how cold it may be outside, in the hay it is always warm. And hay was food for Zlateh. The moment she smelled it, she became contented and began to eat. Outside, the snow continued to fall. It quickly covered the passageway Aaron had dug. But a boy and an animal need to breathe, and there was hardly any air in their hide-out. Aaron bored a kind of a window through the hay and snow and carefully kept the passage clear.

Zlateh, having eaten her fill, sat down on her hind legs and seemed to have regained her confidence in man. Aaron ate his two slices of bread and cheese, but after the difficult journey he was still hungry. He looked at Zlateh and noticed her udders were full. He lay down next to her, placing himself so that when he milked her, he could squirt the milk into his mouth. It was rich and sweet. Zlateh was not accustomed to being milked that way, but she did not resist. On the contrary, she seemed eager to reward Aaron for bringing her to a shelter whose very walls, floor, and ceiling were made of food.

Through the window Aaron could catch a glimpse of the chaos outside. The wind carried before it whole drifts of snow. It was completely dark, and he did not know whether night had already come or whether it was the darkness of the storm. Thank God that in the hay it was not cold. The dried hay, grass, and field flowers exuded the warmth of the summer sun. Zlateh ate frequently; she nibbled from above, below,

Vocabulary
cleft (kleft) *adj.:* split; divided.
chaos (kā'äs') *n.:* total confusion or disorder.
exuded (eg·zyo͞od'id) *v.:* gave off.

"Zlateh, what do you think about what has happened to us?"

"Maaaa," Zlateh answered.

"If we hadn't found this stack of hay, we would both be frozen stiff by now," Aaron said.

"Maaaa," was the goat's reply.

"If the snow keeps on falling like this, we may have to stay here for days," Aaron explained.

"Maaaa," Zlateh bleated.

"What does 'Maaaa' mean?" Aaron asked. "You'd better speak up clearly."

"Maaaa. Maaaa," Zlateh tried.

"Well, let it be 'Maaaa' then," Aaron said patiently. "You can't speak, but I know you understand. I need you and you need me. Isn't that right?"

"Maaaa."

Aaron became sleepy. He made a pillow out of some hay, leaned his head on it, and dozed off. Zlateh too fell asleep.

When Aaron opened his eyes, he didn't know whether it was morning or night. The snow had blocked up his window. He tried to clear it, but when he had bored through to the length of his arm, he still hadn't reached the outside. Luckily he had his stick with him and was able to break through to the open air. It was still dark outside. The snow continued to fall and the wind wailed, first with one voice and then with many. Sometimes it had the sound of devilish laughter. Zlateh too awoke, and when Aaron greeted her, she answered, "Maaaa." Yes, Zlateh's language consisted of only one word, but it meant many things. Now she was saying, "We must accept all that God gives us—heat, cold, hunger, satisfaction, light, and darkness."

Aaron had awakened hungry. He had eaten up his food, but Zlateh had plenty of milk.

For three days Aaron and Zlateh stayed in

from the left and right. Her body gave forth an animal warmth, and Aaron cuddled up to her. He had always loved Zlateh, but now she was like a sister. He was alone, cut off from his family, and wanted to talk. He began to talk to Zlateh. "Zlateh, what do you think about what has happened to us?" he asked.

the haystack. Aaron had always loved Zlateh, but in these three days he loved her more and more. She fed him with her milk and helped him keep warm. She comforted him with her patience. He told her many stories, and she always cocked her ears and listened. When he patted her, she licked his hand and his face. Then she said, "Maaaa," and he knew it meant, I love you too.

The snow fell for three days, though after the first day it was not as thick and the wind quieted down. Sometimes Aaron felt that there could never have been a summer, that the snow had always fallen, ever since he could remember. He, Aaron, never had a father or mother or sisters. He was a snow child, born of the snow, and so was Zlateh. It was so quiet in the hay that his ears rang in the stillness. Aaron and Zlateh slept all night and a good part of the day. As for Aaron's dreams, they were all about warm weather. He dreamed of green fields, trees covered with blossoms, clear brooks, and singing birds. By the third night the snow had stopped, but Aaron did not dare to find his way home in the darkness. The sky became clear and the moon shone, casting silvery nets on the snow. Aaron dug his way out and looked at the world. It was all white, quiet, dreaming dreams of heavenly splendor. The stars were large and close. The moon swam in the sky as in a sea.

On the morning of the fourth day, Aaron heard the ringing of sleigh bells. The haystack was not far from the road. The peasant who drove the sleigh pointed out the way to him—not to the town and Feyvel the butcher, but home to the village. Aaron had decided in the haystack that he would never part with Zlateh.

Aaron's family and their neighbors had searched for the boy and the goat but had found no trace of them during the storm. They feared they were lost. Aaron's mother and sisters cried for him; his father remained silent and gloomy. Suddenly one of the neighbors came running to their house with the news that Aaron and Zlateh were coming up the road.

There was great joy in the family. Aaron told them how he had found the stack of hay and how Zlateh had fed him with her milk. Aaron's sisters kissed and hugged Zlateh and gave her a special treat of chopped carrots and potato peels, which Zlateh gobbled up hungrily.

Nobody ever again thought of selling Zlateh, and now that the cold weather had finally set in, the villagers needed the services of Reuven the furrier once more. When Hanukkah came, Aaron's mother was able to fry pancakes every evening, and Zlateh got her portion too. Even though Zlateh had her own pen, she often came to the kitchen, knocking on the door with her horns to indicate that she was ready to visit, and she was always admitted. In the evening, Aaron, Miriam, and Anna played dreidel.[3] Zlateh sat near the stove, watching the children and the flickering of the Hanukkah candles.

Once in a while Aaron would ask her, "Zlateh, do you remember the three days we spent together?"

And Zlateh would scratch her neck with a horn, shake her white bearded head, and come out with the single sound which expressed all her thoughts, and all her love.

---

3. **dreidel** (drā′dəl): spinning top played with at Hanukkah. Its four sides display Hebrew letters that stand for "A great miracle happened there."

Meet the Writer

Isaac Bashevis Singer

"Time Does Not Vanish"

Isaac Bashevis Singer (1904–1991) was born in a village like the one in this story and grew up in Warsaw, Poland, where his father was a rabbi. As a boy he read constantly and was curious about everything. Both of Singer's parents were skilled storytellers.

Singer listened and watched carefully, storing in his memory scenes, people, and incidents he would write about later in his life. His stories won him the Nobel Prize in literature in 1978.

In "Zlateh the Goat" and many other stories, Singer recalls a way of life that no longer exists. He wrote:

❝Children are as puzzled by passing time as grown-ups. What happens to a day once it is gone? Where are all our yesterdays with their joys and sorrows? Literature helps us remember the past with its many moods. To the storyteller yesterday is still here as are the years and the decades gone by.

In stories time does not vanish. Neither do men and animals. For the writer and his readers all creatures go on living forever. What happened long ago is still present....

I dedicate this book to the many children who had no chance to grow up because of stupid wars and cruel persecutions which devastated cities and destroyed innocent families. I hope that when the readers of these stories become men and women they will love not only their own children but all good children everywhere.❞

For Independent Reading

If you liked "Zlateh the Goat," try reading *The Fools of Chelm and Their History* or *A Day of Pleasure: Stories of a Boy Growing Up in Warsaw.*

Trial by Fire

After battling a blaze in an abandoned auto shop on March 29 last year, New York City firefighters were startled to hear meowing. There, amid the smoke, sat three crying kittens; across the street were two more. Within moments, their mother, a badly injured calico,° was found nearby. "She had done her job and pulled them out one by one," says firefighter David Giannelli, who placed the animals in a box. "Her eyes were burnt shut, but she touched every one of those babies with the tip of her nose."

°**calico** (kal′i·kō′) *n.:* cat with spots and markings of several colors.

Karen Wellen holds her newly adopted cat, Scarlett.

Taken to Long Island's North Shore Animal League, the kittens and their mother—named Scarlett at the shelter—were treated for smoke inhalation and burns. "The instinct to save your young is very strong," says Dr. Bonnie Brown, North Shore's medical director. "This was just an extraordinary example." Sifting through 2,000 adoption applications, administrators finally sent Scarlett home with Karen Wellen, a New York City writer, and her parents. (One kitten died from a viral infection; the others were placed in area homes.) Now three times a day, Scarlett—a plump 15 pounds—receives eye cream to counter damage to her lids but otherwise is healthy and loving. Karen can't believe her own luck: "This cat risked her life to save her kittens. To come out of it with such a sweet personality is amazing."

—from *People Magazine*, July 14, 1997

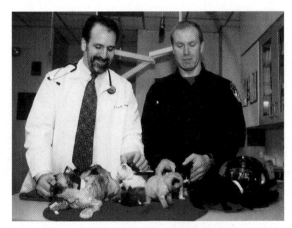

Dr. Larry Cohen and David Giannelli are happy that Scarlett and her kittens are on the road to recovery.

After You Read Response and Analysis

First Thoughts

1. How did you react when the family decided to sell Zlateh to the butcher? How did you feel at the end of the story?

Thinking Critically

2. Think of Aaron's behavior during the storm. What does it tell you about his **character**?

3. List at least two points in the story where you felt **suspense.** Did the next event in the plot happen as you **predicted**? Explain.

4. Singer, who was a dedicated vegetarian, once said, "I love birds and all animals, and I believe men can learn a lot from God's creatures." In this story, what does Aaron learn from Zlateh? What does his family learn?

5. Where in the story does Zlateh express her thoughts and feelings? Did you find Zlateh's methods of communication **credible,** or believable? Why or why not?

North
Carolina
Competency
Goal
1.02; 1.04;
4.01; 4.02;
5.01; 5.02

> ### Reading Check
> Write four questions that deal with the main events of the story's plot. Then, get together with a partner, and ask him or her these questions. Afterward, compare questions and answers. Did you and your partner agree on what was important?

Extending Interpretations

6. Is the **plot** of this story **credible**? Back up your evaluation of the plot with details from the story and from the article "Trial by Fire" (see page 717).

7. Aaron believes that Zlateh tells him, "We must accept all that God gives us—heat, cold, hunger, satisfaction, light, and darkness." What do you think of this attitude?

INTERNET
Projects and
Activities
Keyword: LE5 6-8

WRITING
Comparing Stories

"The Dog of Pompeii" (page 690) and "Zlateh the Goat" have many similarities, even though one story takes place in an ancient Roman city and the other takes place in an eastern European village many centuries later. Write a brief essay comparing the two stories. Focus on the stories' plots, characters, and themes. Use the workshop on writing a **comparison-contrast essay,** pages 404–409, for help with this assignment.

Literary Skills
Analyze suspense; evaluate a plot's credibility.

Reading Skills
Make predictions.

Writing Skills
Write a comparison-contrast essay.

After You Read Vocabulary Development

Clarifying Word Meanings

PRACTICE 1

Show your mastery of the Word Bank words by answering the following questions.

1. Describe three scenes of <u>chaos</u>.
2. Draw a picture of a <u>cleft</u> hoof. Describe the way a <u>cleft</u> in a rock would look.
3. What might you use to <u>penetrate</u> the darkness at night?
4. Name three plants that <u>exude</u> strong odors.

> **Word Bank**
> penetrated
> cleft
> chaos
> exuded

Using Word Parts to Build Meanings: Suffixes

PRACTICE 2

Sometimes you can figure out the meaning of an unfamiliar word if you analyze the meaning of its parts. The more suffixes you know, the more words you'll be able to figure out.

A **suffix** is a word part added to the end of a word or root. The chart below lists common suffixes.

1. Identify the **suffix** in each of the words listed just below. In the chart, find the meaning of the suffix; then, define the whole word.

   fearful   frighten   hopeless   lonely   troublesome

2. Use each word from item 1 in a sentence or two about Aaron and Zlateh.

Common Suffixes		
Suffix	**Meaning**	**Examples**
–able	capable of being	likable, laughable
–en	make	deepen, lengthen
–ful	full of	stressful, doubtful
–ion	act or condition of	inspection, reaction
–less	without	penniless, hopeless
–ly	in a certain way	quickly, smoothly
–ness	quality of being	shyness, happiness
–some	like; tending to be	tiresome, lonesome
–ous	characterized by	luxurious, dangerous

North Carolina Competency Goal
6.01

Vocabulary Skills
Clarify word meanings; use suffixes.

Pronouns and Antecedents Should Always Agree

A pronoun usually refers to a noun or another pronoun, called its **antecedent.** Whenever you use a pronoun, make sure it agrees with its antecedent in number and gender. Doing this is usually easy, except when you use certain pronouns as antecedents.

Use a singular pronoun to refer to *each, either, neither, one, everyone, everybody, no one, anyone, someone,* or *somebody.*

> <u>Nobody</u> would be happy about bringing <u>his</u> or <u>her</u> animal to a butcher.

Nobody is singular, so you use the singular pronouns *his* and *her.* You need both *his* and *her* because the gender of *nobody* can be either masculine or feminine.

> Aaron's mother and sisters were upset about Zlateh; <u>everyone</u> had tears in <u>her</u> eyes.

Everyone is singular, so you use the singular pronoun *her.* You use *her* (rather than *his or her*) because *everyone* refers to Aaron's mother and sisters.

North Carolina Competency Goal 6.01

SKILLS FOCUS

Grammar Skills
Understand pronoun and antecedent agreement.

PRACTICE

Act as an editor: Correct the use of antecedents in the following paragraph about "Zlateh the Goat." Rewrite the sentences if you wish.

Anyone who loves animals will find their interest grabbed by "Zlateh the Goat." It would be hard for someone to take an animal they love to be butchered. No one likes to lose something they love.

For more help, see Problems in Agreement, 2d, in the Language Handbook.

The Village (1973) by Marc Chagall.
©2005 Artists Rights Society (ARS), New York/ADAGP, Paris.

Preparing an Application

Reading Focus
Application Advice

"Trial by Fire" tells the true story of a heroic cat who saved her kittens' lives by carrying them out of a burning building.

Animal shelters give new life to hundreds of cats and dogs every day. Volunteers and veterinarians nurse abandoned animals back to health, in the hope that each one will find a good home.

Taking care of a pet is a serious commitment. Shelter staff try to make sure every adopter is a responsible person who will love and care for the animal. They require anyone seeking to adopt to fill out an application that asks for important personal information. The staff members use the information to determine whether the person would be a good pet owner.

Before you begin filling out any application—whether it's for pet adoption, a job, or admission to college—read it first. You can often learn a great deal about whatever you're applying for by reading through the application. For example, after looking through a shelter application, you may realize you're not really ready to bring Rover or Frisky into your home to live.

■ Here are some other tips for filling out an application:

- Don't leave any line blank. If a question doesn't apply to you, just write *n/a*, which means "not applicable."

- If the form requires a signature, be sure to sign and date it.

- Take your time, and write as neatly as you can.

- After you fill out the application, read it through carefully to make sure you didn't miss anything.

North Carolina Competency Goal
1.04; 2.01

SKILLS FOCUS

Reading Skills
Follow instructions to prepare an application.

Pet Adoption Application

INSTRUCTIONS: **Adopter,** print carefully in **UNSHADED AREAS ONLY**—do not write in shaded areas.

☐ Puppy ☐ Kitten ☐ Dog ☐ Cat

	1	Program

			H T	Adoption Number
			D 0	1
Date / /	Single Adoption / Double Adoption	Age	MTA MTD	L R
			G circle one	2

Day | Time ☐AM ☐PM | Breed | Color | ☐MR. ☐MRS. ☐MS. ☐MISS ☐MR. & MRS.

Sex | ☐Adopter's Last Name   First Name

Voluntary Contribution | Size: S___ M___ L___ | Spay/Neuter

Cash | $ | ☐Pure   ☐Mix | Vaccine Type | Street Address   Apt. #

Check | $ | Pet's Name | Vaccine Date

D V M A circle one | $ | | Rabies Tag

Credit A/R | ($) | ASC Int.   No. | Rabies Date | City   State Zip Code

Total Voluntary Contribution $_____ | Wormed

X_____ | Med. Given | NMR Tech. App. | Home Phone   Business Phone
( )   -   ( )   -

Name of Reference	Address	City	State	Telephone	ID Source
				( )	☐Yes ☐No
				( )	D V ☐Yes
					M A ☐No
				( )	

1. WHOM IS THE PET FOR? Self___ Gift___ For whom?_____ Adopter's age:___

2. IF YOU'RE SINGLE: Do you live alone? Yes___ No___ Do you live with family? Yes___ No___
   Do you work? Yes___ No___ What are your hours?_____

   IF YOU'RE MARRIED: Do both work? Yes___ No___ Husband's hours:_____ Wife's hours:_____
   How many children at home?_____ Ages:_____, _____, _____, _____, _____
   Who will be responsible for the pet? Husband___ Wife___ Children___ Other_____

3. DO YOU: OWN ☐ RENT ☐   HOUSE ☐ APT. ☐ Floor #___ Elevator in the building? Yes___ No___
   (CHECK ONE)   (CHECK ONE)
   If renting, does your lease allow pets? Yes___ No___ Are you moving? Yes___ No___ When?___
   Do you have use of a private yard? Yes___ No___ Is it fenced? Yes___ No___ Fence height:___
   Where will your pet be kept?_____/_____ Any allergy to pets? Yes___ No___
                                DAYTIME   NIGHTTIME

4. DO YOU HAVE OTHER PETS NOW? Yes___ No___ Breed:_____
   Where did you get the pet?_____ How long have you had it?_____

   HAVE YOU EVER HAD A PET BEFORE? Yes___ No___ Breed:_____
   How long did you have the pet?_____ What happened to the pet?_____
   Have you ever adopted from this shelter? Yes___ No___ Where is the pet now?_____

5. YOUR OCCUPATION:_____ Business Phone: ( )_____
   Company:_____ Supervisor's Name:_____

VET'S NAME	CITY, STATE	ZIP CODE

Adopter's Signature:

Preparing an Application

Pet Adoption Application

Test Practice

1. Which of the following people would not be a suitable reference?
   - **A** A teacher
   - **B** A parent
   - **C** A classmate
   - **D** An aunt

2. The main thing the shelter wants to know about an applicant is —
   - **F** whether the applicant will feed the animal the right food
   - **G** whether the applicant plans to let the dog or cat run free through the neighborhood
   - **H** whether the applicant will always keep the pet's best interests in mind
   - **J** what kind of dog or cat the applicant wants

3. The abbreviation *n/a* stands for "not applicable." What does the term *not applicable* mean?
   - **A** None of your business
   - **B** Does not apply to me
   - **C** Not again
   - **D** No answer

4. The application asks for your veterinarian's name. What would be the best thing to do if you didn't already have a vet?
   - **F** Just leave the space blank.
   - **G** Write *n/a*.
   - **H** Ask the shelter to recommend one.
   - **J** Make up a name.

Constructed Response

1. A **reference** is a person who can provide information about you. Why would the adoption shelter want references for an adopter?

2. Why is it important for the adoption shelter to know whether you rent or own your home?

3. What information do you think the shelter is really looking for when it asks what pets you have now?

North Carolina Competency Goal 2.01

SKILLS FOCUS

Reading Skills
Follow instructions to prepare an application.

Becoming a Critical Reader
Analyzing Persuasive Techniques

Persuasion

Persuasion is everywhere. Advertisements urge us to buy things; politicians ask for our votes; editorial writers try to influence our thinking on issues. **Persuasion** is the use of language or of visual images to get us to *believe* or *do* something. Skillful persuaders use a number of techniques to get us to see things their way.

Logical Appeals

Logic is correct reasoning. You're using logic when you put facts together and conclude that "if this is true, then that must be true." A logical persuasive argument is built on opinion supported by **reasons** and **evidence.**

Whenever someone tries to persuade you, ask yourself, "*How* is this person trying to convince me?" Be alert to common kinds of fallacious, or faulty, reasoning. When you see the word *fallacious* (fə·lā′shəs), think of the word *false*. **Fallacious reasoning** is false reasoning. On the surface the person's arguments make sense, but if you look closely, you'll find flaws in the reasoning.

North Carolina Competency Goal
3.01; 3.03; 4.03

SKILLS FOCUS

Reading Skills
Analyze persuasive techniques; analyze fallacious reasoning.

Fallacious Reasoning: Two Plus Two Isn't Three

Here are three kinds of fallacious reasoning:

1 **Hasty generalizations.** A **generalization** is a broad statement that tells about something "in general." Valid generalizations are based on solid evidence. For example, someone who has experience with cats might say, "Most cats love milk." Valid generalizations, like that one, usually include **qualifying words**—*most, some, generally*. Qualifying words allow for exceptions to a generalization (here, cats that don't like milk).

A **hasty generalization** is one that is based on incomplete evidence.

Circular reasoning.

HASTY GENERALIZATION

Jane Goes Overboard

Jane and I went to the Dinner Diner for lunch the other day. Jane ordered a cheeseburger, and it was horrible! She says that she'll never eat in a diner again.

EXPLANATION

Maybe the Dinner Diner's cheeseburgers do taste like shoe leather, but that doesn't mean *every* diner serves a bad cheeseburger. Jane is making a hasty generalization about *all* diners from a single bad experience.

2 **Circular reasoning. Circular reasoning** goes around and around without ever getting anywhere. It says the same thing over and over again, each time using slightly different words.

CIRCULAR REASONING

Too Long Is Too Long Is Too Long

We should cancel these play practices because they are too long. Sometimes they last three hours. We don't need to spend so much time practicing. Three-hour practices are too long.

EXPLANATION

This argument presents no reasons to back up the opinion. At first glance it seems to offer support, but if you look closely, you'll see that the same idea is repeated three times!

3 **Only-cause fallacy.** In the **only-cause fallacy** a situation is seen as the result of only one cause. Situations often have many causes.

ONLY-CAUSE FALLACY

Todd Drops the Ball

Our team lost the game tonight because Todd didn't play well. Todd is usually our best player, but he missed lots of shots and didn't get many rebounds. The blame for this loss lies squarely on Todd's shoulders.

EXPLANATION

Can you see the fallacy in this reasoning? Todd is only one player on a team of many, so his poor playing couldn't be the *only* reason his team lost. Maybe other players on the team didn't play well, either. Maybe the opposing team put their best defender on Todd. Maybe the winning team played a better game.

"We would have won if Todd had gotten that rebound in the first quarter."

Analyzing Fallacious Reasoning

PRACTICE 1

All of the following items illustrate fallacious reasoning. Identify the kind of faulty reasoning in each—**hasty generalization, circular reasoning,** or **only-cause fallacy.** Then, explain why the reasoning is faulty.

1. Students should wear uniforms because they're cheaper than regular clothes. Regular clothes are too expensive. Wearing uniforms means that you don't have to spend lots of money on new clothes.

2. Since Ross started to wear a uniform, he's been getting good grades. He's always studied really hard, and he was on the honor roll three times last year.

3. I love my school uniform. Everyone should wear one.

4. We started wearing uniforms at my school right after spring break. Attendance is much better than it was during the winter.

5. Wearing uniforms will help keep kids from acting up in class and in the halls. Uniforms will make kids behave better.

PRACTICE 2

With a partner or on your own, write one example of each of the following types of fallacious reasoning. Then, read your examples to the class. Can the class identify the fallacy in each one?

1. hasty generalization
2. only-cause fallacy
3. circular reasoning

Becoming a Critical Reader
Analyzing Propaganda

Propaganda

Propaganda is a kind of persuasion designed to keep us from thinking for ourselves. Propaganda relies on appeals to our emotions rather than logical arguments and reasoning. Much propaganda consists of one-sided arguments.

Not all propaganda is bad, however. Most people would agree that a doctor who uses emotional appeals to discourage kids from smoking is using "good propaganda."

Here are several techniques used in propaganda. You'll probably recognize some of them.

1 **Bandwagon appeals.** A **bandwagon appeal** urges you to do something because everyone else is doing it. (The word *bandwagon* refers to a decorated wagon used in a parade. A bandwagon carried—yes—the band. Kids would often jump on the bandwagon for an exciting ride.) A person using a bandwagon appeal takes advantage of our desire to be part of a group. It's the "don't be the last person on your block to have one" technique, and it is often used by advertisers.

A BANDWAGON APPEAL

Eight out of ten people in your area have already signed up for this long-distance phone service. Time is running out, so hurry! Everyone knows what a bargain this is. Shouldn't you save money too?

EXPLANATION

The fact that "everyone is doing it" is not a convincing reason for *you* to do it (or to jump on the bandwagon).

North Carolina Competency Goal
3.01; 3.03; 4.01; 4.03

SKILLS FOCUS

Reading Skills
Analyze propaganda.

2 **Use of stereotypes.** A **stereotype** is a fixed idea about all the members of a group, one that doesn't allow for individual differences. Stereotyping leads to prejudice—evaluating people on the basis of their membership in a group rather than on their individual characteristics.

USE OF A STEREOTYPE

You just can't trust politicians—they'll do anything to get elected.

EXPLANATION

This sentence unfairly lumps all politicians together. As a group, politicians aren't always popular, but not all are untrustworthy.

3 **Name-calling. Name-calling** is using labels to arouse negative feelings toward someone instead of giving reasons and evidence to support an argument.

USE OF NAME-CALLING

Only a liberal tree-hugger would fail to see the importance of building the new supermall. Who needs that rat-infested park, anyway? Let's pave it over!

EXPLANATION

No convincing reasons for building the mall are given. Instead, the person making this argument dismisses any opponents by calling them names.

4 **Snob appeal.** Advertisers use **snob appeal** when they associate their product with wealth, glamour, or membership in a select society. The message they're sending is that using their product sets you apart from the crowd.

USE OF SNOB APPEAL

The average person thinks that any old hair-care product will do. But you know better. Ultra Turbo Hair is designed for people who insist on quality—people like you.

EXPLANATION

This advertisement makes an appeal to people's desire to feel special. It offers no information about the product itself.

5 **Testimonial.** When a football star recommends a breakfast cereal, he's making an emotional appeal to his fans. The message is that you can be just like him if you eat the same cereal. Famous people who recommend a product or a candidate for office are using glamour, talent, and fame to persuade you to part with your money or your vote.

USE OF A TESTIMONIAL

Hello. I'm not a politician, but I play one on television. I'm here today to urge you to vote for Richard Richards as governor of our great state.

EXPLANATION

In this situation a respected state senator or representative would provide a more trustworthy testimonial than an actor who plays a politician on TV.

Analyzing Propaganda

PRACTICE 1

Identify the type of propaganda used in each of the following statements.

1. Women with the finest fashion sense wear Stirrup Earrings.

2. Don't be left out in the cold. Order the vest worn by ninety percent of all ski instructors—the SupraDown hooded vest.

3. The people who want to build the mall are businessmen. All businessmen are selfish and care only about making money.

4. Hi. I'm Dan Nulty, the Olympic gold medalist. I invest all my money with Dansforth Funds. I suggest you go with a winner too!

5. Don't hire Oliver. He's a lazy whiner.

6. Senator Axman is a bleeding-heart liberal and a hypocrite. Vote for Mary Michaels.

7. Come to the protest. Almost everyone will be cutting classes tomorrow to join the march.

PRACTICE 2

With a partner, make up one example of each of the following types of propaganda. Then, read the example to the class, and see if they can identify the kind of propaganda you've used.

1. bandwagon appeal
2. stereotype
3. name-calling
4. snob appeal
5. testimonial

PRACTICE 3

The type of persuasive writing that you come across most often is advertising. Advertisers try to get you to buy their products by using pictures, words, and music. Look through several magazines, and listen critically to advertisements you see and hear on television and the radio. Bring to class advertisements that appeal to your emotions. Try to find advertisements that use some of the techniques discussed in this collection.

Also look for examples of "good propaganda"—advertisements that urge you to do something positive. You might find advertisements from charitable organizations asking you to make a donation, for example. Bring these to class too.

Take notes on the advertisements you bring to class, and discuss the propaganda techniques used in each.

North Carolina Competency Goal
1.02; 1.04; 3.01; 3.03; 4.01; 4.02; 5.01

Reading Skills
Analyze propaganda.

Comparing Literature

Literary Focus
A Writer's Message

A **narrative** is an account of a series of related events. Narratives can be fictional—such as short stories and novels—or true. Most narratives contain a message of some sort. The message is not the same as the **plot,** or what happens in the text. The message is a big idea or truth that goes beyond the specific events of the narrative. When discussing fiction, we refer to a story's message as its **theme.** With nonfiction, the message is called the **main idea.**

A writer's message should be stated in a complete sentence. However, no two readers are likely to ever state it in exactly the same way. In the box at the right are some questions you might consider as you try to figure out a writer's message and state it in your own words.

North Carolina Competency Goal
1.02; 5.01

Reading Skills and Strategies
Comparing and Contrasting

You are about to read and compare two narratives—a fictional story and a true story. Both are about animals in trouble and the people who try to help them.

As you read, look for similarities and differences between the stories. Think about the writer's message in each story. What does the writer want to convey about the relationship between humans and animals? How do the writers' messages compare?

At the end of each story, you'll fill in a chart to keep track of what you've read. You'll use the chart to help you write a **comparison-contrast essay.**

> ### Finding a Writer's Message
>
> You can discover a writer's message by following these steps:
>
> - Look for evidence, or clues, in the text. How do characters change? What do they learn about life?
> - Think of evidence from your own experience. Try to make connections between the narrative and your prior knowledge.
> - Try to state what all this evidence reveals about life and people in general.

SKILLS FOCUS

Literary Skills
Interpret a writer's message.

Reading Skills
Compare and contrast texts.

Before You Read

Every year, millions of dogs are abandoned or born homeless in the United States. "Stray" is a fictional account of what happens to one such puppy. As you read, consider what the story reveals about humans and our relationship to animals.

stray

Cynthia Rylant

In January, a puppy wandered onto the property of Mr. Amos Lacey and his wife, Mamie, and their daughter, Doris. Icicles hung three feet or more from the eaves of houses, snowdrifts swallowed up automobiles, and the birds were so fluffed up they looked comic.

Seated Girl with Dog (1944) by Milton Avery. Oil on canvas (44″ × 32″).
Roy R. Neuberger Collection.

IDENTIFY

❶ What is the setting of this story? How does the setting contribute to the puppy's situation?

The puppy had been abandoned, and it made its way down the road toward the Laceys' small house, its ears tucked, its tail between its legs, shivering. ❶

Doris, whose school had been called off because of the snow, was out shoveling the cinder-block front steps when she spotted the pup on the road. She set down the shovel.

"Hey! Come on!" she called.

The puppy stopped in the road, wagging its tail timidly, trembling with shyness and cold.

Doris trudged through the yard, went up the shoveled drive and met the dog.

"Come on, pooch."

"Where did *that* come from?" Mrs. Lacey asked as soon as Doris put the dog down in the kitchen.

Mr. Lacey was at the table, cleaning his fingernails with his pocketknife. The snow was keeping him home from his job at the warehouse.

"I don't know where it came from," he said mildly, "but I know for sure where it's going." ❷

Doris hugged the puppy hard against her. She said nothing.

Because the roads would be too bad for travel for many days, Mr. Lacey couldn't get out to take the puppy to the pound in the city right away. He agreed to let it sleep in the basement, while Mrs. Lacey grudgingly let Doris feed it table scraps. The woman was sensitive about throwing out food.

By the looks of it, Doris figured the puppy was about six months old and on its way to being a big dog. She thought it might have some shepherd in it.

Four days passed and the puppy did not complain. It never cried in the night or howled at the wind. It didn't tear up everything in the basement. It wouldn't even follow Doris up the basement steps unless it was invited.

It was a good dog. ❸

Several times Doris had opened the door in the kitchen that led to the basement, and the puppy had been there, all stretched out, on the top step. Doris knew it had wanted some company and that it had lain against the door, listening to the talk in the kitchen, smelling the food, being a part of things. It always wagged its tail, eyes all sleepy, when she found it there.

Even after a week had gone by, Doris didn't name the dog. She knew her parents wouldn't let her keep it, that her father made so little money any pets were out of the question, and that the pup would definitely go to the pound when the weather cleared.

Still, she tried talking to them about the dog at dinner one night.

"She's a good dog, isn't she?" Doris said, hoping one of them would agree with her.

Her parents glanced at each other and went on eating.

"She's not much trouble," Doris added. "I like her." She smiled at them, but they continued to ignore her.

"I figure she's real smart," Doris said to her mother. "I could teach her things."

Mrs. Lacey just shook her head and stuffed a forkful of sweet potato in her mouth. Doris fell silent, praying the weather would never clear.

INFER

❷ What do you think Doris plans to do with the puppy? What does her father mean when he says, "I know for sure where it's going"?

ANALYZE

❸ Why do you think the writer puts this sentence into a paragraph of its own?

❹ Why won't Doris's parents let her keep the puppy? Do you think it is an easy decision for them? Explain.

❺ Why do you think Doris dreams about searching for lost things?

But on Saturday, nine days after the dog had arrived, the sun was shining and the roads were plowed. Mr. Lacey opened up the trunk of his car and came into the house.

Doris was sitting alone in the living room, hugging a pillow and rocking back and forth on the edge of a chair. She was trying not to cry but she was not strong enough. Her face was wet and red, her eyes full of distress.

Mrs. Lacey looked into the room from the doorway.

"Mama," Doris said in a small voice. "Please."

Mrs. Lacey shook her head.

"You know we can't afford a dog, Doris. You try to act more grown-up about this." ❹

Doris pressed her face into the pillow.

Outside, she heard the trunk of the car slam shut, one of the doors open and close, the old engine cough and choke and finally start up.

"Daddy," she whispered. "Please."

She heard the car travel down the road, and though it was early afternoon, she could do nothing but go to her bed. She cried herself to sleep, and her dreams were full of searching and searching for things lost. ❺

It was nearly night when she finally woke up. Lying there, like stone, still exhausted, she wondered if she would ever in her life have anything. She stared at the wall for a while.

But she started feeling hungry, and she knew she'd have to make herself get out of bed and eat some dinner. She wanted not to go into the kitchen, past the basement door. She wanted not to face her parents.

But she rose up heavily.

Her parents were sitting at the table, dinner over, drinking coffee. They looked at her when she came in, but she kept her head down. No one spoke.

Doris made herself a glass of powdered milk and drank it all down. Then she picked up a cold biscuit and started out of the room.

"You'd better feed that mutt before it dies of starvation," Mr. Lacey said.

Doris turned around.

"What?"

"I said, you'd better feed your dog. I figure it's looking for you."

Doris put her hand to her mouth.

"You didn't take her?" she asked.

"Oh, I took her all right," her father answered. "Worst-looking place I've ever seen. Ten dogs to a cage. Smell was enough to knock you down. And they give an animal six days to live. Then they kill it with some kind of a shot."

Doris stared at her father.

"I wouldn't leave an *ant* in that place," he said. "So I brought the dog back."

Mrs. Lacey was smiling at him and shaking her head as if she would never, ever, understand him.

Mr. Lacey sipped his coffee.

"Well," he said, "are you going to feed it or not?" **6**

ANALYZE

6 Why does Doris's father change his mind about the puppy? What does this decision show about the kind of person he is?

Meet the Writer

Cynthia Rylant

"Our Lives Are Beautiful, Breathtaking"

Cynthia Rylant (1954–   ) spent part of her childhood with her grandparents in West Virginia. Remembering them fondly, she says:

66 They lived life with strength, great calm, and a real sense of what it means to be devoted to and responsible for other people. The tone of my work reflects the way they spoke, the simplicity of their language, and, I hope, the depth of their own hearts. 99

Why does Rylant—winner of the Newbery and other awards—like to write?

66 I like to show the way our lives are beautiful, breathtaking, in the smallest things: shelling beans on a porch in the evening; sitting in a run-down shoe repair shop; wanting a pretty little lamp; giving saltines to the squirrels. I prefer writing about child characters because they have more possibilities. They can get away with more love, more anger, more fear than adult characters. They can be more moving. I like them more. I sympathize with them more. 99

For Independent Reading

Cynthia Rylant writes poetry, short stories, and novels. If you enjoyed "Stray," try the story collections *Every Living Thing* and *A Couple of Kooks: And Other Stories About Love*.

After You Read "Stray"

First Thoughts

1. Explain your response to Mr. Lacey's decision at the end of the story.

Thinking Critically

2. Why is the **setting**—a cold, snowy January—an important part of the story?

3. After Doris cries, her mother tells her to act more grown-up. Do you think this is good advice? Why or why not?

4. What do you think the **theme** of this story reveals about love and caring? What message does the author convey about the relationship between humans and animals?

Comparing Literature

5. To gather your observations about "Stray," copy the chart below, and fill out the first column. After you read "The Flood," you'll fill out the second column and use the chart to complete an assignment on page 754.

Reading Check

Pretend you are Doris Lacey. Write a diary entry
a. for the day you find the puppy
b. after you've had the puppy for a week
c. about the day your father takes the puppy to the pound

Comparing Stories: Humans and Their Animals		
	"Stray"	"The Flood"
Setting and problem		
How humans help animals		
How humans harm animals		
What humans learn from and about animals		

North Carolina Competency Goal
1.02; 1.04;
4.01; 4.02;
5.01; 5.02

Literary Skills
Analyze a writer's message.

Reading Skills
Compare and contrast stories.

Before You Read

Ralph Helfer spent many years training lions, bears, and other wild animals to perform in movies and on television. Unlike other trainers of his time, who often used beatings and electric shocks to control dangerous animals, Helfer believed in treating his animals with patience and love. (More information about his training technique, called affection training, appears in Meet the Writer on page 753.) At the peak of his career, Helfer became the owner and operator of a large ranch, which was home to hundreds of wild animals. In the following narrative he recounts the time that a terrible flood struck the ranch.

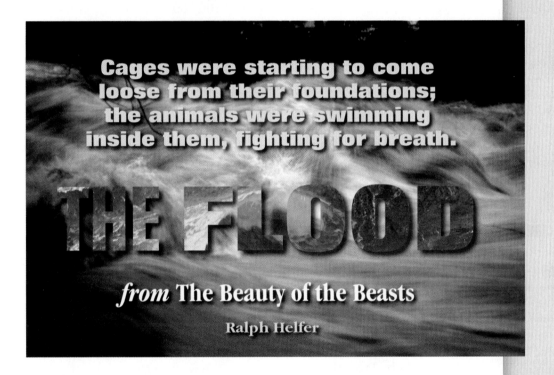

Cages were starting to come loose from their foundations; the animals were swimming inside them, fighting for breath.

THE FLOOD

from The Beauty of the Beasts

Ralph Helfer

It was raining that morning, as usual. For weeks it had been coming down—sometimes heavily, with thunder and lightning, and sometimes with just a mist of light rain. But it was always there, and by now the blankets, the beds, and the whole house were constantly damp.

My career was at a peak. I'd spent twelve years struggling to get to the top, and I had finally made it. My life was pretty good. I had just completed the back-to-back shooting of *Daktari* and *Gentle Ben,* and I was living at our new ranch, Africa U.S.A., with 1,500 wild animals and a crew of dedicated keepers and trainers.

The ranch was beautiful. Nestled at the bottom of Soledad Canyon, about thirty miles north of Los Angeles, the property snaked for a mile down the canyon beside the banks of the Santa Clarita stream. The highway wound above it on one side, the railroad track on the other.

We'd had heavy rains before, and even a few floods, but nothing we couldn't handle. There was a flood-control dam above us, fifteen miles up the canyon, and we weren't too worried about the stream's overflowing. But just to make sure, we had asked the city's flood-control office to advise us. They checked their records for the biggest flood in the office's hundred-year history, and calculated that to handle one that size we would need a channel 100 feet wide, 12 feet deep, and 1 mile long. It cost us $100,000 and three months of hard work, but we built it. It was worth it to feel safe. ❶

Toni and I had grabbed a few hours' sleep before leaving the house, which was located off the ranch up on a hill, and heading out into the rain again early this morning to make sure our animals were dry and safe.

On arriving at the compound, Toni went over to check on the "wild string," a group of lions, tigers, bears, and leopards that had been donated to us by people who never should have had them in the first place. Hopeless animal lovers that we were, we had taken them in, even though we know that very few spoiled mature animals could ever be indoctrinated[1] with affection training. ❷

I checked at the office for messages, then headed for "Beverly Hills," our nickname for the area where our movie-star animals lived—Gentle Ben, Clarence the cross-eyed lion, Judy the chimp, Bullfrog the "talking" buffalo, Modoc the elephant, and many others. The rain had become a steady downpour by the time I arrived there. Everything seemed to be in order, so I went on to the rhinos. No problems there, either.

As I left the rhinos, I noticed that I could no longer jump over the stream that ran beside their barn. I was starting to get a little concerned. The sky was now opening up with a vengeance.[2] I

---

1. **indoctrinated** (in·däk′trə·nāt′id) v.: taught.
2. **with a vengeance** (ven′jəns): with great force.

wrapped my poncho around me and continued my tour of inspection.

I was wondering how Toni was making out with the wild string when Miguel, a Mexican keeper who had been with us for six years, arrived to care for the animals in the Beverly Hills section. He smiled his broad, gold-capped grin, then disappeared around a bend of the stream.

Then my head trainer, Frank Lamping, arrived. He told me that the earthen dam above us was about to go. To prevent the dam from bursting, the flood-control people were opening the flood-gates to release the pressure. We were to watch out for some heavy water coming downstream. ❸

The crew had all been working continuously from morning until night since the rains had begun, to make sure that the ranch was safe. Now we had to redouble our efforts.

I told Frank to check the stock area. A trainer yelled from the roadway above that he had the nursery section under control.

I found some pretty badly undermined cages in my area and set to work with a shovel to fill the erosion. I was looking down at my shovel, working hard, when I heard a noise. It was a low roar, and it was quickly becoming louder and closer. I remember just looking over my shoulder, and suddenly there it was— a wall of water carrying with it full-sized oak trees, sheds, branches. Down it came, crashing and exploding against the compound, uprooting cages, overturning buildings, trucks— anything in its way.

Instantly, everything was in chaos. Sheer panic broke out among the animals in the

INFER

❸ What do you think floodgates are? How will opening them prevent the dam from bursting? Consider where the ranch is located in relation to the dam. What do you think will happen to the ranch when the floodgates are opened?

Ralph Helfer and his family with Zamba the lion.

Beverly Hills section. Lions were roaring and hitting against the sides of their cages; bears were lunging against the bars; chimps were screaming. The water was starting to rock the cages. Some were already floating and were about to be swept downstream.

I didn't know what to do first! I raced for the cages, but was thrown down by the weight of the water. Miguel came running over, yelling half in English and half in Spanish. I told him to grab a large coil of rope that was hanging in a tree nearby. I fastened it around me and, with Miguel holding the other end, I started out into the water. If I could just get to the cages, I could unlock them and set the animals free. At least then they could fend for themselves. It was their only chance. Otherwise, they would all drown in their cages.

The water was rushing past me furiously. I struggled through it to Gentle Ben's cage, fumbling for the key. "Don't *drop* it!" I mumbled to myself. The key turned, I threw open the door, and the great old bear landed right on top of me in his panic for freedom.

I grabbed Ben's heavy coat and hung on as his massive body carried me to a group of cages holding more than twenty animals. The water was now five or six feet deep. Cages were starting to come loose from their foundations; the animals were swimming inside them, fighting for breath. I let go of Ben and grabbed onto the steel bars of one of the cages. My heart sank as I saw Ben dog-paddling, trying to reach the embankment. He never did. I could just barely make out his form as he was carried through some  rough white water and around a bend before he was lost from view.

One by one I released the animals—leopards, tigers, bears— talking as calmly as I could, even managing an occasional pat or kiss of farewell. I watched as they were carried away, swept along with the torrent of water. Some would come together for a moment and would then be whisked away, as though a giant hand had come up and shoved them. Some went under. I strained to see whether any of these came up again, but I couldn't tell.

My wonderful, beloved animals were all fighting for their lives. I felt sick and helpless. ❹

RETELL

❹ In your own words, list the actions Helfer and his employees have taken since the wall of water flooded the ranch. What do you think will happen to the animals they freed?

To my right, about thirty feet out in the water and half submerged, was a large, heavy steel cage on wheels with a row of four compartments in it. I managed to get to it just as the force of the current started to move it. I began to open the compartments, one by one, but now the cage was moving faster downstream, carrying me with it. I looked back to the shore, at Miguel. He saw the problem, and with his end of the rope he threw a dally

around a large tree branch. We were running out of time. If the rope came to the end of its slack before I could get it off me and onto the cage, we would lose the cage. It was picking up speed, and the animals inside were roaring and barking in terror.

I decided to hold the cage myself, with the rope tied around my waist. There were two beautiful wolves in the last cage, Sheba and Rona. Toni and I had raised them since they were pups. I was at their door, fumbling with the lock, when the rope went taut. I thought it would cut me in half. I grabbed the steel bars with both hands, leaving the key in the lock, praying it wouldn't drop out. When I reached down once more to open the lock, the key fell into the water! I was stunned, frozen. I knew I had just signed those animals' death warrants. The water behind the cage was building up a wall of force. I held on as tightly as I could, but finally the cage was ripped out of my hands. ❺

I fell backward into the churning water; when I surfaced, I could see the cage out in the mainstream, racing with the trees, bushes, and sides of buildings, heading on down the raging river. I looked for the last time at Sheba and Rona. They were looking at us quietly as if they knew, but their eyes begged for help. My tears joined the flood as my beloved friends were washed away.

By this time it had become clear to me what had happened. The floodgates on the dam had been opened, all right, but because the ground was already saturated with the thirty inches of rain that had fallen in the last few weeks, it wouldn't absorb any more. At the same time, the new storm had hit, pouring down another fourteen inches in just twenty-four hours. Together, these conditions had caused the flood.

INTERPRET

❺ What words would you use to describe the actions Helfer takes to save the wolves?

RETELL

❻ Explain what caused the ranch to flood. Why did the water come in waves?

It was a larger flood than any that had been recorded in the area in the last hundred years, and it was made worse because the water had been held up occasionally on its fifteen-mile journey down the canyon by debris in its path. When suddenly released, the water that had built up behind the naturally formed logjams doubled in force. By the time it reached us, huge waves had been built up: The water and debris came crashing down on us like a wall, then subsided, only to come crashing down again. We were to struggle through two days and nights of unbelievable havoc and terror, trying desperately to salvage[3] what we could of the ranch. ❻

The storm grew worse. Heavy sheets of rain filled and overflowed our flood channel, undermining its sides until they caved in. By midmorning the Santa Clarita had become a raging, murderous torrent, 150 feet wide and 15 feet deep, moving through Africa U.S.A. with the speed and force of an express train. In its fury it wiped out a two-lane highway, full-grown oak trees, generator buildings— everything. Our sound stage was in a full-sized building, 100 feet long by 50 feet wide, but the water just picked it up like a matchbox and carried it away downstream, end over end,

rolling it like a toy and depositing it on a sand embankment a mile away. Electric wires flared brightly as the water hit them. We rushed for the main switch to the sound stage, shutting everything down for fear of someone being electrocuted. Everywhere, animals and people were in the water, swimming for safety.

We'd be half drowned, and then we'd make our way to the shore, cough and sputter, and go back into the water. You don't think at a time like that—you *do*. My people risked their lives over and over again for the animals.

The waves next hit the elephant pens, hard. We moved the elephants out as the building collapsed and was carried downstream. Then the waves caught the camels' cage, pulling it into the water. One huge camel was turning over and over as he was swept along. (I thought at the time that somewhere, someday, if that animal drowned, some archaeologist would dig up its bones and say, "There must have been camels in Los Angeles!")

---

3. **salvage** (sal′vij) *v.*: save from destruction.

Ranch hands with Raja the tiger on the set of the television series *Daktari*.

We worked frenziedly. Bears, lions, and tigers were jumping out of their cages and immediately being swept downstream. Others were hanging onto our legs and pulling us under, or we were hanging onto them and swimming for shore. I unlocked the cheetah's cage and he sprang out over my head, right into the water, and was gone. Animals were everywhere.

I remember grabbing hold of a mature tiger as he came out of his cage. He carried me on his back to temporary security on the opposite bank as smoothly as if we'd rehearsed it.

Another time I found myself being carried downstream with Zamba, Jr., who was caught in the same whirlpool that I was. I grabbed his mane, and together we swam for the safety of the shore. After resting a bit, I managed to get back to the main area, leaving the lion in as good a spot as any. At least for the moment he was safe.

As the storm rode on, the river was full of animals and people swimming together; there was no "kill" instinct in operation, only that of survival. Men were grabbing fistfuls of fur, clinging for life. A monkey grabbed a lion's tail, which allowed him to make it to safety. ❼

Clarence the cross-eyed lion was in a state of panic. The river had surrounded him and was now flooding his cage. His trainer, Bob,

ANALYZE

❼ What does Helfer mean when he says, "there was no 'kill' instinct in operation, only that of survival"? Are Helfer's animals behaving the way you would expect uncaged wild animals to behave during a disaster? Explain.

The Flood   743

waded across the water, put a chain on Clarence, took him out of his cage, and attempted to jump across the raging stream with him. But the lion wouldn't jump. The water was rising rapidly. Bob threw part of the chain to me. To gain some leverage,[4] I grabbed a pipe that was running alongside a building. As we both pulled, Clarence finally jumped, and just then the pipe I was holding onto came loose. It turned out to be a "hot" electric conduit, for when Clarence leaped and the pipe came loose, we all got a tremendous electric shock!

Fortunately, the pipe also pulled the wires loose, so the shock only lasted for an instant. Had it continued, it would certainly have killed us, as we were standing knee-deep in water.

We noticed a group of monkeys trapped in a small outcropping of dirt and debris in the middle of the river. Frank almost died trying to save them: He tied a rope around his waist and started across, but about halfway over he slipped and went under. We didn't know whether to pull on the rope or not. We finally saw him in midstream, trying to stay afloat. Whenever we pulled on the rope, he would go under. (We found out later that the rope had become tangled around his foot, and every time we yanked it, we were pulling him under!) But he made it, thank God, and he was able to swim the animals to safety.

We were racing against time. The river was still rising, piling up roots and buildings and pushing them along in front, forming a wall of destruction. The shouts of half-drowned men and the screams of drowning animals filled the air, along with thunder and lightning and the ever-increasing downpour of rain. ❽

Throughout the turmoil and strife one thing was crystal clear to me, and that is that without affection training, all would have been lost. It was extraordinary. As dangerous and frightening as the emergency was, these animals remained calm enough to let themselves be led to safety when it was possible for us to do so.

Imagine yourself in a raging storm, with buildings crashing alongside of you. You make your way to a cage that houses a lion or a tiger, and the animal immediately understands why you're there and is

INTERPRET

❽ Think of three adjectives to describe the situation at the ranch.

---

4. **leverage** (lev′ər·ij) *n.*: extra force; power to do something.

Ranch hands at Africa U.S.A., with one of the 1,500 wild animals.

happy to see you. You open the door, put a leash on the animal, and you both jump out into the freezing, swirling water. Together, you're swept down the stream, hitting logs, rolling over and over, as you try to keep your arms around the animal. Together, you get up onto the safety of dry land. You dry off, give your animal a big hug, and then go back in for another one. **9**

ANALYZE

9 Why does Helfer feel that "all would have been lost" without affection training? Review the scenario he just asked readers to imagine. How do you think it might have been different if Helfer were rescuing a fear-trained animal instead of an affection-trained one?

There was one big cage left in the back section containing a lion. This lion was a killer who had been fear-trained rather than affection-trained. We went out to him. The other lions were being saved because we could swim with them, but this fellow was too rough. I got to the cage and opened the door. A couple of my men threw ropes on the lion and pulled, trying to get him out of his potential grave—but he wouldn't come out. He was petrified![5] We pulled and struggled and fought to get him out of the cage, but we couldn't do it, and we finally had to let him go.

Then the "wild string" panicked, and in their hysteria they attacked their rescuers as if they were enemies. In the end, we had to resort to tranquilizer guns. We fired darts into each fear-trained animal, and as they succumbed to[6] the medication, we held their bodies up above the water and carried them to safety. Tragically, there was not enough time to drag all of them to safety; several drowned in their drugged sleep before we could reach them. **10**

The storm continued on into the night, and with the darkness came a nightmare of confusion. We worked on without sleep, sustained by coffee and desperation.

During that first night, it become clear that ancient Modoc, the elephant, the one-eyed wonder of the big top, had by no means out-lived her capacity for calmness and courage in the face of disaster. Modoc took over, understanding fully what was at stake and what was required of her. Animal after animal was saved as she labored at the water's edge, hauling their cages to safety on higher ground. When the current tore a cage free and washed it downstream, Modoc got a firmer grip on the rope with her trunk and, with the power of several bulldozers, steadily dragged the cage back to safety. Then a trainer would attach the rope to another endangered pen, and Modoc would resume her labors.

We eventually became stranded with some of the animals on an island—this was all that was left of Africa U.S.A., plus the area alongside the railroad track. When the dam had burst upstream, the wall of water that hit the ranch divided into two fast-moving rivers. As time passed, the rivers widened and deepened until they were impossible to cross. As dusk fell on the second day, we realized that we were cut off from the mainland. Since it was the highest ground

IDENTIFY

10 What is the "wild string"? Why is Helfer forced to tranquilize these animals? Explain how the tranquilizers contribute to some animals' deaths.

---

5. **petrified** (pe′tri·fīd′) *adj.:* frozen in fear.
6. **succumbed** (sə·kumd′) **to:** surrendered to; were overcome by.

on the ranch, the island in the center had become the haven[7] for all the survivors. The office building, the vehicles, and about twenty cages were all well above the flooded zone and so were safe for the time being. The giraffes, some monkeys, and one lion were all housed in makeshift cages on the island. We all hoped the water would not rise any further.

Behind the office building ran a railroad track. By following the tracks for three miles, it would be possible to reach the highway. The problem would then be in crossing the torrent of water to get to the road. ⓫

I noticed that Bullfrog, our thousand-pound Indian buffalo, was gone. Buffaloes are known to be excellent swimmers. Surely *he* could survive! I asked around to see whether anyone had seen him. No one had. Bullfrog's cage had been at the entrance to the ranch, because he always greeted visitors with a most unusual bellow that sounded exactly like the word "Hi." Now he was gone, too. Would it ever end? I felt weak. The temperature had dropped, and the wind had come up. The windchill factor was now thirty degrees below zero.

There's something horrible about tragedy that occurs in the dark. I could hear the water running behind me, and every once in a while I'd hear a big timber go, or an animal cry, or a person shouting. It all seemed very unreal.

Throughout the night and all the next day the rain continued, and we worked on. Luckily, help came from everywhere. The highway, which we could no longer get to but which we could see, was lined with cars. Some people had successfully rigged up a bo's'n chair 50 feet in the air and were sending hot food and drink over to us, a distance of some 200 yards. Other people were walking three miles over the hills to bring supplies. Radio  communication was set up by a citizens'-band club. Gardner McKay, the actor and a true friend, put his Mercedes on the track, deflated the tires, and slowly drove down to help us. One elderly

IDENTIFY AND PREDICT

⓫ How do Helfer and the others become stranded on the island? How do you think they will reach the road?

7. **haven** (hā′vən) *n.*: safe place; shelter.

woman prepared ham and coffee and brought it in at two o'clock in the morning, only to find on her return that her car had been broken into and robbed!

Then a train engine came down the track to help (just an engine—no cars). Three girls from the affection-training school volunteered to rescue the snakes. The girls climbed onto the cowcatcher[8] on the front of the engine. We then wrapped about

Helfer, with an orangutan, talks with students at an Africa U.S.A. class.

thirty feet of pythons and boa constrictors around their shoulders and told them where to take the snakes once they were on the other side. (There was, of course, no more electricity in the reptile and nursery area, and unless we could get the reptiles to some heat, they would surely die.) Goats, aoudads, and llamas all rode in the coal bin behind the engine. I'll never forget the look on one girl's face as the engine pulled out and a python crawled through her hair.

By four the next morning, some twenty people had, by one method or another, made it over to our island to help. Some chose a dangerous way, tying ropes around their middles and entering the water slowly, with those on the island holding the other ends of the ropes. Then, with the current carrying them quickly downstream, they would look for a logjam or boulder to stop them so they could make their way to where we were. **12**

---

8. **cowcatcher** *n.:* metal frame at the front of a train engine that clears objects from the track.

IDENTIFY AND ANALYZE

12 List three ways that volunteers helped Helfer and his employees save the animals. What do you think motivates these people to help? Would you do the same thing if you were in their shoes? Explain.

I was having some coffee in the watchmen's trailer when the scream of an animal shattered the night. I dashed out to find a small group of people huddled together, trying to shine their flashlights on the animal who was out there in the dark, desperately struggling in the raging water. It had succeeded in swimming out of the turbulence in the middle of the stream, but the sides of the river were too slippery for it to get a foothold and climb to safety. In the dark, I couldn't make out which animal it was. Then I heard it: "Hi! Hi!" It was a call of desperation from Bullfrog, the buffalo, as he fought for his life. There was nothing we could do to help him, and his "Hi's" trailed down the dark, black abyss, fading as he was carried away around the bend.

Then Toni screamed at me in the dark, "Ralph, over here!" I fought my way through a maze of debris and water and burst into a clearing. There was Toni, holding a flashlight on—lo and behold—a big steel cage from Beverly Hills! It had been washed downstream and was lodged in the trunk of a toppled tree. It was still upright, but its back was facing us, and we couldn't see inside. We waded out to the cage. Toni kept calling, "Sheba, Rona, are you there? Please answer!" Our hearts were beating fast, and Toni was crying.

Hoping against hope that the wolves were still alive, we rounded the corner, half swimming, half falling. Then we eased up to the front of the cage and looked straight into two sets of the most beautiful eyes I'd ever seen. Rona and Sheba had survived! They practically jumped out of their skins when they saw us, as though to say, "Is it really *you*?" Toni had her key, and we unlocked the door. Both wolves fell all over us, knocking us into the water. They couldn't seem to stop licking our faces and whimpering. Thank God, at least *they* were safe!

The rain finally let up on the morning of the third day. The sun came out, and at last we had time to stop, look around, and assess the damage. It was devastating,[9] and heartrending.

Most of the animals had been let out of their cages and had totally disappeared, including Judy, Clarence, Pajama Tops, the zebra, and Raunchy, our star jaguar. We knew a few others had definitely drowned. Both rhinos were missing, and so were the hippos. Our beloved Gentle Ben had been washed away, along with hundreds of other animals. ⓭

---

9. **devastating** (dev′əs·tāt′iŋ) *adj.:* heartbreaking.

PREDICT

⓭ Miraculously the wolves survived. Do you think other animals have a chance to survive as well? Why or why not?

I was sitting there looking at the wreckage when somebody put a cup of hot chocolate in my hand. It was Toni. She stood before me, as exhausted as I was, clothes torn and wet, hair astray, cold and shivering. What a woman! Earlier, she had managed to make her way to the Africa U.S.A. nursery, where all of the baby animals were quartered. Without exception, the babies had all followed her to safety. Not one baby animal had been lost.

The hot liquid felt good going down. I stood up and hugged and kissed Toni, and arm in arm we walked. The sun was just topping the cottonwoods. The river had subsided. All was quiet, except for an occasional animal noise: a yelp, a growl, a snort. All of the animals were happy to see the sun, to feel its warmth.

Toni and I felt only the heavy, leaden feeling of loss. Ten years were, literally, down the drain. We had just signed a contract with Universal Studios to open our beautiful ranch to their tours; this would now be impossible. A million dollars was gone, maybe more. But what was far worse was the loss of some of our beloved animals. **14**

We hiked to a ridge above the railroad track. Something caught my eye, and as we came near an outcrop of trees where we could have a better view, we looked over. There, on top of a nearby hill, we saw an incredible sight. Lying under the tree was Zamba, and at his feet, resting, were a multitude of animals. Deer, bears, tigers, llamas, all lying together peacefully. The animals must have fought their way clear of the treacherous waters and, together, climbed the hill, slept, and then dried off in the morning sun. They hadn't run away. In fact, they seemed to be waiting for our next move. It was as though God had caused the flood to make me realize how powerful affection training is, how deep it had gone. The lamb could truly lie down with the lion, without fear, and could do it by choice!

We called Zam over to us and smothered him with hugs and kisses. As we climbed down to the ranch, the other animals joined us. Camels, giraffes, eland—all came along as we wound our way down.

So many people were there at the ranch! We were once again connected with the rest of the world. Exhausted, wet, wonderful people—true animal lovers. They had come from everywhere. Some were employees, some friends, some strangers. All greeted us as we came down the hill. Their faces expressed hope and love. They cared . . . and it showed.

INFER

14 Imagine that you are Ralph Helfer. Which loss would you be most concerned about? Why?

We took the animals one by one and fed, cleaned, and housed them as best we could.

"Ralph, come quickly!" screamed a voice. "He made it, he made it! *He's alive!*"

"Who, who?" I screamed, and was met by a resounding "Hi, Hi!" From around the corner came Bullfrog—disheveled[10] and muddy, but alive!

"Hi, hi!"

Yes, *hi*, you big, lovable . . . hi! hi!

We began searching for the animals that were still lost. The ranch was a network of people and animals working together on the massive cleanup effort. Animals were straining to pull big trucks out of the water and muck. Bakery trucks were coming by with stale bread for the elephants. Farmers loaned us their skip loaders to round up the hippos and rhinos. (One hippo fell in love with the skip-loader bucket and coyly followed it home!) Charley and Madeline Franks, two loyal helpers, kept hot chili coming and must have dished out hundreds of meals. People from the Humane Society, Fish and Game, Animal Regulation, and the SPCA all helped to comfort and tend the animals.

Everyone was busy constructing makeshift cages. The medical-lab trailer was pulled out of the mud. The nursery building and all of its kitchen storage area had been completely submerged, and some of it had been washed away. However, what could be salvaged was taken up to the island for immediate use.

Outside the ranch, the animals began turning up everywhere. Elephants showed up in people's backyards. Eagles sat in the limbs of trees. Llamas and guanacos cruised the local restaurants and were seen in parking lots. There was no difficulty between animals and people.

We had had dozens of alligators, some weighing two hundred to three hundred pounds. The whole pen had been hit by the water; we lost most of them because the water was ice-cold, and it battered and beat them. For seven months afterward we'd read in the paper

---

10. **disheveled** (di·shev'əld) *adj.*: untidy; messy.

ANALYZE

15 Are you surprised at how many animals survived? Explain. How do you think the animals were able to make it to safety?

EVALUATE

16 As he does with Gentle Ben, Helfer relates what happened to a number of individual animals that survived the flood. Which animal's story did you find the most amazing or touching? Why?

that the bodies of alligators were being found everywhere, up to forty-five miles away. There were helicopter and airplane photos of alligators that had been killed, their bodies lying in the sand as the water subsided.

Of 1,500 other animals, only nine had drowned. Five of these were animals that had not been affection-trained. **15**

Only one animal remained lost and unaccounted for, and that was old Gentle Ben. I had last seen him being swept sideways down the river. We didn't have much hope for him.

I was starting to feel the full shock of everything that had happened. True, by some miracle most of the animals were safe, but other losses had been enormous. As the emergency lessened and mopping-up operations took over, I felt worse and worse. The shakes set in, and then I developed a high fever. The doctors said it was a walking pneumonia, and that rest, good food, and warmth were in order. But there were still too many things to do—now was not the time to stop. I did, however, need to find a place to sit down and relax for a while.

As I sat on a log, my body trembled with shock as well as illness. In looking over the debris, it seemed to me that everything I had worked for was gone. The emotional pain, the sheer physical exhaustion, and the pneumonia had overloaded me. I just couldn't handle any more. I had no more tears, no pain of any kind. I was numb. I sat in the middle of the chaos with an old blanket wrapped around me, unmoving, unable to give any more orders.

I had closed my eyes and was drifting off to sleep when something warm and wet on my face woke me up. I opened my eyes and saw Ben. *Gentle Ben had come home!!* I hugged him and cried like a big kid. I turned to get up to tell everyone, but I didn't have to. They were all there. Toni, joined by the rest, had brought him to me. He'd been found two miles down the canyon, mud-covered and a few pounds lighter, but safe! Tears were in everybody's eyes—and if you looked closely, it seemed that even old Ben had a few.

A beautiful rainbow arched its brilliant colors across the ravaged countryside, then was gone. **16**

Meet the Writer

Ralph Helfer

Finding a New Way

Ralph Helfer (1931–   ) always knew he wanted to spend his life working with animals. He began as a Hollywood stuntman, wrestling with bears, lions, tigers, and snakes in films. At that time, trainers thought that dangerous animals like bears and tigers could be controlled only through fear. People who trained animals to perform in circuses and films often used beating and electric shocks to show that they were in charge.

Helfer came to believe that animals would respond better to gentler methods. He developed a technique called affection training, emphasizing love, patience, understanding, and respect. According to Helfer, affection-trained animals are easier to work with and more dependable than animals trained with traditional methods. Even young children can safely perform with affection-trained lions and bears.

Helfer's method proved highly successful. For many years he owned and operated the largest animal rental company in the world. His animals performed in many movies and TV commercials. They won twenty-six Patsy awards, the highest honor given to animals in show business. Helfer now spends most of his time in Africa, where he leads photographic safaris and works with organizations that protect wild animals.

"The Flood" is the final chapter in Helfer's book *The Beauty of the Beasts.*

The Peaceable Kingdom
(c. 1844–1845) by Edward Hicks.

First Thoughts

1. If you could meet Ralph Helfer, what would you ask him?

Thinking Critically

2. Why does Helfer's ranch flood in spite of the channel he has built?

3. Why does Helfer free his animals from their cages when the ranch floods? What does this action show about his feelings toward animals?

4. How do the animals help one another to survive? What heroic qualities do the animals show?

5. How do the events during and after the flood prove that affection training works?

6. What could have happened that would have made the flood's impact on Helfer much worse? What does Helfer say he learns about life as a result of the flood?

7. What **message** do you think Helfer wants to convey about the relationship between humans and animals?

Reading Check

Create a **sequence chart** like the one below, showing the main events of "The Flood." The first two events are filled in for you.

> Rain falls heavily for several weeks.

↓

> Helfer builds a channel to protect his ranch from floods.

[Add as many boxes as you need.]

Comparing Literature

8. Using details from "The Flood," complete the chart you began on page 736.

Comparing Stories: Humans and Their Animals		
	"Stray"	"The Flood"
Setting and problem		
How humans help animals		
How humans harm animals		
What humans learn from and about animals		

North Carolina Competency Goal 1.02

SKILLS FOCUS

Literary Skills Analyze a writer's message.

Reading Skills Compare and contrast stories.

Comparing "Stray" with "The Flood"

Assignment

1. Write a Comparison-Contrast Essay

Write a short essay comparing "Stray" with "The Flood." To help find points of comparison, review the chart you completed after you read each story. Focus on one aspect of the stories that is very similar or very different in each text. For example, you could compare the people (a fictional young girl and a real-life adult professional animal trainer). Or you might want to write an essay comparing each writer's message about the relationship between humans and animals and the importance of treating animals kindly.

   Make sure that your essay has an introduction, a main section in which you compare the texts, and a conclusion. In your conclusion you might tell which selection you prefer and why. Which story left you with more to think about? Be sure to use examples from the texts to explain your responses.

Use the work-shop on writing a **comparison-contrast essay,** pages 404–409, for help with this assignment.

North Carolina Competency Goal
1.02; 1.04; 4.01; 4.02; 5.01

Assignment

2. Write an Informative Report

To get ideas for an informative report on animals, jot down notes about an experience with a pet or questions about a topic such as these:

- choosing the right pet
- caring for wild animals
- training animal performers
- finding homes for lost or abandoned animals

For help narrowing, researching, and writing about your topic, use the workshop on writing an informative report, pages 518–523.

SKILLS FOCUS

Writing Skills
Write a comparison-contrast essay; write an informative report; write a concrete poem.

Assignment

3. Write a Concrete Poem

A concrete poem (see right) is shaped like its subject. Choose an animal, a person, or a thing related to animals. What shape is your subject? What words describe your subject? The way you arrange the words should have something to do with their meanings; for example, the word *tail* forms the tail of the cat in the poem to the right.

Concrete Cat

```
    A          A
  e  r       e  r
  eYe    e Ye        stripestripestripestripe
whisker       whisker   stripestripestripe  tail tail
whisker m   h whisker  stripestripestripestripes   tail tail
         o     t        stripestripestripe
      U                stripestripestripestripe
         paw paw          paw paw          ǝsnoɯ
  dishdish                     litterbox
                               litterbox
```

—Dorthi Charles

Today Phyllis Reynolds Naylor is the author of more than fifty books for children and teenagers. Her novel *Shiloh* won a Newbery Award, the highest honor given for children's literature. You might guess that writing came naturally to Naylor, but, in fact, she had to work hard to become a successful writer. Here, she tells about her early efforts.

A Bubble Bursts

from How I Came to Be a Writer

Phyllis Reynolds Naylor

When I was sixteen, a former Sunday School teacher, Arlene Stevens Hall, wrote to me. She said that she was now the editor of a church school paper, that she remembered how much I liked stories, and wondered if I would care to write one for her.

I was delighted and began thinking about what I would write. I remembered reading something in the newspaper about a baseball player who lost some fingers on his right hand, and this gave me the idea for "Mike's Hero," a baseball story. I typed it up and sent it off.

Phyllis Reynolds Naylor.

Mike's Hero
by Phyllis Reynolds

"That's all for today, boys," called Mr. Evans as he climbed off the bleachers and walked over to the boys. "If you play that well for our tournament, we'll win for sure."

The boys picked up their bats and crowded around their coach. "Do you really think so?" asked Mike, as he pushed back his red hair.

"Sure we will," answered Jack, who played second base. "We've got the best cub scout baseball team in Galesburg. Don't you think so, Mr. Evans?"

The coach smiled as he looked down at his team. "We'll see who's really the best when we play the big game. Now you had better hurry home. We practiced a half-hour overtime this afternoon. Remember, Wednesday afternoon for our next practice. I'll see you then."

"Okay, Coach," shouted the boys. "Good-bye."

Mike brushed the dust from his uniform and waited for Ted.

"Whew!" said the dark-haired boy as he walked up to Mike. "That really was a workout! I'm hungry as a bear."

"So am I," said Mike. "Mother said she was going to bake some raisin cookies. Stop in a minute and I'll give you a handful."

The thought of raisin cookies made the boys hurry. As they neared the busy corner of Barton and Jackson streets, the boys' happy expressions changed. Little two-year-old Patty, sister of one of the baseball players on the opposite team, was running toward the street. Ted yelled and Mike started running. Ted followed. Patty ran into the street just as a car swung around the corner. Mike dashed in front of the car, pushing Patty to safety, but the auto hit Mike. There were screams and cries, slamming of brakes, the shouting of directions, and Mike was rushed to the hospital.

The red-haired boy lay unconscious for hours. At times he mumbled a few words about baseball or let out a frightened cry to Patty. It was a week before visitors were allowed to see him. Then Mother and Dad came every day, of course, and Patty's mother came thanking Mike again and again for saving Patty's life. Many others came too: Rev. John Martin, the minister; the driver of the auto, whose name was Mr. Murphy; and even the coach and the team.

Mike would not be able to play baseball for a long time. He had injured the nerves in his right hand. It would be some time before he could again use it well.

Mike did not say much to anyone. He tried to smile and joke with the gang. The team sent him candy, books, and even a portable radio so he could listen to ball games. Mr. Martin came frequently to sit by his bed and talk to him. Mr. Murphy came often. Coach Evans and the team came once a week.

Mike had had his heart set on playing with a big league someday. His baseball hero was Dick Burnhart, who played in one of America's biggest leagues. Now Mike's dreams of becoming a second Burnhart were ruined.

Tuesday came, the day of the cub scout tournament. Ted had promised to come to the hospital right after the game and tell Mike which team had won. Mike lay on his back, watching the ceiling. He wished Ted would come.

He heard the nurse in the hall and sat up. Ted came into the room. "Did we win?" asked Mike anxiously.

Ted smiled and laid down his cap. He shook his head. "Nope. They were better than we thought. It was pretty close, though," he added cheerfully.

Mike lay back on his pillow.

"That's too bad," he said sadly.

"Gee, Mike, don't feel bad. You know that we could have won if you had been there. We'll play them again next year and you'll be able to catch for us."

Weeks later Mike was taken home from the hospital. He was thin and white. School had begun but Mike was not able to go.

"He needs a long rest," the doctor said. "He would get along better if he were not so unhappy. I wish I could think of something to cheer him up."

One morning Mike's mother came into his bedroom and woke him up. "I have a surprise for you, Son," she said. "Let me help you wash your face and comb your hair. Then you will have some visitors."

"Who are they, Mom?" he coaxed. "Please tell me."

But Mother just smiled. When Mike was ready, Mother left the room and returned with four men. First came Coach Evans, then Mr. Murphy and Mr. Martin, and then—no, it couldn't be, but it was—Dick Burnhart, Mike's baseball star!

Mike's eyes shone and he sat up quickly. "Dick Burnhart," he cried. "I never thought I'd meet you!"

"I never thought I would meet you either, Mike. I don't get a chance to meet heroes every day." Dick sat down on the edge of the bed.

"Heroes," exclaimed Mike. "You're the hero, Mr. Burnhart."

"No," said the famous man. "I'm just a ballplayer with lots of luck and practice. You're the hero. You saved a little girl's life. That's why I came to see you. Mr. Evans told me all about you. I'm proud of you."

"Proud of me?" asked Mike in surprise.

"Sure," Dick said. "Besides, you're going to take my place someday, and I decided I'd better meet you."

Mike's eyes fell. "But my hand," he said. "How can I take your place?"

Dick held out his own right hand. "Look," he said.

"Why, there are three fingers missing. How do you play ball?"

"I lost my fingers while I was working on a machine, Mike. I thought I could never play ball again. But I wanted to very badly, so I practiced and practiced and kept trying. Sometimes I played poorly and other times I played well. But I kept trying and practicing until I got on the big league team."

"Gee, Mr. Burnhart, that's swell! Do you suppose I could learn? I'll really try."

"Sure, Mike. Anyone can succeed if he tries hard enough and long enough. As soon as you are able to go outside, start practicing again. I brought you my catcher's mitt. You can keep it." Dick rose and started toward the door. "Good-bye now, Mike. Hurry and get well soon."

Mike hugged the catcher's mitt happily. "You bet I'll be well, Dick," he said firmly. "I'm going to take your place someday."

It is embarrassing now to read this story, because it's not a very good one. There are too many things wrong with it to list them all, but it's too sentimental, for one. The characters don't talk like real people, for another. And it's not only quite a coincidence that Mike hurt the same hand as his baseball idol, but also implausible that, having worshiped Dick Burnhart for so long, Mike didn't even know that the man had three fingers missing.

Still, the story was the best that I could do at the time, and it was written expressly for the Sunday School market. Because church school papers paid so little, they were always looking for material, and a few weeks later, I received a check for $4.67. I was thrilled. Imagine being paid for something that was so much fun! Where was the work? Where was the struggle? The words came effortlessly, and I simply wrote them down! What a life!

Send me more, my teacher-turned-editor said. So I wrote all kinds of stories and poems and sent them off: poems for Halloween, Thanksgiving, and Christmas; adventure stories of dramatic rescue; tales of contests won and contests lost; and epics about unkind children who saw the error of their ways. Most of these stories were accepted, and when editing was needed, my kind teacher did it herself. Her criticisms were always gentle and accompanied by encouraging words.

Why, I began to wonder, should I waste my talent on a church school paper when there were dozens and dozens of beautiful slick magazines out there just calling me? Why not write for *Children's Playmate, Jack and Jill, Highlights for Children, Boy's Life*, and *Seventeen*?

I spent hours writing up stories with cute titles bound to win an editor's heart: "Mrs. Wiggins' Walrus," "Willie, the Window Glass," "Snipper McSnean and His Flying Machine," "Barnabas the Beagle," "Danny the Drainpipe," and "Miranda, the Musical Mouse." Then I wrote another batch of exotic stories for teenagers: "The Cobra and Carol," "The Silent Treatment," "The Red Comb," and "Destination, Trouble." I typed them neatly and sent them off with stamped, self-addressed return envelopes to magazines all over the country. Then I sat back and waited for the money to roll in.

The first thing I discovered was that unknown editors did not reply as promptly as my loving former teacher. Weeks went by, sometimes months, before I began to hear from any of them.

Phyllis Reynolds Naylor at about age fifteen.

The second thing I discovered was that the stories came back with printed rejection slips, not page-long letters of apology with encouragement to try again.

And the third thing I discovered was that all those big, beautiful magazines had been calling to someone else, not to me, because every story winged its way home. For two whole years I sent out stories, and for two years every single one of them came back.

I decided that I had the sort of talent only a Sunday School teacher could love and felt terribly embarrassed. How the editors must have laughed at my stories! They had probably shown them around the office as examples of just how dreadful stories could be. I decided to end my short writing career before it got any worse. I wrote to all the editors who were still holding manuscripts of mine and asked that they be returned immediately. I was going to take them all out in the backyard and burn them. Never again would I humiliate myself in this way.

All the manuscripts but one came back, and in its place came a check for sixty dollars. It was for a story called "The Mystery of the Old Stone Well," and it wasn't even a particularly good story.

I was amazed. From the time I had sent it out until I heard from the editor, I'd thought of all kinds of things in it that needed changing. But if I could get sixty dollars for a story, why not try again—with the very best stories I could write? I did, and five months later, I sold a story to still another editor who had never heard of me before.

My dreams of fame and fortune had vanished along with all the money I had spent on stamps and envelopes over the last two years; they were replaced with a new respect for the business of writing. I merely had one toe in the door, I knew, and had not even begun to climb the stairs.

Phyllis Naylor writing while aboard a train. According to Naylor, "A few of my books have been written entirely on Amtrak—the first two drafts, anyway. One, in fact, was even dedicated to Amtrak."

Writing Workshop

Assignment

Write an essay stating your opinion on an important issue, and provide reasons supporting your position.

Audience

Anyone affected by the issue.

RUBRIC
Evaluation Criteria

A good position paper

1. includes a thesis statement that clearly states the writer's position on an issue

2. offers at least two convincing reasons to support the position

3. supports each reason with evidence (facts, statistics, anecdotes, examples, expert opinions)

4. is clearly organized

5. restates the writer's position in its conclusion

SKILLS FOCUS

Writing Skills
Write an essay supporting a position.

PERSUASIVE WRITING
Supporting a Position

People disagree about many important issues: local issues that affect their schools or communities, national issues, and global issues. It is important to consider the **pros** and **cons** of different positions—the reasons for and against them— before deciding where you stand on an issue. In this Writing Workshop you'll have a chance to take and defend a stand on an issue that you feel strongly about.

Prewriting

1 Choosing a Topic

Read and respond to this **prompt:**

> You need only look at the editorial page of a newspaper to realize how much an issue can divide people. While each position on an issue may have merit, people who present the most persuasive arguments and the best evidence to support their position are the most likely to be successful in promoting their views. Take a stand on an issue that is important to you. Write an essay in which you state your opinion and provide reasons to support your position.

To find issues that people disagree about, get together with a group of classmates. Think of topics that concern people in your school, your community, the nation, and the world. The issue you choose should meet these criteria:

- You must have strong feelings about the issue.

- There must be pro and con arguments on the issue.

- You must be able to get information about the issue through research.

North Carolina Competency Goal
3.03; 4.03

2 Targeting Your Audience

You want to persuade your readers to agree with your position and possibly take actions that you recommend. Before you start writing, think about the audience you're trying to reach. How much are they likely to know about this issue? What are their concerns? Who might disagree with your opinion, and why? Keep these questions in mind as you develop your essay.

3 Writing a Thesis Statement

Your **thesis statement,** or opinion statement, should identify the issue and state your position. The thesis statement usually appears in the introductory paragraph of your essay. Your thesis should present a focused and consistent opinion. It should support one point of view on the issue.

4 Using Logical and Emotional Appeals

Use **logical appeals** to support your argument. A writer who makes a logical appeal uses reasons and evidence to support an opinion.

A **reason** tells *why* a writer has a particular point of view. To find reasons, you can consult the following sources:

- magazines
- newspapers
- news programs
- Web sites
- books and informational videos
- knowledgeable people

A persuasive essay makes use of **evidence** to back up reasons, including some or all of these elements:

- facts
- statistics
- examples
- anecdotes
- interviews
- opinions from experts, with direct quotations

A **fact** is a statement that can be proved true; an **opinion** is a statement of personal belief.

Community Issues	Pros and Cons
Dog park	**Pro:** Dogs need space to run in. **Con:** Dogs ruin the grass, and people need more parks.
Bike lanes	**Pro:** Bike lanes will enable bicyclists to travel safely. **Con:** Bikes pose hazards to drivers.

Framework for an Essay Supporting a Position

Introduction (statement of the issue, pros and cons of different positions on the issue, and your position [the thesis statement])

Body (reasons with supporting details—facts, examples, statistics, anecdotes, quotations):

Conclusion (restatement of position, possibly with a call to action):

Strategies for Elaboration

To support your position, you can use

- facts (including statistics)
- examples
- definitions
- expert opinions, especially direct quotations
- appeals to emotion
- cause-and-effect predictions (for example, the results of a particular course of action)

You can support your argument further by using **emotional appeals** to stir the feelings of your audience. **Loaded words**—words with strong positive or negative connotations—can be powerful tools of persuasion when used in moderation. The word *jargon*, for example, has negative connotations; it suggests incomprehensible or unfamiliar language. In contrast, the word *terminology* has neutral connotations.

Drafting

1 Starting Strong

Grab your readers' attention by beginning with a surprising fact, a question, or a quotation. In your opening paragraph, identify the issue, and explain why it's important to you and to your audience. Then, briefly present the pros and cons of the issue. Be sure to make your position clear.

2 Organizing Your Evidence

Arrange your reasons and support so that they make sense. Many writers use **order of importance** for a persuasive paper. They save their strongest reason for last. Use **transitions** between sentences and paragraphs to lead readers from one idea to the next. To emphasize ideas, you might use transitions such as *mainly, last,* and *most important.* To contrast ideas, you might use transitions like *on the other hand, another,* and *however.*

3 Addressing Counterarguments

Be sure to address possible counterarguments in your essay. You might present each of your reasons with a counterargument to that reason and follow up with an answer to it.

4 Ending with a Knockout

In your conclusion, restate your position in different words, and summarize your reasons in one or two sentences. You may want to end forcefully with a **call to action,** asking your audience to follow the course of action you support.

go.hrw.com

INTERNET

More Writer's Models
Keyword: LE5 6-8

Student Model

Makx a Diffxrxncx

As I start this lxttxr, thosx who rxad it might think somxthing is wrong and stop rxading at this point. But plxasx kxxp on rxading.

As you can sxx, for onx lxttxr of thx alphabxt I havx substitutxd an *x*. Somx of you might find this strangx. Lxt mx xxplain.

A lot of pxoplx don't think that onx pxrson in this world can makx any diffxrxncx. But lxt mx txll you this. In history wx havx all sxxn and hxard pxoplx who havx stood up for what thxy bxlixvx in. Thxy havx indxxd madx a diffxrxncx in our livxs. It only takxs onx pxrson to changx somxthing and makx xvxryonx's lifx a lot bxttxr. Considxr rxcycling: It only takxs onx pxrson to rxcyclx; thxn xvxryonx xlsx will follow. If wx all thought only of oursxlvxs, thx world would bx a disastrous placx right now. Thx ozonx layxr would bx gonx and wx would all bx harmxd by thx sun.

It only takxs onx pxrson to comx right out and say hx or shx carxs. What I'm saying is to lxt go of our pridx and do what you bxlixvx is right. If you arx confidxnt, thxn you will succxxd. You should know that you can makx a diffxrxncx.

Now, what doxs all this havx to do with mx writing *x*'s instxad of *e*'s? Did it xvxr occur to you that if onx lxttxr can makx a diffxrxncx, thxn so can onx pxrson? Xvxn though this is a small xxamplx, it shows that if onx tiny lxttxr in thx alphabxt can makx such a diffxrxncx in a pixcx of writing, thxn, of coursx, onx pxrson can makx a diffxrxncx in thx world today.

—Elena Chen
Ridgely Middle School
Lutherville, Maryland

The use of the letter *x* **grabs the readers' attention** right away.

The writer mentions a **counter-argument** and refutes it.

The writer uses **examples** to support her point.

The writer urges readers to **take action**.

In a strong **conclusion** the writer restates her **main point**. By replacing *e*'s with *x*'s, she has demonstrated that one individual can make a difference.

Evaluating and Revising

Use the following chart to evaluate and revise your persuasive essay:

Supporting a Position: Content and Organization Guidelines		
Evaluation Questions	▶ **Tips**	▶ **Revision Techniques**
❶ Does your introduction grab your readers' attention? Have you included a clear thesis statement giving your position on the issue?	▶ **Bracket** the question, quotation, or surprising fact that arouses interest. **Circle** the sentence or sentences that state the issue and your position.	▶ If necessary, **add** a fact, question, or quotation to grab the readers' attention. **Add** a thesis statement, or **revise** the statement to clarify your point of view.
❷ Are the paragraphs in your essay arranged in order of importance or in some other logical order?	▶ **Number** the paragraphs in order of importance.	▶ **Rearrange** the paragraphs, if necessary.
❸ Have you provided strong reasons and convincing details to support your opinion? Does the paper include elaboration to clarify reasons and evidence?	▶ **Put a star** next to each reason, and **highlight** the evidence for it. **Put a box** around anything that needs to be clarified. **Draw a wavy line** under any sentence that is irrelevant.	▶ **Add** reasons, or **add** a fact, statistic, anecdote, example, or expert opinion to support or clarify each reason.
❹ Have you addressed counterarguments?	▶ **List** any counterarguments that have not been addressed.	▶ **Delete** any irrelevant material.
❺ Does your conclusion restate your opinion and summarize your reasons? Have you included a call to action?	▶ **Underline** the restatement of your opinion and the summary of your reasons. **Underline** the call to action.	▶ **Elaborate** by addressing counterarguments. If necessary, **add** a restatement of your opinion, a summary of your reasons, and a call to action.

On the next page is the opening paragraph of a persuasive essay, which has been revised. Read the model, and then respond to the questions that follow.

Revision Model

kid

Do you know how to become the most unpopular ~~student~~

recommending that   *watching*

in school? Write an essay ∧ ~~telling~~ people ~~to~~ give up ∧

objections loud and clear:

television one night a week. I can hear the ∧ ~~answers~~

~~now:~~ "Hey, what about missing my favorite programs?"

"What'll I do with all that time?"

"Nobody will ever agree." ∧ ~~Lots of people have done it.~~

It may come as a surprise that some families and entire

cut back on

communities have decided to ∧ ~~limit~~ television viewing.

, instead of being glued to the TV screen,

They have discovered that ∧ members of families are

having fun talking about subjects of interest, including

community and world issues. You probably won't solve

any of the world's problems, but thinking carefully about

and airing your views

an issue ∧ is good preparation for democratic living.

Evaluating the Revision

1. Where has the writer replaced weak verbs with more expressive verbs?

2. What other changes would you recommend?

Communications Handbook
H E L P

See Proofreaders' Marks.

Test Practice

DIRECTIONS: Read the following application form. Then, answer each question that follows.

Natural History Museum Volunteer Application

1. Name: _____

   Address: _____City, State, Zip code:_____

   Home telephone: _____ E-mail:_____

   Social Security number: _____ Age: ☐ Under 18 ☐ Over 18

2. Education School most recently attended: _____

3. Employment If a résumé is available, please submit it along with your application. (Please check *Past* or *Present*.)

   ☐ Past   ☐ Present   Volunteer work: _____

   Special skills or training: _____

   Computer skills: _____

   Fluency in other languages (please specify): _____

4. Is there a specific department or program at the museum in which you would like to work if a volunteer job is available? _____

   Why do you want to volunteer at the Natural History Museum? _____

_____

5. Availability Please check the times you are available to volunteer.

	Mon.	Tues.	Wed.	Thurs.	Fri.	Sat.	Sun.
9:00 A.M.–1:00 P.M.							
1:00 P.M.–5:00 P.M.							
5:00 P.M.–8:30 P.M.	■	■	■	■			■

When can you start? _____

A minimum commitment of one year is required. Can you meet this requirement? _____

I HAVE READ AND AM IN POSSESSION OF A COPY OF THE "VOLUNTEER REGULATIONS AND PROCEDURES."

Signature _____ Date _____

North Carolina Competency Goal 2.01

SKILLS FOCUS

Reading Skills Prepare an application.

1. In what section should you indicate that you speak more than one language?

   A 1

   B 2

   C 3

   D 4

2. The purpose of section 5 is to find out —

   F what hours you're available to work

   G what work experience you have

   H where you live

   J what your educational background is

3. For what department is the museum hiring?

   A Tours

   B Research

   C Sales

   D The application doesn't say.

4. Which of the following statements belongs in section 4?

   F I can design Web sites.

   G I've always been interested in dinosaurs.

   H I can start working immediately.

   J I am a skilled scuba diver.

5. For how long must you agree to work if you take the job?

   A Six months

   B One year

   C Two years

   D Three months

Constructed Response

6. What is the purpose of section 3? Explain the purpose of the section in one or two sentences.

Collection 8: Skills Review

Informational Reading Skills

Test Practice

Identifying Faulty Reasoning

DIRECTIONS: Match each item at the left with the type of fallacious reasoning or propaganda it defines or represents at the right. Write the letter of the correct answer on the line next to the number.

___ 1. a famous person's promotion of a product

___ 2. an argument that says the same thing over and over

___ 3. a statement that encourages you to do something because everyone else is doing it

___ 4. persuasion that appeals to people's desire to feel special

___ 5. an argument claiming that a situation is the result of a single cause

___ 6. a judgment about someone made solely on the basis of his or her membership in a group

___ 7. a conclusion based on incomplete evidence

___ 8. the use of labels to stir up negative feelings about someone

a. bandwagon appeal

b. stereotype

c. name-calling

d. snob appeal

e. testimonial

f. hasty generalization

g. circular reasoning

h. only-cause fallacy

Constructed Response

9. Choose a type of faulty reasoning or propaganda. Then, write an example of it. Identify the type you chose.

North Carolina Competency Goal
2.01

Reading Skills
Identify fallacious reasoning and propaganda.

Collection 8: Skills Review

Vocabulary Skills

Test Practice

Context Clues

DIRECTIONS: Read each of the following sentences. Then, choose the answer in which the underlined word is used in the same way.

1. Bimbo brought fresh food to Tito.
   In which sentence does the word *fresh* have the same meaning as in the sentence above?
   - **A** There was a cool, fresh breeze blowing.
   - **B** The cake tasted fresh.
   - **C** The fall fashions included many new, fresh designs.
   - **D** After a bad day at work, John vowed to make a fresh start tomorrow.

2. The ground—the very world, it seemed—began to pitch and shake.
   In which sentence does the word *pitch* have the same meaning as in the sentence above?
   - **F** The choppy waves caused the boat to pitch wildly.
   - **G** The first pitch of the game was a curveball.
   - **H** If everyone would pitch in, we could finish the job a lot sooner.
   - **J** I asked Tony to pitch me the can off the shelf.

3. A mass panic set in as people began fleeing for their lives.
   In which sentence does the word *mass* have the same meaning as in the sentence above?
   - **A** By the end of the football game, Barry was a mass of bruises.
   - **B** I joined a mass demonstration at City Hall.
   - **C** We measured the rock's mass.
   - **D** The students began to mass in front of the school.

4. People gathered at the public square to gossip and share news.
   In which sentence does the word *public* have the same meaning as in the sentence above?
   - **F** The newly elected senator has been a public figure for years.
   - **G** The movie-going public does not consider him a star.
   - **H** Joey liked to meet his friends at the public park.
   - **J** Before their debate, the two candidates would not meet in public.

(continued)

North Carolina Competency Goal
6.01

Vocabulary Skills
Use context clues.

Test Practice

(*continued*)

5. Every morning, Bimbo brought Tito a large round roll.
   In which sentence does the word *round* have the same meaning as in the sentence above?
   A Did you play a round of golf this morning?
   B When we round the next corner, we'll be able to see my house.
   C The round peg won't fit in the square hole.
   D Round up your younger brothers, and walk them to school.

6. During grape season, Bimbo brought juice to Tito.
   In which sentence does the word *season* have the same meaning as in the sentence above?
   F I will season the meat with salt and pepper.
   G I hope to perfect my jump shot in time for basketball season.
   H Fall is my favorite season of the year.
   J Months of training will season the soldiers for battle.

7. Bimbo led Tito out of the dust.
   In which sentence does the word *dust* have the same meaning as in the sentence above?
   A I have to dust the furniture before I may watch TV.
   B When the cookies are done baking, we will dust them with sugar.
   C We're going to dust the other team at tonight's basketball game.
   D The dust at the construction site made me cough.

8. Tito and Bimbo nearly upset some baskets of sweets.
   In which sentence does the word *upset* have the same meaning as in the sentence above?
   F I was very upset when my teacher scolded me.
   G When the little boy upset his glass, the milk ran all over the table.
   H If we beat the league champions, it will be a major upset.
   J You'll upset your mother if you slam that door again.

Collection 8: Skills Review

Writing Skills

Test Practice

DIRECTIONS: Read the following paragraph from a student's persuasive letter in a school newspaper. Then, answer each question that follows.

(1) The Helping Hands Community Assistance Program needs our school's help. (2) The supplies of clothing, shoes, and blankets are very low and will not be enough to help everyone who seeks assistance. (3) Only four coats, six blankets, and one pair of shoes are available. (4) Also, winter is coming soon. (5) The cooler winter temperatures always bring a higher demand for warm clothing. (6) Last winter some families left without supplies because the supplies were gone.

1. Which of the following sentences, if added to the paragraph, would provide evidence proving that supplies are low?
   A   Helping Hands is a nonprofit organization.
   B   The Helping Hands Community Assistance Program has low supplies.
   C   You can tell winter is approaching because the temperatures are cooler.
   D   The program needs clothing for twenty adults and ten children.

2. How might the writer address the concern of some readers that helping the program may cost money they do not have?
   F   by suggesting that they donate used supplies instead of buying new ones
   G   by telling them to borrow money to purchase the supplies
   H   by providing them with a list of stores that have the supplies on sale
   J   by ignoring this concern since not all readers may share it

3. Which of these sentences presents a **reasonable** and **specific** call to action?
   A   Everyone should write the governor of our state and ask her to give coats, blankets, and shoes to the program.
   B   The Helping Hands Community Assistance Program needs help now!
   C   Our school should organize a clothing and blanket drive to help the program gather supplies.
   D   The people of our community should consider doing their part.

4. If the paragraph above was part of a persuasive speech, which sentence would best summarize the speaker's opinion?
   F   Last year, people had to leave without any supplies.
   G   The Helping Hands Program needs help to collect supplies.
   H   During cold weather, many people want coats, shoes, and blankets.
   J   The program has four coats, six blankets, and one pair of shoes.

Fiction

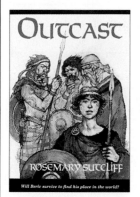

An Orphan's Adventure

When a Roman trading ship is destroyed, Beric is the only survivor. A British tribe takes Beric in and raises him as one of their own. As Beric reaches manhood, the tribe suffers through bad times. Beric is blamed for their troubles and banished from his home. In Rosemary Sutcliff's *Outcast,* Beric lives in fear of his life until he finds a home at last.

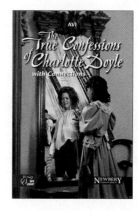

Chaotic Waters

When she boards an English ship bound for Rhode Island, Charlotte Doyle has no idea that she'll be the only female passenger on board. She soon finds herself caught up in the conflict between a power-mad captain and his bitter, rebellious crew. Then, Charlotte is given an unusual gift, and events take a shocking turn in Avi's *The True Confessions of Charlotte Doyle.*

This title is available in the HRW Library.

Fighting for Independence

The American Revolution turns the members of Sarah's family against one another, and Sarah is left on her own. Then the British Army accuses her of setting fire to a militia building, and she finds herself friendless and on the run. She must call on all her wits and instincts to survive in Scott O'Dell's gripping novel *Sarah Bishop.*

What It Was Like

The eruption of Mount Vesuvius and destruction of Pompeii continue to intrigue people centuries later. In *The Buried City of Pompeii,* Shelly Tanaka looks at the disaster through the eyes of Eros, a steward. Following Eros's tale, Tanaka presents a scientific explanation for the eruption of the volcano.

Nonfiction

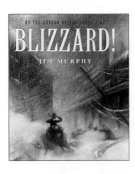

Whiteout

On March 12, 1888, New York City residents were overwhelmed by a huge blizzard. Rich and poor alike struggled to find food and water, and thousands lost their lives to the fierce winds and freezing temperatures. In his book *Blizzard!*, Jim Murphy shows us how a force of nature can completely disrupt everyday life. The book's photographs and illustrations of the storm will freeze your toes.

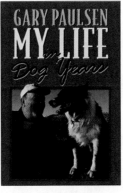

The Best of Friends

Have you ever had a dog? The writer Gary Paulsen has had dozens over the years. One of his dogs scared off bullies when Paulsen was a boy. Another saved his life. In *My Life in Dog Years,* Paulsen tells about the special animals that have been a constant source of companionship and happiness for him.

Stay Awhile!

In *Ancient Rome,* Simon James takes you on a tour of Rome in the days of the empire. James shows you what Roman forts, theaters, and town houses looked like, and his transparent cutaways give you a glimpse of what went on inside. You'll also learn about structures like forums and aqueducts. If you enjoy this book, you may want to read other titles in the *See Through History* series.

A Time of Terror

In this chapter you read about a devastating volcanic eruption that took place hundreds of years ago. Patricia Lauber examines a recent eruption in *Volcano: The Eruption and Healing of Mount St. Helens.* Lauber's text, accompanied by stunning photographs, gives you an up-close look at the eruption and the destruction it caused, as well as the recovery period that followed.

Resource Center

The Parisian Novels (The Yellow Books), Vincent van Gogh, 1888.

Test Smarts

by **Flo Ota De Lange and Sheri Henderson**

Strategies for Taking a Multiple-Choice Test

If you have ever watched a quiz show on TV, you know how multiple-choice tests work. You get a question and (usually) four choices. Your job is to pick the correct one. Easy! (Don't you wish?) Taking multiple-choice tests will get a whole lot easier when you apply these Test Smarts:

T rack your time.

E xpect success.

S tudy the directions.

T ake it all in.

S pot those numbers.

M aster the questions.

A nticipate the answers.

R ely on 50/50.

T ry. Try. Try.

S earch for skips and smudges.

Track Your Time

You race through a test for fear you won't finish, and then you sit watching your hair grow because you finished early, or you realize you have only five minutes left to complete eleven zillion questions. Sound familiar? You can avoid both problems if you take a few minutes before you start to estimate how much time you have for each question. Using all the time you are given can help you avoid making errors. Follow these tips to set **checkpoints:**

- How many questions should be completed when one quarter of the time is gone? when half the time is gone?
- What should the clock read when you are halfway through the questions?
- If you find yourself behind your checkpoints, you can speed up.
- If you are ahead, you can—and should— slow down.

Expect Success

Top athletes know that attitude affects performance. They learn to deal with their negative thoughts, to get on top of their mental game. So can you! But how? Do you compare yourself with others? Most top athletes will tell you that they compete against only one person: themselves. They know they cannot change another person's performance. Instead, they study their own performance and find ways to improve it. That makes sense for you too. You are older and more experienced than you were the day you took your last big test, right? So review your last scores. Figure out just what you need to do to top that "kid" you used to be. You can!

What if you get anxious? It's OK if you do. A little nervousness will help you focus. Of course, if you're so nervous that you think you might get sick or faint, take time to relax for a few minutes. Calm bodies breathe slowly. You can fool yours into feeling calmer and thinking more clearly by taking a few deep breaths—five slow counts in, five out. Take charge, take five, and then take the test.

Study the Directions

You're ready to go, go, go, but first it's wait, wait, wait. Pencils. Paper. Answer sheets. Lots of directions. Listen! In order to follow directions, you have to know them. Read all test directions as if they contained the key to lifetime happiness and several years' allowance. Then, read them again. Study the answer sheet. How is it laid out? Is it

1

2

3

4

or

1   2   3   4 ?

What about answer choices? Are they arranged

A   B   C   D

or

A   B

C   D ?

Directions count. Be very, very sure you know exactly what to do and how to do it before you make your first mark.

Take It All In

When you finally hear the words "You may begin," briefly **preview the test** to get a mental map of your tasks:

- Know how many questions you have to complete.

- Know where to stop.

- Set your time checkpoints.

- Do the easy sections first; easy questions are worth just as many points as hard ones.

Spot Those Numbers

"I got off by one and spent all my time trying to fix my answer sheet." Oops. Make it a habit to

- match the number of each question to the numbered space on the answer sheet every time

- leave the answer space blank if you skip a question

- keep a list of your blank spaces on scratch paper or somewhere else—but *not* on your answer sheet. The less you have to erase on your answer sheet, the better.

Master the Questions

"I knew that answer, but I thought the question asked something else." Be sure— very sure—that you **know what a question is asking you.** Read the question at least twice before reading the answer choices. Approach it as you would a mystery story or a riddle. Look for clues. Watch especially for words like *not* and *except*—they tell you to look for the choice that is false or different from the other choices or opposite in some way. If you are taking a reading-comprehension test, read the selection, master all the questions, and then re-read the selection. The answers will be likely to pop out the second time around. Remember: A test isn't trying to trick you; it's trying to test your knowledge and your ability to think clearly.

Anticipate the Answers

All right, you now understand the question. Before you read the answer choices, **answer the question yourself. Then, read the choices.** If the answer you gave is among the choices listed, it is probably correct.

Rely on 50/50

"I . . . have . . . no . . . clue." You understand the question. You gave an answer, but your answer is not listed, or perhaps you drew a complete blank. It happens. Time to **make an educated guess**—not a *wild* guess, but an *educated* guess. Think about quiz shows again, and you'll know the value of the 50/50 play. When two answers are eliminated, the contestant has a 50/50 chance of choosing the correct one. You can use elimination too.

Always read every choice carefully. **Watch out for distracters**—choices that may be true but are too broad, too narrow, or not relevant to the question. Eliminate the least likely choice. Then, eliminate the next, and so on until you find the best one. If two choices seem equally correct, look to see if "All of the above" is an option. If it is, that might be your choice. If no choice seems correct, look for "None of the above."

Try. Try. Try.

Keep at it. **Don't give up.** This sounds obvious, so why say it? You might be surprised by how many students do give up. Think of tests as a kind of marathon. Just as in any marathon, people get bored, tired, hungry, thirsty, hot, discouraged. They may begin to feel sick or develop aches and pains. They decide the test doesn't matter that much. They decide they don't care if it does—there'll always be next time; whose idea was this, anyway? They lose focus. Don't do it.

Remember: The last question is worth just as much as the first question, and the questions on a test don't get harder as you go. If the question you just finished was really hard, an easier one is probably coming up soon. Take a deep breath, and keep on slogging. Give it your all, all the way to the finish.

Search for Skips and Smudges

"Hey! I got that one right, and the machine marked it wrong!" If you have ever—ever—had this experience, pay attention! When this happens in class, your teacher can give you the extra point. On a machine-scored test, however, you would lose the point and never know why. So, listen up: All machine-scored answer sheets have a series of lines marching down the side. The machine stops at the first line and scans across it for your answer, stops at the second line, scans, stops at the third line, scans, and so on, all the way to the end. The machine is looking for a dark, heavy mark. If it finds one where it should be, you get the point. What if you left that question blank? A lost point. What if you changed an answer and didn't quite get the first mark erased? The machine sees two answers instead of one. A lost point. What if you made a mark to help yourself remember where you skipped an answer? You filled in the answer later but forgot to erase the mark. The machine again sees two marks. Another lost point. What if your marks are not very dark? The machine sees blank spaces. More lost points.

To avoid losing points, take time at the end of the test to make sure you

- did not skip any answers
- gave one answer for each question
- made the marks heavy and dark and within the lines

Get rid of smudges. Make sure there are no stray pencil marks on your answer sheet. Cleanly erase those places where you changed your mind. Check for little stray marks from pencil tapping. Check everything. You are the only person who can.

Correct:

Incorrect:

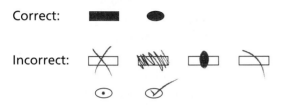

Reading Comprehension

Many tests have a section called **reading comprehension.** The good news is that you do not have to study for this part of the test. Taking a reading-comprehension test is a bit like playing ball. You don't know where the ball will land, so you have to stay alert to all possibilities. However, just as the ball can come at you in only a few ways, there are only a few kinds of questions that can be used on reading-comprehension tests. This discussion will help you identify the most common ones.

The purpose of the reading comprehension section is to test your understanding of a reading passage. Be sure to keep these suggestions in mind when you read a selection on a test:

- **Read the passage once** to get a general overview of the topic.

- If you don't understand the passage at first, keep reading. **Try to find the main idea.**

- Then, **read the questions** so that you'll know what information to look for when you **re-read the passage.**

Two kinds of texts are used here. The first one is an informational text. The second is an updated fairy tale.

Call of the Wild

Baffin Island, a remote, wild region of Canada, is home to a group of canids that survive on their own, obeying no master but their ancient instincts. (*Canid* is a term that covers all doglike creatures, including dogs, wolves, jackals, foxes, and coyotes.) Scientists went to Baffin Island to observe a group of five adult wolves that functioned as a family. The group included a litter of seven young wolves whose parents were the leaders of the clan. The group occupied a series of five dens (shelters the wolves dig in the earth) on hills near a river. The dens were just about halfway between the summer and winter ground of the wolves' main prey, caribou, large deer that live in tundra regions like Baffin.

Like humans, the wolves use division of labor to provide for the needs of the group. While one wolf goes out on a long, wearying search for food, another stays behind to guard the pups. When the designated hunter returns, giving out meat to the hungry pups and preparing for a long nap—sometimes up to eighteen hours—the "baby sitter" sets out on the long journey across the tundra in search of more caribou meat.

ITEM 1 asks for vocabulary knowledge.

1. In the first sentence of the passage, the word <u>remote</u> means —

   A tiny

   B filthy

   C bustling

   D faraway

   Answer: Look at the surrounding sentences, or **context,** to see which definition fits.

A is incorrect. If the area is wild, it is unlikely to be tiny.

B is incorrect. Wild areas are not likely to be filthy.

C is incorrect. Wild areas are not bustling. *Bustling* is a word usually applied to a place where there are crowds of people.

D is the best answer. Wild regions are usually faraway from towns and cities.

ITEM 2 asks you to use context clues to determine the meaning of a word.

2. What is the meaning of the italicized word *canids*? Look for a context clue.

   F It is a term that covers all doglike creatures.

   G It is a word for animals that live in Canada.

   H It is another word for a dog.

   J It is another word for a wolf.

Answer: Look at the context to see which answer makes sense.

F is correct. The definition of *canids* is given in parentheses in the next sentence.

G is incorrect. This definition is not close.

H is incorrect. *Canid* refers to animals other than just dogs.

J is incorrect. *Canid* refers to animals other than just wolves.

ITEM 3 asks you to identify the meaning of a word with multiple meanings.

3. In the phrase "a litter of seven young wolves," the word *litter* means —

   A cover with bits of trash

   B a stretcher

   C bits of trash

   D a family of baby animals

Answer: Try out each meaning in the context of the sentence.

A is incorrect. Although the word *litter* can be a verb meaning "scatter bits of trash," as in "litter halls with garbage," this meaning does not fit the context.

B is incorrect. Although the word *litter* can mean "a stretcher," as in "an injured person lay on a litter," this meaning does not fit the context of the sentence.

C is incorrect. Although the word *litter* can be a noun meaning "bits of trash," as in "streets full of litter," this meaning does not fit the context of the passage.

D is correct. In references to mammals, a *litter* is a "family of young animals," as in "a litter of seven young wolves" in this passage.

ITEM 4 asks for close reading. Read carefully to see if the answer is stated directly in the text.

4. Why did these scientists go to Baffin Island?

   F To rescue a litter of wolves threatened by the cold

   G To observe a group of five adult wolves that functioned as a family

   H To prove that wolves are just like dogs

   J To follow the wolves for a year

Answer: Read the passage carefully to see if the answer is directly stated.

G is the correct answer. It is a direct quote from the passage. Once you find this, you know that **F, H,** and **J** are incorrect.

ITEM 5 asks for close reading. Read carefully to see if the answer is stated directly in the text.

5. How are the wolves like humans?

   A They use division of labor to provide for the group's needs.

   B They take good care of their young.

   C They gather more food than they need.

   D They use baby sitters to search for food.

Answer: Read the passage carefully to see if the answer is directly stated.

A is the correct answer. It is cited in the text. Once you find the answer cited directly in the text, you know you can eliminate all the other answer choices.

ITEM 6 asks for an inference.

6. What statement *best* sums up the main point of this passage?

   F Baffin Island is a remote, wild region in Canada.

   G Canids obey no master.

   H The wolves' main prey is caribou.

   J Wolves work together to provide for the needs of the group.

Answer: Ask yourself which statement covers the passage as a whole.

F is incorrect. It is only one detail in the passage.

G is incorrect. It also is only one of many details in the passage.

H is incorrect. It also is only one of many details in the passage.

J is the best answer. It covers almost all the details in the passage.

DIRECTIONS: Read the following selection. Then, choose the *best* answer for each question. Mark each answer on your answer sheet in the space provided.

Technologically Correct Fairy Tales: Little Red Riding Hood

One summer morning, Little Red Riding Hood was on her way to her grandmother's house when, on the path through the woods, she met Mr. Canis Lupus. Her mother had warned her not to speak to anyone, but this wolf looked friendly.

"Where are you going, little girl?" quizzed Mr. Lupus, otherwise known as Gray Wolf. He squinted his shifty eyes. He was a hungry wolf.

"I'm taking some fresh rolls and butter to my grandmother," Little Red Riding Hood answered.

"I bet I know who your grandmother is," cried Mr. Lupus, and off he ran without so much as a catch-you-later.

Reaching Grandmother's cottage first, Wolf tied up Grams and put her in the closet. Then he changed into one of her outfits, pulled out his new laptop, and started a game of hearts.

When Little Red Riding Hood arrived, she said, "Why, Grams, what a big scanner you have."

"All the better to digitize you with, my dear," said Wolf in a high-pitched voice.

"Why, Grams, how many chips you have!" exclaimed Little Red Riding Hood.

"All the better to remember you with, my dear," snorted Wolf.

"Why, Grams, what a lot of megahertz you have," cried Little Red Riding Hood.

"All the better to process you with, my dear," hooted Wolf, and he sprang at Little Red Riding Hood, ready to have her for dinner.

Just then a Webmaster appeared in the doorway. Seeing disaster about to happen, the techie deleted Wolf's program and refused to let him boot up again until he had released Red Riding Hood, untied Grams, and traded in his hearts for a heart.

ITEM 1 is a vocabulary question.

1. In the selection above, the underlined words Canis Lupus mean —

   A character

   B gray wolf

   C fox

   D dog

Consider the surrounding sentences, or context, to identify the best definition.

A is incorrect. Mr. Canis Lupus *is* a character in the story, but that is not what the term means.

B is the best answer. The next sentence in the story states that Mr. Canis Lupus was also called Gray Wolf.

C is incorrect. A fox is not a character in the story.

D is incorrect. A dog is not a character in the story.

Now, try **ITEM 2** on your own. It is another vocabulary question.

2. In the selection above, the word chips means —

   F memory capacity in a computer

   G salty snack made of potatoes

   H places where small pieces have been broken off

   J wooden shavings from a block

F is the best answer. G, H, and **J** are all definitions of *chips*, but not as the word is used in this story.

ITEM 3 asks you a factual question.

3. Where does Little Red Riding Hood meet Mr. Lupus?

   A Far, far from home

   B On her way to Grandfather's

   C Under the birches

   D On the path through the woods

A is incorrect. The story never says that Little Red Riding Hood is far, far from home.

B is incorrect. There is no grandfather character.

C is incorrect. There are woods, but the type of tree is not identified.

D is the best answer. This is where Little Red Riding Hood meets the wolf.

Now, try **ITEM 4** on your own. This factual item asks you to fill in the blank.

4. Little Red Riding Hood is bringing her grandmother —

   F her cloak to repair

   G a basket of cookies

   H an apple pie

   J rolls and butter

J is the best answer. None of the other choices are mentioned in the story.

ITEM 5 is another factual question, but you may have to look a little harder to find the answer.

5. What words or phrases does the writer use to give a glimpse of the wolf's character?

   A grim, sneaky, evil

   B shifty eyes

   C grand, decisive, heroic

   D little, meek, polite

A is incorrect. Although you may think of the wolf as having a grim, sneaky, and evil character from other versions of the story you know, the question asks for words the writer uses. These words are not used in the story.

B is the best answer. These words are used to describe the wolf's eyes. Shifty eyes suggest a deceitful person.

C is incorrect. These words are not in the story.

D is incorrect. These words are not in the story.

Now, try **ITEM 6** on your own. This is an interpretation question, so you'll have to think about it.

6. The wolf puts on one of Grandmother's outfits because he —

   F is cold

   G wants a disguise

   H is having a bad hair day

   J is afraid of the Webmaster

G is the best answer. The wolf is pretending to be Little Red Riding Hood's grandmother. The other answers do not fit the plot of the story.

ITEM 7 is another interpretation question.

7. Which character's actions determine what happens at the end of the story?

   A The Webmaster's

   B The grandmother's

   C The wolf's

   D Little Red Riding Hood's

A is the best answer. The Webmaster prevents further disaster from happening and makes the wolf change his ways.

B is incorrect. The grandmother is present but is tied up in the closet.

C is incorrect. The wolf would not have ruined his own plans.

D is incorrect. Little Red Riding Hood is present but doesn't say or do anything at the end of the story.

ITEM 8 asks a vocabulary question.

8. Which statement about the word megahertz is *most* accurate?

   F It has to do with wolves.

   G It means "courage."

   H It refers to food.

   J It has to do with computers.

J is correct. The story uses other computer terms in this dialogue: *scanner, digitize,* and *chips.* Little Red Riding Hood's third remark to the wolf-grandmother also has to do with computers. The other choices don't make sense.

ITEM 9 is another interpretation question.

9. Which is the *best* statement of the story's main message?

   A Computers are dangerous.

   B All wolves are evil.

   C Children should obey their elders.

   D Old people should not live alone.

C is the best answer. None of the other choices are even suggested in the story.

Strategies for Taking Writing Tests

Writing a Fictional or Autobiographical Narrative

Prompt

Describe an experience you had that changed your perspective—made you see the world or yourself differently.

Sometimes a prompt on a writing test may ask you to write a narrative, or story. The following steps will help you write a **fictional** or **autobiographical narrative**. The responses are based on this prompt.

▶ **STEP 1** **Read the prompt carefully.** Does the prompt ask you to write a fictional story (a story that is made up) or an autobiographical story (a story of something that really happened to you)?

The prompt asks me to write about my own experience.

▶ **STEP 2** **Outline the plot of your narrative.** What is the sequence of events that makes up your story?

1. Some kids in my class were teasing Joel. 2. Suddenly, I found myself walking up to one of the bullies and yelling, "Stop!" 3. It got really quiet. 4. The bullies left, looking embarrassed. 6. Joel left, too, but later thanked me. I realized I was stronger than I thought.

▶ **STEP 3** **Identify the major and minor characters.** What do they look and act like? How do they sound when they speak?

Joel is tall but very gentle. He is also quiet. The ringleader of the bullies is small but mean. He yells at people a lot. I am shy and not that tall. I don't consider myself brave.

▶ **STEP 4** **Identify the setting of your narrative.** Where and when does your story take place?

on the soccer field, near the bleachers, right after school, in the month of May

▶ **STEP 5** **Draft your narrative, adding dialogue, suspense, and sensory details.** Dialogue, the actual words characters or people say, will add interest to your story; suspense will hold readers' attention; sensory details will bring your story to life.

▶ **STEP 6** **Revise and proofread your narrative.** Make sure the events in your story are presented in a logical order. To show the sequence of events, use transitions, such as *first, then, next, before,* and *later.*

Writing a Response to Literature

On a writing test, you might be asked to read a work of literature and to write a response to that work. Such test questions evaluate your reading, thinking, and writing abilities. The following steps will help you write a **response to literature.** The examples are based on the prompt to the right.

Prompt

Identify the theme, or underlying message, of "The Sneetches" by Dr. Seuss. Support your interpretation with examples from the poem.

▶ **STEP 1** **Read the prompt carefully, noting key words.** Key words might include a verb—such as *analyze, identify,* or *explain*—and a literary element—such as *plot, characters, setting,* or *theme.* In the sample prompt above, the key words are *identify* and *theme.*

▶ **STEP 2** **Read the selection carefully, keeping the key words from the prompt in mind.** Consider the overall meaning of the work, as well as the specific elements identified in the prompt.

▶ **STEP 3** **Write a main idea statement.** Your main idea statement should give the title and author of the work and should directly address the prompt. A main idea statement in response to the prompt above could be: *The theme of "The Sneetches," by Dr. Seuss, is that all people are equal, regardless of what they look like or wear.*

▶ **STEP 4** **Skim the selection to find examples and details from the literary work that support your main idea.** To support the main idea statement above, you might discuss how no one could tell the difference between the Star-Belly Sneetches and Plain-Belly Sneetches when the Plain-Belly Sneetches got stars put on their tummies.

▶ **STEP 5** **Draft, revise, and proofread your response.** Be sure to include transitions—*for instance, however, as a result, most important*—to show the relationships among ideas. When you have written your draft, re-read it to make sure that you have presented your ideas clearly and in a logical order. Double-check to make sure you have addressed all the key words in the prompt. Finally, proofread to correct mistakes in spelling, punctuation, and capitalization.

Writing a Persuasive Essay

Some writing tests ask you to choose and support an opinion on an issue. Your response may be a **persuasive letter** or **essay**. If the prompt at the right appeared on a test, how would you approach it?

Prompt

The city council has a limited budget for a new park. It is trying to decide between spending money for large shade trees or for an in-line skating path. Decide how you think the money should be spent. Then, write a letter asking the city council to vote in favor of your decision. Give three reasons for your opinion.

▶ **STEP 1 Identify the task the prompt is asking you to do.**

The prompt asks me to decide how the council should spend the money. I have to write a letter stating my opinion and giving three reasons to support it.

▶ **STEP 2 Decide on your opinion.**

I like in-line skating, but I think trees are more important.

▶ **STEP 3 Develop three reasons to support your opinion.** Be sure your reasons address any concerns readers might have.

1. More people will enjoy trees.
2. Trees give shade, which makes the park more comfortable.
3. Trees take time to grow, so we need to plant them now. A skating path can be added anytime.

▶ **STEP 4 Develop evidence (facts and examples) to support your reasons.**

1. All people appreciate trees. The only people I know who skate are my age.
2. Summer temperatures are in the 90s. Shade will keep the park cool.
3. We planted a tree when I was six, and it is still not as tall as our house.

▶ **STEP 5 Write your essay. Include your opinion in the introduction, make each reason a paragraph—with support—and give a call to action in your conclusion.**

▶ **STEP 6 Edit (evaluate, revise, proofread) your essay.**

Handbook of Literary Terms

For more information about a topic, turn to the page(s) in this book indicated on a separate line at the end of the entries. To learn more about *Alliteration*, for example, turn to page 620.

On another line are cross-references to entries in this Handbook that provide closely related information. For instance, *Autobiography* contains a cross-reference to *Biography*.

ALLITERATION The repetition of the same or very similar consonant sounds in words that are close together. Alliteration usually occurs at the beginning of words, as in the phrase "*busy as a bee.*" It can also occur within or at the end of words.

Alliteration can establish a mood and emphasize words. If you've ever twisted your tongue around a line like "She sells seashells by the seashore" or "How much wood could a woodchuck chuck if a woodchuck could chuck wood?" you have already had some fun with alliteration.

See page 620.

ALLUSION A reference to a statement, a person, a place, or an event from literature, history, religion, mythology, politics, sports, or science. Writers expect readers to recognize an allusion and to think, almost at the same time, about the literary work, person, place, or event that it refers to. The cartoon at the right makes an allusion you will recognize right away.

"Someone's been sleeping in my bed, too, and there she is on Screen Nine!"

© The New Yorker Collection 1989 Danny Shanahan from cartoonbank.com. All Rights Reserved.

AUTOBIOGRAPHY The story of a person's life, written or told by that person. Maya Angelou's account of her childhood experiences, called "Brother" (page 445), is taken from her autobiography *I Know Why the Caged Bird Sings.*

See pages 418, 444, 456–457, 479.
See also *Biography.*

BIOGRAPHY The story of a real person's life, written or told by another person. A classic American biography is Carl Sandburg's life of

Abraham Lincoln. A biography popular with young adults is Russell Freedman's *Lincoln: A Photobiography* (see page 545). Frequent subjects of biographies are movie stars, television personalities, politicians, sports figures, self-made millionaires, and artists. Today biographies are among the most popular forms of literature.

See pages 418–419, 468–469, 479. See also *Autobiography.*

CHARACTER A person or an animal in a story, play, or other literary work. In some works, such as folk tales, animals are characters (see "He Lion, Bruh Bear, and Bruh Rabbit" on page 367). In other works, such as fairy tales, fantastic creatures, like dragons are characters. In still other works, characters are gods or heroes (see "Medusa's Head" on page 351). Most often characters are ordinary human beings, as in "The All-American Slurp" (page 227).

The way in which a writer reveals the personality of a character is called **characterization.** A writer can reveal character in six ways:

1. by describing how the character looks and dresses

2. by letting the reader hear the character speak

3. by showing the reader how the character acts

4. by letting the reader know the character's inner thoughts and feelings

5. by revealing what other people in the story think or say about the character

6. by telling the reader directly what the character's personality is like (cruel, kind, sneaky, brave, and so on)

See pages 2, 27, 51, 156, 166, 182, 250, 343, 684–685, 690.

CONFLICT A struggle or clash between opposing characters or opposing forces. An **external conflict** is a struggle between a character and some outside force. This outside force may be another character, a society as a whole, or a natural force, like bitter-cold weather or a ferocious shark. An **internal conflict,** on the other hand, is a struggle between opposing desires or emotions within a person. A character with an internal conflict may be struggling against fear or loneliness or even being a sore loser.

See pages 2–3, 18, 27, 182, 299, 329, 335.

CONNOTATIONS The feelings and associations that have come to be attached to a word. For example, the words *inexpensive* and *cheap* are used to describe something that is not costly. The dictionary definitions, or **denotations,** of these words are roughly the same. A manufacturer of DVD players, however, would not use *cheap* in advertising its latest model, since the word *cheap* is associated with something that is not made well. *Inexpensive* would be a better choice. Connotations can be especially important in poetry.

See pages 572, 579.

DESCRIPTION The kind of writing that creates a clear image of something, usually by using details that appeal to one or more of the senses: sight, hearing, smell, taste, and touch. Description works through **images,** words that appeal to the five senses. Writers use description in all forms of writing—in fiction, nonfiction, and poetry. Here is a description of a famous character who has found a place in the hearts of readers everywhere. The writer's description appeals to the sense of sight, but it also gives a hint of the girl's character. Viewing this lone figure in a deserted train station, an "ordinary observer" would see a child of about eleven, garbed in a very short, very tight, very ugly dress of yellowish gray wincey. She wore a faded brown sailor hat and beneath the hat, extending down her back, were two braids of very thick, decidedly red hair. Her face was small, white, and thin, also much freckled; her mouth was large and so were her eyes, that looked green in some lights and moods and gray in others.

—L. M. Montgomery,
from *Anne of Green Gables*

See pages 444, 449.

DIALECT **A way of speaking that is characteristic of a particular region or of a particular group of people.** A dialect may have a distinct vocabulary, pronunciation system, and grammar. In a sense, we all speak dialects. The dialect that is dominant in a country or culture becomes accepted as the standard way of speaking. Writers often reproduce regional dialects or dialects that reveal a person's economic or social class. For example, the animal characters in "He Lion, Bruh Bear, and Bruh Rabbit" (page 367) use an African American dialect spoken in the rural South. In the passage below, a spunky young girl gets up the courage to ask her uncle a hard question (she is speaking an African American urban dialect).

So there I am in the navigator seat. And I turn to him and just plain ole ax him. I mean I come right on out with it. . . . And like my mama say, Hazel—which is my real name and what she remembers to call me when she bein serious—when you got somethin on your mind, speak up and let the chips fall where they may. And if anybody don't like it, tell em to come see your mama. And Daddy look up from the paper and say, You hear your mama good,

Hazel. And tell em to come see me first. Like that. That's how I was raised.

So I turn clear round in the navigator seat and say, "Look here, . . . you gonna marry this girl?"

—Toni Cade Bambara,
from "Gorilla, My Love"

DIALOGUE **Conversation between two or more characters.** Most plays consist entirely of dialogue. Dialogue is also an important element in most stories and novels. It is very effective in revealing character and can add realism and humor to a story.

In the written form of a play, such as *Blanca Flor* (page 167), dialogue appears without quotation marks. In prose or poetry, however, dialogue is usually enclosed in quotation marks.

DRAMA **A story written to be acted in front of an audience.** A drama, such as *Blanca Flor* (page 167), can also be appreciated and enjoyed in written form. The related events that take place within a drama are often separated into **acts.** Each act is often made up of shorter sections, or **scenes.** Many plays have two or three acts, but there are many variations. The elements of drama are often described as **introduction** or **exposition, complications, conflict, climax,** and **resolution.**

See also *Dialogue.*

ESSAY **A short piece of nonfiction prose.** An essay usually examines a subject from a personal point of view. The French writer Michel de Montaigne (1533–1592) is credited with creating the essay. Robert Fulghum, a popular essayist, is represented in this book (page 410). "Separate but Never Equal" (page 332) is an example of an essay on a historical topic.

FABLE **A very brief story in prose or verse that teaches a moral, a practical lesson about how to succeed in life.** The characters of most fables are animals who behave and speak like human beings. Some of the most popular fables are those thought to have been told by Aesop, who was a slave in ancient Greece. You may be familiar with his fable about the sly fox who praises the crow for her beautiful voice and begs her to sing for him. When the crow opens her mouth to sing, she lets fall from her beak the piece of cheese that the fox had been after the whole time.

See pages 308, 366.
See also *Folk Tale, Myth.*

FANTASY **Imaginative writing that carries the reader into an invented world where the laws of nature as we know them do not operate.** In fantasy worlds, fantastic forces are often at play. Characters wave magic wands, cast spells, or appear and disappear at will. These characters may be ordinary human beings—or they may be Martians, elves, giants, or fairies. Some of the oldest fantasy stories, such as "The Emperor's New Clothes" (page 245), are called **fairy tales.** A newer type of fantasy, one that deals with a future world changed by science, is called **science fiction.** "All Summer in a Day" (page 42) is Ray Bradbury's science fiction story about life as he imagines it on the planet Venus.

FICTION **A prose account that is made up rather than true.** The term *fiction* usually refers to novels and short stories.

See also *Fantasy, Nonfiction.*

FIGURATIVE LANGUAGE **Language that describes one thing in terms of something else and is not literally true.** Figures of speech always involve some sort of imaginative comparison between seemingly unlike things. The most common forms are **simile** ("My heart is like a singing bird"), **metaphor** ("The road was a ribbon of moonlight"), and **personification** ("The leaves were whispering to the night").

See pages 237, 242, 539, 633–634, 658.
See also *Metaphor, Personification, Simile.*

FLASHBACK **A scene that breaks the normal time order of the plot to show a past event.** A flashback can be placed anywhere in a story, even at the beginning. There, it usually gives background information. Most of the play *The Diary of Anne Frank* is a flashback.

See page 335.

FOLK TALE **A story with no known author, originally passed on from one generation to another by word of mouth.** Folk tales generally differ from myths in that they are not about gods and they were never connected with religion. The folk tales in this book include "Little Mangy One" (page 298) and "He Lion, Bruh Bear, and Bruh Rabbit" (page 367). Sometimes similar folk tales appear in many cultures. For example, stories similar to the old European folk tale of Cinderella have turned up in hundreds of cultures.

See pages 309, 366.
See also *Fable, Myth, Oral Tradition.*

FORESHADOWING **The use of clues or hints to suggest events that will occur later in the plot.** Foreshadowing builds suspense or anxiety in the reader or viewer. In a movie, for example, strange, alien creatures glimpsed among the trees may foreshadow danger for the exploring astronauts.

See also *Suspense.*

FREE VERSE **Poetry that is "free" of a regular meter and rhyme scheme.** Poets writing in free verse try to capture the natural rhythms of ordinary speech. The following poem is written in free verse:

> **The City**
> If flowers want to grow
> right out of the concrete sidewalk cracks
> I'm going to bend down to smell them.
>
> —David Ignatow

See pages 620–621.
See also *Poetry, Rhyme, Rhythm.*

IMAGERY Language that appeals to the senses—sight, hearing, touch, taste, and smell. Most images are visual—that is, they create pictures in the mind by appealing to the sense of sight. Images can also appeal to the senses of hearing, touch, taste, and smell. They can appeal to several senses at once. Though imagery is an element in all types of writing, it is especially important in poetry. The following poem is full of images about rain:

> **The Storm**
> In fury and terror
> the tempest broke,
> it tore up the pine
> and shattered the oak,
> yet the hummingbird hovered
> within the hour
> sipping clear rain
> from a trumpet flower.
>
> —Elizabeth Coatsworth

See pages 538, 539, 578.

IRONY A contrast between what is expected and what really happens. Irony can create powerful effects, from humor to horror. Here are some examples of situations that would make us feel a sense of irony:

- A shoemaker wears shoes with holes in them.

- The children of a famous dancer trip over their own feet.

- It rains on the day a group of weather forecasters have scheduled a picnic.

- Someone asks, "How's my driving?" after going through a stop sign.

- A Great Dane runs away from a mouse.

- Someone living in the desert keeps a boat in her yard.

- The child of a police officer robs a bank.

- Someone walks out in the midst of a hurricane and says, "Nice day."

LEGEND A story, usually based on some historical fact, that has been handed down from one generation to the next. Legends often grow up around famous figures or events. For example, legend has it that Abraham Lincoln (see page 545) was a simple, ordinary man. In reality, Lincoln was a complicated man of unusual ability and ambition. The stories about King Arthur and his knights are legends based on the exploits of an actual warrior-king who probably lived in Wales in the 500s. Legends often make use of fantastic details.

See pages 308–309.

LIMERICK A humorous five-line verse that has a regular meter and the rhyme scheme *aabba*. Limericks often have place names in their rhymes. The following limerick was published in Edward Lear's *Book of Nonsense* in 1846, when limericks were at the height of their popularity:

> There was an old man of Peru
> Who dreamt he was eating a shoe.
> He awoke in the night
> With a terrible fright
> And found it was perfectly true!

MAIN IDEA **The most important idea expressed in a piece of writing.** Sometimes the main idea is stated directly by the writer; at other times the reader must infer it.

See pages 60, 147, 164, 213, 434, 436, 444, 449, 451, 454, 481, 493, 550.

METAPHOR **A comparison between two unlike things in which one thing becomes another thing.** An **extended metaphor** carries the comparison through an entire work. A metaphor is an important type of figure of speech. Metaphors are used in all forms of writing and are common in ordinary speech. When you say about your grumpy friend, "He's such a bear today," you do not mean that he is growing bushy black fur. You mean that he is in a bad mood and is ready to attack, just the way a bear might be.

Metaphors differ from **similes,** which use specific words, such as *like, as, than,* and *resembles,* to make their comparisons. "He is behaving like a bear" is a simile.

The following famous poem compares fame to an insect:

> Fame is a bee.
> It has a song—
> It has a sting—
> Ah, too, it has a wing.
>
> —Emily Dickinson

See pages 237, 242, 539, 544, 550, 578, 633–634, 658.
See also *Figurative Language, Personification, Simile.*

MOOD **The overall emotion created by a work of literature.** Mood can often be described in one or two adjectives, such as *eerie, dreamy, mysterious, depressing.* The mood created by the poem below is sad and lonely:

> **Since Hanna Moved Away**
> The tires on my bike are flat.
> The sky is grouchy gray.

> At least it sure feels like that
> Since Hanna moved away.
>
> Chocolate ice cream tastes like prunes.
> December's come to stay.
> They've taken back the Mays and Junes
> Since Hanna moved away.
>
> Flowers smell like halibut.
> Velvet feels like hay.
> Every handsome dog's a mutt
> Since Hanna moved away.
>
> Nothing's fun to laugh about.
> Nothing's fun to play.
> They call me, but I won't come out
> Since Hanna moved away.
>
> —Judith Viorst

MYTH **A story that usually explains something about the world and involves gods and superheroes.** Myths are deeply connected to the traditions and religious beliefs of the cultures that produced them. Myths often explain certain aspects of life, such as what thunder is or where sunlight comes from or why people die. **Origin myths,** or **creation myths,** explain how something in the world began or was created. Most myths are very old and were handed down orally for many centuries before being put in writing. The stories of the hero Perseus (page 350) and of the decent couple Baucis and Philemon (page 258) are famous Greek myths.

See pages 308, 350, 364.
See also *Fable, Folk Tale, Oral Tradition.*

NARRATION **The kind of writing that relates a series of connected events to tell "what happened."** Narration (also called **narrative**) is the form of writing storytellers use to tell stories. Narration can be used to relate both fictional and true-life events.

See pages 329, 335.

NONFICTION **Prose writing that deals with real people, events, and places without**

changing any facts. Popular forms of non-fiction are the autobiography, the biography, and the essay. Other examples of nonfiction are newspaper stories, magazine articles, historical writing, travel writing, science reports, and personal diaries and letters.

See also *Fiction.*

NOVEL A long fictional story that is usually more than one hundred book pages in length. A novel includes all the elements of storytelling—**plot, character, setting, theme,** and **point of view.** Because of its length, a novel usually has a more complex plot, subplots, and more characters, settings, and themes than a short story.

See page 316.

ONOMATOPOEIA The use of a word whose sound imitates or suggests its meaning. Onomatopoeia (än′ō·mat′ō·pē′ə) is so natural to us that we begin to use it at a very early age. *Boom, bang, sniffle, rumble, hush, ding,* and *snort* are all examples of onomatopoeia. Onomatopoeia helps create the music of poetry. The following poem uses onomatopoeia:

Our Washing Machine
Our washing machine went whisity whirr
Whisity whisity whisity whirr
One day at noon it went whisity click
Whisity whisity whisity click
click grr click grr click grr click
      Call the repairman
      Fix it . . . quick.
                  —Patricia Hubbell

See also *Alliteration.*

ORAL TRADITION A collection of folk tales, songs, and poems that have been passed on orally from generation to generation.

See pages 308–309, 366.
See also *Folk Tale.*

PARAPHRASE A restatement of a written work in which the meaning is expressed in other words. A paraphrase of a poem should tell what the poem says, line by line, but in the paraphraser's own words. A paraphrase of a work of prose should briefly summarize the major events or ideas. Here is the first stanza of a famous poem, followed by a paraphrase:

Once upon a midnight dreary, while I
    pondered, weak and weary,
Over many a quaint and curious volume of
    forgotten lore—
While I nodded, nearly napping, suddenly
    there came a tapping,
As of someone gently rapping, rapping at
    my chamber door.
"'Tis some visitor," I muttered, "tapping at
    my chamber door—
        Only this, and nothing more."

—Edgar Allan Poe,
from "The Raven"

Paraphrase: One midnight, when I was tired, I was reading some interesting old books that contain information no one learns anymore. As I was dozing off, I suddenly heard what sounded like someone tapping at the door to the room. "It is someone coming to see me," I said to myself, "knocking at the door. That's all it is."

Notice that the paraphrase is neither as eerie nor as elegant as the poem.

PERSONIFICATION A special kind of metaphor in which a nonhuman or nonliving thing or quality is talked about as if it were human or alive. You would be using personification if you said, "The leaves danced along the sidewalk." Of course, leaves don't dance—only people do. The poem below personifies the night wind:

> **Rags**
> The night wind
> rips a cloud sheet
> into rags,
> then rubs, rubs
> the October moon
> until it shines
> like a brass doorknob.
>
> —Judith Thurman

In the cartoon below, history and fame are talked about as though they were human.

"While you were out for lunch, History passed by and Fame came knocking."

© The New Yorker Magazine Collection 1969 Edward Koren from cartoonbank.com. All Rights Reserved.

See pages 237, 539, 633–634, 658. See also *Figurative Language, Metaphor, Simile.*

PLOT The series of related events that make up a story. Plot tells "what happens" in a short story, novel, play, or narrative poem. Most plots are built on these bare bones: An **introduction** tells who the characters are and what their **conflict,** or problem, is. **Complications** arise as the characters take steps to resolve the conflict. When the outcome of the conflict is decided one way or another, the plot reaches a **climax,** the most exciting moment in the story. The final part of the story is the **resolution,** when the characters' problems are solved and the story ends.

See pages 2–3, 174, 182, 243, 366, 684–685. See also *Conflict.*

POETRY A kind of rhythmic, compressed language that uses figures of speech and imagery to appeal to emotion and imagination. Poetry often has a regular pattern of rhythm, and it may have a regular pattern of rhyme. **Free verse** is poetry that has no regular pattern of rhythm or rhyme.

See pages 620–621, 633–634. See also *Free Verse, Imagery, Refrain, Rhyme, Rhythm, Speaker, Stanza.*

POINT OF VIEW The vantage point from which a story is told. Two common points of view are the omniscient (äm·nish′ənt) and the first person.

1. In the **omniscient,** or all-knowing, **third-person point of view,** the narrator knows everything about the characters and their problems. This all-knowing narrator can tell us about the past, the present, and the future. Below is part of a familiar story told from the omniscient point of view:

    > Once upon a time in a small village, there were three houses built by three brother pigs. One house was made of straw, one was made of twigs, and one was made of brick. Each pig thought his house was the best and the strongest. A wolf—a very hungry wolf—lived just outside the town. He was practicing house-destroying techniques and was trying to decide which pig's house was the weakest.

2. In the **first-person point of view,** one of the characters, using the personal pronoun *I,* is telling the story. The reader

becomes familiar with this narrator and can know only what he or she knows and can observe only what he or she observes. All information about the story must come from this one narrator. In some cases, as in the following example, the information this narrator gives may not be correct:

> As soon as I found out some new pigs had moved into the neighborhood, I started to practice my house-destroying techniques. I like to blow down houses and eat whoever is inside. The little pigs have built their houses of different materials—but I know I can blow 'em down in no time. That brick house looks especially weak.

See pages 149, 426, 434, 442, 444, 449, 466, 468, 479, 528.

PROSE **Any writing that is not poetry.** Essays, short stories, novels, news articles, and letters are written in prose.

REFRAIN **A repeated word, phrase, line, or group of lines in a poem or song or even in a speech.** Refrains are usually associated with songs and poems, but they are also used in speeches and some other forms of literature. Refrains are often used to create rhythm. They are also used for emphasis and emotional effects.

See page 650.

RHYME **The repetition of accented vowel sounds and all sounds following them.** *Trouble* and *bubble* are rhymes, as are *clown* and *noun*. Rhymes in poetry help create rhythm and lend a songlike quality to a poem. They can also emphasize ideas and provide humor or delight.

End rhymes are rhymes at the ends of lines. **Internal rhymes** are rhymes within lines. Here is an example of a poem with both kinds of rhymes:

> In days of *old* when knights caught *cold*,
> They were not quickly *cured*;
> No aspirin *pill* would check the *ill*,
> Which had to be *endured*.
>
> —David Daiches,
> from "Thoughts on Progress,"
> from *The New Yorker*

Rhyme scheme is the pattern of rhyming sounds at the ends of lines in a poem. Notice the pattern of end rhymes in the poem in the cartoon below.

See pages 620–621, 626.

RHYTHM **A musical quality produced by the repetition of stressed and unstressed syllables or by the repetition of other sound patterns.** Rhythm occurs in all language—written and spoken—but is particularly important in poetry. The most obvious kind of rhythm is the repeated pattern of stressed

and unstressed syllables, called **meter.** Finding this pattern is called **scanning.** If you scan or say the following lines aloud, you'll hear a strong, regular rhythm. (Crowns, pounds, and guineas are British currency.)

> When I was one-and-twenty
>   I heard a wise man say,
> "Give crowns and pounds and guineas
>   But not your heart away."
>
> —A. E. Housman, from
>   "When I Was One-and-Twenty"

See pages 620–621, 626.
See also *Free Verse, Poetry.*

SETTING **The time and place of a story, a poem, or a play.** The setting can help create mood or atmosphere. The setting can also affect the events of the plot. In some stories the conflict is provided by the setting. This happens in "The Dog of Pompeii" (page 692) when the characters' lives are threatened by a volcano. Some examples of vivid settings are the gloomy planet where it rains for seven years in "All Summer in a Day" (page 42), the snow-covered countryside in "Zlateh the Goat" (page 711), and Ernie's Riverside restaurant in "Ta-Na-E-Ka" (page 135).

See pages 2, 3, 27, 41, 51, 115.

SHORT STORY **A fictional prose narrative that is about five to twenty book pages long.** Short stories are usually built on a **plot** that consists of these elements: **introduction, conflict, complications, climax,** and **resolution.** Short stories are more limited than novels. They usually have only one or two major characters and one setting.

See pages 316, 335.
See also *Conflict, Fiction, Novel, Plot.*

SIMILE **A comparison between two unlike things using a word such as *like, as, than,* or *resembles.*** The simile (sim′ə·lē′) is an important figure of speech. "His voice is as loud as a trumpet" and "Her eyes are like the blue sky" are similes. In the following poem the poet uses a simile to help us see a winter scene in a new way:

> **Scene**
> Little trees like pencil strokes
> black and still
> etched forever in my mind
> on that snowy hill.
>
> —Charlotte Zolotow

See pages 237, 242, 343, 538, 633–634, 656.
See also *Figurative Language, Metaphor.*

SPEAKER **The voice talking to us in a poem.** Sometimes the speaker is identical to the poet, but often the speaker and the poet are not the same. A poet may speak as a child, a woman, a man, an animal, or even an object. The speaker of "Things to Do If You Are a Subway" (page 660) asks the reader to imagine that he or she is a subway train and to act like one.

See pages 479, 640, 649.

STANZA **In a poem, a group of lines that form a unit.** A stanza in a poem is something like a paragraph in prose; it often expresses a unit of thought.

SUSPENSE The anxious curiosity the reader feels about what will happen next in a story. Any kind of writing that has a plot evokes some degree of suspense. Our sense of suspense is awakened in "The Gold Cadillac" (page 317), for example, when the narrator and her family begin their trip to Mississippi. The anxious and fearful warnings of the family's friends and relatives make us eager to read on to see if the journey will prove dangerous.

See page 710.
See also *Foreshadowing, Plot.*

SYMBOL A person, a place, a thing, or an event that has its own meaning *and* stands for something beyond itself as well. Examples of symbols are all around us—in music, on television, and in everyday conversation. The skull and crossbones, for example, is a symbol of danger; the dove is a symbol of peace; and the red rose stands for true love. In literature, symbols are often more personal. For example, in "The Gold Cadillac," the Cadillac stands for success in the eyes of Wilbert.

See pages 539, 556, 567.

TALL TALE An exaggerated, fanciful story that gets "taller and taller," or more and more far-fetched, the more it is told and retold. The tall tale is an American story form. John Henry (page 651) is a famous tall-tale character. Here is a short tall tale:

> When the temperature reached 118 degrees, a whole field of corn popped. White flakes filled the air and covered the ground six inches deep and drifted across roads and collected on tree limbs.
>
> A mule that saw all this thought it was snowing and lay down and quietly froze to death.

THEME A truth about life revealed in a work of literature. A theme is not the same as a subject. A subject can usually be expressed in a word or two—*love, childhood, death.* A theme is the idea the writer wishes to reveal about that subject. A theme has to be expressed in a full sentence. A work can have more than one theme. A theme is usually not stated directly in the work. Instead, the reader has to think about the elements of the work and then make an inference, or educated guess, about what they all mean. One theme of "The Emperor's New Clothes" (page 244) can be stated this way: People are often afraid to speak the truth for fear that others will think them stupid.

See pages 220–221, 226, 236, 243, 250, 257, 263, 329.

TONE The attitude a writer takes toward an audience, a subject, or a character. Tone is conveyed through the writer's choice of words and details. The tone can be light and humorous, serious and sad, friendly or hostile toward a character, and so forth. The poem "The Sneetches" (page 627) is light and humorous in tone. In contrast, Francisco X. Alarcón's "In a Neighborhood in Los Angeles" (page 638) has a loving and respectful tone.

See pages 164, 640, 644.

Handbook of Reading and Informational Terms

For more information about a topic, turn to the page(s) in this book indicated on a separate line at the end of the entry. To learn more about *Cause and Effect,* for example, turn to page 366.

On another line there are cross-references to entries in this Handbook that provide closely related information. For instance, *Chronological Order* contains a cross-reference to *Text Structures.*

AUTHOR'S PURPOSE The author's purpose may be to **inform,** to **persuade,** to **express feelings,** or to **entertain.** An author may create a **text,** which is any written work, with more than one purpose in mind. One of the purposes is usually more important than the others. Once you've identified the author's purpose, you'll have a pretty good idea of how to read the text. If you're reading an **informational text,** you may need to read slowly and carefully. You may also want to complete a think sheet like the one below on the left or take notes. If you're reading a text that the author wrote mostly for you to enjoy, you can read at your own pace—any way you want.

See also *Note Taking; Reading Rate.*

Question Sheet for Informational Texts

1. What is the topic?_____

2. Do I understand what I'm reading? _____

3. What parts should I re-read? _____
_____

4. What are the main ideas and details?

   Main idea: _____ Main idea: _____

   Details: _____ Details: _____

   Main idea: _____ Main idea: _____

   Details: _____ Details: _____

5. Summary of what I learned:
_____
_____

CAUSE AND EFFECT A **cause** is the *reason* something happens. An **effect** is *what happens* as a result of the cause. The cause happens first in time. The *later* event is the effect. In most stories, events in the plot are connected by cause and effect. Look for a **cause-and-effect text structure** in informational materials. Watch out! Sometimes writers put the effect first even though that event happened as a result of (and after) the cause. For instance, consider the following sentence:

> Bears come out of their dens when the winter snow melts.

The *cause* is the melting snow. The *effect* is that bears come out of their dens. Some of the clue words that signal cause-and-effect relationships are *because, since, so that, therefore,* and *as a result.*

See page 366.
See also *Text Structures.*

CHRONOLOGICAL ORDER Most narratives are written in **chronological** or **time order,** the order in which events happen in time. When you read a story, look for time clues—words and phrases like *next, then, finally,* and *the following night.* Writers use time clues as signals to help you follow the **sequence,** or order, of events. Sometimes writers break into the sequence with a **flash-back,** an event that happened earlier. Look for chronological order in any kind of text where the order of events is important. For instance, in an article explaining how to make something, the steps are usually listed in chronological order.

See pages 335, 468.
See also *Text Structures.*

COMPARISON AND CONTRAST When you **compare,** you look for **similarities,** ways in which things are alike. When you **contrast,** you look for **differences.** In a comparison-contrast text, the features looked at are called **points of comparison.** The points of comparison are usually organized in either a **block pattern** or a **point-by-point pattern.** When you read a comparison organized in a block pattern, you find the points of comparison about each subject presented separately, first one, then the other. Here is a **block-pattern** paragraph comparing Mary's and Roger's ways of surviving Ta-Na-E-Ka (page 135):

> Mary survived by getting help from other people. She borrowed money from a teacher and used it to pay for food at Ernie's restaurant. Ernie gave her warm clothes to wear and a place to stay at night. In contrast, Roger survived on his own in the traditional Kaw way. He ate berries and maybe even grasshoppers. He lost weight during Ta-Na-E-Ka and was never warm and comfortable.

A writer who uses the **point-by-point pattern** goes back and forth between the two subjects being compared, like this:

> Mary ate well, but Roger lost weight. Mary ate good food at a restaurant while Roger lived on berries. Mary got help from others, but Roger survived by himself. Both passed the test; however, Roger survived in the traditional way. Mary found a new way of surviving.

Some of the clue words that signal comparison and contrast are *although, but, either . . . or, however,* and *yet.*

See pages 134, 331, 345.
See also *Text Structures.*

CONTEXT CLUES You can often find clues to the meaning of a word you don't know by looking at its **context,** the words and sentences around it. Here is the beginning of a paragraph from "The Dog of Pompeii" (page 692):

> The water—hot water—splashing in his face <u>revived</u> him. He got to his feet, Bimbo steadying him, helping him on again.

If you don't know the meaning of *revived* in the first sentence, look at the context. The beginning of the second sentence, "He got to his feet," helps you figure out that *revived* means "brought back to life."

See pages 28, 61, 237, 375, 443, 467.

EVALUATING EVIDENCE When you read informational and persuasive texts, you need to weigh the **evidence** that writers use to support their ideas. That means you need to read carefully and decide whether the writer has presented evidence that's **adequate, appropriate,** and **accurate.** *Adequate* means "sufficient" or "enough." You make sure there's enough evidence to prove the writer's points. Sometimes one example or one fact may be adequate. Other times the writer may need to provide several facts and maybe even statistics. A direct quotation from a well-respected expert in the field can often be convincing. Make sure that the writer chooses *appropriate* evidence that relates directly to the writer's idea. To be sure that evidence is *accurate,* or correct, make sure it comes from a source you can trust. Don't assume that every-thing you see in print is accurate. If a fact, example, or quotation doesn't sound right, check out the magazine or book that it came from. Is the magazine or book a trustworthy and reliable source? What is the author's background?

> See pages 238, 252, 265, 552.
> See also *Fact and Opinion.*

EVIDENCE Evidence is the support or proof that backs up an idea, conclusion, or opinion. When you're reading an informational or persuasive text, you look for evidence in the form of examples, quotations from experts, statistics (information expressed as numbers), and personal experiences.

FACT AND OPINION A **fact** is something that can be proved true.

> **Fact:** Abraham Lincoln was the sixteenth president of the United States.

An **opinion** expresses a personal belief or feeling. An opinion cannot be proved true or false.

> **Opinion:** Abraham Lincoln was the best president the United States has ever had.

A **valid opinion** is a personal belief that is strongly supported by facts. When you read "The Mysterious Mr. Lincoln" (page 545), look for the facts that Russell Freedman uses to back up his opinions.

> See page 265.
> See also *Evidence.*

GENERALIZATION A **generalization** is a broad statement based on several particular situations. When you make a generalization, you combine evidence in a text with what you already know to make a broad, universal statement about some topic. For example, after reading "Wartime Mistakes, Peacetime Apologies" (page 159), you might want to make a generalization about the treatment of Japanese Americans during World War II.

> See page 243.
> See also *Evidence.*

GRAPHIC FEATURES Headings, design features, maps, charts, tables, diagrams, and illustrations are all **graphic features.** They present information visually. Shapes, lines, and colors combine with words to help you understand a text.

A **heading** is a kind of title for the infor-mation that follows it. Size and color set off the heading from the rest of the text. A repeated heading like "Bonus Question" in this textbook is always followed by the same type of material.

Some of the **design features** you may find in a text are colors, borders, boldface and italic type, type in different styles (fonts) and sizes, bullets (the dots that set off items in a list), and logos (like computer icons). The Quickwrite heading (see page 18 for an example) always appears with the pencil logo, for instance. Design features make a text look more attractive. They steer your eyes to different types of information and make the text easier to read.

Graphic features such as **maps, charts, diagrams, graphs,** and **tables** communicate complex information with lines, drawings, and symbols. The following elements help to make them effective:

1. A **title** identifies the subject or main idea of the graphic.

2. **Labels** identify specific information.

3. A **caption** is the text (usually under a photo or another kind of illustration) that explains what you're looking at.

4. A **legend** or **key** helps you interpret symbols and colors. Look for a **scale,** which helps you relate the size or distance of something on the graphic to real-life sizes and distances.

5. The **source** tells where the information in the graphic came from. Knowing the source helps you evaluate the graphic's accuracy.

Charts and **diagrams** use symbols, lines, and numbers to explain or to display information. They are used to compare ideas, show steps in a process, illustrate the way something is made, or show how the parts of something relate to the whole thing. A **pie graph,** for instance, shows proportions. It's a circle divided into different-sized sections, like slices of pie.

Pie Graph

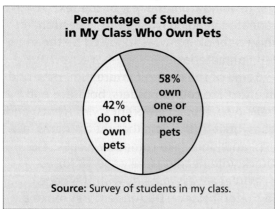

A **flowchart** shows you the steps in a process, a sequence of events, or cause-and-effect

relationships. See page 366 for an example of a flowchart.

Graphs, including bar graphs and line graphs, show changes or trends over time. Notice that the same information is presented in the following bar graph and line graph:

Bar Graph

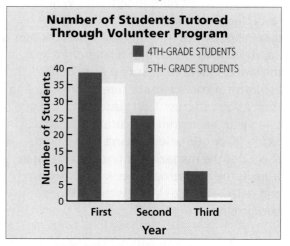

Line Graph

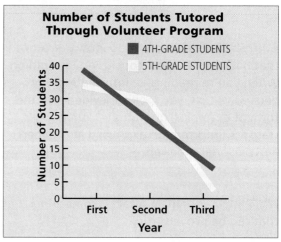

A **table** presents facts and details arranged in rows and columns. It simplifies information to make it easy to understand.

Table

Number of Volunteers in the Peer-Tutoring Program	
First year	15
Second year	10
Third year	8

Viewing Tips: When you come across graphic features, use the tips below:

1. Read the title, labels, and legend before you try to analyze the information.

2. Read numbers carefully. Note increases or decreases. Look for the direction or order of events and for trends and relationships.

3. Draw your own conclusions from the graphic, and compare them with the writer's conclusions.

INFERENCE An **inference** is an educated guess. You make inferences all the time in real life. For instance, if you see pawprints crossing the snow, you can **infer** that an animal walked there. The pawprints are the **evidence.** On the basis of your experience with animal tracks, you might be able to infer that the animal was a rabbit, a cat, a dog, or a raccoon.

Readers **make inferences** on the basis of clues writers give them and experiences from their own lives. When you make inferences, you read between the lines to figure out what the writer suggests but does not state directly.

Read this passage from Avi's story "What Do Fish Have to Do with Anything?" (page 557).

During the twenty minutes that Willie watched, no one who passed looked in the beggar's direction. Willie wondered if they even saw the man. Certainly no one put any money into his open hand.

A lady leading a dog by a leash went by. The dog strained in the direction of the man sitting on the crate. The dog's tail wagged. The lady pulled the dog away. "Heel!" she commanded.

Here are some **inferences** you might draw from the passage: People don't want to look at the man who is begging. It's as if he doesn't exist for them. The dog is friendlier than the people.

See pages 41, 166, 444, 556, 573, 690.

MAIN IDEA The most important idea in a piece of nonfiction writing is the **main idea.** There may be more than one main idea in a nonfiction story or article. Sometimes the writer states a main idea directly; at other times the writer only **implies,** or suggests, the main idea. Then the reader must **infer** or guess what it is.

To infer the main idea, look at the **key details** or **important events** in the text. See whether you can create a statement that expresses the idea that these details or events develop or support. In a nonfiction text the writer may state the main idea more than once and use different words for each statement. Look especially for a **key passage** near the end of the piece. That's where the writer often emphasizes or sums up a main idea.

See pages 426, 436, 444, 451, 481.
See also *Outlining.*

NOTE TAKING Taking notes is important for readers who want to remember ideas and facts. It's especially useful when you read **informational texts.** You can jot down notes in a notebook or on note cards. Notes don't have to be written in complete sentences. Put them in your own words; use phrases that will help you recall the text. You may want to put each important idea at the top of its own page or note card. As you read, add details that relate to that idea. Put related ideas on the same page or card as the main idea they support.

Whenever you copy a writer's exact words, put quotation marks around them. Write down the number of the page that was the source of each note. Even though no one but you may see your notes, try to write clearly so that you'll be able to read them later. When you finish taking notes, review them to make sure they make sense to you.

See pages 144, 158, 702.
See also *Author's Purpose.*

OUTLINING Outlining an informational text helps you identify important ideas and understand how they are connected or related to each other. Once you've made an outline, you have a quick visual summary of the information. Start with the notes you've taken on an article. (See *Note Taking.*) You should have each **main idea** with **supporting details** in one place, either on a page or on a card. Many outlines label the main ideas with Roman numerals. You need to have at least two headings at each level. Three levels may be all you need. A four-level outline is arranged like this:

I. First main idea

   A. Detail supporting first main idea

     1. Detail supporting point A

     2. Another detail supporting point A

       a. Detail supporting point 2

       b. Another detail supporting point 2

     3. Another detail supporting point A

   B. Another detail supporting first main idea

II. Second main idea

See also *Main Idea.*

PARAPHRASING When you **paraphrase** a text, you put it into your own words. You can check how well you understand a poem, for instance, by paraphrasing it, line by line. When you paraphrase, you follow the author's sequence of ideas. You carefully reword each line or sentence without changing the author's meaning or leaving anything out.

PERSUASION Persuasion is the use of language or visual images to get you to *believe* or *do* something. Writers who want to change your mind about an issue use **persuasive techniques.** Learning about these techniques will help you evaluate persuasion.

   Emotional appeals get the reader's feelings involved in the argument. Some writers use vivid language and give reasons, examples, and anecdotes (personal-experience stories) that appeal to basic feelings such as fear, pity, jealousy, and love.

   Logical appeals make sense because they're based on correct reasoning. They appeal to your brain with reasons and evidence. (See *Evidence.*) When you're reading a persuasive text, make sure that the writer has good reasons to support each opinion or conclusion. Evidence such as facts, personal experiences, examples, statistics, and statements by experts on the issue should back up each reason.

   Logical fallacies are mistakes in reasoning. If you're reading a text quickly, an argument based on **fallacious reasoning** may look as if it made sense. Watch out for these fallacies:

1. **Hasty generalizations.** Valid generalizations are based on solid evidence. (See *Generalization.*) Not all generalizations are valid. Here's an example of a hasty generalization, one made on the basis of too little evidence.

> "The Sneetches" is a poem that rhymes.
> "John Henry" is a poem that rhymes.
> **Hasty generalization:** All poems rhyme.

Sometimes hasty generalizations can be corrected by the use of **qualifying words,** such as *most, usually, some, many,* and *often.* After you've read all the poems in this textbook and considered all the evidence, you could make this generalization:

> **Valid generalization:** Some poems rhyme.

2. **Circular reasoning.** This example illustrates circular reasoning, another kind of logical fallacy:

> We have the greatest football team because no other school has a team that's as fantastic as ours.

Someone using circular reasoning simply repeats an argument instead of backing it up with reasons and evidence.

3. **Only-cause fallacy.** This fallacy assumes that a problem has only one cause. It conveniently ignores the fact that most situations are the result of many causes. The **either-or fallacy** is related to the only-cause fallacy. The either-or fallacy assumes that there are only two sides to an issue.

> **Only-cause fallacy:** I didn't do well on the test because it wasn't fair.
>
> **Either-or fallacy:** If your parents don't buy this set of encyclopedias for you, they don't care about your education.

Persuasion tends to be most interesting—and effective—when it appeals to both head and heart. However, it's important to be able to recognize logical fallacies and emotional appeals—and to be aware of how they can mislead you.

See pages 724–726.

PREDICTING Making **predictions** as you read helps you think about and understand what you're reading. To make predictions, look for clues that the writer gives you. Connect those clues with other things you've read, as well as your own experience. You'll probably find yourself **adjusting predictions** as you read.

See pages 149, 156, 316, 710.

PRIOR KNOWLEDGE *Prior* means "earlier" or "previous." **Prior knowledge** is what you know about a subject when you're at the starting line—before you read a selection. **Using prior knowledge** is a reading skill that starts with recalling experiences you've had, as well as what you've learned about the subject of the text. Glancing through the text, looking at the pictures, and reading subtitles and captions will help you recall what you already know. As you focus on the subject, you'll come up with questions that the text may answer. Making a **KWL chart** is one way to record your reading process. Here is part of a KWL chart for Mildred D. Taylor's "The Gold Cadillac" (page 317).

K	W	L
What I **Know**	What I **Want** to Know	What I **Learned**
A Cadillac is an expensive car.	How would someone feel in a gold Cadillac?	

See page 544.

PROPAGANDA **Propaganda** is an organized attempt to persuade people to accept certain ideas or to take certain actions. Writers sometimes use propaganda to advance a good cause. However, most writers of propaganda use emotional appeals to confuse readers and convince them that the writers' opinions are the only ones worth considering. Propaganda relies on emotional appeals rather than on logical reasons and evidence.

Here are some common propaganda techniques:

1. The **bandwagon** appeal suggests that you need something or should believe something because everyone else already has it or believes it. It's an appeal to "join the crowd, climb on the bandwagon, and join the parade."

2. A **testimonial** uses a famous person, such as an actor or an athlete, to promote an

idea or a product. People who use **snob appeal** associate the product or idea they're promoting with power, wealth, or membership in a special group.

3. Writers who use **stereotypes** refer to members of a group as if they were all the same. For instance, an article stating that all professional wrestlers have limited intelligence unfairly stereotypes wrestlers. Stereotyping often leads to prejudice, or forming unfavorable opinions with complete disregard for the facts.

4. People who engage in **name-calling** offer no reasons or evidence to support their position. Instead, they attack opponents by calling them names, such as "busy bodies," "nitpickers," or "rumormongers."

READING RATE Readers adjust the rate at which they read depending on their purpose for reading and the difficulty of the material. The following chart shows how you can adjust your reading rate for different purposes.

Reading Rates According to Purpose

Reading Rate	Purpose	Example
Scanning	Reading quickly for specific details	Finding the age of a character
Skimming	Reading quickly for main points	Previewing a science chapter by reading the headings
Reading slowly and carefully	Reading for mastery (reading to learn)	Reading and taking notes from an article for a research report
Reading at a comfortable speed	Reading for enjoyment	Reading a novel by your favorite writer

See also *Author's Purpose.*

RETELLING Retelling is a reading strategy that helps you recall and understand the major events in a story. From time to time in your reading—for instance, after something important has happened—stop for a few moments. Review what has just taken place before you go ahead. Focus on the major events. Think about them, and retell them briefly in your own words.

See pages 4, 18.

SUMMARIZING When you **summarize** a text, you restate the author's main points in your own words. You include only the important ideas and details. A **summary** of a text is much shorter than the original, while a paraphrase may be the same length as, or even longer than, the original text.

When you're summarizing, stop after each paragraph you read. Try to restate in one sentence what the author wrote. If you're summarizing a story, look for the major events in the **plot,** the ones that lead to the **climax.** If you're summarizing an **essay,** look for the important ideas. Here is a summary of Maya Angelou's "Brother" (page 445):

> Bailey was the person who was most important to the writer when she was a child. She loved Bailey because he was smart, generous, kind, and full of life. He always defended her whenever anyone insulted her. He always came up with ideas to have fun. The author says that Bailey was someone she trusted and loved with all her heart.

See pages 226, 238, 456.

TEXT STRUCTURES Understanding the way a text is structured, or organized, can help you follow the writer's ideas. **Analyzing text structures** will help you understand the information you're reading. The five patterns of organization that writers use most often are cause and effect, chronological order, comparison and contrast, listing, and **problem solution.** Some texts contain just one pattern; others combine two or more patterns. The following guidelines can help you analyze text structure:

1. Look for words that hint at a specific pattern of organization. (See *Cause and Effect, Chronological Order,* and *Comparison and Contrast.*)

2. Look for important ideas. See whether these ideas are connected in an obvious pattern.

3. Draw a graphic organizer that shows how the text is structured. Compare your graphic organizer with the following five diagrams, which illustrate the most common text structures.

A **cause-and-effect pattern** focuses on the relationship between causes and effects. The **causal chain** below shows how the city of Pompeii was destroyed.

Causal Chain

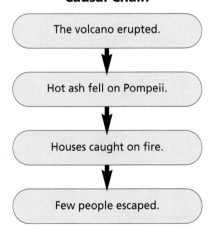

Chronological order shows events in the order in which they happen. The **sequence chain** below is a list of steps for making salsa.

Sequence Chain

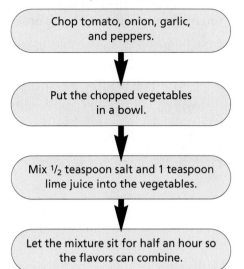

A **comparison-and-contrast pattern** focuses on similarities and differences between things. The Venn diagram below compares and contrasts Mary's and Roger's experiences during Ta-Na-E-Ka (page 135).

Venn Diagram

Mary
- ate well
- got help from others
- found an easy way

proud that they passed the test

Roger
- lost weight
- survived on his own
- followed tradition

Differences   *Similarities*   *Differences*

An **enumeration** or **list pattern** organizes information in a list by order of importance, size, or location or by another order that makes sense. The list below organizes after-school jobs by ranking them in order of difficulty. (You might not agree with this order!)

List

1. Baby-sitting (most difficult)

2. Walking dogs

3. Lawn and garden work

A **problem-solution pattern** focuses on a problem and solutions to the problem. The cluster below shows a problem and some possible solutions:

Cluster

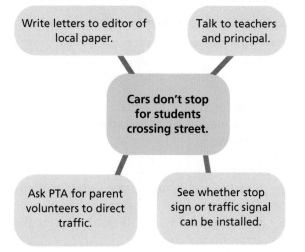

See pages 331, 335, 345.
See also *Cause and Effect, Chronological Order, Comparison and Contrast.*

Language Handbook

1 THE PARTS OF SPEECH

THE NOUN

1a. A *noun* is a word used to name a person, a place, a thing, or an idea.

PERSONS	PLACES	THINGS	IDEAS
grandmother	Cascade Range	braids	courage
Maya Angelou	home	tree	freedom
waiter	Bucktown	cat	luck

Compound Nouns

A *compound noun* is two or more words used together as a single noun. The parts of a compound noun may be written as one word, as separate words, or as a hyphenated word.

ONE WORD	Passover, grasshopper, riverbank
SEPARATE WORDS	U.S. Cavalry, Mary Whitebird, "The Fun They Had"
HYPHENATED WORD	Ta-Na-E-Ka, great-grandparents, eleven-year-old

When you are not sure how to write a compound noun, look in a dictionary.

Common Nouns and Proper Nouns

A *common noun* is a general name for a person, place, thing, or idea. A *proper noun* names a particular person, place, thing, or idea. Proper nouns always begin with a capital letter. Common nouns begin with a capital letter in titles and when they begin sentences.

COMMON NOUNS	PROPER NOUNS
poem	"Things to Do If You Are a Subway"
street	Fifty-first Street
day	Monday

For more about capitalizing proper nouns, see pages 861–866.

QUICK CHECK 1

Identify the nouns in the sentences on the following page. Classify each noun as *common* or *proper*.

EXAMPLE   **1.** The eruption of Mount St. Helens destroyed forests.
        1. *eruption—common; Mount St. Helens—proper; forests— common*

1. According to Patricia Lauber, 230 square miles were involved.
2. People, plants, and animals died in the ash, heat, and smoke.
   3. Spirit Lake was gone, its beauty lost forever.
   4. Darkness covered Yakima, Washington, until noon.
   5. Geologists had predicted the disaster.

Try It Out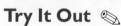

In the following paragraph, replace each vague noun with an exact, specific noun.

[1] Hot and tired from playing a game, the boy wanted a drink. [2] The boy went into the house and discovered a wild animal in a room. [3] The animal was sitting on a table and calmly eating a fruit. [4] Surprised and puzzled, the boy didn't move his body for a while. [5] Then, the boy picked up another fruit and joined the animal at its meal.

Using Specific Nouns

Whenever possible, use specific, exact nouns. Using specific nouns will make your writing more precise as well as more interesting.

EXAMPLE   A woman wrote a poem.
Pat Mora wrote **"Petals."**

THE PRONOUN

1b.   **A *pronoun* is a word used in place of one or more nouns or pronouns.**

EXAMPLE   When Bailey heard the elders' unkind words, **he** [Bailey] spoke up.

The word that a pronoun stands for is called its ***antecedent.*** Avoid the common error of using a pronoun with an unclear antecedent.

UNCLEAR ANTECEDENT   Bailey spoke to Uncle Willie. **He** was angry. [Who was angry?]

CLEAR ANTECEDENT   Even when **Bailey** behaved badly, **he** was rarely punished.

Personal Pronouns

A ***personal pronoun*** refers to the one speaking (*first person*), the one spoken to (*second person*), or the one spoken about (*third person*).

☞ For more information about pronouns and how they are used, see Part 4: Using Pronouns.

PERSONAL PRONOUNS		
	SINGULAR	**PLURAL**
First Person	I, me, my, mine	we, us, our, ours
Second Person	you, your, yours	you, your, yours
Third Person	he, him, his, she, her, hers, it, its	they, them, their, theirs

EXAMPLES   **I** enjoy Maya Angelou's forthright style. [first person]
Have **you** ever heard Angelou speak? [second person]
Please give **them** a copy of the interview. [third person]

Possessive Pronouns

Possessive pronouns are personal pronouns that are used to show ownership. Like personal pronouns, possessive pronouns have singular and plural forms.

POSSESSIVE PRONOUNS		
	SINGULAR	**PLURAL**
First Person	my, mine	our, ours
Second Person	your, yours	your, yours
Third Person	her, hers, his, its	their, theirs

EXAMPLES   Angelou and **her** family doted on Bailey.
Is this notebook **yours**?
The story tells about some of **their** antics.

Reflexive Pronouns

A **reflexive pronoun** refers to the subject and directs the action of the verb back to the subject.

REFLEXIVE PRONOUNS	
First Person	myself, ourselves
Second Person	yourself, yourselves
Third Person	himself, herself, itself, themselves

EXAMPLE   Angelou wrote about Bailey and **herself** in "Brother."

Demonstrative Pronouns

A **demonstrative pronoun** (*this, that, these, those*) points out a person, a place, a thing, or an idea.

EXAMPLE   **This** is a recent picture of Maya Angelou.

Indefinite Pronouns

An **indefinite pronoun** refers to a person, a place, or a thing that is not specifically named.

Common Indefinite Pronouns			
all	either	many	one
any	everybody	none	several
both	everything	no one	some
each	few	nobody	somebody

EXAMPLE   Bailey did **everything** well.

NOTE   Don't confuse the pronoun *its* with the contraction *it's*. The pronoun *its* means "belonging to it." The contraction *it's* means "it is" or "it has."

NOTE   Possessive pronouns are also called *possessive adjectives*.

NOTE   *This, that, these,* and *those* are also used as adjectives.

PRONOUN   *That* is an example of dialect.
ADJECTIVE   **That** word is a colloquialism.

NOTE   Many indefinite pronouns can also serve as adjectives.

INDEFINITE PRONOUN   **Many** of the pickles ended up in his pockets.

ADJECTIVE   **Many** pickles ended up in his pockets.

QUICK CHECK 2

Identify each of the pronouns in the following sentences.

EXAMPLE   **I.** I have a brother like Bailey, but my brother doesn't like pickles.
                I. *I, my*

1. Actually, this is one of my favorite stories.
2. Did each of you compare your brother or sister to Angelou's?
3. How lucky she and I have been!
4. We wonder if her brother still gets pickle juice on himself.
5. Would someone please let us know if they are still friends?

THE ADJECTIVE

1c.   **An *adjective* is a word used to modify a noun or a pronoun.**

To **modify** a word means to describe the word or to make its meaning more definite. An adjective modifies a word by telling *what kind, which one, how much,* or *how many.*

WHAT KIND?	WHICH ONE?	HOW MUCH? *or* HOW MANY?
tired dog	**first** one	**few** others
parlor stove	**that** year	**only** one
early winter	**another** one	**fifty** people

An adjective may come before or after the word it modifies.

EXAMPLES   **Many** dogs could not survive. [*Many* modifies *dogs.*]
                Storm was **tough** and **loyal.** [*Tough* and *loyal* modify *Storm.*]

Articles

The most frequently used adjectives are *a, an,* and *the.* These adjectives are called *articles.* Use *a* before words that begin with a consonant sound. Use *an* before words that begin with a vowel sound.

EXAMPLES   **The** story "Storm" is **a** good example of **an** autobiographical incident.

Proper Adjectives

A ***proper adjective*** is formed from a proper noun and begins with a capital letter.

☞ For more about adjectives and about using modifiers, see Part 5: Using Modifers.

TIPS FOR SPELLING

Some proper nouns, such as *Klondike* and *Hopi,* do not change spelling when they are used as adjectives.

PROPER NOUN	PROPER ADJECTIVE
Alaska	Alaskan crab
Newton	Newtonian physics
Hebrew	Hebraic law
Klondike	Klondike area

Demonstrative Adjectives

This, that, these, and *those* can be used both as adjectives and as pronouns. When these words modify a noun or a pronoun, they are called **demonstrative adjectives.** When they are used alone, they are called **demonstrative pronouns.**

DEMONSTRATIVE ADJECTIVES	Is **this** dog Storm?
	Those dogs are strong.
DEMONSTRATIVE PRONOUNS	**That** is Storm.
	Are **these** your only boots?

☞ For more information about demonstrative pronouns, see page 813.

✓ QUICK CHECK 3

Identify each adjective in the following sentences. Then, give the word the adjective modifies. Do not include the articles *a, an,* and *the*.

EXAMPLE 1. Dogs that pull sleds must be hardy.
   1. *hardy—Dogs*

1. Many types of dogs are used for transportation.
2. You may be familiar with the Siberian type of husky.
3. These dogs can survive in the frigid, bleak Arctic regions.
4. However, Storm didn't like running in the pre-Iditarod race.
5. After a rest, he was ready for another run.

THE VERB

1d. A *verb* is a word used to express action or a state of being.

☞ For more information about verbs and how to use them, see Part 3: Using Verbs.

EXAMPLES Lois Lowry **wrote** "The Tree House."
It **is** a story about friendship.

Action Verbs

1e. An *action verb* may express physical action or mental action.

☞ Every sentence must have a verb. The verb says something about the subject. For more about subjects and verbs, see pages 843–846.

PHYSICAL ACTION	build, climb, yell, say, wash
MENTAL ACTION	plan, think, feel, imagine, remember

For more information about objects, see pages 848–849.

NOTE A verb may be transitive in one sentence and intransitive in another.

TRANSITIVE Leah's father **finished** her treehouse.

INTRANSITIVE Leah's father **finished** quickly.

Transitive and Intransitive Verbs

(1) A *transitive verb* is an action verb that expresses an action directed toward a person or thing.

EXAMPLE Chrissy **decorated** the treehouse. [The action of *decorated* is directed toward *treehouse*.]

With transitive verbs, the action passes from the doer—the subject—to the receiver of the action. Words that receive the action of a transitive verb are called **objects.**

EXAMPLE She made a **sign.** [*Sign* is the object of the verb *made*.]

(2) An *intransitive verb* expresses action (or tells something about the subject) without passing the action to a receiver.

EXAMPLE She **climbed** carefully. [The action of *climbed* is not directed toward a receiver.]

Linking Verbs

If. A *linking verb* links, or connects, the subject with a noun, a pronoun, or an adjective in the predicate.

EXAMPLES One of her best friends **was** Leah.
That day, she **became** an enemy.

 Like intransitive verbs, linking verbs never take direct objects. See page 850 for more information on linking verbs.

Linking Verbs Formed from the Verb *Be*			
am	was being	should be	has been
are	be	would be	was
is	been	must be	were
will be	may be	being	will have been

Other Linking Verbs appear, grow, seem, stay, become, look, smell, taste, feel, remain, sound, turn

Some words may be either linking verbs or action verbs, depending on how they are used.

LINKING Leah **looked** angry.
ACTION Leah **looked** for her father.

NOTE Sometimes the verb phrase is interrupted by other words.

EXAMPLES **Will** Chrissy and Leah **be** friends again?

Chrissy **did** not [*or* didn't] **consider** Leah's feelings.

Helping Verbs

Ig. A *helping verb* (*auxiliary verb*) helps the main verb to express an action or a state of being.

EXAMPLES **could** see **had been** seen **will be** seen

A *verb phrase* consists of a main verb and at least one helping verb.

EXAMPLE Chrissy **should have been** nicer. [The main verb is *been*.]

COMMONLY USED HELPING VERBS	
Forms of *Be*	am, are, be, been, being, is, was, were
Forms of *Do*	do, does, did
Forms of *Have*	have, has, had
Other Helping Verbs	can, could, may, might, must, shall, should, will

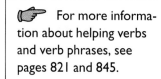 For more information about helping verbs and verb phrases, see pages 821 and 845.

 QUICK CHECK 4

Identify the italicized verb in each of the following sentences as an *action verb*, a *linking verb*, or a *helping verb*. Then, for each action verb, tell whether the verb is *transitive* or *intransitive*.

EXAMPLE   **1.** Grandpa had *made* Chrissy's treehouse.
   1. *action verb, transitive*

1. Chrissy's treehouse *was* beautiful.
2. Leah *walked* away angrily.
3. Leah *wanted* a treehouse, too.
4. Her treehouse *seemed* cozy but lonely.
5. What *would* she do?

 **Using Vivid Verbs**

Using a variety of vivid action verbs can make your writing more interesting. Eliminate dull, vague verbs. Instead, choose vivid verbs that accurately express the specific action you are describing.

DULL, VAGUE   Her treehouse had many admirers.
VIVID   Her treehouse attracted many admirers.

Try It Out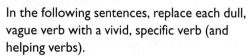

In the following sentences, replace each dull, vague verb with a vivid, specific verb (and helping verbs).

1. Friendship is important in our lives.
2. However, friends may not always be friendly to each other.
3. Conflicts can come between them.
4. Angry words may be said.
5. Yet just as quickly, friends can be forgiven and be friends again.

THE ADVERB

1h.   An *adverb* is a word used to modify a verb, an adjective, or another adverb.

EXAMPLES   The two brothers quarreled **angrily.**

   The Creator became **even** angrier.

   Very soon, there would be war.

An adverb tells *where, when, how,* or *to what extent* (*how much* or *how long*).

WHERE?   The Creator took them **away.**
WHEN?   **Then** they released their arrows.
HOW?   **Obediently,** the brothers did as they were told.
TO WHAT EXTENT?   The Creator's plan **almost** worked.

For more on using adverbs and on using modifiers in general, see Part 5: Using Modifiers.

Adverbs may come before, after, or between the words they modify.

EXAMPLES   They had lived **happily** in the new lands.

They **happily** had lived in the new lands.

They had **happily** lived in the new lands.

 **QUICK CHECK 5**

Identify the adverb (or adverbs) in each of the following sentences. Then, give the word (or words) each adverb modifies.

EXAMPLE   1. Have you ever imagined life without fire?
          1. *ever—have imagined*

1. The people badly needed fire.
2. Without fire, their lives were extremely hard.
3. Then the people lived quite peacefully.
4. Unfortunately, the Creator had made Loo-Wit too beautiful.
5. Not surprisingly, the brothers eventually quarreled again.

Try It Out ✎

For each of the following sentences, replace *very* with a more descriptive adverb, or revise the sentence so that other words carry more of the descriptive meaning.

1. Smith's dragon is *very* modern.
2. His dragon is *very* tame.
3. I was *very* surprised at its name.
4. Can a *very* old dragon learn to cook?
5. It can if you believe Smith's *very* humorous poem in this book.

Using Descriptive Adverbs

The adverb *very* is overused. Try to replace *very* with more descriptive adverbs. You may also revise the sentence so that other words carry more of the descriptive meaning.

EXAMPLE   The poem "The Toaster" is very short.
REVISED   The poem "The Toaster" is the shortest poem I've ever read.
          or
The poem "The Toaster" has only four lines.

THE PREPOSITION

11.   A *preposition* is a word used to show the relationship of a noun or a pronoun to another word in the sentence.

Notice how a change in the preposition changes the relationship between the snake and the chair in each of the following sentences.

A snake is **on** your chair.   A snake is **next to** your chair.
A snake is **under** your chair.   A snake is **near** your chair.

NOTE The word *but* is a preposition when it means "except."

EXAMPLE My little brother can be nothing **but** a pest sometimes.

Commonly Used Prepositions			
aboard	before	in	over
about	behind	in addition to	past
above	below	in front of	since
according to	beneath	inside	through
across	beside	like	throughout

The Prepositional Phrase

A preposition is usually followed by a noun or a pronoun. This noun or pronoun is called the **object of the preposition.** All together, the preposition, its object, and any modifiers of the object are called a **prepositional phrase.**

EXAMPLE   Rattlesnakes can be found **in the desert.**

A preposition may have more than one object.

EXAMPLE   Rattlesnakes can be found **in the desert or the forest.**

Adverb or Preposition?

Some words may be used as either prepositions or adverbs. To tell an adverb from a preposition, remember that a preposition always has a noun or a pronoun as its object.

ADVERB   The snake slithered **along.**
PREPOSITION   The snake slithered **along** the path.

☑ QUICK CHECK 6

Identify the preposition (or prepositions) in each of the following sentences. Then, give the object of each preposition.

EXAMPLE   **1.** The rattlesnake rested beside the rocks.
    1. *beside—rocks*

1. The sound of its rattles frightens animals away.
2. Even large animals like buffalo or deer fear it.
3. Without that sound, rattlers might waste their venom.
4. Do not rouse a rattler from its sleep.
5. Like people, rattlers can awake in a bad mood.

THE CONJUNCTION

1j.   **A *conjunction* is a word used to join words or groups of words.**

The most common conjunctions are called *coordinating conjunctions*.

Coordinating Conjunctions						
and	but	or	nor	for	so	yet

EXAMPLES   Have you ever heard of Buck Jones, Tom Tyler, **or** Hoot Gibson?
    Did you buy the cards **and** get a present for Father?
    He was confused, **but** he made a choice.

 For more about prepositional phrases, see pages 839–842.

 NOTE Do not confuse a prepositional phrase that begins with *to* (*to town*) with a verb form that begins with *to* (*to run*).

 For information on using commas in a series of words, see page 868. For information on using commas when joining sentences, see page 868.

THE INTERJECTION

1k. An *interjection* is a word used to express emotion. An interjection does not have a grammatical relation to other words in the sentence. Usually an interjection is followed by an exclamation point but sometimes may be set off by a comma.

EXAMPLES **Oh!** Is that a President Cleveland card?
Why, this must be your lucky day!

Common Interjections				
aha	goodness	hooray	ouch	wow
alas	gosh	oh	well	yikes
aw	hey	oops	whew	yippee

✓ QUICK CHECK 7

Identify the *conjunctions* and *interjections* in the following sentences.

EXAMPLE **1.** Well, Armand did seem kind and thoughtful.
1. *Well—interjection; and—conjunction*

1. Gosh, that family had hard times but stuck together.
2. Hey! Rollie's not your friend, yet you sold him your card.
3. Hooray! I have thirty-five cents, so I can get a new card.
4. Wow! You certainly know a lot about presidents and cowboys.
5. Oh, Rollie or Roger knows just as much about them.

DETERMINING PARTS OF SPEECH

The part of speech of a word is determined by the way the word is used in a sentence. Many words can be used as more than one part of speech.

EXAMPLES The boys were angry at Jerry, **for** he had sold the card. [conjunction]
He had sold the card **for** five dollars. [preposition]

The bucket fell to the bottom of the **well.** [noun]
Well, don't you look nice today! [interjection]
Suddenly, I did not feel **well.** [adjective]
How **well** did you do on the test? [adverb]

His warm jacket was filled with **down.** [noun]
Attendance is **down** at our soccer games. [adjective]
She slowly came **down** the stairs. [preposition]
Don't look **down.** [adverb]
The team will **down** more water in this heat. [verb]

NOTE When *for* is used as a conjunction, it connects groups of words that are sentences, and it is preceded by a comma. On all other occasions, *for* is used as a preposition.

✓ QUICK CHECK 8

Identify the part of speech of the italicized word in each sentence.

EXAMPLE   **1.** His *search* led him to the closet.
              1. *noun*

1. Armand's *need* was more important.
2. *Goodness*! That was a kind thing to do.
3. In confusion, he looked *away.*
4. I'm *so* happy!
5. May I borrow your *baseball* glove?

2 AGREEMENT

NUMBER

Number is the form of a word that indicates whether the word is singular or plural.

2a. When a word refers to one person, place, thing, or idea, it is *singular* in number. When a word refers to more than one, it is *plural* in number.

SINGULAR	road	goat	child	he	each
PLURAL	roads	goats	children	they	all

☞ For more about forming plurals, see pages 882–883.

AGREEMENT OF SUBJECT AND VERB

2b. A verb agrees with its subject in number.

A subject and verb *agree* when they have the same number.

(1) Singular subjects take singular verbs.

EXAMPLES   **Hanukkah comes** once a year.
              Aaron loves Zlateh the goat.

(2) Plural subjects take plural verbs.

EXAMPLES   Isaac Bashevis Singer's **stories celebrate** ordinary life.
              His **characters seem** real.

The first helping verb in a verb phrase must agree with its subject.

EXAMPLES   **Reuven is** selling the family's beloved goat.
              The **sisters are** crying at the news.
              Does he know the way to the town?
              Do you have a pet?

✓ QUICK CHECK I

For each of the following items, choose the correct form of the verb in parentheses.

EXAMPLE **1.** (*Do, Does*) Aaron have any trouble on his trip?
   1. *Does*

1. A sudden storm (*covers, cover*) the roads with snow.
2. Icicles (*forms, form*) on the goat's beard.
3. (*Has, Have*) Aaron gotten lost?
4. They (*is, are*) seeking shelter from the storm.
5. I (*is, am*) not telling the end of the story.

PROBLEMS IN AGREEMENT

Prepositional Phrases Between Subjects and Verbs

2c. **The number of a subject is not changed by a prepositional phrase following the subject.**

EXAMPLE **Drifts** of snow **cover** the roads.

Indefinite Pronouns

Some pronouns do not refer to a definite person, place, thing, or idea and are therefore called *indefinite pronouns.*

2d. **The following indefinite pronouns are singular:** *anybody, anyone, each, either, everybody, everyone, neither, nobody, no one, one, somebody, someone.*

EXAMPLE **No one knows** where the boy and the goat are.

2e. **The following indefinite pronouns are plural:** *both, few, many, several.*

EXAMPLE **Both** of them **were** safe.

2f. **The following indefinite pronouns may be either singular or plural:** *all, any, most, none, some.*

The number of the subject *all, any, most, none,* or *some* is often determined by the number of the object in a prepositional phrase following the subject. If the subject refers to a singular object, the subject is singular. If the subject refers to a plural object, the subject is plural.

EXAMPLES **Some** of the hay **has been eaten.** [*Some* refers to *hay*.]
   Some of his dreams **were** of warm days. [*Some* refers to *dreams*.]

Compound Subjects

2g. Subjects joined by *and* usually take a plural verb.

EXAMPLE   **Aaron** and **Zlateh are** sleeping in the haystack.

2h. When subjects are joined by *or* or *nor,* the verb agrees with the subject nearer the verb.

EXAMPLES   Neither **Aaron** nor his **sisters want** to sell Zlateh.
Neither Aaron's **sisters** nor **he wants** to sell Zlateh.

✓ *QUICK CHECK 2*

Most of the following sentences contain an error in agreement. Correct each error. If a sentence is correct, write *C.*

EXAMPLE   **I.** The grass in the meadows were growing at Hanukkah.
I. *was*

1. Furriers like Reuven has no work.
2. Reuven and Leah sends Aaron to the town.
3. A cap and earmuffs keeps Aaron warm.
4. Both of Aaron's younger sisters cry at the news.
5. None of the children wants to see Zlateh go.

2i. When the subject follows the verb, find the subject, and make sure the verb agrees with it. The subject usually follows the verb in sentences beginning with *here* or *there* and in questions.

EXAMPLES   There **is food** for Zlateh in the haystack. [food is]
Does Aaron dream of flowers? [Aaron does dream]

The contractions *here's, there's,* and *where's* contain the verb *is* and should be used only with singular subjects.

NONSTANDARD   Here's the books.
STANDARD   Here **are** the **books.**
STANDARD   Here's the **book.**

2j. The contractions *don't* and *doesn't* must agree with their subjects.

Use *don't* with plural subjects and with the pronouns *I* and *you.*

EXAMPLES   **They don't** need anything else.
I don't like goat's milk.
Don't you like goat's milk?

Use *doesn't* with other singular subjects.

EXAMPLE   **She doesn't** understand his worries.

NOTE   When the subject of a sentence follows the verb, the word order is said to be *inverted*. To find the subject of a sentence with inverted order, restate the sentence in normal word order.

INVERTED   There **goes** **Zlateh.**
NORMAL   **Zlateh goes** there.
INVERTED   **Does** **Zlateh go** there?
NORMAL   **Zlateh does** **go** there.
INVERTED   Into the kitchen **goes Zlateh.**
NORMAL   **Zlateh goes** into the kitchen.

☞ For more about contractions, see page 877.

✓ QUICK CHECK 3

For each of the following sentences, correct each error in agreement.

EXAMPLE   **1.** Poems like "Steam Shovel" ends on a humorous note.

      1. *Poems like "Steam Shovel" end on a humorous note.*

1. Here's several poems about pets.
2. Don't he have a pet?
3. His mother don't want one for a number of reasons.
4. Doesn't you and your brother want a pet?
5. All over the house is dog hairs.

Try It Out

Revise each of the following sentences. If a subject and verb are plural, change them to singular. If they are singular, change them to plural.

1. The theme of this story is simple.
2. Has she looked in the glossary?
3. I find some interesting information there.
4. Here's your copy.
5. Both my pencils are broken.

Using Singular and Plural Forms

Generally, nouns ending in *s* are plural (*candles, ideas, neighbors, horses*), and verbs ending in *s* are singular (*sees, writes, speaks, carries*). However, verbs used with the singular pronouns *I* and *you* often do not end in *s*.

EXAMPLES   **Winter arrives** early there.
           The **seasons change** quickly.
           I like Singer's stories.
           Do you like them, too?

3 USING VERBS

THE PRINCIPAL PARTS OF A VERB

The four basic forms of a verb are called the **principal parts** of the verb.

3a.   **The principal parts of a verb are the** *base form,* **the** *present participle,* **the** *past,* **and the** *past participle.*

BASE FORM	PRESENT PARTICIPLE	PAST	PAST PARTICIPLE
work	(is) working	worked	(have) worked
sing	(is) singing	sang	(have) sung

The principal parts of a verb are used to express the time when an action occurs.

PRESENT TIME   Ray Bradbury **writes** science fiction.
           I **am writing** a report on "All Summer in a Day."

PAST TIME   I **wrote** the first paragraph last night.
           I finally **had written** a thesis statement.

FUTURE TIME   I **will write** the rest of it this weekend.
           By Monday, I **will have written** the whole report.

 NOTE   Present participles and past participles always require helping verbs (forms of *be* and *have*).

Regular Verbs

3b. A *regular verb* forms its past and past participle by adding *–d* or *–ed* to the base form.

BASE FORM	PRESENT PARTICIPLE	PAST	PAST PARTICIPLE
use	(is) using	used	(have) used
suppose	(is) supposing	supposed	(have) supposed
attack	(is) attacking	attacked	(have) attacked
drown	(is) drowning	drowned	(have) drowned
rely	(is) relying	relied	(have) relied

One common error in forming the past or past participle of a regular verb is to leave off the *–d* or *–ed* ending.

NONSTANDARD   The sun was suppose to come out.

STANDARD   The sun **was supposed** to come out.

If you are not sure about the principal parts of a verb, look in a dictionary. Entries for irregular verbs give the principal parts of the verb.

 QUICK CHECK 1

For each of the following sentences, supply the correct past or past participle form of the verb given in italics.

EXAMPLE   **1.** *crush*   On Venus, heavy rain _____ all the new plants.
               1. *crushed*

1. *watch*   Many of the children have never _____ the sun set.
2. *look*   How they _____ forward to it!
3. *remember*   Only Margot _____ the sun.
4. *live*   However, she has _____ on Venus for many years.
5. *like*   She and the other children have not always _____ each other.

Irregular Verbs

3c. An *irregular verb* forms its past and past participle in some other way than by adding *–d* or *–ed* to the base form.

An irregular verb forms its past and past participle
• by changing vowels or consonants

BASE FORM	PAST	PAST PARTICIPLE
ring	rang	(have) rung
make	made	(have) made
hold	held	(have) held

• by changing vowels and consonants

BASE FORM	PAST	PAST PARTICIPLE
eat	ate	(have) eaten
go	went	(have) gone
be	was/were	(have) been

• by making no changes

BASE FORM	PAST	PAST PARTICIPLE
spread	spread	(have) spread
burst	burst	(have) burst
cost	cost	(have) cost

COMMON IRREGULAR VERBS			
BASE FORM	PRESENT PARTICIPLE	PAST	PAST PARTICIPLE
begin	(is) beginning	began	(have) begun
blow	(is) blowing	blew	(have) blown
break	(is) breaking	broke	(have) broken
bring	(is) bringing	brought	(have) brought
choose	(is) choosing	chose	(have) chosen
come	(is) coming	came	(have) come
do	(is) doing	did	(have) done
drink	(is) drinking	drank	(have) drunk
drive	(is) driving	drove	(have) driven
fall	(is) falling	fell	(have) fallen
freeze	(is) freezing	froze	(have) frozen
give	(is) giving	gave	(have) given

☑ QUICK CHECK 2

For each of the following sentences, give the correct past or past participle form of the verb in parentheses.

EXAMPLE 1. Margot had (*come, came*) from Ohio.
    1. *come*

1. Rain had (*fell, fallen*) for years on Venus.
2. Their teacher has (*gave, given*) them a brief recess.
3. Happily, the children (*gone, went*) to see the sun.
4. Sunlight (*burst, bursted*) out of the clouds.
5. What terrible thing have they (*did, done*)?

COMMON IRREGULAR VERBS			
BASE FORM	**PRESENT PARTICIPLE**	**PAST**	**PAST PARTICIPLE**
know	(is) knowing	knew	(have) known
ride	(is) riding	rode	(have) ridden
run	(is) running	ran	(have) run
see	(is) seeing	saw	(have) seen
shrink	(is) shrinking	shrank	(have) shrunk
sing	(is) singing	sang	(have) sung
sink	(is) sinking	sank	(have) sunk
speak	(is) speaking	spoke	(have) spoken
steal	(is) stealing	stole	(have) stolen
swim	(is) swimming	swam	(have) swum
take	(is) taking	took	(have) taken
throw	(is) throwing	threw	(have) thrown
wear	(is) wearing	wore	(have) worn
write	(is) writing	wrote	(have) written

✓ QUICK CHECK 3

For each of the following sentences, give the correct past or past participle form of the verb in parentheses.

EXAMPLE **I.** Who (*wrote, written*) this version of Medusa's story?
      I. *wrote*

1. The oracle (*knew, known*) the future of King Acrisios.
2. He (*threw, throw*) poor Danae into an underground room alone.
3. Danae and the boy have (*rode, ridden*) inside a chest for days.
4. Dictys the fisherman (*took, taken*) them out.
5. Danae must have (*sing, sung*) many songs to young Perseus.

VERB TENSE

3d. The *tense* of a verb indicates the time of the action or state of being that is expressed by the verb.

This time line shows how the six tenses of every verb are related.

Past	*Present*	*Future*
existing or happening in the past	existing or happening now	existing or happening in the future

Past Perfect	*Present Perfect*	*Future Perfect*
existing or happening before a specific time in the past	existing or happening sometime before now, or starting in the past and continuing now	existing or happening before a specific time in the future

EXAMPLES   present perfect   present
She **has read** "Petals" and **has** a topic for her paper.

past perfect   past
She **had chosen** another poem but **decided** against it.

future perfect   future
She **will have written** it by Friday and **will proofread** it on Monday.

Listing all the forms of a verb in the six tenses is called *conjugating* a verb.

CONJUGATION OF THE VERB *WRITE*	
PRESENT TENSE	
SINGULAR	***PLURAL***
I write	we write
you write	you write
he, she, *or* it writes	they write
PAST TENSE	
SINGULAR	***PLURAL***
I wrote	we wrote
you wrote	you wrote
he, she, *or* it wrote	they wrote
FUTURE TENSE	
SINGULAR	***PLURAL***
I will write	we will write
you will write	you will write
he, she, *or* it will write	they will write
PRESENT PERFECT TENSE	
SINGULAR	***PLURAL***
I have written	we have written
you have written	you have written
he, she, *or* it has written	they have written
PAST PERFECT TENSE	
SINGULAR	***PLURAL***
I had written	we had written
you had written	you had written
he, she, *or* it had written	they had written
FUTURE PERFECT TENSE	
SINGULAR	***PLURAL***
I will have written	we will have written
you will have written	you will have written
he, she, *or* it will have written	they will have written

NOTE   In the future tense and the future perfect tense, the helping verb *shall* is sometimes used in place of *will*.

 QUICK CHECK 4

Change the tense of the verb in each of the following sentences to the tense given in italics.

EXAMPLE   **1.** *past*   In "Petals," Pat Mora writes about an old woman.
                 1. *In "Petals," Pat Mora wrote about an old woman.*

1. *future*   The woman sells baskets and paper flowers.
2. *present perfect*   Her stall was there for many years.
3. *past perfect*   Straw hats are popular there.
4. *present*   She will remember the days of her youth.
5. *future perfect*   By day's end, many people saw her flowers.

SIX CONFUSING VERBS

Sit and *Set*

(1) **The verb *sit* means "to rest in an upright, seated position." *Sit* seldom takes an object.**

(2) **The verb *set* means "to put (something) in a place." *Set* often takes an object. Notice that *set* has the same form for the base form, the past, and the past participle.**

BASE FORM	PRESENT PARTICIPLE	PAST	PAST PARTICIPLE
sit (to rest)	(is) sitting	sat	(have) sat
set (to put)	(is) setting	set	(have) set

EXAMPLES   She **sits** in the market. [no object]
           Sellers **set** their goods on the tables.
             [Set what? *Goods* is the object.]
           The children **sat** quietly. [no object]
           She **set** them there. [Set what? *Them* is the object.]

 QUICK CHECK 5

For each of the following sentences, choose the correct verb in parentheses.

EXAMPLE   **1.** Tapahonso's grandmother (*sat, set*) on a wild horse.
            1. *sat*

1. Where did she (*sit, set*) her saddle?
2. Was the saddle (*sitting, setting*) on the fence?
3. Her family (*sat, set*) and waited for her.
4. Only then, did she (*sit, set*) down.
5. She (*set, sat*) the place mats on the table.

Lie and *Lay*

(1) The verb *lie* means "to rest," "to recline," or "to be in a place." *Lie* never takes an object.

(2) The verb *lay* means "to put (something) in a place." *Lay* usually takes an object.

BASE FORM	PRESENT PARTICIPLE	PAST	PAST PARTICIPLE
lie (to rest)	(is) lying	lay	(have) lain
lay (to put)	(is) laying	laid	(have) laid

EXAMPLES   Puppets **are lying** under the table. [no object]
A girl **is laying** a puppet down. [Is laying what? *Puppet* is the object.]

One flower **lies** on the ground. [no object]
A child **laid** it there. [Child laid what? *It* is the object.]

COMPUTER NOTE   Most word processors can help you check to be sure that you have used verbs correctly. For example, a spellchecker will highlight misspelled verb forms such as *drownded* or *costed*. Style-checking software can point out inconsistent verb tense. It may also highlight uses of problem verb pairs such as *lie/lay* or *rise/raise*. Remember, though, that the computer is just a tool. You still need to make all the style and content choices that affect your writing.

✓ QUICK CHECK 6

For each sentence, choose the correct verb in parentheses.

EXAMPLE   **1.** Her hair (*lay, laid*) neatly against her head.
    1. *lay*

1. The kitchen utensils (*laid, lay*) in their places.
2. Where have you (*lain, laid*) Grandmother's picture?
3. The foals have (*lain, laid*) down for a nap.
4. She (*lay, laid*) the blanket on the pony's back.
5. She was (*lying, laying*) in the dirt where the horse had thrown her.

Rise and *Raise*

(1) The verb *rise* means "to go up" or "to get up." *Rise* seldom takes an object.

(2) The verb *raise* means "to lift up" or "to cause (something) to rise." *Raise* usually takes an object.

BASE FORM	PRESENT PARTICIPLE	PAST	PAST PARTICIPLE
rise (to go up)	(is) rising	rose	(have) risen
raise (to lift up)	(is) raising	raised	(have) raised

EXAMPLES   She **rises** very early on market days. [no object]
She **raises** her eyes to the hills. [She raises what? *Eyes* is the object.]

She **has risen** from her seat. [no object]
A man **has raised** a basket up high. [A man has raised
what? *Basket* is the object.]

✔ QUICK CHECK 7

For each sentence, choose the correct verb in parentheses.

EXAMPLE   **I.** She must have (*raised, risen*) the saddle carefully.
         I. *raised*

1. The horses' heads (*raised, rose*) at her step.
2. They (*raised, rose*) their heads when she called.
3. She must have (*risen, raised*) early in the morning.
4. The horse's hooves were (*rising, raising*) in the air.
5. She (*raised, rose*) clouds of dust behind her.

Using Consistent Verb Tense

When writing about events that take place in the present, use verbs in the present tense. Similarly, when writing about events that occurred in the past, use verbs in the past tense. Do not change needlessly from one tense to another.

INCONSISTENT   When she read "Petals," she thinks of
you. [*Read* is past tense, and *thinks* is
present tense.]

PRESENT   When she **reads** "Petals," she **thinks**
of you.

PAST   When she **read** "Petals," she **thought**
of you.

Try It Out ✎

Read the following paragraph, and decide whether you think it should be rewritten in the present or past tense. Then, change the appropriate verb forms to make the verb tense consistent.

[1] We frequently go to the flea market just outside town. [2] The sellers had some unique merchandise. [3] At lunch, we stop and get a sandwich there. [4] Usually, someone like the woman in Pat Mora's poem "Petals" was there. [5] I enjoyed talking with these interesting people.

4 USING PRONOUNS

THE FORMS OF PERSONAL PRONOUNS

The form of a personal pronoun shows its use in a sentence. Pronouns used as subjects and predicate nominatives are in the **subject form.**

EXAMPLES   **I** read "A Glory over Everything." [subject]
The author is **she.** [predicate nominative]

Pronouns used as direct objects and indirect objects of verbs and as objects of prepositions are in the **object form.**

EXAMPLES   Harriet Tubman asked **her** for help. [direct object]
Many people gave **her** help. [indirect object]
Have you read about **her**? [object of preposition]

NOTE Possessive pronouns (such as *my, your,* and *our*) are also called *possessive adjectives.*

☞ For more about possessive pronouns, see pages 813 and 876.

 NOTE Notice that the pronouns *you* and *it* are the same in the subject form and object form.

The ***possessive form*** (*my, your, his, her, its, their, our*) is used to show ownership or relationship.

EXAMPLES With **her** help, many escaped slavery.

The first report about Harriet Tubman was **ours.**

PERSONAL PRONOUNS		
SINGULAR		
SUBJECT FORM	**OBJECT FORM**	**POSSESSIVE FORM**
I you he, she, it	me you him, her, it	my, mine your, yours his, her, hers, its
PLURAL		
SUBJECT FORM	**OBJECT FORM**	**POSSESSIVE FORM**
we you they	us you them	our, ours your, yours their, theirs

☑ QUICK CHECK 1

Classify each of the following pronouns as the *subject form* or *object form.* If the pronoun can be the subject form or the object form, write *either.*

EXAMPLE   **1.** she
          1. *subject form*

1. them **5.** he **9.** me
2. I **6.** him **10.** it
3. us **7.** they
4. you **8.** her

The Subject Form

4a. **Use the subject form for a pronoun that is the subject of a verb.**

EXAMPLES **She** and **they** set out on their journey. [*She* and *they* are the subjects of *set.*]

Can **we** imagine such a thing? [*We* is the subject of *can imagine.*]

To choose the correct pronoun in a compound subject, try each form of the pronoun separately.

EXAMPLE: Liza or (*me, I*) will play Harriet Tubman.

Me will play Harriet Tubman.

I will play Harriet Tubman.

ANSWER: Liza or **I** will play Harriet Tubman.

4b. Use the subject form for a pronoun that is a predicate nominative.

EXAMPLES   Her husband was **he.** [*He* identifies the subject *husband.*]

Her betrayers were **they.** [*They* identifies the subject *betrayers.*]

✔ QUICK CHECK 2

For each of the following sentences, choose the correct form of the pronoun in parentheses.

EXAMPLE   **1.** Did her brothers and (*she, her*) succeed?
1. *she*

1. In the fields, (*them, they*) sang songs with hidden meanings.
2. Harriet Tubman and (*he, him*) did not agree about leaving.
3. (*Her, She*) and many others helped the Underground Railroad.
4. The conductor is (*she, her*).
5. The next reader will be (*him, he*).

The Object Form

4c. Use the object form for a pronoun that is the direct object of a verb.

EXAMPLES   Her story amazed **us.** [*Us* tells *who* was amazed.]
Vines were plentiful, but the men did not see **them.** [*Them* tells *what* the men did not see.]

To choose the correct pronoun in a compound direct object, try each form of the pronoun separately in the sentence.

EXAMPLE   Did anyone help (*she, her*) and the others? [Did anyone help *she*? Did anyone help *her*? *Her* is the correct form.]

4d. Use the object form for a pronoun that is the indirect object of a verb.

EXAMPLE   Harriet gave **her** a quilt. [*Her* tells *to whom* Harriet gave a quilt.]

To choose the correct pronoun in a compound indirect object, try each form of the pronoun separately in the sentence.

4e. Use the object form for a pronoun that is the object of a preposition.

EXAMPLES   to **them**   in front of **me**   according to **her**

To choose the correct pronoun when the object of a preposition is compound, try each form of the pronoun separately in the sentence.

NOTE When choosing the correct form of a pronoun used as a predicate nominative, remember that the pronoun could just as well be used as the subject in the sentence.

EXAMPLE   The one in the wagon was **she.**
or
She was the one in the wagon.

☞ For more about predicate nominatives, see page 850.

☞ For more information about direct objects, see page 848.

☞ For more about indirect objects, see pages 848–849.

☞ For a list of prepositions, see page 818. For more information about prepositional phrases, see pages 839–842.

✓ QUICK CHECK 3

For each of the following sentences, identify the correct personal pronoun in parentheses.

EXAMPLE   **1.** At each stop, new directions were given to (*she, her*).
   1. *her*

1. Tubman's journey took (*her, she*) far away from (*them, they*).
2. She would have taken (*they, them*) with (*she, her*).
3. Will you read (*me, I*) these lines for the Reader's Theater?
4. Between you and (*I, me*), Viola should be playing Harriet.
5. Who will play (*he, him*) and (*they, them*)?

Try It Out ✎

Revise the following sentences to show standard, polite usage of pronouns.

1. That was them in the blue sedan.
2. May I and Rhoda ride with you?
3. The one doing the dishes is always me.
4. Call me, and tell me if it was her.
5. Save a seat for me and Larry.

Revising for Polite Usage

Expressions such as *It's me, That's her,* and *It was them* are accepted in everyday speaking. In writing, however, such expressions should generally be avoided.

STANDARD   It is **I.**   That is **she.**   It was **they.**

Additionally, remember that in English it is considered polite to put first-person pronouns (*I, me, mine, we, us, ours*) last in compound constructions.

EXAMPLE   My friends and **I** will design the set.

SPECIAL PRONOUN PROBLEMS

Who and Whom

The pronoun *who* has two different forms. *Who* is the subject form. *Whom* is the object form. When deciding whether to use *who* or *whom* in a question, follow these steps:

STEP 1:   Rephrase the question as a statement.

STEP 2:   Decide how the pronoun is used—as subject, predicate nominative, object of the verb, or object of a preposition.

STEP 3:   Determine whether the subject form or the object form is correct according to the rules of standard English.

STEP 4:   Select the correct form of the pronoun.

EXAMPLE: (*Who, Whom*) did Harriet Tubman tell?

STEP 1:   The statement is *Harriet Tubman did tell* (*who, whom*).

STEP 2:   The subject of the verb is *Harriet Tubman,* the verb is *did tell,* and the pronoun is the direct object.

STEP 3:   A pronoun used as a direct object takes the object form.

STEP 4:   The object form is *whom.*

ANSWER: **Whom** did Harriet Tubman tell?

NOTE   In spoken English, the use of *whom* is becoming less common. In fact, when you are speaking, you may correctly begin any question with *who* regardless of the grammar of the sentence. In written English, however, you should distinguish between *who* and *whom.*

Pronouns with Appositives

Sometimes a pronoun is followed directly by an appositive. To decide which pronoun to use before an appositive, omit the appositive, and try each form of the pronoun separately.

EXAMPLE: (*We, Us*) boys will read for the parts. [*Boys* is the appositive identifying the pronoun.]

We will read for the parts.

Us will read for the parts.

ANSWER: **We** boys will read for the parts.

✓ QUICK CHECK 4

For each of the following sentences, choose the correct pronoun in parentheses.

EXAMPLE   **1.** Four of (*we, us*) girls want to play Harriet.

1. *us*

1. (*Who, Whom*) is Ann Petry?
2. The behavior of Tubman's brothers angered (*we, us*) girls.
3. For (*who, whom*) did Tubman work?
4. (*Whom, Who*) do you like to read about?
5. The readers will be (*us, we*) boys.

☞ For more informa-
tion about appositives, see
page 869.

5 USING MODIFIERS

COMPARISON OF MODIFIERS

A *modifier* is a word or a phrase that describes or limits the meaning of another word. Two kinds of modifiers—adjectives and adverbs—may be used to compare things. In making comparisons, adjectives and adverbs take different forms. The form that is used depends on how many sylla-bles the modifier has and how many things are being compared.

5a. The three degrees of comparison of modifiers are *positive*, *comparative*, and *superlative*.

The *positive degree* is used when only one thing is being described.

EXAMPLES   Perseus's discus flew **high.**
The discus flew **quickly.**

The *comparative degree* is used when two things are being compared.

EXAMPLES   Perseus's discus flew **higher** than the course.
The discus flew **more quickly** than the wind.

The **superlative degree** is used when three or more things are being compared.

EXAMPLES Which athlete's discus flew **highest** of all?
Which discus flew **most quickly**?

To show decreasing comparisons, all modifiers form their comparative and superlative degrees with *less* and *least*.

POSITIVE	swift	fully
COMPARATIVE	less swift	less fully
SUPERLATIVE	least swift	least fully

Regular Comparison

(1) **Most one-syllable modifiers form their comparative and superlative degrees by adding –er (less) and –est (least).**

POSITIVE	dark	warm	swift
COMPARATIVE	darker	warmer	less swift
SUPERLATIVE	darkest	warmest	least swift

(2) **Some two-syllable modifiers form their comparative and superlative degrees by adding –er and –est. Other two-syllable modifiers form their comparative and superlative degrees by using more (less) and most (least).**

POSITIVE	angry	helpful	eager
COMPARATIVE	angrier	more helpful	less eager
SUPERLATIVE	angriest	most helpful	least eager

(3) **Modifiers that have three or more syllables form their comparative and superlative degrees by using more (less) and most (least).**

POSITIVE	hideous	fearfully	intelligent
COMPARATIVE	more hideous	more fearfully	less intelligent
SUPERLATIVE	most hideous	most fearfully	least intelligent

☑ **QUICK CHECK 1**

Give the comparative forms and the superlative forms for each of the following modifiers. You may use a dictionary if necessary.

EXAMPLE **1.** easy
1. *easier (less easy), easiest (least easy)*

1. furious
2. wise
3. quickly
4. helpless
5. poor
6. lucky
7. beautifully
8. swiftly
9. handsome
10. terrible

For more information about spelling words when adding suffixes, see page 881.

Irregular Comparison

Some modifiers do not form their comparative and superlative degrees by using the regular methods.

POSITIVE	bad	far	good	well	many	much
COMPARATIVE	worse	farther	better	better	more	more
SUPERLATIVE	worst	farthest	best	best	most	most

You do not need to add anything to an irregular comparison. For example, *worse*, all by itself, is the comparative form of *bad. Worser* and *more (less) worse* are nonstandard forms.

✓ QUICK CHECK 2

For each blank in the following sentences, give the correct form of the italicized modifier.

EXAMPLE **1.** *well*   I liked "Medusa's Head" _____ than "The Fly."
            1. *better*

1. *far*   Perseus threw the discus _____ of all the athletes.
2. *many* Athene helped Perseus through _____ trials than Zeus did.
3. *much* King Polydectes was _____ cruel than Dictys.
4. *good* This drawing of Medusa's head is the _____ in the class.
5. *bad*   Which of the three sisters looked _____?

SPECIAL PROBLEMS WITH MODIFIERS

5b. **The modifiers *good* and *well* have different uses.**

(1) Use *good* to modify a noun or a pronoun.

EXAMPLE   The three old women had only one **good** eye among them.

(2) Use *well* to modify a verb.

EXAMPLE   Perseus listened **well** to Athene's advice.

Well can also mean "in good health." When *well* has this meaning, it acts as an adjective.

EXAMPLE   In spite of their ordeal, Danae and her son were **well.**

5c. **Avoid using double comparisons.**

A ***double comparison*** is the use of both *–er* and *more (less)* or both *–est* and *most (least)* to form a comparison. A comparison should be formed in only one of these two ways, not both.

EXAMPLE   To Nereus, no one was **lovelier** [*not* more lovelier] than his daughters.

QUICK CHECK 3

The following sentences contain incorrect forms of comparison. Revise each sentence, using the correct form.

EXAMPLE   **1.** Andromeda was the most beautifulest person in the land.
     1. *Andromeda was the most beautiful person in the land.*

1. Who could have been more braver than Perseus?
2. He did good on his quest.
3. Medusa's head was the most horriblest sight in the world.
4. Perseus became more angrier at the king's insult.
5. All of the presents were well, but Perseus had given none.

Double Negatives

5d.   **Avoid the use of double negatives.**

A **double negative** is the use of two negative words to express one negative idea.

Common Negative Words			
barely	never	none	nothing
hardly	no	no one	nowhere
neither	nobody	not (–n't)	scarcely

NONSTANDARD   Polydectes shouldn't never have laughed at Perseus.

STANDARD   Polydectes **should never** have laughed at Perseus.

STANDARD   Polydectes should**n't** have laughed at Perseus.

 QUICK CHECK 4

Revise each of the following sentences to eliminate the double negative. Some double negatives may be corrected in more than one way.

EXAMPLE   **1.** Without the gods' help, there wasn't no hope for him.
     1. *Without the gods' help, there was no hope for him.*
     or
     1. *Without the gods' help, there wasn't any hope for him.*

1. Perseus had rashly made a promise with hardly no thought at all.
2. I couldn't hardly look at Medusa in the movie.
3. There wasn't nobody to help Andromeda.
4. Neither Acrisios nor Perseus could hardly avoid the fate that befell each of them.
5. Didn't no one there in Larissa know nothing about Acrisios?

6 THE PREPOSITIONAL PHRASE

PHRASES

6a. **A *phrase* is a group of related words that is used as a single part of speech. A phrase does not contain both a verb and its subject.**

Phrases cannot stand alone. They must always be used with other words as part of a sentence.

PHRASE   from the Persian culture

SENTENCE   "Ali Baba and the Forty Thieves" is a tale that comes **from the Persian culture.**

THE PREPOSITIONAL PHRASE

6b. **A *prepositional phrase* includes a preposition, a noun or a pronoun called the *object of the preposition,* and any modifiers of that object.**

EXAMPLES   This tale is the story **of a simple woodcutter.** [The noun *woodcutter* is the object of the preposition *of.*]

In the distant past, great things happened **to him.**
[The noun *past* is the object of the preposition *in.* The pronoun *him* is the object of the preposition *to.*]

A preposition may have more than one object.

EXAMPLE   The tale is the story **of a man and a treasure.** [The nouns *man* and *treasure* are both objects of the same preposition *of.*]

☞ For a list of commonly used prepositions, see page 818.

✓ QUICK CHECK 1

Identify the prepositional phrase or phrases in each of the following sentences. Underline each preposition, and circle its object. A preposition may have more than one object.

EXAMPLE   1. In ancient Persia lived two brothers.

   1. *In ancient* (Persia)

1. Cassim was one of the richest merchants in the city.
2. His brother Ali Baba loaded wood onto donkeys.
3. One day in the woods, Ali Baba discovered a great treasure.
4. Inside a cave were heaps of gold and silver.
5. Ali Baba filled some sacks with treasure and returned home.

The Adjective Phrase

A prepositional phrase used as an adjective is called an **adjective phrase.**

ADJECTIVE	**Buffalo** herds roamed a few miles away.
ADJECTIVE PHRASE	Herds **of buffalo** roamed a few miles away.

6c. An *adjective phrase* is a prepositional phrase that modifies a noun or a pronoun.

Adjective phrases answer the same questions that single-word adjectives answer: *What kind? Which one? How many?* or *How much?*

EXAMPLES   Long ago, a group **of people** called the Toltecs lived there. [What kind of group?]

The boy **with the headphones** did not hear the news. [Which boy?]

Notice in these examples that an adjective phrase generally follows the word it modifies.

More than one adjective phrase may modify the same noun or pronoun.

EXAMPLE   Huynh Quang Nhuong's journey **from Vietnam to the United States** makes an interesting read. [Both phrases modify the noun *journey.*]

An adjective phrase may modify the object of another adjective phrase.

EXAMPLE   The name **of the hero in this myth** is Quetzalcoatl. [The phrase *in this myth* modifies *hero,* which is the object in the other adjective phrase.]

☑ QUICK CHECK 2

Identify the adjective phrase or phrases in each of the following sentences. Then, give the word that each phrase modifies.

EXAMPLE   **I.** Quetzalcoatl was an old man with a beard.

I. *with a beard—man*

1. All of the people from the neighboring states were jealous.
2. Quetzalcoatl buried his treasures of gold and silver.
3. The "medicine" in Tezcatlipoca's cup was strong wine.
4. A train of pages and musicians accompanied Quetzalcoatl.
5. The other gods hoped to gain some of his secrets.

The Adverb Phrase

A prepositional phrase used as an adverb is called an **adverb phrase.**

ADVERB	He woke **early.**
ADVERB PHRASE	We woke **in the morning.**

6d. An *adverb phrase* is a prepositional phrase that modifies a verb, an adjective, or an adverb.

An adverb phrase tells *how, when, where, why,* or *to what extent* (that is, *how long, how far,* or *how many*).

EXAMPLES   Ali Baba stared **in amazement.** [How?]

In front of him was a heap of gold, silver, and fine silks. [Where?]

His life changed **on that morning.** [When?]

For years, Ali Baba kept his secret. [How long?]

The gold pieces he found numbered **in the thousands.** [How many?]

The thieves traveled together **over many miles.** [How far?]

An adverb phrase may come before or after the word it modifies.

EXAMPLES   **In the story "All Summer in a Day,"** children on Venus experience sunshine for the first time.

Children on Venus experience sunshine for the first time **in the story "All Summer in a Day."**

More than one adverb phrase may modify the same word or words.

EXAMPLE   **Without any guidance,** Richard's Shetland pony can lead him **to the apple orchard.** [Both adverb phrases modify *can lead.*]

An adverb phrase may be followed by an adjective phrase that modifies the object of the preposition in the adverb phrase.

EXAMPLE   **In their rush to the door,** the other children forget Margot. [The adverb phrase *in their rush* modifies the verb *forget.* The adjective phrase *to the door* modifies *rush,* which is the object in the adverb phrase.]

 ## QUICK CHECK 3

Identify the prepositional phrase or phrases in each of the following sentences. Then, label each phrase as an *adjective phrase* or an *adverb phrase.* Give the word or words the phrase modifies.

EXAMPLE   1. Forests on Venus had been crushed under the rain.

1. *on Venus*—adjective phrase, *Forests; under the rain—* adverb phrase, *had been crushed*

1. In a quiet voice, Margot read her poem.
2. The other children in the class edged away.
3. Margot beat against the closet door.
4. The forest was the color of rubber and ash.
5. The children played in the sun for an hour.

Try It Out ✎

Use prepositional phrases to combine each of the following pairs of choppy sentences into one smooth sentence.

1. The Lins emigrated to the United States. China had been their homeland.
2. Mrs. Gleason offered the Lins celery. The celery was on a relish tray.
3. The celery strings got caught. The strings got caught in the Lins' teeth.
4. The Lins dined out. The restaurant served French food.
5. Mr. Gleason chased a pea on his plate. He chased it with his chopsticks.

Combining Sentences Using Prepositional Phrases

Knowing how to use prepositional phrases can help you improve your writing. For example, you can use prepositional phrases to combine short, choppy sentences. Take a prepositional phrase from one sentence, or turn one sentence into a prepositional phrase. Then, add the phrase to the other sentence.

CHOPPY   The pony was waiting. It was near the hill.

REVISED   The pony was waiting near the hill.

CHOPPY   Rachel and I wanted to swim. The lake was cool and inviting.

REVISED   Rachel and I wanted to swim **in the cool, inviting lake.**

7 SENTENCES

SENTENCE OR SENTENCE FRAGMENT?

7a.   **A *sentence* is a group of words that has a subject and a verb and expresses a complete thought.**

A sentence begins with a capital letter and ends with a period, a question mark, or an exclamation point.

EXAMPLES   Vo-Dinh retold the story of "The Fly**.**"
Read it for Monday**.**
Did the ending surprise you**?**
What a clever boy he was**!**

A ***sentence fragment*** is a group of words that either does not have a subject and verb or does not express a complete thought.

SENTENCE FRAGMENT	The boy's mother and father. [What about the boy's parents?]
SENTENCE	The boy's mother and father were away from the house.
SENTENCE FRAGMENT	With its twist at the end. [What about the twist at the end?]
SENTENCE	With its twist at the end, this story will surprise you.

NOTE   In speech, people often use sentence fragments. Professional writers may use sentence fragments to create specific effects. However, in your writing at school, you will find it best to use complete sentences.

COMPUTER NOTE   Some computer programs can help you identify sentence fragments. Such programs are useful, but they aren't perfect. The best way to eliminate fragments from your writing is to make sure that each sentence has a subject and a verb and that it expresses a complete thought.

QUICK CHECK I

Tell whether each group of words is a *sentence* or a *sentence fragment*. If the word group is a sentence, correct it by adding a capital letter and end punctuation. If the word group is a sentence fragment, correct it by adding words to make a complete sentence.

EXAMPLE 1. in a huge house with a beautiful garden
1. *sentence fragment—In a huge house with a beautiful garden lived a rich man.*

1. playing in the dirt in the peasant couple's yard
2. a rich man in his fancy clothes
3. the clever boy posed a riddle
4. about the sun and the moon and about living and dead trees
5. could he solve the boy's riddle

THE SUBJECT AND THE PREDICATE

A sentence consists of two parts: a *subject* and a *predicate*.

The Subject

7b. A *subject* tells whom or what the sentence is about. A *complete subject* may be one word or more than one word.

EXAMPLES **The fly in the story** has only a small part.
It has only a small part.

Finding the Subject

The subject does not always come at the beginning of a sentence. The subject may be in the middle or even at the end. To find the subject of a sentence, ask *Who?* or *What?* before the predicate.

EXAMPLES The **boy** saw the stick. [Who saw it? The boy saw it.]
In his hand was a **stick**. [What was in his hand? A stick was.]
Did **you** read this story? [Who did read it? You did.]

 QUICK CHECK 2

Identify the complete subject in each of the following sentences.

EXAMPLE 1. The moneylender in this story was not an honest man.
1. *The moneylender in this story*

1. He cared only about material things.
2. The welfare of others was not his concern.
3. Didn't the rich moneylender lie to the boy?
4. At the end of the story is a surprise.
5. What a curious story "The Fly" is!

☞ For more about sentence fragments, see page 855.

NOTE In this book, the term *subject* refers to the simple subject unless otherwise indicated.

7c. A *simple subject* is the main word or words in the complete subject.

EXAMPLES The **boy** did not become upset. [The complete subject is *the boy.*]

"**Dragon, Dragon**" by John Gardner is in this book. [The complete subject is *"Dragon, Dragon" by John Gardner.*]

What a clever boy was **he**! [The complete and the simple subject is *he.*]

The simple subject is *never* part of a prepositional phrase.

EXAMPLE **Many** of the students laughed at the ending. [Who laughed? You might be tempted to say *students,* but *students* is part of the prepositional phrase *of the students. Many* laughed. *Many* is the subject.]

✓ QUICK CHECK 3

Identify the simple subject in each of the following sentences.

EXAMPLE **1.** The poor son of the peasant couple was playing.
1. *son*

1. His only playthings were stones and sticks.
2. Much of his time must have been spent in thought.
3. In the poor boy's yard were no witnesses for the promise.
4. Even one witness would have been enough.
5. Did they find one?

The Predicate

NOTE In this book, the term *verb* refers to the simple predicate unless otherwise indicated.

7d. The *predicate* of a sentence is the part that says something about the subject. A *complete predicate* consists of a verb and all the words that describe the verb and complete its meaning.

In the following examples, the vertical line separates the complete subject from the complete predicate.

EXAMPLES The boy's mother and father | **owed a debt.**
From a traditional story comes | this surprising tale.

Finding the Predicate

The predicate usually comes after the subject. Sometimes, however, the predicate comes before the subject. Part of the predicate may even appear on one side of the subject and the rest on the other side.

EXAMPLES **On a bamboo pole near them was** a fly.
In a few sentences, the boy **solved the riddle.**
Could a fly **be a witness**?

QUICK CHECK 4

Identify the complete predicate in each of the following sentences. Keep in mind that parts of the complete predicate may come both before and after the complete subject.

EXAMPLE　**1.** His father was planting dead trees.
　　　　　　1. *was planting dead trees*

1. These trees would be part of a fence.
2. The boy answered with a riddle.
3. Perhaps the boy should have been more polite to the man.
4. Do you think so?
5. I wonder about the future of a boy with such an ability at riddles.

7e. A *simple predicate, or verb,* is the main word or group of words in the complete predicate.

A simple predicate may be a one-word verb, or it may be a verb phrase. A *verb phrase* consists of a main verb and its helping verbs.

EXAMPLES　The moneylender **is** angry at the boy.
　　　　　　He **should** not **have made** such a promise to the boy.

Notice in the second example that the word *not* is not part of the verb phrase. The words *not* and *never* and the contraction *–n't* are adverbs, not verbs.

 For more information about helping verbs and verb phrases, see pages 816–817.

 QUICK CHECK 5

Identify the verb in each of the following sentences.

EXAMPLE　**1.** Such a boy may well get into trouble.
　　　　　　1. *may get*

1. He might succeed beyond his wildest dreams.
2. Couldn't he become a lawyer?
3. No doubt, he will be wealthy.
4. Surely, the moneylender must not have been thinking clearly.
5. Was the fly really on his nose?

The Compound Subject

7f. A *compound subject* consists of two or more connected subjects that have the same verb.

The usual connecting word between the subjects is the conjunction *and, or,* or *nor.*

EXAMPLES　Neither the **boy** nor the **moneylender** had been honest.
　　　　　　Among the people at court were the **boy,** his **parents,** and the **lender.**

The Compound Verb

7g. A *compound verb* consists of two or more verbs that have the same subject.

A connecting word—usually the conjunction *and, or,* or *but*—is used between the verbs.

EXAMPLES   This weekend I **will read** "Baucis and Philemon" or **prepare** my report on Medusa.

The mandarin **listened, asked** questions, and **made** a decision.

Both the subject and the verb of a sentence may be compound.

EXAMPLES
        S   S   V   V
The **mother** and **father laughed** and **went** home. [The mother laughed and went home. The father laughed and went home.]

     S   S   V   V
Jose or **she made** dinner and **set** the table. [Jose made dinner and set the table. She made dinner and set the table.]

✓ QUICK CHECK 6

Identify the *subjects* and *verbs* in each of the following sentences.

EXAMPLE   1. The poem "Things to Do If You Are a Subway" is short but is also funny.
      1. *poem—subject; is—verb; is—verb*

1. Dragons and subways sound alike and have many things in common.
2. They both live underground and roar.
3. Caves and tunnels are their homes and hide them from view.
4. Darkness and speed protect them from danger.
5. Both dragons and modern trains seemingly swallow people and carry them off.

Try It Out ✎

Use a compound subject or verb to combine each of the following pairs of sentences.

1. A metaphor is a figure of speech. A simile is a figure of speech.
2. Compare the modern world with the ancient world. Contrast the modern world with the ancient world.
3. Motorcycles carry people. Horses carry people.
4. Saddles can express the personality of their owners. Bridles can do so, too.
5. Horses require much care. Horses give joy to their owners.

Using Compound Subjects and Verbs

TIPS FOR WRITERS

Sometimes you may choose to repeat a subject or a verb for special emphasis. Most of the time, however, you will want to communicate as efficiently as possible. Using compound subjects and verbs, you can combine ideas and reduce wordiness in your writing. Compare the examples below.

WORDY   Under the city are dragons. Subways are there, too.

REVISED   Under the city are dragons and subways.

8 COMPLEMENTS

RECOGNIZING COMPLEMENTS

8a. A *complement* is a word or a group of words that completes the meaning of a verb.

Every sentence has a subject and a verb. Sometimes the subject and the verb can express a complete thought without a complement.

EXAMPLES   Fish swim.

Each evening my grandfather walks for an hour with his neighbor Mr. Silverstone.

Many verbs, however, need complements. A complement may be a noun, a pronoun, or an adjective. Each of the following subjects and verbs needs a complement to complete the meaning of the verb and create a complete sentence.

		S	V
INCOMPLETE	John Gardner	became	[*what?*]

		S	V	C
COMPLETE	John Gardner	became	a **writer.**

| **INCOMPLETE** | His stories are [*what?*] |
| **COMPLETE** | His stories are **wonderful.** |

| **INCOMPLETE** | Rachel will tell [*whom? what?*] |
| **COMPLETE** | Rachel will tell **us** the **story.** |

A complement is never in a prepositional phrase.

COMPLEMENT   A dragon was **loose.**

OBJECT OF A PREPOSITION   A dragon was on the **loose.**

 QUICK CHECK 1

Identify the subjects, verbs, and complements in the sentences in the following paragraph. A sentence may have more than one subject, verb, or complement.

EXAMPLE   [1] Many traditional tales have a foolish son for a hero.
   1. *tales—subject; have—verb; son—complement*

[1] Often, the silly son is the youngest child in the family. [2] Sometimes he appears stupid to everyone. [3] Supernatural or magical helpers give him special powers. [4] With their help, he becomes a hero. [5] Frequently, this character later marries a beautiful princess and becomes a king.

 NOTE   An adverb is never a complement.

ADVERB   He writes **humorously.** [*Humorously* describes how he writes.]

COMPLEMENT   His writing is **humorous.** [The adjective *humorous* describes the subject *writing.*]

For more information about adverbs, see pages 817–818.

For more about prepositional phrases, see pages 839–842.

DIRECT OBJECTS

8b. **A *direct object* is a noun or pronoun that receives the action of the verb or that shows the result of the action. A direct object tells *what* or *whom* after a transitive verb.**

EXAMPLES A fierce dragon threatens **them.** [The pronoun *them* receives the action of the transitive verb *threatens* and tells *whom.*]

The king made a **bargain.** [The noun *bargain* shows the result of the action verb *made* and tells *what.*]

A direct object may be compound.

EXAMPLE The dragon stole **jewels, treasure,** and the wizard's **book.** [The nouns *jewels, treasure,* and *book* receive the action of the transitive verb *stole* and tell *what.*]

A direct object never follows a linking verb.

LINKING VERB The king **seems** cowardly. [The verb *seems* does not express action; therefore, it has no direct object.]

A direct object is never part of a prepositional phrase.

DIRECT OBJECT He needs **volunteers.**

OBJECT OF A PREPOSITION He calls for **volunteers.**

☑ *QUICK CHECK 2*

Identify the direct object (or objects) in each of the following sentences.

EXAMPLE **I.** The wizard had lost his book of spells.
      I. *book*

1. He could not help the king.
2. The dragon was frightening people and breaking things.
3. Did he take the spark plugs from cars' engines?
4. A cobbler makes shoes and leather goods.
5. This man had a wife and three sons.

INDIRECT OBJECTS

8c. **An *indirect object* is a noun or a pronoun that comes between the verb and the direct object and tells *to what* or *to whom,* or *for what* or *for whom,* the action of the verb is done.**

EXAMPLE The king gave the young **man** a chance. [The noun *man* tells *to whom* the king gave the chance.]

☞ For more about transitive verbs, see page 816.

☞ For more about linking verbs, see page 816. For more about prepositional phrases, see pages 839–842.

NOTE If a sentence has an indirect object, it always has a direct object also.

Linking verbs do not have indirect objects. Also, an indirect object is never in a prepositional phrase.

LINKING VERB	A dragon **is** a fearsome beast.
INDIRECT OBJECT	It causes **people** trouble.
OBJECT OF A PREPOSITION	It causes trouble for many **people.**

An indirect object may be compound.

EXAMPLE   The dragon caused the **king** and his **subjects** a great deal of trouble.

✓ QUICK CHECK 3

Identify the indirect object in each of the following sentences. If a sentence has no indirect object, write *none*.

EXAMPLE   **1.** The cobbler told each of his sons a special poem.
　　　　　　1. *each*

1. The first two sons gave little thought to the poem.
2. However, the youngest son always showed his father respect.
3. A friend lent the youngest son a suit of armor.
4. The youngest son got himself a sword from another friend.
5. The cobbler had taught him well.

Revising to Avoid *Be* Verbs

Overusing the linking verb *be* can make writing dull and lifeless. As you evaluate your writing, you may get the feeling that nothing is *happening,* that nobody is *doing* anything. That feeling is one indication that your writing may contain too many *be* verbs. Wherever possible, replace a dull *be* verb with a verb that expresses action. Remember that most action verbs take direct objects, and some can have indirect objects, too.

***BE* VERB**	His voice **was** loud and confident.
ACTION VERB	He **shouted** loudly and confidently.

Try It Out ✎

Revise each of the following sentences by substituting an interesting action verb for the dull *be* verb.

1. The queen was a rosebush.
2. The king was not really upset about this transformation.
3. The rosebush is in need of water.
4. The wizard has not been helpful.
5. His book of spells will be in the dragon's cave.

SUBJECT COMPLEMENTS

A *subject complement* completes the meaning of a linking verb and identifies or describes the subject.

EXAMPLES   The youngest son became a **hero.** [*Hero* identifies the subject *son.*]

His task was **difficult.** [*Difficult* describes the subject *task.*]

👉 For information about linking verbs, see page 816.

👉 See page 816 for more about verbs that may be used as either linking verbs or action verbs.

NOTE In conversation, many people say *It's me* and *That was him.* Such nonstandard expressions may one day become acceptable in writing as well as in speech. For now, however, it is best to follow the rules of standard English in your writing.

Common Linking Verbs					
appear	become	grow	remain	smell	stay
be	feel	look	seem	sound	taste

Some verbs, such as *look, grow,* and *feel,* may be used as either linking verbs or action verbs.

LINKING VERB   The dragon **looked** fierce. [*Looked* links the adjective *fierce* to the subject *dragon.*]

ACTION VERB   The youngest son **looked** in the cave. [*Looked* expresses the youngest son's action.]

The two kinds of subject complements are the *predicate nominative* and the *predicate adjective.*

Predicate Nominatives

8d.   A *predicate nominative* is a noun or a pronoun that follows a linking verb and identifies the subject or refers to it.

EXAMPLES   The queen became a **rosebush.** [The noun *rosebush* is a predicate nominative that identifies the subject *queen.*]

The son who marries the princess is **he.** [The pronoun *he* is a predicate nominative that refers to the subject *son.*]

Predicate nominatives never appear in prepositional phrases.

EXAMPLE   His father's advice was only two **lines** of poetry. [*Lines* is a predicate nominative that identifies the subject *advice. Poetry* is the object of the preposition *of.*]

Predicate nominatives may be compound.

EXAMPLE   The troublesome dragon was a **thief,** a **vandal,** and a **mischief-maker.**

✓ QUICK CHECK 4

Identify the predicate nominative or predicate nominatives in each of the following sentences.

EXAMPLE   **1.** In the right situation, a coward may be a hero.
     1. *hero*

1. Did the oldest son and the middle son become the dragon's lunch?
2. The wizard was not a young man.
3. A sense of humor can be a weakness.
4. This cobbler was a shoemaker and wise teacher.
5. It was they in the dragon's belly.

Predicate Adjectives

8e. A *predicate adjective* is an adjective that follows a linking verb and describes the subject.

EXAMPLE The dragon felt **confident.** [*Confident* is a predicate adjective that describes the subject *dragon.*]

Predicate adjectives may be compound.

EXAMPLE The youngest son was neither **clever** nor **strong.** [*Clever* and *strong* are predicate adjectives that describe the subject *son.*]

✓ QUICK CHECK 5

Identify the *predicate adjective* (or *adjectives*) or *predicate nominative* (or *nominatives*) in each of the following sentences.

EXAMPLE 1. Is "Dragon, Dragon" a true story?
            1. *story—predicate nominative*

1. A story may reveal a truth but not be factual.
2. To the dragon, the poem seemed laughable.
3. The youngest son became frustrated and angry at the dragon's laughter.
4. At the end, the queen was all wet and ungrateful.
5. Did the princess become a happy bride?

9 KINDS OF SENTENCES

SIMPLE SENTENCES AND COMPOUND

The Simple Sentence

9a. A *simple sentence* has one subject and one verb. A compound subject has two or more parts, but it is still considered one subject. Likewise, a compound verb or verb phrase is considered one verb.

EXAMPLES "**Baucis and Philemon**" **is** an ancient Greek story. [single subject and single verb]

You will be reading it soon. [single subject and verb phrase]

Baucis and **Philemon lived** in a cottage near a marsh. [compound subject and single verb]

For more about compound subjects and compound verbs, see pages 845–846.

> S   V   V
> The **cottage was** small and **had been thatched** with dried weeds. [single subject and compound verb]
>
> S   S   V   V
> **Zeus** and **Hermes were visiting** earth and **asking** for food. [compound subject and compound verb]

✓ QUICK CHECK 1

Identify the *subject* (or *subjects*) and *verb* (or *verbs*) in each of the following sentences.

EXAMPLE 1. Baucis and Philemon were quite poor.
1. *Baucis—subject; Philemon—subject; were—verb*

1. They did have a few goats and grew their own vegetables.
2. The man and woman welcomed the strangers and asked them in.
3. Their couch and old table had seen their best days years ago.
4. Baucis kept the table clean and scented it with mint.
5. Soon, olives, cherries, and many other fine foods were placed on the table and offered to the strangers.

The Compound Sentence

9b. A *compound sentence* consists of two or more simple sentences usually joined by a connecting word.

In a compound sentence, the conjunction *and, but, for, nor, or, so,* or *yet* often connects the simple sentences. A comma usually comes before the conjunction in a compound sentence. The simple sentences in a compound sentence may also be joined by a semicolon.

>   S   V
> **EXAMPLES** Olivia Coolidge **wrote** the book *Greek Myths*, **but**
>   S   V
> Edouard Sandoz **illustrated** it.
>
> S V   S   V
> **It had been** a good season; **they had** a good harvest.

Do not confuse a compound sentence with a simple sentence that contains a compound subject, a compound verb, or both.

>   S   S   V
> **SIMPLE SENTENCE** **Zeus** and **Hermes ate** and
>   V
> **drank** heartily.
>
>   S   V   S
> **COMPOUND SENTENCE** **Zeus smiled,** and **Hermes**
>   V
> **spoke** to the couple.

COMPUTER NOTE A computer can help you analyze your writing for sentence length and structure. Programs that tell you the average number of words in your sentences are now available. Such programs also tell you how many of each kind of sentence you have used. This information can help you decide whether you need to revise some of your sentences to add variety to your writing.

Identify each of the following word groups as either a *simple sentence* or a *compound sentence*.

EXAMPLE **1.** The gods punish the unkind but reward the kind.
1. *simple sentence*

1. Baucis and Philemon were afraid, but Zeus and Hermes smiled.
2. You gave us shelter and fed us, yet many others did not.
3. What were the requests and desires of the old couple?
4. Did they want money, or did they want splendor?
5. Philemon thought and then answered the gods.

TIPS FOR WRITERS

Using Varied Sentence Structure

Variety is the spice of life. It's also the spice of writing. By varying the length and the structure of sentences, you can make your writing clearer and more interesting to read.

Simple sentences with single subjects and verbs are best used to express fairly simple ideas. To present more complicated ideas and to show relationships between them, use compound subjects, compound verbs, and compound sentences.

SIMPLE SENTENCES   The bowl was almost empty. He brought the wineskin. He discovered the bowl was full.

COMPOUND SENTENCE   The bowl was almost empty, so he brought the wineskin but discovered that the bowl was full again.

Try It Out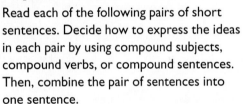

Read each of the following pairs of short sentences. Decide how to express the ideas in each pair by using compound subjects, compound verbs, or compound sentences. Then, combine the pair of sentences into one sentence.

1. Olives lay on the table. Baked eggs lay on the table.
2. The goose cackled. The goose ran away.
3. The guests were hungry. Baucis fed them.
4. Baucis and Philemon loved each other. They would never be parted.
5. Zeus and Hermes rewarded the couple. Baucis and Philemon were together forever.

SENTENCES CLASSIFIED BY PURPOSE

In addition to being classified by structure, a sentence is also classified according to its purpose: *declarative, interrogative, imperative,* or *exclamatory.*

9c. **A *declarative sentence* makes a statement. It is followed by a period.**

EXAMPLE   Their home became a temple**.**

9d. **An *interrogative sentence* asks a question. It is followed by a question mark.**

EXAMPLE   How did the gods reward them**?**

9e. An *imperative sentence* gives a command or makes a request. It is followed by a period. A strong command is followed by an exclamation point.

EXAMPLES   Bring the wine. [command]
Please light the candles, Baucis. [request]
Catch that goose! [strong command]

In an imperative sentence, the "understood" subject is always *you*.

EXAMPLES   **(You)** Watch out!
Rita, **(you)** tell us your opinion.

9f. An *exclamatory sentence* shows excitement or expresses strong feeling. An exclamatory sentence is followed by an exclamation point.

EXAMPLES   Wow, that was fun!
What a fortunate couple they were!

☑ QUICK CHECK 3

Classify each of the following sentences according to its purpose—*declarative, interrogative, imperative,* or *exclamatory*.

EXAMPLE   **1.** Have you read "Baucis and Philemon" yet?
1. *interrogative*

1. Myths sometimes explain natural phenomena.
2. Kyle, does a myth always include a god as a character?
3. What marvelous stories these are!
4. Sharon, please read the next paragraph aloud.
5. Thank goodness!

10 WRITING EFFECTIVE SENTENCES

WRITING CLEAR SENTENCES

A **complete sentence** has both a subject and a verb, and it expresses a complete thought.

EXAMPLES   I often dream of a secret garden.
Do you dream about a garden, too?
What a wonderful dream that was!

Two stumbling blocks to the development of clear sentences are *sentence fragments* and *run-on sentences.*

NOTE   Be careful not to use too many exclamation points. Save exclamation points for sentences that express especially strong emotion. When exclamation points are overused, they lose their impact.

☞ For more information about complete sentences, see pages 842–846.

Sentence Fragments

10a. **Avoid using sentence fragments.**

A *sentence fragment* is a part of a sentence that has been capitalized and punctuated as if it were a complete sentence.

FRAGMENT	Traveled far away to England. [The subject is missing. *Who* traveled?]
SENTENCE	Mary traveled far away to England.
FRAGMENT	After the death of her parents, the girl. [The verb is missing. What did the girl *do*?]
SENTENCE	After the death of her parents, the girl lived at Misselthwaite Manor.
FRAGMENT	As soon as she arrived in England. [*What happened* as soon as she arrived?]
SENTENCE	As soon as she arrived in England, she met Mrs. Medlock.

 QUICK CHECK I

Identify each of the following word groups as either a *complete sentence* or a *sentence fragment*.

EXAMPLE   **I.** The swift and deadly spread of cholera.
       I. *sentence fragment*

1. Killing Mary's parents with amazing speed.
2. With no family left in India and absolutely alone in the world.
3. In what way did Mary's behavior change?
4. No one knows in advance his or her reaction to shocking events.
5. Although she was only a child.

 Revising Sentence Fragments

Usually, a sentence fragment is closely related to the sentence that comes before or after it. In most cases, you can correct the fragment by attaching it to the related sentence.

SENTENCE AND FRAGMENT	Mary was often troubled during her days on the estate. Because many strange events occurred.
REVISED	Mary was often troubled during her days on the estate **because many strange events occurred.**

☞ For more information about sentence fragments, see page 842.

Try It Out ✎

Each of the following numbered items contains a sentence fragment. Correct each item by connecting the two word groups to create a complete sentence.

1. In mourning after the death of her parents. Mary has no appetite for food in the hotel dining room.
2. The woman was Mrs. Medlock. A tall, thin housekeeper more than sixty years old.
3. According to Mrs. Crawford, Mary's mother did not care for the girl. Because Mary was not beautiful.
4. Because they are strange and unfamiliar to her. Mary apparently dislikes everyone and everything in England.
5. With her attitude of cold, rude, and rejecting silence. Mary offends just about everyone.

Run-on Sentences

10b. **Avoid using run-on sentences.**

If you run together two complete sentences as if they were one sentence, you create a *run-on sentence.*

RUN-ON   Mr. Craven will be Mary's guardian the girl has no other relatives.

REVISED   Mr. Craven will be Mary's guardian. The girl has no other relatives.

REVISED   Mr. Craven will be Mary's guardian, **for** the girl has no other relatives.

REVISED   **Because** Mary has no other relatives, Mr. Craven will be her guardian.

You also create a run-on sentence if you use only a comma between two complete sentences.

RUN-ON   Mrs. Medlock offers Mary sandwiches, Mary refuses them.

REVISED   Mrs. Medlock offers Mary sandwiches. Mary refuses them.

REVISED   Mrs. Medlock offers Mary sandwiches, **but** Mary refuses them.

To spot run-ons, try reading your writing aloud. A natural pause in your voice usually marks the end of one thought and the beginning of another. If you pause at a place where you don't have any end punctuation, you may have found a run-on sentence.

Here are two ways you can revise run-on sentences.

1. You can make two sentences.
2. You can use a comma and a coordinating conjunction, such as *and, but, for,* or *or.*

RUN-ON   The manor had been built long ago it was a beautiful place.

REVISED   The manor had been built long ago. It was a beautiful place.

REVISED   The manor had been built long ago, **and** it was a beautiful place.

 QUICK CHECK 2

The following paragraph is confusing because it contains fragments and run-ons. Identify the *fragments* and *run-ons.* Then, revise each fragment and run-on to make the paragraph clearer.

EXAMPLE   [1] The house seems dark to Mary tapestries hang from the walls.

        1. *run-on—The house seems dark to Mary, and tapestries hang from the walls.*

[1] Her first night at the manor. [2] On orders issued by Mrs. Medlock, may not go into the rest of the house. [3] The sound of

☞ For a list of coordinating conjunctions, see page 819.

crying fills the air Mary cannot sleep. [4] Mary is frightened by the sound, she sits up in bed. [5] The sound may be a ghost it may be something else entirely.

Revising Stringy Sentences

For variety, you'll sometimes want to join sentences and sentence parts with *and*. But if you string too many ideas together with *and*, you create a **stringy sentence.** Stringy sentences ramble on and on. They don't give the reader a chance to pause between ideas.

STRINGY   Dickon is a boy at the manor and he seems nice and he always smiles and there is something magical about him and many animals follow him.

REVISED   Dickon is a boy at the manor**. He** seems nice, **and** he always smiles**. There** is something magical about him**, and** many animals follow him.

In the revised version, only two groups of ideas are linked by *and*. These ideas can be joined in one sentence because they are closely related to each other. Also, notice that a comma has been added before the *and*. The comma is necessary to show a slight pause between the two complete ideas.

> ### Try It Out ✎
>
> The following sentences are stringy. Revise them in any way you choose.
>
> 1. At dawn, Ben sees Dickon on the moors and Dickon has a crow, a lamb, a fox, and a squirrel with him and because Ben and Dickon are good friends, Ben puts his work aside for a while so that Dickon can show him a trick.
> 2. Dickon plays the pipe and walks on his hands and Ben laughs at the sight and then must resume work and Dickon goes off with the animals.

COMBINING SENTENCES

10c.   **Improve choppy sentences by combining them to make longer, smoother sentences.**

Good writers usually use some short sentences, but an entire paragraph of short sentences makes writing sound choppy. Notice how dull and choppy the following paragraph sounds.

> Mary's parents die. She must go to England. She arrives at Misselthwaite Manor. The manor is beautiful but mysterious. She first meets Mrs. Medlock. The woman tries to be friendly. Mary is unhappy at the manor. She hears about the locked garden.

Now, see how the writer has revised the paragraph.

> Mary's parents die, and she must go to England. She arrives at the beautiful but mysterious Misselthwaite Manor, where she first meets Mrs. Medlock. The woman tries to be friendly, but Mary is unhappy at the manor until she hears about the locked garden.

When you change the forms of words, you often add endings such as *–ed, –ing, –ful,* and *–ly* to make adjectives and adverbs. When adding the suffix *–ly* to most words, do not change the spelling of the word itself. However, for words that end in *y,* you usually need to change the *y* to *i* before adding *–ly.*

EXAMPLES slow + ly = slowly
easy + ly = easily

Inserting Words

One way to combine two sentences is to take a key word from one sentence and insert it into the other sentence. Sometimes you can simply add the key word to the other sentence. Other times, you'll need to change the form of the key word before you can insert it.

ORIGINAL	A wind blows across the moors. The wind is mournful.
COMBINED	A **mournful** wind blows across the moors.
COMBINED	A wind blows **mournfully** across the moors.

✓ QUICK CHECK 3

Each of the following items contains two sentences. Combine the sentences by taking the italicized word from the second sentence and inserting it into the first sentence. The directions in parentheses will tell you how to change the form of the italicized word if you need to.

EXAMPLE **1.** What was this sound? This sound was *eerie.*
1. *What was this eerie sound?*

1. Sad and alone, Mary speaks to Dickon of her desire for a friend. She speaks *wistfully.*
2. Dickon will be Mary's friend. Dickon is *gentle.*
3. Mary hides her tears. Mary is *proud.* (Add *–ly.*)
4. Each day, Mary searches for the garden. The garden is *locked.*
5. Tucked in her bed, she listens to the wind outside. The wind makes a *howl.* (Add *–ing.*)

Inserting Groups of Words

Often, you can combine two related sentences by taking an entire group of words from one sentence and adding it to the other sentence. In some cases, you will need to add or change a word to make the group of words fit smoothly into the sentence.

ORIGINAL	Dickon eats dinner. He does so on the moors.
COMBINED	Dickon eats dinner **on the moors.**
COMBINED	**On the moors,** Dickon eats dinner.
ORIGINAL	The hidden garden has a wall. The wall goes all the way around it.
COMBINED	The wall goes all the way **around the hidden garden.**
COMBINED	The hidden garden has a wall **that goes all the way around it.**

Sometimes you will need to put commas around the group of words you are inserting. To determine whether a comma is needed, ask yourself whether the group of words renames or explains a noun or pronoun in the sentence. If it does, use a comma or commas to set off the word group from the rest of the sentence.

ORIGINAL	Martha is kind to Mary. Martha is a maid at the manor.
COMBINED	Martha**,** **a maid at the Manor,** is kind to Mary.
ORIGINAL	Lilias loved the garden. She was the wife of Mr. Craven.
COMBINED	Lilias**,** **the wife of Mr. Craven,** loved the garden.

☞ For more about using commas to set off phrases, see page 869.

✓ QUICK CHECK 4

Combine each of the following pairs of sentences by taking the italicized word or word group from the second sentence and inserting it into the first sentence. Be sure to add commas if they are needed.

EXAMPLE   1. Mary explores the house. Mary is *a curious child.*
              1. *Mary, a curious child, explores the house.*

1. Mary investigates the gallery. It is *a long hall full of portraits.*
2. She discovers a room. The room is *beautifully furnished.*
3. In it are flowers. The flowers are *in bowls and vases.*
4. The scent of the perfume triggers a memory. The perfume has a *familiar* scent.
5. For a moment, a memory takes Mary to Delhi. The memory is *of her mother.*

Using Connecting Words

Another way you can combine sentences is by using connecting words called *conjunctions.* Conjunctions such as *and, but,* and *or* allow you to join closely related sentences and sentence parts.

☞ For a list of coordinating conjunctions, see page 819.

ORIGINAL	Dead leaves litter the ground. Dead branches do, too.
COMBINED	Dead **leaves and branches** litter the ground.
ORIGINAL	The key was there all along. It was hidden by debris.
COMBINED	The key **was** there all along **but was hidden** by debris.
ORIGINAL	Mary could replace the key. She could find a new hiding place for it.
COMBINED	Mary **could replace** the key **or find** a new hiding place for it.

Combining Sentences

When you connect two sentences by using *and, but,* or *or,* place a comma before the conjunction.

☞ For more about using commas with conjunctions, see page 868.

ORIGINAL	The roses are ugly now. They must have been lovely at one time.
COMBINED	The roses are ugly now**,** **but** they must have been lovely at one time.

When you are combining sentences, you may find that one sentence helps explain the other sentence by telling *how, where, why,* or *when.* A good way to combine these sentences is to add a connecting word that shows the special relationship. Some connecting words that you can use are *after, although, as, because, before, if, since, so that, until, when, whether,* and *while.* The word that you choose will depend on the relationship between the sentences you are combining.

ORIGINAL The door was shut. No one could see the entrance.

COMBINED **When** the door was shut, no one could see the entrance.

 QUICK CHECK 5

The following paragraph sounds choppy because it has too many short sentences. Use the methods you've learned in this section to combine some of the sentences.

CHOPPY A gust of wind reveals the door. The door leads to the garden.

COMBINED *A gust of wind reveals the garden door.*

Mary is joyful. She places the key in the lock. Layers of dead leaves cover the ground. The leaves are wet and brown. The grass is dead. The plants are dead. High on the walls, ivy climbs. Rose vines climb there, too. Mary explores the garden. Mary sees something green. A small, tender shoot is growing. It is growing in the dead grass. The garden seems dead. There are many tiny plants.

Revising Wordy Sentences

Unnecessary words and phrases tend to make writing sound awkward and unnatural. As you revise your writing, read each of your sentences aloud to check for wordiness. If you run out of breath before the end of a sentence, chances are the sentence is wordy. You can revise wordy sentences by

1. replacing a group of words with one word

    WORDY With great happiness, she began her work.

    REVISED **Happily,** she began her work.

2. replacing a clause with a phrase

    WORDY She always felt happier when she was in the garden.

    REVISED She always felt happier **in the garden.**

3. taking out a whole group of unnecessary words

    WORDY What I mean to say is that *The Secret Garden* was suspenseful.

    REVISED *The Secret Garden* was suspenseful.

11 CAPITAL LETTERS

11a. Capitalize the first word in every sentence.

EXAMPLE   **H**ave you ever heard the song "John Henry"?

The first word of a sentence that is a direct quotation is capitalized even if the quotation begins within a sentence.

EXAMPLE   At John Henry's grave, passing trains say, "**T**here lies a steel-driving man."

Traditionally, the first word in a line of poetry is capitalized. However, some modern poets do not follow this style. When you are quoting, follow the capitalization used in the source of the quotation.

EXAMPLE   **J**ohn Henry was about three days old
Sittin' on his papa's knee.
He picked up a hammer and a little piece of steel
Said, "Hammer's gonna be the death of me, Lord, Lord!
Hammer's gonna be the death of me."
                                    —Traditional African American song

☞ For more on using capital letters in quotations, see page 873.

11b. Capitalize the pronoun *I*.

EXAMPLE   Mark and **I** made our own music video of "John Henry."

✓ QUICK CHECK 1

Most of the following sentences contain errors in capitalization. If a sentence is correct, write *C*. If there are errors in the use of capitals, correct the word or words that should be changed.

EXAMPLE   **1.** Did you see the set i designed for "John Henry"?
                1. *I*

1. who will be designing the costumes?
2. Pearl and Lisa want to do a rap voice-over during the dance.
3. no way, i think we should keep the traditional lyrics.
4. well, couldn't i modernize a few lines?
5. how would you change a line like "his hammer was striking fire"?

11c. Capitalize proper nouns.

A **common noun** is a general name for a person, place, thing, or idea. A **proper noun** names a particular person, place, thing, or idea. A common noun is capitalized only when it begins a sentence or is part of a title. A proper noun is always capitalized. Some proper nouns consist of more than one word. In these names, short prepositions (those of fewer than five letters) and articles (*a, an, the*) are not capitalized.

☞ For more about proper nouns, see page 811.

COMMON NOUNS	statue	man
PROPER NOUNS	Colossus of Rhodes	Attila the Hun

(1) Capitalize the names of persons and animals.

EXAMPLES   Cindy Chang, Nick de Vries, Black Beauty, Wilbur

(2) Capitalize geographical names.

> **NOTE** In a hyphenated street number, the second part of the number is not capitalized.
>
> **EXAMPLE**
> West Fifty-fourth Street

TYPE OF NAME	EXAMPLES
Towns, Cities	San Jose, New York City
Islands	Isle of Hispaniola, Ellis Island
Counties, States	Polk County, Wyoming
Countries	Nigeria, France
Bodies of Water	San Francisco Bay, Dead Sea
Forests, Parks	Black Forest, Everglades National Park
Streets, Highways	Route 41, Keltner Street
Mountains	Mount St. Helens, Camelback Mountain
Continents	South America, Antarctica
Regions	the Northwest, the Sun Belt

> **NOTE** Words such as *north, east,* and *southwest* are not capitalized when they indicate direction.
>
> **EXAMPLES**   flying north, south of Boise

(3) Capitalize the names of planets, stars, and other heavenly bodies.

EXAMPLES   Mercury, Antares, Sagittarius, the Southern Cross

(4) Capitalize the names of teams, organizations, businesses, institutions, and government bodies.

> **NOTE** The word *earth* should not be capitalized unless it is used along with the names of other heavenly bodies. The words *sun* and *moon* are not capitalized.
>
> **EXAMPLE**   Venus and Mars are the two planets closest to Earth.

TYPE OF NAME	EXAMPLES
Teams	Baltimore Orioles, Indiana Pacers
Organizations	Glee Club, Home Builders Association
Businesses	Wallpaper World, Kellogg Company
Institutions	Bay Memorial Hospital, Houston High School
Government Bodies	Internal Revenue Service, Department of Health

✓ QUICK CHECK 2

Correct all errors in capitalization in each of the following sentences.

EXAMPLE   **1.** Life on venus was often dismal for a child from ohio.
   1. *Life on Venus was often dismal for a child from Ohio.*

1. Up early, Mary saw the sun rise over the Missouri river and thought of her grandfather, amos deer leg.
2. She was raised in the salinas valley and had family in mexico.

3. The baseball cards were at lemire's drugstore, next to st. jude's parochial school.

4. Rollie Tremaine lived on laurel street and wasn't much use to the frenchtown tigers during a football game.

5. Didn't you ever pretend you were robin hood in sherwood forest?

(5) Capitalize the names of historical events and periods.

TYPE OF NAME	EXAMPLES
Historical Events	**B**attle of **B**ritain, **C**old **W**ar
Historical Periods	**D**ark **A**ges, **I**ndustrial **R**evolution

(6) Capitalize the names of special events, holidays, and calendar items.

TYPE OF NAME	EXAMPLES
Special Events	**O**hio **S**tate **F**air, **M**ardi **G**ras
Holidays	**M**emorial **D**ay, **I**ndependence **D**ay
Calendar Items	**S**aturday, **D**ecember

(7) Capitalize the names of nationalities, races, and peoples.

EXAMPLES   Italian, Sudanese, Caucasian, Hispanic, Cherokee

(8) Capitalize the names of religions and their followers, holy days, sacred writings, and specific deities.

TYPE OF NAME	EXAMPLES
Religions and Followers	**Z**en **B**uddhism, **C**atholic
Holy Days	**C**hristmas, **R**amadan
Sacred Writings	**K**oran, **T**orah
Specific Deities	**V**ishnu, **Y**ahweh

(9) Capitalize the names of buildings and other structures.

EXAMPLES   Trump Towers, Golden Gate Bridge, the Pyramids

(10) Capitalize the names of monuments and awards.

TYPE OF NAME	EXAMPLES
Monuments	**T**omb of the **U**nknowns, **L**incoln **M**emorial
Awards	**C**aldecott **M**edal, **D**istinguished **F**lying **C**ross

NOTE The name of a season is not capitalized unless it is part of a proper name.

EXAMPLES   the first day of **s**ummer, the Carson **S**ummer Festival

NOTE The word *god* is not capitalized when it refers to a mythological god. The names of specific gods, however, are capitalized.

EXAMPLE   The **g**od of war in ancient Rome was **M**ars.

(11) Capitalize the names of trains, ships, airplanes, and spacecraft.

TYPE OF NAME	EXAMPLES
Trains	*Orange Blossom Special*, *Orient Express*
Ships	*USS Saratoga*, *Yarmouth Castle*
Airplanes	*Glamorous Glennis*, *Spirit of Columbus*
Spacecraft	*Telstar 1*, *Eagle*

(12) Capitalize the brand names of business products.

EXAMPLES   **P**ilot pens, **C**orvette convertible, **L**ee jeans [Notice that the names of the types of products are not capitalized.]

 **QUICK CHECK 3**

Correct each of the following expressions, using capital letters as needed. If an item is correct, write *C*.

EXAMPLE   **1.** passages in the bible
         1. *Bible*

1. congressional medal of honor
2. a Mattel toy
3. the friday before easter sunday
4. the last flight of the *hindenburg*
5. the great wall of China

6. Jason's ship, the *argo*
7. a baptist minister
8. the age of chivalry
9. strawberry festival
10. the battle of gettysburg

11d.   **Capitalize proper adjectives.**

A **proper adjective** is formed from a proper noun and is almost always capitalized.

PROPER NOUN   China   Pawnee
PROPER ADJECTIVE   Chinese porcelain   **P**awnee customs

11e.   **Capitalize titles.**

(1) Capitalize the title of a person when it comes before a name.

EXAMPLES   **D**r. Washington, **G**overnor Hill wants to talk to you.

(2) Capitalize a title used alone or following a person's name only when you want to emphasize the position of someone holding a high office.

EXAMPLES   Everyone was waiting for the **R**abbi's decision.
         How long have you wanted to become a **r**abbi?

A title used alone in direct address is usually capitalized.

EXAMPLES   May I speak to you for a moment, **D**octor?
What can I do for you, **S**ir [*or* sir]?

(3) Capitalize a word showing a family relationship when the word is used before or in place of a person's name.

EXAMPLES   Hey, **M**om, **A**unt Lisa and **U**ncle John are here!

Do not capitalize a word showing a family relationship when a possessive comes before the word.

EXAMPLES   Bill's **m**other and my **g**randfather Ned lived in Nigeria.

 QUICK CHECK 4

Correct each of the following expressions, using capital letters as needed. If an item is correct, write *C*.

EXAMPLE   **1.** a British school
1. *C*

1. my cousin Jane
2. latin
3. Amy's Uncle Joe
4. jewish rye bread
5. senator Daniels
6. the mayor of Seattle
7. a dance with mexican music
8. Grandfather Paul
9. president Clinton
10. a shakespearean sonnet

(4) Capitalize the first and last words and all important words in titles of books, magazines, newspapers, poems, short stories, historical documents, movies, television programs, works of art, and musical compositions.

Unimportant words in titles include

- prepositions of fewer than five letters (such as *at, of, for, from, with*)
- coordinating conjunctions (*and, but, for, nor, or, so, yet*)
- articles (*a, an, the*)

TYPE OF NAME	EXAMPLES
Books	*The Land I Lost, Science in Ancient China*
Magazines	*Horse and Pony, Family Circle*
Newspapers	*Milwaukee Journal, The Miami Herald*
Poems	"Jimmy Jet and His TV Set," "The Sneetches"
Short Stories	"The Southpaw," "The Golden Serpent"
Historical Documents	Magna Carta, Declaration of Independence
Movies	*The Lion King, Roots*
Television Programs	*Home Improvement, Paleoworld*
Works of Art	*Nocturne in Blue and Silver, The Gulf Stream*
Musical Compositions	*West Side Story,* "La Bamba"

For more information about words used in direct address, see rule 12i(2) on page 869.

NOTE   The article *the* before a title is not capitalized unless it is the first word of the title.

EXAMPLES   Was your picture really in **t**he *New York Post*?
Send your letter to *The Atlantic Monthly.*

For information on when to italicize (underline) a title, see page 872. For information on using quotation marks for titles, see page 875.

11f. Do *not* capitalize the names of school subjects, except language courses and course names followed by a number.

EXAMPLES Next semester I am planning to take **S**panish, **m**ath, and **M**usic II.

✓ QUICK CHECK 5

The following sentences contain words that should be capitalized. Correct the words requiring capitals.

EXAMPLE **1.** Did you read "All summer in a day" yet?
1. *Summer, Day*

1. I read in the television listing that tonight *Ancient warrior*s is about the romans.
2. I am calling the poem that I wrote about Dickon in *the secret garden* "nature's magic."
3. For my project in French class, I wrote a paper about La Fontaine's "The fox and the crow."
4. Wasn't there a photo in *Time* of *Ducks in a stream* and some other paintings of Hokusai's?
5. How about reading *The old man and the sea* for your report?

12 PUNCTUATION

END MARKS

An **end mark** is a mark of punctuation placed at the end of a sentence. The three kinds of end marks are the *period*, the *question mark*, and the *exclamation point*.

12a. Use a period at the end of a statement.

EXAMPLE Huynh Quang Nhuong is a writer**.**

12b. Use a question mark at the end of a question.

EXAMPLE Didn't he write *The Land I Lost***?**

12c. Use an exclamation point at the end of an exclamation.

EXAMPLES Wow**!** What a life he has led**!**

12d. Use a period or an exclamation point at the end of a request or a command.

EXAMPLES Please tell us about it**.** [request]
Give me a chance**!** [command]

QUICK CHECK I

Add an appropriate end mark to each of the following sentences.

EXAMPLE   **I.** Is that story about the crocodile actually true

       I. *Is that story about the crocodile actually true?*

1. I thought so

2. Just imagine it

3. Was Lan brave

4. How frightened she must have been

5. Please read me that part again

12e. **Use a period after most abbreviations.**

TYPES OF ABBREVIATIONS	EXAMPLES
Personal Names	Herbert S. Zim W.E.B. Du Bois
Titles Used with Names	Mr. Ms. Jr. Sr. Dr.
States	N.Y. Fla. Tenn. Calif.
Addresses	St. Rd. Blvd. P.O. Box
Organizations and Companies	Co. Inc. Corp. Assn.
Times	A.M. P.M. B.C. A.D.

When an abbreviation with a period ends a sentence, another period is not needed. However, a question mark or an exclamation point is used as needed.

EXAMPLES   Hello, P.J.

            Have you been introduced to Yoshiko, P.J.?

 ## QUICK CHECK 2

Insert punctuation where it is needed in the following sentences.

EXAMPLE   **I.** "The Sneetches" is one of my favorite Dr Seuss stories

       I. *"The Sneetches" is one of my favorite Dr. Seuss stories.*

1. Did J R tell you about our plans for a play about the Sneetches

2. We need 10 ft of felt to make stars for the Star-Belly Sneetches

3. Write to the Tim P Smith Co, 101 W Sixth Ave, St. Louis, MO 64505

4. The PTA's address is 412 E Oak Rd

5. We'll meet at 10:00 AM on Monday at the Savings and Loan Assoc on Elm Blvd

COMMAS

An end mark is used to separate complete thoughts. A ***comma*** is used to separate words or groups of words *within* a complete thought.

 NOTE A two-letter state abbreviation without periods is used only when it is followed by a ZIP Code.

EXAMPLE
Atlanta, **GA** 30327

 NOTE Abbreviations for government agencies and some widely used abbreviations are written without periods. Each letter of the abbreviation is capitalized.

EXAMPLES   UN, FBI, PTA, NAACP, PBS, CNN, YMCA, VHF

 NOTE Abbreviations for most units of measure are written without periods.

EXAMPLES   cm, kg, ml, ft, lb, mi, oz, qt

EXCEPTION   in.

Items in a Series

12f. **Use commas to separate items in a series.**

Make sure that there are three or more items in a series; two items do not need a comma.

EXAMPLES Joey had been to Hawaii, Venezuela, and Panama. [words in a series]

We looked for our cat Jeffrey under the beds, in the closets, and under the porch. [phrases in a series]

If all items in a series are joined by *and* or *or,* do not use commas to separate them.

EXAMPLE I miss him **and** our talks **and** our walks.

12g. **Use a comma to separate two or more adjectives that come before a noun.**

EXAMPLE He was a good, true friend.

Do not place a comma between an adjective and the noun immediately following it.

INCORRECT His new, house is far from here.

CORRECT His new house is far from here.

Sometimes the last adjective in a series is closely connected in meaning to the noun. In that case, do not use a comma before the last adjective.

EXAMPLE He was my only best friend.

 QUICK CHECK 3

Rewrite each of the following sentences, correcting any comma error. If a sentence is correct, write *C.*

EXAMPLE **1.** Lara Joe and Mike admire Langston Hughes's poetry.
1. *Lara, Joe, and Mike admire Langston Hughes's poetry.*

1. Hughes's poems often have short simple direct lines.
2. Wasn't he one of the modern African American poets?
3. Hughes's career began when he was elected Class Poet wrote a poem about his school and received loud applause when he read it at his graduation.
4. Hughes often memorized his poems and took a walk and recited them aloud.
5. What gives this poem a "soft," end?

12h. **Use a comma before *and, but, or, nor, for, so,* or *yet* when it joins the parts of a compound sentence.**

EXAMPLE I liked *Owls*, **but** I did my report on *Volcano*.

 NOTE You may omit the comma before *and, but, or,* or *nor* if the clauses are very short and there is no chance of misunderstanding.

Interrupters

12i. Use commas to set off an expression that interrupts a sentence.

Two commas are needed if the expression to be set off is in the middle of a sentence. One comma is needed if the expression comes first or last.

EXAMPLES   The author of this story, **Ray Bradbury,** sometimes appears on television.

Yes, he's a science fiction writer.

Isn't one of his stories in our book, **Bess**?

(1) Use commas to set off appositives and appositive phrases that are not needed to understand the meaning of a sentence.

An *appositive* is a noun or pronoun that identifies or explains another noun or pronoun beside it. An *appositive phrase* is an appositive with its modifiers.

EXAMPLE   Her illustration, **a sketch of a volcano,** is well drawn.

Do not use commas when an appositive is needed to understand the meaning of a sentence.

EXAMPLES   My sister **Paula** drew it. [I have more than one sister and am giving her name to identify which one I mean.]

My sister, **Paula,** drew it. [I have only one sister and am giving her name simply as extra information.]

(2) Use commas to set off words used in direct address.

Using the name of the person to whom you are speaking is using *direct address.*

EXAMPLE   **Mona,** tell us about yourself.

(3) Use a comma after such words as *well, yes, no,* and *why* when they begin a sentence.

EXAMPLE   **Well,** I have always liked drawing.

Conventional Situations

12j. Use commas in certain conventional situations.

(1) Use commas to separate items in dates and addresses.

EXAMPLES   They married on June 1, 1965, in Taos, New Mexico.

The plant opens in Reno, Nevada, next week.

Summer vacation begins on Friday, May 20.

My new address will be 110 Oak Drive, Minneapolis, MN 55424. [Notice that a comma is not used between a two-letter state abbreviation and a ZIP Code.]

(2) Use a comma after the salutation of a friendly letter and after the closing of any letter.

EXAMPLES   Dear Uncle Rollo,   Sincerely yours,   Yours truly,

✓ QUICK CHECK 4

Add commas where they are needed in the following sentences.

EXAMPLE   **1.** Maya Angelou a major modern poet wrote "Brother."
            1. *Maya Angelou, a major modern poet, wrote "Brother."*

1. Nicky tell us about Bailey the title character.
2. Yes Ms. Walsh I'd be glad to.
3. Isn't your brother's address 12 Linden Road Atlanta Georgia?
4. Well it has been for years but he may have moved by now.
5. No he won't move until Monday October 10.

SEMICOLONS

12k. **Use a semicolon between parts of a compound sentence if they are not joined by *and, but, or, nor, for, so,* or *yet.***

EXAMPLE   The Rum Tum Tugger is quite a character; he, not his owner, is the boss.

✓ QUICK CHECK 5

Write the following sentences, adding semicolons as needed.

EXAMPLE   **1.** Try to read "The Rum Tum Tugger" soon it's funny.
            1. *Try to read "The Rum Tum Tugger" soon; it's funny.*

1. This cat is at home in a drawer he hides behind the door.
2. No one can stop his antics this cat makes up his own mind.
3. His eating habits are finicky yes, even cream may not suit him.
4. Fish may revolt him cream may disgust him.
5. Perhaps you have a cat like him perhaps you know of one.

COLONS

12l. **Use a colon before a list of items, especially after expressions like *as follows* or *the following.***

EXAMPLES   Poets may use the following: rhyme, metaphor, and imagery.

            One poetic device is rhyme: end rhyme and internal rhyme.

12m. Use a colon in certain conventional situations.

(1) Use a colon between the hour and the minute.

EXAMPLES   1**:**15 P.M.   6**:**32 A.M.

(2) Use a colon after the salutation of a business letter.

EXAMPLES   Dear Ms. Cruz**:**   Dear Sir or Madam**:**

Dear Sales Manager**:**   To Whom It May Concern**:**

(3) Use a colon between a title and a subtitle.

EXAMPLE   "Snakes**:** The Facts and Folklore"

 QUICK CHECK 6

The following items contain errors in the use of colons. Rewrite each item, correcting each error.

EXAMPLE   **1.** The following poets use cats as a subject T. S. Eliot, Gary Soto, and Suki Lehman-Becker.

1. *The following poets use cats as a subject: T. S. Eliot, Gary Soto, and Suki Lehman-Becker.*

1. Poetry may be composed on any subject; common subjects include the following love, grief, special moments.
2. Characteristics of successful poets are as follows love of words, love of sound, dedication to their poetry.
3. Did you ever watch *Star Trek; The Next Generation?*
4. Some writers get up at 5 30 in the morning.
5. Dear Sir or Madam

 Using Semicolons

Semicolons are most effective when they are not overused. Sometimes it is better to separate a compound sentence or a heavily punctuated sentence rather than to use a semicolon.

ACCEPTABLE   Like so many pets, the kitten had been abandoned; luckily, Gary Soto found it, just a few weeks old, and carried it to his home, a safe harbor at last for the hungry kitten.

BETTER   Like so many pets, the kitten had been abandoned. Luckily, Gary Soto found it, just a few weeks old, and carried it to his home, a safe harbor at last for the hungry kitten.

 NOTE   Never use a colon directly after a verb or a preposition. Omit the colon, or reword the sentence.

INCORRECT   The devices Eliot uses in the poem are: rhyme, repetition, and alliteration.

CORRECT   The devices Eliot uses in the poem are rhyme, repetition, and alliteration.

CORRECT   In the poem, Eliot uses the following devices: rhyme, repetition, and alliteration.

Try It Out ✎

Decide how the information in each of the following sentences could be most clearly and effectively expressed. If you think the information can be better presented, revise the sentence.

1. Soto's cat loves the crunchy rattle of dry cat food; equally appetizing are pieces of soft, cold, aromatic cheese taken from the writer's own hand.
2. Some cats hunt mice and small birds; we have a cat.
3. For this skinny kitten, Soto, unlike many cat owners, cooked eggs; eggs, rich in nutrients, helped the kitten back to health.
4. Some cats enjoy a nap on an article of their owners' clothing, in this case, slippers; other cats prefer the privacy and darkness of a closet.
5. Soto's family protected, fed, and cuddled the kitten; in turn, the kitten responded with love and happiness.

13 PUNCTUATION

UNDERLINING (ITALICS)

COMPUTER NOTE If you use a computer, you may be able to set words in italics yourself. Most word-processing software and many printers are capable of producing italic type.

Italics are printed letters that lean to the right, such as *the letters in these words*. In your handwritten or typewritten work, indicate italics by underlining.

HANDWRITTEN *The Land I Lost is an autobiography.*

TYPEWRITTEN The Land I Lost is an autobiography.

13a. Use underlining (italics) for titles of books, plays, periodicals, works of art, films, television programs, recordings, and long musical compositions, and for the names of trains, ships, aircraft, and spacecraft.

 For examples of titles that are not italicized but are enclosed in quotation marks, see page 875.

TYPE OF TITLE	EXAMPLES	
Books	*Hank the Cowdog*	*Barrio Boy*
Plays	*The Secret Garden*	*Brian's Song*
Periodicals	*TV Guide*	*Sports Illustrated*
Works of Art	*The Pietà*	*View of Toledo*
Films	*Toy Story*	*The Land Before Time*
Television Programs	*Ancient Warriors*	*The Magic School Bus*
Recordings	*Unforgettable*	*Ave Maria*
Long Musical Compositions	*Don Giovanni* *The Mikado*	*The Four Seasons* *Water Music*
Ships	*Calypso*	USS *Nimitz*
Trains	*Orient Express*	*City of New Orleans*
Aircraft	*Spruce Goose*	*Spirit of St. Louis*
Spacecraft	*Friendship 7*	USS *Enterprise*

✓ QUICK CHECK 1

Write and underline the words that should be italicized in each of the following sentences.

EXAMPLE 1. Who wrote the book Greek Myths?
     1. *Greek Myths*

1. How many people did the Mayflower carry?
2. Did the Kansas City Star review the film Pocahontas?
3. My copy of The Stories of Ray Bradbury is overdue.
4. I love the show Where in the World Is Carmen Sandiego?
5. Why are you calling your painting Silver Suite 682?

QUOTATION MARKS

13b. Place quotation marks before and after a *direct quotation*—a person's exact words.

EXAMPLES "Has everyone read the story?" she asked.
"I read it last night," said Carlos.

Do not use quotation marks for an **indirect quotation**—a rewording of a direct quotation.

DIRECT QUOTATION Carlos said, "I enjoyed it very much."
INDIRECT QUOTATION Carlos said that he enjoyed it very much.

13c. A direct quotation begins with a capital letter.

EXAMPLE Nicole added, "**It**'s based on an Indian folk tale."

13d. When the expression identifying the speaker interrupts a quoted sentence, each part of the quotation is enclosed in quotation marks.

EXAMPLE "This story by Rudyard Kipling," said Tanya, "is my favorite so far."

Notice in the example above that the second part of the divided sentence begins with a lowercase letter.

When the second part of a divided quotation is a new sentence, it begins with a capital letter.

EXAMPLE "Rudyard Kipling is famous for this type of story," said Mrs. Perkins. "**H**ave any of you read *The Jungle Book*?"

13e. A direct quotation is set off from the rest of the sentence by a comma, a question mark, or an exclamation point, but not by a period.

If a quotation comes at the beginning of a sentence, a comma follows it. If a quotation comes at the end of a sentence, a comma comes before it. If a quoted sentence is interrupted, a comma follows the first part and comes before the second part.

EXAMPLES "Well, we could write a fable about how the elephant got its tusks," Alyssa said.
Mark said, "Didn't somebody do that?"
"Maybe somebody did," Alyssa pointed out, "but we could, too."

When a quotation ends with a question mark or with an exclamation point, no comma is needed.

EXAMPLES "Didn't he write *Just So Stories*?" asked Delia.
"What an imagination!" exclaimed Mark.

✓ QUICK CHECK 2

Revise the following sentences by adding commas, end marks, and quotation marks where necessary.

EXAMPLE **1.** "Hey, what did you think of that poem asked Mary.
1. *"Hey, what did you think of that poem?" asked Mary.*

1. Sam replied Kipling must have been a workaholic."
2. I don't know about him, Mary said, but I have lots to do already.
3. Just doing my homework keeps me busy Ken interjected. Doing yardwork and other chores takes up the rest of my time.
4. Humph! I hate yardwork Mary said.
5. Yeah, and Kipling says that we should work until we sweat! I don't think so," Sam retorted.

13f. **A period or a comma is always placed inside the closing quotation marks.**

EXAMPLES Mrs. Alaniz said, "Read this for tomorrow**.**"
"I'll get started right away**,**" replied Chip.

13g. **A question mark or an exclamation point is placed inside the closing quotation marks when the quotation itself is a question or an exclamation. Otherwise, it is placed outside.**

EXAMPLES "Why does the camel have such a bad attitude**?**" asked **Mario.** [The quotation is a question.]
Did Ms. Johnson say, "All reports are due on Friday"**?**
[The sentence, not the quotation, is a question.]

13h. **Use single quotation marks to enclose a quotation within a quotation.**

EXAMPLE "What happened to the **'**steel-driving man**'** John Henry?" Mr. Zinn asked.

13i. **When a quotation consists of several sentences, place quotation marks at the beginning and at the end of the whole quotation.**

EXAMPLE **"**Read the story by Thursday. Gather your thoughts and make notes. Please be prepared to discuss your idea in class,**"** said Mr. Ellis.

13j. **When you write dialogue (conversation), begin a new paragraph each time you change speakers.**

EXAMPLE "He says 'Humph!'" said the Dog; "and he won't fetch and carry."
"Does he say anything else?"

> "Only 'Humph!'; and he won't plow," said the
> Ox.
> "Very good," said the Djinn.
> —Rudyard Kipling, "How the Camel Got His Hump"

✔ QUICK CHECK 3

Revise the following sentences by adding commas, end marks, and quotation marks where necessary.

EXAMPLE   1. Ms. Ash asked What, class, is this story's moral?
             1. *Ms. Ash asked, "What, class, is this story's moral?"*

1. Work! yelled Austin.
2. What about work? mused Ms. Ash. Is it good or bad for you?
3. Kipling says that if you're unhappy, work's good for you, Laura said.
4. I wonder why the Djinn called the camel 'Bubbles,' Austin said.
5. Serena Ms. Ash said would you tell us about your ride on a camel?

13k. **Use quotation marks to enclose titles of short works such as short stories, poems, articles, songs, episodes of television programs, and chapters and other parts of books.**

TYPE OF TITLE	EXAMPLES	
Short Stories	"All Summer in a Day"	"The Fun They Had"
Poems	"The Sidewalk Racer"	"The Lawn Mower"
Articles	"Volcano"	"The Survivors"
Songs	"The Star-Spangled Banner"	"Amazing Grace"
Episodes of TV Programs	"Heart of a Champion"	"The Trouble with Tribbles"
Chapters and Other Parts of Books	"Learning About the Lungs" "Chapter Summary"	"Parts of Speech" "Appendix 1: Maps of the World"

☞ For examples of titles that are italicized, see page 872.

✔ QUICK CHECK 4

Revise the following sentences by adding commas, end marks, and quotation marks where necessary.

EXAMPLE   1. Will you play John Henry on your guitar for us? asked Ed.
             1. *"Will you play 'John Henry' on your guitar for us?" asked Ed.*

1. Read the next chapter, Food for Health, by Monday, said Mr. Carl.
2. I'm calling my poem Wind at Morning.
3. My sister and she are like the girls in that story The Tree House.
4. I'll be playing So Rare at my recital; it's an old tune.
5. Wow! Read this review titled Too Little, Too Late exclaimed Paul.

14 PUNCTUATION

APOSTROPHES

Possessive Case

The **possessive case** of a noun or a pronoun shows ownership (**Harriet's** courage) or relationship (**her** brother).

14a. To form the possessive case of a singular noun, add an apostrophe and an *s*.

> **EXAMPLES** a person**'s** best friend   a day**'s** time

> A proper name ending in *s* may take only an apostrophe to form the possessive case if the addition of *'s* would make the name awkward to pronounce.

> **EXAMPLES** Marjorie Kinnan Rawlings**'** novels
> Hercules**'** feats

> **TIPS FOR SPELLING**
> Do not use an apostrophe to form the *plural* of a noun. Remember that the apostrophe shows ownership or relationship.

14b. To form the possessive case of a plural noun ending in *s*, add only the apostrophe.

EXAMPLES dreams**'** meanings   wolves**'** caves

14c. To form the possessive case of a plural noun that does not end in *s*, add an apostrophe and an *s*.

EXAMPLES people**'s** habits   mice**'s** holes

14d. Do *not* use an apostrophe with possessive personal pronouns.

EXAMPLES The cat was **hers.**   That is **his** dog.

14e. To form the possessive case of some indefinite pronouns, add an apostrophe and an *s*.

EXAMPLES anyone**'s** guess   no one**'s** report

✓ QUICK CHECK I

Add an apostrophe to any word that needs one in the following sentences.

EXAMPLE   **I.** Cat would go to Adams house.
            I. *Adam's*

1. Dog heard a gorillas footsteps and barked his loudest.
2. According to Cats thinking, his promise was most important.
3. Cats have always been mices enemies.
4. In most cases, cats enemies are dogs.
5. Somebodys cat was scratching loudly at the back door; I think it must have been hers.

Contraction

14f. **To form a contraction, use an apostrophe to show where letters have been left out.**

A *contraction* is a shortened form of a word, a number, or a group of words. The apostrophe in a contraction shows where letters, numerals, or words have been left out.

EXAMPLES	I am .... I'm	1997 .... '97
	where is .... where's	of the clock .... o'clock

The word *not* can be shortened to *n't* and added to a verb, usually without changing the spelling of the verb.

EXAMPLES	has not ...... hasn't	are not ..... aren't
	had not ...... hadn't	do not ...... don't
	should not ... shouldn't	were not ... weren't
EXCEPTIONS	will not ...... won't	cannot ..... can't

Do not confuse contractions with possessive pronouns.

CONTRACTIONS	POSSESSIVE PRONOUNS
It's an African fable. [*It is*]	**Its** explanation of dogs and cats amuses me.
Who's Eve's favorite? [*Who is*]	**Whose** home was the cave?
There's not much food. [*There is*]	This home was **theirs.**
They're not home. [*They are*]	**Their** dog warned them.

Plurals

14g. **Use an apostrophe and an *s* to form the plurals of letters, numerals, and signs, and of words referred to as words.**

EXAMPLES Your *T*'s look like *F*'s.
He always crosses his 7's with a horizontal line.
Don't use so many *!*'s and *oh*'s.

✓ QUICK CHECK 2

Write the correct form of each item that requires an apostrophe in the following sentences.

EXAMPLE   1. Cat wouldnt come to an agreement.
1. *wouldn't*

1. Were reading "The Fun They Had" next.
2. Its not right to break a promise.
3. Do #s mean "pounds"?
4. Lets ask him if hes going there, too.
5. "Whos its owner?" I asked.

HYPHENS

14h. **Use a hyphen to divide a word at the end of a line.**

When dividing a word at the end of a line, remember the following rules:

(1) Divide a word only between syllables.

INCORRECT Both Dog and Cat had agreed that they would, unfort-unately, separate, and Cat went to Adam's house.

CORRECT Both Dog and Cat had agreed that they would, unfor-tunately, separate, and Cat went to Adam's house.

(2) Do not divide a one-syllable word.

INCORRECT Without any warning, Gorilla reached down and pick-ed Dog up angrily.

CORRECT Without any warning, Gorilla reached down and picked Dog up angrily.

(3) Do not divide a word so that one letter stands alone.

INCORRECT After some discussion with his friend, Dog set out a-lone on his search for food.

CORRECT After some discussion with his friend, Dog set out alone on his search for food.

14i. **Use a hyphen with compound numbers from *twenty-one* to *ninety-nine* and with fractions used as adjectives.**

EXAMPLES **twenty-two** verbs, **one-half** pint, **fifty-first** state

 QUICK CHECK 3

Proofread each of the following sentences for errors in the use of hyphens. Correct each error.

EXAMPLE 1. Have you read the poem on page thirty nine yet?
   1. *Have you read the poem on page thirty-nine yet?*

1. Unhappy at first, Dog and Cat did not like being a-part from each other.
2. However, after several days of being apart had pass-ed, Cat was quite content.
3. They sat together and thought, and Dog and Cat scr-atched fleas.
4. Do you remember, Elizabeth, which animal's loud fo-otsteps Dog heard?
5. Is your report actually twenty three pages long?

COMPUTER NOTE Some word-processing programs will automatically break a word at the end of a line and insert a hyphen. Occasionally, such a break will violate one of the rules given under rule 14h. Always check a printout of your writing to see how the computer has hyphenated words at the ends of lines. If a hyphen is used incorrectly, revise the line by moving the word or by rebreaking the word and inserting a "hard" hyphen (one that the computer cannot move).

15 SPELLING

USING WORD PARTS

Many English words are made up of various word parts. Learning to spell frequently used parts can help you spell many words correctly.

Roots

15a. The *root* of a word is the part that carries the word's core meaning.

COMMONLY USED ROOTS		
WORD ROOT	**MEANING**	**EXAMPLES**
–ped–	foot	pedal, pedestrian
–port–	carry	porter, portable
–vid–, –vis–	see	video, visual

Prefixes

15b. A *prefix* is one or more letters or syllables added to the beginning of a word or word part to create a new word.

COMMONLY USED PREFIXES		
PREFIX	**MEANING**	**EXAMPLES**
dis–	away, opposing	disarm, disagree
il–, im–, in–, ir–	not	illegal, incomplete
semi–	half	semicircle

Suffixes

15c. A *suffix* is one or more letters or syllables added to the end of a word or word part to create a new word.

COMMONLY USED SUFFIXES		
SUFFIX	**MEANING**	**EXAMPLES**
–en	made of, become	wooden, broaden
–ful	full of	joyful, hopeful
–ness	quality	kindness, goodness

NOTE When you are not sure about the spelling of a word, look it up in a dictionary. A dictionary will also tell you the correct pronunciation and syllable divisions of a word.

ie and *ei*

15d. Except after *c*, write *ie* when the sound is long *e*.

EXAMPLES ceiling   receive   piece   believe   chief   field
EXCEPTIONS either   sheik   protein   seize   weird

15e. Write *ei* when the sound is not long *e*, especially when the sound is long *a*.

EXAMPLES eighteen   sleigh   neigh   vein   their
EXCEPTIONS ancient   mischief   pie   friend   conscience

This time-tested verse may help you remember when to use *ie* and when to use *ei*.

I before *e*
Except after *c*
Or when sounded like *a*,
As in *neighbor* and *weigh*.

> **NOTE** Rules 15d and 15e and the rhyme following rule 15e apply only when the *i* and the *e* are in the same syllable.

✓ QUICK CHECK I

Add the letters *ie* or *ei* to spell each of the following words correctly.

EXAMPLE **I.** bel . . . ve
          I. *believe*

1. f . . . rce
2. conc . . . t
3. perc . . . ve
4. h . . . r
5. . . . ght
6. h . . . ght
7. pr . . . st
8. rel . . . f
9. rev . . . w
10. fr . . . nd

–cede, –ceed, and *–sede*

15f. The only word ending in *–sede* is *supersede*. The only words ending in *–ceed* are *exceed*, *proceed*, and *succeed*. Most other words with this sound end in *–cede*.

EXAMPLES concede   intercede   precede   recede   secede

Adding Prefixes

15g. When adding a prefix to a word, do not change the spelling of the word itself.

EXAMPLES pre + view = **pre**view   post + script = **post**script
          mis + spell = **mis**spell   im + mature = **im**mature

Adding Suffixes

15h. When adding the suffix *–ly* or *–ness* to a word, do not change the spelling of the word itself.

EXAMPLES quick + ly = quick**ly**   near + ness = near**ness**

EXCEPTIONS For words that end in *y* and have more than one syllable, change the *y* to *i* before adding *-ly* or *-ness*.
tardy + ly = tard**ily**   ready + ly = read**ily**

15i. Drop the final silent *e* before a suffix beginning with a vowel.

EXAMPLES strange + er = strang**er**   close + ing = clos**ing**

EXCEPTIONS Keep the final silent *e* in a word ending in *ce* or *ge* before a suffix beginning with *a* or *o*.
change + able = chang**eable**
service + able = servic**eable**

15j. Keep the final silent *e* before a suffix beginning with a consonant.

EXAMPLES false + ly = false**ly**   pride + ful = pride**ful**

EXCEPTIONS nine + th = nin**th**   argue + ment = argu**ment**

15k. For words ending in *y* preceded by a consonant, change the *y* to *i* before any suffix that does not begin with *i*.

EXAMPLES empty + ness = empt**iness**   dry + ed = dr**ied**

15l. For words ending in *y* preceded by a vowel, keep the *y* when adding a suffix.

EXAMPLES stay + ing = staying   pay + ment = pay**ment**

EXCEPTIONS day—da**ily**   lay—la**id**   pay—pa**id**   say—sa**id**

15m. Double the final consonant before a suffix beginning with a vowel if the word

(1) has only one syllable or has the accent on the last syllable

and

(2) ends in a single consonant preceded by a single vowel.

EXAMPLES wed + ing = we**dd**ing   begin + er = begi**nn**er

Do not double the final consonant in words ending in *w* or *x*.

EXAMPLES bow + ing = bow**ing**   tax + ed = tax**ed**

Also, the final consonant is usually not doubled before a suffix beginning with a vowel.

EXAMPLES send + er = send**er**   final + ist = final**ist**

 NOTE *Vowels* are the letters *a, e, i, o, u,* and sometimes *y*. All other letters of the alphabet are **consonants.**

NOTE When adding *–ing* to words that end in *ie*, drop the e and change the *i* to *y*.

EXAMPLES
tie + ing = **tying**
lie + ing = **lying**

 NOTE In some cases, the final consonant either may or may not be doubled.

EXAMPLE travel + ed = travel**ed** *or* travel**led**

QUICK CHECK 2

Spell each of the following words, adding the prefix or suffix given.

EXAMPLE   **1.** display + ed
   1. *displayed*

1. im + mobile   **6.** force + able
2. re + set   **7.** shop + er
3. un + lucky   **8.** dirty + ness
4. happy + ly   **9.** hurry + ed
5. semi + precious   **10.** outrage + ous

Forming the Plurals of Nouns

15n. For most nouns, add *–s.*

SINGULAR	log	thought	pen	hoe	soda	Baker
PLURAL	log**s**	thought**s**	pen**s**	hoe**s**	soda**s**	Baker**s**

15o. For nouns ending in *s, x, z, ch,* or *sh,* add *–es.*

SINGULAR	lass	box	waltz	pinch	blush	Ruíz
PLURAL	lass**es**	box**es**	waltz**es**	pinch**es**	blush**es**	Ruíz**es**

15p. For nouns ending in *y* preceded by a consonant, change the *y* to *i* and add *–es.*

SINGULAR	fly	puppy	cry	lady
	enemy	remedy		
PLURAL	fl**ies**	pupp**ies**	cr**ies**	lad**ies**
	enem**ies**	remed**ies**		

EXCEPTIONS   For proper nouns ending in *y,* just add *–s.*
Nicky—Nicky**s**   Kelly—Kelly**s**

However, for nouns ending in *y* preceded by a vowel, add *–s.*

SINGULAR	joy	replay	key	Wiley
PLURAL	joy**s**	replay**s**	key**s**	Wiley**s**

15q. For some nouns ending in *f* or *fe,* add *–s.* For others, change the *f* or *fe* to *v* and add *–es.*

SINGULAR	belief	wife	tariff	life	giraffe
PLURAL	belief**s**	wi**ves**	tariff**s**	li**ves**	giraffe**s**

15r. For nouns ending in *o* preceded by a vowel, add *–s.*

SINGULAR	radio	patio	stereo	cameo	Nunzio
PLURAL	radio**s**	patio**s**	stereo**s**	cameo**s**	Nunzio**s**

TIPS FOR SPELLING

In some names, marks that show pronunciation are just as important as the letters themselves.

PEOPLE   Raúl   Thérèse   Muñoz
PLACES   Skíros   Lünen   Châteauroux

If you're not sure about the spelling of a name, ask the person whose name it is, or check in a reference source.

15s. For nouns ending in *o* preceded by a consonant, add *–es*.

SINGULAR	torpedo	potato	echo	hero
PLURAL	torpedo**es**	potato**es**	echo**es**	hero**es**

EXCEPTIONS For musical terms and proper nouns, add *-s*.

alto—alto**s**	soprano—soprano**s**
Palombo—Palombo**s**	Soto—Soto**s**

15t. A few nouns form their plurals in irregular ways.

SINGULAR	ox	child	foot	tooth	man
PLURAL	ox**en**	child**ren**	f**ee**t	t**ee**th	m**e**n

15u. For some nouns, the singular and the plural forms are the same.

SINGULAR AND PLURAL Sioux Japanese salmon deer moose

15v. For numbers, letters, symbols, and words used as words, add an apostrophe and *–s*.

EXAMPLES *3*'s *z*'s *!*'s *or*'s

✓ QUICK CHECK 3

Spell the plural form of each of the following items.

EXAMPLE **1.** *$*
1. *$'s*

1. rodeo	**3.** Gómez	**5.** child	**7.** shelf	**9.** *L*
2. dairy	**4.** toy	**6.** push	**8.** Chinese	**10.** 200

Writing Numbers

15w. Spell out a number that begins a sentence.

EXAMPLE **Thirteen** people helped stage *The Secret Garden.*

Within a sentence, spell out numbers that can be written in one or two words.

EXAMPLE More than **sixty-five** people came for the opening performance.

15x. If you use several numbers, some short and some long, write them all the same way. Usually, it is better to write them all as numerals.

EXAMPLE In all, we spent **23** days rehearsing and sold **250** tickets.

15y. Spell out numbers used to indicate order.

EXAMPLE This was our **third** stage play of the year.

16 GLOSSARY OF USAGE

The Glossary of Usage is an alphabetical list of words and expressions with definitions, explanations, and examples. Some examples are labeled *Standard* or *Formal*. These labels identify language that is appropriate in serious writing or speaking, such as in compositions for school or in speeches. Expressions labeled *Informal* are acceptable in conversation and in everyday writing. *Nonstandard* expressions do not follow the guidelines of standard English.

---

a, an   Use *a* before words or expressions that begin with consonant sounds. Use *an* before words or expressions that begin with vowel sounds.

EXAMPLES   Tom Sawyer was **a** friend of Huckleberry Finn.
The two boys had quite **an** adventure.
Mark Twain certainly created **a** unique character.
Was Tom **an** honest person?

Notice in the last two examples that a word may begin with a vowel that has a consonant sound or with a consonant that has a vowel sound.

accept, except   *Accept* is a verb that means "receive." *Except* may be either a verb or a preposition. As a verb, *except* means "leave out" or "exclude." As a preposition, *except* means "other than" or "excluding."

EXAMPLES   The Lins **accept** a dinner invitation from the Gleasons.
No guest was **excepted** from the Gleasons' hospitality.
No one **except** the Lins zipped the strings from the
   celery.

affect, effect   *Affect* is a verb meaning "influence." As a noun, *effect* means "the result of some action."

EXAMPLES   One error will not greatly **affect** your score on the test.
What **effect** did Rosa Parks's action have on the civil
   rights movement?

ain't   Avoid this word in speaking and writing. It is nonstandard English.

all ready, already   *All ready* means "completely prepared." *Already* means "before a certain point in time."

EXAMPLES   Mary was **all ready** for the test of endurance.
Her grandfather had **already** passed the test.

all right   Used as an adjective, *all right* means "unhurt" or "satisfactory." Used as an adverb, *all right* means "well enough." *All right* should always be written as two words.

EXAMPLES   Mary wondered if she would be **all right.** [adjective]
She did **all right** during her time away from home.
   [adverb]

a lot   *A lot* should always be written as two words.

EXAMPLE   She certainly learned **a lot** during those few days.

among   See **between, among.**

anywheres, everywheres, nowheres, somewheres   Use these words without the final *s*.

EXAMPLE   She didn't want to go **anywhere** [*not* anywheres].

at   Do not use *at* after *where.*

EXAMPLE   Where was Roger? [*not* Where was Roger at?]

bad, badly   *Bad* is an adjective. *Badly* is an adverb.

EXAMPLES   The berries taste **bad.** [*Bad* modifies the noun *berries.*]
Roger's eyes had swollen **badly.** [*Badly* modifies the verb *had swollen.*]

between, among   Use *between* when referring to two things at a time, even though they may be part of a group containing more than two.

EXAMPLES   A deal was made **between** Ernie and Mary.
Between explorations in the forest, lessons in cooking, and hearty meals, Mary told Ernie about Kaw legends. [The storytelling occurs only *between* any two of these activities.]

Use *among* when referring to a group rather than to the separate individuals in the group.

EXAMPLE   She walked **among** the many flowers.

bring, take   *Bring* means "come carrying something." *Take* means "go carrying something." Think of *bring* as related to *come.* Think of *take* as related to *go.*

EXAMPLES   Please **bring** your new puzzle when you come over.
Take your bathing suit when you go to the beach.

bust, busted   Avoid using these words as verbs. Use a form of either *burst* or *break.*

EXAMPLES   The dam **burst** [*not* busted], causing a flood.
Did you **break** [*not* bust] that window?
If you **break** [*not* bust] anything, you have to pay for it.

choose, chose   *Choose* is the present tense form of the verb *choose.* It rhymes with *whose* and means "select." *Chose* is the past tense form of *choose.* It rhymes with *grows* and means "selected."

EXAMPLES   What story did you **choose** for your report?
I **chose** a Greek myth.

 NOTE   Many writers overuse *a lot.* Whenever you run across *a lot* as you revise your own writing, try to replace it with a more exact word or phrase.

EXAMPLE   The dinner guests ate a lot.
REVISED   The dinner guests piled their plates with food.

could of   Do not write *of* with the helping verb *could*. Write *could have*. Also avoid using *ought to of, should of, would of, might of,* and *must of.*

EXAMPLE   Roger **could have** [*not* could of] done as Mary did.

Of is also unnecessary with *had*.

EXAMPLE   If he **had** [*not* had of] done so, he would have had a better time.

doesn't, don't   *Doesn't* is the contraction of *does not*. *Don't* is the contraction of *do not*. Use *doesn't* with most singular subjects and *don't* with plural subjects and with *I* and *you*.

EXAMPLES   He **doesn't** look well.
Mary's feet **don't** have very many cuts.
I **don't** think so.

double subject   See **he, she, they.**

effect   See **affect, effect.**

everywheres   See **anywheres,** etc.

except   See **accept, except.**

fewer, less   *Fewer* is used with plural words. *Less* is used with singular words. *Fewer* tells "how many"; *less* tells "how much."

EXAMPLES   My family has **fewer** traditions than Mary's family.
Next time, use **less** chili powder.

good, well   *Good* is always an adjective. Never use *good* as an adverb. Instead, use *well*.

EXAMPLE   Mary did **well** [*not* good] on her endurance ritual.

Although *well* is usually an adverb, *well* may also be used as an adjective to mean "healthy."

EXAMPLE   She looked **well** after her test.

had of   See **could of.**

had ought, hadn't ought   Unlike other verbs, *ought* is not used with *had*.

EXAMPLE   Mary **ought to** [*not* had ought to] tell the truth.

hardly, scarcely   The words *hardly* and *scarcely* are negative words. They should never be used with other negative words.

EXAMPLES   Grandfather **could** [*not* couldn't] **hardly** believe it.
He **had** [*not* hadn't] **scarcely** begun his Ta-Na-E-Ka when he found a dead deer.

NOTE   *Feel good* and *feel well* mean different things. *Feel good* means "feel happy or pleased." *Feel well* means "feel healthy."

EXAMPLES   She felt **good** [*happy*] about her Ta-Na-E-Ka.
But Roger didn't feel **well** [*healthy*] at all and had lost weight.

he, she, they   Avoid using a pronoun along with its antecedent as the subject of a verb. This error is called the **double subject.**

NONSTANDARD   Ray Bradbury he wrote "All Summer in a Day."

STANDARD   Ray Bradbury wrote "All Summer in a Day."

hisself   *Hisself* is nonstandard English. Use *himself.*

EXAMPLE   He fed **himself** [*not* hisself] on that deer the whole time.

how come   In informal situations, *how come* is often used instead of *why*. In formal situations, *why* should always be used.

INFORMAL   I don't know how come Roger didn't think of it.

FORMAL   I don't know **why** Roger didn't think of it.

its, it's   *Its* is a personal pronoun in the possessive form. *It's* is a contraction of *it is* or *it has*. See page 877.

EXAMPLES   **Its** purpose is to build confidence. [possessive pronoun]
It's called Ta-Na-E-Ka. [contraction of *it is*]
It's been practiced for many years. [contraction of *it has*]

kind, sort, type   The words *this, that, these*, and *those* should agree in number with the words *kind, sort*, and *type*.

EXAMPLES   Have you ever read **that kind** of story before?
Have you ever read **those kinds** of stories before?

kind of, sort of   In informal situations, *kind of* and *sort of* are often used to mean "somewhat" or "rather." In formal English, *somewhat* or *rather* is preferred.

INFORMAL   Mary seemed kind of upset about the ritual.

FORMAL   Mary seemed **somewhat** upset about the ritual.

learn, teach   *Learn* means "gain knowledge." *Teach* means "instruct" or "show how."

EXAMPLES   The young people **learned** how to survive in the wilderness.
Their parents **taught** them what foods to eat.

less   See **fewer, less.**

lie, lay   See page 830.

might of, must of   See **could of.**

nowheres   See **anywheres,** etc.

of   Do not use *of* with other prepositions such as *inside, off*, and *outside.*

EXAMPLES   She waited **outside** [*not* outside of] the restaurant.
Jesse dared me to jump **off** [*not* off of] the dock.

☑ QUICK CHECK I

Revise each of the following sentences to correct any error in usage. A sentence may contain more than one error.

EXAMPLE 1. How come cultures need rituals?
       1. *Why do cultures need rituals?*

1. A ritual marks time and personal changes, and it's tradition holds a society together.
2. Perhaps you have all ready participated in a ritual and found it was quite a exciting experience.
3. A ritual don't always involve danger, though.
4. However, alot of rituals can be dangerous.
5. I wonder if I could of done as good as Mary.

ought to of See **could of.**

rise, raise See pages 830–831.

scarcely See **hardly, scarcely.**

should of See **could of.**

sit, set See page 829.

somewheres See **anywheres,** etc.

sort See **kind, sort, type.**

sort of See **kind of, sort of.**

take See **bring, take.**

teach See **learn, teach.**

than, then *Than* is a conjunction used in making comparisons. *Then* is an adverb that means "at that time."

EXAMPLES Are dogs friendlier **than** cats?
       Back **then,** Dog and Cat were best friends.

that See **who, which, that.**

that there See **this here, that there.**

their, there, they're *Their* is used to show ownership. *There* is used to mean "at that place" or to begin a sentence. *They're* is a contraction of *they are.* See page 877.

EXAMPLES Won't **their** parents be pleased?
       They will go into the woods over **there.**
       There are many ways to gain self-confidence.
       They're leaving today for their Ta-Na-E-Ka.

theirself, theirselves *Theirself* and *theirselves* are nonstandard English. Use *themselves*.

EXAMPLE Dog and Cat found **themselves** [*not* theirself *or* theirselves] a home with Adam and Eve.

them *Them* should not be used as an adjective. Use *those*.

EXAMPLE Have you read all **those** [*not* them] poems about machines?

this here, that there *Here* and *there* are not necessary after *this* and *that*.

EXAMPLES **This** [*not* this here] cricket doesn't taste much worse than **that** [*not* that there] berry.

this kind, sort, type See **kind, sort, type.**

use to, used to Be sure to add the *–d* to *use*. *Used to* is in the past tense.

EXAMPLE Kaw young **used to** [*not* use to] paint themselves white before their journey.

way, ways Use *way*, not *ways*, in referring to a distance.

EXAMPLE They were quite a **way** [*not* ways] from home.

well See **good, well.**

when, where Do not use *when* or *where* incorrectly in writing a definition.

NONSTANDARD The ritual Ta-Na-E-Ka is when young men and women journey alone into the wilderness for several days.

STANDARD The ritual Ta-Na-E-Ka is a journey taken by young men and women, who go alone into the wilderness for several days.

where Do not use *where* for *that*.

EXAMPLE I read **that** [*not* where] Ta-Na-E-Ka is still practiced today.

who, which, that The relative pronoun *who* refers to people only; *which* refers to things only; *that* refers to either people or things.

EXAMPLES The man and woman **who** were sitting next to us cheered.
The player dropped the ball, **which** was wet from the rain.
He made an error **that** allowed the other team to score.

would of See **could of.**

your, you're   *Your* shows possession. *You're* is the contraction of *you are.*

EXAMPLES   **Your** story was very interesting.
You're part of a long tradition.

QUICK CHECK 2

Revise each of the following sentences to correct any error in usage. A sentence may contain more than one error.

EXAMPLE   1. This here story tells about a Kaw ritual.
1. *This story tells about a Kaw ritual.*

1. The Kaw people treated one another good.
2. Take the time to research you're own culture's past.
3. Perhaps your a member of more then one culture.
4. Your family's traditions can learn you about yourself.
5. My family use to celebrate births and christenings in special ways.

Using a Variety of Adverbs

In informal situations, the adjective *real* is often used as an adverb meaning "very" or "extremely." In formal situations, *very, extremely,* or another adverb is preferred.

INFORMAL   Ta-Na-E-Ka is a real important event in the Kaw culture.

FORMAL   Ta-Na-E-Ka is an **extremely** important event in the Kaw culture.

Try It Out

Revise each of the following sentences by substituting an adverb for the word *real.*

1. In Grandfather's time, Ta-Na-E-Ka was *real* dangerous.
2. Life alone in the wilderness was *real* hard.
3. However, the endurance trial was *real* exciting, too.
4. These traditions have survived a *real* long time.
5. Ernie doesn't understand that people must learn self-sufficiency *real* young.

Spelling Handbook

COMMONLY MISSPELLED WORDS

Some words that cause spelling problems need to be memorized. The list of fifty "demons" below contains words that you should be able to spell automatically, without pause. Note the letters that are underlined. These letters are the ones that students most often miss when attempting to spell each word correctly.

FIFTY SPELLING DEMONS

ache	cough	guess	ready	though
again	could	half	said	through
always	country	hour	says	tired
answer	doctor	instead	seems	tonight
blue	does	knew	shoes	trouble
built	don't	know	since	wear
busy	early	laid	straight	where
buy	easy	minute	sugar	women
can't	every	often	sure	won't
color	friend	once	tear	write

ONE HUNDRED SPELLING WORDS

The list that follows includes words that you should know. They are grouped by tens so that you may study them group by group. Again, the underlining points out places in the words that may give you the most trouble.

ONE HUNDRED SPELLING WORDS

absence	century	explanation	myth	rumor
achieve	choice	fantasy	nuclear	safe
adjective	communicate	faucet	occurrence	seize
advertisement	conservation	fiction	ounce	separate
against	constitution	fourth	passage	similar
aisles	courteous	gasoline	pesticide	solar
angle	criticism	gene	physical	solemn
apology	curiosity	genuine	pieces	species
arithmetic	decimal	grammar	poisonous	surface
assignment	delicate	height	popularity	temporary
autobiography	disguise	heir	population	theme
average	divide	humorous	practice	tragedy
bacteria	early	imitation	preferred	treasure
ballad	ecology	interview	prejudice	trial
benefit	eighth	legislature	pyramid	tropical
brief	environment	liter	recipe	vegetable
brilliant	equipment	magazine	remainder	veil
career	exact	medicine	rescue	weapon
careless	excellent	message	resources	wonder
ceased	experience	musician	review	wrestle

Communications Handbook

The Reference Section

Every library has materials you can use only in the library. Some examples are listed below. (Some reference works are available in both print and electronic form.)

Encyclopedias
Collier's Encyclopedia
The World Book Encyclopedia

General Biographical References
Current Biography Yearbook
The International Who's Who
Webster's New Biographical Dictionary

Special Biographical References
American Men & Women of Science
Biographical Dictionary of American Sports
Mexican American Biographies

Atlases
Atlas of World Cultures
National Geographic Atlas of the World

Almanacs
Information Please Almanac
The World Almanac and Book of Facts

Books of Quotations
Bartlett's Familiar Quotations

Books of Synonyms
Roget's International Thesaurus
Webster's New Dictionary of Synonyms

RESEARCH STRATEGIES

Using a Media Center or Library

To find a book, audiotape, film, or video in a library, start by looking in the **catalog.** Most libraries use an **online,** or computer, **catalog.**

Online catalogs vary from library to library. With some you begin searching for resources by **title, author,** or **subject.** With others you simply enter **keywords** for the subject you're researching. With either system, you enter information into the computer and a new screen will show you a list of materials or subject headings relating to your request. When you find an item you want, write down the title, author, and **call number,** the code of numbers and letters that shows you where to find the item on the library's shelves.

Some libraries still use card catalogs. A **card catalog** is a collection of index cards arranged in alphabetical order by title and author. Nonfiction is also cataloged by subject.

Electronic Databases. Electronic databases are collections of information you can access by computer. You can use these databases to find such resources as encyclopedias, almanacs, and museum art collections.

There are two kinds of electronic databases: **Online databases** are accessed at a computer terminal connected to a modem. The modem allows the computer to communicate with other computers over telephone lines. **Portable databases** are available on CD-ROM.

A **CD-ROM** (compact disc-read only memory) is played on a computer equipped with a CD-ROM player. If you were to look up *Maya Angelou* on a CD-ROM guide to literature, for example, you could see and hear her reading passages from her books and also read critical analyses of her work.

Periodicals. Most libraries have a collection of magazines and newspapers. To find up-to-date magazine or newspaper articles on a topic, use a computerized index, such as *InfoTrac* or *EBSCO.* Some of these indices provide a summary of each article. Others provide the entire text, which you can read on-screen or print out. *The Readers' Guide to Periodical Literature* is a print index of articles that have appeared in hundreds of magazines.

Using the Internet

The **Internet** is a huge network of computers. Libraries, news services, government agencies, researchers, and organizations communicate and share information on the Net. The Net also lets you chat online with students around the world. For help in using the Internet to do research or to communicate with someone by computer, explore the options on the following page.

The World Wide Web

The easiest way to do research on the Internet is on the World Wide Web. On the Web, information is stored in colorful, easy-to-access files called **Web pages.** Web pages usually have text, graphics, photographs, sound, and even video clips.

Using a Web Browser. You look at Web pages with a **Web browser,** a program for accessing information on the Web. Every page on the Web has its own address, called a **URL,** or Uniform Resource Locator. If you know the address of a Web page you want to go to, just enter it in the location field on your browser.

Hundreds of millions of Web pages are connected by **hyperlinks,** which let you jump from one page to another. These links usually appear as underlined or colored words or images, or both, on your computer screen. With hundreds of millions of linked Web pages, how can you find the information you want?

Using a Web Directory. If you're just beginning to look for a research topic, click on a **Web directory,** a list of topics and subtopics created by experts to help users find Web sites. Think of the directory as a giant index. Start by choosing a broad category, such as Literature. Then, work your way down through the subtopics, perhaps from Poetry to Poets. Under Poets, choose a Web page that looks interesting, perhaps one on Robert Frost.

Using a Search Engine. If you already have a topic and need information about it, try using a **search engine,** a software tool that finds information on the Web. To use a search engine, just go to an online search form and enter a **search term,** or keyword. The search engine will return a list of Web pages containing your search term. The list will also show you the first few lines of each page.

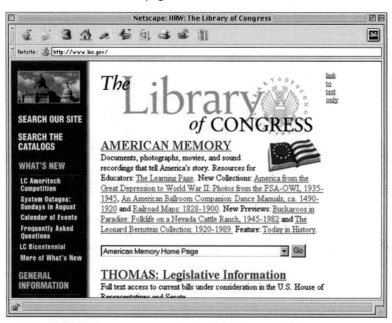

Techno Tip

- If you get too few hits, use a more general word or phrase as your search term.

- If you get too many hits, use a more specific word or phrase as your search term.

COMMON TOP-LEVEL DOMAINS AND WHAT THEY STAND FOR	
.edu	Educational institution. Site may publish scholarly work or the work of elementary or high school students.
.gov	Government body. Information should be reliable.
.org	Usually a nonprofit organization. If the organization promotes culture (as a museum does), information is generally reliable; if it advocates a cause, information may be biased.
.com	Commercial enterprise. Information should be evaluated carefully.
.net	Organization offering Internet services.

COMMON SEARCH OPERATORS AND WHAT THEY DO	
AND	Demands that both terms appear on the page; narrows search
+	Demands that both terms appear on the page; narrows search
OR	Yields pages that contain either term; widens search
NOT	Excludes a word from consideration; narrows search
–	Excludes a word from consideration; narrows search
NEAR	Demands that two words be close together; narrows search
ADJ	Demands that two words be close together; narrows search
" "	Demands an exact phrase; narrows search

A search term such as *Frost* may produce thousands of results, or **hits,** including weather data on frost. If you're doing a search on the poet Robert Frost, most of these thousands of hits will be of no use. To find useful material, you have to narrow your search.

Refining a Keyword Search. To focus your research, use **search operators,** such as the words AND or NOT, to create a string of keywords. If you're looking for material on Robert Frost and his life in Vermont, for example, you might enter the following search terms:

Frost AND Vermont NOT weather

The more focused search term yields pages that contain both *Frost* and *Vermont* and nothing about weather. The chart at the bottom left explains how several search operators work.

Evaluating Web Sources

Since anyone—you, for example—can publish a Web page, it's important to evaluate your sources. Use these criteria to evaluate a source:

Authority. Who is the author? What is his or her knowledge or experience? Trust respected sources, such as the Smithsonian Institution, not a person's newsletter or home page.

Accuracy. How trustworthy is the information? Does the author give his or her sources? Check information from one site against information from at least two other sites or print sources.

Objectivity. What is the author's **perspective,** or point of view? Find out whether the information provider has a bias or a hidden purpose.

Currency. Is the information up-to-date? For a print source, check the copyright date. For a Web source, look for the date on which the page was created or revised. (This date appears at the bottom of the site's home page.)

Coverage. How well does the source cover the topic? Could you find better information in a book? Compare the source with several others.

Listing Sources and Taking Notes

When you write a research paper, you must **document,** or identify, your sources so that readers will know where you found your material. You must avoid **plagiarism,** or presenting another writer's words or ideas as if they were your own.

Listing Sources

List each source, and give it a number. (You'll use these source numbers later, when you take notes.) Here's where to find the publication information (such as the name of the publisher and the copyright date) you'll need for different types of sources:

- **Print sources.** Look at the title and copyright pages of the book or periodical.
- **Online sources.** Look at the beginning or end of the document or in a separate electronic file. For a Web page, look for a link containing the word *About.*
- **Portable electronic databases.** Look at the start-up screen, the packaging, or the disk itself.

There are several ways to list sources. The chart on page 897 shows the style created by the Modern Language Association.

Taking Notes

Here are some tips for taking notes:

- Put notes from different sources on separate index cards or sheets of paper or in separate computer files.
- At the top of each card, sheet of paper, or file, write a label that briefly gives the subject of the note.
- At the bottom, write the numbers of the pages on which you found the information.
- Use short phrases, and make lists of details and ideas. You don't have to write full sentences.
- Use your own words unless you find material you want to quote. If you quote an author's exact words, put quotation marks around them.
- Include in your notes opinions from experts and analogies (or comparisons to more familiar topics or situations).
- Take notes from a variety of sources, including those with different perspectives, or opinions, on your topic.

The sample note card at the right shows how to take notes.

Techno Tip

To evaluate a Web source, look at the top-level domain in the URL. Here is a sample URL with the top-level domain—a government agency—labeled.

top-level domain

http://www.loc.gov

Sample Note Card

Bradbury on Education   3

—Teach "tools" of reading & writing at
  gr. K–2; no Internet till gr. 3

—"Teach students to be in love with life,
  to love their work, to create at the
  top of their lungs."   p. F1

Preparing a List of Sources

Use your source cards to make a **works cited** list at the end of your report. List your sources in alphabetical order, following the MLA guidelines for citing sources (see the chart below). Note the sample that follows:

Works Cited

"Bradbury, Ray." The World Book Encyclopedia. 2003 ed.

Geirland, John. "Interview with Ray Bradbury." The Fresno Bee 3 Jan. 1999: F1.

Mogen, David. Ray Bradbury. New York: Macmillan, 1986.

The chart below shows citations of print, audiovisual, and electronic sources:

MLA GUIDELINES FOR CITING SOURCES	
Books	Give the author, title, city of publication, publisher, and copyright year. Mogen, David. Ray Bradbury. New York: Macmillan, 1986.
Magazine and newspaper articles	Give the author, title of the article, name of the magazine or newspaper, date, and page numbers. Geirland, John. "Interview with Ray Bradbury." The Fresno Bee 3 Jan. 1999 F1.
Encyclopedia articles	Give the author (if named), title of the article, name of the encyclopedia, and edition (year). "Bradbury, Ray." The World Book Encyclopedia. 2003 ed.
Films, videotapes, and audiotapes	Give the title, producer or director, medium, distributor, and year of release. Ray Bradbury: Tales of Fantasy. Listening Library Productions. Audiocassette. Filmic Archives, 1992.
CD-ROMs and DVDs	In many cases, not all the information is available. Fill in what you can. Give the author, title of document or article; database title; publication medium (use the term *CD-ROM* or *DVD*); city of publication; publisher; date. "Science Fiction." Britannica Student Encyclopedia 2004. DVD. Chicago: Encyclopedia Britannica, 2004.
Online sources	In many cases, not all the information is available. Fill in what you can. Give the author, title of document or article; title of complete work or database; name of editor; publication date or date last revised; name of sponsoring organization; date you accessed the site; the full URL in angle brackets. Jepsen, Chris. *Ray Bradbury Online*. 2001. 20 Dec. 2003. <http://www.spacecity.com/bradbury/bradbury/>.

PROOFREADERS' MARKS

Symbol	Example	Meaning
≡	New mexico	Capitalize lowercase letter.
/	next $\cancel{S}$pring	Lowercase capital letter.
∧	a book∧quotations *of*	Insert.
℘	A good go℘d idea	Delete.
∩∪	a grape ∪fruit tree	Close up space.
∿	does'∿t	Change order (of letters or words).
¶	¶"Who's there," she asked.	Begin a new paragraph.
⊙	Please don't forget⊙	Add a period.
∧	Maya∧did you call me?	Add a comma.
⟨:⟩	Dear Mrs. Mills⟨:⟩	Add a colon.
∧̦	Columbus, Ohio∧̦ Dallas, Texas	Add a semicolon.
ᵛ ᵛ	ᵛAre you OK?ᵛ he asked.	Add quotation marks.

Giving and Listening to an Oral Narrative

Choosing a Narrative

To choose a story to tell, first consider your **audience, purpose,** and **occasion.** Ask yourself

- *Who will listen to my narrative?*
- *What effect do I want to have on my audience?*
- *When and where will I present my narrative?*

Answering these questions will help you choose the right **message.** For example, if your purpose is to scare your classmates, you might choose to tell a ghost story. If your purpose is to amuse young children, then you might choose a very different narrative, such as the tale of the three little pigs.

Once you have chosen an appropriate story, jot down the basic **plot** events in a **time line.** The **organizational structure** of most stories will be in **time order.**

Planning Your Presentation

An introduction will help prepare listeners to understand your oral narrative. In your introduction, do the following.

- Make a **connection** between your listeners and the story. Use what you know about your audience to ask them a question or mention a common experience that relates to the subject of the story.
- Explain your **reasons** for choosing the narrative you are presenting.
- Establish the **context** of the narrative, telling listeners any important information about the **setting** and identifying the **point of view** from which you will tell the story (for example, a narrator may tell the story or the story may be told by one of its characters).

To plan how to tell the story you have chosen, first think about the events that make up the plot and about the characters. Then, consider these techniques for telling about the events and characters in a vivid, entertaining way.

Sensory Details and Concrete Language You should use **descriptive strategies** to bring the characters and events in your oral narrative to life. These strategies include using *sensory details* and *concrete language*. **Sensory details** appeal to the senses—describing sights, sounds, smells, tastes, or sensations. **Concrete language** uses specific words to give readers an exact mental image of what you are describing.

Rhetorical Devices **Rhetorical devices** can add to your presentation's impact on listeners and make it more memorable. Think about where you might add some of the rhetorical devices in the following chart to the story you have chosen.

TYPES OF RHETORICAL DEVICES	
Rhetorical Device	**Effect**
Rhythm (Cadence): the beat of the words, created through the words' stressed syllables, their arrangement, and sentence length	Creates mood and can build suspense
Onomatopoeia: a word whose sound imitates its meaning	Helps listeners to hear the sounds you are describing
Repetition: repeating key words, phrases, or sounds	Emphasizes important ideas or events, can add humor, provides coherence

Delivering an oral narrative means more than just talking. When you present **dialogue** from a story, you adjust your own voice to re-create the characters' speech and communicate a different personality for each character. You can also use your voice to keep listeners involved in the narrative by communicating *tone, mood,* and *emotion*.

- **Tone** is the overall feeling of an oral communication. The sound of your voice and your choice of words will indicate the tone of the **message** to your listeners.

- **Mood** is the general emotional state of a particular character or speaker.

- **Emotion** is a speaker's or character's feeling about a particular thing or event.

Making Delivery Notes

To help you remember all of the elements of your oral narrative, add delivery notes to your time line. Imagine yourself telling your story to an audience, and jot down ideas about the items listed at the bottom of page 900 and about *verbal* and *nonverbal elements* you want to include. **Verbal elements** include **rate, volume,** and **vocal modulation,** or **pitch**—the high or low sounds of your voice. **Nonverbal elements** include **gestures, facial expressions, posture,** and **eye contact**.

Rehearsing and Presenting

An entertaining oral narrative doesn't just happen—it takes lots of practice. Follow these guidelines:

- Practice the gestures and facial expressions you will use. Use your body and your voice to show the characters in distinctive ways.
- Practice speaking slowly, clearly, and loudly enough so that someone in the back of the classroom will be able to understand you.
- If possible, record your practice session on audiotape or videotape. Then, carefully evaluate it. Make any necessary changes. If you do not have access to a tape recorder or a video camera, practice in front of a mirror.

When you feel comfortable with all of the elements of your presentation, present your oral narrative to the class.

Listening to an Oral Narrative

When you listen to an oral narrative, consider the **verbal elements**—*volume, pitch,* and *rate*—of the presentation. Notice also the speaker's use of **nonverbal elements**—*gestures, posture, eye contact,* and *facial expressions.* Watch to see whether the verbal and nonverbal elements match. For example, the speaker may gesture and raise his or her voice at the same time to emphasize an important event. To evaluate a narrative and provide feedback to the speaker, make notes in response to these questions as you listen:

- What is the overall **tone** of the oral narrative? Explain how the words and the voice and gestures the speaker used to communicate those words helped you figure out the tone.
- What is the general **mood** of each character? What verbal and nonverbal elements helped communicate each character's mood?
- What specific **feelings,** or **emotions,** can you identify in the narrative? What verbal and nonverbal elements helped you identify each emotion?
- Where and why does the speaker use rhetorical devices such as **rhythm, onomatopoeia,** or **repetition**? How effective is each device?

Giving and Listening to an Oral Response to Literature

Planning Your Oral Response

Giving an **oral response** to a piece of literature allows you to share information about a written work. The information here will help you prepare an oral response to a short story. Your **focus** will be your interpretation of the story's theme.

Choose a story you'd like to speak about. (You may want to adapt an essay you've already written on a short story.) Start to prepare your oral response by writing brief sentences about the characters, setting, plot, and your **interpretation** of the theme on note cards to help you remember each idea you want to share. Include also **evidence** to support your ideas about the story's theme. (Leave plenty of space on each note card. You will need that space for other notes that will help you deliver your ideas effectively.)

Once you have your ideas on the note cards, you can **organize** them in a logical order. Number your note cards in the order that you want to present your ideas.

Since the **occasion,** or the situation that prompts you to speak, is a class assignment, your **audience** will be your teacher and classmates. To present your **message** in an effective way, you need to consider your audience's backgrounds and interests. For example, if your audience is not familiar with the short story you are sharing, you may want to provide more details about the plot or characters. If you know that your audience will not understand a particular word, you will want to define it. Making the content of your oral response match your audience will help you achieve your **purpose**—to share information.

Delivering Your Oral Response

To become a good public speaker, you must use more than just words. **Nonverbal** communication, or body language, adds to your message. The chart below lists some ideas on how you can include nonverbal elements in your oral response:

USING NONVERBAL ELEMENTS

Nonverbal Element	Examples
Eye contact	Look into the eyes of your audience to keep your audience's attention.
Facial expression	Smile, frown, or raise an eyebrow to show your feelings or to emphasize parts of your message.
Gestures	Give a thumbs up, shrug, nod, or shake your head to emphasize a point or to add meaning to your speech.
Posture	Stand tall and straight to show that you are sure of yourself.

How you use your voice can also affect the message that you give your audience. Consider the **verbal elements** in the chart below as you practice and deliver your speech:

USING VERBAL ELEMENTS

Verbal Element	Explanation
Feeling	Show enthusiasm through your voice so that your audience will become enthusiastic about your response.
Pitch (or vocal modulation)	Your voice rises and falls naturally when you speak. Capture the audience's attention by using the pitch of your voice to emphasize key points.
Rate (or tempo)	In conversations you may speak at a fast rate, or speed. When you make a speech, you should talk more slowly to help listeners understand you.
Tone (or mood)	The mood of your presentation should be informative. Strive to maintain an objective point of view. The tone of your voice should show that you are knowledgeable about the short story.
Volume	You will need to speak loudly when giving your oral response. The listeners at the back of the room should be able to hear you clearly.

To help you remember all of the verbal and nonverbal elements you want to include in your oral response, make delivery notes. Consider writing your delivery notes on your note cards in a color different from that of your speaking notes.

Practice your oral response out loud and standing up. Practice it over and over until all the words are familiar and you are comfortable with all the gestures, movements, and facial expressions you want to include. Practice with a friend or in front of a mirror, or use a tape recorder or videorecorder to figure out what parts of your presentation need work.

Listening to an Oral Response

An effective listener considers not only the words being said but also the speaker's verbal and nonverbal messages. When you listen to an oral response to literature, you can gain a deeper understanding of the story and evaluate the speaker's techniques at the same time.

As you listen to an oral response, make notes on content and delivery. You might ask the following questions:

Content

- What is the main idea in the speaker's response?

- What support does the speaker provide for the main idea?

Delivery

- Does the speaker talk loudly and clearly? Explain.

- How would you describe the speaker's tone? Does it fit the speaker's purpose?

- Do the speaker's nonverbal techniques (posture, gestures) relate to the speaker's verbal techniques (pitch, mood, tone)? Explain.

- Does the speaker emphasize key points with his or her voice or gestures? Explain.

Giving and Listening to an Informative Speech

Preparing a Report for a Speech

What makes a good speech? As you get ready to make an informative speech, focus on these elements:

- **Think about the purpose and occasion.** Are you giving an informal speech to your class, or is your speech part of a formal evaluation? Think about how these factors affect your word choice and delivery.

- **Limit your speech to your report's major ideas and the evidence you need to clarify and support** those ideas. When giving evidence, make sure you tell your audience where you found that information.

- **Adjust your word choice** so that your audience can easily understand your ideas and learn from your speech.

- **Use a simple outline** to deliver your speech, rather than simply reading your report. Speaking from a simple outline will make your speech sound more conversational and natural.

- **Avoid speaking too quickly or too slowly or too loudly or too softly.** In other words, use an effective **rate** and **volume** for your audience.

- **Use the pitch, or the highs and lows, of your voice to create an enthusiastic tone.** If the tone of your voice suggests that you do not care about your speech, your audience is likely to feel the same.

Using Visuals in an Informative Speech

Avoid getting caught up in "chartmania," the mysterious disease that affects speakers who use too many visuals. Having one or two well-chosen visuals is better than having too many. Whatever the number of visuals you decide to use, each one should have the same purpose: to complement and extend the meaning of an important point.

Posters, Pictures, Charts, and Graphs If you decide that using a poster, picture, chart, or graph is essential to your presentation, follow these tips:

- Make sure all words and pictures are large enough to be seen clearly from the back of the room.

- Be sure to describe in words what the visual means.

- When explaining a visual, face the audience.

Overhead Projectors or Presentation Software One of the best ways to use visuals that everyone can see is to use a projector. By creating transparencies of your visuals, you can make them large or small by moving the projector away from or closer to the screen. Some projectors even project images from a word-processing program or presentation software. If you choose to use a projector, consider these tips:

- Use dark colors for your text and pictures.

- Make your graphic simple. A cluttered design is confusing.

- Have a backup plan in case the projector breaks or is unavailable.

Video- or Audiotaped Segments Sometimes the best way to demonstrate your point is by using a video- or audiotaped segment. Here are some tips for using a video or audio clip:

- The clip should be fairly short; it should support your presentation, not replace it.

- Have your tape cued up before you speak so that the audience does not have to wait for you to rewind or fast-forward it.

- Test your equipment before your audience arrives.

Running through your entire presentation—visuals and all—a few times will help you avoid making mistakes on speech day. Practice delivering your speech as if you were in front of the class. If you are using note cards or visuals, practice using them too. Keep practicing until you are able to get through the speech once without stopping.

Listening to an Informative Speech

An informative speech often contains so much information that you might have trouble absorbing it all. To make the most of the informative speeches you hear, follow the steps listed in the chart below:

QUESTIONS FOR EVALUATING AN INFORMATIVE SPEECH	
Content	• **Determine your purpose.** Identify what you want to learn from listening to this speech.
	• **Make Predictions.** Identify two or three points you expect the speaker to cover.
	• **Get ready.** Have pen or pencil and paper ready for taking notes.
Delivery	• **Devote your full attention to the speaker.** Looking around the room or doing another assignment is discourteous and will prevent you from learning all you can.
	• **Listen for cues that signal main points.** Cues can also include these words and phrases: *first, second,* and *finally; there are many reasons or causes; the most important thing is;* and *in conclusion.* Hearing these cues is the key to understanding, interpreting, and organizing the information you hear in the speech.
	• **Summarize the main points of the speech.** As you listen, take notes by summarizing the speaker's main points and supporting details.
Credibility (Believability)	• **Monitor your understanding.** Ask yourself if the speaker covered all of the points you expected. If not, what did he or she leave out? Ask the speaker to clarify.

Giving and Evaluating a Persuasive Speech

Adapting a Persuasive Essay

You may want to adapt the persuasive essay you wrote for the Writing Workshop on pages 762–767. If so, the **position** (or **point of view**) at the heart of your speech will be the same one you took in the essay. Your specific **purpose** for arguing your position may change, depending on your speech **audience.** Before you adapt your essay, consider the **occasion,** or situation that prompts you to speak. Since the occasion for your speech is a class assignment, you know your audience will be your classmates. To match your specific purpose to this audience, ask yourself these questions:

- *Will my audience tend to agree or disagree with my opinion?*
- *Are they willing to get involved in a cause?*

The answers to these questions will help you figure out whether you should push for action on your issue or simply try to open your audience members' minds.

Relevant Reasons and Evidence If your classmates were not part of the audience for your persuasive essay, you may need to change elements of your **message** to appeal to their interests and backgrounds.

Visual and Media Displays You can make your speech more convincing by using visual and media displays, such as charts, graphs, illustrations, or video segments. These displays may be made by hand or with technology.

You want your message to be clear, but you also want it to be memorable. **Rhetorical devices,** effective writing and speaking techniques, can help you emphasize your major points and develop a memorable message. As you plan your message, think about where you might include the following devices:

- **Cadence** refers to the rhythmic rise and fall of your voice as you speak. Varying your sentence lengths will allow you to achieve a rhythmic cadence. Without cadence your voice may become a monotone, and your words may sound dull and uninteresting.
- **Repetitive patterns** are words or phrases that are repeated to stress their importance. By repeating a word or phrase throughout a speech, you make it easier for your audience to remember your main points.

Organizing Your Speech You have a clear opinion, relevant evidence to support it, and rhetorical strategies to make your points memorable. Now you will need to be sure your information is organized in a way that will persuade your audience. Whether your speech includes reasons and evidence from your essay or new information, plan to place your most appealing reasons at the point in your speech where they will pack the biggest punch. You can either

- begin with your most important reason and supporting evidence to grab your listeners' attention

or

- end with your most important reason and supporting evidence to leave your listeners with a strong impression

Also, plan to make your ideas **coherent,** or clearly connected, for listeners by using **transitions,** such as *for this reason* and *most important.*

Developing Your Delivery

Your ideas may not be persuasive if you do not deliver them effectively—for example, if you get rattled by distractions, mumble, or have trouble operating the audio or visual equipment. To avoid these types of problems, practice your speech before delivering it. As you practice, concentrate on using *nonverbal* and *verbal elements,* using visual and media displays, and handling distractions.

When you speak, you communicate a message not only with the words you say but also with **verbal elements** (how your voice expresses those words) and **nonverbal elements** (what your face and body do as you say the words). Aligning these elements by matching your voice and movements can add to the impact of your message and make you a more effective and persuasive speaker.

Verbal Elements *Rate, volume, pitch,* and *tone* are all examples of verbal elements. When you give a persuasive speech, it is important to speak at a slow **rate** so your audience can keep up with what you are saying. You should also speak at a loud enough **volume** so the people in the back of the room can hear you. Varying your **vocal modulation,** or **pitch**—the high or low notes of your speaking voice—can help keep your audience interested. Adjusting the **tone,** or attitude, of your voice to match your message helps the audience know your feelings about the issue. When giving a persuasive speech, your tone should be enthusiastic and believable so your audience will accept your opinion.

Nonverbal Elements Your **posture, eye contact** with the audience, **gestures,** and **facial expressions** are examples of nonverbal elements. Standing tall while looking directly at your audience shows that you are confident, and using appropriate gestures and facial expressions can **emphasize** important ideas. For example, if you were to ask a question such as *Is this the best way to solve the problem?* you could demonstrate your own uncertainty by shrugging your shoulders and raising your eyebrows.

Visual and Media Displays Visual and media displays can make a powerful case for your opinion. Use these tips as you prepare to deliver your speech:

- Make sure all audience members can see your displays.

- Make sure you have all the audio and visual equipment that you need and that it is working properly. Cue your video or audio clips to the correct starting point ahead of time.

- Use an easel, if available, for graphs, charts, and other hand-held visuals.

- If you use presentation software, make sure your computer is loaded with the necessary program. Make sure the computer and program are running properly.

Listening and Evaluating

As your classmates deliver their speeches, listen carefully. Your purpose for listening to a persuasive speech will be to understand the speaker's position and evaluate his or her ideas. To listen effectively, you must consider the *content* and *delivery* of the speech.

As you listen to the speeches of your classmates, ask yourself the following questions about the **content** of the speech, and note your responses on a sheet of paper:

- What is the speaker's opinion? Is it clearly stated?

- How effectively does the speaker support his or her opinion with relevant evidence and visual or media displays? How strong is the evidence? How well do the visuals support the message?

- Which rhetorical devices, such as **cadence, repetitive patterns,** and **onomatopoeia,** does the speaker use? How do these devices help the speech achieve its purpose?
- How is the speech organized? Does this organization seem logical to you? Why or why not?

As you listen to your classmates' speeches, you will also need to evaluate their **delivery** skills. Ask yourself the following questions about each speaker's delivery, and note your responses on a sheet of paper:

- Does the speaker talk loudly and slowly enough?
- How effectively does the speaker vary the **pitch** of his or her voice?
- What is the speaker's **tone,** or attitude toward the issue? How well does the tone match the speaker's message?
- Do the speaker's **posture** and **eye contact** show confidence and make the message seem believable?
- How well do the speaker's nonverbal messages, such as **gestures** and **facial expressions,** match the verbal message?

Giving and Listening to a Problem-Solution Speech

A **problem-solution speech** is a type of **oral exposition**—an explanation given out loud to an audience. The first step in planning a problem-solution speech is to identify a problem. (You may want to adapt the problem-solution essay you wrote for the Writing Workshop on pages 206–211.) Follow the guidelines below for selecting a problem:

- The problem should directly affect your audience.
- The solutions you propose should be ones your listeners can use.

Avoid selecting a problem your listeners are not affected by or cannot help solve.

Defining the Problem A focused problem-solution speech should define the problem and provide **evidence** to prove the existence of the problem. You can research the problem by interviewing people, viewing Web sites, and reading newspaper and magazine articles.

Explaining Causes and Effects Once you have defined the problem, identify the problem's most important **causes** and **effects.** To identify causes and effects, think about or research the problem. Make note of one or two causes of the problem as well as the one or two most common or noticeable effects of the problem.

Solving the Problem After explaining the problem and its causes and effects, plan to provide your listeners with two solutions that they could use themselves. A good solution should

- limit the causes of the problem, or
- reduce the effects of the problem

Introduction
> Problem: sibling rivalry
>> *example of typical behavior*
> Causes: feelings of competition; parent favoritism
>> *facts from book: Siblings Without Rivalry*
> Effects: hurt feelings; loss of adult relationship w/ sibling
>> *quote from Siblings. . . on emotional damage*

Solution 1: share feelings
describe behavior
- reduces competitiveness
opinion of school counselor
- strengthens relationships
anecdote from experience

Solution 2: focus on strengths
describe behavior
- reduces competitiveness
anecdote from experience
- makes sibling feel better, not worse
make comparison

Conclusion
- summary of the problem and solutions

In order for listeners to accept your solutions, you will need to support your explanation of each solution with **evidence.** Evidence includes facts, examples, descriptions, and statements made by experts. You can find evidence by doing research and by thinking of your own experience with the problem.

Avoid trying to persuade the audience to choose a particular solution, though; your **purpose** for speaking is simply to provide information.

Planning Your Speech   Your next step in planning a speech is to organize the problem, causes, effects, solutions, and evidence you have gathered. Consider creating note cards or a graphic organizer such as the example on this page.

In the introduction, explain the problem's causes and effects. In the body, provide evidence, as shown in blue in the example. To leave listeners with a strong impression, put the best solution last. (This organizational structure is known as **reverse order of importance.**) Finally, conclude your speech by summarizing your problem and your solutions. You may also want to explain the benefits of solving the problem.

Practicing Your Speech Run through your speech several times, relying only on your graphic organizer or note cards and your memory to practice elaborating on the ideas you have noted. Once you are comfortable with the content of your speech, it is time to rehearse as if you were delivering that content to your audience.

Listening to a Problem-Solution Speech Your job is not finished when your presentation ends. You should listen carefully and politely to your classmates' presentations in order to learn from them. As you watch and listen to your classmates' presentations, notice both **content**—what the speaker says—and **delivery**—how the speaker says it.

Content A speaker's ideas should be clear, well supported, and appropriate to the audience—in other words, his or her ideas should matter to listeners.

Delivery A good speaker provides a strong message and uses his or her voice and body language together effectively to present that message. Pay attention to each speaker's **verbal** and **nonverbal elements.**

Asking questions like the ones on the next page can help you organize your ideas about a classmate's speech. You might refer to the instruction on pages 910–911 to come up with additional criteria for evaluating the content and delivery of a presentation. As you listen, take notes about how well the speaker meets those criteria.

EVALUATION QUESTIONS	
Content	• How clear was the explanation of the problem and its causes and effects? • How useful and well supported did the solutions seem to you?
Delivery	• What was the speaker's tone? • How effective was the speaker's use of verbal and non-verbal elements such as volume, rate, facial expressions, and eye contact? • What techniques did the speaker use to emphasize important points?

Interviewing

Interviews—conversations in which one person asks another person questions to obtain information—are more common than you might think. You've probably been interviewed—by a teacher, the school nurse, or a neighbor wanting you to baby-sit or mow the lawn.

Sometime you may need to conduct an interview yourself. Here's how to get off to a good start:

Preparing for the Interview

A good interviewer is well prepared. Before you take out your pencil and notepad, follow these steps:

- **Research your topic.** If your interview focuses on a topic—kayaking, say—go to a library, and find out all you can about it. The more you know, the better your questions will be.

- **Know your subject.** If your interview focuses on the ideas and life of the person you're interviewing (your subject), see if any newspaper or magazine articles have been written about him or her. If your subject is a writer, read her latest book; if he's an architect, go see—or find a picture of—a building he designed.

- **Make a list of questions.** Ask obvious questions rather than pretend you know the answers. Don't ask questions that can be answered with a simple yes or no. Avoid questions that might influence your subject, like *You hate losing, don't you?*

- **Set up a time and place for the interview.** Choose a place that's comfortable and familiar to your subject—interview a horse trainer at her ranch or a chemistry teacher in his lab. Be on time.

Conducting the Interview

You're seated across from your subject, pencil poised. How do you make the most of your opportunity? Follow these guidelines:

- **Set the ground rules.** If you want to tape-record the interview, ask your subject's permission before you begin. If you plan to quote your subject's exact words in a newspaper article or in an essay, you must ask permission to do that too.

- **Be courteous and patient.** Allow your subject plenty of time to answer your questions. Try not to interrupt. Respect the person's ideas and opinions, even if you disagree.

TIP Team up with a classmate, and come up with a situation in which an interviewer and a subject have opposing points of view (a dog hater interviews the director of the Humane Society; a vegetarian interviews the owner of a cattle ranch). Then, act out two versions of the interview. In the first version the interview is tense and hostile, full of insults, interruptions, and accusations. In the second the interview is polite and constructive, and the interviewer refrains from directly expressing his or her point of view. What did you learn from the two scenarios?

- **Listen carefully.** Don't rush on to your next question. If you're confused, ask for an explanation. If an answer reminds you of a related question, ask it—even if it isn't on your list.
- **Focus on your subject, not on yourself.** Avoid getting off on tangents, such as "Something like that happened to me. . . ."
- **Wrap things up.** A good interview is leisurely but doesn't go on forever. Know when to stop. You can always phone later to check a fact or ask a final question. Be sure to thank your subject.

Following Up the Interview

Your notebook is filled, and your mind is bursting with ideas. How do you get your thoughts in order? Follow these steps:

- **Review your notes.** As soon as possible, read through your notes, and make sure your information is complete and clear.
- **Write a summary.** To make sure you understand what was said, write a summary of the main points of the interview.
- **Check your facts.** If you can, check the spelling of all names and technical facts against another source, such as an encyclopedia.

Turning the Tables: Being Interviewed

Sometime someone may want to interview you. Here are some tips:

- **Stay relaxed.** Listen carefully to each question before you begin your answer. If a question confuses you, ask the interviewer to reword it or repeat it. Take your time. Long, thoughtful answers are better than short, curt ones.
- **Be accurate.** Don't exaggerate. If you're not sure of something, say so.
- **Keep a sense of humor.**

Analyzing Propaganda on TV

Persuasive messages are everywhere—in essays, letters, and speeches. You also find them in television, radio, and movies. The persuasive messages you listen to and view usually contain *persuasive techniques* or *propaganda techniques*. **Persuasive techniques** convince an audience by providing sound reasons. These reasons persuade through strong, relevant supporting evidence. **Propaganda techniques,** though, appeal primarily to an audience's emotions and may contain false or misleading information. When you unquestioningly listen to or view messages that contain propaganda techniques, you may make poor decisions. The information presented here will help you identify persuasive and propaganda techniques, including false and misleading information. These skills will help you make well-informed decisions when watching TV.

Persuasive Techniques

To be persuasive, you must make sense. Signs of persuasive techniques include

- a clearly stated opinion, or claim
- logical reasons for the opinion supported by relevant evidence
- an appeal to the interests and backgrounds of a particular audience

Watch for these signs as you view, but don't automatically accept a message that includes them. First, check for propaganda techniques.

Propaganda Techniques

Propaganda techniques appeal more to your emotions than to common sense or logic. Like persuasive techniques, they are used to convince you to think, feel, or act a certain way. The difference is that a **propagandist,** a person who uses propaganda techniques, does not want you to think critically about the message.

For example, when you hear the name of a product or see its logo associated with your favorite football team, your excitement about that team is being used to sell that product. If you connect your excitement about the team with the product enough times, this propaganda technique, known as **transfer,** may eventually persuade you to buy the product. Your decision would be based not on logical reasons for buying the product but on your emotional response to the propaganda technique.

A persuasive message that includes propaganda techniques may be sound—as long as it also provides strong and accurate supporting evidence. The term *propaganda* describes a message that relies too heavily on any particular idea. Propaganda may also contain false or misleading information. (See pages 920–921.)

The following chart gives definitions and examples of other common propaganda techniques found in television ads and programs. As you watch TV, look for the given clues to identify these techniques in every kind of programming you watch:

PROPAGANDA TECHNIQUES USED ON TELEVISION

Techniques	Clues	Examples
Bandwagon tries to convince you to do something or believe something because everyone else does.	Listen for slogans that use the words *everyone, everybody, all,* or in some cases, *nobody.*	While being interviewed on a talk show, an author might encourage viewers to join the thousands of other people who have benefited from his new diet book.
Loaded language uses words with strongly positive or negative meanings.	Listen for strongly positive or negative words, such as *perfect* or *terrible.*	*Wake-up Juice is a fantastic way to start your day!*
Product placement uses brand-name products as part of the scenery. The products' companies may pay producers for this seemingly unintended advertising.	As you watch TV, keep your eyes peeled for clearly visible brand names. Ask yourself if the brand names have anything to do with the plot of the show.	In the middle of a TV movie, an actor may drink a bottle of juice. The juice is not an important part of the plot, but the brand name of the juice is clearly visible.
Snob appeal suggests that a viewer can be special or part of a special group if he or she agrees with an idea or buys a product.	Listen for words such as *exclusive, best,* or *quality.* Look for images of wealth, such as big houses, expensive cars, and fancy boats.	*Treat your cat like a queen; give her the cat food preferred exclusively by discriminating cats.*

(continued)

Techniques	Clues	Examples
Symbols associate the power and meaning of a cultural symbol with a product or idea.	Look for flags, team mascots, state flowers, or any other symbol that people view with pride.	A political candidate might use a national flag as a backdrop for a speech on TV.
Testimonials use knowledgeable or famous people to endorse a product or idea.	Look for famous actors, athletes, politicians, and experts. Listen for their names or titles as well.	*TV star Zen Williams actively supports alternative-energy research—shouldn't you?*

False and Misleading Information

As you know, a propagandist counts on you to be led by your emotions and not by your intelligence. Even if you wanted to think critically about a propagandist's message, you would not have much to go on because propaganda is so strongly **biased.** That is, it favors one point of view and ignores information that supports another point of view. Here are some signals that a persuasive message contains misleading information:

Presenting Opinions as Facts **Opinions** are beliefs, judgments, or claims that cannot be tested and proved true. Watch out for opinions presented as if they were facts. For example, a news report may quote an expert who says, "Space exploration is necessary for the future of human survival." How could such a statement be proved? Opinions presented as facts and not supported with evidence can be misleading.

Missing Information A persuasive message may downplay or leave out negative information. For example, car commercials often downplay the high price of the car. Instead, the commercials focus on the comfort, design, speed, and other positive features of the car. To avoid believing false information, consider the source of any fact or statistic. An authoritative source such as a respected research institution—for example, the Smithsonian Institution—probably provides accurate facts. If the information comes from a source you suspect may be strongly biased—for example, an oil company providing information that "proves" environmental regulations don't work—look for a more reliable source that can confirm the facts before you accept them.

Media Handbook

Analyzing False and Misleading Information

The following steps will help you identify and analyze examples of false and misleading information on TV:

▶ STEP 1 **Focus on a specific program or advertisement. Briefly describe the message you have chosen and how it makes you feel.** You might pick an interview on a talk show, a segment of a newscast, a sports broadcast, or a commercial shown during your favorite TV program.

▶ STEP 2 **Identify the main message or claim of the program or ad.**

▶ STEP 3 **Ask yourself, "Is the claim a fact, which can be proved true, or is it someone's opinion?"** Remember that scientific-sounding words do not necessarily point to factual information.

▶ STEP 4 **Ask yourself, "What is missing from the message?"** Is there any information you still do not know after watching the program or advertisement? Are there other parts of the event, product, service, or idea that were not presented?

▶ STEP 5 **Using your answers from the previous questions, decide whether or not you think the TV program or advertisement is misleading.** Explain your answer.

Using Electronic Texts to Locate Information

Types of Electronic Texts

When you think of electronic sources of information, your first thought may be the Internet, but do not limit your searches to the Web alone. Explore the other electronic options at your library—the online library catalog, library databases, encyclopedias on CD-ROM, even e-mail. To choose the best source for your search, consider the purposes and limitations of each type of electronic text listed below:

Online Library Catalog

Purpose: The online catalog will tell you whether a book is available for checkout and where in the library the book is located.

Limitation: If your library's collection is small, you may not find much information in the catalog.

CD-ROM Encyclopedia

Purpose: Use a CD-ROM encyclopedia for the same purpose as a printed encyclopedia. The only difference is that, using a CD-ROM, you can more easily move from one entry to another than you might with a large set of printed encyclopedias.

Limitation: Like a printed encyclopedia, a CD-ROM encyclopedia may not include the most up-to-date information, depending on the date of the edition you are using.

Library Databases

Purpose: A periodical index is a good place to start (and narrow) your search. It can direct you to the specific issue of a periodical that contains the information you need.

Limitation: A database may include listings for a large pool of books or periodicals; you might find a listing for an interesting book but not find a copy of the book in your library.

Web Sites

Purpose: The variety of sites available can help you find many different perspectives on your topic.

Limitation: Web sites are not checked for accuracy. Try to stick with sites sponsored by trustworthy organizations, which often have addresses ending in *edu, gov,* or *org.*

E-Mail

Purpose: You can use e-mail to ask experts directly for information.

Limitation: Like Web sites, e-mail does not necessarily provide accurate information. Make sure anyone you consult really does know about your topic.

Features of Electronic Texts

When you use nearly any electronic text to search for information, you need to think of a *keyword*. A **keyword** is a word or phrase, such as *giant panda,* that identifies your specific topic. You may need to experiment with keywords in order to find the information you need. Any time you use an electronic source, be prepared to think of all the ways your topic might be listed in order to get the most useful information.

Each type of electronic text is organized in a slightly different manner. To use electronic texts effectively, you need to understand the features of each type of text and the methods for using each type. Here are examples of four different types of electronic texts along with descriptions, explanations, and search tips:

Electronic Encyclopedia You might find this record by typing the keyword *panda* in the encyclopedia's search box:

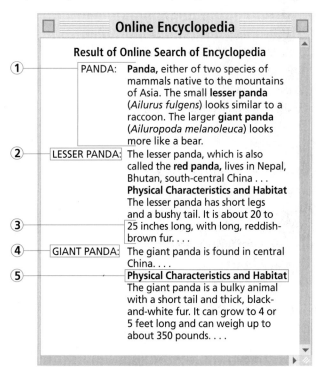

Online Encyclopedia

Result of Online Search of Encyclopedia

① PANDA: **Panda,** either of two species of mammals native to the mountains of Asia. The small **lesser panda** (*Ailurus fulgens*) looks similar to a raccoon. The larger **giant panda** (*Ailuropoda melanoleuca*) looks more like a bear.

② LESSER PANDA: The lesser panda, which is also called the **red panda,** lives in Nepal, Bhutan, south-central China . . .
Physical Characteristics and Habitat The lesser panda has short legs and a bushy tail. It is about 20 to ③ 25 inches long, with long, reddish-brown fur. . . .

④ GIANT PANDA: The giant panda is found in central China. . . .
⑤ **Physical Characteristics and Habitat** The giant panda is a bulky animal with a short tail and thick, black-and-white fur. It can grow to 4 or 5 feet long and can weigh up to about 350 pounds. . . .

① **First search result** finds two different entries about pandas.

② **Heading** for the entry about the first type of panda, the lesser panda

③ Since you are interested in pandas with black-and-white fur, skip to the next entry.

④ **Heading** for the entry about the second type of panda, the giant panda

⑤ **Subheadings** introduce smaller sections of the entry. As you read, take notes. You can search for additional information by using details, such as names of places pandas inhabit, as keywords.

Web Site You can use a *directory* or a *search engine* to find Web sites relevant to your search. A **directory** organizes sites into categories, such as Sports. Each category is then broken down into smaller and smaller categories to help you narrow your search. A **search engine** allows you to type in your keyword and then provides you with a list of Web sites that include your keyword. In searching for information on giant pandas, you can eliminate irrelevant listings in most search engines by

- putting the words *giant panda* in quotation marks to find sites that include those words, next to each other and in that order
- using *AND* to find sites that include two terms (though not necessarily right next to each other), such as *computer AND games*
- using *NOT* to rule out irrelevant sites that commonly come up using your keyword. For example, in searching for sites on the human heart, you can eliminate the sites on romance by searching for *heart NOT love.*

Here is an example of a Web page in a browser frame:

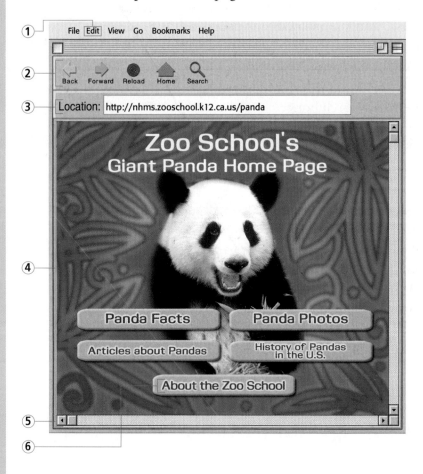

1. **Pull-down menu buttons** allow you to perform a variety of functions. Use the Find command on the pull-down Edit menu to locate quickly individual uses of a word in a text-heavy Web page.

2. **Toolbar buttons** help you navigate the Web.

3. The **Uniform Resource Locator** (URL) is the address of the Web page.

4. **Content area** of the Web page contains text, photos, and sometimes audio or video clips.

5. The horizontal and vertical **scroll bars** allow you to move side-to-side or up and down on a Web page.

6. When you click on underlined text or **hyperlink** buttons, your browser jumps to another part of the current page, a different page on the same Web site, or a page on a different Web site.

Online Library Catalog Like a traditional card catalog, an online catalog allows you to search for books and other information in a library by author, title, or subject. In most cases, when you are doing research, you will search by subject. Look at the example of a subject entry below:

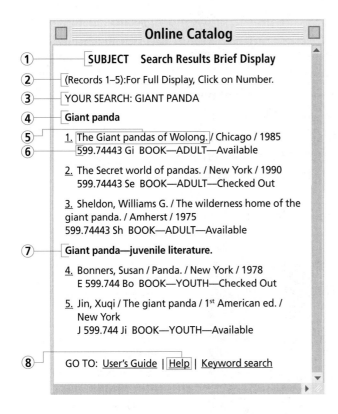

(1) This line shows what kind of search (title, author, or subject) you performed. "Brief Display" means that just the basic information about each book is listed here.

(2) Click on the number next to a listing to bring up a record containing more detailed information about the book.

(3) The keyword you entered is noted here.

(4) This is the first subject heading that matches your search request. (Compare it with item 7 below.)

(5) This is the title of the first book on the subject of giant pandas.

(6) This line notes the book's **call number,** which indicates where in the library the book is located and tells whether the book is available for checkout.

(7) This next subject heading starts a section of children's books about giant pandas.

(8) Click on the Help button for instructions on using the library catalog. If on-screen help or an instruction sheet is not available, ask a librarian for help.

Database Record from a Periodical Index Your library may carry hundreds of periodicals containing articles on every subject you can imagine. To search efficiently for articles about a particular topic in magazines, newspapers, or journals, refer to an online periodical index. You can search a periodical index, such as the *Readers' Guide to Periodical Literature,* to find a listing of magazine articles that fit your subject keyword. An example of a search result appears on the next page.

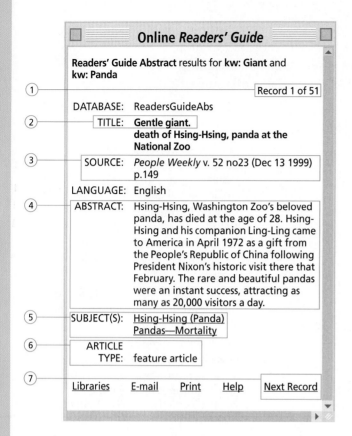

Media Handbook

Online *Readers' Guide*

Readers' Guide Abstract results for **kw: Giant** and **kw: Panda**

(1) Record 1 of 51

DATABASE: ReadersGuideAbs

(2) TITLE: **Gentle giant.**
death of Hsing-Hsing, panda at the National Zoo

(3) SOURCE: *People Weekly* v. 52 no23 (Dec 13 1999) p.149

LANGUAGE: English

(4) ABSTRACT: Hsing-Hsing, Washington Zoo's beloved panda, has died at the age of 28. Hsing-Hsing and his companion Ling-Ling came to America in April 1972 as a gift from the People's Republic of China following President Nixon's historic visit there that February. The rare and beautiful pandas were an instant success, attracting as many as 20,000 visitors a day.

(5) SUBJECT(S): Hsing-Hsing (Panda)
Pandas—Mortality

(6) ARTICLE TYPE: feature article

(7) Libraries   E-mail   Print   Help   Next Record

(1) Your search for the keywords ("kw") *Giant* and *Panda* produced 51 records. This is the first record in the database.

(2) Each line in a database is called a *field*. The **title field** contains the title of an article about giant pandas.

(3) The **source field** indicates the name, issue number, and page number of the magazine in which the article was published.

(4) An **abstract** gives you a summary of the article's contents.

(5) The database shows **additional subject headings** related to your search.

(6) Examining the **type of article** will also help you decide if the article will be useful for your research.

(7) To see information about the next article that fits your search, click on the words *Next Record*.

Glossary

The glossary that follows is an alphabetical list of words found in the selections in this book. Use this glossary just as you would use a dictionary—to find out the meanings of unfamiliar words. (Some technical, foreign, and more obscure words in this book are not listed here but instead are defined for you in the footnotes that accompany many of the selections.)

Many words in the English language have more than one meaning. This glossary gives the meanings that apply to the words as they are used in the selections in this book. Words closely related in form and meaning are usually listed together in one entry (for instance, *compassion* and *compassionate*), and the definition is given for the first form.

The following abbreviations are used:

adj.	adjective
adv.	adverb
n.	noun
v.	verb

Each word's pronunciation is given in parentheses. A guide to the pronunciation symbols appears at the bottom of this page. For more information about the words in this glossary or for information about words not listed here, consult a dictionary.

A

aghast (ə·gast′) *adj.:* shocked; horrified.
alien (āl′yən) *n.:* foreigner.
ambitious (am·bish′əs) *adj.:* eager to succeed.
animation (an′i·mā′shən) *n.:* liveliness.
anonymous (ə·nän′ə·məs) *adj.:* unknown; unidentified.
audacity (ô·das′ə·tē) *n.:* boldness; daring.
avenge (ə·venj′) *v.:* get even for; get revenge for.

C

chaos (kā′äs′) *n.:* total confusion or disorder.
cleft (kleft) *adj.:* split; divided.
contemplate (kän′təm·plāt′) *v.:* study carefully.
controversial (kän′trə·vur′shəl) *adj.:* debatable; tending to stir up argument.
crusade (krōō·sād′) *n.:* struggle for a cause.

D

defiant (dē·fī′ənt) *adj.:* disobedient; boldly resisting.
defy (dē·fī′) *v.:* resist; oppose.
descend (dē·send′) *v.:* move to a lower place; come down.
determine (dē·tur′mən) *v.:* decide.
devastate (dev′ə·stāt′) *v.:* cause great damage. —**devastating** *v.* used as *adj.*
diagnosis (dī′əg·nō′sis) *n.:* act of identifying a disease by examining symptoms.
diligence (dil′ə·jəns) *n.:* steady effort.
disengage (dis′in·gāj′) *v.:* unfasten.

---

at, āte, cär; ten, ēve; is, īce; gō, hôrn, look, tōol; oil, out; up, fur; ə *for unstressed vowels, as* a *in* ago, u *in* focus; ′ *as in* Latin (lat′′n); chin; she; zh *as in* azure (azh′ər); thin; the; ŋ *as in* ring (riŋ)

E

elude (ē·lōōd′) *v.:* escape the notice of; avoid detection by.

emit (ē·mit′) *v.:* give out; send forth.

etiquette (et′i·kit) *n.:* acceptable manners and behavior.

evacuate (ē·vak′yōō·āt′) *v.:* remove from an area.

evident (ev′ə·dənt) *adj.:* obvious.

exposure (ek·spō′zhər) *n.:* state of being unprotected.

exude (eg·zyōōd′) *v.:* give off.

F

feral (fir′əl) *adj.:* untamed; wild.

formidable (fôr′mə·də·bəl) *adj.:* fearsome.

forsaken (fôr·sā′kən) *adj.:* abandoned; deserted.

furtive (fʉr′tiv) *adj.:* done in a sneaky or secretive way.

G

gawky (gô′kē) *adj.:* clumsy; awkward.

gorge (gôrj) *v.:* fill up; stuff (oneself).

grating (grāt′iŋ) *adj.:* irritating.

grimace (grim′is) *v.:* twist the face to express pain, anger, or disgust.

H

hallucination (hə·lōō′si·nā′shən) *n.:* sight or sound of something that isn't really there.

hazardous (haz′ər·dəs) *adj.:* dangerous; risky.

heedful (hēd′fəl) *adj.:* attentive; keeping in mind.

hover (huv′ər) *v.:* remain suspended in the air.

I

ignorance (ig′nə·rəns) *n.:* lack of knowledge.

inexplicable (in·eks′pli·kə·bəl) *adj.:* not explainable.

infest (in·fest′) *v.:* inhabit in large numbers (said of something harmful).

intent (in·tent′) *adj.:* closely attentive. —**intently** *adv.*

intern (in·tʉrn′) *v.:* imprison or confine.

J

jubilant (jōō′bə·lənt) *adj.:* joyful.

L

laud (lôd) *v.:* praise highly.

lavish (lav′ish) *adj.:* generous; plentiful. —**lavishly** *adv.*

legitimate (lə·jit′ə·mət) *adj.:* here, reasonable; justified.

listless (list′lis) *adj.:* lifeless; lacking in interest or energy.

lofty (lôf′tē) *adj.:* noble; high.

lure (lʊr) *v.:* tempt; attract.

M

marvel (mär′vəl) *v.:* wonder.

melancholy (mel′ən·käl′ē) *adj.:* mournful; gloomy.

milestone (mīl′stōn′) *n.:* significant event.

mortify (môrt′ə·fī′) *v.:* make ashamed; embarrass deeply. —**mortified** *v.* used as *adj.*

N

nurture (nʉr′chər) *v.:* promote the growth of; nurse.

O

omen (ō′mən) *n.:* thing believed to be a sign of future events.

P

paramount (par′ə·mount′) *adj.:* main; most important.

penetrate (pen′i·trāt′) *v.:* pierce; make a way through.

perpetual (pər·pech′ōō·əl) *adj.:* permanent; constant.

perplexity (pər·plek′sə·tē) *n.:* bewilderment; confusion.

placate (plā′kāt′) *v.:* calm or soothe (someone who is angry).

ponder (pän′dər) *v.:* think over carefully.

precision (prē·sizh′ən) *n.:* exactness; accuracy.

proverb (präv′ərb) *n.:* short traditional saying that expresses a truth.

prudent (prōō′dənt) *adj.:* wise; sensible.

R

recess (rē′ses) *n.:* inner place.

regain (ri·gān′) *v.:* recover.

repose (ri·pōz′) *n.:* state of rest or inactivity.

resilient (ri·zil′yənt) *adj.:* springy; quick to recover.

reticent (ret′ə·sənt) *adj.:* reserved; tending to speak little.

revive (ri·vīv′) *v.:* awaken; bring back to life.

rural (rŏŏr′əl) *adj.:* having to do with country life.

S

savor (sā′vər) *v.:* delight in.

servitude (sʉr′və·tōōd′) *n.:* condition of being under another person's control.

shrewd (shrōōd) *adj.:* sharp; clever. —**shrewdest** *adj.* used as *n.*

sinewy (sin′yōō·ē) *adj.:* strong; tough.

slacken (slak′ən) *v.:* lessen; slow down. —**slackening** *v.* used as *adj.*

spectacle (spek′tə·kəl) *n.:* remarkable sight.

surge (sʉrj) *v.:* move in a wave.

T

tolerant (täl′ər·ənt) *adj.:* patient; accepting of others.

U

urgency (ʉr′jən·sē) *n.:* pressure; insistence.

V

vague (vāg) *adj.:* not clear or definite; general. —**vaguely** *adv.*

vapor (vā′pər) *n.:* gas; fumes.

W

wily (wī′lē) *adj.:* sly; clever in a sneaky way.

Spanish Glossary

A

aghast/espantado, da *adj.* horrorizado; pasmado.

alien/extranjero *s.* forastero; ajeno.

ambitious/ambicioso *adj.* que ansia el éxito; anheloso; insatisfecho.

animation/animación *s.* excitación; viveza; acción.

anonymous/anónimo *adj.* desconocido; incógnito.

audacity/audacia *s.* osadía; intrepidez; valentía; coraje.

avenge/vengar *v.* castigar; escarmentar; reivindicar.

C

chaos/caos *s.* anarquía; confusión total; babel.

cleft/grietado *adj.* hendido; abierto; partido.

contemplate/contemplar *v.* meditar; considerar; examinar de cerca.

controversial/controvertido *adj.* discutido; debatido; polémico; contencioso; que lleva a desacuerdos.

crusade/cruzada *s.* lucha; campaña; empresa.

D

defiant/provocativo *adj.* provocador; desafiante; tono de voz retador.

defy/retar *v.* desafiar; provocar; resistir; oponer.

descend/descender *v.* bajar; decrecer.

determine/determinar *v.* decidir; precisar; concretar.

devastate/devastar *v.* asolar; arrasar.

diagnosis/diagnosis *s.* pronóstico; identificación de una enfermedad por sus síntomas.

diligence/diligencia *s.* encargo; esmero; atención.

disengage/desenganchar *v.* soltar; liberar; desengranar; retirar.

E

elude/eludir *v.* evitar; esquivar; rodear.

emit/emitir *v.* difundir; producir; irradiar.

etiquette/etiqueta *s.* protocolo; ceremonial; comportamiento y modales aceptables.

evacuate/evacuar *v.* vaciar; desocupar; expulsar; desalojar.

exposure/exposición *s.* revelación; abandono; falta de protección.

exude/exudar *v.* rezumar; emitir.

F

feral/feroz *adj.* salvaje; fiero.

formidable/formidable *adj.* tremendo; terrible; impresionante; que inspira la admiración de otros; que causa pavor.

forsaken/abandonado *adj.* desertado; largado; largado.

furtive/furtivo *adj.* que actúa a escondidas; que se hace en secreto.

G

gawky/torpe *adj.* desgarbado; larguirucho.

gorge/atiborrar *v.* hartar; llenar; rellenar.

grating/irritante *adj.* insoportable; fastidioso; molesto.

grimace/mueca *s.* gesto; mohín.

H

hallucination/alucinación *s.* sueño; visión; espejismo.

hazardous/peligroso *adj.* arriesgado; azaroso; inseguro.

heedful/acatador *adj.* obediente; observante; respetuoso.

hover/flotar en el aire *v.* revolotear; aletear; rondar; dar vueltas alrededor de un mismo paraje; esbozar una sonrisa.

I

ignorance/ignorancia *s.* inexperiencia; incompetencia; falta de conocimientos.

inexplicable/inexplicable *s.* misterioso; enigmático; incomprensible; que no se puede explicar.

infest/infestar *v.* plagar; poblar en grandes números (de algo nocivo).

intent/atento *adj.* que presta atención; dispuesto; vigilante. —**intently/ atentamente** *adv.*

intern/internar *v.* encerrar; recluir; encarcelar.

L

laud/alabar *v.* levantar hasta las nubes; ensalzar.

lavish/pródigo *adj.* generoso; extravagante; profuso.

legitimate/legítimo *adj.* razonable; justificado; genuino; legal.

listless/decaído *adj.* indiferente; sin energía ni interés.

lofty/alto *adj.* noble; ilustre; distinguido.

lure/atraer *v.* tentar; cautivar.

M

marvel/maravilla *s.* portento; fenómeno; prodigio.

melancholy/melancólico *adj.* triste; sombrío.

milestone/hito *s.* poste; jalón; evento significante.

mortify/mortificar *v.* vejar; humillar; afligir.

N

nurture/fomentar *v.* mantener; alimentar; sostener; proteger.

O

omen/presagio *s.* auspicio; augurio; profecía.

P

paramount/supremo *adj.* dominante; sumo.

penetrate/penetrar *v.* entrar; invadir; infiltrar.

perpetual/perpetuo *adj.* imperecedero; perenne; eterno.

perplexity/perplejidad *s.* confusión; duda; titubeo.

placate/apaciguar *v.* aplacar; tranquilizar; sosegar.

ponder/considerar *v.* reflexionar; meditar; pensar.

precision/precisión *s.* exactitud; puntualidad; claridad.

proverb/proverbio *s.* máxima; aforismo; dicho tradicional que exprime una verdad.

prudent/prudente *adj.* sensato; moderado; cauteloso.

R

recess/recinto *s.* cercado; nicho; alcoba.

regain/recobrar *v.* recuperar; redimir.

repose/reposo *s.* estado de inactividad; descanso; respiro.

resilient/elástico *adj.* resistente; elástico; flexible.

reticente/reticente *adj.* parco; evasivo; circunspecto.

revive/revivir *v.* resucitar; reanimar; restablecer.

rural/rural *adj.* campestre; pastoral; aldeano; sencillo.

S

savor/saborear *v.* paladear; probar; deleitarse.

servitude/servidumbre *s.* sujeción; servicio; hallarse bajo el control de otro.

shrewd/avispado *adj.* listo; astuto; penetrante.

sinewy/vigoroso *adj.* nervudo; fuerte; vigoroso.

slacken/reducir *v.* aminorar; disminuir, aflojar; soltar las riendas.

spectacle/espectáculo *s.* fausto; circo; exhibición.

surge/ondear *v.* encresparse; ondear; levantar.

T

tolerant/tolerante *adj.* comprensivo; paciente; benévolo; pasivo.

U

urgency/urgencia *s.* premura; necesidad; apremio.

V

vague/vago *adj.* impreciso; indeciso; poco claro.

vapor/vapor *s.* gas; efluvio; humo.

W

wily/astuto *adj.* taimado; avisado; listo.

Acknowledgments

For permission to reprint copyrighted material, grateful acknowledgment is made to the following sources:

The Albion Press, Ltd.: From "Rapunzel" from *Fairy Tales of the Brothers Grimm,* retold and introduced by Neil Philip. Copyright © 1997 by Neil Philip.

Arcade Publishing, New York, New York: "A Balmy Spring Wind" from *Haiku: This Other World,* edited by Richard Wright. Copyright © 1998 by Ellen Wright.

Arte Público Press: "En la Sangre" and "In the Blood" from *Chants* by Pat Mora, www.patmora.com. Copyright © 1985 by Pat Mora. Published by Arte Público Press–University of Houston, Houston, TX, 1985.

Atheneum Books for Young Readers, an imprint of Simon & Schuster Children's Publishing Division: "A Bubble Bursts" from *How I Came to Be a Writer* by Phyllis Reynolds Naylor. Copyright © 1978, 1987 by Phyllis Reynolds Naylor. "The Bracelet" by Yoshiko Uchida from *The Scribner Anthology for Young People,* edited by Anne Diven. Copyright © 1976 by Yoshiko Uchida. "Since Hannah Moved Away" and "Weird!" from *If I Were in Charge of the World and Other Worries* by Judith Viorst. Copyright © 1981 by Judith Viorst.

Catherine Beston Barnes: "The Storm" by Elizabeth Coatsworth.

Susan Bergholz Literary Services, New York: "Good Hot Dogs" from *My Wicked, Wicked Ways* by Sandra Cisneros. Copyright © 1987 by Sandra Cisneros. Published by Third Woman Press and in hardcover by Alfred A. Knopf. All rights reserved. "Eleven" from *Woman Hollering Creek* by Sandra Cisneros. Copyright © 1991 by Sandra Cisneros. Published by Vintage Books, a division of Random House, Inc., New York, and originally in hardcover by Random House, Inc. All rights reserved.

Georges Borchardt, Inc. for the Estate of John Gardner: "Dragon, Dragon" from *Dragon, Dragon and Other Tales* by John Gardner. Copyright © 1975 by Boskydell Artists Ltd.

Geoffrey Bownas and Anthony Thwaite: "Winter Rain" by Nozawa Bonchō and "Bad-tempered, I got back" by Ōshima Ryōta from *The Penguin Book of Japanese Verse* translated by Geoffrey Bownas and Anthony Thwaite, Penguin Books, 1964. Translation copyright © 1964 by Geoffrey Bownas and Anthony Thwaite.

Brooks Permissions: "Cynthia in the Snow" from *Bronzeville Boys and Girls* by Gwendolyn Brooks. Copyright © 1956 by Gwendolyn Brooks Blakely.

Curtis Brown, Ltd.: "The Camel," "The Panther," "The Duck," "The Octopus," and "A Caution to Everybody" by Ogden Nash. Copyright © 1935, 1940, 1942, 1953 by Ogden Nash; copyright renewed.

Candlewick Press, Cambridge, MA: "What Do Fish Have to Do with Anything?" from *What Do Fish Have to Do With Anything?* by Avi. Copyright © 1997 by Avi.

Carus Publishing Company: "Wartime Mistakes, Peacetime Apologies" by Nancy Day from *Cobblestone: Japanese Americans,* April 1996. Copyright © 1996 by Cobblestone Publishing Company. All rights reserved.

CBS News Archives, a division of CBS Inc.: From "One Child's Labor of Love" from *60 Minutes II,* October 5, 1999. Copyright © 1999 by CBS Inc.

Laura Cecil, Literary Agent, on behalf of The James Reeves Estate: "The Sea" from *Complete Poems for Children* by James Reeves. Copyright 1950 by James Reeves.

Children's Express Foundation, Inc.: From "Too Much TV Can Equal Too Much Weight" by Jamie Rodgers from *Children's Express* web site, accessed September 22, 2000, at http://www.cenews.org/news/200007obesetv.htm. Copyright © 2000 by Children's Express Foundation.

Children's Press/Franklin Watts, a Grolier Publishing Company, a division of Scholastic Incorporated: From "Nilou" from *Newcomers to America: Stories of Today's Young Immigrants* by Judith E. Greenberg. Copyright © 1996 by Judith E. Greenberg.

Chronicle Books, San Francisco: "In a Neighborhood in Los Angeles" from *Body in Flames/Cuerpo en Llamas* by Francisco X. Alarcón. Copyright © 1990 by Francisco X. Alarcón.

Clarion Books/Houghton Mifflin Company: "The Mysterious Mr. Lincoln" from *Lincoln: A Photobiography* by Russell Freedman. Copyright © 1987 by Russell Freedman. All rights reserved.

Coffee House Press: "Forty-One Seconds on a Sunday in June, in Salt Lake City, Utah" from *Choruses: Poems* by Quincy Troupe. Copyright © 1999 by Quincy Troupe.

Ruth Cohen for Lensey Namioka: "The All-American Slurp" by Lensey Namioka from *Visions,* edited by Donald R. Gallo. Copyright © 1987 by Lensey Namioka. All rights reserved by the author.

Don Congdon Associates, Inc.: "All Summer in a Day" by Ray Bradbury. Copyright © 1954 and renewed © 1982 by Ray Bradbury.

Richard Curtis Associates, Inc.: From "The Flood" from *The Beauty of the Beasts* by Ralph Helfer. Copyright © 1990 by Ralph Helfer.

David Daiches: From "Thoughts on Progress" by David Daiches from *The New Yorker,* August 28, 1954. Copyright © 1954, 1982 by The New Yorker Magazine, Inc.

Dial Books for Young Readers, a Member of Penguin Group (USA) Inc.: From *The Gold Cadillac* by Mildred D. Taylor. Copyright © 1987 by Mildred D. Taylor.

Doubleday, a division of Random House, Inc.: "The Fun They Had" from *Earth Is Room Enough* by Isaac Asimov. Copyright © 1957 by Isaac Asimov.

Dramatists Play Service, Inc.: *The Hitchhiker* by Lucille Fletcher. Copyright © 1946 by Lucille Fletcher. CAUTION: The reprinting of *The Hitchhiker* included in this volume is by permission of Dramatists Play Service, Inc. The Engligh language stock and amateur stage performance rights in this Play are controlled exclusively by Dramatists Play Service, Inc., 440 Park Avenue South, New York, NY 10016. No professional or nonprofessional performance of the play may be given without obtaining, in advance, the written permission of the Dramatists Play Service, Inc., and paying the requisite fee.

Gwen Everett: From *John Brown: One Man Against Slavery* by Gwen Everett. Text copyright © 1993 by Gwen Everett.

Farrar, Straus & Giroux, LLC: "The Toaster" from *Laughing Time: Collected Nonsense* by William Jay Smith. Copyright © 1990 by William Jay Smith.

Dorothy Geiger: *In the Fog* by Milton Geiger.

Greenwood Publishing Group, Westport, CT: Adapted from "Blanca Flor/White Flower" from *¡Teatro! Hispanic Plays for Young People* by Angel Vigil. Copyright © 1996 by Teacher Ideas Press.

Harcourt, Inc.: "Ugly Duckling or Little Mermaid?" from *Lives of the Writers: Comedies, Tragedies (and What the Neighbors Thought)* by Kathleen Krull. Copyright © 1994 by Kathleen Krull. "La Bamba" from *Baseball in April and Other Stories* by Gary Soto. Copyright © 1990 by Gary Soto. "Ode to Mi Gato" from *Neighborhood Odes* by Gary Soto. Copyright © 1992 by Gary Soto. Text from *King Long Shanks* by Jane Yolen, illustrated by Victoria Chess. Text copyright © 1998 by Jane Yolen.

HarperCollins Publishers, Inc.: From "The Inside Search" (retitled "I Kept on Probing to Know…") from *Dust Tracks on a Road* by Zora Neale Hurston. Copyright 1942 by Zora Neale Hurston; copyright renewed © 1970 by John C. Hurston. From "Searching for Stories" and excerpts (retitled "How the Snake Got Poison," "How the Possum Lost the Hair on Its Tail" and "Why the 'Gator Is Black") adapted from *Mules and Men* by Zora Neale Hurston. Copyright 1935 by Zora Neale Hurston; copyright renewed © 1963 by John C. Hurston and Joel Hurston. Excerpt (retitled "The Landlord's Granddaughter") from *Red Scarf Girl: A Memoir of the Cultural Revolution* by Ji-Li Jiang. Copyright © 1997 by Ji-Li Jiang; foreword copyright © 1997 by HarperCollins Publishers. From *The Land I Lost* by Huynh Quang Nhuong. Copyright © 1982 by Huynh Quang Nhuong. "Jimmy Jet and His TV Set" from *Where the Sidewalk Ends* by Shel Silverstein. Copyright © 1974 by Evil Eye Music, Inc. "Zlateh the Goat" from *Zlateh the Goat and Other Stories* by Isaac Bashevis Singer, illustrated by Maurice Sendak. Text copyright © 1966 by Isaac Bashevis Singer.

Harvard University Press and the Trustees of Amherst College: 1763 "Fame is a bee" from *The Poems of Emily Dickinson,* edited by Thomas H. Johnson. Copyright © 1951, 1955, 1979 by the President and Fellows of Harvard College. Published by The Belknap Press of Harvard University Press, Cambridge, Mass.

Henry Holt and Company, LLC: "The Stone" from *The Foundling and Other Tales of Prydain* by Lloyd Alexander. Copyright © 1973 by Lloyd Alexander. "Steam Shovel" from *Upper Pasture* by Charles Malam. Copyright 1930, © 1958 by Charles Malam.

Houghton Mifflin Company: "Baucis and Philemon" and "Medusa's Head" from *Greek Myths* by Olivia Coolidge. Copyright © 1949 and renewed © 1977 by Olivia E. Coolidge. All rights reserved.

Jet Propulsion Laboratory, California Institute of Technology: From "Solar System Bodies: Venus" from the *NASA Solar System Exploration* Web site accessed July 21, 2000, at http://sse.jpl.nasa.gov/features/planets/venus/venus.html. From the *NASA Solar System Exploration* Web site accessed August 10, 2000, at http://sse.jpl.nasa.gov. Copyright © 2000 by the Jet Propulsion Laboratory, California Institute of Technology.

John Johnson Ltd.: "The Bridegroom" from *The Bronze Horseman and Other Poems* by Alexander Pushkin, translated by D. M. Thomas. Translation copyright © 1982 by D. M. Thomas.

Bobbi Katz, www.bobbikatz.com: "Things to Do If You Are a Subway" by Bobbi Katz from *Upside Down and Inside Out: Poems for All Your Pockets.* Copyright © 1973 by Bobbi Katz. Bobbi Katz controls all reprint rights.

David Kherdian: "About 'That Day'" by David Kherdian. Copyright © 1991 by David Kherdian.

Alfred A. Knopf, a division of Random House, Inc.: Text from "He Lion, Bruh Bear, and Bruh Rabbit" from *The People Could Fly* by Virginia Hamilton. Copyright © 1985 by Virginia Hamilton. "Motto" and "Poem" from *Collected Poems of Langston Hughes.* Copyright © 1994 by The Estate of Langston Hughes.

Brian Lanker: Excerpt (retitled "I Was Not Alone") by Rosa Parks from *I Dream a World: Portraits of Black Women Who Changed America* by Brian Lanker. Copyright © 1989 by Brian Lanker.

Lescher & Lescher, Ltd.: Text from "The Southpaw" by Judith Viorst from *Free to Be …You and Me* by Marlo Thomas and Associates. Copyright © 1974 by Judith Viorst.

Edward Lueders: "Your Poem, Man…" by Edward Lueders from *Some Haystacks Don't Even Have Any Needle: and Other Complete Modern Poems,* compiled by Stephen Dunning, Edward Lueders, and Hugh Smith. Copyright © 1969 by Scott, Foresman and Company.

Margaret K. McElderry Books, an imprint of Simon & Schuster Children's Publishing Division: "Hard on the Gas" from *Behind the Wheel: Poems About Driving* by Janet S. Wong. Copyright © 1999 by Janet S. Wong.

Alice P. Miller: "All Aboard with Thomas Garrett" by Alice P. Miller from *Cobblestone,* February 1981, vol. 2, no. 2. Copyright © 1981 by Alice P. Miller.

North Shore Animal League, Port Washington, New York: North Shore Animal League Pet Adoption Application. Copyright © 2000 by North Shore Animal League.

The Overlook Press: "That Day" from *I Remember Root River* by David Kheridan. Copyright © 1978 by David Kheridan.

Pantheon Books, a division of Random House, Inc.: "Little Mangy One" from *Arab Folktales* by Inea Bushnaq. Copyright © 1986 by Inea Bushnaq.

People Weekly: From "Brave Hearts" (retitled "Trial by Fire") by Dan Jewel and Sephronia Scott Gregory from *People Weekly,* July 14, 1997. Copyright © 1997 by Time Inc.

Pets.com: "Animal Instincts" by Gina Spadafori from *Pets.com, The Magazine for Pets and Their Humans,* vol. 1, issue 4, June 2000. Copyright © 2000 by www.pets.com.

Random House, Inc.: Excerpt (retitled "Brother") from *I Know Why the Caged Bird Sings* by Maya Angelou. Copyright © 1969 and renewed © 1997 by Maya Angelou. From *Gorilla, My Love* by Toni

Cade Bambara. Copyright © 1971 by Toni Cade Bambara. "The Sneetches" from *The Sneetches and Other Stories* by Dr. Seuss. TM and copyright © 1953, 1954, 1961 and renewed © 1989 by Dr. Seuss Enterprises, L.P.

Random House Children's Books, a division of Random House, Inc.: From *Bud, Not Buddy* by Christopher Paul Curtis. Copyright © 1999 by Christopher Paul Curtis. "Just Once" by Thomas Dygard from *Ultimate Sports,* edited by Donald R. Gallo. Copyright © 1995 by Thomas Dygard.

Marian Reiner for Lillian Morrison: "The Sidewalk Racer or On the Skateboard" from *The Sidewalk Racer and Other Poems of Sports and Motion* by Lillian Morrison. Copyright © 1965, 1967, 1968, 1977 by Lillian Morrison.

Marian Reiner: "An Old Silent Pond" by Bashō from *Cricket Songs: Japanese Haiku,* translated by Harry Behn. Copyright © 1964 by Harry Behn; copyright renewed © 1992 by Prescott Behn, Pamela Behn Adam, and Peter Behn. "Our Washing Machine" from *The Apple Vendor's Fair* by Patricia Hubbell. Copyright © 1963 and renewed © 1991 by Patricia Hubbell. "Rags" from *Flashlight and Other Poems* by Judith Thurman. Copyright © 1976 by Judith Thurman.

Russell & Volkening as agents for Ann Petry: "A Glory over Everything" from *Harriet Tubman: Conductor on the Underground Railroad* by Ann Petry. Copyright © 1955 and renewed © 1983 by Ann Petry.

The Saturday Review: "The Path Through The Cemetery" by Leonard Q. Ross from *The Saturday Review,* November 29, 1941. Copyright © 1941 by General Media International, Inc.

Scholastic Inc.: Adaptation of "Why Dogs Chase Cats" from *How Many Spots Does a Leopard Have? and Other Tales* by Julius Lester. Copyright © 1989 by Julius Lester. "Ta-Na-E-Ka" by Mary Whitebird from *Scholastic Voice,* December 13, 1973. Copyright © 1973 by Scholastic Inc.

Scribner, an imprint of Simon & Schuster Adult Publishing Group: "Earth" from *The Gardener and Other Poems* by John Hall Wheelock. Copyright © 1961 by John Hall Wheelock. Excerpt (retitled "Two Frogs and the Milk Vat") from *Manchild in the Promised Land* by Claude Brown. Copyright © 1965 by Claude Brown.

Robert Silverberg: From "Pompeii" from *Lost Cities and Vanished Civilizations* by Robert Silverberg. Copyright © 1962 and renewed © 1990 by Agberg, Ltd.

Simon & Schuster Books for Young Readers, an imprint of Simon & Schuster Children's Publishing Division: "The Nightingale" from *The Nightingale* by Hans Christian Andersen, translated by Anthea Bell. Copyright © 1984 by Neugebauer Press, English translation copyright © 1988 by Picture Book Studio. Excerpt (retitled "Storm") from *Woodsong* by Gary Paulsen. Copyright © 1990 by Gary Paulsen. "Stray" from *Every Living Thing* by Cynthia Rylant. Copyright © 1985 by Cynthia Rylant.

Stone Soup, the magazine by young writers and artists: "The Brother I Never Had" by Gim George, 13 years old, from *Stone Soup, the magazine by young writers and artists,* vol. 21, no. 5, May/June 1993. Copyright © 1993 by the Children's Art Foundation.

Teen Ink: "Summer Diamond Girl" by Toni Janik from *Teen Ink,* October 2002. Copyright © 2002 by The Young Authors Foundation, Inc. All rights reserved.

Time Inc.: Text from "What Will Our Towns Look Like? (If We Take Care of Our Planet)" from *Time for Kids,* January 21, 2000. Text copyright © 2000 by Time Inc. "His Gift to Girls" by Ritu Upadhyay from *Time for Kids,* vol. 5, no. 16, February 4, 2000. Copyright © 2000 by Time Inc.

Sc©tt Treimel NY: "Scene" from *River Winding* by Charlotte Zolotow. Copyright © 1970 by Charlotte Zolotow.

Laurence S. Untermeyer on behalf of the Estate of Louis Untermeyer, Norma Anchin Untermeyer, c/o Professional Publishing Services Company: "The Dog of Pompeii" from *The Donkey of God* by Louis Untermeyer. Copyright 1932 by Harcourt Brace & Company.

Viking Penguin, a Member of Penguin Group (USA) Inc.: "Rumpelstiltskin" by Rosemarie Künzler, translated by Jack Zipes from *Spells of Enchantment,* edited by Jack Zipes. Copyright © 1991 by Jack Zipes.

Villard Books, a division of Random House, Inc.: From *All I Really Need to Know I Learned in Kindergarten* by Robert L. Fulghum. Copyright © 1986, 1988 by Robert L. Fulghum.

Wesleyan University Press: "The City" from *David Ignatow: Poems 1934–1969* by David Ignatow. Copyright © 1970 by David Ignatow. All rights reserved.

West End Press: "Yes, It Was My Grandmother" from *A Breeze Swept Through* by Luci Tapahonso. Copyright © 1987 by Luci Tapahonso.

Picture Credits

The illustrations and/or photographs on the Contents pages are picked up from pages in the textbook. Credits for those can be found either on the textbook page on which they appear or in the listing below.

permission of Marian Reiner. (bottom left) © Royalty-Free/CORBIS, (center) © Royalty-Free/CORBIS; 667, Bardinet/Photo Researchers, Inc.; 668, (bottom left) Menny Borovski; 669, © UPI/CORBIS; 675, © Dana White/PhotoEdit; 680, (top left) Cover Art copyright © 2000 by Ashley Bryan. Used by permission of HarperCollins Publishers., (top right) Cover from I'm Nobody! Who Are You? Poems of Emily Dickinson for Young People, by Emily Dickinson, illustrated by Rex Schneider, edited by Barbara Holdridge, by permission of Stemmer House Publishers, Inc. Cover illustration copyright © 1978 by Rex Schneider., (bottom left) Jacket used with permission of Harcourt, Inc. All rights reserved., (bottom right) From It's a Woman's World edited by Neil Philip, selection and introduction. Volume copyright © 2000 by The Albion Press Ltd. Used with permission from Dutton Children's Books. A division of Penguin Young Readers Group, A Member of Penguin Group (USA) Inc., 345 Hudson St., New York, NY 10014. All rights reserved.; 681, (top left) Used by permission of the Grolier Publishing Company, a division of Scholastic, Inc., (top right) THE STONE AGE NEWS. Text © 1998 Fiona MacDonald. Illustrations © 1998 Walker Books Ltd. Reproduced by permission of the publisher Candlewick Press, Inc., Cambridge, MA, on behalf of Walker Books Ltd., London., (bottom left) From Street Smart: Cities of the Ancient World. Copyright 1994 by Runestone Press, an imprint of the Lerner Publishing Group. Used by permission of the publisher. All rights reserved., (bottom right) Cover painting of mammoth skull © 1999 by Kristen Kest. Photo courtesy of the Maryland Historical Society. Jacket © 1999 by HarperCollins Publishers. Used by permission of HarperCollins Publishers.; 682, Digital Image © The Museum of Modern Art/Licensed by Scala/Art Resource, NY; 687, Used by permission of HarperCollins Publishers.; 688, Cover from The Watsons Go to Birmingham—1963 by Christopher Paul Curtis with Connections, © HRW; HRW photos by Mavournea Hay (car) and Sam Dudgeon (people), map background courtesy of Michigan Department of Transportation, photo of young boy courtesy of the Alexander Family. Cover photo by John Fei Photography.; 691, © Scala/Art Resource, NY; 701, © Phil Burchman/Getty Images; 702, © Steve O'Meara/Volcano Watch International; 704, © Bettmann/CORBIS; 707, Eric Anderson/PictureQuest; 716, © Susan Greenwood/Getty Images; 717, (left) North Shore Animal League, Photo by Mary Bloom (right) Chris Kasson/AP/Wide World Photos; 721, 723, © PhotoDisc/Getty Images; 731, © Vince Streano/Getty Images; 732, Jim Frank; 737, Mark Antman/The Image Works; 738, © PhotoDisc/Getty Images; 739, Richard R. Hewett/Shooting Star; 740-742, © PhotoDisc/Getty Images; 743, Richard R. Hewett/Shooting Star; 744, © PhotoDisc/Getty Images; 745, Richard R. Hewett/Shooting Star; 747, © PhotoDisc/Getty Images; 748, Richard R. Hewett/Shooting Star; 751, 752, © PhotoDisc/Getty Images; 753, © Art Resource/NY; 756, National Education Association, Carolyn Salisbury; 757, 759, Digital Image Copyright © 2005 Artville; 760, Courtesy of Phyllis Reynolds Naylor; 761, Courtesy of Phyllis Reynolds Naylor; 774, (top left) Jacket design by Victor Ambrus from OUTCAST by Rosemary Sutcliff. Cover art © 1995 by Victor Ambrus. Reprinted by permission of Farrar, Straus and Giroux, LLC., (top right) Cover from The True Confessions of Charlotte Doyle by Avi with Connections, © HRW; HRW photo by Andrew Yates Photography, (bottom left) Illustration from the cover of SARAH BISHOP by Scott O'Dell.

Published by POINT, an imprint of Scholastic, Inc. Illustration copyright © 1995 by Scholastic, Inc. Reprinted by permission., (bottom right) Design © 1997 The Madison Press Limited. A Hyperion/Madison Press Book.; 775, (top left) Cover illustration by Leonid Gore from BLIZZARD! by Jim Murphy. Published by Scholastic Press, a division of Scholastic, Inc. Illustration copyright © 2000 by Leonid Gore. Reprinted by permission., (top right) From MY LIFE IN DOG YEARS (Jacket Cover) by Gary Paulsen, copyright © 1998 by Gary Paulsen. Used by permission of Dell Publishing, a division of Random House, Inc., (bottom left) Jacket by Bill Le Fever, from ANCIENT ROME by Simon James, copyright © 1992 by Reed International Books Ltd. Used by permission of Viking Penguin, A division of Penguin Young Readers Group, A Member of Penguin Group (USA) Inc., 345 Hudson St., New York, NY 10014. All rights reserved., (bottom right) Cover photo by Lyn Topinka, courtesy of the USGS/Cascades Volcano Observatory, Vancouver, WA.; 777, The Parisian Novels (The Yellow Books), Vincent van Gogh, 1888, © Christie's Images/CORBIS; 924, Keren Su/Stone/Getty Images.

Illustrations

All art, unless otherwise noted, by Holt, Rinehart & Winston.

Borovski, Menny 495, 495, 496, 498, 499, 500, 506
Britt, Tracy 659, 664
Callanan, Brian 469
Chess, Victoria 283, 283, 284, 285, 286, 288, 289, 290
Chesworth, Michael 6, 8, 10, 11, 12
Davis, Nancy 227, 228, 231, 235
Day, Sam 724, 725, 726, 727
Diaz, David 468, 470, 471, 472, 475
Dryden, Jim 336, 337, 338, 339, 340, 341
Duranceau, Suzanne 243, 244, 247, 248
Gil, Mariano 371, 372
Granmoe, Kristine 377, 387, 388, 397
McMullan, James 396
Morris, Burton 398, 400, 401, 402
Park, Chang 150, 152, 153
Pappas, Lou 467
Papoulas, Ted 199, 201
Pavey, Jerry 366, 367, 369, 375
Pelavin, Daniel 192
Prato, Rodica 260, 261, 262, 351
Sauber, Robert 278, 280, 282
Sawchuk, Peter 66, 70, 73
Schrier, Fred 660, 664, 664
Slomowitz, Marsha 165, 264, 269, 451, 572
Spector, Joel 690, 692, 695, 696, 700
Stankiewicz, Steve 507, 543
Vazquez, Carlos 167, 170, 173, 177, 179, 180
Wenzel, David 30, 32, 34, 35, 37
Zimmerman, Jerry 344, 349, 634

Index of Skills

Historical fiction, 691
Imagery, **538**, 539, **573**, 578, 622, 644, 661, 663, 794
    contrasting, 644
Independent Reading, 15, 26, 38, 50, 103, 120, 131, 155, 181, 190, 205, 216, 235, 249, 262, 304, 328, 342, 370, 414, 433, 448, 517, 534, 549, 566, 577, 587, 605, 616, 631, 648, 669, 680, 716, 735, 774
Inference, 51
    about character traits, 479
Internal conflict, 134, 142
Internal rhyme, 620, 632
Irony, **580**, 585, 588, 592, 593, 594, 598, 602, 794
Key details, 426, 456
Key passages, 426
KWL chart, 544
Legend, **309**, 794
Limerick, 794
Literary criticism, **684–685**
    evaluating characters, **684–685**
    evaluating plot, **685**
    glossary of terms, 685
Literary devices, **538–539**
    figurative language, **539**
    imagery, **538**
    metaphor, **539**
    personification, **539**
    simile, **539**
    symbol, **539**
Main character, 93
Main events, 39, 456
    sequence chart, 655, 754
Main idea, **426**, 730, 795
Message, 644
    writer's, **730**, 736, 754
Metamorphosis, **257**, 263
    chart, 263
Metaphor, 505, **539**, **544**, 550, 578, **633**, **658**, 795
    extended, 640, **658**, 661, 663, 667
Meter, **620–621**, 626
Mood, 795
Moral, 374, 632
Moral lesson, **29**, 39
Motif, 182
Motive, 250
Myth, **308**, 350, 795
Mythic hero, **350**
Narration, 795
    first-person, **418**, **426**, **456**, 466, 528
    third-person, **418**, **456**, 466
Narrative, 466

details chart, 329
Narrator
    first-person, **456**
    third-person, **456**
Nonfiction, 418, 795
Novel, 796
Novella, **316**
Ode, **635**
    gift diagram, 635
Onomatopoeia, 622, 796
Oral tradition, 796
Paraphrasing, 501, 796
Personification, **539**, 622, **633–634**, 640, 796
Plot, **2–3**, 27, 124, 366, 797
    and character, 124, 182
    credibility of, **685**, 718
    diagram, 3, 191
    story map for, 27, 85
    theme and, **243**
Plot diagram, 3, 191
Poetry, **620–621**, **633–635**, 797
    alliteration in, **620**, 677
    comparison chart, 498, 501, 505, 640, 661, 666
    comparisons in, 622
    extended metaphor in, 640, **658**, 661, 667
    figures of speech in, **633–634**
    free verse, **621**
    haiku, **641**
    how to read, **622**
    imagery in, 622, 644, 661
    metaphor in, **633**, **658**
    meter in, **620–621**, 626
    ode, **635**
    onomatopoeia in, 622
    personification in, 622, **633–634**, 640
    punctuation in, 622
    refrain, **650**, 655
    repetition, **650**
    rhyme in, **620**, **626**, 632, 666
    rhyme scheme in, **626**, 632
    rhythm in, 622, 666
    scanning, 626
    simile in, **633**, 640, 677
    speaker in, **635**, 649
    stanzas in, 632
    title of, 505, 622
    tone of, **635**, 640, 644, 649, 677
    word choice in, 622, **641**
Point of view, **149**, 434, 449, 797
    character and, **149**
    first-person, **149**, **418**, **426**, 444
    third-person, **418**, **468**
Predictions, 39, 236
Problem, 115

Prose, 798
Punctuation in poetry, 622, 625
Refrain, **650**, 655, 798
Repetition, **650**
Resolution, 3, 115, 142, 156, 182, 466, 602
Retelling, 602
Rhyme, **620**, **626**, 632, 666, 798
    end, 620
    internal, 620, 632
    scheme, **626**, 632
Rhyme scheme, **626**, 632
Rhythm, 622, 666, 798
Scanning, in poetry, 626
Sequence chart, 655, 754
Setting, **2–3**, 27, 39, **41**, 51, 104, 115, 705, 736, 799
Short story, **335**, 799
    structure chart, 335
Simile, 343, **539**, **633**, 640, 677, 799
Speaker, 649, 799
    and tone, **635**
Stanza, 632, 799
Story map, 27, 85, 281, 456, 588
Subject,
    subject-versus-theme chart, 226
    theme and, **226**
Summary, 364, 456, 567
    story map, 456
Suspense, 74, 78, **710**, 718, 800
    comparison chart, 85, 104
    elements of, 74
Symbol, 271, 274, **539**, **556**, 800
Symbolism, **556**, 567
Tall Tale, 800
Theme, 27, **220–221**, 236, **243**, 250, 257, 263, 268, 329, 730, 736, 800
    complications and, 221
    plot and, **243**
    subject and, **226**
    subject-versus-theme chart, 226
    universal, **257**
Think-pair-share, 710
Third-person narration, 418, **456**, 466
Third-person point of view, **418**, **468**
Time clues, 335
Time line
    of your life, 419
    Zora Neale Hurston, 388–389
Title, 505, 622
Tone, **494**, 501, 505, **635**, 646
    in poetry, **635**, 640, 644, 649, 677, 800
    in songs, 655
Traits, character, **184**, 250, 479
    chart, 125
Trickster, **366**, 374

Universal themes, 257
Visualizing, 449
Word choice in poetry, 622, **641**
Writer's message, **730**, 736, 754

INFORMATIONAL READING SKILLS

Adequate evidence, 268
Anecdote, 442
Application
    advice on, **721**
    filling in, **707**
    preparing an, **707, 721**
    reading an, 707
    references for, **707**, 723
    revising an, 707
    signing and dating an, 707
    spelling and, 707
    truthful answers and, 707
Appropriate evidence, 268
Assertions, **552**, 554, **569**, 571, 613
    assertion-citation graphic
        organizer, 569
    assertion-evidence chart, 552
    citations and, **569**
    evidence and, **552**, 554, 613
    supporting, 554
Author's purpose, 801
Bandwagon appeal, **727**, 807
Block pattern of organization, **345**,
    348
    chart, 345
Caption, 53
Case study, 252
Circular reasoning, **725**, 726
Citations, **569**, 571
    assertion-citation graphic
        organizer, 569
    assertions and, **569**
Clarifying questions, 144
Compare-and-contrast, 802
    block pattern, **345**, 348
    block pattern chart, 345
    organization, **345**, 348
    point-by-point pattern, **345**, 348
    point-by-point pattern chart,
        345
Comparing, 60, 331, 334, 345, 348
    main ideas, **451**
Comparison and contrast, **331**, 334,
    411
Conclusion, 241, 255
    support for, 255
Conclusions, evaluating writer's, **238**
Conflict, 164
Connecting main ideas across texts,

481, 493
    chart, 482
Contents page of magazine, 53
Contrasting, 331, 334, 345, 348
Cover of magazine, 53
Direct quotation, 252
Evaluating evidence, **252, 265**, 802
Evidence, **252, 265**, 268, **552**, 554,
    613, 724, 803
    adequate, 268
    appropriate, 268
    assertion-evidence chart, 552
    assertions and, **552**, 554, 613
    evaluating, **252, 255, 265**
    inadequate, 265
    inappropriate, 265
    logical appeal and, 724
Fact, 60, 442, 530, 571
    and opinion, **265**
Fact and opinion, 803
Fallacious reasoning, 724, **725–726**
    circular reasoning, **725**, 726
    hasty generalization, **725**, 726
    logical appeal and, 724
    only-cause fallacy, **726**
Faulty reasoning, 770
Generalization, **243, 725**, 803
    hasty, **725**, 726
    qualifying words in, 725
Graphic features, 803
Graphic organizers
    assertion-citation graphic
        organizer, 569
    assertion-evidence chart, 552
    block pattern chart, 345
    connecting main ideas across
        texts chart, 482
    main-idea cluster diagram, 452
    point-by-point-pattern chart,
        345
Hasty generalization, **725**, 726
Heading, 53, 56
Home page, 57
Illustration, 53
Inadequate evidence, 265
Inappropriate evidence, 265
Independent Reading, 121, 217, 305,
    415, 535, 617, 681, 775
Inference, 454, 493, 805
Informational text, 331
Internet, **57**
    home page, 57
    links, 57
    search engine, 57
    structural features of, **57**
    table of contents in, 57
    Web sites on, **57**
Links, 57

Logic, 724
Logical appeal, **724**
    evidence, 724
    fallacious reasoning and, 724
    reasons, 724
Magazine, **53**
    contents page, 53
    cover, 53
    structure, **53**
Magazine article, **53**
    caption, 53
    heading, 53, 56
    illustration, 53
    outlining, 53
    subtitle, 53, 56
    title, 53, 56
Main idea, 144, 147, 164, 213,
    451–452, 454, 481, 530, 805
    cluster diagram, 452
    comparing, **451**
    connecting across texts, **481**, 493
    connecting across texts chart,
        482
    finding, **451**
    in related texts, **452**
    title and, 451, 454
    of Web page, 60
Maps
    China, 507
    Greek myths, 351
    Harriet's Route to Freedom, 469
    India, 614
    Kaw homeland, 134
    Underground Railroad, 483
    Vietnam, 457
Metaphor, 241
Name-calling, **728**, 808
Note taking, 144, **158**, 805
    logical, **158**
Only-cause fallacy, **726**
Opinion, 268, 613
    fact and, **265**
    valid, 265
Organizational patterns, 411
    compare and contrast, 345, 348
Outlining, 53, **144**, 147, 213, 806
    clarifying questions, asking, 144
    main ideas, getting, 144
    note taking, 144
    subheads, 144
Paraphrasing, 806
Persuasion, **724**, 806
Persuasive techniques, **724–726**
    fallacious reasoning, 724,
        725–726
    logical appeal, **724**
Point-by-point pattern of
    organization, **345**, 348

VOCABULARY SKILLS

READING SKILLS

WRITING SKILLS

SPEAKING AND LISTENING MEDIA SKILLS

LANGUAGE (GRAMMAR, USAGE, AND MECHANICS) SKILLS

INDEPENDENT READING

Index of Authors and Titles

Student Authors and Titles